32-Bit Microprocessors

A Primer Plus

Dedicated to

Rochelle,
David,
Matthew,
Jeremy
    and my parents

Gary J. Bronson

Ronnie,
Sharon,
Michael,
    and to the memory
    of my parents

Howard I. Silver

32-Bit Microprocessors

A Primer Plus

Gary J. Bronson
Fairleigh Dickinson University

Howard I. Silver
Fairleigh Dickinson University

with contributions by
Stephen J. Menconi
AT&T

AT&T Advanced Technology Series

AT&T Customer Information Center
Indianapolis, Indiana, U.S.A.

PRODUCTION CREDITS

Text Design: Stephen Menconi
Copy Editor: Rose Van Heest
Line Art: Donna Guettler
Composition: Vincent Mattaliano

International Standard Book Number 0-932764-10-X

Library of Congress Catalog Number 88-071953

AT&T Customer Information Center Select Code 311-027

For inquiries, contact:

AT&T Customer Information Center
2855 North Franklin Road
Indianapolis, IN 46219

Telephone: 1-800-432-6600

Acknowledgments

We acknowledge the contributions of the many people who have assisted in making this book a reality. These include the encouragement and support of Ron Hoth and Yolanda Hardin, the insightful comments and suggestions made by Paul Guettler, and the vision and dedication of Stephen Menconi that inspired the writing of this text and brought it to completion.

Additionally we would like to thank the AT&T Document Development Organization (DDO) production staff assigned to this project for their enthusiastic and professional support. They include Rose Van Heest, copy editor; Donna Guettler, line-art illustrator; and Vincent Mattaliano (Victory Graphics), compositor/graphics designer.

Also to be recognized are the technical support groups at AT&T, Intel, and Motorola that generously provided us with information; and the reviewers of the manuscript for their many constructive suggestions. Additionally, we thank Dr. G. Lansing Blackshaw, Dr. J. Warren Blaker, Dr. Paul Lerman, Dr. William Schick, and Dr. William Walker, all of Fairleigh Dickinson University, and Dr. Frederick Kelly of Seton Hall University for their indispensable encouragement and support.

Finally, we deeply appreciate the patience and understanding provided by our wives, Rochelle and Ronnie, throughout this project.

Gary J. Bronson
Howard I. Silver

A Word About Trademarks . . .

DEC, PDP, and UNIBUS are trademarks of Digital Equipment Corporation.
IBM is a trademark of International Business Machines, Inc.
INTEL, MULTIBUS, and ICE are trademarks of Intel Corporation.
MOTOROLA and VERSAbus are trademarks of Motorola, Inc.
WE is a registered trademark of AT&T.
ZILOG and Z80 are trademarks of Zilog, Inc.

Contents

Acknowledgements v
A Word About Trademarks vi
Preface xiv

PART ONE Fundamentals 1

CHAPTER ONE Basics 3

1.1 Computer Architecture 4
      Why 32 bits? 7
1.2 Buses 8
      Data Bus 8
      Address Bus 9
      Control Bus 10
      Single Bus Architectures 11

Microprocessors and Microcomputers 12

Support Devices and Coprocessors 13

Signal Groups 15

1.3 Packaging 15

1.4 Timing Conventions 18

Timing Signals 18

Timing Definitions 20

Standard Time Intervals 22

Timing Reference Points 24

1.5 Microprocessor Timing and Clock Signals 24

Bus Cycles 27

1.6 Fabrication 32

1.7 Chapter Highlights 35

CHAPTER TWO 32-Bit Microprocessor Architectures 41

2.1 Basic CPU Operations and Capabilities 42

Instruction Requirements 44

Pipelining 45

Multitasking 45

Additional Capabilities 46

2.2 Register Sets 48

Program Model Register Set 50

System Model Register Set 60

2.3 Memory Management Concepts 61

Segments and Offsets 63

INTEL 80386 CPU Real Memory Management Mode 66

2.4 Memory Management Implementations 69

Segmentation 69

INTEL 80386 CPU Protected Mode 71

Fragmentation 75

Paging 77

INTEL 80386 CPU Protected Mode Page Operation 79

2.5 Chapter Highlights 82

CHAPTER THREE Operating System Support Features 85

3.1 Privilege Levels 86

3.2 Tasks 87

INTEL 80386 CPU Task State Segment 88

Task State Segment Descriptor 88

Task Register 90
Hidden Descriptor Registers 90
Task Switches 92
The Sharing of Address Spaces 92
3.3 System Calls - The Gate Mechanism 95
Passing Parameters 97
3.4 Interrupts 100
Interrupt Gates 100
3.5 Exceptions 102
Processor Exceptions 103
Programmed Exceptions 104
3.6 Chapter Highlights 106

PART TWO Specific Microprocessors 109

CHAPTER FOUR INTEL 80386 Microprocessor 111

4.1 Register Sets 112
Program Register Model 112
System Register Model 116
4.2 Data Types 123
4.3 Addressing Modes 128
Register Operand Storage 128
Immediate Operand Storage 129
Memory and I/O Operand Storage 130
High-Level Language Support 137
Address Mode Restrictions 138
4.4 Instruction Encoding 139
Opcode Bytes 141
Addressing Mode Bytes 143
Override Prefix Bytes 150
4.5 Instruction Set 156
Data Transfer Instructions 156
Arithmetic Instructions 164
Logical, Shift, and Rotate Instructions 170
Program Control Instructions 173
String/Character Translation Instructions 175
High-Level Language Support and Systems Instructions 178
4.6 Programming Examples 181
An Averaging Routine 182

A Data String Move and Verify Routine 184
A Sorting Routine 186
4.7 Chapter Highlights 190

CHAPTER FIVE AT&T *WE* 32100 Microprocessor 197

5.1 Register Sets 199
Program Register Model - Conventional Group 199
Program Register Model - Special Purpose Registers 201
System Model Register Set 202
5.2 Data Types 203
Sign and Zero Extension 205
Data Storage in Memory 205
Register Data Storage 206
5.3 Instruction Set 207
Data Transfer Instructions 208
Arithmetic Instructions 209
Logical Instructions 211
Program Control Instructions 213
Coprocessor Instructions 218
Stack and Miscellaneous Instructions 220
5.4 Addressing Modes 220
Register Mode 224
Register Deferred Mode 225
Displacement Mode 226
Deferred Displacement Mode 227
Immediate Mode 229
Absolute Mode 230
Absolute Deferred Mode 230
Expanded Operand Mode 231
5.5 AT&T *WE* 32200 Microprocessor Enhancements 233
Auto Pre/Post Increment/Decrement 235
Indexed Register Modes 236
5.6 Chapter Highlights 241

CHAPTER SIX MOTOROLA MC68020 Microprocessor 247

6.1 Register Sets 248
Program Model Registers 248
System Model Registers 251
6.2 Data Types 255

6.3 Addressing Modes 258

   Absolute Addressing Mode 259

   Immediate Addressing Mode 260

   Register Direct Addressing Mode 260

   Register Indirect Addressing Mode 261

   Indexed Register Indirect Addressing Mode 263

   Memory Indirect Addressing Mode 264

   Program Counter Relative Addressing Modes 266

6.4 Instruction Set 267

   Data Transfer Instructions 268

   Arithmetic Instructions 268

   Binary Coded Decimal Instructions 271

   Logical, Shift, and Rotate Instructions 271

   Bit Management Instructions 273

   Program and System Control Instructions 273

   Coprocessor Instructions 278

6.5 Instruction Encoding 280

   Single Effective Address Instruction Format 280

   Brief Extension Word 284

   Full Extension Word Format 285

6.6 Chapter Highlights 287

PART THREE Interfacing 295

CHAPTER SEVEN Memory Interfacing 297

7.1 Memory Devices 298

   Read Only Memories 298

   Read/Write Memories 299

   Memory Structure 300

   Device Examples 302

7.2 Address Decoding and Buffering 308

   Address Decoders 309

   Address Decoding for 32-Bit CPUs 317

   Read/Write Control 324

   Buffering 328

   Voltage and Current Specifications for 32-Bit Microprocessors 331

7.3 Timing 332

   Read and Write Cycles 333

   Timing Examples 334

80386 Address Pipelining 338
Wait States 340
Wait State Circuit 343
Cache Systems 344
Other Examples of Cache Implementation 349
7.4 DRAM Interfacing 350
Address Multiplexing, Reading and Writing DRAMs 351
DRAM Refreshing 352
Interleaved DRAM Banks 353
DRAM Controller Devices 354
7.5 Memory Management Revisited 362
Segmented and Paged Addressing 362
Memory Management Implementations 364
INTEL 80386 CPU Memory Management 364
MOTOROLA 68020 and MC68030 CPU Memory Management 365
Memory Management for the AT&T *WE* 32100/32200 CPU 369
7.6 Chapter Highlights 371

CHAPTER EIGHT I/O Interfacing 379

8.1 Overview of Data Transfer Techniques 380
Programmed I/O 381
Interrupt Controlled I/O 381
Direct Memory Access 383
8.2 Programmed I/O 384
Data Transfer Without Status Checking 385
Status Checking 386
8.3 Interrupts 391
Interrupt Control Signals 392
Transferring Control to Interrupt Service Routines 394
Multiple Device Interrupt Handling 398
Programmable Interrupt Controller 401
MOTOROLA MC68020 CPU Interrupt Handling 404
AT&T *WE* 32100 CPU Interrupt Handling 407
8.4 Direct Memory Access (DMA) 409
CPU Bus Request and Acknowledge Signals 409
DMA Transfer Modes 410
Introduction to Single-Chip DMA Controllers 412
INTEL 8237A High Performance Programmable DMA Controller 412
INTEL 82258 Advanced DMA Coprocessor 414
AT&T *WE* 32104 DMA Controller 416
8.5 Interfacing to Parallel I/O 419

8255A PPI Basic Operation 420

Interfacing the INTEL 8255A PPI to the 80386 CPU 420

Programming the 8255A for Basic I/O Mode 424

8255A PPI Strobed I/O Mode Used With Interrupt 429

IEEE-488 Parallel Data Transfer Standard Bus - A Brief Overview 432

8.6 Serial I/O Interfacing 434

Serial Signal Formats 435

Data Transmission Standards and Modems 438

Serial Interfacing - A Software Approach 442

Serial Interfacing - the INTEL 8251A USART 444

8.7 Chapter Highlights 450

CHAPTER NINE Coprocessors and Multiprocessing 457

9.1 Coprocessors 458

An Overview of Coprocessor Operation 458

Numeric Coprocessors for the INTEL 80386 CPU 459

Numeric Coprocessor for the MOTOROLA MC68020 CPU 463

Math Accelerator Units for the AT&T *WE* 32100 and 32200 CPUs 465

Programming Example Using the AT&T *WE* 32106 Math Accelerator Unit 466

9.2 Multiprocessing 473

Resource Sharing in Multitasking and Multiprocessing 474

Multiprocessing with Local and System Buses 478

INTEL MULTIBUS I 478

INTEL MULTIBUS II 480

VMEbus 481

9.3 Chapter Highlights 483

Appendices 487

A. Numeric Data Formats 488

B. Digital Logic 495

C. Microprocessor Signal Descriptions 524

D. Manufacturers' Addresses 535

E. Acronyms and Abbreviations 536

F. Answers to Selected Exercises 539

Index 543

Preface

Current microprocessing interests and the rapid adoption of 32-bit microprocessors motivated the writing of this textbook. We felt that the unique capabilities of these complex CPUs warranted a textbook devoted entirely to 32-bit devices. In writing this text, our goals are to provide:

- A clear tutorial explanation of 32-bit architectures and features they support
- Information on specific 32-bit processors
- Actual hardware and software interface design examples.

Our point of view is that students need all three — explanation, specifics, and design examples. To meet these goals, the text is divided into three major parts:

- Fundamentals
- Specific Microprocessors
- Interfacing.

Although the emphasis in each part is indicated by its title, there is a constant interplay between tutorial and specifics within each section. For example, though Part One is primarily a tutorial, specific examples illustrating each new concept, using Intel, AT&T, and Motorola 32-bit CPUs, are used throughout. This clarifies the concept presented and introduces the actual 32-bit processor. Keeping in mind that each part contains an interweaving of both theory and specific examples, the primary emphasis of each is:

- Part One Fundamentals is intended as a true tutorial that presents the architecture of 32-bit CPUs, memory management concepts and practices, pipelining, and operating system support features.

- Part Two Specific Microprocessors presents a more detailed description and extensive coverage of the three CPUs that were used in Part I. Specifically, the INTEL 80386 CPU, AT&T *WE* 32100 CPU, and MOTOROLA MC68020 CPU are presented. Reference is also made to features of the MOTOROLA MC68030 CPU and the AT&T *WE* 32200 Microprocessor.
- Part Three Interfacing presents a design-oriented approach to interfacing with specific examples of memory, I/O, and coprocessors. Both the hardware and software aspects of interfacing are presented. Due to the current and expected future popularity of the INTEL 80386 CPU, the text emphasizes this device.

In addition to the three major parts of the text, appendices are provided on binary number systems, digital logic, microprocessor signal descriptions, manufacturer's addresses, acronyms and abbreviations, and answers to selected exercises.

The following briefly summarizes the topics covered in each chapter:

Chapter 1 - Basics

Topics: Evolution of microprocessor architecture, bus structure, device packaging, and timing conventions.

Chapter 2 - 32-Bit Microprocessor Architecture

Topics: Basic fetch and execute operations; an introduction to pipelining, multitasking, and numeric coprocessor support; register architectures of the INTEL 80386 CPU, the AT&T *WE* 32100 Microprocessor, and the MOTOROLA MC68020 CPU; and memory management implementations.

Chapter 3 - Operating System Support Features

Topics: Privilege levels, task switching, and interrupts and exceptions.

Chapter 4 - INTEL 80386 Microprocessor

Topics: 80386 CPU registers, data types, and addressing modes; assembly language and machine encoding of the 80386 instruction set; instruction examples; and examples of data manipulation programs.

Chapter 5 - AT&T *WE* 32100 Microprocessor

Topics: AT&T *WE* 32100 Microprocessor registers, data types, and addressing modes; assembly language instructions; and *WE* 32200 Microprocessor enhancements.

Chapter 6 - The MOTOROLA MC68020 Microprocessor

Topics: MOTOROLA MC68020 registers, data types, and addressing modes; assembly language and machine encoding of the MC68020 instruction set.

Chapter 7 - Memory Interfacing

Topics: ROM and RAM devices; address decoding, buffering, and timing considerations; use of wait states, address pipelining, and cache memory; DRAM interfacing concepts; memory management hardware implementation.

Chapter 8 - I/O Interfacing

Topics: Data transfer via programmed I/O, interrupt, and DMA; interrupt and DMA controllers; parallel and serial data transmission using programmable parallel interface and USART devices.

Chapter 9 - Coprocessors and Multiprocessing

Topics: Interfacing and control of numeric processors, use of shared resources by multiple CPUs, standard multiprocessing system buses.

It is recommended that this text be used in a one-semester or two-semester advanced undergraduate or graduate course in 32-bit microprocessors. Ideally, this course should be preceded by a more fundamental 8-bit or 16-bit microcomputer course that stresses architecture, assembly language programming, and interfacing. However, since the text does not require extensive assembly language-level programming background, it can be used as a first course in the subject. Prior experience with digital hardware and computer fundamentals is recommended, although the appendices on number systems and logic design contain the basic information required.

For a one-semester course concentrating on the INTEL 80386 CPU alone, it is recommended that coverage be limited to Chapters 1, 2, and 4 with appropriate portions of Chapters 7, 8, and 9. A two-semester course can include the operating system features presented in Chapter 3, and a survey of the other two CPUs using portions of Chapters 5 and 6. Exercises are provided at the end of each chapter.

Gary J. Bronson
Howard I. Silver

Fundamentals

Part One

Basics

Chapter One

1.1   Computer Architecture
1.2   Buses
1.3   Packaging
1.4   Timing Conventions
1.5   Microprocessor Timing and Clock Signals
1.6   Fabrication
1.7   Chapter Highlights

In less than a decade since 1975, microprocessor architecture has evolved from 4 bits and 8 bits to 32 bits. This progression followed the same path as the earlier electronic evolution from larger to smaller as represented by the transition from vacuum tubes to transistors to integrated circuits. Each forward step has been spurred by advancements in both circuit design techniques and manufacturing technologies. These advances have enabled significantly more electronic circuitry to be included in a diminishing space.

The continual reduction in the size of the components used in producing electronic circuits is quite visible. This reduction in size is matched by equally dramatic changes within the integrated circuits themselves. The significant differences between the 8-bit, 16-bit, and 32-bit microprocessors are graphically displayed in Figure 1-1.

This chapter reviews the history of the microprocessor and introduces the major functional and architectural changes that have occurred during the progression to 32 bits. The three 32-bit microprocessors discussed are the INTEL 80386 Microprocessor, the AT&T *WE* 32100 Microprocessor, and the MOTOROLA MC68020 Microprocessor.

1.1 Computer Architecture

All computer systems, from general-purpose programmable systems to dedicated real-time controllers, provide a minimum set of capabilities and perform a minimum set of functions. These are the same for desktop personal computers, minicomputers, mainframes, computer-controlled automobile ignition systems, robotic systems, etc., and include the capability to:
- accept input to the system
- provide output from the system
- store information in a logically consistent format (traditionally binary)
- perform arithmetic and logic operations on either the input or stored data
- monitor, control, and effectively direct the overall operation and sequencing of the system.

Large mainframe computer systems and the smaller minicomputers relegated each of these capabilities to separate units. Figure 1-2 illustrates a classical block diagram of a computer system and the interconnection of these various units: arithmetic and logic, control, memory, and input/output.

The internal architecture of early minicomputers almost exactly mirrored this classical unit-based concept of a computer system. The key to this structure is the specific function(s) performed by each unit.

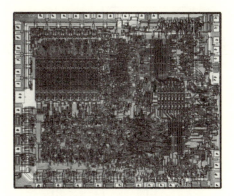

FIGURE 1-1a   8-Bit INTEL 8080 Microprocessor Chip

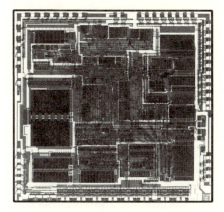

FIGURE 1-1b   16-Bit INTEL 80286 Microprocessor Chip

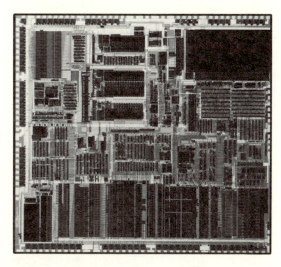

FIGURE 1-1c   32-Bit INTEL 80386 Microprocessor Chip
Photographs courtesy of Intel Corporation.

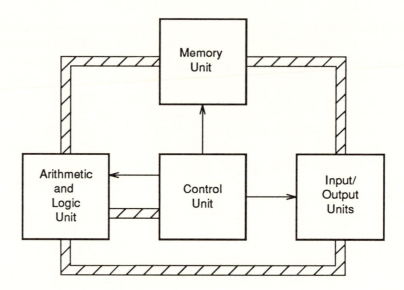

ZZZZ Address and Data Lines

———➤ Control

FIGURE 1-2   Basic Hardware Units of a Computer System

Memory Unit. This unit stores information in a logically consistent format and is capable of being written to and read from. Typically, both instructions and data are stored in memory, usually in separate and distinct areas.

Control Unit. The control unit directs and monitors the overall operation and sequencing of the system. It keeps track of where in memory the next instruction resides, decodes instructions, issues the signals needed to read data from and write data to other units in the system, executes an instruction and sequences through a series of instructions. To accomplish sequencing and timing tasks usually requires external clock circuitry.

Arithmetic and Logic Unit (ALU). The ALU performs all the arithmetic and logic functions required by the system. The ability to add, subtract, and compare two numbers is the minimum function needed.

Input/Output (I/O) Unit. This unit provides access to and from the computer system. It is the interface to which other digital or analog units may be attached. Devices typically connected to the I/O Unit's interfaces are keyboards, displays, printers, recording devices, and transducers that convert external signals into machine acceptable formats or, conversely, convert internal digital signals into an external analog or digital form.

At first, the various units comprising commercially developed computer systems were built with relays and vacuum tubes. In these systems, a basic binary flip-flop circuit required two vacuum tubes that occupied a space that could hold a standard six-ounce tea cup. In the late 1950s, this same circuit was built with transistors and occupied the space of a one-cent postage stamp. This savings in space allowed computer manufacturers to combine the arithmetic and logic unit with the control unit onto a single board called the central processing unit (CPU). This was a natural combination since many processing control functions were concerned with the passing of control information to the arithmetic and logic unit. Combining the ALU with the control unit simplified the interface between these two units and provided faster processing speed since the control unit no longer had to access a separate unit for each arithmetic operation. Of course, the remaining control functions required to direct the flow of information between either the CPU and memory or between the CPU and the I/O devices, were still needed.

The mid-1960s saw the introduction of integrated circuits (ICs) that resulted in a further reduction in the space required to produce a CPU. The early integrated circuits contained up to 100 transistors on a single chip of silicon and were called small-scale integrated (SSI) circuits. From the late 1960s to the mid-1970s, medium scale integrated (MSI) circuits predominated, each chip containing 100 to 1000 transistors. Large scale integrated (LSI) circuits, containing more than 1000 transistors, were introduced in the mid-1970s. Current versions of LSI chips, referred to as very large scale integrated (VLSI) circuits, contain from hundreds of thousands to over a million transistors on a single silicon substrate. VLSI circuits have provided the means of transforming the giant computers of the 1950s into today's desktop personal computers. Each individual unit required to form a computer (CPU, memory, and I/O) can now be manufactured on single chips. A single-chip CPU providing arithmetic, logic, and control functions is called a *microprocessor*.

Why 32 Bits?

Advancements in VLSI technology resulted in the circuitry needed to process more bits of data on each chip. The number of bits that a microprocessor's internal circuitry can process as a single, complete entity at one time is referred to as *word size*. Current leading-edge microprocessors have internal word sizes of 32 bits and can internally process and route 32-bit addresses and 32-bit data.

The choice of an internal 32-bit word size is not dictated solely by the VLSI technology available. Before this technology was available, 32 bits was the word size of choice for mainframes and minicomputers. It represented an ideal trade-off between speed and efficiency. Speed dictates a larger bit width to allow more bits to be simultaneously processed in parallel, while efficiency limits the bit width size to avoid wasted bits being processed and routed for each operation.

The rate at which individual instructions can be processed is as important as word size. Here too, microprocessors approach, and sometimes exceed, the processing rate of their larger mainframe and minicomputer relatives. The execution speed of a CPU is measured in millions of instructions per second (MIPs). The approximately 2 to 5 MIPs performance rate of current 32-bit microprocessors is equivalent to that of a mainframe. Today's 32-bit

7

microprocessors truly provide a mainframe on a chip, or "maxicomputing in microspace" capability.

1.2 Buses

The functional units within a computer system are physically interconnected using address, data, and control buses. A bus is simply a set of parallel wires or conductors used to connect two or more devices. Except for propagation delays, all devices on the bus receive the same signals at the same time. The number of lines in a bus is called the *bus width*. For example, a 32-bit bus consists of 32 separate lines and can transmit 32 bits at a time. In this case, the bus width, or size, is said to be 32 bits.

Data Bus

The data bus carries data between units. A 32-bit data bus consists of 32 lines capable of simultaneously transmitting 32 bits of data in parallel. The size of the data bus generally defines the external word size of the computer and usually is the same as the internal word size of the microprocessor. The AT&T, Intel, and Motorola 32-bit microprocessors have 32-bit data buses and internal word sizes of 32 bits.

Figure 1-3a illustrates a microprocessor with a 32-bit data bus. All 32 individual data lines are shown. A data bus is usually illustrated graphically using the more compact forms given in Figures 1-3b and 1-3c.

The arrows in Figure 1-3 indicate that the data bus is *bidirectional*. All data, regardless of the bus width, are received and sent using the same bus. The process of sending data from the microprocessor to another device is called a write operation; the process of receiving data is called a read operation. Bidirectional data bus operation requires at least one microprocessor control line to set the direction of operation for the data bus (read or write). For example, both the AT&T *WE* 32100 Microprocessor and the MOTOROLA MC68020 Microprocessor have a control line labeled $R/\overline{W}$ that establishes a write operation (output direction) when at a low logic (0) state, and a read operation (input direction) when at a high logic (1) state.

Data transmitted on the data bus are always ordered to form a binary number. For example, the INTEL 80386 and MOTOROLA MC68020 Microprocessor data pins are labeled D0 through D31, where the least significant bit (LSB) of the binary word is transmitted on D0 and the most significant bit (MSB) is transmitted on D31. The data pins on the AT&T *WE* 32100 Microprocessor are labeled DATA00 through DATA31, where DATA00 represents the LSB and DATA31 the MSB.

Address Bus

The address bus carries addresses from the microprocessor to all other devices connected to it. When a separate address bus is present, the bus is a single-direction (unidirectional) output bus. Many 16-bit microprocessors use the same bus lines for both data and addresses. In this situation, the bus is configured for output-only operation when addresses are transmitted and for the appropriate input or output operation when data is handled. The INTEL 8086 CPU is typical of these processors.

The size of the address bus defines the *physical address space* of the microprocessor. Since each individual address bus line can be at either a high (1) or a low (0) state, a bus consisting of 32 lines can address 2^{32} unique locations.

FIGURE 1-3   Data Bus Representations

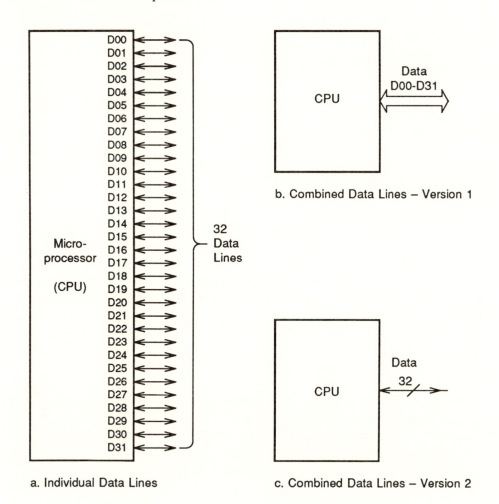

a. Individual Data Lines

b. Combined Data Lines – Version 1

c. Combined Data Lines – Version 2

This includes all binary addresses from

$$\text{MSB} \Rightarrow 00000000000000000000000000000000 \Leftarrow \text{LSB}$$
$$\text{to}$$
$$\text{MSB} \Rightarrow 11111111111111111111111111111111 \Leftarrow \text{LSB}$$

In the hexadecimal number system, these addresses are represented as 00000000 to FFFFFFFF inclusive, where 00000000 is the lowest address and FFFFFFFF is the highest. Each individual address in the range is unique and can refer to a single location, either in memory or to another device connected to the address bus. The physical address space defined by this address range is 4,294,967,296 locations (2^{32}).

The three microprocessors considered in this book have full 32-bit address buses. As each address refers to an individual byte location these microprocessors are said to be byte-addressable machines.

Address bits transmitted on the address bus are always ordered to form a positive integer. For example, the address pins of the MOTOROLA MC68020 CPU are labeled A0 through A31, where the least significant bit (LSB) of the binary address is transmitted on A0 and the most significant bit (MSB) is transmitted on A31. The address pins on the AT&T *WE* 32100 CPU are labeled ADDR00 through ADDR31, where ADDR00 represents the LSB and ADDR31 the MSB of the transmitted address. The INTEL 80386 CPU uses a slightly different arrangement of address lines, and is described in detail in the next chapter.

Control Bus

The control bus transmits the control, status, and power signals required to synchronize the operation of the microprocessor with the devices connected to it. A typical 8-bit microprocessor might require approximately one dozen control lines for proper operation; a 32-bit microprocessor usually requires thirty or more control lines. This increase in the number of required control lines reflects the added complexity and increased capabilities provided by 32-bit microprocessors.

The control signals and their functions make evident the variability among the microprocessors. Although each 32-bit microprocessor performs similar functions, the signal names used by their respective manufacturers can differ greatly. Nevertheless, certain control functions are common to most microprocessors considered, regardless of the name given to the control signal. For example, the three 32-bit microprocessors considered have control signals that indicate the size of the data being transmitted on the data bus, and also have a read/write control signal that defines the direction of data transfer. Additionally, the three microprocessors have control signals to request and acknowledge interrupts, and to provide direct memory access (DMA) for external I/O devices without processor intervention. In general, most of these control signals are also required for 8-bit and 16-bit microprocessors.

Unlike 8-bit and 16-bit microprocessors, the 32-bit microprocessors also provide extensive support for operating systems, development systems, bus arbitration, and bus exceptions. For example, all the 32-bit microprocessors have features directly supporting advanced multiuser and multitasking operating system requirements, such as task-switching and privilege levels, to control access between tasks. These processors also support some form of memory management and have interfaces to dedicated numerical coprocessors. Due to their increased complexity, these microprocessors require efficient development systems. Additional capabilities and features, such as caches and pipelining, demand their own control signals. All the signals needed to manage these are transmitted on the control bus.

Single Bus Architectures

Prior to the introduction of the Digital Equipment Corporation (DEC) PDP-11 Minicomputer in 1974, each unit in a computer had its own individual set of buses to connect it to the other units in the system. With the introduction of the PDP-11 Minicomputer, the concept of using a single bus to interconnect all of the units in the computer system was introduced. The PDP-11 UNIBUS Bus consisted of a series of fifty-six wires separated into three distinct groups - an address group, a data group, and a control group. What made the UNIBUS Bus special was that all units in the computer were connected to the same bus and all the individual buses that previously ran between communicating units were eliminated. Each unit on the bus was assigned a unique address (or set of addresses), and only responded if the correct address was present on the address section of the bus.

Each unit attached to the bus could be switched on or off. In addition, each unit had a third state that allowed it to be physically on when the unit was not being addressed, but to not affect the bus in any way. This third state was a high-impedance state that effectively prevented the unit from drawing any current from the bus, thereby significantly reducing the loading on the bus. Devices used in the units that could switch to this third state were called tristate devices. Tristate devices were essential to the single bus concept. They assured that bus signals were not affected by devices that were simply attached to the bus. Figure 1-4 illustrates the PDP-11 UNIBUS Bus architecture.

The UNIBUS Bus concept firmly established the importance of the central processing unit (CPU) as the dominant element in a computer system. Communication between any two units on the UNIBUS Bus was on a master/slave or handshaking basis, where the CPU was the master device that controlled access to the bus. Each control signal issued by the CPU had to be acknowledged by a response from the designated slave device for a complete transfer of data. This type of communication between devices is called asynchronous data transfer. Asynchronous means that the time interval between data transfers is variable, and the signal to start one operation is provided by a signal designating the completion of a previous operation.

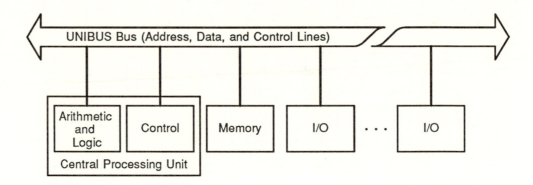

FIGURE 1-4   The UNIBUS Bus — Unique Feature of the DEC PDP-11 Minicomputer

Although the operation of most current CPUs is synchronous, which means that an operation starts as the result of a signal generated by a clock, the UNIBUS Bus firmly established the commercial usefulness of a single bus to which all devices could be connected. Since the introduction of the UNIBUS Bus, different bus standards have evolved (General Purpose Interface Bus, VMEbus, etc.), but all these have adhered to the concept of a single uniform bus which connects to many devices.

Microprocessors and Microcomputers

The evolution to a standard microcomputer bus architecture was a small step from the unified bus introduced by the DEC PDP-11 Minicomputer. This basic microcomputer bus structure is illustrated in Figure 1-5. Although slight variations of this model exist, these variations are easily understood within the context of the basic model. Viewed as a computer, the architecture of a microcomputer must still contain the same functional elements illustrated in Figure 1-2. A close comparison of these two figures shows this to be the case.

The CPU illustrated in Figure 1-5 is, of course, a microprocessor IC. The data, address, and control buses are variations of their respective data, address, and control lines on the UNIBUS Bus. Like the original UNIBUS Bus, each of these buses presents a set of standard electrical characteristics to which different devices (VLSI chips) can be connected. Since the crystal controlling the microprocessor's clock circuitry is manufactured from a quartz material, it is not on the silicon microprocessor chip. The crystal is a separate unit; however, for convenience it is not shown as such in Figure 1-5.

Any system that incorporates the structure illustrated in Figure 1-5, regardless of manufacturer, is classified as a microcomputer. A microcomputer is a computer that has a microprocessor as its central processing unit. The term "microcomputer," however, does not infer that the system is a general-purpose, programmable computer. Depending on the I/O peripherals and software used, a microcomputer

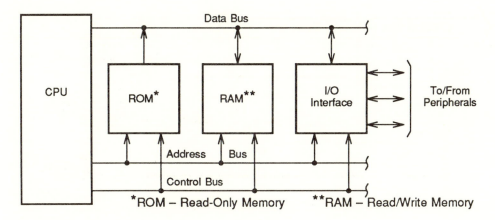

FIGURE 1-5   Basic Microcomputer Architecture

can be either a general purpose computer or a dedicated control unit. This apparent dual nature of the same system is clarified by considering Figure 1-6.

Figure 1-6 shows the distinction between the I/O interface units that are an integral part of a microcomputer and the I/O peripherals that are connected to these interface units. In Figure 1-6a, a keyboard and cathode ray tube (CRT) screen have been connected to the basic microcomputer system. This combination, with the appropriate software support, results in a general-purpose desktop computer.

In Figure 1-6b, the input unit is a keypad and the output unit is an eight-digit, seven-segment light emitting diode (LED) display. With the appropriate software, the resulting system is a handheld calculator. To a digital circuit designer, the microcomputer in this example is really a specialized logic circuit.

The input unit in Figure 1-6c is a temperature sensing thermistor; the output unit is an LED display. When the appropriate software is used, this system becomes an electronic thermometer in which the microcomputer performs a dedicated logic function.

Depending on the I/O peripherals and software used with the microcomputer, the same functional units can be configured as either a general-purpose programmable computer, or as a programmed digital circuit for process control and dedicated applications.

Support Devices and Coprocessors

An advantage to the configuration in Figure 1-6 is that the CPU, memory, and I/O units can be purchased as off-the-shelf components. These can be mounted on a motherboard or on printed circuit boards that are plugged into a backplane containing the system bus structure. Any device having the required electrical characteristics can be connected to the bus for each bus structure. (Each manufacturer has its own standards.)

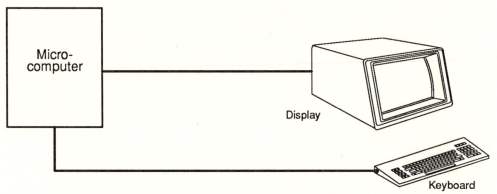

a. General-Purpose Desktop Computer

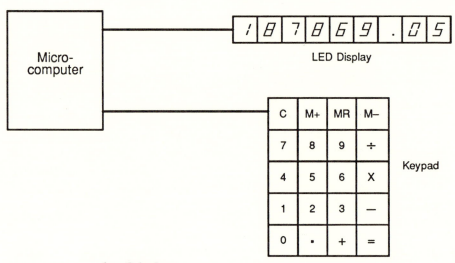

b. Calculator

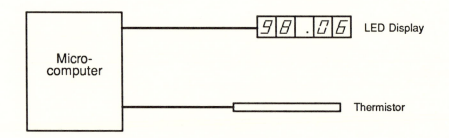

c. Electronic Thermometer

FIGURE 1-6 Microprocessor Applications

More typical is the situation where the other VLSI devices connected to the system buses are sophisticated peripheral chips that perform specialized tasks for the CPU. These include memory management units (MMUs), math accelerator units (MAUs) that perform floating-point arithmetic operations, direct memory access controllers (DMACs), and dynamic random access memory controllers (DRAMCs). The MAU is referred to as a coprocessor because it has its own instruction set. These devices perform specific tasks for the CPU without direct CPU intervention. The elimination of CPU involvement results in increased system performance.

Signal Groups

The AT&T, Intel, and Motorola 32-bit microprocessors have true 32-bit address and 32-bit data buses. These devices have 32 address and 32 data pins, with the remaining pins on the package dedicated to control, timing (clock), power, and ground signals. Figures 1-7 through 1-9 illustrate the functional signal groups provided by each of these microprocessors. As shown, all three microprocessors have clearly identifiable 32-bit data buses. The AT&T and Motorola microprocessors have clearly identified 32-bit address buses. The Intel microprocessor has byte-enable signals ($\overline{BE0}$ through $\overline{BE3}$) that are used to specify the physical size (1, 2, 3, or 4 bytes) of the addressed operand.

Reviewing Figures 1-7 through 1-9 reveals that all three microprocessors have the same basic functional control signals. For example, they have bus arbitration, bus exception, interrupt, and clock signals. In addition, these microprocessors have signals that define the bus cycle operation (read memory, write memory, etc.). These signals for the AT&T, Intel, and Motorola devices are named access status, bus cycle definition, and asynchronous bus control, respectively.

The total number of signals used by each microprocessor is:

AT&T *WE* 32100 Microprocessor   125 signals
INTEL 80386 Microprocessor   124 signals
MOTOROLA MC68020 Microprocessor   114 signals

1.3 Packaging

Since the introduction of the first SSI chips in the early 1960s, packaging for these chips has been continually modified to allow more pins to be accommodated in a given amount of space.

The dual in-line package (DIP), one of the earliest IC packages, accounts for approximately 80% of all ICs sold. As illustrated in Figure 1-10, DIPs consist of either a plastic or ceramic body with plated metal pins on each side of the package.

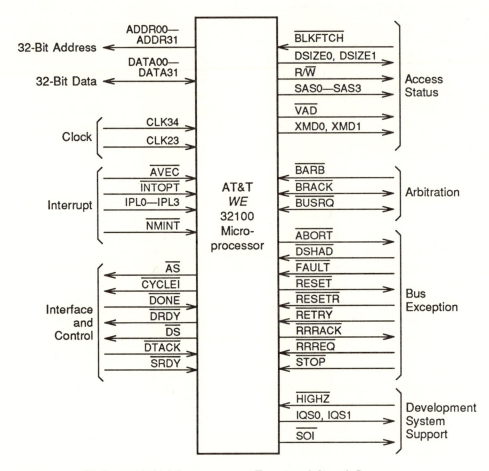

FIGURE 1-7   AT&T *WE* 32100 Microprocessor Functional Signal Groups

The integrated circuit resides in a cavity in the middle of the body of the package. Fine gold wire is used to connect the chip's connection pads to the pins on the DIP.

The placement of the pins on the sides of the DIP results in an inherent restriction of the number of pins that can be provided without making the package unduly large. A maximum of 64 external pins can be provided on a DIP. For gating circuits (NAND and NOR), line drivers, and buffer ICs that require 64 or less leads, this pin limit on DIPs presents no restriction. A 32-bit microprocessor requires 64 pins alone for its address and data buses, making the 64-pin package unsuitable.

In 1975, the Joint Electronic Device Engineering Council (JEDEC) approved a standard leadless ceramic chip carrier (LCCC) package. A chip carrier (see Figure 1-11) is essentially a modified version of the sealed chip cavity portion of a DIP.

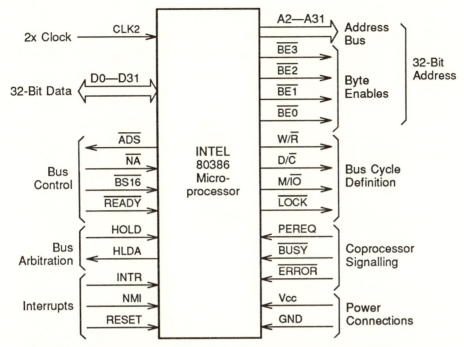

FIGURE 1-8 INTEL 80386 Microprocessor Functional Signal Groups

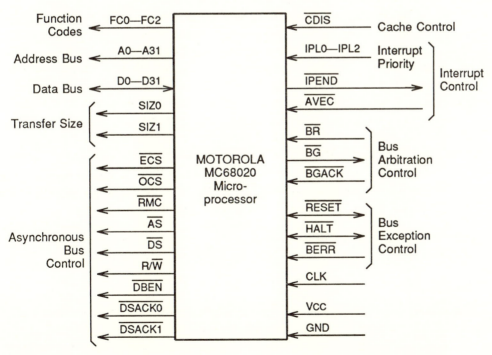

FIGURE 1-9 MOTOROLA MC68020 Microprocessor Functional Signal Groups

The gold wires that would normally connect the chip to the pins on the DIP now go directly to flush contact pads located on the four sides of the package.

As its name implies, the leadless chip carrier has no external pins. The package itself is flush-mounted in a socket and secured by the tension provided by the socket's contacts. These packages are ideal for testing ICs, where quick mounting and removal from the test fixture is required. The LCCC provides a signal count on an order of magnitude greater than twice that of a DIP. The LCCC packaging concept was extended to include a leaded version implemented in either plastic or ceramic (see Figure 1-11).

The chip carrier package was soon followed by a pin grid array (PGA) package (see Figure 1-12). Using a typical square package size of 1.35 inches and a spacing of 0.1 inches (2.54 millimeters) between pin centers, the PGA package can accommodate a maximum of 258 pins. The PGA package has become the de facto packaging standard for 32-bit microprocessors.

1.4 Timing Conventions

Understanding the hardware interactions of a microprocessor requires knowledge of the operation and timing of the signals used by the microprocessor. Some signals are active (true) at a high logic level; some are active at a low logic level. To avoid confusion, the term *asserted* is used to indicate that a signal is driven to its active state, independent of whether this state is a high or low level. Similarly, the terms *nonasserted* or *negated* indicate a signal is in the inactive (false) state. Active-low signals are designated or flagged in the manufacturer's documentation either by a bar over the signal name or by a pound symbol (#). For consistency, signals throughout this textbook that are asserted by a low logic level are flagged using a bar over the signal name. For example, the INTEL 80386 CPU $\overline{ADS}$ signal is active low. In this case, asserting this signal drives it to its logical low state. For positive logic circuits, a nonflagged signal is asserted using a high voltage level, and negated by a low voltage. Similarly, a flagged signal is asserted by a low voltage and negated by a high voltage. The opposite voltage levels are required for the assertion states for negative logic circuits.

The terms, definitions, and standards adopted by the Institute of Electrical and Electronic Engineers (IEEE) are used throughout this textbook except in those cases where they conflict with the manufacturer's documentation.

Timing Signals

Different graphical symbolism is used to represent the high, low, and high-impedance logic states that can occur. Signals can also be shown to be in a valid or an undetermined state. Figure 1-13 shows the symbols used to express these logic states.

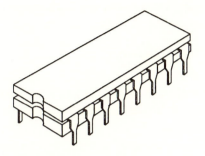

Plastic Package — Exterior

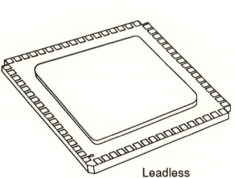

Plastic Package — Interior

FIGURE 1-10 Typical DIP (16-Pin Plastic)

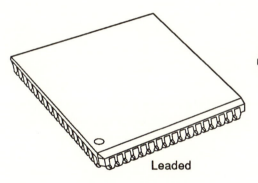

Leaded

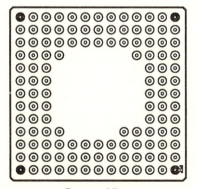

Leadless

FIGURE 1-11 Typical Chip Carrier Packages

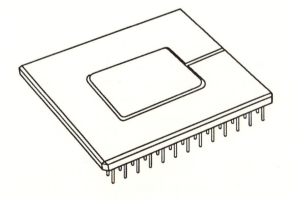

Bottom View

FIGURE 1-12   Typical 125-Pin PGA Package

Transitions from one state to another are shown by connecting the levels indicating previous and current states with a sloped line. This sloped connecting line represents the finite, nonzero, transition time that occurs from one state to the next. Figure 1-14 illustrates the transition from a low to a high to a high-impedance state; Figure 1-15 shows the transition from a high state to a don't care state.

Transition times that vary or are unimportant are shown using a series of parallel transition lines as illustrated in Figure 1-16. These transition lines always correspond to the region in which the transition may occur.

Timing Definitions

Five transition symbols are used by the IEEE to indicate the changes or transitions of a signal from its initial state to its final state:

Symbol	Indication
H	transition to a high logic level
L	transition to a low logic level
V	transition to a valid, steady-state level
X	transition to an unknown, changing, or don't care level
Z	transition to a high-impedance state.

The measurement of elapsed time between a transition on one pin and a transition on another pin, or transitions on the same pin, is designated using the notation

$$tAwCy$$

where:

t   indicates time

A   is the name of the signal used as the reference to mark the beginning of the specified time interval. The signal name generally should not exceed five characters; typically, it is two or three characters long.

w   designates the type of transition used for the reference signal. It must be one of the five transition symbols (H, L, V, X, or Z) followed by no more than one number.

C   is the name of a signal used to mark the end of the specified time interval. This signal name generally should not exceed five characters; it is frequently limited to two or three characters.

y   designates the type of transition used to mark the end of the specified time interval. It must be one of the five transition symbols (H, L, V, X, or Z) followed by no more than one number.

For example, the notation tSIHREL refers to the time interval that starts when signal SI goes to its high state and ends when signal RE goes to its low state. Similarly, the term tSILREH represents the interval of time from SI going low to RE going high. Figure 1-17 illustrates how these two signals and the time intervals between them might appear on a typical manufacturer's data sheet. Actual signal

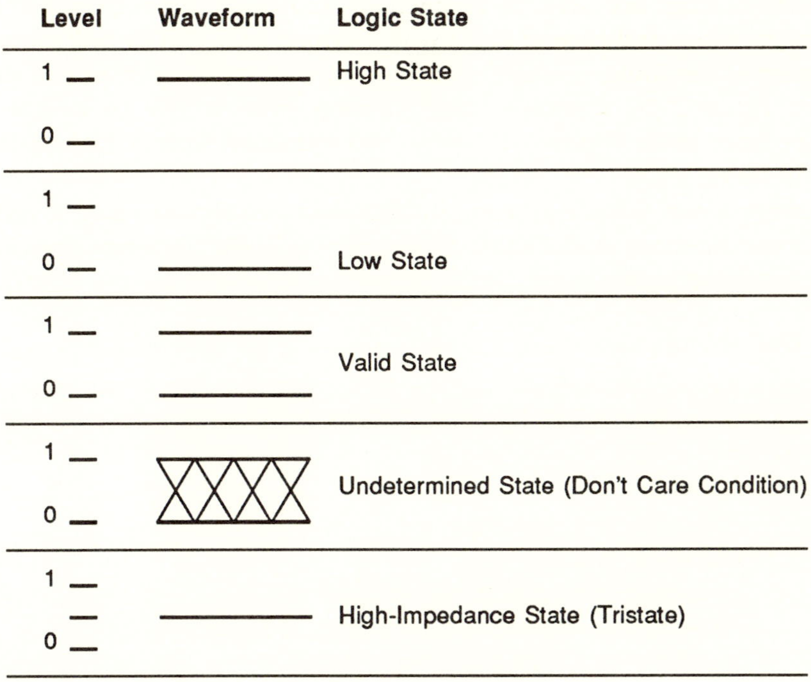

Level	Waveform	Logic State
1 — 0 —	————————	High State
1 — 0 —	————————	Low State
1 — 0 —	———————— ————————	Valid State
1 — 0 —	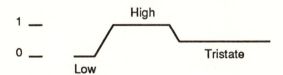	Undetermined State (Don't Care Condition)
1 — — 0 —	————————	High-Impedance State (Tristate)

FIGURE 1-13   Graphical Representation of Logic States

```
      High
1 _    ___
      /   \
0 _ _/     _____
  Low        Tristate
```

FIGURE 1-14   Transitions From Low to High to High-Impedance State

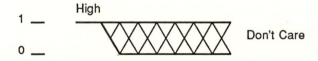

FIGURE 1-15   Transition From High to Don't Care Condition

FIGURE 1-16   A Variable High-to-Low Transition Time

names, such as SI for strobe input and RE for read enable, are usually selected either by the circuit designer or designated by the manufacturer according to accepted industry conventions. These names are meant to convey information about the type of signal being used. For example, the terms ADDR, ADD, or A are typically used for address signals, and the terms DAT, DD, or D are used for data signals. The reference points used for the transitions shown on Figure 1-17 are the 50% points. In general, transition reference points may be any two points on the waveform as long as they are clearly indicated on the waveform diagram. Other commonly used references are the 10% point and 90% point.

Standard Time Intervals

The timing notation introduced can be used to describe any time interval between two signal waveforms. Certain standard timing intervals, such as delay, set-up, hold, access, and cycle times, are common to all microprocessor-based systems. A description of these conventional timing intervals follows.

Delay Time: The time interval between a reference point on one waveform and a reference point on another waveform.

For example, time intervals tSIHREL and tSILREH in Figure 1-17 represent delay times. A delay time designation can be used as the designation for any time interval not described below.

When the delay time interval references the time delay between an input and subsequent output waveform, the delay time is referred to as a propagation delay time. For example, if SI represented the input to a circuit and RE the output of the same circuit, the delay times illustrated in Figure 1-17 would be propagation delay times.

Set-Up Time: The time interval between the application of a signal at one input and a subsequent active transition at another input.

Figure 1-18 illustrates the set-up time interval for the data lines of an AT&T WE 32100 Microprocessor. Interval tDATVC34H refers to the time between the transition of valid data being applied to the data lines and the transition of the CLK34 line going high. Prior to data being placed on the individual data lines, the data lines are tristated. This is denoted by the line drawn between the high

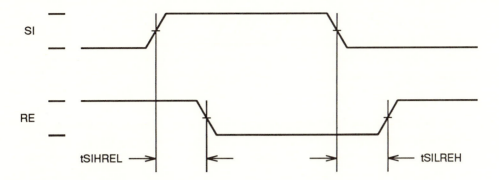

FIGURE 1-17 Timing Notations

and low levels. The 32 individual data lines are represented by the notation
DAT00-DAT31. The first transition for these lines represents a transition from the
tristate condition to valid data being on the 32 individual lines. Since each
individual data line can be either high or low, the term *valid* within the diagram
signifies that each line is at a state (high or low) representing an actual valid bit
of data. The final transition for these lines represents a transition from valid data
to a don't care state. Any data on the lines within the don't care time frame
(indicated by crosshatching) are ignored by the system.

Hold Time: The time interval during which a signal must be retained after an
active transition occurs at another input signal.

Figure 1-19 illustrates the hold time required for data placed on the data bus
after the $\overline{\text{WRITE}}$ signal is negated (goes high).

Access Time: The time interval between the application of an input signal and
the availability of valid data at an output.

FIGURE 1-18 Sample Set-Up Time Between Two Input Signals

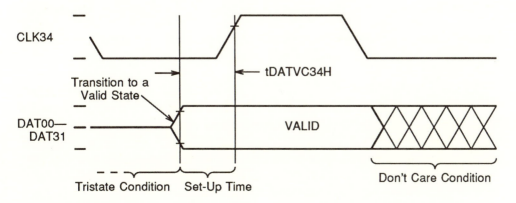

Figure 1-20 illustrates the access time, tADDVDATV, between a valid address being available on address lines ADD00-ADD31 and valid data being available on data lines DAT00-DAT31. Access times can be referenced from a variety of signals. For example, the time interval between a chip-enable signal to the availability of valid data from the chip represents an access time.

Cycle Time: The time interval between an input transition and the next occurrence of the same transition.

All microprocessors define a memory read and memory write cycle. Other cycles may also be defined.

Pulse Width: The time interval between specified reference points on two transitions of a waveform (also referred to as pulse duration).

Figure 1-21 illustrates the pulse widths for a clock signal. The waveform shown is symmetrical; the symmetry requirements depend on the microprocessor being used.

In addition to the time intervals defined, many other time intervals are needed to describe circuits using microprocessors. These additional time intervals include enable, disable, precharge, recovery, and refresh times. These additional time intervals will be introduced in the context of specific examples as we explore various microprocessors.

Timing Reference Points

Waveform transitions are always measured from clearly defined voltage levels. For example, the levels 1.5 volts or (VDD – 1.0) volts represent valid reference voltages.

Often it is necessary to define more than one timing point on a single waveform. When this occurs, numbers are used to designate the respective points. For example, Figure 1-22 illustrates the use of numbers to designate rise and fall time intervals. In general, the number 1 is used to designate a point at or near the low-level logic state defined for the device and a 2 is used to designate the high-level logic state.

1.5 Microprocessor Timing and Clock Signals

All microprocessors require a central clock or timing signal for proper operation. Typically, the clock signal is either a single-phase or multiphase signal that is provided by a separate LSI circuit. For example, AT&T provides a *WE* 32102 Clock for its *WE* 32100 Microprocessor, Intel provides an 82384

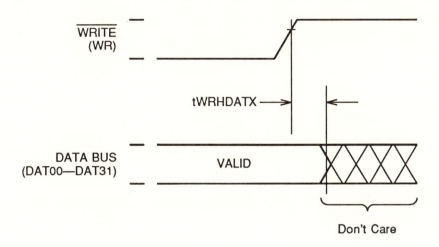

FIGURE 1-19   Data Hold Time

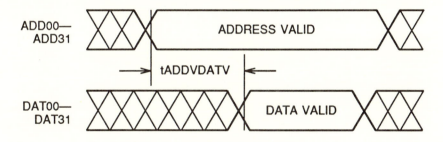

FIGURE 1-20   Access Time from a Valid Address State

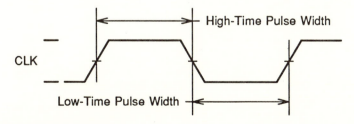

FIGURE 1-21   Pulse Width Illustration

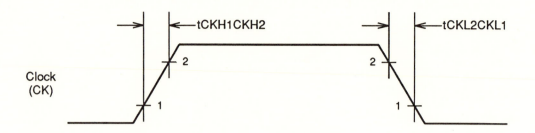

FIGURE 1-22 Using Numbers for Multiple Reference Points

Clock Generator chip for use with its 80386 microprocessor, and Motorola provides an MC68020RC16 clock for its MC68020 microprocessor.

The waveform(s) produced by the clock circuit are needed to provide timing for the flow of address, data, and control signals both internally to the microprocessor and externally between the microprocessor and the other devices connected to it.

The clock signal(s) required for each microprocessor is either a single-phase or multiphase signal. A single-phase signal consists of a single clock output, similar to that illustrated for the MOTOROLA MC68020 Microprocessor in Figure 1-23. Notice the Motorola clock waveform does not use the H and L transition designators. The clock period, rise and fall times, and pulse widths for this signal are listed in Table 1-1.

A multiphase clock signal consists of two or more periodic signals with a fixed phase difference between them. An example of this is the two-phase clock signal required by the AT&T *WE* 32100 Microprocessor, illustrated in Figure 1-24. Table 1-2 contains the timing specifications for Figure 1-24.

FIGURE 1-23 Motorola Single-Phase Clock

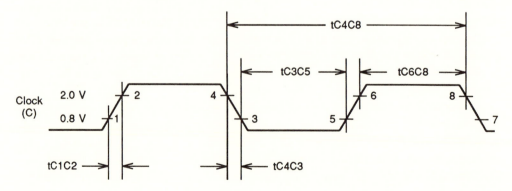

TABLE 1-1 MOTOROLA MC68020 CPU Clock Specifications (see Figure 1-23)

Characteristic	Symbol	Min. Value	Max. Value
Period	tC4C8	60 ns	125 ns
Pulse Width	tC3C5	24 ns	95 ns
Pulse Width	tC6C8	24 ns	95 ns
Rise Time	tC1C2	-	5 ns
Fall Time	tC4C3	-	5 ns

Note: All timing measurements are referenced from a low voltage of 0.8 volt and a high voltage of 2.0 volts.

The addition of a second clock signal may appear to complicate the timing; but, in fact, the reverse is true. The second timing signal provides two additional timing reference points (the rising and falling edges of the second signal) plus a reference consisting of the relative timing difference between the two clock signals. These provide sufficient reference points to synchronize the various data transfers required in a microcomputer system. The INTEL 80386 Microprocessor needs only a single-phase clock input since it derives its second clock from this input. Intel also has an 82384 clock generator, a two-phase clock source, that provides both signals directly.

Bus Cycles

Communication between a microprocessor and another device is always completed within a bus cycle. Although the time required for a bus cycle can vary depending on the type of data transfer occurring, a bus cycle always begins with the initiation of a request for data and ends when the data transfer has been completed. For example, fetching an instruction from memory requires one bus cycle, and storing the result of an instruction into memory requires another bus cycle. Although the time to complete these two different types of data transfer is different, each cycle involves the microprocessor's address bus, data bus, and various control signals required for the data transfer.

The prevalent transfer of information between a microprocessor and memory requires manufacturers to specify the timing requirements for memory read and write operations. A CPU memory read cycle refers to a bus cycle initiated by the microprocessor that results in data being read from a memory device. As illustrated in Figure 1-25, a read cycle occurs when the CPU places a valid address on the address bus and asserts the required control signals. It is then the responsibility of the memory unit to decode the address, place the referenced

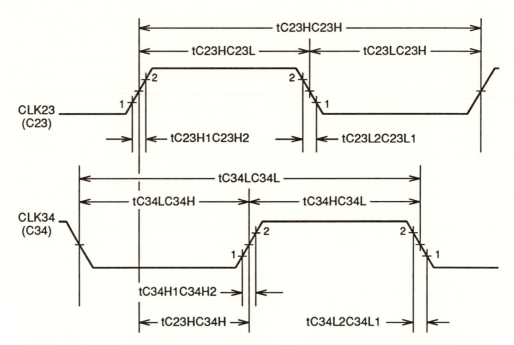

FIGURE 1-24   Two-Phase Clock Signals Required by AT&T *WE* 32100 Microprocessor

TABLE 1-2 AT&T *WE* 32100 CPU Clock Specifications (see Figure 1-24)

Characteristic	Symbol	Min.	Nominal	Max.
Period				
Clock 23	tC23HC23H	-	-	55.6 ns
Clock 34	tC34LC34L	-	-	55.6 ns
Pulse Widths				
Clock 23 High Width	tC23HC23L	26.1	27.8	29.5 ns
Clock 34 High Width	tC34HC34L	26.1	27.8	29.5 ns
Clock 23 Low Width	tC23LC23H	26.1	27.8	29.5 ns
Clock 34 Low Width	tC34LC34H	26.1	27.8	29.5 ns
System Clock				
Clock 23 Rise Time	tC23H1C23H2	-	-	4 ns
Clock 34 Rise Time	tC34H1C34H2	-	-	4 ns
Clock 23 Fall Time	tC23L2C23L1	-	-	4 ns
Clock 34 Fall Time	tC34L2C34L1	-	-	4 ns
Phase Difference	tC23HC34H	11.9	13.9	15.9 ns

data on the data bus, and assert any required acknowledge signals. To complete the read bus cycle, the CPU must acquire the data on the data bus and then negate all previously asserted control signals. Finally, the memory unit terminates the cycle by removing the data from the data bus and negates any of its previously asserted control signals. Table 1-3 summarizes the read cycle transactions for a microprocessor system with a memory unit consisting of decoders, control circuitry, and memory devices.

Figure 1-25 illustrates the timing for a simplified CPU memory read cycle. It assumes that a single read control signal, R/$\overline{W}$, is used by the microprocessor to initiate a read request, and that a single data ready control signal, READY, is used to inform the microprocessor that data is available on the data bus. Although 32-bit microprocessors require considerably more control signals than shown for the initiation, acknowledgment, and termination of a read cycle, the timing shown in Figure 1-25 does illustrate the five timing intervals required to understand 32-bit CPU memory cycles. These are:

Address Set-Up Time: The time required by the CPU to place a valid address on the address bus, referenced to either a clock or control signal.

FIGURE 1-25   Basic Read Cycle Timing

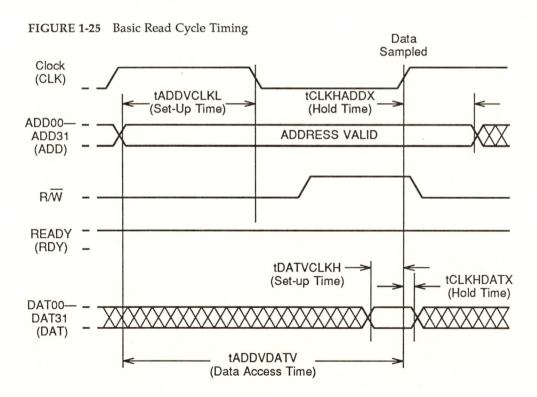

29

TABLE 1-3 Typical CPU Memory Read Cycle Transactions

Step 1. Microprocessor addresses memory.
CPU places an address on the address bus.
CPU asserts the required read control signal(s).
Step 2. Memory responds to the address on the address bus.
a. Memory unit decodes the address.
b. Memory unit places the data on the data bus.
c. Memory unit asserts the required acknowledge signal(s).
Step 3. Microprocessor acquires the data on the data bus.
a. CPU latches the data.
b. CPU negates its previously asserted control signal(s).
Step 4. Memory terminates the read cycle.
a. Memory unit removes the data from the data bus.
b. Memory unit negates its previously asserted control signal(s).

Address Hold Time: The time the address must remain on the address bus; referenced to either a clock or control signal.

Data Set-Up Time: The time required by the memory unit to supply stable and valid data on the data bus before the data is to be sampled by the CPU.

Data Access Time: The time after a valid address has been placed on the address bus to the time that the data on the data bus is latched into the CPU.

Data Hold Time: The time the data must remain on the data bus after it has been sampled by the CPU.

TABLE 1-4 Typical Read Cycle Timing for a 16 MHz 32-bit CPU (see Figure 1-25)

Symbol	Description	Typical Value
tADDVCLKL	Address set-up time	17 ns
tCLKHADDX	Address hold time	15 ns
tDATVCLKH	Data set-up time	12 ns
tCLKHDATX	Data hold time	7 ns
tADDVDATV	Data access time	150 ns

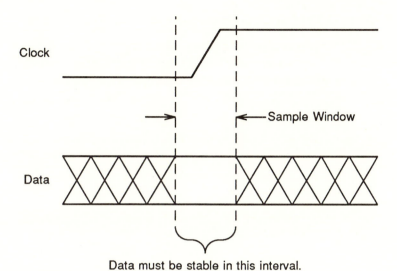

FIGURE 1-26   A Sample Window

Table 1-4 contains read cycle times for a typical 32-bit microprocessor operating at 16 MHz.

The ready signal in Figure 1-25 is used by the memory interface circuitry to alert the CPU that the data is not available on the data bus. Negating this signal causes the CPU to go into an idle condition, or wait state, preventing the CPU from sampling the data lines until the ready signal is asserted. All microprocessors have a signal that is used to introduce wait states if memory cannot respond within the required data access time.

Data acceptance during a CPU read cycle is typical of all inputs accepted by a microprocessor. Each input signal presented to the microprocessor is latched into the processor during a time interval called the sample window. Figure 1-26 illustrates a sample window during which data is latched on the rising edge of a clock signal. During the sample window, all signal levels being sampled must be held stable. Any signals that change during the sample window will be resolved by the processor as either a high or low logic state, but the actual level accepted will be unpredictable.

A CPU memory write cycle is similar to a memory read cycle, except that data is written to memory rather than read from memory. As stated in Table 1-5, a write cycle occurs when the CPU places a valid address on the address bus and asserts the required control signals. In this case, however, the CPU also places valid data on the the data bus. The memory unit must then decode the address, copy the data on the data bus into memory, and assert any required acknowledge signals. At the conclusion of the write cycle, the CPU removes the address, data, and control signals from the system and the memory unit negates its previously asserted signals.

TABLE 1-5 Typical CPU Memory Write Cycle Transactions

Step 1. Microprocessor addresses memory.
a. CPU places an address on the address bus.
b. CPU asserts the required write control signal(s).
c. CPU places the data on the bus.
Step 2. Memory responds to the address on the address bus.
a. Memory unit decodes the address.
b. Memory unit latches the data on the data bus.
c. Memory unit asserts the required acknowledge signal(s).
Step 3. Microprocessor terminates the data transfer.
a. CPU negates its previously asserted control signal(s).
b. The data is removed from the data bus.
Step 4. Memory unit terminates the write cycle.
The memory unit negates its previously asserted acknowledge signal(s).

1.6 Fabrication

The 32-bit microprocessors considered in this book are fabricated using a metal-oxide semiconductor (MOS) process. The basic fabrication model of a MOS device is illustrated in Figure 1-27. As shown, a basic MOS transistor consists of two n-type or p-type wells embedded in a silicon substrate of the opposite type. A p-type well is a region with a surplus of electrons, whereas an n-type well has a shortage of electrons relative to the silicon substrate material. MOS transistors with n-type wells are called NMOS transistors, and those constructed with p-type wells are called PMOS transistors.

Regardless of type, one well forms the source of the transistor and the other well the drain. The space between the two wells is called the channel. The width of the channel is an important parameter for chip designers. As the channel width is decreased, the number of transistors that can be manufactured on the same chip of silicon increases. Currently, channel widths are on the order of 1 micron. On top of the channel is an insulating material with a deposit of metal on its top surface. The metal layer forms the gate of the transistor.

In addition to PMOS and NMOS technologies, additional MOS technologies, such as complementary metal-oxide semiconductors (CMOS), high-performance

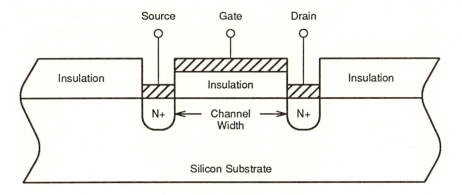

Basic NMOS Transistor Structure

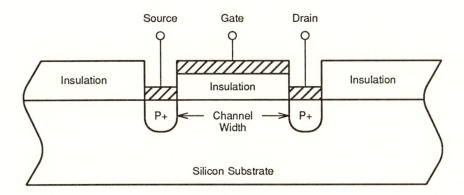

Basic PMOS Transistor Structure

FIGURE 1-27 Basic MOS Transistor Structure

MOS (HMOS), and a combination of these two technologies (CHMOS), are in current use. The technology used significantly influences the performance characteristics of the final device. Specifically, these characteristics include:

Gate Switching Speed: The speed at which the basic gate circuit can change its state. The higher the switching speed, the higher the overall operating frequency of the chip and the lower the overall propagation delay through the device as a whole. The speed is typically expressed in terms of the propagation delay, in nanoseconds, through the basic gate circuits used in the device.

Power Dissipation: The power dissipation determines the amount of heat generated by the device. The less heat that is dissipated, the more gates that can be contained in a given space without concern for heat build-up and its effect on system reliability. Power dissipation is measured in milliwatts.

Speed-Power Product: There is usually a direct relationship between the power dissipated by a gate circuit and its switching speed. Higher switching speeds (lower propagation delay) result in greater power dissipation. The speed-power product, measured in picojoules (nanoseconds times milliwatts) is obtained by multiplying the propagation delay with the power dissipation. This product provides a useful measure of overall gate speed and power dissipation.

Density: Device density is the number of transistors that can be accommodated in a given space. It is directly related to the channel width that can be manufactured and is measured by the number of gates that can be accommodated on a square millimeter of silicon substrate.

Noise Immunity (Margin): The noise immunity is the amount of noise, in the form of voltage levels, that can be tolerated before the transistor incorrectly interprets a logic level. High noise immunity is desirable.

Drive Capability (Fan-out): The ability of a transistor or gate circuit to provide current to drive a number of other gates connected to it. The fan-out is the precise number of gates that an output can drive. Transistors with high fan-outs (output drive capability) that require little input drive current are desirable.

Noise immunity and fan-out are discussed, and examples for different technologies are presented in Chapter Seven. Table 1-6 lists the typical values of propagation delay, gate power dissipation, speed-power product, and density associated with current fabrication technologies. While important to chip designers, such fabrication technology is not nearly as critical to system designers who are more concerned with the speed of the processor, device operating characteristics and timing, the instruction set provided, the number of general-purpose and special-purpose registers available, and other features that will increase overall system performance. These features depend on the technology used, but are fixed from the standpoint of the end-user. Equally important to a user are:

- quality of supplied documentation
- availability of support devices, development systems, development and application software, and technical support services.

TABLE 1-6 Comparison of Fabrication Technology Characteristics

Characteristic	NMOS	PMOS	CMOS	HMOS	Unit
Propagation Delay	20	60	25	4	nanoseconds
Power Dissipation	1	1.5	1	.6	milliwatts
Speed-Power Product	20	90	25	2.4	picojoules
Density	150	100	75	200	gates/sq. mm

1.7 Chapter Highlights

1. A *microprocessor* is a single-chip central processing unit (CPU) that provides arithmetic, logic, and control functions.

2. The number of bits that a microprocessor can process as a complete entity is referred to as its *word size*. The AT&T *WE* 32100 Microprocessor, MOTOROLA MC68020 Microprocessor, and INTEL 80386 Microprocessor have 32-bit word sizes.

3. The 32-bit word sizes present a current trade-off between speed and efficiency. Speed requires large word sizes for simultaneous multibit processing, while efficiency limits the word size to avoid transmitting and processing unused bits.

4. A *bus* consists of a set of parallel wires, or lines, that connect two or more devices. A data bus is bidirectional and carries or transmits data between devices. An address bus is unidirectional and carries address information. The control bus consists of a set of unidirectional lines for transmitting control signals between devices.

5. Current very large scale integrated (VLSI) technology permits hundreds of thousands of transistors to be manufactured on a single integrated circuit (IC) chip. VLSI is the latest step in the evolution of IC technology that started in the late 1960s with a small scale integrated (SSI) technology that provided 10 to 100 transistors per chip. Next came medium scale integrated (MSI) technology that yielded 100 to 1000 transistors per chip. This was followed by large scale integrated (LSI) technology with more than 1000 transistors per chip.

6. Package technology has evolved along with IC technology. The dual in-line package (DIP) still accounts for approximately 80% of all ICs sold. Current 32-bit microprocessors are housed in either leadless chip carriers, leaded chip carriers, or pin grid array (PGA) packages.

7. Time intervals between two signal waveforms can be defined using IEEE standard notation. In this notation, the time interval being defined begins with the lowercase letter t, followed by the name of the first reference signal, followed by a transition symbol, followed by the second reference signal and its transition symbol. Valid transitions are defined as transitions to the:
- high state (H)
- low state (L)
- valid state (V)
- don't care state (X)
- high-impedance state (Z).

For example, the notation tSIHREL designates the time interval between the SI signal going to a high state (H) and the RE signal going to a low state (L).

8. Address set-up, address hold, data set-up, data hold, and data access times refer to time intervals required by microprocessors to perform read or write operations. These intervals are defined as:

Address Set-Up Time: The time required by the microprocessor to place a valid address on the address bus relative to either a clock or control signal.

Address Hold Time: The time the address must remain on the address bus relative to either a clock or control signal.

Data Set-Up Time: The time required by the memory unit to supply stable and valid data on the data bus before it is sampled by the microprocessor.

Data Hold Time: The time the data must remain on the data bus after it has been sampled by the microprocessor.

Data Access Time: The time after a valid address has been placed on the address bus to the time that the data on the data bus is sampled by microprocessor.

Exercises

1a. List the functions that must be performed by a computer.
1b. List the functions that must be performed by a microprocessor.
1c. Describe the differences between a microprocessor and a microcomputer.

2a. Describe the differences between synchronous and asynchronous data transmission.
2b. Would synchronous or asynchronous operation be the logical choice for transmitting data between two devices, one of which can operate at a very high speed compared to the other? Why?
2c. Would synchronous or asynchronous operation be the logical choice for transmitting data between two devices, both of which operate at the same nominal speed? Why?

3. What do SSI, MSI, LSI, and VLSI mean? Describe the differences implied by these terms.

4. The 8-bit INTEL 8080 Microprocessor has 16 address lines. Determine the number of bytes that can be directly addressed by this microprocessor.

5. The 16-bit INTEL 8086 Microprocessor has 20 address lines, where each address can reference one byte in memory. Determine the number of bytes in memory that can be directly addressed by this microprocessor. To how many words of memory does this

correspond?

6. The 16-bit INTEL 80286 Microprocessor has 24 address lines, where each address can reference one byte of memory. Determine the number of bytes in memory that can be directly addressed by this microprocessor. To how many words of memory does this correspond?

7. The 32-bit INTEL 80386 Microprocessor has 32 address lines, where each address can reference one byte of memory. Determine the number of bytes in memory that can be directly addressed by this microprocessor. To how many words of memory does this correspond?

8. Obtain the data sheet for the MOTOROLA MC68020 Microprocessor, INTEL 80386 Microprocessor, or AT&T *WE* 32100 Microprocessor and verify the address, data, and control signals shown in Figures 1-9, 1-8, and 1-7, respectively. (The address of each of these manufacturers is listed in Appendix D.)

9. Figure 1-28 is a sample of a CPU read cycle timing diagram based on the AT&T *WE* 32100 Microprocessor. Using this figure, complete the table below by matching the numbered time intervals with the symbols listed. For example, the symbol tDATVC34H corresponds to interval number 16 on the figure.

Symbol	Numbered Interval	Symbol	Numbered Interval	Symbol	Numbered Interval
tDATVC34H	16	tDSHDATX		tC34HDRYH	
tC34HASL		tADDVASL		tASLADDV	
tC34HASH		tASHADDX		tC34HDSL	
tC34HDSH		tC34LCYCL		tC34LCYCH	
tC34HDATX		tSRYLC34L		tC34LSRYH	
tDTALC34H		tDSHDATH		tIPLVC23L	
tC34LADDV		tC23HADDZ		tC34LSASV	
tC34LDSZV		tDSHDATX		tC34HDRYL	

10. Figure 1-29 is a sample of a write cycle timing diagram based on the AT&T *WE* 32100 Microprocessor. For each of the numbered timing intervals shown, write the correct timing signal notation. For example, the notation for time interval 1 is tC34HDSL.

11a. Figure 1-30 is part of the read cycle timing diagram for an INTEL 80386 Microprocessor. Write correct timing signal notations for the waveforms shown.
11b. Figure 1-31 illustrates the typical relationship between address and write enable waveforms for a 32-bit microprocessor. Write correct timing signal notations for the waveforms shown.

12a. Which of the timing intervals illustrated on Figure 1-30 represents a data set-up time? Which represents a data hold time?

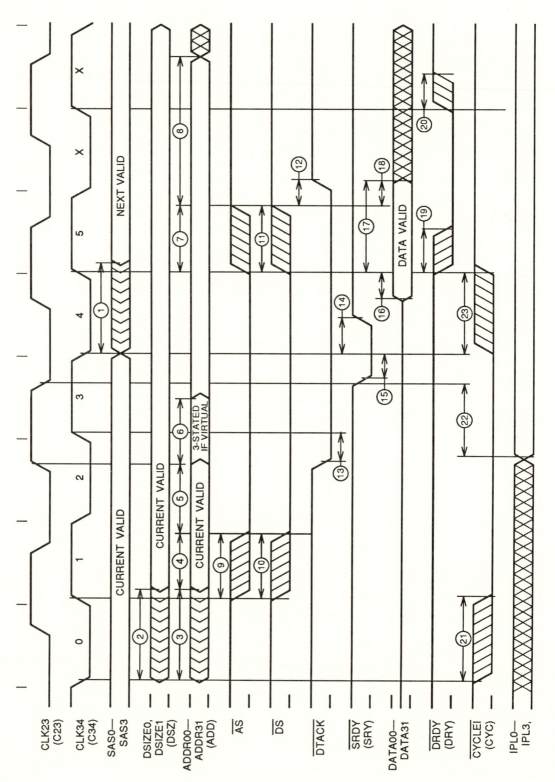

FIGURE 1-28 Sample CPU Read Cycle Timing Diagram

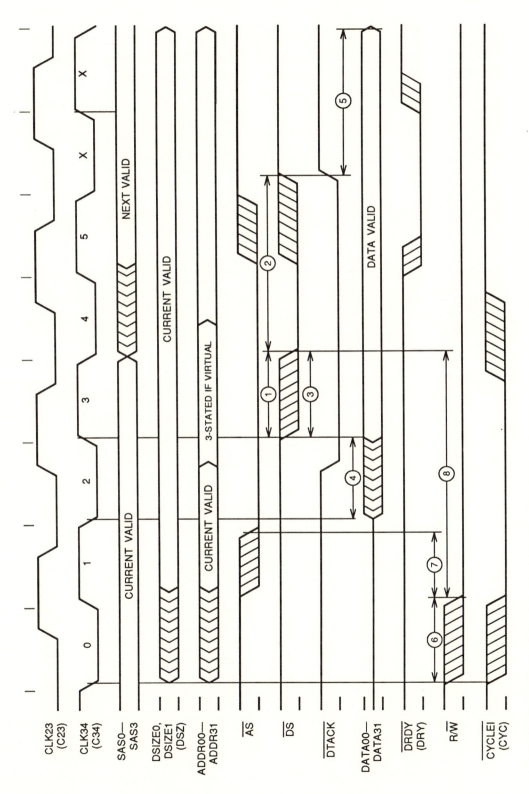

FIGURE 1-29 Sample CPU Write Cycle Timing Diagram

12b. Which of the timing intervals illustrated on Figure 1-31 represents an address set-up time? Which represents an address hold time?

13. Figure 1-32 illustrates two-phase clocking. Write the correct timing signal notation for each of the numbered time intervals shown.

14. Construct a timing diagram for the write bus cycle described in Table 1-5. Your timing diagram should be similar to the read cycle timing diagram illustrated in Figure 1-25.

FIGURE 1-30   Part of a Read Cycle

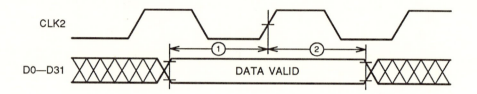

FIGURE 1-31   Address and Write Enable Relationship

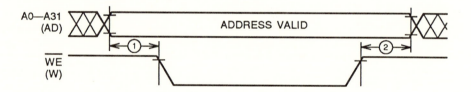

FIGURE 1-32   Two-Phase Clocking

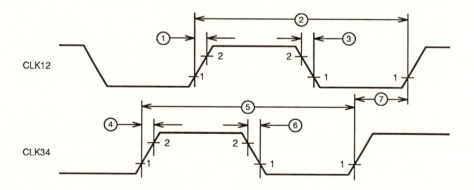

32-Bit Microprocessor Architectures

2.1 Basic CPU Operations and Capabilities
2.2 Register Sets
2.3 Memory Management Concepts
2.4 Memory Management Implementations
2.5 Chapter Highlights

The term microprocessor architecture refers to the structure or on-chip arrangement of the microprocessor's hardware components and the interactions between these components. In this chapter we introduce the on-chip hardware components common to most 32-bit microprocessors and the features these components support. The topics range from the basic components used to fetch, decode, and execute program instructions to the more advanced pipelining, multitasking, and memory management features. Subsequent chapters deal with the specific hardware implementations and software coding schemes used by the Intel, AT&T, and Motorola 32-bit microprocessors to realize these features.

2.1 Basic CPU Operations and Capabilities

The CPU performs and controls the fetching, decoding, and execution of instructions. These three operations, as shown in Figure 2-1, are done in a sequential manner for an individual instruction; that is, the next operation begins upon completion of the current one. Memory operands needed by the instruction are retrieved as part of the execution phase of the instruction.

Sequential instruction operation (fetch, decode, and execute) in which both the instructions and the required data are stored in the same memory unit was developed by the mathematician John Von Neumann in the 1940s. The architecture that implements this type of operation is referred to as a Von Neumann architecture. Figure 2-2 illustrates the basic internal units of current standard 32-bit microprocessors that implement this type of architecture. These units are the fetch, decode, execution, and bus interface units.

The *fetch unit* obtains the instructions and data to be used by the CPU. The operation of this unit is transparent to the user and provides features that enhance microprocessor performance significantly. One of these is the ability to fetch and store into the CPU the next instruction during the execution phase of the current instruction. This type of operation is called prefetching. The prefetching of

FIGURE 2-1   Sequential Fetch/Decode/Execute Operation

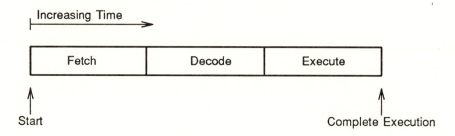

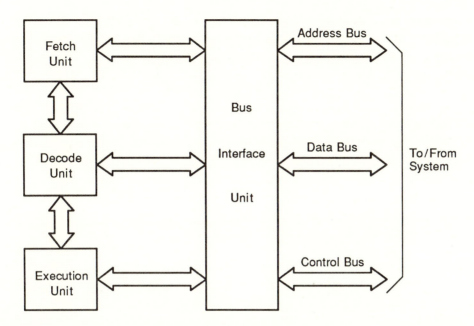

FIGURE 2-2   Typical Internal Units of a 32-Bit Microprocessor

instructions in parallel with the execution of another instruction is known as pipelining. Pipelining produces a significant increase in overall effective CPU processing speed when the next instruction to be executed is available in the prefetch storage area.

The *decode unit* deciphers the instructions from the prefetch storage area and prepares them for processing by the execution unit. Decode units use separate storage areas, called instruction queues, for storing the bit fields required by the execution unit.

The *execution unit* is responsible for performing the operation indicated by each instruction that is presented to it. This unit obtains a fully decoded instruction from the decode unit and performs the specified arithmetic, logical, data-movement, or program-control operations. This unit also contains the user-accessible, general-purpose data registers and address registers.

The *bus interface unit* controls all the address, data, and control signals between the CPU and all other external units. It performs all the bus operations required by the fetch and execution units. These include addressing and accessing memory for the fetching of instructions, as determined by the prefetch unit, and the fetching of operands and transferring of data as determined by the execution unit. The bus interface unit is responsible for prioritizing these various bus requests. For example, a prefetch instruction bus request is given a lower priority than an execution-related bus request, and the prefetching of an instruction must always wait for the bus to become available.

Instruction Requirements

The execution of an instruction requires a direct interplay between the information contained within the instruction and the hardware available to fetch, decode, and execute it. In this regard, the hardware not only supports the execution of an instruction but also defines and limits what instructions are possible. For example, a fetched instruction is transferred from memory to the CPU over the data bus. This limits the maximum number of bits for an instruction fetched in a single bus cycle to the size of the data bus. Although larger instructions are frequently needed, their use is restricted because they require multiple bus cycles for retrieval and a consequent increase in instruction fetch time. This limitation on instruction size has important ramifications on both the internal units of the microprocessor and the various encoding schemes used to "pack" information within an instruction.

The fetch unit must have information on the location of the instruction to initiate an instruction fetch. The decode unit must have the hardware needed to correctly decode and interpret the information contained within the fetched instruction. This information includes the operation desired (add, subtract, compare, etc.), the location of required operands, and where the result of the operation is to be stored.

Consider a hypothetical instruction that tells the CPU to add the contents of memory locations 25 and 26 and store the result in memory location 55. Also assume the next instruction to be executed is stored in memory location 1257. Figure 2-3 illustrates a possible single-instruction format for this information.

The instruction illustrated in Figure 2-3 is an example of a complete *two-operand* instruction. It requires two operands for the indicated addition operation. The two operands, located in memory locations 25 and 26, are referred to as *source* operands. Memory location 55 receives the result of the operation and is referred to as the *destination* location.

Although the general instruction format of Figure 2-3 could be used for any two-operand operation, this is impractical because of the 32-bit bus limitation. For example, an instruction containing four 32-bit addresses would need 128 bits (4 times 32) plus additional bits to encode the actual operation command. Fetching such instructions from memory requires either a data bus width of over 128 bits or four individual read bus cycles just to bring the addresses within the instruction into the CPU.

FIGURE 2-3   A Complete Binary Instruction Format

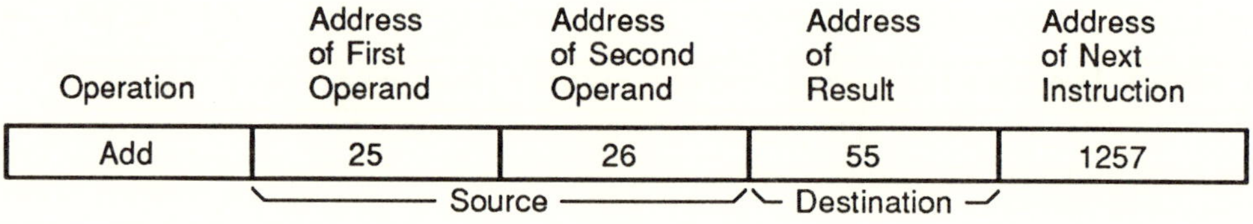

Operation	Address of First Operand	Address of Second Operand	Address of Result	Address of Next Instruction
Add	25	26	55	1257

Source ————————— Destination

Although the CPU requires the information illustrated in Figure 2-3 to execute a two-operand instruction, it does not require that this information be contained within the instruction itself. To eliminate large instructions, each unit within a CPU contains special purpose hardware and uses specific operation and address coding methods. The codes, which include special bit codes to designate each possible operation (add, subtract, compare, move, etc.) are called *operation codes*, or *opcodes*. *Addressing modes* are used to specify the location of an instruction's operands. Specific addressing modes for the Intel, AT&T, and Motorola CPUs are presented in Chapters Four, Five, and Six, respectively.

Pipelining

The sequential fetch, decode, and execute phases needed to execute a single instruction in a Von Neumann architecture do not have to wait for completion of the previous instruction, as is the case in Figure 2-4. Overlapping the fetch, decode, and execution stages of one instruction with the same operations of a second instruction (see Figure 2-5) results in enhanced performance. This method of overlapped instruction execution is the same pipelined instruction processing introduced earlier.

The ability to simultaneously overlap the phases of instructions is possible because the CPU's internal fetch, decode, and execute units can operate autonomously and in parallel. Prefetching requires that the fetch unit have a facility for storing the prefetched instructions. The INTEL 80386 Microprocessor stores these instructions in a 16-byte storage queue, whereas both the AT&T *WE* 32100 Microprocessor and MOTOROLA MC68020 Microprocessor use a 256-byte storage queue. The storage queue of these processors consists of high-speed internal storage registers that are read by the decode unit. Prefetching, however, is always suspended whenever the execution unit needs the bus interface unit to either retrieve an operand or store a result in memory.

Multitasking

Another feature of 32-bit CPUs is their ability to support multitasking. A single task, referred to as a process, is any activity that can be scheduled and executed as an independent unit by the CPU. Each task defines the context within which the CPU operates and consists of one or more routines that are executed while the task is in operation.

FIGURE 2-4 Simplified Nonoverlapped Program Execution

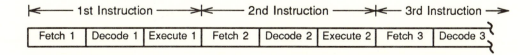

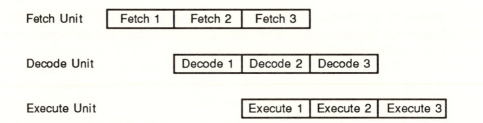

FIGURE 2-5 Instruction Pipelining

Multitasking is the ability to run several different tasks concurrently. Since only one task can control a CPU's operation at a time, multitasking is achieved by interleaving the execution of the different tasks. This interleaving of tasks requires that individual tasks be rapidly switched into and out of the CPU while they are being executed, whether or not they have been completed. This fast switching between tasks effectively gives the appearance of simultaneous, parallel task processing. For example, if multitasking is used to execute three different programs, with each program producing an output on a different CRT screen, the output on all three screens would appear to be displayed at the same time.

From each task's point-of-view, the CPU appears to be a dedicated processor under the task's control. This illusion is maintained by the rapid starting, halting, and switching of task executions. Although the scheduling of each task is determined by the operating system, the CPU must provide the hardware to support a multitasking operating system. Essentially this requires hardware capable of rapidly saving the contents of all internal registers when a task is suspended and reinstating the contents when the task is resumed. Current 32-bit microprocessors have both hardware registers and instructions to do this. The specific registers, instructions, and data structures required for implementing task switching are described more fully in Chapter Three.

Additional Capabilities

In addition to pipelining and multitasking, current 32-bit CPUs typically provide privilege and protection mechanisms, exception and interrupt processing support, coprocessor support, and block move capabilities. These features, along with memory management, are introduced below and are presented in detail in the remaining chapters.

Privilege and Protection

Multitasking requires a security mechanism to restrict access between tasks, to prevent errors in one program from affecting other programs running under the same task, and to separate system tasks from user tasks. User programs operating under a task are generally confined to accessing only their own data and code areas, while operating system tasks have access to all system resources.

One means of providing this security is by supplying the CPU with different privilege levels or states. These privilege states are used by the operating system to manage differing layers of user accesses.

Current 32-bit CPUs provide such privilege capabilities. A *privilege* is the degree to which one task or program can access or affect another task or program. Both the AT&T and Intel 32-bit CPUs provide four distinct privilege levels—the highest level permits access to all code and data segments and is limited to certain operating system instructions; the lowest level permits restricted code and data accesses. The Motorola 32-bit CPU provides three privilege levels.

Privilege levels are essentially software generated states that can be used by an operating system to identify and monitor task accesses. As such, privilege levels are but one aspect of a more comprehensive protection mechanism. Complete system protection requires a means of enforcing the privileged states. This includes alerting the operating system when an illegal access is attempted and providing corrective procedures when such an exception to accepted processing occurs. These additional protection mechanisms are provided by the system's memory management capabilities and the CPU's exception handling facilities. Privilege levels are discussed in detail in Chapter Three.

Exceptions and Interrupts

Exceptions and interrupts require actions that alter the normal flow of program control. Exceptions are processor or operating system detected errors, whereas interrupts are externally generated events. For example, the processor may detect an invalid opcode or illegal access attempt (both are exceptions), or a printer might signal the CPU of a malfunction (an interrupt).

The 32-bit microprocessors support exception and interrupt processing by providing facilities for determining whether or not the interrupt or exception will be recognized, how the interrupt or exception will be acknowledged, and how the servicing of the exception or interrupt will be accomplished. In addition, servicing an interrupt or exception requires that the CPU be capable of rapidly saving and later resuming the interrupted task when possible, or aborting execution when normal processing cannot be resumed. Specific mechanisms for supporting interrupt and exception processing are described in Chapter Three.

Numeric Coprocessor Support

Current 32-bit microprocessors perform floating point arithmetic using software algorithms. The execution speed of these arithmetic operations is significantly increased using numeric coprocessors. A *numeric coprocessor* is a separate LSI device with hardware capable of directly performing floating point arithmetic and logic operations. As such, numeric coprocessors are really math acceleration units (MAUs), and the two terms are used interchangeably.

When a 32-bit microprocessor connected to a numeric coprocessor encounters a floating point operation, the microprocessor relinquishes control to the coprocessor to perform the operation. The 32-bit CPUs provided by Intel, AT&T,

47

and Motorola all have hardware and software features to implement this interface with a numeric coprocessor. Numeric coprocessors are discussed in Chapter Nine.

Block Moves

The AT&T and Intel 32-bit CPUs provide hardware support for the automatic manipulation of blocks of data. This hardware capability is augmented by a set of instructions that directly operate on blocks of data. The MOTOROLA MC68020 CPU has no such dedicated instructions, although its internal hardware supports the construction of similar operations using its standard instruction set.

2.2 Register Sets

The primary purpose of a microprocessor is the execution of instructions. This is true regardless of the final system application, whether it is for a dedicated controller or a general-purpose computer. From this perspective the fetch, decode, and bus interface units of a CPU can be regarded as support units required to enhance the operation of the execution unit. It is not surprising that most of the user-accessible hardware within a 32-bit CPU is found in the execution unit.

This user-accessible hardware consists of two sets of registers where a register is simply a very-fast access storage location implemented directly on the CPU chip. One set of these registers is called the *program model* register set. This register set contains the registers typically needed by applications programmers for performing data calculations and manipulations. These include both general-purpose registers, which can be used for a variety of data processing tasks, and special-purpose registers, which perform specific and dedicated CPU functions needed by an application program. Besides providing applications programmers with the flexibility of directly accessing and using fast on-chip storage locations, most of the program model registers have a second, equally significant role. Having a small set of general purpose registers that can be used for source and destination operands permits replacing 32-bit source and destination memory addresses within an instruction with 3-bit or 4-bit register addresses. This reduction of instruction address information is an important function of many of the program model registers.

The second set of user accessible registers is referred to as the *systems model* or *supervisor model* register set. This set contains special purpose registers needed by operating systems programmers for performing such tasks as memory management, restricting application program access to data areas, checking and restricting the range of application program transfers of control, multitasking, and controlling the exception and interrupt mechanisms of the CPU. Figures 2-6 through 2-8 show the register sets for the INTEL 80386 CPU, AT&T *WE* 32100 CPU, and MOTOROLA MC68020 CPU. The registers in both the program model

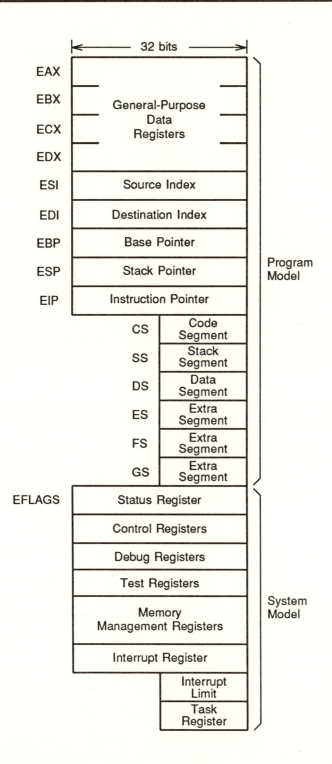

FIGURE 2-6   INTEL 80386 Microprocessor Register Set

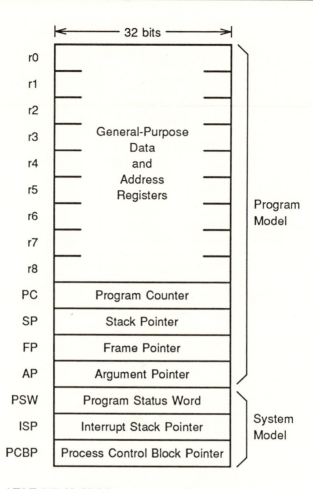

FIGURE 2-7 AT&T *WE* 32100 Microprocessor Register Set

and system model register sets that are common to 32-bit CPUs are described below.

Program Model Register Set

Minimally, the program model register set consists of a set of general-purpose registers, an instruction pointer, a stack pointer, and a flag register (see Figure 2-9). The general-purpose registers are sometimes, as in the case of the INTEL 80386 CPU and MOTOROLA MC68020 CPU, further subdivided into data and address registers. This distinction is not made by the AT&T Microprocessor since all its general purpose registers can be used interchangeably between data and address with no restrictions. The INTEL 80386 CPU provides an additional set of segment registers for handling memory management functions. Since some applications (for example, a dedicated controller) do not need this feature, both AT&T and Motorola provide the equivalent of these registers in a separate memory management unit (MMU) chip.

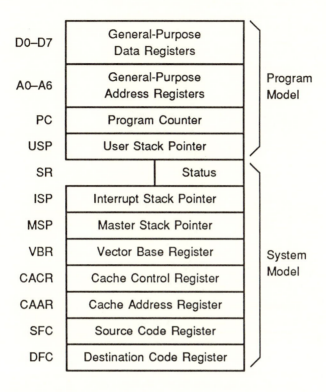

D0–D7	General-Purpose Data Registers
A0–A6	General-Purpose Address Registers
PC	Program Counter
USP	User Stack Pointer
SR	Status
ISP	Interrupt Stack Pointer
MSP	Master Stack Pointer
VBR	Vector Base Register
CACR	Cache Control Register
CAAR	Cache Address Register
SFC	Source Code Register
DFC	Destination Code Register

Program Model

System Model

FIGURE 2-8   MOTOROLA MC68020 Microprocessor Register Set

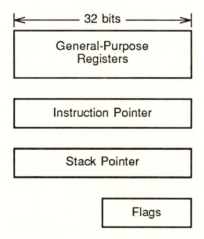

← 32 bits →

General-Purpose Registers

Instruction Pointer

Stack Pointer

Flags

FIGURE 2-9   Program Model Register Set (Minimum Configuration)

51

General-Purpose Data Registers

General-purpose data registers may contain any source or destination operands used by an instruction. These registers may also be used for arithmetic calculations, logical calculations, data storage, data movement, or any other function supported by the microprocessor instruction set. Since their specific function in an applications program is determined by the programmer, they are always referred to as general-purpose data registers. Instruction execution time is significantly decreased by maintaining data in these on-chip registers because they eliminate the need for additional memory read cycles to obtain source operands and memory write cycles to store destination operands.

The AT&T 32-bit CPU provides nine general-purpose data registers, called r0 through r8. The MOTOROLA MC68020 CPU provides eight general-purpose registers referred to as D0 through D7. The INTEL 80386 CPU provides four such registers, called EAX, EBX, ECX, and EDX. Although all these registers are 32-bits wide, each CPU provides a means of accessing both single byte (8-bits) and double bytes (16-bits) of data from any register.

Besides decreasing instruction execution time, the use of general purpose data registers for both source and destination operands also significantly reduces the bit length of an instruction. AT&T CPU instructions, for example, require four bits to correctly specify the desired general purpose register. Motorola instructions require 3 bits (1 of 8), while an Intel instruction requires 2 bits (1 of 4). This is significantly less than the number of bits needed to specify a complete memory address.

To ensure this type of instruction length savings, the INTEL 80386 CPU requires that at least one source operand in each two operand instruction be stored in one of its general-purpose registers. The AT&T and Motorola 32-bit CPUs are less restrictive in this regard and permit both operands to be memory resident. Both the AT&T and Motorola CPUs, however, require that the address of each memory operand either be stored in a general-purpose register or included in an instruction as immediate data. The inclusion of on-chip general-purpose registers, however, has a software cost – additional instructions must be provided to both initially load these registers with data obtained from memory and to subsequently store the contents of these registers in memory.

General-Purpose Address Registers

Instructions contain two types of information: the operation to be performed and the location of the required operand(s). When an operand is located in memory, various methods are used for encoding the memory address within a limited number of bits. Collectively, the various schemes used for encoding an operand's address, be it a register or memory location, are referred to as *addressing modes*.

No matter how they are constructed, an addressing mode used to code a memory address requires expansion of the encoded operand address into a full

32-bit quantity. Quite frequently this expansion includes a 32-bit value contained within a register. The value in the register can be used in a variety of ways: as the final operand address by itself, as a base address to which an offset is added, as an offset, or as an index value to a table or data structure. Registers that can be used for a variety of addressing modes are referred to as *general-purpose address registers*.

The MOTOROLA MC68020 CPU provides seven general-purpose address registers; the INTEL 80386 CPU provides four such registers. The AT&T CPU allows any of its nine general-purpose data registers to be used as general-purpose address registers. Although many of the Motorola and Intel address registers can also be used as general-purpose data registers, their primary function is to provide full 32-bit address values. In many cases, a specific instruction requires that a correct address value be placed into one of these registers.

Address registers are required by the Motorola and Intel CPUs to make them compatible with earlier Motorola and Intel microprocessors that used specific address registers and had their own addressing schemes. The AT&T CPU uses a conceptually simpler and more powerful register addressing scheme that does not require specific address registers. This simpler scheme was made possible because the AT&T processor had no commercial predecessors with which it had to be compatible. The particular addressing modes used by the Intel, AT&T, and Motorola CPUs are presented in detail in Chapters Four, Five, and Six, respectively.

Instruction Pointer

This special-purpose register contains the address of the next instruction to be executed. The AT&T and Motorola 32-bit microprocessors both refer to this register as a *program counter*, while the INTEL 80386 CPU refers to this register as the *instruction pointer*. In all three CPUs, this register is a full 32-bits wide. Unless instructed otherwise, the address in this register is automatically incremented during the execution of the current instruction. Assume that program instructions are stored sequentially in memory and that the address of the first program instruction was correctly loaded into the program counter. Incrementing this register by the byte or word size of the current instruction correctly updates its address to the byte or word address of the next instruction. In the case of the INTEL 80386 CPU, the address in the instruction pointer is combined with an address in one of its segment registers to obtain the final instruction address.

The instruction pointer illustrates the close association between hardware and software and the interplay between them. By placing the address of the next instruction to be executed in this hardware register, this address is eliminated from an instruction resulting in a dramatic reduction in instruction length. Using an instruction pointer does require additional instructions to load and change the addresses within the register. These instructions, called load, jump, and branch instructions, are needed to initially set an address into the program counter and alter the address in the creation of program loops and subroutine transfers. These instructions also directly affect the prefetch facility of 32-bit CPUs. When the address in the instruction pointer is reset by any of these instructions, the prefetch unit begins refilling its storage queue starting from the newly addressed location.

Stack Pointer

A user *stack pointer* is a 32-bit address register that allows users rapid access to a memory stack. A memory stack, also called a *last-in-first-out* (LIFO) *buffer* or a *push-down stack* provides the means of storing information by order of occurrence. This stack is conceptually similar to a stack of trays in a cafeteria, where the last tray placed on top of the stack is the first tray removed. A memory stack is simply an area of memory used for rapidly storing and retrieving data in the same last-in, first-out sequential manner. The stack pointer register is used to store the address of the top location in a stack and is automatically incremented or decremented each time an item on the stack is added or removed.

The only item on a stack that is immediately available through the stack pointer is the top of the stack. Placing a data item on the stack is called a *push* operation; removing a data item from the top of the stack is called a *pop* operation. These terms are retained from early 8-bit CPUs and larger mainframe processors that implemented a stack as a dedicated set of internal CPU registers. With this early type of implementation, putting a new data item in the top register of the stack required moving each data item directly into the register immediately below. This effectively looked like each data item was being pushed down one level. Similarly, removing the contents of the top register required moving each data item up by one register, which looked like a popping up of the register contents. Push and pop operations are illustrated in Figures 2-10 and 2-11.

Although register stacks provide faster operation than memory stacks, the number of items that can be stored in a register stack is limited by the number of registers in the stack. As a result of this limitation, register stacks are not used and memory stacks are implemented by 32-bit microprocessors. This allows the memory stack to grow as large as the memory available and permits the storing of as much data as is required.

FIGURE 2-10   Pushing an Operand Onto the Stack

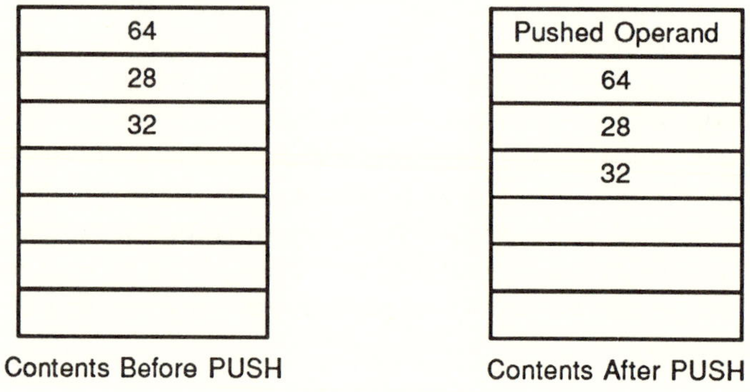

64
28
32

Contents Before PUSH

Pushed Operand
64
28
32

Contents After PUSH

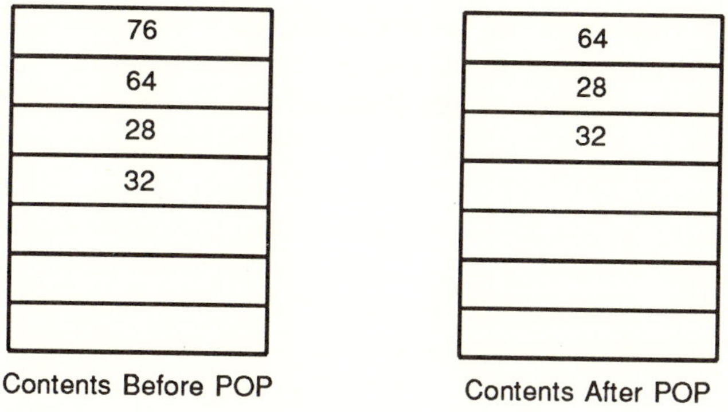

76	
64	
28	
32	

64	
28	
32	

Contents Before POP   Contents After POP

FIGURE 2-11   Popping an Operand From the Stack

All 32-bit CPUs provide a dedicated user stack pointer to access the memory stack. The address in both the Motorola and Intel stack pointers is the memory address of the last pushed operand; the AT&T stack pointer contains the address of the next available location. On a push operation the AT&T stack pointer already points to the correct location, whereas the Intel and Motorola stack pointer addresses must first be adjusted to point to the next available location. The opposite is true on a pop operation. The Intel and Motorola stack pointers contain the correct address and the pop can be implemented immediately; the AT&T CPU must first adjust its stack pointer address before the data can be retrieved. The user stacks for these microprocessors are shown in Figures 2-12 and 2-13.

As shown in Figure 2-12, the AT&T CPU also differs from its Intel and Motorola counterparts in how its stack grows in memory as data is pushed onto it. The memory stack used by the AT&T CPU fills from low-to-high addresses, whereas the Intel and Motorola stacks grow down in memory address as data is pushed on them. The way the stack expands and contracts as items are pushed and popped, respectively, is determined by how the addresses in the stack pointer are automatically adjusted by the CPU when push and pop instructions are encountered. A push by the AT&T CPU is accompanied by an automatic increment in the stack pointer address, and a pop results in an automatic decrement to the address. The opposite is true for the Intel and Motorola CPUs.

Flag Register

The flag register consists of a set of individual bits that reflect the result of the most recently executed instruction. This register is part of a larger processor status register, which is used by systems programmers to monitor overall system performance. In the Intel, AT&T, and Motorola CPUs this system register is called the EFLAGS, processor status word (PSW), and status register (SR), respectively. While the full capabilities of these registers are required by systems programmers, the individual flag bits are useful to applications programmers in comparison and test instructions.

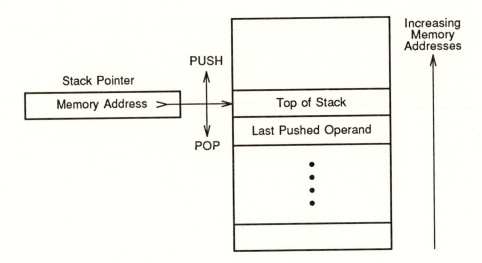

FIGURE 2-12   The AT&T *WE* 32100 Microprocessor User Stack

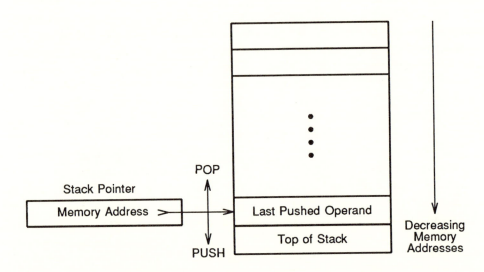

FIGURE 2-13   INTEL 80386 Microprocessor and MOTOROLA MC68020 Microprocessor
User Stacks

Most instructions set individual flag bits according to specific criteria defined by each manufacturer, and the available flag bits for each processor are described individually in the chapters devoted to each CPU. The four flag bits common to the Intel, AT&T, and Motorola CPUs are:

N **(Negative) Flag Bit:** This bit is set (1) if the result of the last computation is negative, or cleared (0) if it is positive or zero. This bit is effectively a copy of the most significant bit (MSB) of the result.

Z **(Zero) Flag bit:** This flag is set (1) if the result of the last computation is zero, or cleared (0) if it is a nonzero value.

V **(Overflow) Flag bit:** This flag bit is set (1) if the result of the last computation is either too large a positive number or two small a negative number to fit into the destination operand. If the result of the last computation is within the range of acceptable values, this bit is cleared (0).

C **(Carry) Flag Bit:** This flag bit is set (1) if a carry out of the most significant bit (MSB) occurs for an addition operation or if a borrow occurs for a subtraction, comparison, or negation operation. If a carry or borrow does not occur, this bit is cleared (0).

Table 2-1 lists the names of these bits for the Intel, AT&T, and Motorola microprocessors. For the Intel CPU, these four flags are contained within bits 0, 6, 7, and 11 of the EFLAGS register. For the AT&T CPU, these four flag bits correspond to bits 21, 20, 19, and 18 of the processor status word (PSW) register. For the Motorola CPU, they correspond to bits 3, 2, 1, and 0 of the status register (SR).

TABLE 2-1 Flag Bit Names

Processor	Negative Flag	Zero Flag	Overflow Flag	Carry Flag	Register
INTEL 80386 CPU	SF	ZF	OF	CF	EFLAGS
AT&T WE 32100 CPU	N	Z	V	C	PSW
MOTOROLA MC68020 CPU	N	Z	V	C	Status

Segment Registers

A unique feature of the INTEL 80386 CPU is its segment registers. The segment registers support the CPU's on-chip memory management capabilities and make it compatible with programs written for the earlier INTEL 8086 and 80286 Microprocessors. Although Intel stresses the on-chip memory management aspects of its CPU as an added and distinct feature, the compatibility requirement with earlier CPUs made the inclusion of the segment registers a necessity. As many applications do not require memory management, AT&T and Motorola provide separate memory management chips to perform the memory management functions.

The 16-bit internal address bus of the earlier 16-bit INTEL 8086 Microprocessor would have restricted the addressing capability to 65,536 (2^{16}) memory locations. To extend the usable programming space of this processor to the full 20-bits of its external address bus, Intel introduced a rather simple on-chip memory segmentation capability for the 8086 CPU using four segment registers (see Figure 2-14). The INTEL 80286 CPU retained the segment registers, making the 80286 CPU compatible with the 8086 CPU, and extended their function to provide a more complete memory segmentation capability. The INTEL 80386 CPU retained compatibility with both the 8086 and 80286 CPUs, expanded the allowable addressing range, and included paging features within its memory management capabilities. The complete segmentation and paging capabilities of the 80386 CPU are described in Sections 2.3 and 2.4. A description of the more limited capabilities that make the 80386 memory management features compatible with the earlier 8086 memory management approach is presented below.

The six 80386 segment registers shown in Figure 2-14 are 16-bit address registers. Each segment register stores the starting address of a section of memory. This provides the CPU with direct access to six segments at one time, with the starting address of each segment stored in an individual segment register. When segment registers are used to directly store an address, the INTEL 80386 CPU is operating in its *real mode,* as opposed to its *protected mode* (described later in Section 2.4) in which it uses segment register values as indices into memory tables that provide the actual addresses needed to locate a segment.

The address stored in the code segment (CS) register is the starting address of the current section of memory used for code; instructions are fetched from this section. The address in the stack segment (SS) register points to the starting address of the section of memory used for the stack, and the data segment registers (DS, ES, FS, and GS) are used to store the starting addresses of up to four individual data segments.

FIGURE 2-14   INTEL 8086 and 80386 CPU Segment Registers

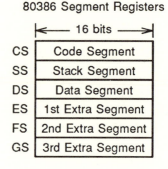

From a programming perspective, segment registers provide an elegant way of isolating programming from physical storage considerations. All programs can be written and subsequently translated into machine language assuming that they are going to be located in memory starting at physical location zero with any address calculations or offsets computed relative to this base address. Figure 2-15 shows that when the program is actually stored in memory, regardless of where each segment is finally located, the address of the first location in each program segment is stored in the appropriate segment register.

Since all instruction addresses internal to the program are calculated relative to location zero, actual instruction addresses are found by adding the contents of the instruction pointer to the starting address in the CS register. Figure 2-16 illustrates the calculation of an instruction's physical address. In this address calculation the address in the instruction pointer is interpreted as an offset value into the code segment pointed to by the CS register.

Actual physical addresses for the stack and data segments are determined in a similar manner. For example, the actual physical address of the top-of-stack is determined by adding the address in the stack pointer to the address contained in the stack segment (SS) register. Once a segment has been loaded into memory and its correct starting address is stored in the appropriate segment register, the determination of a physical address is straightforward and automatically performed by the CPU.

Although six separate segments can be accessed by the INTEL 80386 CPU, with each segment in a separate and distinct location, this is only one of many possible segmentation arrangements. For example, if a modest size program and

FIGURE 2-15 Relating Segment Register Addresses to Storage Areas

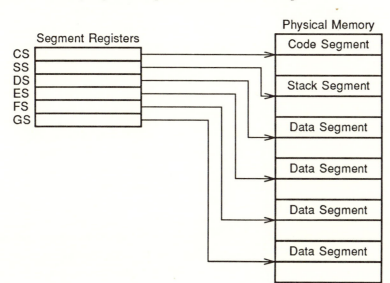

59

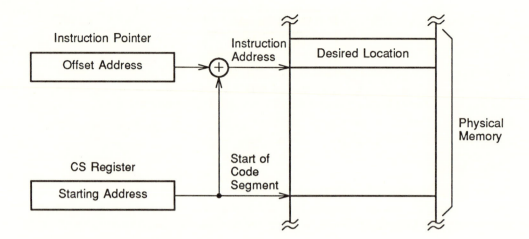

FIGURE 2-16   Calculating an Instruction's Physical Address

its data can be contained in a single segment, all segment registers would be loaded with the same starting address. In general, any number of segments can overlap. The final segmentation is determined by the application, and complete control over the segments is available to assembly language programmers. The 8086 segment registers operate in the same manner as just described for the 80386 CPU, except the 8086 CPU provides only two data segment registers.

Perhaps the most important aspect of segmentation is that it permits *dynamic relocation* of segments by the operating system. In dynamic relocation, the program is not bound to specific physical locations while it is being executed. The operating system can stop the program, relocate it to another area of memory, and restart it without the necessity of further compilation or assembly to adjust internal program addresses. This type of relocation is critical in multiuser systems to make effective use of memory; inactive programs are removed and other programs relocated to make room for programs waiting to be run. Using segment registers, the moving of a program segment is accomplished by physically relocating the segment in memory and updating the address in the appropriate segment register.

System Model Register Set

The registers in the system model register set provide control and monitoring capabilities for overall system functions, as opposed to the individual application functions performed by the program model register set. Although each CPU has its own specialized registers, all CPUs contain system registers for performing status, task, and interrupt functions (see Figure 2-17). The status, task, and interrupt registers are presented below. The complete set of system registers provided by the Intel, AT&T, and Motorola 32-bit CPUs is presented in Chapters Four, Five, and Six, respectively.

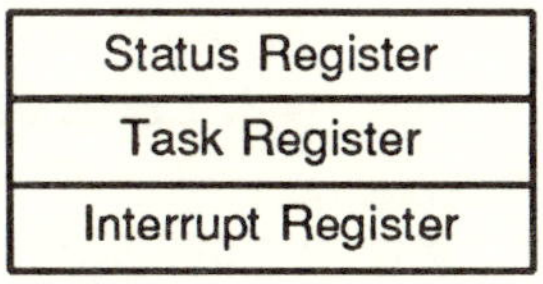

Status Register
Task Register
Interrupt Register

FIGURE 2-17   System Model Register Set (Minimum Configuration)

Status Register

This 32-bit register stores status information about the microprocessor and the current task. In addition, selected bits of this register are used to control system interrupt priorities and processor states (supervisor or user mode). Other bits within this register are used as flag bits for applications programmers (flags register). In the INTEL 80386 CPU the status register is referred to as the EFLAGS register; in the AT&T *WE* 32100 CPU as the processor status word (PSW); and in the MOTOROLA MC68020 CPU as the status register (SR).

Task Register

This 32-bit register stores the starting address of a task control block for the currently executing process. A task control block is a memory-resident data structure used to store the state of a task whenever it is suspended. This information permits the task to be reinstated at a later time as scheduled by the operating system. In the INTEL 80386 CPU this register is referred to as the task register; in the AT&T *WE* 32100 CPU it is called the process control block pointer (PCBP). In the MOTOROLA MC68020 CPU, the functions of this register are performed by the master stack pointer (MSP) register.

Interrupt Register

This 32-bit register stores the starting address of either a memory interrupt stack or table of interrupt handler routines. In both the AT&T *WE* 32100 CPU and the MOTOROLA MC68020 CPU, this register is referred to as the interrupt stack pointer (ISP). In the INTEL 80386 CPU, the interrupt register is referred to as the interrupt descriptor table register (IDTR); the address in this register points to a table containing addresses of various interrupt handler routines.

2.3 Memory Management Concepts

Memory management refers to how a computer system administers its memory resources. This management includes such activities as the translation of addresses from the CPU into physical memory addresses, and the assignment of the protection and privilege features needed by multiuser operating systems that require large amounts of memory.

This section describes the fundamentals of memory management and introduces the concepts of segment and offset addressing. The *real mode* of the INTEL 80386 CPU is used to illustrate the concepts presented.

To understand what is involved with address translation and why it is needed, consider the simple case of fetching a single instruction from memory. The instruction must be stored in a physical location in memory at the time of the fetch; however, the instruction does not have to be stored in memory either before or after the moment in time that it is actually needed. In theory, we could construct a computer with a much smaller physical memory than that required to store a complete program. The complete program could be stored on some external storage medium, such as a disk, and could contain millions of instructions and require billions of bytes of disk storage. The full range of storage addresses required by a program is called the *program's address space*. All that is required to successfully execute a program is that the computer's memory be properly managed so that the relevant portions of a program are resident within physical memory at the proper times.

The maximum physical memory size possible in a computer system, as contrasted to the actual size of any one program, is determined by the width of the system's address bus. This maximum memory size is referred to as the system's *real address space*. For example, the INTEL 8080 Microprocessor has an address bus width of 16 bits. If this processor is used in a system with a 16-bit wide address bus, a total of 2^{16} (or 65,536) memory locations can be addressed (see Figure 2-18) and the system is said to have a real address space of 64 Kbytes of memory (1 Kbyte equals 1024 bytes). Naturally, only that portion of a system's

FIGURE 2-18   The Real Address Space of an INTEL 8080 Microprocessor Based System

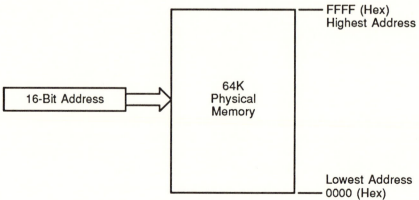

FFFF (Hex)
Highest Address

16-Bit Address

64K
Physical
Memory

Lowest Address
0000 (Hex)

real address that has physical memory components attached can actually be used. In this context, a real address space represents the theoretical maximum *physical address space*. The physical address space represents the subset of real address space actually populated by memory components.

In systems that bring in sections of software from a disk as needed, a program's address space can be larger than either the system's real or physical address space. The physical address space naturally limits the amount of the program that can be physically resident in memory at one time. The total size of the program, however, is not limited to either the real address space or physical address space, and can be determined by the application.

Consider the hypothetical CPU shown in Figure 2-19. This CPU has a 4-bit wide external address bus. Assuming that this bus width is maintained throughout the system, the system's real address space is restricted to 2^4 or 16 addressable locations. The lowest addressable memory location in the real address space is binary address 0000; the highest memory location is binary address 1111.

Internally, this hypothetical microprocessor is capable of holding a 10-bit address in its instruction pointer register. The address space that can be referenced by this register is 2^{10} or 1024 locations, which is considerably more than the 16 location real address space. The maximum addressable space that can be formulated internal to a CPU is referred to as the CPU's *virtual address* or *virtual storage space*. Generally this virtual storage space is larger than the real address space, but it need not be. The instruction pointer register used in this example does not define the CPU's virtual address space and has been used only to illustrate how an internal CPU address can be larger than the address presented to its external address bus. A CPU's virtual address space is defined by the maximum address that can be manipulated internal to the CPU, regardless of how that address is created. These addresses can be formulated internally using a combination of registers, as is done in the INTEL 80386 CPU.

The practical implication of having a virtual storage space of 1024 addresses is that it limits the maximum program that can be executed to this size. This is true regardless of the size of the virtual storage — a program's address space must always be less than the virtual address space of the CPU used to execute the program. As virtual address spaces currently tend to exceed 4 Gigabytes (2^{32}), this does not constitute a practical limitation on program sizes.

Segments and Offsets

Each virtual address must ultimately be translated into a real address. This translation always occurs prior to referencing the desired location from physical memory and can be accomplished either by the CPU itself or by a separate device called a memory management unit (MMU). Where the virtual storage space is larger than the real address space, either translation must occur within the CPU or additional address lines must be provided to write the virtual address to the external MMU. This allows the CPU to either present the correct size real address on its external address bus or let the MMU downsize the address to the appropriate system address bus size. To see how this can be accomplished, let us take a closer look at our hypothetical CPU with a 10-bit virtual address space and a 4-bit real address space (see Figure 2-19).

A 10-bit virtual address space encompasses 2^{10} or 1024 addresses, with the lowest binary address in the address space being 0000000000 or 0_{10} and the highest binary address being 1111111111 or 1023_{10} (see Figure 2-20). Rather than treat this virtual address space as a series of 1024 continuous addresses, as is done in Figure 2-20, it is more convenient to view the address space as a series of segments, with each segment consisting of the same number of identically addressed locations. This view of the virtual space is reinforced if the 10-bit virtual address is itself considered as consisting of two parts: a segment specifier and an offset.

For example, partitioning our 10-bit virtual address into a 6-bit segment specifier and a 4-bit offset, as illustrated in Figure 2-21, allows a maximum of 2^6 or 64 different segments to be specified, with each segment consisting of 2^4 or 16 locations. Using this partitioning, an address such as 0000010111 would be read as "offset location 7 within segment 1," rather than as absolute virtual address 23_{10} (see Figure 2-22). Although both address designations reference the same location, the segment/offset interpretation is more useful for memory management purposes. If segment number 1 is not physically located in memory, the operating system would first locate this segment on the external disk and load it into physical memory. The offset, which represents a displacement within the segment, is then used to correctly access the desired location.

The partitioning makes each segment equal in size to the real memory space. If the 16-location real address space is fully populated with memory devices and the correct segment is loaded into memory starting at physical address 0, placing the offset value directly on the 4-bit external bus as a physical address results in the correct memory location access. Segments with the same size as physical memory, however, are almost never used because they require that the complete

FIGURE 2-19   A Hypothetical CPU Illustrating Two Address Spaces

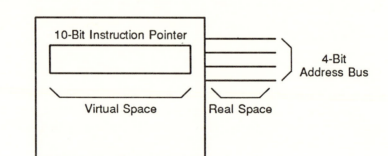

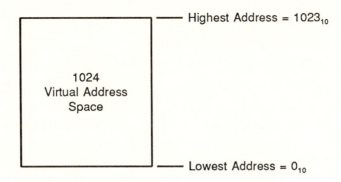

FIGURE 2-20   A 10-bit Virtual Address Space

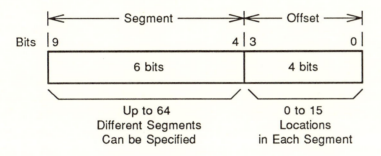

FIGURE 2-21   A Partitioned Address Structure

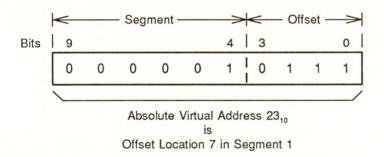

FIGURE 2-22   The Virtual Address 23_{10} as a Segment/Offset Address

physical memory be rewritten each time a segment is loaded from an external disk. For systems having physical address spaces in the megabyte (Mbyte) and gigabyte (Gbyte) range this is unrealistic. For these systems the actual segment size is typically much smaller than physical memory. Although the maximum possible segment size is determined by the number of bits in the offset portion of the virtual address, the application program and/or the operating system typically limit the actual segment size used.

INTEL 80386 CPU Real Memory Management Mode

The concept of an internal segment and offset address, which forms the basis of all memory management approaches, is used by the *real memory management mode* addressing mechanism of the INTEL 80386 CPU. This memory management approach is the same as the addressing scheme employed by the earlier INTEL 8086 CPU and allows the 80386 CPU to execute existing 8086 software. The INTEL 80386 CPU enters this memory management mode whenever it is initially activated or reset.

When the INTEL 80386 CPU operates in real mode it uses only 20 of its external address lines. This is in keeping with the earlier INTEL 8086 CPU, which had a 20-bit external address bus. Using 20 address lines permits addressing of up to 1 Mbyte (2^{20}) of physical memory. Operating in real mode, the INTEL 8086 CPU and 80386 CPU construct their 20-bit addresses internally using a 16-bit segment register value and a 16-bit offset.

To access code segments, the starting code segment address must be loaded into the CS register (see Figure 2-23). Similarly, a data segment is accessed by loading one of the four segment registers (DS, ES, FS, or GS) with the starting address of a data segment (the 8086 CPU has only two data segment registers, DS and ES) and the SS register is loaded with the starting address of the stack segment. Each of these registers is loaded with appropriate segment starting addresses using special instructions for this purpose. The offset address can be generated in a variety of ways. Regardless of the particular method used to create an offset, it is always a 16-bit quantity representing a displacement address within the selected segment. For code segments the real mode offset is provided by the lower-order 16 bits of the instruction pointer.

FIGURE 2-23   INTEL 80386 CPU Segment Registers

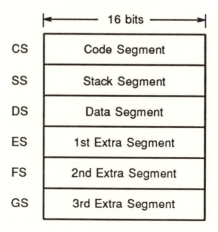

All Intel microprocessors are byte addressable machines. The 16-bit segment address permits a maximum of 2^{16} or 64K segments to be defined. The 16-bit offset defines a maximum segment size of 2^{16} or 64 Kbytes. Thus, if the virtual address was formulated as the concatenation of the segment and offset addresses, a true 2^{32} or 4 Gbytes of virtual address space would be defined. However, the virtual address is not formulated this way.

The virtual address created in real mode is constructed by first shifting the address in the segment register by 4 bits, which produces the true 20-bit starting address of the segment. For example, if the hexadecimal address 2046 were contained in the code segment register, left shifting this address by 4 bits is equivalent to adding four low-order binary zeros, and results in the starting hexadecimal address of the segment being 20460. The offset value is added to this left-shifted segment base address and the resulting address is transmitted to the 20-bit address bus (see Figure 2-24).

Although the real memory management mode of the INTEL 80386 CPU illustrates segment and offset addressing, this mode neither exploits the full virtual address possible with a 16-bit segment register and 16-bit offset, nor does it realize the full potential of a virtual address system. Rather than achieving the complete 4 Gbytes (2^{32}) of virtual address space theoretically possible (2^{16} segments x 2^{16} bytes per segment), only 1 Mbyte of virtual storage addresses (2^{20}) is created. This is a result of shifting the segment address by 4 bits to obtain a 20-bit base segment address rather than shifting it by 16 to obtain a full 32-bit address before adding the offset.

The smaller shift of four bits also results in an interaction between the lower-order 12 bits of the segment starting address and the upper 12 bits of the offset as shown in Figure 2-25. This bit overlap implies that many combinations of segment and offset addresses can produce the same virtual address. This has both positive and negative consequences.

A positive consequence of the overlap is that it permits two separate data segments with differing starting segment addresses to share a common, partially overlapped address space. For example, a segment with a decimal starting address of 0 and a maximum decimal offset of 64,000 shares half its address space with

FIGURE 2-24 Real-Mode Address Translation

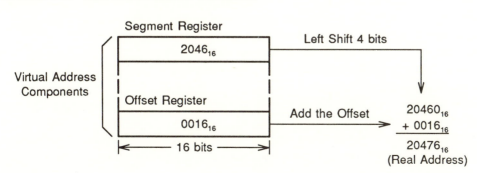

This overlap would not occur if
a full 16-bit shift were used.

CS Register (shifted):	0100	1000	1111	0010	0000	= $48F20_{16}$
Offset:		0111	0010	0101	0101	= 07255_{16}

Final Address:	0101	0000	0001	0111	0101	= 50175_{16}

FIGURE 2-25 Real-Mode Overlap Bits

a segment having a starting address of 32,000. The first 32,000 bytes of the initial segment, however, are inaccessible to the second segment. The last 32,000 bytes of the second segment are inaccessible to the first segment.

A negative consequence of the overlap is a problem that can occur when comparing the same address composed of different segment and offset values. For example, a segment starting at decimal address 0 with a decimal offset of 33,000 references the same location as offset 1000 in a segment starting at address 32,000. Clearly then, just comparing segment and offset addresses individually does not adequately indicate whether the same address is being referenced.

A further consequence of the shifting of the segment address by four is that segments must always be located in memory starting at addresses whose four lower-order bits are zero. This ensures that when the address in the segment register is shifted by four, the resulting segment address can match the actual location of the segment. In other words, the starting address of each segment in memory must be evenly divisible by sixteen. Such addresses are called paragraph addresses and this explains why all assembly language programs written for the INTEL 8086 CPU had to be paragraph aligned. This effect, which places a restriction on the location of segments in memory, is essentially transparent to an applications programmer.

From a wider perspective, the real-mode memory management scheme supplies the rudiments for a more complete and comprehensive programming protection scheme. For example, by selectively using starting segment addresses that do not lie within the range of the starting address and maximum offset of any other segment, the six segment registers provide a means of totally isolating all code, data, and stack segments into separate, nonoverlapped memory areas. The opposite effect, in which all segments totally coincide, can be produced by loading all six segment registers with the same address. Between these two extremes is the case where segments partially overlap.

The fuller possibilities of a more complete memory management scheme are not realized precisely due to the way the segment and offset addresses are formulated in real mode. The shifting of the segment address and the addition of the offset value effectively collapses a possible 32-bit virtual address (16 segment bits and 16 offset bits) into a 20-bit real address, which is then put on the address bus, unaltered, as a physical address. This explains why Intel describes this memory management mode as a real, rather than virtual mode. In using segment and offsets, the real mode address translation does not include the additional features needed to support the memory swapping capabilities of a true multiuser and multitasking system. This was not a problem for the INTEL 8086 CPU, compatible with the real mode of the INTEL 80386 CPU, because this earlier microprocessor was essentially developed as a single-user system. It did, however, prevent the expansion of the INTEL 8086 CPU into a true multitasking system. This also is not a problem for the INTEL 80386 CPU because this processor has a second memory management mode for supporting a complete virtual memory address space and implementing a true multitasking capability, called the *protected mode*. The additional memory management features necessary to support this mode, beyond segment and offset addressing, are the topics of the next section.

2.4 Memory Management Implementations

A 32-bit CPU with over 4 billion bytes of real address space (4 Gbytes) places no practical limitation on a program's size. Thus, the need to provide a virtual storage area sufficient to accommodate a single large program address space is not the motivation for memory management in these systems. Here memory management requirements stem from the need to protect various code and data segments inherent in a multiuser environment from unauthorized access and the need to efficiently allocate physical memory space among many tasks.

Operating system software must be protected from user-generated software and each user's software must be protected from other users. This generally entails several layers of protection. For example, a system may allow execution of a code segment only; or reading and execution access to a section of code; or reading, execution, and modification (writing) privileges. Attempts to transfer program control into a data segment or to write data into an instruction area must also be prohibited. The ability to provide this protection forms the basis of a complete memory management scheme that goes beyond the simple segment and offset addressing mechanism described in the last section. The segment/offset address translation furnishes the foundation on which a full segmented memory management system is based.

Segmentation

A complete memory management approach requires that both a CPU's hardware and its operating system software accommodate loading and removing program segments in an efficient manner. From an operating systems perspective, the system must keep track of where each segment of a program is loaded into real memory, what sections of real memory are still available for new segments, and what sections of real memory are out-of-bounds for each memory access requested. As we have seen, a key component of memory management is that each program be divided into one or more segments. Figure 2-26 illustrates the segmentation of a program address space into five segments and shows how these segments might reside within a system's physical address space.

As shown in Figure 2-26, only three of the program's segments currently reside in memory. The operating system can keep track of the starting address of each segment in a number of ways. One of the simplest is to load the starting segment address into a dedicated segment register, as is done in the real memory management mode of the INTEL 80386 CPU. The limitation of this approach is that the number of possible segments is limited by the number of available segment registers. For example, with six segment registers, the INTEL 80386 CPU can keep track of six segments and a maximum storage area of 384 Kbytes (6 segments x 64 Kbytes/segment). This is out of a total real storage address space of over 4 billion bytes. This limitation is acceptable when the 80386 CPU is used in real mode, which effectively emulates a single-user 8086 CPU. To support a

FIGURE 2-26　A Hypothetical Program Segmentation

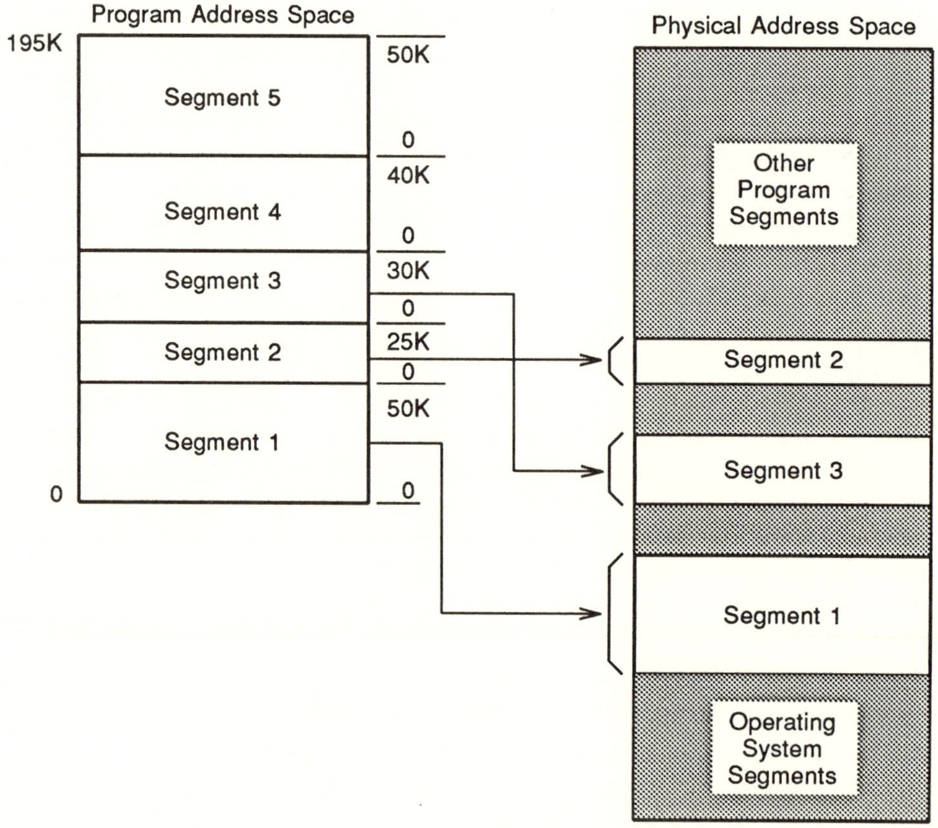

multiuser operating system, this limitation on the total number of monitored segments must be overcome.

A more flexible scheme is to use segment registers to keep track of only the currently operating segments and for the operating system to maintain a more comprehensive table that keeps track of all segments, whether or not the segments are physically present in memory or not. This table, called a *segment descriptor table*, contains the actual starting physical address for each segment residing in memory. In addition, this table contains descriptive data about each segment, including its actual size, privilege levels, and whether or not the segment resides in memory. This additional data is used by the operating system to perform access privilege and bounds checking each time a memory location is accessed.

Although the creation and maintenance of a segment descriptor table is the responsibility of the operating system, it does require that the CPU have a number of dedicated registers and features needed to support such a table. One such register is called a *descriptor table origin register*, which is used to store the starting memory address of the descriptor table itself. As before, segment registers are also used, but in this case the value in the segment register is equivalent to an index or subscript used to locate the desired entry in the descriptor table.

The address translation of a fully segmented virtual storage system proceeds as shown in Figure 2-27. Using the value in the segment register as an index into the descriptor table, the operating system locates the segment's descriptor entry and checks whether the segment is physically loaded in memory. If the segment is not physically located in memory, the operating system signals a program exception, which initiates the actual loading of the desired segment into an available memory area and the updating of the descriptor entry to reflect the correct segment starting address. If the segment is present, address translation continues, with the offset added to the starting address contained within the descriptor. This results in a real address, which can either be placed on the address bus as a physical address or be further translated if *paging* is used. Before discussing paging, a specific example of the segmentation approach described is illustrated using the *protected mode* of the INTEL 80386 CPU.

INTEL 80386 CPU Protected Mode*

In addition to the real memory management mode described in the previous section, the INTEL 80386 CPU provides a full virtual memory management and protection mode, called the *protected mode*. Figure 2-28 illustrates the segment address translation algorithm used in this mode.

The segment translation used in protected mode (upper portion of Figure 2-28) corresponds almost exactly to our theoretical virtual address translation algorithm illustrated in Figure 2-27, taking into account the different notation used by Intel. Intel refers to virtual addresses as logical addresses, which reinforces the

---

*This topic can be omitted on a first reading without loss of subject continuity.

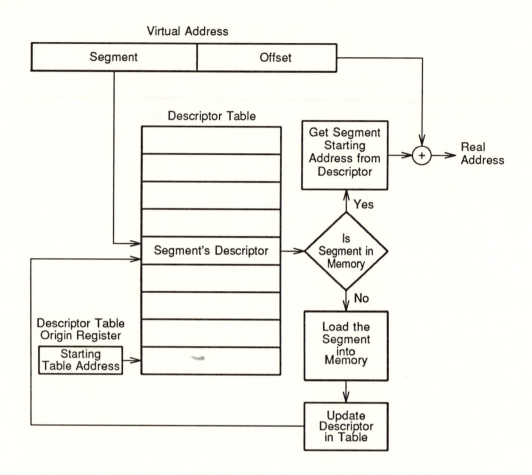

Virtual Address

Segment	Offset

Descriptor Table

Get Segment Starting Address from Descriptor

Real Address

Segment's Descriptor

Is Segment in Memory

Yes

No

Descriptor Table Origin Register

Starting Table Address

Load the Segment into Memory

Update Descriptor in Table

FIGURE 2-27   Virtual Address Translation

concept that this internal address is used for referencing logically consistent addresses within a program address space. As with a traditional virtual address, the logical address consists of a segment selector and an offset. Within the INTEL 80386 CPU, a segment selector value is stored within one of the CPU's segment registers (CS, DS, ES, FS, GS, or SS).

Unlike our theoretical virtual address system that maintained only one descriptor table, the Intel CPU supports two types of such tables, called local and global descriptor tables, respectively. Segments described in the global descriptor table are system-wide segments that can be shared among all users. Typically these consist of operating system code segments that all user programs might require. A local descriptor table contains descriptions of all segments in each task's address space. The starting address of the local descriptor table for the currently running task is referenced using the CPU's 16-bit *local descriptor table register* (LDTR). This system register is used in the same manner as the six segment registers and is explained more fully in Section 4.1. The starting address of the

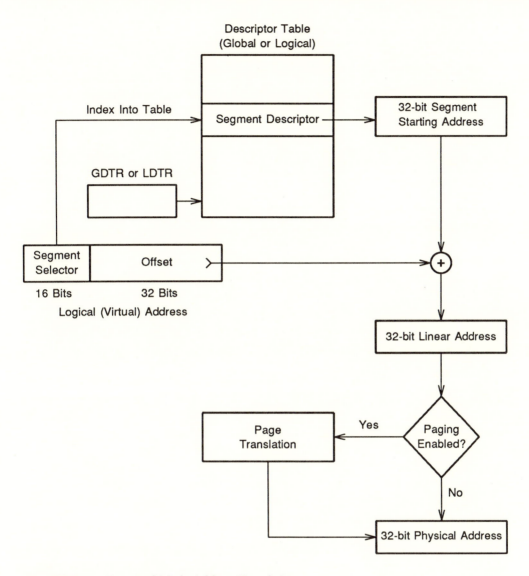

FIGURE 2-28 Protected Mode Address Translation

global descriptor table is stored in the CPU's 48-bit *global descriptor table register* (GDTR), which contains a 32-bit starting address and a 16-bit limit value. These two registers perform the role provided by the descriptor table origin register in our theoretical virtual storage system.

Each segment descriptor in a descriptor table requires 8 bytes of storage and includes the starting address of the segment, the actual size of the segment, whether the segment is physically located in memory, and other information that can be used by an operating system to control memory management. Figure 2-29 shows the descriptor format used for applications code segments.

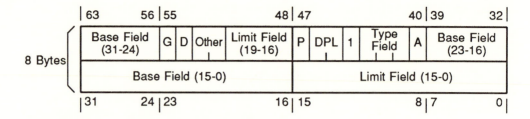

FIGURE 2-29 Code Segment Descriptor Format

As illustrated in Figure 2-29, code descriptors consist of various bit fields. The relevant bit fields for our purposes are:

Base Field: The starting segment address in this field consists of three base fields that are concatenated by the processor to form a full 32-bit segment starting address.

Limit Field: The limit field defines the actual size of the segment and consists of two fields that are concatenated and interpreted based on the value of the G bit.

G Bit: This is the *granularity* bit. When this bit is cleared (0), the value of the limit is interpreted in units of one byte. Thus, the 20 bit limit defines a maximum segment size of 2^{20} or 1 Mbyte. When the granularity bit is set (1), the limit is shifted left by 12 bits to define a maximum segment size of 2^{32} or 4 Gbytes.

D Bit: This is the *default* operand size bit that determines the size of operands accessed by the code and the implied offset address length. When set (D = 1), 32-bit operands and 32-bit offset addresses are specified. When cleared (D = 0), 16-bit operands and offset addresses are specified.

Type Field: The three bits in the type field are used to distinguish between various descriptor types. These include standard data and code segment descriptors, special operating system descriptors, and gate descriptors.

DPL Field: *The descriptor privilege level* bits determine the access privileges of the segment.

P Bit: The P bit is used to indicate that the segment is present in physical memory. An attempt to access a segment when this bit is cleared (0) results in the operating system being alerted to locate and load the requested segment.

A Bit: The *access* bit is set (1) whenever the segment has been referenced. By periodically clearing (0) all access bits and checking them later, the operating system can determine which segments have been recently referenced. This can be used to determine which segment areas to use when new segments must be loaded into memory.

Data segment descriptors have the same format as shown in Figure 2-29 for code segments, except for variations in the type field bit assignments and the default operand size (D) bit. Data segment descriptors do not contain a D bit.

When a segment descriptor is referenced by the value in a segment register, the CPU first determines if the segment is physically present in memory (P bit is a 1). If the P bit is zero, the operating system must locate and load the correct segment. When the segment is present, the CPU compares the offset in the logical address to the segment's limit value to prevent addressing a location outside the segment. An illegal reference within the segment results in a protection fault to the operating system. A valid reference results in the offset being added to the starting segment address in the descriptor to form a 32-bit real address, called a linear address by Intel. When paging is disabled, this linear address is transmitted directly to the address bus as a physical address.

As with our theoretical virtual storage system, the segment and offset portions of a virtual address define the maximum number of segments possible and the maximum size of a segment, respectively. The 32-bit offset used in Intel's logical address defines a maximum segment size of 2^{32} or over 4 billion bytes (4 Gbytes). A 16-bit segment register's contents consists of 13 address bits, one table indicator bit, and two privilege level bits (see Figure 2-30). The 13 address bits permit selection of one of 8192 possible segments (2^{13}) and the table indicator bit permits selection of one of two tables. When this bit is zero, the global descriptor table is selected; when it is one, the local descriptor table for the currently executing task is selected. In total then, 16,384 different segments may be accessed by each task, with each segment composed of a maximum of 4 Gbytes. This defines a virtual storage space for each task of 64 Terabytes or Tbytes ($2^{14} \times 2^{32} = 2^{46}$).

Fragmentation

Program segment size has an enormous effect on system performance. Large segments require smaller descriptor tables and subsequently less total look-up time than do smaller segments. The use of large segments can result in long waits

FIGURE 2-30   A Segment Register's Contents

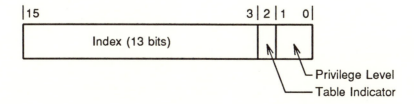

while the necessary segments are loaded into physical memory. Large segments can also result in unusable fragments between segments as various size segments are loaded into memory over a period of time. Figure 2-31 illustrates a case where a program consisting of three segments and a total of 86 Kbytes is ready to be run. Although the system has over 90 Kbytes of memory available, not enough contiguous space is available for any one of the program's segments. This *fragmentation* problem occurs frequently in multiuser systems. One solution to the fragmentation problem is to periodically purge the system. Execution of all programs is stopped and the unused sections or gaps in memory are eliminated by relocating all memory resident segments to one large contiguous area of memory. The appropriate descriptor tables are then updated. This is referred to as "garbage collection" and can significantly increase system overhead time.

A second solution to the fragmentation problem is to create smaller segments. Since segments are constructed to correspond to a program's logical code and data structure, this solution destroys the initial conceptual basis for creating segments. The third and more frequently employed approach is to partition segments into smaller fixed-size blocks called *pages*. If only part of a segment is needed in memory, the page corresponding to the needed part can be loaded. Paging can significantly reduce memory fragmentation by loading only small sections of memory with a program's address space as needed.

FIGURE 2-31   The Fragmentation Problem

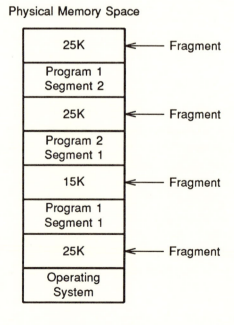

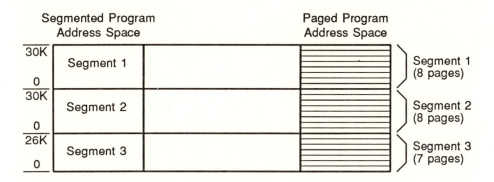

FIGURE 2-32   A Paged Program Address Space

Paging

Figure 2-32 illustrates the division of a program's address space into segments, and the segments into pages. Typically, pages are a fixed size of 4 Kbytes. Using this standard page size, a 30 Kbyte segment requires 8 pages. Since the segment's size is not evenly divisible by a page, the last page in the segment will be only partially full.

The process of loading individual segment pages into memory as they are required is called *demand paging*. In demand paging, physical memory is maintained as a set of smaller units. These units are typically either 2K or 4K bytes and each is called a page frame. The process of physically loading a page from a program's address space into a physical memory page frame is referred to as a *page-in* operation. For consistency, the size of a memory page frame is always the same as the size of a page stored on a disk or any other external storage medium.

Demand paging requires that the operating system keep track of where pages are stored on disk, which pages are loaded into memory, and which memory page frames are available to accept a new page, either because they have never been used or because they contain pages that have not been used recently and can be overwritten with a new page. This process is very similar to the process needed in maintaining nonpaged segments within memory, and simply adds another level of refinement to the address translation process. One method of implementing demand paging is to provide each program segment with its own page table. Using this approach, the entries in a segment's page table contain the starting physical addresses of each page associated with the segment (see Figure 2-33).

Providing each segment with its own page table requires that an additional table be maintained. This additional table contains a directory of all page tables and is used to locate the specific page table associated with a particular segment (see Figure 2-34). Additionally, paging requires that each address used internal

Page Table
(One per Segment)

Page 1 Descriptor
Page 2 Descriptor
• • •
Page m Descriptor
• • •

FIGURE 2-33 An Individual Page Table

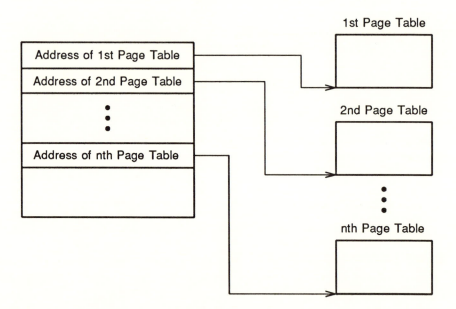

FIGURE 2-34 A Page Directory Table

to the CPU, before or after the segment translation stage, contain sufficient information to identify the page associated with the referenced location. The various page tables use this information to locate the desired page and load it into memory if it is not currently memory resident.

Although particular implementations of paging vary, the need for page tables, either one per segment or one per system, and the need for identification of the

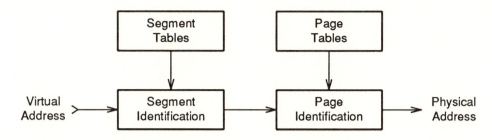

FIGURE 2-35 Virtual Address Translation for a Paged System

proper page within an address, are universal for all paged systems. The complete address translation, regardless of the particular implementation, follows the general pattern illustrated in Figure 2-35.

INTEL 80386 CPU Protected Mode Page Operation*

As with segmentation, paging requires that the operating system and CPU hardware provide certain features needed to support a paged environment. For the INTEL 80386 CPU, the special registers and protection features available for paging are invoked when the operating system sets the PG bit in control register 0 (CR0).

Figure 2-36 illustrates the segment translation previously described for the INTEL 80386 Microprocessor. As noted earlier, Intel refers to the address produced by its segment translation process as a *linear address*. When paging is in effect,

FIGURE 2-36 Protected Mode Segment Translation

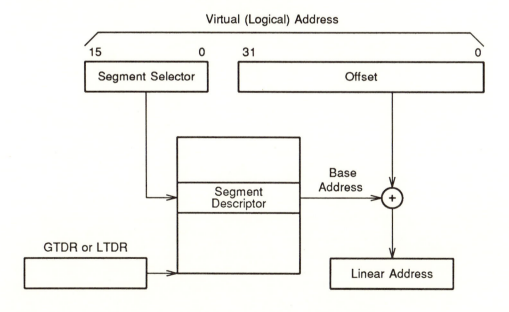

---

*This topic can be omitted on a first reading without loss of subject continuity.

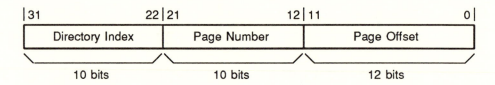

FIGURE 2-37   Linear Address Format

the CPU interprets this address as consisting of three fields - a directory index field, a page number field, and an address offset field (see Figure 2-37).

Figure 2-38 illustrates how the linear address produced by the segmentation unit is translated into a physical address. As shown on this figure, two levels of tables are used to access a page of memory. The index field in the linear address is used to access the page directory table and the page number is used to access an individual segment's page table.

As shown in Figure 2-38, the 10-bit index value is used to locate a single entry in the page directory table, where the entry in this table contains the starting physical address of the segment's page table. The starting address of the page directory table itself is loaded into the CPU's page directory base register (PDBR) by the operating system. (The PDBR register is contained within system register CR3.) Each page directory table can contain a maximum of 1024 entries, which

FIGURE 2-38   Page Translation

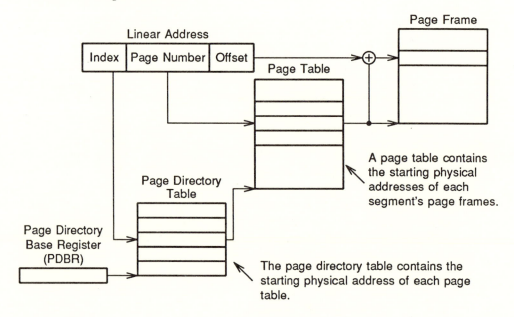

corresponds to the maximum number of entries that can be referenced by a linear address directory index field.

Once the appropriate page table has been located, the page number field within the linear address is used to locate the desired page. Each page table consists of a maximum of 1024 entries that, along with other information, contain the starting physical address of the desired page frame. The page offset value is then added to the starting page frame address to yield an absolute 32-bit physical address. As each page directory can hold 1024 starting page table addresses, each page table can hold 1024 starting page frame addresses, and each frame consists of 2^{12} bytes. A single page directory table can reference the entire 4 Gbyte physical address space of the INTEL 80386 CPU (2^{10} x 2^{10} x 2^{12}). This permits the operating systems designer to use one page directory for all tasks, or one page directory for each task, or any combination between these two extremes.

The paging facilities of the INTEL 80386 CPU allow it to support four basically different types of memory management in protected mode. These include segmentation with paging, segmentation without paging, no segmentation at all (called the flat model), and paging without segmentation (called the linear model). The relationship between address spaces for these modes is:

Segmentation with Paging: A logical address is translated to a linear address that is translated to a physical address.

Segmentation without Paging: A logical address is translated to a linear address that is treated as a physical address with no further translation.

No Segmentation or Paging (Flat Model): A logical address is treated directly as a physical address with no intervening address translation. Strictly speaking, segmentation is always in effect in protected mode. The flat model is created by turning the paging feature off and giving each segment the same starting address. This results in the same address being output by the segment translation algorithm as was input, which is equivalent to turning the segmentation unit off.

Paging Only (Linear Model): A logical address is treated directly as a linear address by turning the segmentation feature off as in the flat model. Paging is enabled and is used to further translate the linear address to a physical address.

Two further points need to be mentioned. First, the procedures described for segmentation and paging require multiple comparisons and table look-ups. If done individually for each memory reference access, these comparisons and table look-ups could add substantially to system overhead and significantly reduce overall system performance. To reduce this overhead and ensure that system performance is not adversely affected, the INTEL 80386 CPU has dedicated on-chip address translation registers and special *associative array registers* and *translation look-aside buffers*. Both of these are high speed devices that can do multiple comparisons in parallel. Secondly, the actual creation and maintenance of the various segment and page tables are always handled by the operating system in conjunction with compilers, linkers, and loaders. From an application programmer's perspective, address translation is always transparent, except as it affects total program size in high-level languages and segment alignment in assembly-level languages.

2.5 Chapter Highlights

1. The AT&T, Intel, and Motorola 32-bit microprocessors, or central processing units (CPUs), have similar architectures consisting of internal fetch, decode, execution, and bus interface units. These architectures support pipelined operation, multitasking, privilege and protection schemes, coprocessor operation, and advanced memory management.

2. The ability of the fetch, decode, and execution units to operate semiautonomously permits the prefetching of instructions in parallel. Thus, as a previously fetched instruction is being executed, another instruction can be fetched, decoded, and loaded into an instruction queue. This overlapping of fetch, decode, and execution operations is referred to as pipelining.

3. 32-bit CPUs support multitasking. Multitasking is the ability to run several tasks concurrently and is achieved by interleaving the execution of different tasks. By supplying dedicated registers, such as task and process control block pointers, support for rapidly switching tasks into and out of the CPU is provided.

4. The register sets of each 32-bit CPU are conveniently separated into a program and system model set. Program model registers consist, at a minimum, of a program counter register, a stack pointer register, a flags register, and multiple general-purpose data and address registers. These registers are typically used by applications programs for data calculation and manipulation. The system model register set provides task, status, and interrupt registers required in the support of operating system functions.

5. An essential feature of 32-bit CPUs is their ability to address a large address space (2^{32}). To effectively manage this space requires advanced memory management techniques. The central feature of all memory management is the ability to translate the program addresses manipulated by the CPU into physical

memory addresses. Additional capabilities include subdividing programs into smaller sections called segments and then allocating each program segment to physical memory locations. In paged memory management, program segments are further subdivided into fixed divisions called pages. This facilitates moving small sections of code into and out of memory as needed.

Exercises

1a. Define the term computer architecture.
1b. Describe a Von Neumann computer architecture.

2a. Describe the operation of the fetch, decode, execution and bus interface units internal to 32-bit CPUs.
2b. Describe how pipelined operation works.

3a. Define the term addressing mode.
3b. What is a task?
3c. Define the term multitasking.

4a. Describe how privilege levels provide a measure of overall system security from a user's viewpoint.
4b. Describe how privilege levels provide a measure of overall system security from an operating system's viewpoint.
4c. Determine if privilege levels are necessary in a single-user environment.

5. Describe the difference between an exception and an interrupt.

6a. Describe the functions of a numeric coprocessor.
6b. Must a coprocessor be a numeric coprocessor? Explain.

7a. What is a program model register set?
7b. List the types of registers typically included in a program model register set.
7c. List the capabilities associated with general-purpose data registers.
7d. List the capabilities associated with general-purpose address registers.
7e. Describe the function of an instruction pointer.

8a. Describe the function of a stack pointer register.
8b. What steps are involved in a push operation?
8c. What steps are involved in a pop operation?
8d. Determine the minimum number of operands required in either a push or pop operation.

9. List the four flag bits common to all flag registers and describe the functions of each bit.

10a. Describe the primary function performed by the segment registers of the INTEL 8086 CPU.

10b. What additional functions did the segment registers of the INTEL 80286 CPU provide that were not available on the 8086 CPU?

10c. What additional functions did the segment registers of the INTEL 80386 CPU provide that were not available on the 80286 CPU?

10d. List the segment registers provided by the INTEL 80386 CPU.

11. List the types and functions of the registers typically associated with a system model register set.

12a. Define what is meant by memory management.

12b. Define the terms program address space, real address space, and physical address space.

12c. Define the term virtual address space and determine the relationship between virtual and program address spaces.

13. Determine the real-mode addresses specified by the following hexadecimal segment and offset values:

a. segment value = 0AB25 and offset value = 00777

b. segment value = 0376F and offset value = 073C4

c. segment value = 01492 and offset value = 00100

d. segment value = 0F216 and offset value = 01950

14a. Describe the information provided by a segment descriptor table.

14b. Determine the mode in which the INTEL 80386 CPU must be operating if segmentation is in effect.

15. Describe the purpose of the D bit within a code segment descriptor. Why is the bit provided on the INTEL 80386 CPU and not required for the INTEL 80286 CPU?

16. Determine the maximum amount of memory that can be addressed by the following Intel microprocessors:

a. 8080 CPU

b. 8086 CPU

c. 80286 CPU

d. 80386 CPU

17. Determine the relationship between the logical, linear, and physical addresses used by the INTEL 80386 CPU when:

a. Segmentation and paging are in effect.

b. Segmentation is used without paging.

c. Neither segmentation nor paging is in effect.

Operating System Support Features

Chapter Three

3.1   Privilege Levels
3.2   Tasks
3.3   System Calls - The Gate Mechanism
3.4   Interrupts
3.5   Exceptions
3.6   Chapter Highlights

In addition to memory management provisions, 32-bit microprocessors provide system designers with special-purpose operating system instructions and architectures that support task-oriented operating systems. This chapter presents these operating system support features.

3.1 Privilege Levels

Operating systems for 32-bit microprocessors are generally multitasking systems that schedule and initiate all tasks, handle error conditions (exceptions to normal processing), and provide system and file security. As we have already seen, an individual task is a separately scheduled, independently executed activity. Generally, a set of tasks is used to perform a major function (such as a program manager, a file manager, or a memory manager). Tasks are scheduled through common scheduling algorithms initiated through a task switch. A task switch is a change in the task controlling the microprocessor invoked by either an implicit or explicit request. Explicit task switches occur in response to instructions that cause either a jump, call, or return to a task. Implicit task switches occur as a result of reset and interrupt requests, or can be caused by the processing of certain exception conditions.

As part of its architecture, a 32-bit microprocessor provides multiple privilege levels for tasks. In the INTEL 80386 Microprocessor and the AT&T *WE* 32100 Microprocessor there are four privilege levels, ranging from the most privileged (level 0) to the least privileged (level 3). One of the functions of the memory management system is to enforce the assigned privilege levels and ensure that code and data at a particular level are accessed only by code or tasks having the right permissions. The four privilege levels used by the Intel and AT&T microprocessors are defined as:

Kernel (level 0): The most privileged level, it is assigned to the operating system's most privileged services (e.g., device drivers and interrupt handlers).

Executive (level 1): This level, sometimes called the system service level, provides a less privileged state for operating system functions.

Supervisor or Custom Extensions (level 2): Common library routines can operate at this level and be safe from corruption by level 3 activities. Typically, any input or output data buffers are assigned to this level.

Applications (level 3): The least privileged level, most user programs are assigned this level.

In addition to the privilege levels that are assigned to tasks, each 32-bit processor has a two-level hierarchy for its instruction set: privileged and nonprivileged. Privileged instructions may only be executed if the processor is executing a kernel level task. These instructions are used by the operating system to perform task switches, to enable or disable memory management segmentation and paging, or to suspend fetching of instructions.

Many privileged instructions automatically cause a built-in sequence of actions, called a *microsequence*, to be executed by the CPU. These microsequences change the hardware state of the CPU for a new task. For example, a task-switching instruction causes a microsequence to be executed that automatically stores into memory the contents of selected CPU registers and loads the registers with values appropriate to the new task. This machine execution feature removes many of the actions required for task switching from the operating system software, permitting quicker and more efficient operating system design and execution.

Nonprivileged instructions may be executed by all tasks regardless of their privilege level. Included within the nonprivileged instruction set is a unique instruction called a gate. A *gate instruction* provides restricted entry into higher level tasks by lower level tasks. This allows a nonoperating system task to access an operating system task in a limited manner that does not breach the security of the operating system.

3.2 Tasks

A task determines the context under which the CPU operates. This includes the machine (hardware) state, which consists of the CPU's register values, and the software state, which consists of any operating system data structures such as descriptor tables. Each program executed by the CPU is regulated and monitored by the current task controlling the CPU. As such, a task provides an umbrella under which programs are allowed to operate. At any one time, however, only one task may define the context under which the CPU operates. To support this type of operation, a task in a multitasking operating system must include the following two elements:

Task State Control Block: This data structure is stored in the external memory that contains the hardware context of a task. When an executing task is stopped, sufficient information about the contents of selected CPU registers needed to reinstate the task later are stored in this data structure. The INTEL 80386 CPU stores each task state control block in its own segment referred to as a task state segment (TSS). The AT&T *WE* 32100 CPU refers to this block as a process control block (PCB).

Task State Control Block Pointer: This system model CPU register identifies the starting location of the task state control block for the currently executing task. This register can only be written by a privileged instruction when the CPU is operating in the kernel privilege level.

To make the discussion of these two elements more tangible, let us consider their implementation using the INTEL 80386 CPU.

INTEL 80386 CPU Task State Segment

Figure 3-1 illustrates an INTEL 80386 task state segment (TSS). The items stored in a TSS consist of both dynamic and static information fields. The dynamic fields of the currently executing task are updated by the CPU when a task switch occurs during its execution. The values stored in these fields are subsequently reloaded into the CPU whenever a task switch is used to reinstate the task. These dynamic fields include storage for the contents of:
- general registers EAX, EBX, ECX, EDX, EBP, ESP, ESI, and EDI
- segment registers CS, DS, SS, ES, FS, and GS
- flag register EFLAGS
- instruction pointer EIP, and
- address information to locate the previously executing task.

The static fields include information that can be read by the processor but that does not normally change. This includes operating system data stored in the system model registers and address information for various stacks used by programs operating under the task. The purpose of these static fields, as they relate to task management, is presented in this section.

Task State Segment Descriptor

The 80386 task state segment is identified and located by a task state segment descriptor. This TSS descriptor is almost identical to the descriptors used for code and data segments and is illustrated in Figure 3-2. The granularity (G) bit; the present (P) bit; and the base, limit, and descriptor privilege level (DPL) fields of the TSS descriptor provide the same functions that they perform in the code and segment descriptors. The busy (B) bit is used to indicate a busy task. When the B bit is one, the task is currently executing; when it is zero, the task is not being executed. A task is forbidden to call itself (tasks are not re-entrant) and the state of the B bit is used to detect this type of illegal task switch.

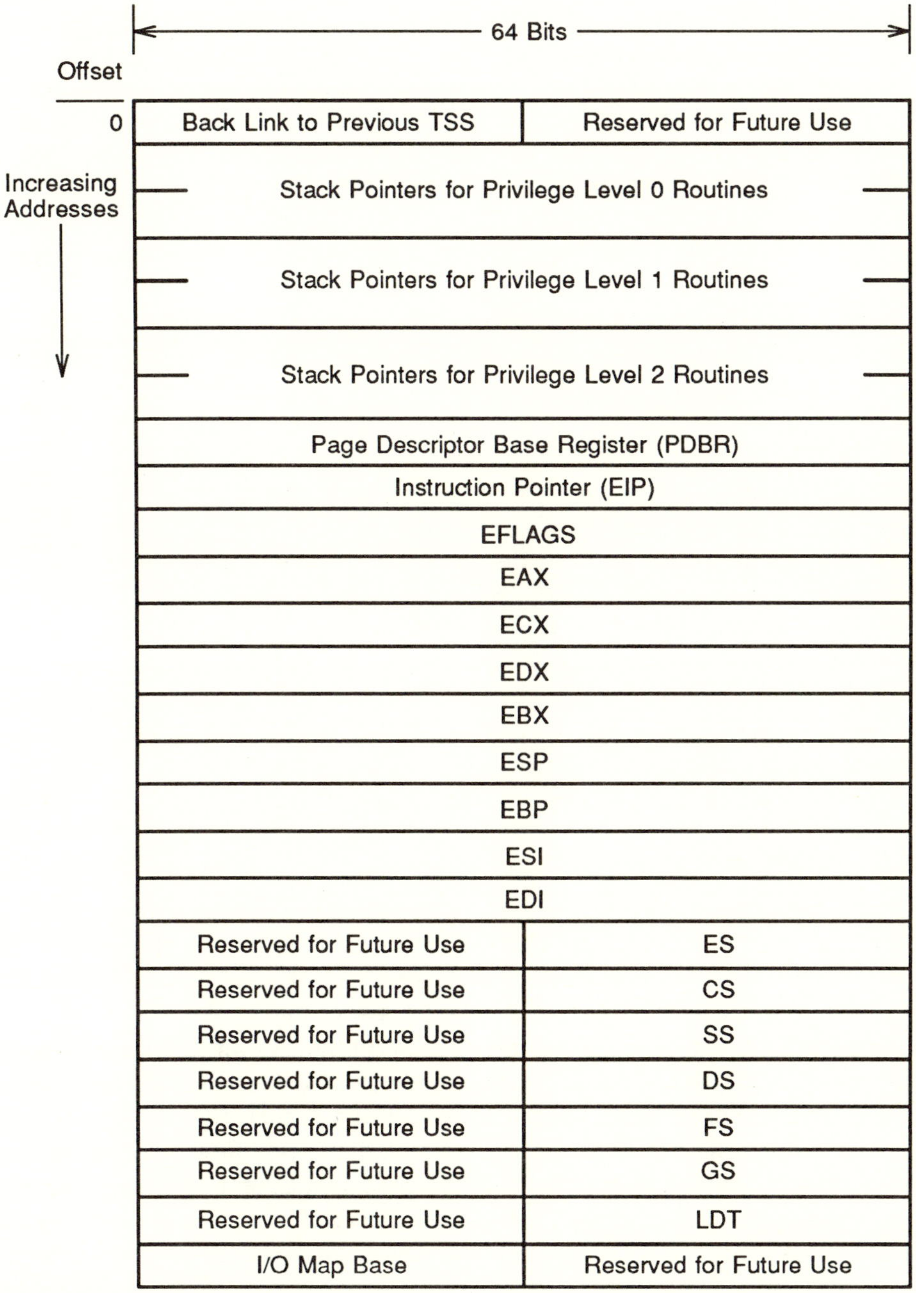

```
                    |←————————————— 64 Bits —————————————→|
Offset
  0    | Back Link to Previous TSS    | Reserved for Future Use    |
       |——  Stack Pointers for Privilege Level 0 Routines      ——|
       |——  Stack Pointers for Privilege Level 1 Routines      ——|
       |——  Stack Pointers for Privilege Level 2 Routines      ——|
       |       Page Descriptor Base Register (PDBR)            |
       |              Instruction Pointer (EIP)                |
       |                     EFLAGS                            |
       |                      EAX                              |
       |                      ECX                              |
       |                      EDX                              |
       |                      EBX                              |
       |                      ESP                              |
       |                      EBP                              |
       |                      ESI                              |
       |                      EDI                              |
       | Reserved for Future Use      | ES                     |
       | Reserved for Future Use      | CS                     |
       | Reserved for Future Use      | SS                     |
       | Reserved for Future Use      | DS                     |
       | Reserved for Future Use      | FS                     |
       | Reserved for Future Use      | GS                     |
       | Reserved for Future Use      | LDT                    |
       | I/O Map Base                 | Reserved for Future Use|
```

Increasing Addresses ↓

FIGURE 3-1 INTEL 80386 Microprocessor Task State Segment (TSS)

89

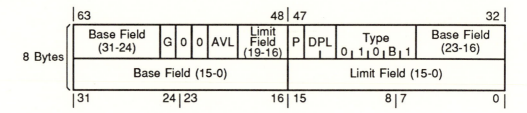

FIGURE 3-2 80386 Task State Segment (TSS) Descriptor

Unlike code and data segment descriptors that can be located in either the global descriptor table or a local descriptor table, TSS descriptors must be located in the global descriptor table (GDT) for the INTEL 80386 CPU.

Task Register

The current task segment is located using a task segment register, which is referred to as the task register (TR) in the INTEL 80386 CPU. Using the task register, the operation for locating the current task state segment is identical to that used to locate code, data, and stack segments.

As illustrated in Figure 3-3, the task register contains an index value that specifies the location of the TSS descriptor within the global descriptor table. This index value is referred to as a *selector*. Selectors contained in the task register are used in the same manner as the selectors stored in the code, data, and stack segment registers: they select a descriptor within a descriptor table. The descriptor contains the actual starting address of the desired segment.

Hidden Descriptor Registers

All descriptor tables are located in memory. The table look-up shown in Figure 3-3 implies a time-consuming memory reference each time a selector is used. To circumvent the need for this memory reference, the INTEL 80386 CPU supplies the task, code, stack, and data segment registers with individual, 64-bit "hidden" descriptor registers as shown in Figure 3-4. The contents of the hidden descriptor registers are maintained by the CPU and are a copy of the appropriate descriptors stored within the complete descriptor tables located in memory. The descriptors contained within these registers cannot be read or modified directly by any program instruction; they are effectively invisible or hidden to the programmer.

Programs affect the contents of the hidden descriptor registers whenever the contents of a segment or task register are changed. Each time a program changes the selector in either a segment register or the task register, the CPU automatically locates the associated descriptor in the descriptor table and loads this descriptor into the corresponding hidden descriptor register. Subsequently, any reference using a segment or task register results in the descriptor being obtained from the CPU's hidden descriptor register rather than from a direct table look-up.

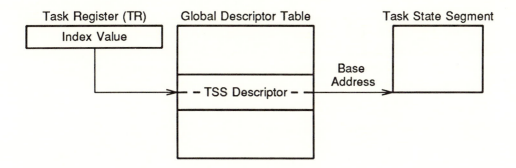

FIGURE 3-3 Locating the Current Task State Segment

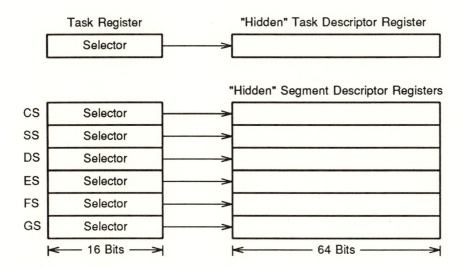

FIGURE 3-4 Segment Registers and Their Associated Hidden Descriptor Registers

The presence of hidden registers requires that a change to a descriptor made in the memory descriptor table also be made to the copy in the hidden register if the changed descriptor corresponds to a currently used segment. This update is the responsibility of the operating system. Without this explicit update the contents of the hidden register would continue to reflect the value of the descriptor prior to the change. Only when a selector change is made directly to either the task or segment registers does the CPU automatically update the descriptor register without further operating system intervention.

Task Switches

An explicit task switch is invoked by either unconditionally jumping to a new task or by calling a task. In both cases, the context under which the CPU operates is switched by the saving of the current TSS and the loading of the new TSS. This includes:

- saving the state of the outgoing task by storing the contents of the general, segment, EFLAGS, and EIP registers in the current TSS
- clearing the busy bit in the outgoing TSS descriptor
- loading the task register (TR) with the incoming task's selector. This includes loading the hidden section of the TR with the task's descriptor.
- setting the busy bit in the incoming TSS descriptor
- resetting the state of the CPU by loading the general, segment, EFLAGS, EIP, LDT, and PDBR registers from the new TSS.

A primary difference between unconditionally changing a task through a jump or by calling a task is that a called task can reinstate the calling task using a privileged return instruction. The return instruction forces an explicit task switch similar to an unconditional jump, except the incoming task is identified by the return address provided by the calling task.

In the case of unconditionally jumping to a new task, the CPU automatically checks that the privilege level of the outgoing task is equal to or higher than the privilege level of the designated task. This prevents a less privileged task from entering a more privileged task. Should such an invalid task switch be attempted, an exception is signaled (see Section 3.5).

In the case of a call, a less privileged task is permitted to access a more privileged task. As might be expected, the means of doing this is highly regulated to ensure that overall system integrity is not compromised. Entry into more privileged tasks, or more privileged procedures (code segments) operating under the same task, is provided by means of gate descriptors, which is the topic of the next section.

Whenever a task switch occurs as a result of either an explicit switch due to a jump, call, or return instruction or an implicit switch due to a reset, interrupt, or exception condition, certain CPU system model registers are neither saved nor reloaded. These include the global descriptor table register (GDTR), which contains information required by all tasks, and the local descriptor table (LDT) register. Although the LDT register is not saved, it is updated from the LDT field of the incoming task when a task switch is invoked. The LDT selector does not have to be saved because this selector value is never altered under normal task control. Should the operating system modify a task's LDT selector, the change would be made directly within the task's TSS. The next task switch to this task would then update correctly the CPU's LDT register.

The Sharing of Address Spaces

Since each task has access to the same global descriptor table, the sharing of code and data segments can always be accomplished by having each task use

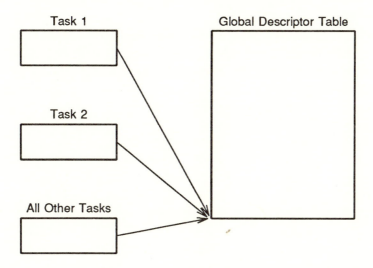

FIGURE 3-5 Sharing Segments Using a Global Descriptor Table

descriptors located in this system table. For example, if two tasks use only code and data descriptors contained within the global descriptor table, as illustrated in Figure 3-5, the address space for both tasks will be identical.

A more selective method of restricting segment-sharing among a limited number of tasks is to have each task use the same local descriptor table. As previously shown in Figure 3-1, each task state segment (TSS) includes a selector that is loaded in the CPU's local descriptor table (LDT) register when the task is invoked. By having each task's LDT selector point to the same table, both tasks will share the same local address space for all of their segments (see Figure 3-6).

Another method of sharing segments between tasks is to give each task its own unique local descriptor table with at least one descriptor that is identical in each table. Since the same descriptor resides in both tables, both tasks will share access to the same segment. Descriptors that point to the same segment are referred to as aliased descriptors. Any number of individual segments can be shared by providing an aliased descriptor for each segment.

The sharing of address spaces can be further refined when paging is enabled. In this case, a task's page directory base register (PDBR) selector value is loaded from the TSS. With a page directory entry (PDE) in each page directory pointing to a common page table, both tasks can share the same page frames in the common page table. The sharing of page frames using this method is illustrated in Figure 3-7.

Finally, complete isolation of address spaces between tasks can be accomplished by giving each task its own local descriptor table and ensuring that each table has no aliased descriptors.

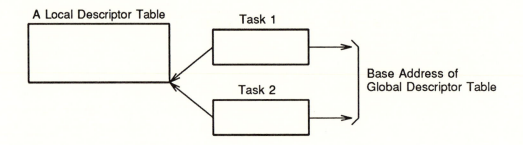

FIGURE 3-6 Sharing Segments Using the Same Local Descriptor Table

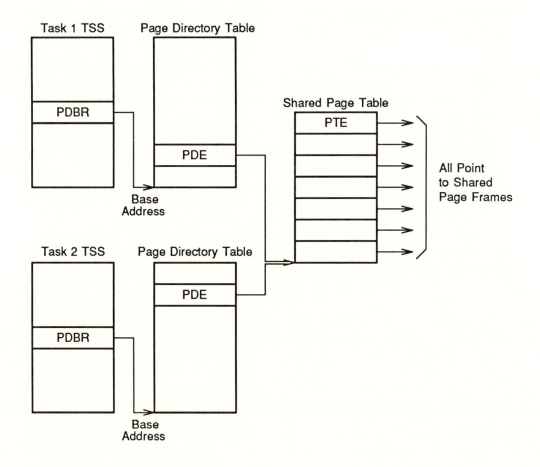

FIGURE 3-7 Sharing Page Frames

3.3 System Calls - The Gate Mechanism

Assigning a privilege level (0, 1, 2, or 3) to a task effectively prohibits a less privileged task from calling a more privileged task. This same restriction applies to procedures within a task or between two different tasks: under normal circumstances, code located in a segment having a lower privilege level cannot access code located in a higher-level segment. This assignment of privilege levels makes it necessary to have some means of "jumping" around the assigned levels in a selected and controlled manner. For example, code located in a less privileged user code segment must occasionally access procedures located in more privileged operating systems code segments. The means for doing this is provided by *gate descriptors.*

There are four types of gate descriptors: task gates, call gates, interrupt gates, and trap gates. Essentially, these gates all perform the same function and allow lower-level tasks or procedures to call higher-level tasks or procedures. These lower-level to higher-level calls are referred to as *system calls.*

The name of the gate is indicative of the function that it performs. A task gate provides entry into a more privileged task; a call gate provides entry into more privileged code; and interrupt and trap gates provide entry into the operating systems interrupt and trap handler routines.

The call, interrupt, and trap gate descriptor format shown in Figure 3-8 consists of a selector and offset. The selector determines the base address of a code segment; the offset determines the entry point into the code segment by a calling procedure. For interrupt and trap gates, the entry point corresponds to an interrupt handling routine. The DPL field of the gate determines the minimum privilege level needed by the calling task in order to use the gate.

Figure 3-9 shows the format for a task gate descriptor. Since entry to a task state segment must begin at the starting address of the segment, a task gate descriptor does not contain an offset address.

FIGURE 3-8   Call, Interrupt, and Trap Gate Descriptor Format

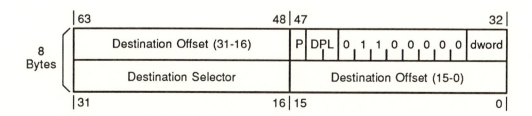

95

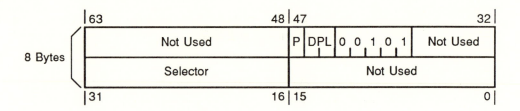

FIGURE 3-9 A Task Gate Descriptor

Figure 3-10 illustrates indirect access to a protected code segment via a call gate descriptor. (A similar indirect access to a task state segment is provided by a task gate descriptor, except no offset into the task state segment is used). Although the DPL field of the code segment descriptor defines the segment's security level, the DPL field of the gate defines the level needed to use the gate for entry into the code segment descriptor. As such, the gate descriptor provides a secondary and controlled entry into the segment, hence the name gate. Gate descriptors are used by a calling program or task using a call instruction (also referred to as a call gate instruction). The call instruction references a gate and the gate indirectly specifies the final code or task segment called.

FIGURE 3-10 Using a Call Gate Descriptor

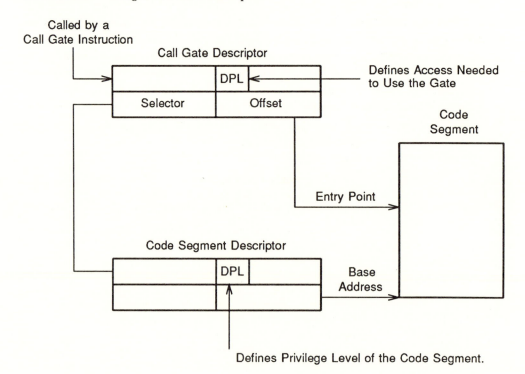

Although call gate descriptors can reside in either the global descriptor table or any local descriptor table, call gates used for entry into operating system procedures are always placed in the global descriptor table. This makes the code pointed to available to all code segments. Task gates are typically located in local descriptor tables but point to task state segment descriptors stored in the global descriptor table. Interrupt and trap gates are located in the interrupt descriptor table described in the next section.

Besides providing alternate entry into a segment or task, using gates provides a further advantage in that the calling code or task need only reference the memory address of the gate and not the ultimate address of the called segment or task. Consider a modification to the operating system that requires relocating a code or task segment into another section of memory. The modified operating system must be compatible with application code written for the older version. All that has to be done to meet this requirement is to update the selector and offset information in all gate descriptors. The locations of the gate descriptors within the global descriptor table must not, of course, be modified. Using this method, existing user programs need not be relinked to run under the modified operating system.

Passing Parameters

Call, interrupt, and trap gates can only point to code segments and the referenced code always executes within the context of the currently controlling task. The contents of the task register are not altered; all that is effectively switched is the currently executing code segment.

Using gates to access procedures (code segments) requires that some means be provided for the passing of data and a return address to the called procedure. The INTEL 80386 CPU is unique in that separate stacks are provided for each privilege level of the currently active code segment. This ensures that higher-level called procedures do not have to depend on a lower-level procedure to provide sufficient stack space.

When the target procedure and the calling procedure have the same privilege level, both procedures share the same execution stack. This is referred to as an *intralevel* system call. In this case, the passed parameters and the return address are placed on the current stack, as illustrated in Figure 3-11.

The number of bytes required to store the passed parameters on the stack must be specified by the dword field of the gate descriptor that provides entry into the called procedure. For example, if two parameters are placed on the stack, the gate descriptor contains a double word count of 2. Since the dword field can contain a maximum value of 31, the passing of more than 31 doubleword parameters requires passing an address. The called procedure can then use the address to reference the memory area where the parameters are stored. Additionally, the called procedure must have information as to the number of parameters located at the starting address passed.

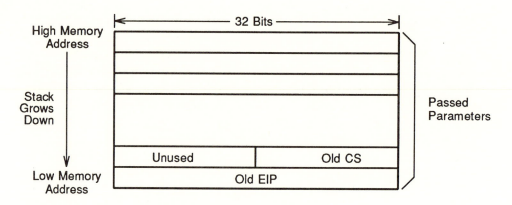

FIGURE 3-11   Stack Contents for an Intralevel System Call

When the target procedure has a higher privilege level than the calling procedure, both the passed parameters and the return address are placed on a stack. In this case, the stack is not the caller's stack but the execution stack of the more-privileged called procedure. The values for the new stack segment and offset (SS and ESP, respectively) that point to the new stack are provided by the currently active task state segment.

Recall that each task state segment contains three pairs of stack pointers (refer to Figure 3-12). Each of these pointers consists of a 16-bit stack segment address and a 32-bit offset address. Which stack is active depends on the privilege level of the called procedure (its DPL value) relative to the privilege level of the calling procedure (its CPL value). When a system call to a level 0 procedure is made from a less-privileged procedure, the privilege level 0 stack pointers are used. Similarly, a system call to a privilege level 1 or 2 procedure from a less-privileged procedure causes the SS and ESP registers to be loaded with the appropriate values from the task state segment. Since a privilege level 3 procedure cannot be called from a lower-level procedure (none exist), the TSS segment does not contain SS and ESP values for a switch to this privilege level.

Since system calls to higher-level procedures, referred to as *interlevel* calls, involve altering the execution stack, the SS and ESP contents of the calling procedure must be stored for later reinstatement. The method for constructing the new stack requires that the calling procedure place the parameters to be passed onto its own stack, as is done in an intralevel system call. The call gate instruction then locates the new stack from the task state segment. This is done because the privilege level of the requested procedure (its DPL) is lower than the privilege level of the currently operating procedure (its CPL). The caller's SS, ESP, and the parameters on its stack are copied onto the new stack. Following these, the caller's return address, consisting of the caller's CS and EIP register values, is placed on the stack. See Figure 3-12.

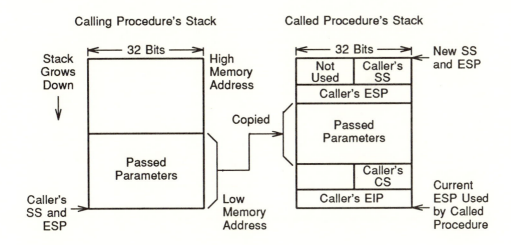

FIGURE 3-12 Stack Contents for an Interlevel System Call

A return from a called procedure is accomplished using a return instruction. This instruction includes the number of bytes used in storing the passed parameters on the stack, regardless of the privilege level under which the stack was created. For example, if four double-word parameters were stored on the stack, the return instruction would specify a byte count of 16.

The purpose of a return is to restore the caller's stack to its original state as it existed before the call was made. A return:

- Pops the old CS and EIP values from the stack into the appropriate registers.
- Pops the old SS and ESP values from the stack into the appropriate registers if a gate to a more-privileged procedure was used. (The caller's privilege level, contained in bits 0 and 1 of the its CS selector, is compared to the CPL of the new procedure to determine if a privilege level switch occurred).
- Increments the old ESP by the correct number of passed parameter bytes to restore the pointer to its value before the system call was issued.

Because of this return procedure, calls to lower-level procedures using gates are not permitted by the INTEL 80386 CPU. If such a call were allowed, the less-privileged procedure could alter the return address on the stack. This would provide a return to any location within the more-privileged procedure and effectively circumvent the restricted access procedure provided by the gate mechanism. Obviously, such an unrestricted access into higher-level procedures could wreak havoc with the operating system.

Call, interrupt, and trap gates provide restricted entry and return to code segments; a task gate provides restricted entry into a task. When the task is entered through a gate using a call instruction, an explicit task switch occurs. Unlike a task switch invoked by an unconditional jump to a task, an explicit task switch through a gate permits the called task to return to the calling task using a return instruction. This requires that the return address be available to the new task.

The return to the original task is accomplished by writing the calling task's selector (the value in the task register) into the back-link field of the new TSS and setting the nested task (NT) bit in the new task's EFLAGS register. The NT bit indicates to the processor that the current back-link field is valid. The CPU examines the NT bit upon encountering a return instruction. If this bit is set, the 80386 CPU performs a task switch to the task indicated by the back-link field. Notice that this return procedure does not use a stack as was used for the call, interrupt, or trap gates. Since the stack is not involved in a task switch, the direct passing of parameters between tasks is not facilitated. This is not a disadvantage because tasks, by definition, are independently-executing units of activity.

3.4 Interrupts

Interrupts are externally generated requests for CPU attention. A *maskable interrupt* is a request that can be ignored (or masked) by the CPU depending on the setting of a flag bit in the CPU's condition register. For the INTEL 80386 CPU, the interrupt flag is bit 9 in the EFLAGS register. A requested interrupt is accepted when this bit is set (1) and an external device drives the interrupt request (INTR) pin high. When this bit is cleared (0), the CPU ignores the state of the INTR pin and no interrupts are accepted.

A *nonmaskable interrupt* is a hardwired interrupt request that cannot be masked and ignored by the CPU. Interrupts are made nonmaskable by asserting the CPU's nonmaskable interrupt pin. For example, nonmaskable interrupt requests are presented to the INTEL 80386 CPU by setting its nonmaskable interrupt (NMI) pin high (1). The nonmaskable interrupt is used to provide immediate service for high-priority requests. For example, the detection of a sudden voltage drop by external monitoring equipment would signal the CPU of an impending power failure via the nonmaskable interrupt line.

Interrupt Gates

An operating system's interrupt handlers, whether separate tasks or procedures executing under the currently running task, are accessed using an interrupt vector table. The interrupt vector table's entries can be used to locate all interrupt handler routines. In the INTEL 80386 CPU, this vector table is called an interrupt descriptor table, and each entry is either an interrupt gate, task gate, or trap gate. The interrupt descriptor table is a global table accessible by all tasks and any procedure running under a task. To locate this memory table, the INTEL

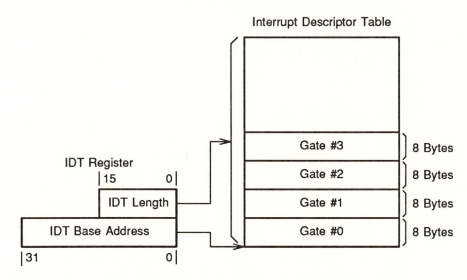

FIGURE 3-13   Intel IDT Register and Associated Interrupt Descriptor Table

80386 CPU stores the base address and length of the table in its interrupt descriptor table (IDT) register (see Figure 3-13).

Actual switching to an interrupt handler is accomplished using the addresses provided in the interrupt vector table. Figure 3-14 illustrates how this is done by the INTEL 80386 CPU when a task gate is used. The desired interrupt handler is identified by an interrupt number corresponding to the cause of the interrupt as identified by the operating system. The interrupt number is used as an index into the interrupt descriptor table to locate the correct gate. Within the gate descriptor is a selector (shown in Figure 3-9). This selector is used as an index to the operating system's global descriptor table to locate a TSS descriptor. The TSS

FIGURE 3-14   A System Call to an Interrupt Task

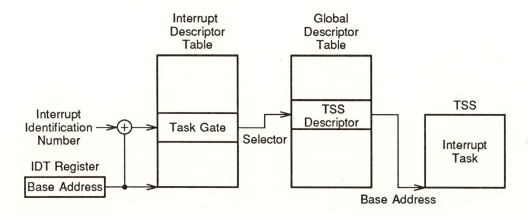

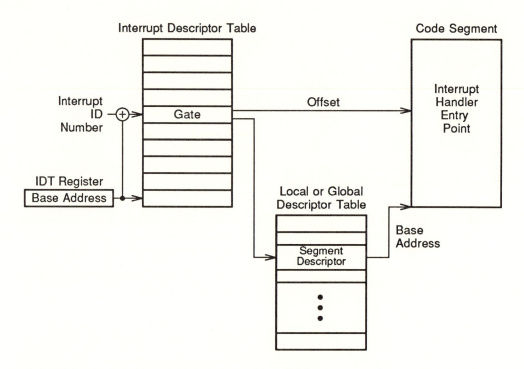

FIGURE 3-15 A System Call to an Interrupt Procedure

descriptor contains the base address of the new task state segment. The mechanism used to return to the calling code was described in the last section.

Figure 3-15 illustrates the process used when a system call is made to an interrupt procedure. This is the identical gate mechanism described in the previous section for call gates. Unlike call gates which can reside in either the global or local descriptor tables, an interrupt gate must be located in the interrupt descriptor table. In all other regards, both gates are identical.

3.5 Exceptions

Exceptions are error conditions generated by the action of the CPU. An interrupt is generated independently of the currently executing instruction and is caused by an event external to the CPU. By definition, exceptions are caused by error conditions resulting from the execution of an instruction. Exceptions are classified as either *processor* or *programmed* exceptions.

Processor Exceptions

There are three types of processor exceptions: faults, traps, and aborts. These are defined as:

Faults: A fault is an error condition caused by an instruction either before or during its execution. After the fault is serviced, execution typically resumes with the instruction that caused the fault. Faults can be further classified as internal or external. Internal faults are detected by the processor; external faults are caused by an instruction but are recognized outside the processor, typically when an illegal memory access is attempted.

Traps: Traps are internal error conditions which are the result of an instruction and are detected by the processor. After the trap is serviced, execution typically resumes with the next instruction that would have been executed had no trap occurred.

Aborts: Aborts are exceptions caused by severe system errors, such as illegal system table values or CPU hardware errors that preclude continuing execution of the current code.

Table 3-1 lists the more commonly detected processor exceptions. Like interrupts, processor exceptions alert the operating system to the need for service. This service consists of suspending operation of the current instruction and invoking an exception service routine, referred to as an *exception handler.*

Unlike interrupt handlers, exception handlers are almost always implemented as procedures operating under the context of the currently executing task. This allows the exception handler to access the running task's data and to use the resources of the current task. The entry to the exception handler is accomplished using the same gate mechanism shown in Figure 3-15, except the gate descriptor is formally referred to as a trap gate instead of an interrupt gate. Both interrupt and trap gate descriptors, shown in Figure 3-8, have the same format.

To correctly access an exception handler, the CPU requires that the operating system place gates to specific exception handlers in specified places within its interrupt vector table. Then, when the CPU identifies an exception using an identification number, the exception handler corresponding to the specified condition will be accessed correctly. Table 3-2 lists the gate descriptors that the INTEL 80386 CPU expects the operating system to load into its interrupt descriptor table. The table can contain 256 gate descriptors; the first 32 are reserved for the listed exception handler gates. Table 3-3 lists the gate assignments defined by the MOTOROLA MC68020 CPU. A similar table is required by the AT&T processor.

TABLE 3-1 Common Exception Summary

Exception	Cause	Type
Integer zero divide	An attempt to divide by zero.	Fault
Illegal opcode	Use of an undefined opcode.	Fault
Gate Error	An exception when accessing a gate descriptor.	Fault
Illegal level change	An attempt to increase the current execution privilege level on a return from a gate.	Fault
Integer overflow	An attempt to write data into a destination that is too small.	Trap
Privileged opcode	An attempt to execute an opcode defined for kernel level from a different execution level.	Fault
Privileged register	An attempt to write system registers when not in kernel level.	Fault
Stack bound	A stack pointer outside the upper or lower stack boundary.	Fault
Interrupt ID fetch	A memory exception when accessing a TSS on a task switch.	Fault
Breakpoint	Detection of breakpoint.	Trap

Programmed Exceptions

In addition to processor detected exceptions, the INTEL 80386 CPU, MOTOROLA MC68020 CPU, and the AT&T *WE* 32100 CPU all have instructions specifically designed to generate exceptions. These are termed *programmed exceptions* and are sometimes referred to as *software interrupts*. These programmed exceptions are caused by an event internal to the CPU; however, they are always classified as exceptions and are handled accordingly.

In the INTEL 80386 CPU, a programmed exception is caused by the execution of an instruction having the form INT n, where n is used as an index value into the interrupt descriptor table. For example, the instruction INT 0 would reference the first gate stored in the interrupt descriptor table. As listed in Table 3-2, this causes a system call to the exception handler reserved for a divide error. The equivalent instruction for the AT&T CPU is an explicit GATE instruction to the desired exception handler. The equivalent instruction for the MOTOROLA MC68020 CPU is the TRAP n instruction, where n refers to the corresponding gate in the Motorola interrupt vector table.

TABLE 3-2 INTEL 80386 CPU Interrupt and Exception Assignments

Identifier	Description
0	Divide error
1	Debug exceptions
2	Non maskable interrupt
3	Breakpoint (one-byte INT 3 instruction)
4	Overflow (INTO instruction)
5	Bounds check (BOUND instruction)
6	Invalid opcode
7	Coprocessor not available
8	Double fault
9	Reserved
10	Invalid TSS
11	Segment not present
12	Stack exception
13	General protection
14	Page fault
15	Reserved
16	Coprocessor error
17-31	Reserved
32-255	For external interrupts via INTR pin

TABLE 3-3 MOTOROLA MC68020 CPU Interrupt and Exception Assignments

Vector Number	Assignment
0	Reset: Initial interrupt Stack Pointer
1	Reset: Initial Program Counter
2	Bus Error
3	Address Error
4	Illegal Instruction
5	Zero Divide
6	CHK, CHK2 Instruction
7	cpTRAPcc, TRAPcc, TRAPV Instructions
8	Privilege Violation
9	Trace
10	Line 1010 Emulator
11	Line 1111 Emulator
12	(Unassigned, Reserved)
13	Coprocessor Protocol Violation
14	Uninitialized Interrupt
15	Format Error
16–23	(Unassigned, Reserved)
24	Spurious Interrupt
25	Level 1 Interrupt Auto Vector
26	Level 2 Interrupt Auto Vector

TABLE 3-3 MOTOROLA MC68020 CPU Interrupt and Exception Assignments (Continued)

Vector Number	Assignment
27	Level 3 Interrupt Auto Vector
28	Level 4 Interrupt Auto Vector
29	Level 5 Interrupt Auto Vector
30	Level 6 Interrupt Auto Vector
31	Level 7 Interrupt Auto Vector
32–47	TRAP #0-15 Instruction Vectors
48	FPCP Branch or Set on Unordered Condition
49	FPCP Inexact Result
50	FPCP Divide by Zero
51	FPCP Underflow
52	FPCP Operand Error
53	FPCP Overflow
54	FPCP Signaling NAN
55	Unassigned, Reserved
56	PMMU Configuration
57	PMMU Illegal Operation
58	PMMU Access Level Violation
59–63	(Unassigned, Reserved)
64–255	User Defined Vectors (192)

3.6 Chapter Highlights

1. A task determines the context under which the CPU operates. This includes the hardware (machine) state consisting of the CPU's register values, and the software state consisting of operating system data structures.

2. A multitasking operating system must schedule, initiate, suspend, and restart individual tasks that control the computer system. The operating system also must provide communication between tasks in a manner that ensures one task does not degrade or interfere with the operation of another task.

3. The Intel, AT&T, and Motorola 32-bit microprocessors provide hardware capabilities that support multitasking operating systems. These capabilities include multiple privilege levels, task-related registers, task data structure support, and task call mechanisms that allow controlled accesses between tasks.

4. A task switch is a change in the task controlling the microprocessor. An explicit task switch is invoked by either a call or jump-to-task instruction. An implicit task switch occurs in response to a reset, interrupt, or exception condition.

5. The three microprocessors described in this chapter all have a two-level instruction hierarchy. Privileged instructions may be executed only by operating system tasks. Nonprivileged instructions may be executed by both operating system and applications tasks.

6. A microsequence is a sequence of instructions executed by the CPU in response to a single program instruction. All task switch instructions invoke a microsequence to automatically store the contents of selected CPU registers for the outgoing task and to load these registers with the values for the incoming task. This alleviates the operating system from explicitly performing these instructions, permitting quicker and more efficient operating system design and execution.

7. System calls allow lower privileged tasks and procedures (code segments) operating under a task to access higher privileged tasks and procedures. The entry mechanism to the higher privileged states is called a gate. Task gates provide entry into more privileged tasks; call gates provide entry into more privileged code segments; and interrupt and trap gates provide entry into the operating system interrupt and trap handler procedures.

8. Interrupts are externally generated requests for CPU attention. Software instructions can be used to direct the CPU to ignore maskable interrupts. Nonmaskable interrupts are hardware generated requests that cannot be ignored by the CPU under software control.

9. An exception is an error condition generated by the action of the CPU. There are three types of exceptions: faults, traps, and aborts. Faults are exceptions detected either before or during an instruction's execution. Traps are exceptions caused as a result of an instruction's execution. Aborts are error conditions caused by the CPU, such as a CPU hardware error.

Exercises

1a. Describe the purpose of a task state control block.
1b. Describe the purpose of a task state control block pointer.

2a. What is the purpose of the granularity, present, base, limit, and DPL fields of the INTEL 80386 CPU task state segment descriptor?
2b. What is the purpose of the hidden descriptor registers associated with each INTEL 80386 CPU segment register?

3. Assume that a task must manipulate a linked list of data elements. If an interrupt were allowed while the task was updating a link address, the correct linkage between data elements would be destroyed. Determine what the task must do to ensure that this does not happen.

4. Assume that two tasks share a common data area. Prior to accessing the data area, each task tests a shared "in use" flag to determine that the data area is not being used by the other task. If the test indicates that the data area is available, the requesting task sets the "in use" flag; this prevents the other task from accessing the data area until the first task clears the flag. Using this protection technique, determine what occurs if the second task interrupts the first task immediately after the flag has been tested and before it is set by the first task.

5. Assume that two tasks share a common data area and that each task maintains a separate "in use" flag. Prior to accessing the data area, a task sets its own "in use" flag to prevent the other task from accessing the data, and then tests the other task's flag before proceeding. Using this protection technique, determine what can occur if the first task is interrupted by the second task after the first task has set its own flag and before it has tested the second task's flag.

6a. Define the function of a gate.
6b. List four different types of gates.
6c. Describe how the gate mechanism works.

7. Explain why call gates from higher privilege levels to lower privilege levels are not permitted by most operating systems.

8a. Describe the difference between an INTEL 80386 CPU intralevel system call and interlevel system call.
8b. Determine the limitation imposed on the number of arguments that can be passed directly in an INTEL 80386 CPU intralevel system call due to the size of the dword field.
8c. What two items must be passed during an INTEL 80386 CPU intralevel system call to remove the limitation determined in Exercise 8b?

9a. What data structure is used for passing parameters in INTEL 80386 CPU system calls?
9b. Determine why direct parameter-passing between INTEL 80386 CPU task calls is not permitted.
9c. Does the lack of a direct interlevel parameter-passing facility present a problem to multitasking operating systems?

10a. What is the difference between a maskable and nonmaskable interrupt?
10b. What is the purpose of an interrupt gate?

11a. What is the difference between an interrupt and an exception?
11b. What is the difference between a fault, a trap, and an abort?

12a. Given the nature of an exception, is it more advisable to implement an exception handler as a separate task or within the context of the task that incurred the exception?
12b. Given the nature of an interrupt, is it more advisable to implement an interrupt handler as a separate task or within the context of the task that was interrupted?

Specific Microprocessors

Part Two

INTEL 80386
Microprocessor

Chapter Four

4.1   Register Sets
4.2   Data Types
4.3   Addressing Modes
4.4   Instruction Encoding
4.5   Instruction Set
4.6   Programming Examples
4.7   Chapter Highlights

The INTEL 80386 Microprocessor consists of six major sections or units - bus interface, code prefetch, instruction decode, control and execution, segmentation, and paging. The arrangement of these sections is shown in Figure 4-1; their functions have been described in Chapter Two. This chapter presents the register sets, data types, instruction set, and instruction formats supported by this basic 80386 architecture. Programming examples are also included.

4.1 Register Sets

The complete set of user-accessible 80386 registers is shown in Figure 4-2. For descriptive purposes it is useful to separate these registers into the conventional program and system model register sets.

Program Register Model

The program register model consists of eight 32-bit general-purpose registers, six 16-bit segment registers, one 32-bit flags register, and one 32-bit instruction pointer (see Figure 4-3).

FIGURE 4-1   INTEL 80386 Microprocessor Block Diagram

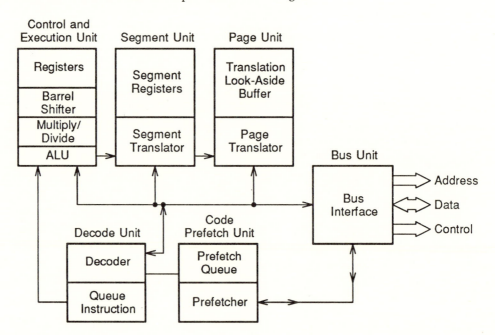

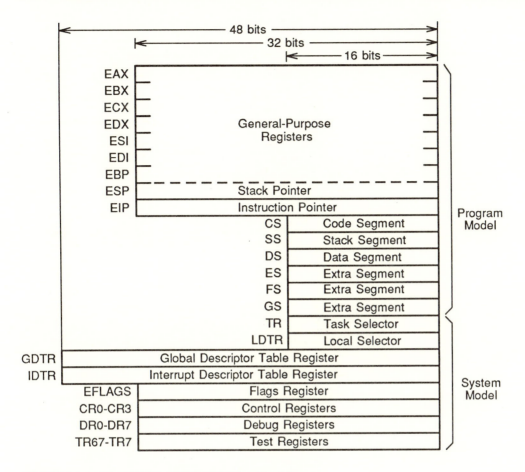

FIGURE 4-2 The INTEL 80386 CPU User Registers

General-Purpose Registers

The INTEL 80386 CPU has eight general-purpose registers named EAX, EBX, ECX, EDX, EBP, ESP, ESI, and EDI. Except for the ESP register, which cannot be used as an index register, each of these 32-bit registers may be used interchangeably as either accumulators, address registers, data registers, base registers, or index registers. The ESP is also the user's stack pointer.

As shown in Figure 4-3, the low-order 16-bits of each 32-bit general-purpose register can be treated as a unique 16-bit register. These 16-bit registers are the AX, BX, CX, DX, BP, SP, SI, and DI registers. These registers are used for 16-bit data and for emulating the earlier INTEL 8086 and 80286 CPUs, which used identically named 16-bit registers. The prefix E on the 80386 register names signifies that these registers have been extended to 32 bits.

In addition to their 16-bit components, the EAX, EBX, ECX, and EDX registers also allow unique 8-bit register operations. As shown in Figure 4-3, the lower

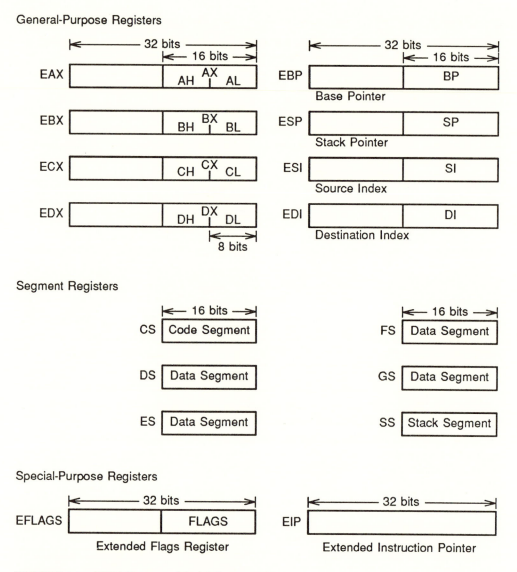

General-Purpose Registers

Segment Registers

Special-Purpose Registers

FIGURE 4-3 80386 Program Model Register Set

bytes of these registers are named the AL, BL, CL, and DL registers, respectively. The next higher bytes are named the AH, BH, CH, and DH registers, respectively. These registers are used for 8-bit data and for emulating the earlier 8080 CPU, which used 8-bit registers.

Although each of the 32-bit general-purpose registers can be used interchangeably for storing the results of arithmetic and logical instructions, the encoding of certain instructions is compressed significantly by selecting certain registers for specific addressing modes. The impact of register selection on instruction encoding is described in Section 4.4. Additionally, string, stack, I/O, translation, loop, and certain double-precision arithmetic instructions implicitly reference specific general-purpose registers. These instructions are presented in Section 4.5.

Segment Registers

The six 16-bit segment registers provide immediate access for one code segment, one stack segment, and up to four data segments. The currently active code segment is specified by the code segment (CS) register, the currently active stack segment by the stack segment (SS) register, and the currently active data segment by the data segment (DS) register. In addition, three extra data segments can be specified by the ES, FS, and GS segment registers. These extra data segments provide areas for storing and sharing selected data structures.

Recall that a complete INTEL 80386 CPU memory address consists of a segment and offset address. For instructions, the segment address is located using the CS register, and the offset address is the address contained within the 32-bit instruction pointer (EIP) register. For data operands, the segment address is implicitly located using the DS register, unless the ES, FS, or GS registers are explicitly specified by an instruction. The offset is computed from a combination of addresses that can be located both within an instruction and in two general-purpose registers. The exact determination of data offset addresses is described in Section 4.3.

As described in Section 3.2, the value stored in a segment register is referred to as a selector. In real mode, the selector is a segment's starting address. In protected mode, the selector is actually an index value that is used to locate a segment's descriptor in either the operating system's global descriptor table or a task's local descriptor table. The descriptor contains the actual starting address of the segment and its associated privilege levels and size.

To bypass the need to access a descriptor table each time a selector is used, each segment register has a 64-bit "hidden" descriptor register associated with it. Each hidden register contains a copy of the descriptor associated with the selector in a segment register. This makes the descriptor directly accessible, on chip, without the need for an external memory fetch, whenever a segment register is referenced. The hidden registers are automatically maintained and accessed by the CPU and cannot be directly read or modified by any program instruction.

Special Purpose Registers

The extended instruction pointer (EIP) and EFLAGS registers are two special-purpose 80386 registers.

Extended Instruction Pointer (EIP): The 32-bit EIP register contains the offset address of the next executable instruction relative to the starting address of the current code segment. (In other microprocessors, this register is referred to as the program counter.)

115

FLAGS Register: The lower 16 bits of the 32-bit EFLAGS system model register is the 80386 FLAGS register. These 16 bits store the same flag bits used to monitor and control certain operations in the 8086/80286 CPU. The EFLAGS register contains thirteen flags: six status flags, six system flags, and one control flag. Figure 4-4 shows the EFLAGS register; Table 4-1 lists the function of each flag.

System Register Model

In addition to the EFLAGS register, the 80386 system register model consists of four sets of registers as shown in Figure 4-5. In general, these registers may only be accessed by privileged instructions and are inaccessible to application programs. Typically these registers are initialized by the operating system.

Memory Management Registers

The memory management registers (see Figure 4-6) consist of the global descriptor table register (GDTR), local descriptor table register (LDTR), interrupt descriptor table register (IDTR), and task register (TR). The global descriptor table and interrupt descriptor table registers are collectively referred to as *system address registers* because they contain the starting memory addresses of the global descriptor and interrupt descriptor tables available to all tasks.

FIGURE 4-4   The EFLAGS Register

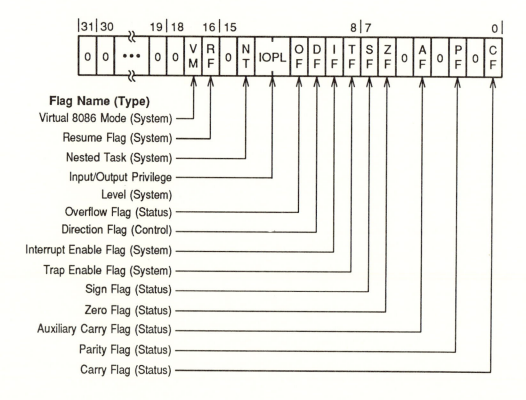

TABLE 4-1 Flag Descriptions

Symbol	Name	Bit	Description
Status Flags			
CF	Carry flag	0	Set (1) on high-order carry or borrow; otherwise cleared (0).
PF	Parity flag	2	Set (1) if low-order 8-bits results contain an even number of 1 bits; otherwise cleared (0).
AF	Auxiliary carry flag	4	Used for BCD arithmetic. Set (1) on a borrow or carry from the lower-order 4-bits of AL; otherwise cleared (0).
ZF	Zero flag	6	Set (1) if the result is zero; otherwise cleared (0).
SF	Sign flag	7	State determined by MSB of the results; cleared (0) if positive, set (1) if negative.
OF	Overflow flag	11	Set (1) if the result is too large a positive number or too small a negative number to fit the destination.
System Flags			
TF	Trap enable flag	8	When set (1), forces CPU into a single-step mode.
IF	Interrupt enable flag	9	When set (1), CPU recognizes maskable interrupt requests. When cleared (0), maskable interrupts are disabled (ignored).
IOPL	I/O privilege level	12, 13	Determines the privilege level needed to execute all I/O instructions. A code segment can only execute the I/O instructions if the current privilege level (CPL) is at least as privileged as the I/O privilege level.
NT	Nested task	14	Set (1) indicates a nested task is operating.
RF	Resume flag	16	When set (1), the CPU allows debug exceptions to a restarted instruction. When cleared (0), debug exeptions are disabled.
VM	Virtual 8086 mode	17	Set (1) indicates the current task is executing a real mode 8086 program within a protected mode task.
Control Flags			
DF	Direction flag	10	When set (1), strings are processed from high address characters to low address characters; otherwise from low-to-high address characters.

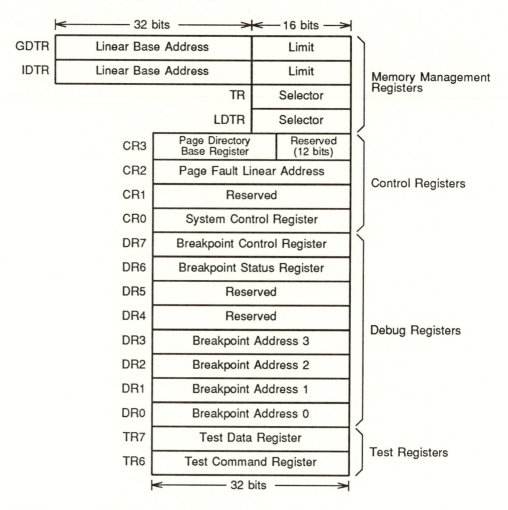

FIGURE 4-5   80386 System Registers

The local descriptor table register and task register are referred to collectively as the *system segment registers* because they contain selector values. These selectors are identical in format to the selectors contained within the set of six program model segment registers and are used in the same manner. The two system selectors are task specific, point to descriptors contained within the global descriptor table, and change each time a new task is invoked. The descriptor pointed to by the task register contains the starting address of the current task state segment (TSS). The descriptor pointed to by the local descriptor table register contains the starting address of the task's local descriptor table.

Associated with each of these two system segment registers are "hidden" descriptor registers that are transparent or invisible to the user. These hidden descriptor registers, like their counterparts in the program model register set, contain copies of the descriptors associated with their respective selector value.

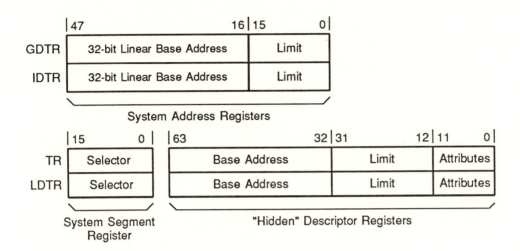

FIGURE 4-6 Memory Management Registers

Control Registers

Figure 4-7 illustrates the formats of system control registers CR0, CR1, CR2, and CR3. Control register 0 (CR0) contains six system flags that are used to control and monitor system conditions. The functions of the system flags are given in Table 4-2. Control register 1 (CR1) is currently reserved for future use. Control registers 2 and 3 (CR2 and CR3) are used only when the paging flag (PG) is set in control register 0. CR2 is used when a page fault occurs to store the linear

FIGURE 4-7 Control Registers

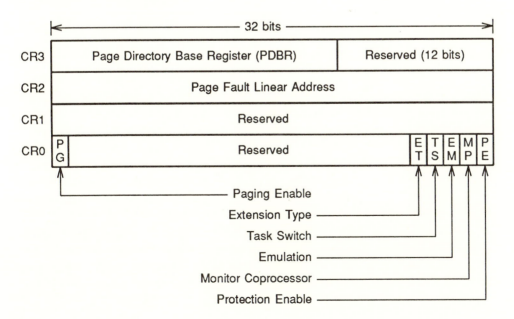

TABLE 4-2 Flag Descriptions

Exception	Type	Bit	Description
PE	Protection enable	0	A set (1) causes execution in protected mode (see Section 2.4); a clear (0) causes execution in real mode (See Section 2.3).
MP	Monitor coprocessor	1	A set (1) causes the TS flag to be tested to determine whether there has been a task switch since the execution of the last coprocessor instruction. If clear (0), does not test the TS flag.
EM	Emulate coprocessor	2	A set (1) indicates math coprocessor instructions are being emulated by software; otherwise math coprocessor instructions are not being emulated.
TS	Task switch	3	A set (1) indicates a task switch has occurred. Used to coordinate coprocessor and CPU tasks.
ET	Processor extension type	4	If set (1) and a coprocessor is present (MP = 1, set), indicates an 80387 coprocessor is present; otherwise indicates an 80287 coprocessor is present.
PG	Paging	31	A set (1) indicates that paging is enabled and that linear addresses must be translated into physical addresses using page tables. A clear (0) indicates paging is disabled.

address that caused the fault. Control register 3, also called the page directory base register (PDBR), contains the physical starting address of the current page directory (see Section 2.4).

Debug Registers

The debug registers provide the ability to set breakpoint addresses for either data or code segments. A *breakpoint* is a user-selected point in a computer program at which execution is temporarily suspended. In the early stages of program development, breakpoints provide a convenient means of determining whether specified instructions or memory addresses have been accessed. In the later stages of program development, the debug registers provide for the examination of register and memory contents when the breakpoint has been reached.

The INTEL 80386 CPU has eight debug registers (see Figure 4-8). These consist of four address registers (DR0 through DR3), two reserved registers (DR4 and DR5), one status register (DR6) and one control register (DR7).

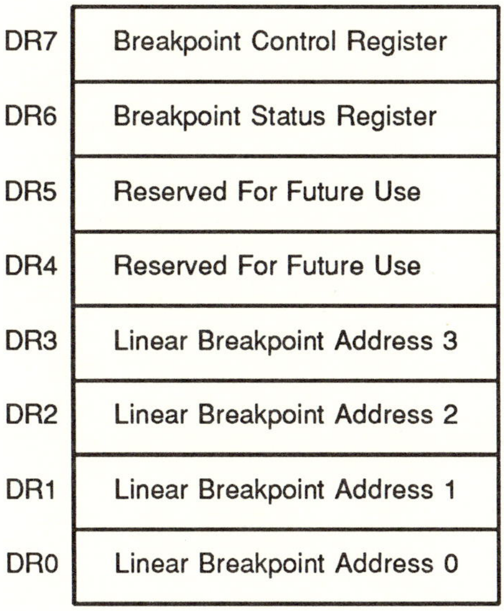

DR7	Breakpoint Control Register
DR6	Breakpoint Status Register
DR5	Reserved For Future Use
DR4	Reserved For Future Use
DR3	Linear Breakpoint Address 3
DR2	Linear Breakpoint Address 2
DR1	Linear Breakpoint Address 1
DR0	Linear Breakpoint Address 0

FIGURE 4-8 The Debug Registers

Debug Address Registers

The four debug address registers store the addresses of four memory locations used for breakpointing, where the contents of each location can be either an instruction or data. Each address is a 32-bit linear address. When paging is enabled, the linear address is automatically translated into a physical address as previously described in Section 2.4. If paging is not enabled, the linear address is treated as a physical address.

Debug Control Register

The debug control register, DR7, selectively enables specific debug conditions for the addresses contained in the debug address registers, DR0-DR3. Table 4-3 lists the functions of the bits contained in this register.

Debug Status Register

The debug status register, DR6, defines 7 of its 32 bits as status flags. These are called B0-B3, BT, BS and BD.

The B0, B1, B2, and B3 flags record the status of each breakpoint address set in the debug address registers. These bits can then be tested to cause execution of a debug exception (interrupt vector 1 in the Interrupt Descriptor Table). The BT flag is set prior to entering the debug exception handler if a task switch has been made

TABLE 4-3 Debug Control Register Fields

Symbol	Bit(s)	Name	Description
L0-L3	0,2, 4,6	Local active	If set (1), the breakpoint address in the associated debug address register is active for the current local task only. A task switch automatically clears these bits.
G0-G3	1,3, 5,7	Global active	If set (1), the breakpoint address in the associated debug address register is active for all tasks. These bits are unaffected by task switches.
LE	8	Local enable	When set (1), causes all local breakpoint interruptions to be reported in the debug status register. This bit is cleared on a task switch.
GE	9	Global enable	When set (1), causes all global breakpoint interruptions to be reported in the debug status register. This bit is unaffected by task switches.
R/W0 R/W1 R/W2 R/W3	16,17 20,21 24,25 28,29	Read/ write	Determines the type of action causing a breakpoint for the address in the associated debug address register. The codes are: 00 - Break only on instruction execution 01 - Break only on data writes 10 - Undefined 11 - Break only on data reads and writes
LEN0 LEN1 LEN2 LEN3	18,19 22,23 26,27 30,31	Length field	Determines the range of sequential bytes to be monitored starting from the address in the corresponding debug address register. The codes are: 00 - One-byte length 01 - Two-byte length 10 - Undefined 11 - Four-byte length

and the T bit of the entering task state segment is set. The BS bit is set when the TF (trap flag) in the EFLAGS register indicates a single-step exception (TF = 1). The BD bit is set when the next instruction is to read or write one of the eight registers in the INTEL ICE-386 In-Circuit Emulator debugger system.

By monitoring the state of the various status and control register bits listed in Table 4-4, various breakpoint conditions can be recognized for further processing by an exception handler.

TABLE 4-4 Debug Exception Conditions

Tested Bits	Condition Indicated
B0 = 1 AND (G0 = 1 OR L0 = 1)	Breakpoint occurred as defined by DR0, LEN0, and R/W0 (Table 4-3)
B1 = 1 AND (G1 = 1 OR L1 = 1)	Breakpoint occurred as defined by DR1, LEN1, and R/W1 (Table 4-3)
B2 = 1 AND (G2 = 1 OR L2 = 1)	Breakpoint occurred as defined by DR2, LEN2, and R/W2 (Table 4-3)
B3 = 1 AND (G3 = 1 OR L3 = 1)	Breakpoint occurred as defined by DR3, LEN3, and R/W3 (Table 4-3)
BS = 1	Single-step exception
BD = 1	Debug registers are not not available due to use by ICE-386 debugger
BT = 1	Task switch has occurred

Test Registers

Two test registers are available for testing the on-chip translation look-aside buffer (TLB) cache. The CPU uses the TLB when translating linear addresses to physical addresses with paging enabled (see Section 2.4). Essentially, these two registers are used for writing test addresses and flag bits to the TLB and storing addresses and flag data that has been read from the TLB.

Typically, the test registers are used by the operating system only for a power-up confidence test of the 80386 CPU. As such, these two registers perform an extremely specialized function and are not normally considered part of the 80386's operating architecture.

4.2 Data Types

The basic data types supported by the INTEL 80386 Microprocessor are bytes, words, and double words. The instruction set has provisions that allow these data types to be interpreted as either signed integers or unsigned integers. In addition, the CPU supports bit fields, bit strings, 32-bit and 48-bit addresses, and binary-coded decimal (BCD) numbers. Although software algorithms can be programmed for floating-point data, floating-point operands are not directly supported by the 80386 hardware architecture. Hardware implementation of floating-point data is provided by the INTEL 80287 and 80387 Numeric Processor Extension devices, more commonly referred to as numeric or math coprocessors.

Using standard terminology, Intel defines a byte as eight contiguous bits. As shown in Figure 4-9, bits within a byte are numbered from right to left, starting with 0 and ending with 7. Bit 0 is the least significant bit (LSB) in the byte. In unsigned (integer) bytes, bit 7 is the most significant bit (MSB). The range of unsigned byte values is 0 through 255. For signed bytes, bit 7 is the sign bit and bit 6 is the MSB. The value range of signed bytes is from –128 to +127. Since the 80386 CPU can address any byte in memory, a byte datum can be located at any memory address.

A word is a 16-bit quantity that is stored in memory at any two consecutive byte locations. Bits within a word are numbered from right to left starting with 0, the LSB, and ending with 15 (see Figure 4-10.) In unsigned (integer) words, bit 15 is the MSB and the range of values is from 0 through 65,535. For signed words, bit 15 is the sign bit and bit 14 is the MSB. The value range of signed words is from –32,768 to +32,767.

Words are stored in memory with their lower-order bytes at lower-order addresses and their higher-order bytes at higher-order addresses. For example, the hexadecimal word AABB is stored in memory with the lower-order memory byte containing the value BB and the higher-order memory byte containing the value AA. When a word is accessed from memory, the address of the lower-order byte is used as the address of the word.

Since the 80386 CPU data paths are 32-bits, the definition of 16-bits as a word is contrary to the conventional usage of this term. Intel defines an 80386 16-bit

FIGURE 4-9   Byte Data

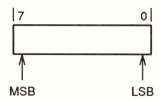

FIGURE 4-10   Word Data Storage in Memory

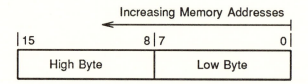

quantity as a word to retain notational compatibility with the earlier 8086 and 80286 microprocessor definitions.

Other 32-bit CPU manufacturers define 32-bit quantities as words, but Intel refers to these as double-words. A double-word is stored in memory at any four consecutive byte locations. Bits within a word are numbered from right to left starting with 0, the LSB, and ending with 31 (see Figure 4-11). As with unsigned bytes and words, the leftmost bit of an unsigned integer double-word is referred to as the MSB. An integer double-word has a value range of from 0 through 4,294,967,295 (2^{32} − 1). In a signed double-word, bit 31 is the sign bit and bit 30 is the MSB. A signed integer double-word has a value range of from −2,147,483,648 (-2^{31}) to +2,147,483,647 ($+2^{31}$ − 1).

Double-words are stored in memory with their lower-order bytes at lower-order addresses and their higher-order bytes at higher-order addresses. For example, the hexadecimal double-word AABBCCDD is stored in memory with the lowest-order memory byte containing the value DD and the highest-order memory byte containing the value AA. When a double-word is accessed from memory, the address of the lowest-order byte is used as the address of the double-word.

When used with either an INTEL 80287 or 80387 Numeric Processor Extension (numeric coprocessor), the INTEL 80386 CPU supports single-precision (32-bits), double-precision (64-bits), or extended double-precision (80-bits) floating-point numbers. Figure 4-12 illustrates these floating-point data types. (See also Appendix A.)

In addition to bytes, words, and double-words, the 80386 microprocessor supports near pointer, far pointer, bit field, bit string, unpacked binary-coded decimal (BCD) digit, packed BCD digit, and string data types.

Near Pointer: A near pointer is a 32-bit offset address (see Figure 4-13). This address can be used either with segmentation and paging or without segmentation and paging ("flat" model). In all cases, the near pointer refers to an address within a segment defined by one of the segment registers (CS, SS, DS, ES, FS, or GS).

Far Pointer: A far pointer consists of a 32-bit offset and a 16-bit selector (see Figure 4-14). The selector in real mode is a starting segment address, and in

FIGURE 4-11 Double-Word Storage in Memory

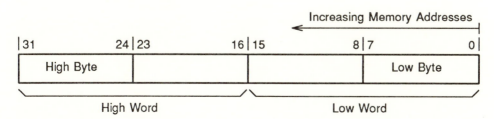

125

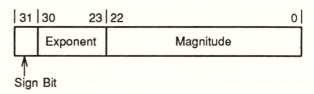

FIGURE 4-12a   Single Precision Floating-Point Format

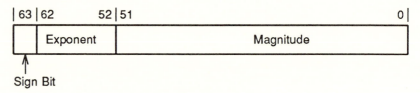

FIGURE 4-12b   Double Precision Floating-Point Format

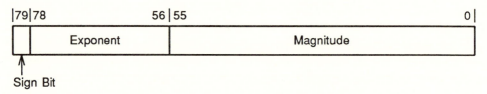

FIGURE 4-12c   Extended Double Precision Floating-Point Format

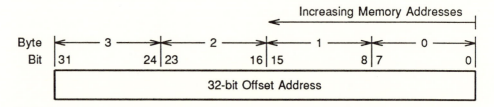

FIGURE 4-13   Near Pointer Format

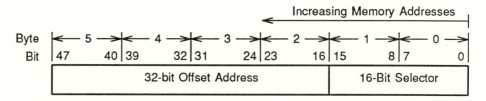

FIGURE 4-14   Far Pointer Format

protected mode is an index. The index is used to locate a descriptor within a designated descriptor table, which provides the base address of the desired segment. The offset is used as an offset address within the selected segment.

Bit Field and Bit String: A bit field is any contiguous sequence of up to 32 bits. A bit string is any contiguous sequence of bits containing up to 4,294,967,295 $(2^{32} - 1)$ bits. The bit field and bit string may begin at any bit position in any byte. A bit field, or bit fields, may be contained within a larger bit string.

Unpacked Binary Coded Decimal (BCD) Digits: In unpacked BCD, each individual decimal digit is stored in the lower-order 4 bits of a byte using the binary representation for the decimal digits 0 through 9. For example, the decimal number 4869 in unpacked BCD requires four bytes of storage (one byte per decimal digit) and it is stored as illustrated in Figure 4-15. The high-order 4 bits of each byte must contain zeros when unpacked BCD data types are multiplied or divided; otherwise they may contain any values.

Packed BCD: In packed BCD, a byte is used to store two decimal digits; one digit per each half-byte. The least-significant decimal digit is stored in the low-order half byte of the byte with the lowest address. For example, the decimal number 4869 in packed BCD requires two bytes of storage (one byte for every two decimal digits) and is stored as illustrated in Figure 4-16.

FIGURE 4-15 Unpacked BCD Representation of 4869

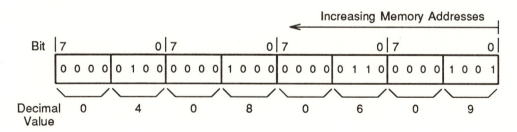

FIGURE 4-16 Packed BCD Representation of 4869

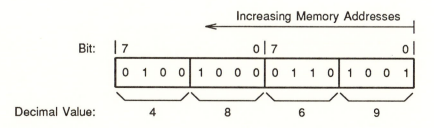

Strings: A string is a contiguous sequence of either bytes, words, or double-words having a maximum length of 4,294,967,295 ($2^{32} - 1$) bytes.

The 80386 CPU supports each of its data types by supplying instructions for manipulating and operating them in various ways. Table 4-5 lists the basic instruction types that can be applied to each data type. The specific instructions within each instruction type, instruction formats, and addressing modes available for locating data operands are presented in the next three sections.

TABLE 4-5 Data Type Instruction Support

Instruction Type	Unsigned Integer	Signed Integer	BCD	Bit Fields	Strings
Data Movement	Yes	Yes	Yes	Yes	Yes
Compare	Yes	Yes	Yes	Yes	Yes
Logical AND, OR, etc.	Yes	Yes	No	No	No
Arithmetic*	Yes	Yes	Yes	No	No

* Includes add, subtract, multiply, divide, negate, etc.

4.3 Addressing Modes

An individual 80386 instruction can explicitly reference two operands at most. Individual operands are located using either register, immediate, or memory addressing modes, depending on where the operand is stored. This section describes the three basic operand storage locations and the various addressing modes available to reference them.

Register Operand Storage

Operands can be stored directly in any of the 8-bit, 16-bit, or 32-bit registers listed in Table 4-6. Additionally, if a segmented memory model is in effect, the six 16-bit segment registers (CS, SS, DS, ES, FS, GS) can be referenced directly by 80386 instructions. The 80386 CPU also has instructions that use individual flags in the EFLAGS register as operand data.

Register operands are specified in assembly language by listing the appropriate

TABLE 4-6 Allowable Operand Registers

32-Bit Operand Registers	16-Bit Operand Registers	8-Bit Operand Registers
EAX	AX	AL
EBX	BX	AH
ECX	CX	BL
EDX	DX	BH
ESI	SI	CL
EDI	DI	CH
ESP	SP	DL
EBP	BP	DH

register name after the mnemonic for the desired operation. This is called the *register addressing mode*. For example, in the single-operand instruction

INC EAX

INC is the mnemonic for the *increment* instruction and the operand is located in the 32-bit EAX register. In the two-operand instruction

MOV EAX,EBX

both of the operands are located in registers. This instruction causes the 32-bit contents of the EBX register (the source operand is always the second operand listed) to be moved into the EAX register (the destination operand is always the first operand listed). The contents of the EBX register remains unchanged after the move operation.

Immediate Operand Storage

Immediate data may be either 8-bit, 16-bit, or 32-bits long and is specified in assembly language by including the data with the instruction. Immediate hexadecimal data must have a trailing H after the hexadecimal number and a leading 0 if it starts with A through F. For example, the instruction

MOV EAX,0ABCDEF99H

loads the EAX register with the hexadecimal number ABCDEF99.

Immediate data can only be used as the source operand in a two-operand instruction. It can be either positive or negative and is always sign-extended to produce an operand having the bit-width of the destination operand.

Memory and I/O Operand Storage

In addition to register and immediate data, operands can also be stored in either memory or I/O ports, areas external to the CPU (off-chip). From an addressing viewpoint, these are accessed using the address of the desired location. For convenience, and where the context is clear, both memory and I/O operands will collectively be referred to as either external operands, or simply as memory operands.

The INTEL 80386 CPU has a variety of methods of specifying an external operand's address. Recall that this address consists of two parts: a segment address and an offset address. The segment address is determined using one of the six segment registers. The choice of segment register is by default unless a specific segment register is explicitly referenced by an instruction. Table 4-7 lists the default segment register assignments made by the 80386 CPU.

TABLE 4-7 Default Segment Register Assignments

Memory Reference Type	Default Segment Register
Instructions	CS (Code)
Data	DS (Data)
Stack	SS (Stack)
String Destinations	ES (Extra)

An operand's offset address represents the desired memory location within a segment relative to the segment's starting address. This offset, also referred to as an *effective address*, is computed by taking the sum of three individual components:

1. Base address
2. Scaled index
3. Displacement

Figure 4-17 illustrates the composition of an effective address (offset) using these three components. Effective addresses can consist of any combination of these three components and the various component combinations form the basis for the majority of the 80386 memory addressing modes. When present, 32-bit base addresses are usually stored in either the EBX or EBP registers; however, any of the registers in Table 4-8 may also be used to store base addresses. This differs from the earlier 8086 and 80286 CPUs, which required that the 16-bit BX or BP registers be used for base addresses. Similarly, 32-bit index values, when present, are typically stored in either the ESI or EDI registers; however, any of the registers

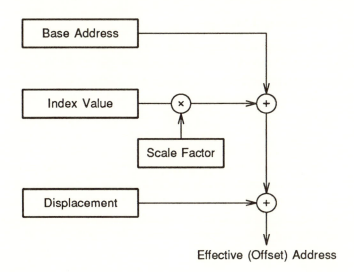

FIGURE 4-17 Effective Address Calculation

in Table 4-8 may be used also. Again, this differs from the 8086 and 80286 CPUs, which restricted index values to either the SI or DI registers only.

TABLE 4-8 Allowable Base and Index Registers

Allowable Base Registers	Allowable Index Registers
EAX, EBX, ECX, EDX, EBP, ESI, EDI, ESP	EAX, EBX, ECX, EDX, EBP, ESI, EDI

When a register in Table 4-8 is used to store a base address or index value, it is referred to as a *base* or *index register*, respectively. The distinction between these two terms is determined solely by the context in which the register is used and not by the name of the register. For example, when a register is used to store a base address such as the starting address of an array, the register is referred to as a base register. When the register is used to store an index such as a subscript value designating a specific element of an array, the register is referred to as an index register. The use of the EBX and EBP registers as base registers and ESI and EDI registers as index registers (or their equivalent 8086/80286 registers) results in an instruction storage size that is one byte less than when other registers are used. This will be explained in the next section.

The various combinations of base, index, and displacement components used to construct an effective (offset) address produce the conventional microprocessor memory-addressing modes. The more traditional combinations and their corresponding addressing mode names are given in Table 4-9.

TABLE 4-9 Common Memory-Addressing Modes

Effective Address Components	Addressing Mode Name
Displacement only	Direct memory
Base or index register only	Register indirect
Base and displacement	Register relative (base relative)
Index and displacement	Register relative (direct indexed)
Base and index	Based index
Base, index, and displacement	Based index relative

Direct Memory Addressing

In direct memory addressing, the effective address of the desired operand consists of a displacement either as a near pointer or in the context of a far pointer (see Figure 4-18). In assembly language, a direct memory address is usually equated with a label (in high-level languages a direct memory address is equivalent to the address of a scalar variable). For example, the instruction

INC MEMDATA

would increment the contents of the address associated with MEMDATA. An additional assembler directive is required to set the size to either 8, 16, or 32 bits (see Section 4.6).

Register Indirect Addressing

In register indirect addressing, the address of the memory operand is contained within a register. When a register is used in this manner it is also called a pointer register because its contents are used to point to the desired operand. Figure 4-19 illustrates the relationship between the address contained in a pointer register and the operand obtained. The term indirect addressing is used to describe this procedure. The operand is obtained indirectly by first going to the register for an address that is then used to access the desired operand.

FIGURE 4-18   Direct Memory Addressing

Displacement Value = Operand's Address ⟶ A Memory Location | Operand

FIGURE 4-19   Register Indirect Addressing

Indirect register addressing is designated in assembly language by enclosing the designated register name within square brackets. For example, the instruction

   MOV EAX,[EBX]

causes a copy of the 32-bit contents starting at the location whose address is in EBX to be placed into register EAX. The address in EBX remains unchanged.

Register Relative Addressing

This is another indirect memory-addressing mode in which the effective memory operand address is formed by adding a displacement to the contents of either a base or index register (see Figure 4-20).

The displacement used in register relative mode may be either 8-bit, 16-bit, or 32-bits. Two's complement, negative displacements are also valid. Displacements smaller than the size of the register contents to which the displacement will be added are always sign-extended to the appropriate size.

Register relative addressing is specified in assembly language by enclosing the designated register name within square brackets and including a displacement either within or outside the brackets. The following instructions are equivalent:

   MOV EAX,[EBX]+5
   MOV EAX,[EBX+5]
   MOV EAX,5[EBX]

FIGURE 4-20   Register Relative Addressing

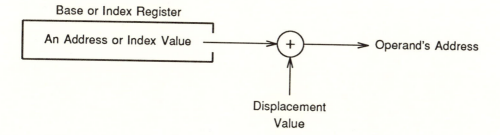

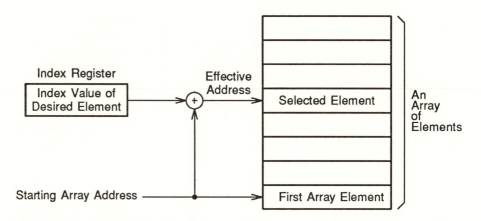

FIGURE 4-21 Referencing Array Elements

Each of these instructions causes the 32-bit contents of memory starting at the address 5 above the address in EBX to be copied into EAX. The address in EBX remains unchanged.

The use of either an index or base register with a displacement depends on the application and determines the context in which the displacement is viewed. Index registers are typically used to reference elements of an array. Base registers are preferred for referencing items in a record. This preference reflects the interpretation placed on the displacement address.

In referencing an array element, the displacement value is used to store the direct memory address of the beginning of the array. This is a natural interpretation for arrays because the starting array address is fixed. The value in the index register, which can change, is then used to locate any desired array element (see Figure 4-21). This allows individual array elements to be located rapidly by simply altering the value in the index register.

If each element of the array in Figure 4-21 is exactly one byte in length, the index register value equals the element's subscript value. This correspondence is lost if each element requires more than a byte of storage. For the case where an element is either 2, 4, or 8, bytes in length, the automatic index scaling feature of the 80386 can be used. The default scale factor of one can be altered by including the desired scale factor within the square brackets containing the index register. For example, consider the array in Figure 4-22. Each element requires two bytes of storage and the first array element, A[0], resides at memory address 600 relative to the start of the data segment. Assuming register CX contains the number 4, the assembly language instruction

MOV AX,[CX*2+600]

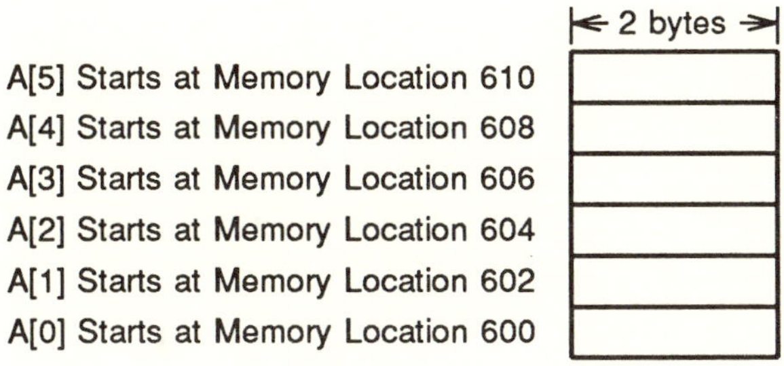

|← 2 bytes →|

A[5] Starts at Memory Location 610

A[4] Starts at Memory Location 608

A[3] Starts at Memory Location 606

A[2] Starts at Memory Location 604

A[1] Starts at Memory Location 602

A[0] Starts at Memory Location 600

FIGURE 4-22   An Array Stored in Memory

references A[4] as the source operand and copies the 16-bit contents of this location to register AX. The effective address of the source operand is calculated as 4*2+600 = 608, which is the address of A[4]. The advantage of using a scale factor is that the value contained in the index register CX continues to equal the array element's subscript value. This correspondence is especially useful for correctly keeping track of the element being referenced by the index register and provides a means for efficiently converting high-level language subscripts into memory references.

When an index register is used in register-relative mode, the addressing mode is frequently referred to as *direct indexing*. This terminology stresses the use of the displacement as the primary direct address and the index value as an adjustment to this address. The opposite interpretation is taken when a base register is used. The address in the base register is considered an indirect address, as in register-indirect mode, to which the displacement value is added as an adjustment. This interpretation is useful when referencing individual items of a record.

A record, sometimes called a structure, consists of a set of elements which need not be of the same data type. For example, the record illustrated in Figure 4-23 consists of a 2-byte identification item, a 20-byte name field, and a 4-byte year-of-hire item. Here, each item is conveniently located as a fixed distance from the start of the record. Any item can be conveniently located by storing the starting address of the record in a base register and using the displacement to represent the number of bytes to the desired item. The advantage of this

FIGURE 4-23   A Single Record

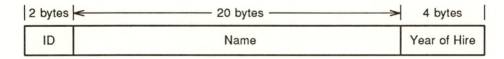

2 bytes	←————————— 20 bytes —————————→	4 bytes
ID	Name	Year of Hire

arrangement is more obvious if several records of the same form exist. A change in the value of the base register by an integral multiple of the record's byte size effectively selects another record, while the fixed displacement continues to select the same item within each record.

When a base register is used in register relative mode, the addressing mode is also referred to as *base relative* addressing. Both base relative addressing and direct index addressing are intrinsically the same, with the difference resulting from how each mode is conceptually used.

An extremely useful and special case of base relative addressing occurs when either the EBP or BP register is used as the base register. When either of these registers is used, the default segment register is the SS register, which references the stack segment. This mode of register relative addressing is called the *stack-frame-relative* address mode and is extremely useful for passing data between subroutines. As each subroutine is called, the passed operands can be placed on the stack by the calling routine and retrieved by the called routine, as long as each routine uses the same starting stack address relative to the beginning of the stack segment. Using the EBP or BP register forces the CPU to access the stack segment, with the EBP or BP storing the starting stack address within this segment. The displacement value acts as an adjustment to locate the desired element on the stack (see Figure 4-24).

Based Index Addressing

In based index address mode, the effective address is obtained using both a base and index register without any displacement (see Figure 4-25). In assembly language this form of addressing is specified by either enclosing both register names within separate square brackets or by combining register names with a

FIGURE 4-24 Stack-Frame-Relative Addressing

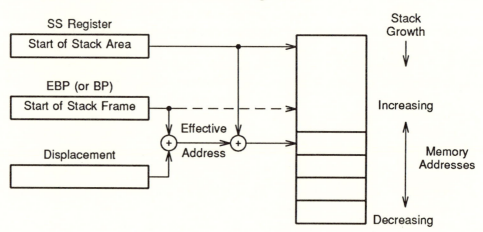

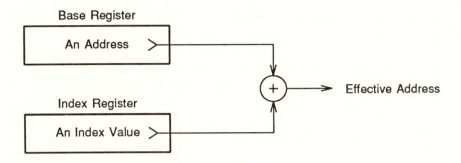

FIGURE 4-25   Based Index Addressing

plus sign and enclosing the complete expression within one square bracket. For example, both instructions

        MOV EAX,[EBX][ESI]
        MOV EAX,[EBX+ESI]

use based index addressing to specify the source operand. Here, the contents of memory whose address is the sum of the values contained within the EBX and ESI registers is copied into the EAX register.

Based Index Relative Addressing

This mode of addressing is the most inclusive of all of the indirect addressing modes. In this mode an instruction must specify a base register, index register, and displacement. This mode is extremely useful for referencing a single element within a two dimensional array or for accessing a single item in an array of identically sized records. When used for two-dimensional arrays, the displacement becomes the address of the beginning of the array, one of the registers is used for the row index, and the other array for the column index. When used to access a single item in an array of records, the displacement is used to designate the location of the item relative to a single record, the base register is used to store the starting address of the entire array, and the index register is used to store the subscript value of the desired record.

High-Level Language Support

At first glance, the multitude of the 80386 CPU's effective address combinations can be overwhelming. However, each address mode is ideally suited for accessing commonly used data structures, such as scalar variables, pointers, arrays, records, and arrays of records. These are the same data structures that are supported by structured high-level languages such as PASCAL, ADA, Modula 2, and C. Since the 80386 CPU provides addressing modes that conform quite naturally to these high-level language data structures, compilers can translate programs written in high-level languages into extremely efficient 80386 machine code.

With the more restricted set of addressing modes common to 8- and 16-bit CPUs, this almost one-to-one correspondence between addressing modes and individual elements within a high-level language data structure did not exist. This forced compilers to translate high-level code using the more restrictive addressing modes, producing less than optimum code. Alternatively, the performance sensitive sections of application programs could be coded directly in assembly language to obtain the desired execution speed and final program byte counts.

With the larger set of addressing modes, many performance sensitive tasks for 32-bit CPUs can be coded directly in a high-level language. This high-level code is compiled with little or no degradation in either execution speed or final program byte count compared to hand-written assembly code. Increased programmer productivity, resulting from the significant decrease in software development time, was one of the prime motivations for providing the address modes available on the INTEL 80386 CPU.

Address Mode Restrictions

Some restrictions do apply to 80386 address mode combinations. An 80386 CPU can explicitly reference, at most, two operands in any one instruction. Due to the way address modes are encoded within an instruction, there are combinations of address modes that are not permissible with two-operand instructions. The permissible combinations of addressing modes for two-operand instruction are restricted by the 80386 CPU to:

- Immediate source operand to register destination. Example: Move the hexadecimal number FFEE1987 into register EAX.
- Immediate source operand to memory/output port destination. Example: Move the hexadecimal number CF198601 into hexadecimal location 00001852.
- Register source operand to register destination. Example: Move the contents of register EAX to register EDX.
- Register source operand to memory/output port destination. Example: Move the contents of register EAX to hexadecimal location 19530001.
- Memory/input port source operand to register destination. Example: Move the contents of hexadecimal location 19530001 to register EAX.

Missing from this list are memory source operands combined with memory destinations. Except for memory-to-memory string operations, the 80386 CPU does not support instructions that directly move or arithmetically combine the contents of one memory location to another memory location. To achieve a memory- to-memory move, for example, the source operand must first be moved into a register (memory-to-register operation) followed by a move from the register to the final memory destination (register-to-memory operation). The reason for this is the encoding of address modes within an instruction, which is presented in the next section.

In a broader sense, the limitations of two-operand instructions also requires that one of the operands act as an accumulator for arithmetic operations. For example, in the instruction

ADD EAX,EBX

the destination is the EAX register. However, there are two source operands: one located in EBX and the other being the original contents of EAX. The operand located in EBX is called the *explicit source* operand; the original contents of EAX is called the *implicit* or *implied source* operand. The final contents of EAX is the sum of its original contents and the contents of the EBX register. In this regard, EAX acts as an accumulator. It is both the implied source for one of the operands and the explicit destination for the result of the computation.

4.4 Instruction Encoding

An INTEL 80386 CPU machine-language instruction consists of a maximum of 16 bytes and can explicitly reference, at most, two operands. Most instructions are encoded using a basic subset of only 12 bytes as shown on Figure 4-26. The remaining 4 bytes are used to override common default assignments. The basic 12 bytes specify the operation to be performed, the addressing mode (ModR/M and SIB bytes), a displacement address (if present), and a maximum 32-bit immediate datum. The bits designating the operation to be performed are called the instruction's *opcode*. Sometimes opcode and addressing mode information are combined together within the same byte. The opcode, in the absence of override bytes, is always stored at the lowest byte address used by an instruction stored in memory. Immediate data, if present, is always stored at the highest memory byte address (see Figure 4-26).

When displacement addresses and immediate data are present, they are coded within an instruction stored in memory with the lower-order bytes located at lower-order memory addresses. For example, the hexadecimal value 12345678H is stored as illustrated on Figure 4-27. Notice that the storing of lower-order bytes at lower-order addresses results in the complete value being stored in a "backwards" manner. This reverse storage is consistently applied, whether the data is 16-bits or 32-bits wide. For example, the 16-bit data 0ABCDH is stored in two consecutive bytes as 0CDH followed by 0ABH.

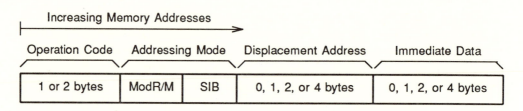

FIGURE 4-26   General INTEL 80386 CPU Instruction Format in Memory

The presence of displacement addresses is always signified by information contained within the ModR/M address byte. Immediate data is data that is included directly within an instruction and is immediately available. Immediate data can be either 8-bits, 16-bits, or 32-bits wide. It can only be the source operand of a two-operand instruction and its presence is always indicated by the opcode.

In addition to the information contained within the general instruction format of Figure 4-26, the INTEL 80386 CPU requires information on operand size (8-bits, 16-bits, or 32-bits), operand type (signed, unsigned, etc.), and address size (16-bits or 32-bits). This information is needed to retrieve and store operands correctly and to manipulate operand data internal to the CPU. The code segment descriptor's D bit selects the default size of both addresses and operands accessed by a program. When the D bit is cleared (D = 0), the 80386 assumes all addresses and operands are 16-bits wide. When this bit is set (D = 1), the default size for both addresses and operands is assumed to be 32-bits wide. Two specific assembler directives exist that allow programmers to set and clear the code segment descriptor's D bit. The 80386 assembler (ASM386) provides a *use16* directive to clear the D bit. Use of this directive creates 80286 compatible 16-bit operands and offsets. The *use32* assembler directive causes the D bit to be set (1), and produces 32-bit operands and offset addresses.

Regardless of the default sizes specified by the D bit, overrides for individual instruction operands (8-bits, 16-bits, or 32-bits) and addresses (16-bits or 32-bits) also exist. The overrides between 16-bit and 32-bit addresses and operands is provided by two override bytes that always precede the opcode byte. These *opcode prefix bytes* are described at the end of this section. The override to specify 8-bit data is designated by a bit within the instruction's opcode.

FIGURE 4-27   Sample Displacement and Immediate Data Storage

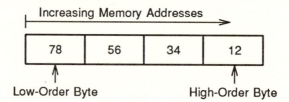

Figures 4-28a through 4-28g illustrate several variations on the basic 80386 instruction format. These variations distinguish primarily between instructions referencing zero, one, or two operands and the addressing modes used to locate each operand. For example, instructions with zero operands, such as a halt instruction, typically consist of a single opcode byte and have the form illustrated in Figure 4-28a.

Like zero-operand instructions, single-operand instructions that use the contents of either 16-bit or 32-bit general-purpose registers are also encoded with a single-byte format. This single-byte instruction format includes a 5-bit opcode field and a 3-bit register field (see Figure 4-28b). The register field designates one of eight possible registers, as listed in the last two rows of Table 4-10. For example, assuming the 80386 is in 32-bit mode (D bit is 1), the assembly language instruction INC EAX would be encoded as shown in Figure 4-29. This same encoding is produced by the instruction INC AX when the 80386 is in 16-bit mode (D bit is 0). Single-operand instructions using one of the 8-bit registers listed in Table 4-10 require the longer two-byte form illustrated in Figure 4-28c.

TABLE 4-10 Register Selection Codes

Register	Register Field (reg) Value							
Size	000	001	010	011	100	101	110	111
8-bit	AL	CL	DL	BL	AH	CH	DH	BH
16-bit	AX	CX	DX	BX	SP	BP	SI	DI
32-bit	EAX	ECX	EDX	EBX	ESP	EBP	ESI	EDI

Opcode Bytes

Each instruction has at least one opcode byte, called the primary opcode byte. A few instructions also require a second opcode byte, called the supplemental opcode byte. In addition, many single-operand instructions can be encoded with both opcode and addressing mode bits contained within the same byte (see Figure 4-28, parts b and c).

Unlike the AT&T and Motorola 32-bit CPUs, the INTEL 80386 CPU uses many more opcodes for the same operation. For example, there are over ten opcodes for a move operation depending on the storage location of the operands being moved. The instruction set for the INTEL 80386 CPU is presented in the next section. The reader should refer to the *INTEL 80386 Programmer's Reference Manual* for a complete listing of opcodes (see Appendix D). Two bits within the opcode field are directly related to addressing mode information. These are the destination and operand width bits, called the d and w bits, respectively. When present, these bits are always the last two bits of the opcode.

```
+------------------+
|     Opcode       |
+------------------+
|7               0|
```

Key:
Reg — Register
mod — Mode
r/m — Register/Memory

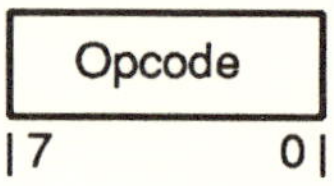

FIGURE 4-28a Single-Byte Zero-Operand Instruction

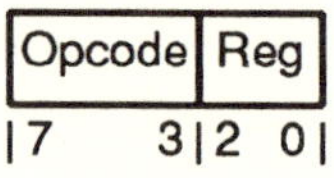

```
+--------+------+
| Opcode | Reg  |
+--------+------+
|7     3|2   0|
```

FIGURE 4-28b Single-Byte Register-Operand Instruction

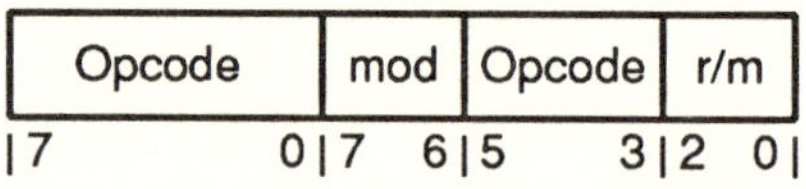

```
+----------+-----+--------+-----+
|  Opcode  | mod | Opcode | r/m |
+----------+-----+--------+-----+
|7       0|7  6|5     3|2  0|
```

FIGURE 4-28c Two-Byte Register or Memory-Operand Instruction

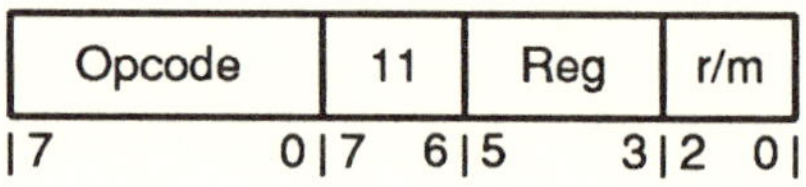

```
+----------+-----+-------+-----+
|  Opcode  | 11  |  Reg  | r/m |
+----------+-----+-------+-----+
|7       0|7  6|5    3|2  0|
```

FIGURE 4-28d Two-Operand Register to Register Instruction

```
+----------+-----+-------+-----+------------------+
|  Opcode  | mod |  Reg  | r/m |   Displacement   |
+----------+-----+-------+-----+------------------+
|7       0|7  6|5    3|2  0| 0, 1, 2 or 4 bytes |
```

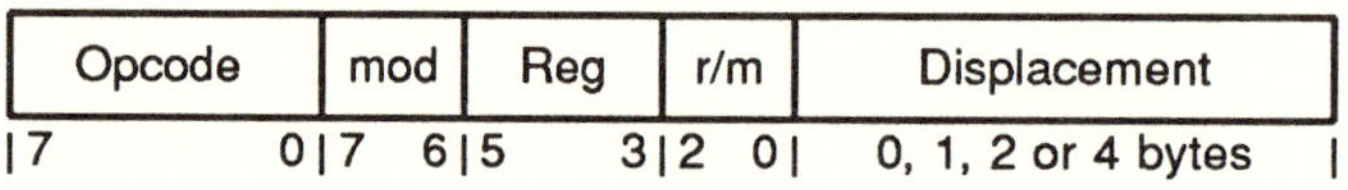

FIGURE 4-28e Two-Operand Register to/from Memory Instruction

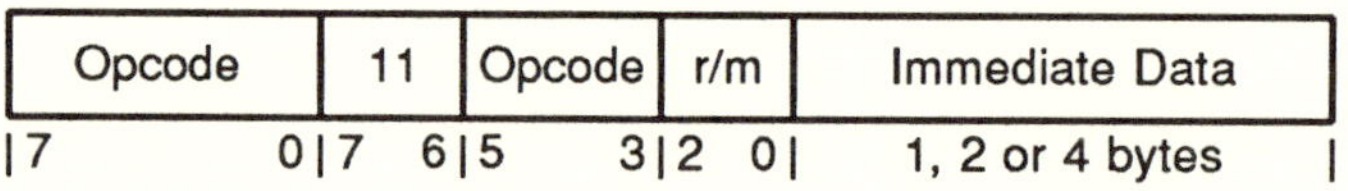

```
+----------+-----+--------+-----+------------------+
|  Opcode  | 11  | Opcode | r/m |  Immediate Data  |
+----------+-----+--------+-----+------------------+
|7       0|7  6|5     3|2  0|  1, 2 or 4 bytes |
```

FIGURE 4-28f Two-Operand Immediate to Register Instruction

```
+----------+-----+--------+-----+------------------+------------------+
|  Opcode  | mod | Opcode | r/m |   Displacement   |  Immediate Data  |
+----------+-----+--------+-----+------------------+------------------+
|7       0|7  6|5     3|2  0| 0, 1, 2 or 4 bytes |  1, 2 or 4 bytes |
```

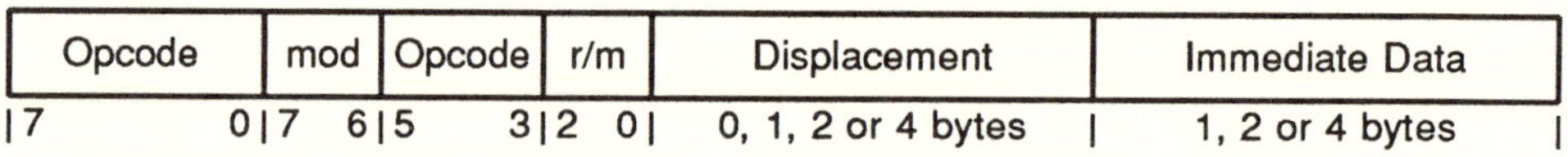

FIGURE 4-28g Two-Operand Immediate to Memory Instruction

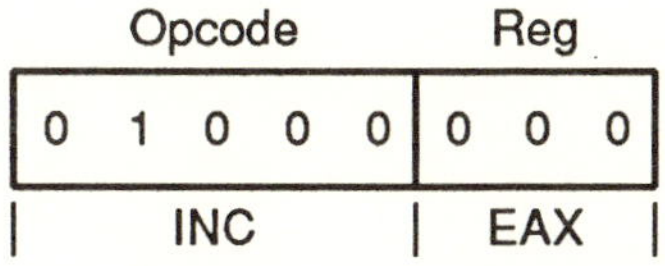

```
           Opcode           Reg
        ┌─────────────────┬───────────┐
        │ 0   1   0   0   0 │ 0   0   0 │
        └─────────────────┴───────────┘
        |      INC        |    EAX    |
```

FIGURE 4-29 Single-Byte Encoding of the INC EAX Instruction

The w bit distinguishes between 8-bit and 16-bit/32-bit operands. When the w bit is set (1), the 16-bit/32-bit default operand size is in effect for all operands unless an override byte is present. When the w bit is cleared (0), operands are 8-bits wide regardless of the setting of the D bit in the segment-descriptor register or the presence of an override byte. The d bit is used by two-operand instructions to distinguish between source and destination operands, as described below.

Addressing Mode Bytes

Although addressing mode information can be contained within the opcode byte, as illustrated in Figure 4-28b, this information is more typically encoded within two separate addressing mode bytes. The first addressing byte, called the ModR/M byte, is the primary addressing mode byte and is present in most 80386 instructions. The second addressing byte, called the SIB (scale, index and base) byte, supplies additional data required for certain 32-bit addressing modes. When the INTEL 80386 CPU is operated using 16-bit addressing modes (for example, when emulating the 8086 microprocessor), the SIB byte is never present.

ModR/M Byte

The term ModR/M byte is derived from register or memory (R/M) addressing mode (Mod). This is the primary addressing mode byte for the majority of 80386 instructions and it has the two formats illustrated in Figure 4-30. The two-operand format is used for addressing both operands in a two-operand instruction. One of the operands is specified by the combination of the mode and r/m fields; the other operand is specified by the register (reg) field. The register field encodings are the same as those contained in Table 4-10. One operand of every two-operand instruction must be directly located in a register as specified by the register field. This ensures that addressing mode information for both operands can be encoded within one ModR/M byte, keeping 80386 instructions as short as possible.

The ModR/M byte does not include the distinction between source and destination operands. This specification is always made by the destination (d) bit in the instructions opcode. When the d bit is set (1), the operand specified in the register field is the destination operand and the operand specified by the mode and r/m fields is the source operand. The reverse is true when the opcode's d bit is cleared (0).

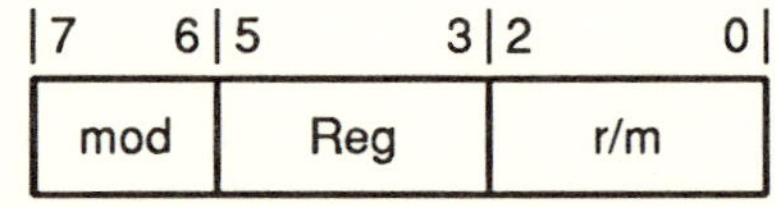

```
|7    6|5        3|2      0|
 ┌──────┬─────────┬────────┐
 │ mod  │   Reg   │  r/m   │
 └──────┴─────────┴────────┘
```

a. Two-Operand Format for ModR/M Byte

```
|7    6|5        3|2      0|
 ┌──────┬─────────┬────────┐
 │ mod  │ Opcode  │  r/m   │
 └──────┴─────────┴────────┘
```

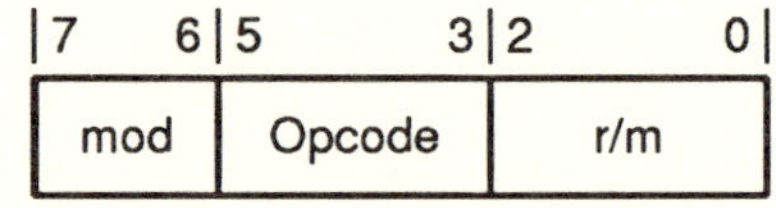

b. One-Operand Format for ModR/M Byte

FIGURE 4-30   Operand Formats for the Addressing Mode (ModR/M) Byte

Single-operand instructions use the ModR/M byte format shown in Figure 4-30b. Here the mode and r/m fields locate the single memory or register operand and the opcode field contains additional opcode bits supplementing those contained in the primary opcode byte. Single-operand instructions that use either a 16-bit or 32-bit register, such as INC EAX, may be encoded also by using the shorter one-byte instruction format shown in Figure 4-28b. This provides two possible formats for this type of instruction.

mod and r/m Bits

The INTEL 80386 Microprocessor uses three primary operand storage locations: registers, immediate data, and external locations (memory or I/O ports). The opcode indicates the presence of immediate operands for all 80386 instructions. Immediate data is never specified by distinct addressing mode bits within the ModR/M byte. When a ModR/M addressing byte is present, the distinction between the remaining operand locations, register or memory, is determined by the setting of the mode (mod) bits. This is also true for the INTEL 8086, 8088, and 80286 Microprocessors.

A mod value of 11 designates register direct addressing mode with the operand located in the register specified by the r/m bits. Table 4-11 lists all possible values for the r/m bits and the corresponding register selected when the mod field is

TABLE 4-11 r/m Register Codes for mod = 11

Register	r/m Value (mod = 11)							
Size	000	001	010	011	100	101	110	111
8-bit	AL	CL	DL	BL	AH	CH	DH	BH
16-bit	AX	CX	DX	BX	SP	BP	SI	DI
32-bit	EAX	ECX	EDX	EBX	ESP	EBP	ESI	EDI

11. Notice that these encodings are the same as those used for the reg field previously listed in Table 4-10.

For example, the mod and r/m combination of 11 000 specifies an operand located in either the 16-bit AX register or the 32-bit EAX register. The choice of registers depends on the data size in effect as determined by the D bit of the segment descriptor. If the D bit is 0, the 16-bit registers listed are referenced; otherwise, the 32-bit registers are selected. Regardless of the state of the D bit, the 8-bit registers are selected by the state of the width (w) bit within the opcode. When w is present and is 0, it always overrides the 16-bit or 32-bit default operand size in effect.

Note that in all cases the final bit encoding is created by the compiler or assembler used to translate a programmer's instructions. For example, the instruction INC AL causes the mod and r/m bit encoding illustrated in Figure 4-31. In this case, the w bit is the least significant bit of the opcode byte and the ModR/M address byte uses the one-operand format shown in Figure 4-30b.

Just as a mod field of 11 designates a register operand, mod values of 00, 01, and 10 specify memory operands. For these operands, the r/m field specifies the base and index registers used in calculating the effective memory address. Instructions referencing memory operands do not have the one-byte, short format available to single-operand register instructions. Again, a distinction must be made between 16-bit and 32-bit memory operands.

16-Bit Memory Address Modes

Tables 4-12, 4-13, and 4-14 list the addressing modes that correspond to mod fields of 00, 01, and 10, respectively, for an 80386 CPU operating in 16-bit mode (the D bit is 0). Included are all possible encodings of the r/m field. In these tables the r/m field designates the base register, index register, and default segment for one operand. The only difference in the r/m encodings is that an r/m value of 110 specifies the BP register as the base register for mods 01 and 10 (Tables 4-13 and 4-14, respectively), whereas in Table 4-12 (mod = 00) this encoding designates a direct memory address mode. For this mode, the direct-memory address (relative to the beginning of the data segment) is encoded as a displacement address within the instruction. For example, Figure 4-32

FIGURE 4-31 Encoding of the INC AL Instruction

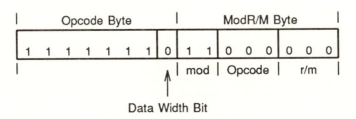

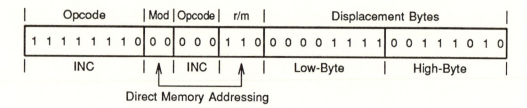

FIGURE 4-32 A Sample Direct-Memory-Address Increment Instruction

illustrates the encoding used to increment the byte at displacement address 0011 1010 0000 1111.

Except for the direct memory address mode designated by the mod and r/m combination of 00 110, the mod values 00, 01, and 10 differentiate between displacement addresses encoded within an instruction. A mod value of 00 designates no displacement address, except when r/m is 110, a mod value of 01 designates an 8-bit displacement value (one displacement byte), and a value of 10 designates a 16-bit displacement value (two displacement bytes), which is the default operand size when the D bit is 0.

Consider the ModR/M byte illustrated in Figure 4-33. The operand specified by the mod and r/m combination of 00 000 indicates an operand in memory whose effective address is the sum of the addresses contained in the BX base register and SI index register. Since a mod value of 00 indicates that there is no displacement value in the effective address, an instruction containing this ModR/M byte will have no displacement bytes. The second operand, specified by reg the field, is located in the DX register (see Table 4-10). The distinction between source and destination operands is determined by the state of the opcode's d bit.

32-Bit Memory Address Modes

The 16-bit address mode structure defines the BX and BP registers as base registers and the DI and SI registers as index registers. The 32-bit structure allows almost any register to be used for either purpose making encoding of 32-bit memory address modes within the ModR/M simpler conceptually than that used for 16-bit mode.

When the 80386 CPU is operated in 32-bit mode (D bit is 1), the mod values 00, 01, and 10 perform the same function as when in 16-bit mode; they differentiate between displacement addresses encoded within an instruction. A mod value of 00 designates no displacement bytes are present (except when r/m is 101, which differs from the 16-bit encoding for direct-memory address mode); a value of 01 designates an 8-bit displacement value (one displacement byte) is present; and a value of 10 designates a displacement equal to the default operand size. In 32-bit mode (D = 1), the default operand size is a four-byte displacement.

TABLE 4-12 16-Bit Memory Addressing Modes - No Address Displacement

mod Value	r/m Value	Base Register	Index Register	Default Segment
Based Index Addressing Mode				
00	000	BX	SI	DATA
00	001	BX	DI	DATA
00	010	BP	SI	STACK
00	011	BP	DI	STACK
Register Indirect Addressing Mode				
00	100	None	SI	DATA
00	101	None	DI	DATA
00	111	BX	None	DATA
Direct Memory Addressing Mode				
00	110	None	None	DATA

TABLE 4-13 16-Bit Memory Addressing Modes - One Displacement Byte

mod Value	r/m Value	Base Register	Index Register	Default Segment
Based Index Addressing Mode				
01	000	BX	SI	DATA
01	001	BX	DI	DATA
01	010	BP	SI	STACK
01	011	BP	DI	STACK
Register Relative Addressing Mode				
01	100	None	SI	DATA
01	101	None	DI	DATA
01	111	BX	None	DATA
01	110	BP	None	STACK

TABLE 4-14 16-Bit Memory Addressing Modes - Two Displacement Bytes

mod Value	r/m Value	Base Register	Index Register	Default Segment
Based Index Addressing Mode				
10	000	BX	SI	DATA
10	001	BX	DI	DATA
10	010	BP	SI	STACK
10	011	BP	DI	STACK
Register Relative Addressing Mode				
10	100	None	SI	DATA
10	101	None	DI	DATA
10	111	BX	None	DATA
10	110	BP	None	STACK

mod	Reg	r/m
0　0	0　1　0	0　0　0

FIGURE 4-33 A Sample ModR/M Byte

The major difference between 16-bit and 32-bit addressing resides in the encodings represented by the r/m bits. Table 4-15 lists these encodings for 32-bit addressing.

TABLE 4-15 r/m Bit Encodings

r/m	Specified Register
000	EAX
001	ECX
010	EDX
011	EBX
100	SIB address byte is present
101	EBP, except if mod = 00
110	ESI
111	EDI

Several comments are in order concerning Table 4-15. First, the encodings and registers specified in Table 4-15 are almost identical to those listed in Table 4-11 for register mode (mod = 11). For memory operands (mods 00, 01, and 10), the registers specified in Table 4-15 are used as pointer registers whose contents are treated as addresses within the context of the 80386 indirect address modes. For example, Figure 4-34 illustrates the encoding of the instruction

MOV ECX,[EBX]

FIGURE 4-34 The Encoding of the MOV ECX,[EBX] Instruction

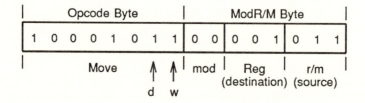

Second, notice that when the mod bits are 00 an r/m value of 101 does not designate the EBP register. In 32-bit mode a mod and r/m combination of 00 101 designates the direct memory address mode. For example, Figure 4-35 illustrates the encoding used to increment the 32-bit double-word located at offset address

0011 1010 0000 1111 1010 0101 1100 1110

when the CPU is in 32-bit mode (D = 1).

Finally, the codes listed in Table 4-15 permit encoding of only one register that is to be used as either a base or index register, as the application requires. For the use of both a base and index register, the r/m encoding 100 must be used. This encoding specifies that a second address mode byte: the scale, index, and base (SIB) byte, will be used to specify both a base and index register.

Figure 4-36 shows the format for a SIB byte. The first two bits (ss) specify a scale factor, the next three bits specify an index register, and the last three bits specify a base register. Table 4-16 lists the scale factors specified by the scale field; Table 4-17 lists the index registers specified by the index field; and Table 4-18 lists the base registers specified by the base field.

With the use of Tables 4-16, 4-17, and 4-18, encoding an SIB byte is rather straightforward. For example, the encoding of the instruction

    MOV EAX,[ECX + 4*EDX]

is illustrated in Figure 4-37.

FIGURE 4-35   A Sample 32-Bit Direct-Memory Address Instruction

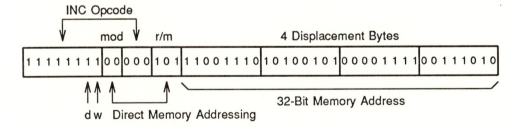

FIGURE 4-36   SIB Byte Format

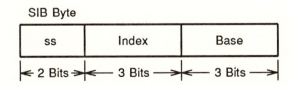

TABLE 4-16 Scale Factor Encoding

ss Code	Scale Factor
00	1
01	2
10	4
11	8

TABLE 4-17 Index Register

Index Code	Index Register
000	EAX
001	ECX
010	EDX
011	EBX
100	None, scale factor must be 00
101	EBP
110	ESI
111	EDI

TABLE 4-18 Base Register Encoding

Base Code	Base Register
000	EAX
001	ECX
010	EDX
011	EBX
100	ESP
101	EBP, except if mod = 00
110	ESI
111	EDI

As per Table 4-18, if a SIB byte is present and the base field is encoded as 101 when the mod field is 00, the EBP register is not used as a base register. In this case, no base register is used and the effective address is calculated as the sum of a displacement and scaled index address (this is the direct index mode described in Section 4.3).

Override Prefix Bytes

Although the majority of 80386 instructions are encoded using variations of the basic 12 bytes shown in Figure 4-26, in its most general form an 80386

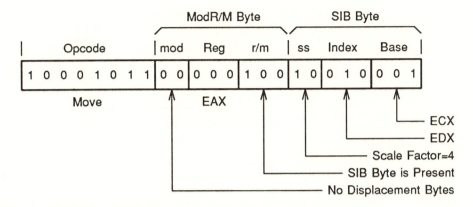

FIGURE 4-37   Encoding of the MOV EAX, [ECX+4*EDX] Instruction

instruction can consist of up to 16 bytes. The additional 4 bytes, shown in Figure 4-38, are called prefix bytes. Three of these prefix bytes are used to alter the default segment, operand size, and address size associated with an instruction. The instruction prefix byte is essentially used for string instructions.

Segment Override Prefix Byte

Each instruction referencing a memory operand assumes implicitly the default segments given in Table 4-19. Memory operands are not restricted to these default segments and can be located in any of the six segments supported by the 80386 CPU. In assembly language a segment override is specified by listing the desired segment register, followed by a colon. For example, the instruction

MOV EAX, ES:[ECX]

causes the source operand's effective address to be determined by the contents of the ECX register. This is done relative to the segment designated by the ES register rather than the default DS segment register. The double word (32-bits) located at this address is then moved into the EAX register.

When a segment override is specified, a segment override byte is present within an instruction. This byte explicitly designates the segment register to be

FIGURE 4-38   The Prefix Bytes

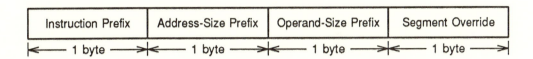

Instruction Prefix	Address-Size Prefix	Operand-Size Prefix	Segment Override
← 1 byte →	← 1 byte →	← 1 byte →	← 1 byte →

TABLE 4-19 Default Segment Registers

Memory Reference	Default Segment Register
Stack Operation	SS
String Source Location	DS
String Destination Location	ES
Nonstring Data	DS
Operand Address in EBP or BP	SS

used for the instruction's memory operand and overrides the default segment register normally assumed by the CPU. Table 4-20 lists the override prefix codes. Each of these prefix codes is unique in that no opcode has these values. These prefix codes identify the byte as a segment prefix override rather than an opcode that is usually the first byte of an instruction.

TABLE 4-20 Segment Override Prefix Codes

Prefix Code (Hex)	Destinated Segment Register
2E	CS
36	SS
3E	DS
26	ES
64	FS
65	GS

Operand-Size Prefix Byte

The operand-size prefix byte acts as a toggle switch to reverse the default operand size set by the D bit segment descriptor bit. This byte can only have a value of 66H, which represents a unique bit pattern identifying the presence of this byte. When the 80386 CPU is operating in protected mode as a 16-bit machine (D bit is 0), the presence of the operand-size prefix code switches to 32-bits the operand size accessed and manipulated by the instruction. When the D bit is 1, indicating a 32-bit default operand size, the presence of the operand-size prefix code switches to 16-bits the operand size accessed and manipulated by the instruction. The operand-size prefix byte affects only the size of the operand used by the instruction; it does not modify the default address size used to locate the operand.

Address-Size Prefix Byte

The address-size prefix byte acts as a toggle switch to reverse the default addressing size set by the D bit segment descriptor bit. This byte can only have a value of 67H, which represents a unique bit pattern identifying the presence of this byte. When the 80386 CPU is operating in protected mode as a 16-bit machine (D bit equal to zero), the presence of the address-size prefix code switches to 32-bits the addresses generated and used by the instruction. When the D bit is a 1, indicating a 32-bit default address size, the presence of the address-size prefix code switches to 16-bits the addresses generated and used by the instruction. The address-size prefix byte affects only the size of the address used by the instruction to locate an operand; it does not modify the default operand size.

Instruction Prefix Byte

The instruction prefix byte has three unique codes that identify this byte as an instruction prefix. Two of these codes (F2 and F3) are repeat prefixes that can be used only with string instructions (these are described in the next section). The third code (F0) causes the $\overline{\text{LOCK}}$ signal of the 80386 CPU to be asserted when the instruction is being executed. This signal is used in a multiprocessor environment to ensure that the CPU executing the instruction has exclusive use of any shared memory while the instruction is being executed.

Notation: The multiplicity of available 80386 addressing modes mandates the establishment and use of consistent and concise notation to specify both the operand sizes and addressing modes supported by an instruction. We will use the Intel notation presented in Table 4-21 to describe the 80386 instruction set. The notation r/m followed by the data size (8, 16, or 32) is the same form that we have already used: the operand is either a register or a memory operand of the designated size addressable in the modes previously presented.

The notation presented in Tables 4-22 and 4-23 is used to differentiate between the allowable addressing mode combinations. These tables provide the complete list of addressing modes available for single-operand and double-operand instructions, respectively. The notation given is used extensively in the next section to indicate permissible addressing modes supported by individual 80386 instructions.

A semicolon is used in Tables 4-22 and 4-23 to separate individual cases. For example, in Table 4-22 the notation imm8; imm16; imm32 listed for mode 3 indicates that the single operand may be either immediate 8-bit, 16-bit, or 32-bit data. Additionally, a comma is used in Table 4-23 to separate the first permissible operand addressing mode from the second. For example, the notation r16,imm16; r32,imm32 indicates that the first operand can be either a 16-bit or 32-bit register. When the first operand is a 16-bit register, the second operand must be immediate 16-bit data; similarly, when the first operand is a 32-bit register, the second operand must be immediate 32-bit data.

TABLE 4-21 Operand Notation

Symbol	Description
r8	Byte register AL,AH,BL,BH,CL,CH,DL, or DH.
r16	Word register AX,BX,CX,DX,SP,BP,SI, or DI.
r32	Double-word register EAX, EBX, ECX, EDX, ESP, EBP, ESI, or EDI.
Sreg	Segment register CS, DS, ES, FS, GS, or SS.
r/m8	Byte register or memory byte (provided by effective address computation).
r/m16	Word register or memory word.
r/m32	Double word register or memory double word.
imm8	Immediate signed byte ranging from –128 to +127.
imm16	Immediate signed word ranging from –32768 to +32767.
imm32	Immediate signed double word ranging from -2^{31} to $(+2^{31}-1)$.
moffs8	Memory byte at simple offset relative to segment base.
moffs16	Memory word at simple offset relative to segment base.
moffs32	Memory double word at simple offset relative to segment base.
CR	Control register CR0, CR2, or CR3.
DR	Debug register DR0, DR1, DR2, DR3, DR6, or DR7.
TR	Test register TR6 or TR7.
m16&16	16-bit and 16-bit data item pairs, using any memory-addressing mode.
m16&32	16-bit and 32-bit data item pairs, using any memory-addressing mode.
m32&32	32-bit and 32-bit data item pairs, using any memory-addressing mode.
rel8	Relative address ranging from –128 to +127 bytes from the end of the instruction.
rel16	Relative address within same code segment as current instruction with 16-bit operand size attribute.
rel32	Relative address within same code segment as current instruction with 32-bit operand size attribute.
ptr16:16	Far pointer, typically in a different code segment than current instruction. Pointer consists of 16-bit selector, or value for CS followed by 16-bit offset. Operand size attribute is 16-bits.
ptr16:32	Same as ptr16:16, except that offset is 32-bits corresponding to operand size attribute of 32-bits.
m16:16	Memory operand, containing far pointer which consists of 16-bit segment selector and 16-bit offset.
m16:32	Same as m16:16, except that pointer offset is 32-bits.

TABLE 4-22 Permissible Single-Operand Addressing Modes

Symbol	Designated Combination
1	r/m8
2	r/m16; r/m32
3	imm8; imm16; imm32
4	Sreg
5	rel8
6	rel16; rel32
7	r/m16; r/m32
8	prt16:16; ptr16:32
9	m16:16; m16:32

TABLE 4-23 Permissible Double-Operand Addressing Mode Combinations

Symbol	Designated Combination
a	r/m8,r8
b	r8, r/m8
c	r/m16,r16; r/m32,r32
d	r16,r/m16; r32,r/m32
e	r/m8,imm8
f	r/m16,imm16; r/m32,imm32
g	r/m16,imm8; r/m32,imm8
h	r/m16,Sreg; Sreg,r/m16
i	AL,moffs8; AX,moffs16; EAX,moffs32; moffs8,AL; moffs16,AX; moffs32,EAX
j	r16,r/m8; r32,r/m8; r32,r/m16
k	r32,CR/DR/TR; CR/DR/TR,r32
m	r/m8,1; r/m16,1; r/m32,1
n	r/m8,CL; r/m16,CL; r/m32,CL
p	r16,m16:16; r32,m16:32
q	r16,m16&16; r32,m32&32

4.5 Instruction Set

The INTEL 80386 CPU Instruction set consists of six functional groups: data transfer, arithmetic, logical, program control, string/character translation, and high-level and system support instructions. This section describes each group and lists its mnemonics.

Recall that an 80386 instruction can reference at most two operands. When a double-operand instruction is given, the first operand represents the destination operand and the second operand the source operand. The notation used to indicate permissible operand register and addressing modes is the same as that presented in Tables 4-21, 4-22, and 4-23. All numbers used in instruction examples are hexadecimal.

Data Transfer Instructions

Data transfer instructions permit the transfer of data between on-chip CPU registers, and between these registers and external locations (memory and I/O ports). Table 4-24 lists all the instructions within the data transfer group. Included are the instruction's mnemonic, operand, allowable addressing modes, and description. Additional descriptive information and specific examples of their operation are presented after the table.

The MOV instruction (MOV) allows 8-bit, 16-bit, or 32-bit data to be moved using a large number of addressing modes. These addressing modes include register to register, register to/from memory, immediate to register or memory, register or memory to/from segment register, and memory-offset-address to accumulator. In addition, this instruction is used to transfer data between a general-purpose 32-bit register and a control, debug, or test register. The exchange (XCHG) instruction allows swapping data between registers or between a register and memory.

The stack manipulation group permits general-purpose register, segment register, flag register, and memory data to be saved on the stack using a push operation (PUSH, PUSHF, PUSHFD), and retrieved from the stack using a pop operation (POP, POPF, POPFD). If all the general-registers (16-bit or 32-bit) are to be saved, a single "push all" (PUSHA, PUSHAD) operation can be used; likewise POPA or POPAD replaces all the registers.

Type conversion instructions include the convert instructions CBW, CWD, CWDE, and CDQ, which sign-extend an accumulator byte, word, or double word (dword) to twice its size. The extended bits occupy the upper part of the accumulator for CBW and CWDE, the DX register for CWD, or EDX for CDQ if 32-bits is extended to a 64-bit quadword (qword). Move with sign-extend (MOVSX) and move with zero-extend (MOVZX) are listed here, since they convert a byte to a word or double word before moving it. The flag transfer operations LAHF and SAHF move the lower byte of FLAGS to/from AH.

TABLE 4-24 Data Transfer Instruction Group (See Notes)

Instruction	Mnemonic	Operands	Modes	Description
Move				
Move data/special registers	MOV	dst,src	a-f,h,i,k	dst←src
Exchange				
Exchange register/memory with register	XCHG	dst,src	a-d	dst↔src
Stack Manipulation				
Push operand	PUSH	src	2,3,4	stack←src
Push all general registers	PUSHA			stack←all16
	PUSHAD			stack←all32
Push flag register	PUSHF			stack←FLAGS
	PUSHFD			stack←EFLAGS
Pop operand	POP	dst	2,4	src←stack
Pop all general registers	POPA			all16←stack
	POPAD			all32←stack
Pop flag register	POPF			FLAGS←stack
	POPFD			EFLAGS←stack
Type Conversion				
Convert byte to word	CBW			AX←seo AL
Convert word to dword	CWD			DX:AX←seo AX
	CWDE			EAX←seo AX
Convert dword to qword	CDQ			EDX:EAX←seo EAX
Move with sign extend	MOVSX	dst,src	j	dst←seo src
Move with zero extend	MOVZX	dst,src	j	dst←zeo src
Flag Transfer				
Load flags into AH	LAHF			AH←FLAGS(LO)
Store AH into flags	SAHF			FLAGS (LO)←AH
Data Pointer				
Load full pointer	LDS	dst,src	p	DS:dst←src
	LES	dst,src	p	ES:dst←src
	LFS	dst,src	p	FS:dst←src
	LGS	dst,src	p	GS:dst←src
	LSS	dst,src	p	SS:dst←src
Address Calculate				
Load effective address	LEA	dst,src		r16/r32←oa16/oa32
Translate				
Table look-up translation	XLAT	[mem8]		AL←DS:(BX/EBX
	XLATB			+zeo AL)
Input/Output				
Input from port	IN	dst,src		AL/AX/EAX← port(imm8/DX)
Output to port	OUT	dst,src		port(imm8/DX)← AL/AX/EAX

TABLE 4-24 Data Transfer Instruction Group (See Notes) (Continued)

Notes

1. Mode symbols are defined in Tables 4-21, 4-22, and 4-23.
2. all16 - all 16-bit registers: AX, BX, CX, DX, SP, BP, SI, DI.
3. all32 - all 32-bit registers: EAX, EBX, ECX, EDX, ESP, EBP, ESI, EDI.
4. PUSHA saves the original values of SP, BP, SI, and DI.
5. PUSHAD saves the original values of ESP, EBP, ESI, and EDI.
6. seo - sign extension of
7. zeo - zero extension of
8. LO - lower 8-bits
9. oa - offset address
10. [mem8] - 8-bit memory operand used only for the segment override case
11. port(imm8/DX) - 16-bit I/O port address (8-bit immediate data zero extended to 16-bits, or the contents of DX).

The data pointer instructions LDS, LES, LFS, LGS, and LSS permit the simultaneous loading of a 16-bit segment register and a 16-bit or 32-bit bit general register from a memory operand. Load effective address (LEA) transfers the source's offset, rather than its contents, to a 16-bit or 32-bit register. The table look-up translation instruction (XLAT) uses AL as an offset to a base address in BX or EBX, and replaces AL by the byte at the offset address.

Finally, the input and output instructions (IN, OUT) are included in the data transfer group. These instructions permit direct transfer of byte, word, or dword data between the accumulator and an I/O port. The port address, which is a 16-bit address separate from the space of memory addresses, is either an 8-bit immediate number zero extended to 16-bits or is taken from register DX. The use of a separate set of input and output instructions for I/O ports is a direct result of the INTEL 80386 CPU's discrimination between memory address space and I/O address space (this is described in more detail in Chapters 7 and 8).

Examples of the operations performed by data transfer instructions for 8-bit, 16-bit, and 32-bit register-to-register moves are:

Example	Operation
MOV BL,AL	BL $\leftarrow$ AL (8 bit)
MOV BX,AX	BX $\leftarrow$ AX (16 bit)
MOV EBX,EAX	EBX $\leftarrow$ EAX (32 bit)

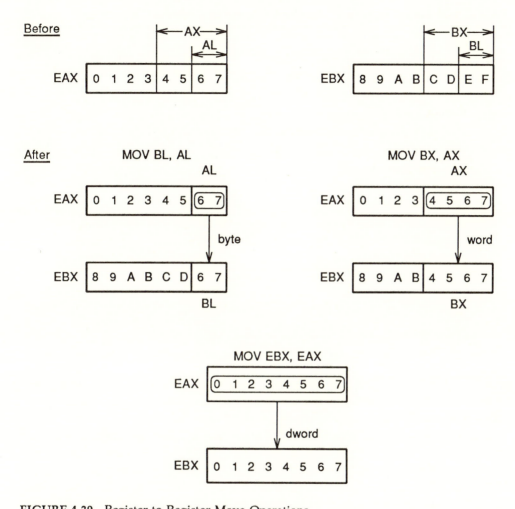

FIGURE 4-39 Register-to-Register Move Operations

Figure 4-39 illustrates the transfer of byte, word, and double-word data from EAX to EBX. The assumed register contents before instruction execution are given as

EAX = 01234567   EBX = 89ABCDEF

The final contents of register EBX after execution of each instruction (EAX is unchanged in each case) are:

Instruction	Result
MOV BL,AL	EBX = 89ABCD67
MOV BX,AX	EBX = 89AB4567
MOV EBX,EAX	EBX = 01234567

Consider the following examples of 8-bit, 16-bit, and 32-bit register-indirect to register moves:

Example	Operation
MOV BL,[EAX]	BL ← DS:EAX (8-bit)
MOV BX,[EAX]	BX ← DS:EAX (16-bit)
MOV EBX,[EAX]	EBX ← DS:EAX (32-bit)

Notice that DS:EAX points to memory data in the segment corresponding to DS (default case), starting at the offset address contained in register EAX.

Figure 4-40 illustrates the transfer of byte, word, and double-word data from DS:EAX to EBX. The assumed register and memory contents before instruction execution are given as

EBX = 89ABCDEF   DS:EAX = 6C 73 A2 ED

The final contents of register EBX after execution of each instruction are:

Instruction	Result
MOV BL,[EAX]	EBX = 89ABCD6C
MOV BX,[EAX]	EBX = 89AB736C
MOV EBX,[EAX]	EBX = EDA2736C

In each case, the contents of EAX and all memory locations remain unchanged. As shown in Figure 4-40, a byte is transferred from the physical address to the low byte of EBX, namely BL. For a word transfer, the byte at the physical address and the byte located at the next highest address are transferred to the lower half of EBX, namely BX. A double word is fetched starting from the physical address given in the instruction and replaces EBX in its entirety.

Example of a table look-up translation:

Example	Operation
XLAT	AL ← DS:(EBX+AL)

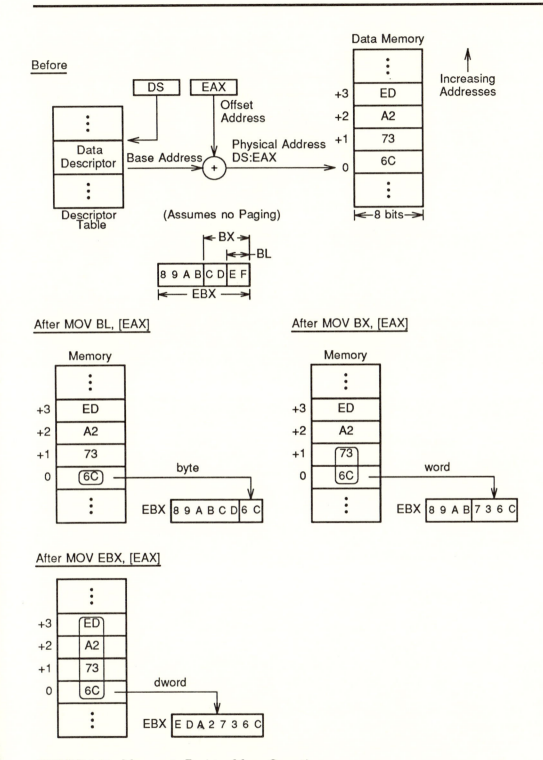

FIGURE 4-40   Memory-to-Register Move Operations

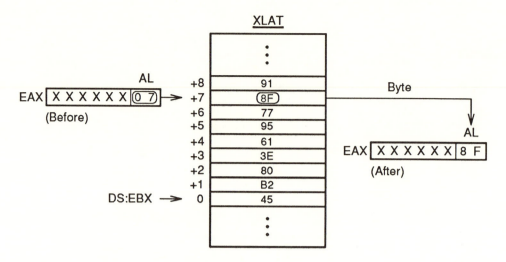

FIGURE 4-41 Table Look-Up Operation

Figure 4-41 illustrates the table look-up operation. The assumed register and memory contents before the instruction is executed is given as

AL = 07   DS:EBX = 45 B2 80 3E 61 95 77 8F 91 ...

The change in register contents after instruction execution is

AL = 8F

The EBX and memory contents are unchanged. The low byte of EAX, namely AL, provides an offset to the physical address defined by DS:EBX. Since AL contains 07, the byte stored seven locations above the physical address DS:EBX is transferred to AL. Thus, the table offset address in AL has been replaced by the table's content at that location.

Example of 8-bit, 16-bit, and 32-bit input using indirect port addressing:

Example	Operation
IN AL,DX	AL ← Port(DX) (8-bit)
IN AX,DX	AX ← Port(DX) (16-bit)
IN EAX,DX	EAX ← Port(DX) (32-bit)

Figure 4-42 illustrates the input operation for byte, word, and double-word data. It is assumed that the hardware is configured such that each port address corresponds to a byte (similar to a memory address in this respect). The port address is 16-bits in length; in this example the DX register stores the port address and indirect addressing is used.

162

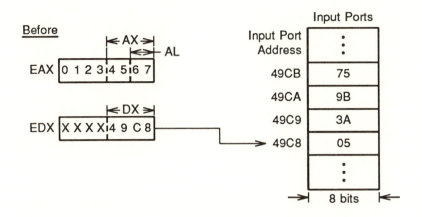

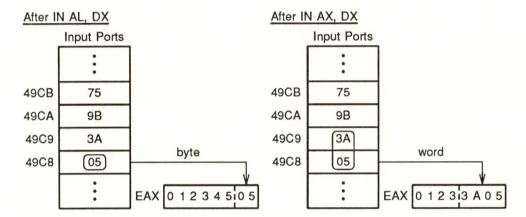

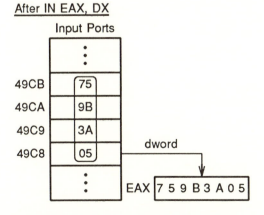

FIGURE 4-42   Input From Port Operation

Before each instruction is executed, the assumed register and input port contents, starting with the highest byte, are:

EAX = 01234567   DX = 49C8
            Port 49C8 =   05   (8-bit)
            Port 49C8 =   3A 05   (16-bit)
            Port 49C8 =   75 9B 3A 05   (32-bit)

The final register contents after each instruction is executed are shown below. In each case the contents of register DX and the input port remain unchanged.

Instruction   Result

IN AL,DX   EAX = 01234505
IN AX,DX   EAX = 01233A05
IN EAX,DX   EAX = 759B3A05

As in memory-to-register transfers, a byte transfer replaces only the low byte of the 32-bit register, a word transfer replaces only the low word, and a double-word transfer replaces the entire register content. Thus, either a byte from Port 49C8 replaces the contents of AL, a word from port addresses 49C8 and 49C9 replaces the contents of AX, or a double word from port addresses 49C8 to 49CB replaces the contents of EAX.

Arithmetic Instructions

The arithmetic instruction group is presented in Table 4-25. Add (ADD, ADC), subtract (SUB, SBB), and compare (CMP) are operations performed on byte, word, or dword source and destination operands. With the exception of the compare instruction, which only affects the status flags, arithmetic operations replace the destination operand with the result of the computation. The source and destination can be either a register or memory; however, memory cannot be both a source and destination. The source may also be immediate data; an immediate source byte can be sign extended to operate with a word or dword. The increment (INC), decrement (DEC), and negate (NEG) operations add 1, subtract 1, and perform two's complement negation, respectively, on any single byte, word, or dword. The operand may reside in a general register or in memory.

Multiply (MUL, IMUL) can be performed on bytes, words, and dwords. In the most general case, the product may be twice as large as the individual numbers multiplied and the destination must hold either a word, dword, or quad word (64-bits). The unsigned version, MUL, multiplies the accumulator (AL, AX, or EAX) by the same size operand in another register or in memory; the accumulator is also the destination. For 16-bit or 32-bit multiplications, the upper half of the

TABLE 4-25 Arithmetic Instruction Group (See Notes)

Instruction	Mnemonic	Operand	Modes	Description
Addition				
Add	ADD	dst,src	a-g	dst←dst+src
Add with carry	ADC	dst,src	a-g	dst←dst+src+CF
Increment by 1	INC	dst	1,2	dst←dst+1
Subtraction				
Integer subtract	SUB	dst,src	a-g	dst←dst−src
Integer subtract with borrow	SBB	dst,src	a-g	dst←dst−src−CF
Decrement by 1	DEC	dst	1,2	dst←dst−1
Multiplication				
Unsigned multiply	MUL	src1,src2		dst←src1*src2
Signed multiply	IMUL	1, 2, or 3 Operands		dst←src1*src2
Division				
Unsigned divide	DIV	dst,src2		dst←src1/src2
Signed divide	IDIV	dst,src2		dst←src1/src2
Decimal Arithmetic				
Decimal add adjust	DAA			AL←BCD p.d.
Decimal subtract adjust	DAS			AL←BCD p.d.
ASCII adjust after add	AAA			AX←u.d.
ASCII adjust after subtract	AAS			AX←u.d.
ASCII adjust after multiply	AAM			AX←u.d.
ASCII adjust before divide	AAD			AX←p.d.
Compare				
Compare two operands	CMP	dst,src	a-g	dst − src
Negate				
Two's complement negation	NEG	dst	1,2	dst←(−dst)

Notes

1. Mode symbols are defined in Tables 4-21, 4-22, and 4-23.

2. p.d. denotes packed digits and u.d. denotes unpacked digits

3. The source and destination operands for the multiply and divide instructions are in subtables 25a, 25b, and 25c.

Continued

165

TABLE 4-25 Arithmetic Instruction Group (Continued)

25a. Multiply (MUL and IMUL src2)

	8 Bit	16 Bit	32 Bit
src1	AL	AX	EAX
src2	r/m8	r/m16	r/m32
dst	AX	DX:AX	EDX:EAX

25b. Divide (DIV and IDIV)

		8 Bit	16 Bit	32 Bit
	src1	AX	DX:AX	EDX:EAX
	src2	r/m8	r/m16	r/m32
Quotient	dst	AL	AX	EAX
Remainder	dst	AH	DX	EDX

25c. Signed Multiply (2 and 3 Operands)

IMUL dst,src				IMUL dst,src1, src2			
dst←dst*src				dst←src1*src2			
dst	src			dst	src1	src2	
r16	r/m16	imm8	imm16	r16	r/m16	imm8	imm16
r32	r/m32	imm8	imm32	r32	r/m32	imm8	imm32

product is stored in DX or EDX respectively. The signed multiply, IMUL, has several addressing options. A single register or memory operand multiplied by the implied accumulator content is equivalent to the two operand MUL, except that the numbers are treated as signed. Two and three operand versions of IMUL permit 16-bit or 32-bit multiplications; however, the destination is a 16-bit or 32-bit general register, which means that the product cannot exceed the length of the multiplied numbers. The source for the two-operand case can be a register, memory, or immediate data (sign extended to 16-bits or 32-bits if specified as a byte). The three-operand IMUL multiplies a register or memory operand by an immediate operate, and again stores the result in any general register.

Divide (DIV, IDIV) is the inverse of multiplication. The 16-bit, 32-bit, or 64-bit dividend is stored in either AX, DX:AX, or EDX:EAX, respectively. It is divided by 8-bit, 16-bit, or 32-bit register/memory data. The quotient is then placed into AL, AX, or EAX, and the remainder into AH, DX, or EDX.

To facilitate decimal arithmetic, decimal-adjust after add (DAA) and before subtract (DAS) instructions are provided, along with ASCII-adjust after add (AAA), after subtract (AAS), after multiply (AAM), and before divide (AAD) instructions. These operations convert numbers to either packed binary-coded decimal (BCD), or to unpacked BCD (also called ASCII). As discussed in Section 4.2, a packed byte contains two decimal digits (0-9), each represented by a nibble (4 bits). In contrast, an unpacked BCD number represents a single decimal digit by its low-order nibble. The high-order nibble must be zero when used in multiplication and division operations.

The following examples illustrate the operation of the 32-bit arithmetic instructions.

Example of a 32-bit addition:

Instruction	Operation
ADD [EDX+5],EBX	DS:(EDX+5)←DS:(EDX+5) + EBX

Figure 4-43 illustrates the addition of a double word in memory to a 32-bit register, and the replacement of memory by the arithmetic sum. The assumed register and memory contents before the instruction is executed are:

EBX = 11223344
DS:EDX = DD CC BB AA 99 88 77 66 55 44 ....

As shown in Figure 4-43, the following addition is performed:

$$\begin{array}{r} 1122\ 3\ 3\ 4\ 4 \\ +\ 5566\ 7\ 7\ 8\ 8 \\ \hline 6688\ AACC \end{array}$$

The memory contents after instruction execution is given by

DS:EDX = DD CC BB AA 99 CC AA 88 66 44 ...

Registers EBX and EDX are unchanged. The double word added to EBX is fetched from memory starting at an address five above the physical address defined by DS:EDX, where +5 is the displacement provided with the instruction. The result of the addition replaces the double word at displacement locations +5 to +8, with respect to DS:EDX.

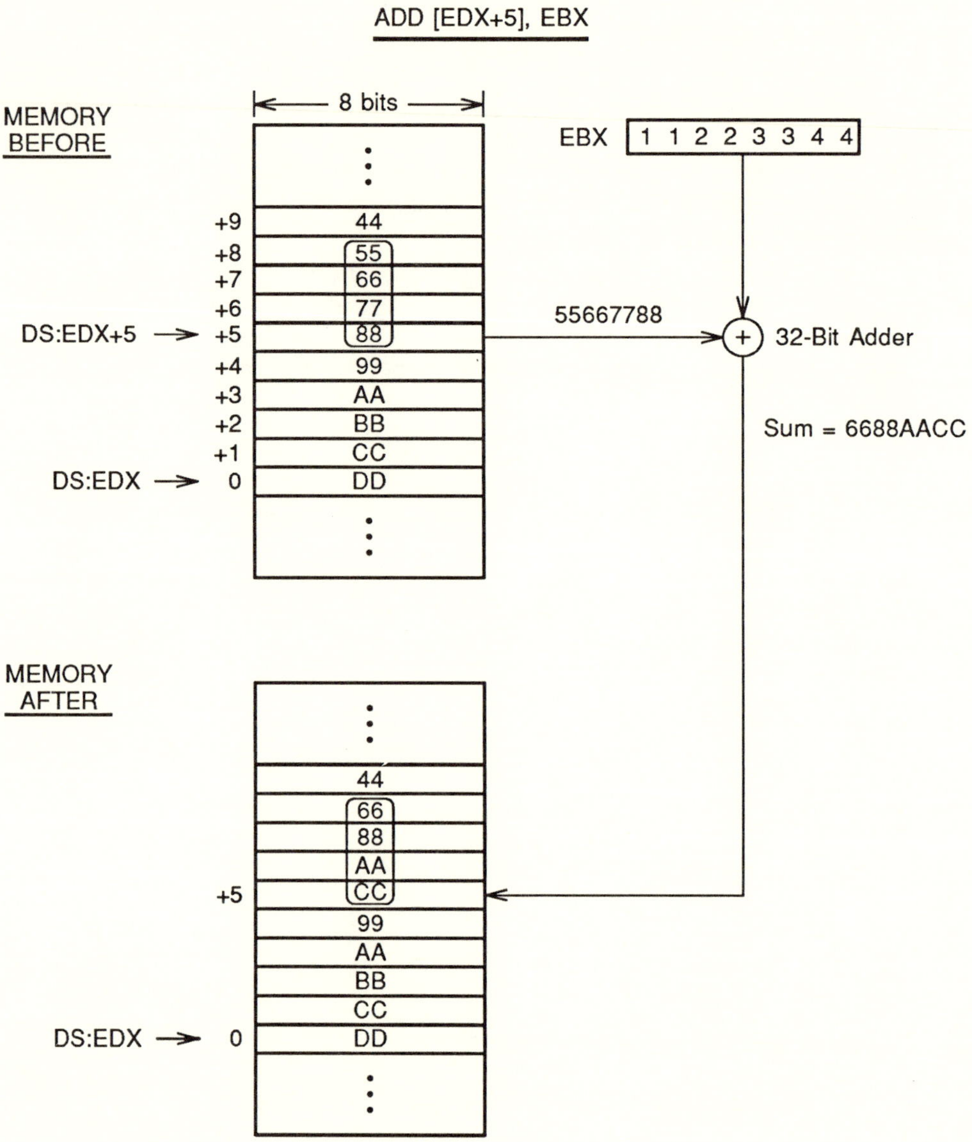

ADD [EDX+5], EBX

MEMORY
BEFORE

8 bits

EBX 1 1 2 2 3 3 4 4

+9	44
+8	55
+7	66
+6	77
+5	88
+4	99
+3	AA
+2	BB
+1	CC
0	DD

DS:EDX+5 → +5

DS:EDX → 0

55667788

(+) 32-Bit Adder

Sum = 6688AACC

MEMORY
AFTER

	44
	66
	88
	AA
+5	CC
	99
	AA
	BB
	CC
0	DD

DS:EDX → 0

FIGURE 4-43   32-bit Addition Operation

Example of a 32-bit multiplication:

Instruction   Operation

MUL EAX,EBX   EDX:EAX ← EAX ∗ EBX

The notation EDX:EAX identifies a 64-bit register to store the product, where the high 32-bits are stored in EDX. The assumed register contents before the instruction is executed are:

EAX = 12121212   EBX = 40000000   EDX = 00000000

The multiplication illustrated in Figure 4-44 is performed as:

              12121212
           x 40000000
          ─────────────────
          0484848480000000

The change in register contents after instruction execution is

EAX = 80000000   EDX = 04848484

The contents of register EBX remains unchanged.

FIGURE 4-44   32-bit Multiplication Operation

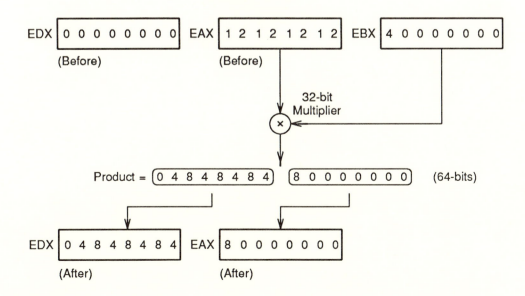

MUL EAX, EBX

Logical, Shift, and Rotate Instructions

The logical instruction group is presented in Table 4-26. The two-operand Boolean logical operations (AND, OR, XOR) are analogous to arithmetic add and subtract in that they operate on 8-bit, 16-bit, or 32-bit data and replace the dst operand with the result. The logical operation is performed on a bit-wise basis. A logical compare (TEST) performs a bit-wise logical AND of src and dst, but is analogous to the arithmetic compare in that it only affects the flags. The single-operand NOT complements each bit of the data, thereby converting a number to its one's complement (in contrast to the arithmetic NEG which converts to two's complement form).

The bit test/modify instructions test a register or memory word, or dword, where the bit position is defined by an offset in another register of the same size, or by an immediate byte. The bit value is placed into the carry flag CF, and is either unaltered (BT), set to 1 (BTS), reset to 0 (BTR), or complemented (BTC). Bit scan locates the position of the first set bit in the source operand (r/m16 or r/m32), and places its bit number into the destination operand (r16 or r32). The scan can be done in a forward direction, starting from the lowest order bit (BSF), or in reverse starting with the most significant bit (BSR). A numerical example illustrating the forward bit scan is presented after Table 4-26. A set byte on condition (SETcc) instruction replaces a register or memory byte with all ones if a flag condition is met.

The shift instructions permit rapid multiplying (SAL, SHL) or dividing (SAR, SHR) of a byte, word, or dword by a power of 2. The count operand specifies the number of bits shifted, and may be explicitly set (1), or may use the number in byte register CL. An additional mode permits a byte to be shifted by a count specified as any immediate byte. The bits shifted out are always replaced by 0s, and the last bit shifted replaces CF. Arithmetic and logical shifts are synonyms for the same operation. The double-precision shifts (SHLD,SHRD) permit shifting two linked word or dword operands (r/m16:r16 or r/m32:r32) as a single 32-bit or 64-bit operand. The count is either an immediate byte or the value of CL.

Rotate (ROL, ROR) and rotate-through-carry (RCL, RCR) instructions are similar to shifts except that the bits shifted out are replaced by bits from the opposite end. The rotates use the same addressing modes as the shifts, and the rotate-through-carry operations treat CF as an extension to the operand.

TABLE 4-26 Logical Instruction Group (See Notes)

Instruction	Mnemonic	Operands	Modes	Description
Boolean				
Logical AND	AND	dst,src	a-g	dst←dst AND src
Logical inclusive OR	OR	dst,src	a-g	dst←dst OR src
Logical exclusive OR	XOR	dst,src	a-g	dst←dst XOR src
One's complement negation	NOT	dst	1,2	dst←NOT dst
Bit Test/Modify				
Bit test	BT	src1,src2	c,g	CF←bit
Bit test and set	BTS	src1,src2	c,g	CF←bit, bit←1
Bit test and reset	BTR	src1,src2	c,g	CF←bit, bit←0
Bit test and complement	BTC	src1,src2	c,g	CF←bit, bit←NOT bit
Bit Scan				
Bit scan forward	BSF	dst,src	d	dst←forward bix
Bit scan reverse	BSR	dst,src	d	dst←reverse bix
Shift/Rotate				
Shift arithmetic left	SAL	dst,count	e,m,n	dst←dst∗(2∗count)
Shift logical left	SHL	dst,count	e,m,n	dst←dst∗(2∗count)
Shift arithmetic right	SAR	dst,count	e,m,n	dst←dst/(2∗count)
Shift logical right	SHR	dst,count	e,m,n	dst←dst/(2∗count)
Shift left double	SHLD	dst1,dst2, count		⟲ dst1:dst2
Shift right double	SHRD	dst1,dst2, count		⟳ dst1:dst2
Rotate left	ROL	dst,count	e,m,n	⟲ dst
Rotate right	ROR	dst,count	e,m,n	⟳ dst
Rotate through carry left	RCL	dst,count	e,m,n	⟲ CF:dst
Rotate through carry right	RCR	dst,count	e,m,n	⟳ CF:dst
Byte Set on Condition				
Set byte on condition	SETcc	dst	1	if cc then dst←ones
Test				
Logical compare	TEST	dst,src	a,c, e,f	dst AND src
Flag Control				
Set carry flag	STC			CF←1
Clear carry flag	CLC			CF←0
Complement carry flag	CMC			CF←NOT CF
Clear direction flag	CLD			DF←0
Set direction flag	STD			DF←1
Clear interrupt flag	CLI			IF←0
Set interrupt flag	STI			IF←1

TABLE 4-26 Logical Instruction Group (Continued)

Notes

1. Mode symbols are defined in Tables 4-21, 4-22, and 4-23.
2. bit denotes the src1 bit position defined by src2 offset.
3. bix denotes the bit index. This is defined as the index of the first bit set starting from the least significant bit for BSF instruction, and from most significant bit for BSR instruction.
4. ⟲ denotes rotate left number of bit positions contained in count.

   ⟳ denotes rotate right number of bit positions contained in count.
5. cc denotes the flag condition as defined by:

Condition	Alternative	True	False	Alternative True	Alternative False
Above (U)	Not below or equal	A	NA	NBE	BE
Below (U)	Not above or equal	B	NB	NAE	AE
Below (U)	Carry	B	NB	C	NC
Equal (U)	Zero	E	NE	Z	NZ
Greater (S)	Not less or equal	G	NG	NLE	LE
Less (S)	Not greater or equal	L	NL	NGE	GE
Overflow (S)		O	NO		
Parity (U)	Parity even	P	NP	PE	PO
Sign (S)		S	NS		

where:
   (U) - used with unsigned numbers   (S) - used with signed numbers

6. The source and destination operands for the double-precision shift instructions are:

Shift double	dst1	dst2	count
(SHLD, SHRD)	r/m16	r16	imm8; CL
	r/m32	r32	imm8; CL

Flag control instructions enable explicit manipulation of individual flag bits. These include set, clear, and complement carry (STC, CLC, CMC), as well as set and clear direction flag (STD, CLD) or interrupt flag (STI, CLI).

The following programming example illustrates a bit scan forward operation.

Instruction	Operation
BSF ECX,[3A5614H]	ECX←bit index of 32-bit memory data (first set bit)

The assumed register and memory contents before the instruction is executed are:

$$\text{ECX} = 00000000 \qquad \text{DS:003A5614} = 00\ 00\ 00\ 58$$

The bit index calculation is shown below. The scan is done in the forward direction starting with bit 0, the least significant bit of the double word in memory starting at the physical address defined by DS:003A5614. Note that in contrast to previous instruction examples, the segment offset address is explicitly given in the instruction rather than located in a 32-bit pointer register.

```
Memory data = 58000000H =    01011000   00000000   00000000   00000000
                             ↑ ↑           ↑          ↑          ↑
     Bit number (decimal) →  27 24        16          8          0
```

Bit index = 27_{10} = 1BH

The final contents of register ECX is 0000001B, with the contents of memory remaining unchanged by the instruction. Notice that ECX contains the bit position corresponding to the first single digit found in the 32-bit memory word. For this example, the first one does not appear until the highest order byte is reached (bit 27 position).

Program Control Instructions

The program control instructions are summarized in Table 4-27. The jump (JMP) and call procedure (CALL) operations permit unconditional transfer of a program to a different instruction; in the case of call, the return address is saved on the stack. Both jumps and calls can be made to different segments as well as within the current code segment. For transfers within the segment, a relative 16-bit or 32-bit address (depending on the address-size attribute) adds an offset to EIP. For the jump only, an 8-bit offset is also permitted. A jump or call can be made indirectly within the segment, where the destination address is a register or memory operand (word or dword). A 4-byte or 6-byte long pointer operand, consisting of a selector word and offset word or dword, can be supplied directly or indirectly from memory. In real address mode the pointer loads its selector into CS and offset into EIP. In protected mode the selector indexes the appropriate segment descriptor, and the subsequent action depends on the descriptor's access rights (AR) byte. For example, the jump or call may transfer to a code segment at the same privilege level, or may involve a task switch (as detailed in Chapter 3).

The return from procedure (RET) instruction, is used to return from a called procedure to the calling program. The address, and possibly the segment

TABLE 4-27 Program Control Instruction Group (See Notes)

Instruction	Mnemonic	Operands	Modes	Description
Unconditional				
Jump	JMP	addr	5-9	CS:IP/EIP←addr
Call procedure	CALL	addr	6-9	stack←CS:IP/EIP CS:IP/EIP←addr
Return from procedure	RET			CS:IP/EIP←stack
	RET	imm16		CS:IP/EIP←stack ESP←ESP+imm16
Interrupt return	IRET			CS:IP←stack FLAGS←stack
	IRETD			CS:EIP←stack EFLAGS←stack
Conditional				
Jump on flag condition	Jcc	addr	5,6	if cc then CS:IP/EIP←addr
Jump on counter condition	JCXZ	addr	5	if CX=0 then CS:IP/EIP←addr
	JECXZ	addr	5	if ECX=0 then CS:IP/EIP←addr
Loop control with counter	LOOP	addr	5	ECX←ECX–1 if ECX=0 then CS:IP/EIP←addr
	LOOPzc	addr	5	ECX←ECX–1 if (ECX=0 AND zc) then CS:IP/EIP←addr
Software Interrupts				
Call interrupt procedure	INT	imm8		IF←0, stack←CS:IP/EIP stack←FLAGS/EFLAGS CS:IP/EIP←IDT(imm8)
	INTO			if OF=1 then INT 4
Check array index against bounds	BOUND	src1, src2	q	if src1>bound(src2) then INT 5

Notes

1. Mode symbols are defined in Tables 4-21, 4-22, and 4-23.

2. cc denotes flag condition (see Notes for Table 4-26).

3. zc denotes a zero condition.
   True condition: Equal (E) or Zero (Z)
   False condition: Not Equal (NE) or Not Zero (NZ)

4. IDT(imm8) denotes an Interrupt Descriptor Table entry with offset proportional to the immediate byte.

5. bound(src2) denotes a data item pair providing an operand that contains an upper and lower bound for the signed array index in src1.

descriptor, saved on the stack by the call instruction, is restored by the return. An optional immediate word operand can be used to adjust the stack pointer when input parameters have been passed to the called procedure.

Conditional branches include jump on flag conditions (Jcc), jump on counter condition (JCXZ, JECXZ), and loop control with counter (LOOP, LOOPzc). The flag conditions, summarized in Note 5 for Table 4-26, are the results of operations on unsigned or signed numbers. These include the true and false conditions denoting above, below (or carry), equal (or zero), greater, less, overflow, parity, and sign. The counter condition is CX or ECX containing all zeroes. The loop control operation, LOOP, is a combination of decrement count followed by jump on counter condition. The zero condition version, LOOPzc, requires additionally that the zero (equal) flag condition be met (true or false); otherwise the branch is not taken.

Interrupt procedure calls (INT, INTO) and returns (IRET, IRETD) are also provided. As previously described in Chapter 3, the operand for an INT instruction is an immediate byte that permits accessing any one of the 256 interrupt descriptors stored in the system interrupt descriptor table (see Table 3-2). Interrupt on overflow (INTO), for example, accesses descriptor 4 on an overflow condition. In addition to saving the return address on the stack, as was the case for a call procedure instruction, the interrupt call also saves the flags and disables further interrupts by clearing the interrupt flag (IF). The interrupt return placed at the end of the interrupt handling routine then restores the instruction address and flags. Restoring the original flags pushed on the stack automatically re-enables the interrupt system. An interrupt may also be generated by checking a signed array index against 16-bit or 32-bit address bounds (BOUND), defined by any memory addressing mode. The index is stored in a word or dword register; if the array index is outside the specified limits, an INT 5 results and descriptor 5 of the interrupt table is accessed.

String/Character Translation Instructions

String and character manipulation instructions are presented in Table 4-28. The instructions in this group are double-operand instructions that transfer and compare data, but differ from the data movement instructions presented earlier in two respects: both operands can be in memory, and the addresses are automatically updated to facilitate repeated operations. All instructions in this group can reference 8-bit, 16-bit, or 32-bit data. Memory source data is identified by the data segment selector in DS, and the segment offset address in ESI. If the destination is also memory, then ES:EDI defines its physical location.

The data transfer string operations include move (MOVSB, MOVSW, MOVSD), load (LODSB, LODSW, LODSD), store (STOSB, STOSW, STOSD), input (INSB, INSW, INSD), and output (OUTSB, OUTSW, OUTSD). Move instructions transfer memory to memory and the I/O instructions between the port addressed by DX and memory. Load transfers memory (DS:ESI) to accumulator (AL,AX, or EAX depending on operand size), and store from accumulator to memory

TABLE 4-28 String/Character Translation Group (See Notes)

Instruction	Mnemonic	Description
Move Data from String to String		
Move byte	MOVSB	ES:EDI←DS:ESI (byte)
Move word	MOVSW	ES:EDI←DS:ESI (word)
Move double word	MOVSD	ES:EDI←DS:ESI (dword)
		Update ESI and EDI (all cases)
Compare String Operands		
Compare byte	CMPSB	DS:ESI–ES:EDI (byte)
Compare word	CMPSW	DS:ESI–ES:EDI (word)
Compare double word	CMPSD	DS:ESI–ES:EDI (dword)
		Update ESI and EDI (all cases)
Compare String Data		
Compare byte	SCASB	AL–ES:EDI (byte)
Compare word	SCASW	AX–ES:EDI (word)
Compare double word	SCASD	EAX–ES:EDI (dword)
		Update EDI (all cases)
Load String Operand		
Load byte	LODSB	AL←DS:ESI (byte)
Load word	LODSW	AX←DS:ESI (word)
Load double word	LODSD	EAX←DS:ESI (dword)
		Update ESI (all cases)
Store String Operand		
Store byte	STOSB	ES:EDI←AL (byte)
Store word	STOSW	ES:EDI←AX (word)
Store double word	STOSD	ES:EDI←EAX (dword)
		Update EDI (all cases)
Input from Port to String		
Input byte	INSB	ES:EDI←port(DX) (byte)
Input word	INSW	ES:EDI←port(DX) (word)
Input double word	INSD	ES:EDI←port(DX) (dword)
		Update EDI (all cases)
Output String to Port		
Output byte	OUTSB	port(DX)←DS:ESI (byte)
Output word	OUTSW	port(DX)←DS:ESI (word)
Output double word	OUTSD	port(DX)←DS:ESI (dword)
		Update ESI (all cases)
Repeat Following String Operation		
Repeat	REP	While (ECX <> 0)
Repeat while equal	REPE,REPZ	perform string operation,
Repeat while unequal	REPNE,REPNZ	ECX←ECX–1

Notes

1. Mode symbols are defined in Tables 4-21, 4-22, and 4-23.

2. Descriptions are shown for 32-bit address size attribute. For 16-bit address size attribute: ESI becomes SI, EDI becomes DI, ECX becomes CX.

TABLE 4-28 String/Character Translation Group (Continued)

3. Update of ESI and EDI:

   ESI ← ESI+incr/decr

   EDI ← EDI+incr/decr

   where incr/decr is either 1, 2, 4, –1, –2, or –4 as determined by the state of the direction flag and the operand size as follows:

	Operand Size		
Direction Flag	8-bit	16-bit	32-bit
DF=0	1	2	4
DF=1	–1	–2	–4

4. If repeat instructions precede string compare operations, the operation is repeated until either ECX=0, or result of the comparison is unequal (using REP, REPE, REPZ); or either ECX=0, or the result of the comparison is equal (using REPNE, REPNZ).

(ES:EDI). Compare string operands (CMPSB, CMPSW, CMPSD) adjust the flags based on a memory-to-memory data comparison, while compare string data (SCASB, SCASW, SCASD) compare accumulator with memory (ES:EDI).

All the string operations update the address offset in ESI and/or EDI after performing the indicated operation. The update depends on the state of the direction flag (DF) and the operand size. If DF is set, the addresses are incremented by 1 for byte, 2 for word, or 4 for dword; for DF=0, the addresses are decremented by those values.

If the repeat prefix (REP) precedes any of the instructions, the operation is performed repeatedly, decrementing the count in ECX by 1 for each repetition, until the count reaches zero. An example of a string-to-string move with and without the repeat prefix is illustrated. The repeat-while-equal (REPE, REPZ) is equivalent to REP, and for string compare operations the operation is repeated until the comparison is unequal or the count reaches zero. Likewise, repeat-while-unequal (REPNE, REPNZ) continues the comparison until equal data is found, or the count reaches zero. These conditional repeats allow continuous examination of a data block until a match (or no match) is found, or until the end of the block is reached.

The following programming example illustrates 8-bit, 16-bit, and 32-bit string-to-string move operations. The use of the REP prefix is also shown.

Example	Operation
MOVSB, MOVSW, MOVSD	ES:EDI←DS:ESI (byte, word, or dword) Update ESI, EDI
REP (prefix)	Repeat operation until ECX=0

The assumed register, direction flag, and memory contents before these instructions are executed are:

ESI = 00001000   EDI = 00002000   ECX = 00000003
                        DF = 0 (forward)

DS:1000 = 11 22 33 44 55 66 77 88 99 AA BB CC DD
ES:2000 = 00 00 00 00 00 00 00 00 00 00 00 00 00

The final register and memory contents after the instructions are executed are given below. The memory contents at physical addresses starting at DS:1000 remain unchanged.

Instruction	ESI	EDI	ECX	ES:2000
MOVSB	1001	2001	3	11 00 00 00 00 00 00 00 00 00 00 00 00
MOVSW	1002	2002	3	11 22 00 00 00 00 00 00 00 00 00 00 00
MOVSD	1004	2004	3	11 22 33 44 00 00 00 00 00 00 00 00 00
REP MOVSB	1003	2003	0	11 22 33 00 00 00 00 00 00 00 00 00 00
REP MOVSW	1006	2006	0	11 22 33 44 55 66 00 00 00 00 00 00 00
REP MOVSD	100C	200C	0	11 22 33 44 55 66 77 88 99 AA BB CC 00

Without the REP prefix, a single byte, word, or dword move occurs from the memory segment identified by DS to the segment corresponding to ES. A move within the same segment is specified if the contents of both DS and ES are the same. After the move, both index registers ESI and EDI are incremented by 1, 2, or 4 respectively. If the direction flag had been set (1) instead, the index registers would have been decremented by the appropriate value.

The count in ECX is not used unless the REP prefix is applied. In this case the number of data items moved is equal to the initial count in ECX. Thus, for a count of three as illustrated, either three bytes, words, or dwords are moved. The index registers are then incremented by 3, 6, or 12, respectively, corresponding to the number of bytes moved. The count is also decremented upon each move, so that its final value is always zero, independent of the data size.

High-Level Language Support and Systems Instructions

The high-level language support and systems instructions are summarized in Table 4-29. High-level language support includes the ENTER and LEAVE instructions, which are somewhat analogous to high-level procedure call and return instructions, respectively. The ENTER instruction, when placed at the beginning of a called procedure, creates the stack frame required to implement block-structured high-level languages. The LEAVE instruction reverses the effect of the ENTER at the end of the called procedure.

The coprocessor and multiprocessing instructions include the escape prefix (ESC), a wait instruction (WAIT), a lock prefix (LOCK), and an operation to clear the task-switched flag of control register CR0 (CLTS). ESC and WAIT permit interaction with a numeric coprocessor. The ESC code pattern causes the CPU to send the opcode and operand addresses of the next instruction to the coprocessor, rather than to the CPU. The WAIT instruction suspends execution of CPU instructions until the $\overline{\text{BUSY}}$ input to the CPU is inactive. This allows the coprocessor to complete its operation before the next CPU instruction begins.

The LOCK instruction asserts the CPU's $\overline{\text{LOCK}}$ signal during an instruction preceded by a LOCK prefix code. This signal can be used in a multiprocessing environment to ensure exclusive access of one CPU to a shared memory resource while $\overline{\text{LOCK}}$ remains asserted. The use of ESC, WAIT, and LOCK are detailed in Chapter 9.

CLTS is a privilege level 0 operating system instruction. The task switch flag (TS) in CR0 is set whenever a task switch occurs. A trap results when an ESC occurs while TS is set. Since it may be necessary to save the coprocessor's context before a new ESC occurs, the fault handler can save the context and then reset TS with this instruction.

System security is provided by operations which adjust the requested privilege level field of a selector (ARPL), load access rights byte (LAR) and segment limit (LSL), and verify segments for reading and writing (VERR, VERW). ARPL checks the requested privilege level of a 16-bit register/memory selector operand against that in a 16-bit register. It is used to guarantee that a selector parameter to a subroutine does not request more privilege than allowed to the caller. LAR reads a 16-bit or 32-bit segment descriptor from register/memory and places various bits (other than segment base address and limit) into a register of the same size. The segment limit part of the descriptor can be loaded in a similar fashion by the LSL instruction. VERR and VERW verify the accessibility of a segment for reading or writing; the segment descriptor is a 16-bit register/memory operand.

Descriptor table addressing is facilitated by the ability to load or store local, global, or interrupt descriptors (LLDT, SLDT, LGDT, SGDT, LIDT, SIDT). The LDT is loaded or stored via a 16-bit register/memory operand. The base and limit fields of the GDT and IDT are stored in six successive memory locations via SGDT and SIDT, respectively. If the data size attribute is 32-bits, the same size operand is loaded via LGDT and LIDT. If the data size attribute is 16-bits, a 24-bit base address is loaded to maintain 80286 compatibility.

For multitasking and other system control, the task register and control register 0 (CR0) machine status word can be loaded or stored via a 16-bit register/memory operand (LTR, STR, LMSW, SMSW). Finally, the no operation (NOP) instruction takes a byte of code space but does not affect machine status when executed, and the privileged halt operation (HLT) places the CPU in the halt state.

TABLE 4-29 High Level Language Support and Systems Instructions
(See Notes)

Instruction	Mnemonic	Operands	Modes	Description
High-Level Language Support				
Enter procedure	ENTER	imm16,imm8		Create stack frame
Leave procedure	LEAVE			ESP←EBP, EBP←stack
Coprocessor and Multiprocessing				
Escape (ESC)				if (ESC opcode) coproc ← instr
Wait	WAIT			if (BUSY=1) next instruction
Assert $\overline{\text{LOCK}}$	LOCK			$\overline{\text{LOCK}}$←0 during next instr
Clear CR0 task switched flag	CLTS			CR0 (TS flag)←0
Verification of Pointer Paramaters				
Adjust requested privilege level field of selector	ARPL	r/m16,r16		if r/m16 (bits 1,0) < r16 (bits 1,0) then r/m16 (bits 1,0) ← r16 (bits 1,0),ZF←1 else ZF←0
Load access rights	LAR	dst,src	d	dst←(src AND mask)
Load segment limit	LSL	dst,src	d	dst←segment limit (from descriptor selected by src)
Verify segment for reading	VERR	r/m16		(See Notes)
Verify segment for writing	VERW	r/m16		(See Notes)
Addressing Descriptor Tables				
Load LDT register	LLDT	r/m16		LDTR←r/m16
Store LDT register	SLDT	r/m16		r/m16←LDTR
Load GDT register	LGDT	m16&32		GDTR←m16&32
Store GDT register	SGDT	m16&32		m16&32←GDTR
Load IDT register	LIDT	m16&32		IDTR←m16&32
Store IDT register	SIDT	m16&32		m16&32←IDTR
Multitasking				
Load task register	LTR	r/m16		task reg←r/m16
Store task register	STR	r/m16		r/m16←task reg
System Control				
Load machine status word	LMSW	r/m16		CR0(MSW)←r/m16
Store machine status word	SMSW	r/m16		r/m16←CR0(MSW)
No operation	NOP			Only affects EIP
Halt	HLT			Enter halt state

TABLE 4-29 High Level Language Support and Systems Instructions (Continued)

Notes

1. Mode symbols are defined in Tables 4-21, 4-22, and 4-23.
2. ENTER creates a stack frame. Operand imm16 specifies the number of bytes of dynamic storage allocated on the stack for the routine being entered. Operand imm8 specifies the nesting level (0 to 31) of the routine within the high-level language source code.
3. VERR, VERW verify a segment for reading or writing. If the segment corresponding to the descriptor selected by r/m16 is accessible with current privilege level, and the segment is readable (for VERR) or writable (for VERW), then ZF ← 1; else, ZF ← 0.
4. Mask = (0000 0000 1111 xxxx) 1111 1111 0000 0000

4.6 Programming Examples

This section presents programming examples illustrating the use of arithmetic, program transfer, and string manipulation instructions. These examples are programmed using assembly statements from the 80386 assembly language (INTEL MASM386 Macro Assembler language). Consistent with almost all assembly languages, the general format of an 80386 assembler statement may contain up to four fields (a label field, operation [mnemonic] field, operand field, and a comment field) having the form:

label: mnemonic operand(s); comment

The mnemonic field must appear in each assembly language statement; the other fields need not be present. For example, the instruction HLT contains only a mnemonic field and the instruction INC EAX contains a mnemonic and operand field. In addition, when an instruction contains a source and destination operand, the destination operand is listed first and is separated from the source operand by a comma. For example, in the instruction

MOV EAX,EBX

the destination operand is the EAX register and the source operand is the EBX register.

Also notice the mnemonic does not specify the data size of the instruction's operand(s), as it does in some other assembly languages. For example, in the AT&T *WE* 32100 Microprocessor assembly language there are MOVB, MOVH, and MOVW mnemonics that designate a byte, halfword (16-bits), and word

(32-bits) copy, respectively. In 80386 assembly language, the operand size is specified by the operand itself. Thus, an 80386 statement such as

INC MEMADD

could either increment the byte, word (16 bits), or dword (32 bits) specified by the symbolic name MEMADD. To remove the ambiguity, the assembler requires that the size of all symbolic names be defined with a special assembler statement in the program that uses the symbolic name. If absolute addresses are used directly in a statement, the statement must indicate the size of the data being referenced. For example, the statement

INC dword ptr[19ABH]

increments the 32-bits (dword) starting at hexadecimal address 19AB, and the statement

INC word ptr[19ABH]

increments the word (16-bits) starting at hexadecimal address 19AB. Similarly, the instruction

INC word ptr[EBX]

increments the word where the starting address is located in EBX. No such additional designation must be supplied with an instruction such as INC EBX because the register name specifies the data size used by the register.

Each of the examples is presented as if it were a subroutine called from a main program. The first line has a label that would be used by a CALL instruction in the main routine and the program terminates with the return (RET) instruction. The CALL saves the main program's current address on the stack, and RET subsequently pops it from the stack, allowing resumption of the main program at the correct point. Additionally, all the examples use a loop to process individual data entries in a table. The symbolic names BASE and SIZE are also used to refer to the base address and size, respectively, of either a data string or table stored in memory.

An Averaging Routine

Program 4-1 adds the elements of a table composed of 16-bit unsigned numbers, and then divides by the table size to produce a numerical average (see Figure 4-45).

Program 4-1 initially loads the base address into register EBX and the size of the table into register CX. Subsequently, the contents of EBX is used as a pointer, using indirect addressing, to reference the next element in the table to be added to the total. The size (number of words) initially loaded into the 16-bit CX register restricts the table size that can be processed to a maximum of 64K words. By limiting the table size to 64K words, the total cannot exceed 32 bits in the worst case.

Program 4-1

Averaging Program Assembly Language Listing

```
AVG:        MOV   EBX,BASE    ; Load base address
            MOV   CX,SIZE      ; Load table size
            MOV   AX,0         ; Start with zero sum
AGAIN:      ADD   AX,[EBX]     ; Add current 16-bit number to
            JNC   NEXT         ;    previous sum
            INC   DX           ; Add carry bit to DX
NEXT:       INC   EBX          ; Repeat until all numbers
            INC   EBX          ;    added
            LOOP  AGAIN
            DIV   AX,SIZE      ; Divide sum by table size to
            RET                ;    get average
```

It should be clear that it is necessary to provide 32-bits to hold the accumulated entries and that the average is obtained by dividing this 32-bit sum (dividend) by the 16-bit table size (divisor). Notice from the summary of the arithmetic instruction group (Table 4-25), that for this division the dividend must be stored in the combined register DX:AX. After the divide, the quotient (average) occupies AX and the remainder is in DX.

The routine effectively "links" DX to AX by incrementing DX only when the addition generates a carry. The carry-out from the addition of the most significant bit of AX to that of the memory operand, therefore, becomes a carry-in to the least significant bit of DX. As a result, DX:AX forms a 32-bit "accumulator" as required by the divide operation. This "linking" is accomplished by the instruction sequence

```
            JNC   NEXT
            INC   DX
NEXT:       INC   EBX
```

If the carry bit has not been set by the previous addition, the JNC (jump on no carry) causes a branch to the NEXT label, thereby omitting execution of the INC DX instruction. If the addition did result in a carry, the DX register is incremented by one.

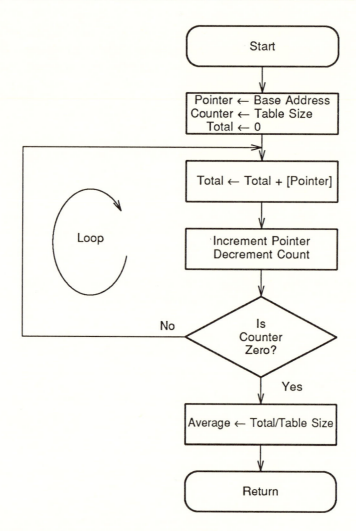

FIGURE 4-45 Flowchart for Averaging Program

The sequencing through all the elements of the table is provided by the LOOP instruction. This instruction automatically decrements the count in CX by 1 (or ECX by 1 when the address size attribute is set to 32 bits), and then branches back to AGAIN unless the count in CX is zero. It is thus equivalent to a decrement of CX followed by a jump on nonzero operation. The division is therefore not done until all the words in the table have been added. Since words rather than bytes are being added, the table address in EBX is incremented by two each time (i.e. recall that each address corresponds to a byte).

A Data String Move and Verify Routine

Operating systems frequently transfer programs and data between different parts of memory, and then verify the transfer to ensure that the memory devices have read and written the information correctly. Program 4-2 illustrates the efficient accomplishment of this task using memory-to-memory string move and string-compare instructions, along with repeat prefixes. The symbolic name BASE1 is the base (lowest) address of the original location of the string, and BASE2 is the base address to which the string will be moved. To accomplish the

Program 4-2

Data String Move and Verify Routine
Assembly Language Listing

```
MOVVER:    MOV    ESI,BASE1     ; Load source and destination
           MOV    EDI,BASE2     ;    base addresses
           MOV    ECX,SIZE      ; Load string size
           CLD                  ; Set to forward direction
           REP    MOVSD         ; Repeatedly move 32 bits
                                ;    until entire string moved
           MOV    ESI,BASE1     ; Reinitialize base addresses
           MOV    EDI,BASE2     ;    and string size
           MOV    ECX,SIZE
           REPE   CMPSD         ; Repeatedly compare dwords
                                ;    until string finished or
                                ;    nonmatch found
           JNZ    ERROR         ; Branch to error handler only
           RET                  ;    if nonmatch occurs
ERROR:
                     :
           (Error Handling Routine)
                     :
           RET
```

operation in as short a time as possible, the move and verify is done using 32-bit operands (four bytes at a time). Thus, the symbolic name SIZE that is loaded into ECX corresponds to the number of double words comprising the string.

Notice from the summary of string/character translation instructions (Table 4-28) that MOVSD moves a double word from the location identified by DS:ESI to that corresponding to ES:EDI. It is assumed that the main program has properly initialized the data segment registers, DS and ES. Note that by using different segment registers for source and destination, the move can be done within the same segment (if DS and ES are set to the same value), or between different segments. Since the direction flag is cleared (CLD instruction) prior to the move, the base addresses are both incremented (rather than decremented) by 4 after each move. The repeat (REP) prefix preceding the string move causes the operation to be performed and ECX to be decremented by one, and then repeated until ECX reaches zero. Thus the entire string is transferred, 32 bits at a time, by the operation REP MOVSD.

The verify operation is done after the entire string has been moved, illustrating the use of another repeated string operation. The base addresses and string size values are first reloaded into the appropriate registers, a necessary step since these registers were obviously altered by the repeated move operation. The repeat-while-equal (REPE) prefix, along with CMPSD, repeatedly compares the corresponding double words as long as they match (are equal). When used with a string move instruction, the REP prefix repeats the operation until the string is completed (string size in ECX reaches zero). When used with string compare, however, the REPE (syntactically equivalent to REP) prefix repeats the operation until the string ends, or until a nonmatch is found, whichever occurs first.

Since the double words being compared in this example are expected to match (one is a copy of the other), a nonmatch indicates an error in reading or writing during the string move or the string compare operation. The zero flag is set each time the compare produces an equal result; the jump on not-equal (JNE) branches only if the zero flag is clear, indicating a nonequal or nonzero. The program then branches to the error handling routine only if a nonmatch occurs anywhere in the string. If all double words match, the program exits from the string compare when the string ends (ECX reaches zero). It then bypasses the error handler, returning directly to the main program.

A Sorting Routine

Data sorting routines are widely used to arrange data in numerical order or to alphabetize character strings (this is equivalent to numerical ordering, since ASCII codes are in numerical order when characters are alphabetized). A sorting algorithm called the "bubble sort" is popular because it is easy to understand and to program. There are faster algorithms for sorting but this subject is beyond the scope of this text.

Two very similar versions of the bubble sort algorithm are presented in Program 4-3, Versions 1 and 2. As in Program 4-2, these routines illustrate move and compare operations. The programs are written without the use of string operations to allow demonstration of the concepts of indexing, use of displacements, and scaling, which were discussed earlier in the chapter.

To understand the two versions and how they differ, consider an array of N values of an arbitrary size called X. In a high-level language, such as BASIC, the individual values are assigned to array variable names X(1), X(2), X(3), ..., X(N − 1), X(N). A general index I identifies the array variable X(I). To sort these in ascending numerical order requires that the smallest value be assigned to X(1), the next smallest to X(2), the next to X(3), etc. The largest value is to be identified with X(N).

One approach to the sort is to compare X(1) successively to X(2), X(3), ..., and X(N). If X(1) is larger than any value compared to it, simply exchange the two values. After completion, the smallest number has "bubbled to the top" and becomes X(1). This process is then repeated, comparing X(2) to X(3), X(4), ..., and X(N), and swapping values where necessary. The second smallest number is then in X(2). Each succeeding array variable is compared to all those with a higher index, with the final comparison being between X(N − 1) and X(N). The BASIC language statements that accomplish the sort after the array has been properly dimensioned and assigned values are:

```
FOR I = 1 TO N − 1
   FOR J = I+1 TO N
      IF X(I) > X(J) THEN
         TEMP = X(I):
         X(I) = X(J):
         X(J) = TEMP
   NEXT J
NEXT I
```

Observe that two loops are required to keep track of which two array variables X(I) and X(J) are being tested (where J > I in all cases). A temporary variable (TEMP) is required since there is no exchange statement in the language.

An equivalent 80386 assembly language routine is shown below. The data size is assumed to be 8-bits with 32-bit addresses. Register EBX is initialized with the base address, which is the address of X(1). Since this register is incremented before the program loops to START, the address corresponds to the array index I (initially I = 1). The counter, ECX, is loaded with one less than the array size, since the number of passes around this outer loop is N − 1. The source index register, ESI, keeps track of the difference between the J and I indices. It is initialized to one so that initially J = I + 1 as required. It is repeatedly incremented and compared to the count (which is decremented by LOOP on each pass through the outer loop), so that the last value of J is always N. The inner loop is finally exited by ignoring JLE CHECK when ESI exceeds the count.

The array variable X(I) is accessed by register indirect addressing using the base register, using the syntax [EBX]. The operand X(I) is placed in AL temporarily. The other operand, X(J), is then addressed by [EBX + ESI], the based index mode. If X(J) is greater than or equal to X(I), the two numbers are in the right order and are not swapped. The jump on greater than or equal (JGE) transfers control to NEXT in this case. If swapping is required, the exchange (XCHG) instruction places X(I) into the memory location formerly occupied by X(J) and replaces AL with X(J). The next instruction

```
MOV [EBX],AL
```

then places X(J) into the memory position vacated by X(I). Notice the accumulator has to be used because neither the compare nor the exchange operation can be done between two memory operands.

Program 4-3 Version 1

Bubble Sort by Locating Smallest Values Routine
Assembly Language Listing

```
SORT1:    MOV    EBX,BASE       ; Load base address (I=1)
          MOV    ECX,SIZE-1     ; Load array size minus one (N-1)
START:    MOV    ESI,1          ; Start with J=I+1
CHECK:    MOV    AL, [EBX]      ; Compare X(J) to X(I)
          CMP    [EBX+ESI],AL
          JGE    NEXT           ; If X(J) < X(I), then
          XCHG   [EBX+ESI],AL   ;   swap bytes
          MOV    [EBX],AL
NEXT:     INC    ESI            ; Increment J
          CMP    ESI,ECX        ; After comparing X(N) to X(I),
          JLE    CHECK          ;   increment base address
          INC    EBX
          LOOP   START          ; Repeat to end of array
          RET
```

An alternative bubble sort involves comparing adjacent pairs of array variables, that is X(J) and X(J + 1). Starting with the first variable, X(1) is compared with X(2), then X(2) to X(3), X(3) to X(4), ..., until X(N − 1) to X(N). If the appropriate pairs are swapped as before, this procedure bubbles the largest value to the end each time; that is, X(N) will contain the highest value. Repeating this causes the second highest value to occupy X(N − 1). It is not necessary to compare X(N − 1) with X(N) on the second pass, since the largest number was previously placed in the X(N) location. The third pass will then terminate with X(N − 3) compared to X(N − 2). It is repeated until the last pass occurs, which needs only to compare X(1) to X(2) to correctly order the two smallest values. This algorithm is implemented in BASIC as:

```
FOR I = N − 1 TO 1 STEP −1
   FOR J = 1 TO I
      IF X(J) > X(J + 1) THEN
         TEMP = X(J):
         X(J + 1) = TEMP
   NEXT J
NEXT I
```

Observe the outer loop index I is used only to control the upper limit of index J; thus, decrementing I by 1 each time reduces the upper limit of J by the same amount. This avoids the unnecessary comparisons mentioned previously.

The equivalent assembly language version for byte sorting is shown below. The based index mode [EBX + ESI] is again identified with index J. Since X(J) is being compared to X(J + 1) each time, the more complicated base index relative mode is useful here; thus the operand [EBX + ESI + 1] always points to X(J + 1). Since each set of comparisons start with X(1) again it is not necessary to increment the base address as was the case for the Version 1 algorithm.

Program 4-3 Version 2

Bubble Sort by Locating Largest Value Routine
Assembly Language Listing

```
SORT2:    MOV    EBX,BASE        ; Load base address
          MOV    ECX,SIZE-1      ; Load array size minus 1 (N-1)
START:    MOV    ESI,0           ; Start with J=1
CHECK:    MOV    AL,[EBX+ESI]    ; Compare X(J+1) to X(J)
          CMP    [EBX+ESI+1],AL
          JGE    NEXT            ; If X(J+1) < X(J) then
          XCHG   [EBX+ESI+1],AL  ;    swap bytes
          MOV    [EBX+ESI],AL
NEXT:     INC    ESI             ; Increment J
          CMP    ESI,ECX         ; After comparing X(N) to
          JL     CHECK           ;    X(N – 1) decrement size
          LOOP   START           ; Repeat to end of array
          RET
```

It is also instructive to illustrate the modification of this Version 2 program if longer length data items are to be sorted. The two routines in Program 4-4 sort 16-bit and 32-bit numbers. The different data sizes are handled very simply. The temporary storage of the numbers, which used AL for bytes, now uses either AX for words or EAX for double words. Since words occupy two successive memory locations, and double words have four addresses, the pointers must be incremented either twice or four times during each pass. The use of the automatic scaling feature of the 80386 CPU alleviates the need for multiple increment instructions. As noted in the listings, the index register is scaled by either two or four. Thus, whenever ESI is incremented once, the factor ESI*2 adds two to the pointer address. Similarly, ESI*4 adjusts the pointer by four for the double-word size case.

Program 4-4

Sorting Routines for Longer Length Data Items
Assembly Language Listing

Sorting 16-bit Numbers			Sorting 32-bit Numbers		
SORT3:	MOV	EBX,BASE	SORT4:	MOV	EBX,BASE
	MOV	ECX,SIZE–1		MOV	ECX,SIZE-1
START:	MOV	ESI,0	START:	MOV	ESI,0
CHECK:	MOV	AX,[EBX+ESI*2]	CHECK:	MOV	EAX,[EBX+ESI*4]
	CMP	[EBX+ESI*2+2],AX		CMP	[EBX+ESI*4+4],EAX
	JGE	NEXT		JGE	NEXT
	XCHG	[EBX+ESI*2+2],AX		XCHG	[EBX+ESI*4+4],EAX
	MOV	[EBX+ESI*2],AX		MOV	[EBX+ESI*4],EAX
NEXT:	INC	ESI	NEXT:	INC	ESI
	CMP	ESI,ECX		CMP	ESI,ECX
	JL	CHECK		JL	CHECK
	LOOP	START		LOOP	START
	RET			RET	

4.7 Chapter Highlights

1. The program model register set for the INTEL 80386 Microprocessor consists of eight 32-bit general-purpose registers, six 16-bit segment registers, one 16-bit flag register, and one 32-bit instruction pointer.

2. The INTEL 80386 CPU constructs off-chip addresses as a combination of a segment and offset component. The six segment registers individually specify the starting address of a code, stack, and up to four external data segments. The offset address specifies the position of the desired location relative to the segment's starting address.

3. The value stored in a segment register is formally referred to as a selector. In protected addressing mode the selector is an index into a table of segment starting addresses. In real addressing mode the selector is the segment's starting address.

4. Offset addresses are also referred to as effective addresses. By selectively including or excluding the various components of an effective address, the conventional direct, indirect, base relative, indexed, base-indexed, and base-index-relative addressing modes are supported by the CPU.

5. The 80386 system model register set consists of system flags, four memory management registers, four control registers, eight debug registers, and two test registers. These registers are accessed by privileged operating system instructions.

6. The INTEL 80386 CPU supports signed and unsigned byte, word (16-bit), and double-word (32-bit) memory fetches. In addition, the CPU recognizes bit-field, packed and unpacked BCD digits, and pointer addresses. Within memory, the CPU assumes that lower-order bytes are stored at lower-order memory addresses.

7. An individual INTEL 80386 CPU instruction can explicitly reference, at most, two operands. Operands can be stored either directly within the general-purpose data registers, as immediate data encoded within an instruction, or external to the CPU in memory and I/O ports.

8. All INTEL 80386 CPU instructions are encoded using a maximum of 16 bytes. Typically, a machine instruction consists of less than 12 bytes. Each instruction may contain one or more opcode bytes, one or more addressing mode bytes, a displacement address, and a 32-bit immediate datum.

9. The ModR/M byte is the primary addressing mode byte in an 80386 machine language instruction. This byte encodes addressing mode information for both single- and double-operand instructions. An additional SIB byte is used for addressing modes requiring a scale factor, index value, or base register.

10. The instruction set of the INTEL 80386 CPU consists of data transfer, arithmetic, logical, shift, rotate, string, program control, and high-level language and systems level instructions. Two-operand instructions within each group require that the destination operand be listed before the source operand.

11. The wide variety of instructions and addressing modes make possible efficient data manipulation routines. Subroutines that total and average, move and verify, and sort numerical tables require no more than ten to fifteen assembly language instructions.

Exercises

1a. What registers comprise the INTEL 80386 CPU program register set and what are the functions that these registers can perform?

1b. What registers comprise the 80386 system register set and what are the functions that these registers perform?

2a. What data types are supported by the INTEL 80386 CPU?

2b. What is the difference between a near pointer and a far pointer?

3. How would the 32-bit data 0ABEF19CCH be stored in memory starting at address 1620H?

4a. What are the three operand storage locations permitted by 80386 instructions?

4b. Are memory-to-memory addressing modes provided by the 80386 instruction set?

5a. What is meant by the term effective address?

5b. What are the three individual components that can be included in an effective address?

5c. Determine the individual components required to form an effective address for a memory operand whose address is stored in a general-purpose address register.

5d. What are the six basic addressing modes supported by the INTEL 80386 CPU?

6. The format for various 80386 MOVE instructions are shown in Figure 4-46. Using both the information in the figure and in Tables 4-10 and 4-15, determine the bit encoding for:

6a. MOV EAX,EBX

6b. MOV [EAX],ECX

6c. MOV EAX,[ECX]

6d. MOV EAX,738291ABH

6e. MOV [EAX],1953FFEEH

7. Using the information shown in Figure 4-46, encode the instruction

        MOV EBX,7A19H

two different ways.

8. As illustrated in Figure 4-46, the direction (d) bit distinguishes between source and destination operands. By altering the setting of the d bit, encode the instruction

        MOV ECX,EDX

two different ways.

9. Using Figure 4-46, determine the bit encoding for:

9a. MOV EAX,[EBX + ECX]

9b. MOV EAX,[EBX + 2*ECX]

9c. MOV EAX,[EBX + 0FFEEH]

Register to Register/Memory
Register/Memory to Register

1	0	0	0	1	0	d	w	mod	reg	r/m

d = 0 implies reg field designates source operand.
d = 1 implies reg field designates destination operand.
The w bit applies to both operands, including immediate data.

Immediate to Register/Memory

1	1	0	0	0	1	1	w	mod	0	0	0	r/m	Immediate Data

Immediate to Register (Short Form)

1	0	1	1	w	reg	Immediate Data

FIGURE 4-46 Move Instruction Formats

9d. MOV EAX,[EBX + 1950ABDFH]
9e. MOV EAX,[EBX + 4*ECX]
9f. MOV [EBX+8*ECX], EDX
9g. MOV [EBX + 8*ECX], 1860ABCDH
9h. MOV ECX, [ESI + 2*EBX]
9i. MOV EAX, [ECX + 4*EBX + 0ABH]
9j. MOV EBX, [EAX + 8*ECX + 1860ABCDH]
9k. Identify the operand addressing modes used for the source and destination operands
used in each instruction encoded in Exercises 9a. through 9j.

10. The format for various 80386 ADD instructions is illustrated in Figure 4-47. Using
Figure 4-47, determine the bit encoding for:
10a. ADD EBX,ECX
10b. ADD [EBX],ECX
10c. ADD EBX,[ECX]
10d. ADD EBX,19H
10e. ADD [EBX],19ABH
10f. ADD EAX,[EBX + ECX]
10g. ADD EAX,[EBX + 2*ECX]
10h. ADD EAX,[EBX + 0FFEEH]
10i. ADD EAX,[EBX + 1950ABDFH]
10j. ADD EAX,[EBX + 4*ECX]
10k. ADD [EBX+8*ECX], EDX
10l. ADD [EBX + 8*ECX], 1860ABCDH

11. Write assembly language instructions to perform the following operations:
11a. Move the number 0FFEEH into AX.
11b. Move the number 0AAEFH into BX.
11c. Move the number 19 into AL.

Register to Register
Register to Memory
Register to Register

0	0	0	0	0	0	d	w	mod	reg	r/m

d = 0 implies mod and r/m fields designate destination operand.
d = 1 implies reg field designates destination operand.

Immediate to Register/Memory

1	0	0	0	0	0	s	w	mod	0	0	0	r/m	Immediate Data

s = 1 when 8-bit immediate data is used with either
16-bit or 32-bit destination operand; otherwise s = 0.

FIGURE 4-47   Add Instruction Formats

11d. Shift the contents of EAX one bit to the left.
11e. Multiply AX by BX.

12. Assuming that 8-bit codes for the characters Hello World! are stored in memory starting at location 1690H, write one or more instructions to individually perform the following operations:
12a. Move a copy of the characters into memory starting at location 0AACDH.
12b. Move a reverse copy of the characters into memory starting at location 0AACDH.
12c. Load the last four characters (rld!) into the EBX register.

13a. An array of ten signed 16-bit integers is stored in memory starting at address 0AB190000H. Write a sequence of 80386 assembly language instructions to sum the ten elements, providing sufficient room for a sum greater than 16-bits.
13b. Modify the instructions written in Exercise 13a so that the sums of the positive and negative elements are produced individually.

14. An array of nonzero, 16-bit unsigned integers is stored in memory starting at address 1620H. A trailing value of zero is used to indicate the end of the list. Write a sequence of 80386 assembly language instructions to sum the numbers in the list and to terminate when the zero value is accessed. Assume that the sum does not exceed 32-bits.

15a. The unsigned 16-bit operands, 0AB60H and 3587H, are to be multiplied. Write a series of 80386 assembly language instructions to load these operands into registers AX and BX, respectively, and to generate a 32-bit product.
15b. In which registers will the product produced in Exercise 15a reside?

16a. Write a series of 80386 assembly language instructions to locate the maximum value in a set of twenty-five 32-bit signed integers. The first integer is stored in memory at address 6000H.

16b. Modify the instructions written for Exercise 16a to locate the minimum value.

17. Write a series of 80386 assembly language instructions to produce the cube of a signed 8-bit integer number located in the AL register.

18. The binary and ASCII codes for the digits 0 through 9 are listed in Table 4-30. To convert the binary code for these digits to the corresponding ASCII code requires adding a value of 30H to each digit's binary value. Using this information, write a series of 80386 assembly language instructions to convert a binary number (representing 0-9) stored in the AL register into its equivalent ASCII representation.

19. The binary and ASCII codes for the hexadecimal digits A through F are listed in Table 4-31. To convert the binary code for these digits to the corresponding ASCII code requires adding a value of 37H to each digit's binary value. Using this information, write a series of 80386 assembly language instructions to convert a binary number representing A to F, stored in the AL register into its equivalent ASCII representation.

20. Using the results of Exercises 18 and 19, write a series of 80386 assembly language instructions for converting the binary representation of the hexadecimal digits 0 - F into their equivalent ASCII codes. (Hint: Recall that the letter codes require an additional value of 7H to be added for proper conversion to ASCII).

TABLE 4-30 Binary and ASCII Digit Codes (0 - 9)

Digit	Binary	ASCII Binary	ASCII Hex
0	00000000	011 0000	30H
1	00000001	011 0001	31H
2	00000010	011 0010	32H
3	00000011	011 0011	33H
4	00000100	011 0100	34H
5	00000101	011 0101	35H
6	00000110	011 0110	36H
7	00000111	011 0111	37H
8	00001000	011 1000	38H
9	00001001	011 1001	39H

TABLE 4-31 Binary and ASCII Digit Codes (A - F)

Digit	Binary	ASCII Binary	ASCII Hex
A	00001010	100 0001	41H
B	00001011	100 0010	42H
C	00001100	100 0011	43H
D	00001101	100 0100	44H
E	00001110	100 0101	45H
F	00001111	100 0110	46H

AT&T *WE* 32100 Microprocessor

Chapter Five

5.1 Register Sets
5.2 Data Types
5.3 Instruction Set
5.4 Addressing Modes
5.5 *WE* 32200 Microprocessor Enhancements
5.6 Chapter Highlights

The AT&T *WE* 32100 Microprocessor is comprised of four major sections as shown in Figure 5-1. These are the bus interface control, main controller, fetch unit, and execute unit.

The bus interface control provides all the strobes and control signals necessary to implement the interface to all peripheral devices.

The main controller is responsible for directing the action of both the fetch and execute controllers. This unit also responds to, and directs the handling of, interrupt and exception conditions.

The fetch unit handles the instruction stream and performs memory-based operand accesses. It consists of a fetch controller, an instruction cache, an instruction queue, an immediate and displacement extractor, and an address arithmetic unit. The fetching and decoding of instructions and the fetching of memory-based operands are handled by this unit as directed by the main controller.

The execute unit performs all arithmetic and logical operations, and all shift and rotate operations, and determines the state of the condition flags. It consists of an execute controller, sixteen 32-bit user-accessible registers, working registers, and a 33-bit wide arithmetic logic unit (ALU). The sixteen 32-bit registers include nine general-purpose registers (r0–r8) and seven dedicated registers. The working registers are used exclusively by the microprocessor and are not user-accessible.

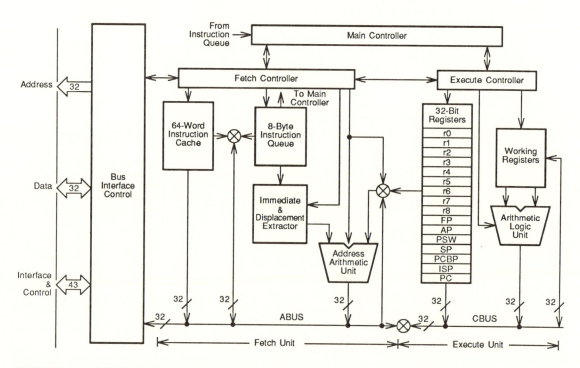

FIGURE 5-1   *WE* 32100 Microprocessor Block Diagram

5.1 Register Sets

Figure 5-2 shows the complete set of sixteen 32-bit user-accessible registers. When describing these registers, it is useful to separate them into the traditional program and system model register sets. The program model can additionally be subdivided into conventional and special-purpose register groups.

Program Register Model - Conventional Group

The program register model's conventional register group consists of nine general-purpose registers, a stack pointer, a program counter, and a flags register (see Figure 5-3). The flags register is contained within the processor status word register.

General-Purpose Registers

The WE 32100 CPU has nine true general-purpose registers, designated r0 through r8. Each of these registers can be used with all arithmetic, data transfer, logical, and program control operations. These can be used as data registers to store source and destination operands directly or as address registers containing operand addresses. The modes in which these registers are used to store and locate operands is described in Section 5.4.

FIGURE 5-2 *WE* 32100 Microprocessor User CPU Registers

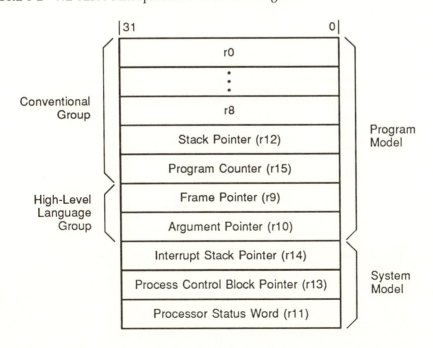

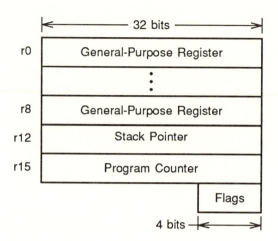

FIGURE 5-3   Conventional Program Model Registers

Stack Pointer

The stack pointer (SP), register r12, contains the 32-bit address of the top of the current execution stack. As illustrated in Figure 5-4, the stack pointer points to the next available memory location. A PUSH instruction immediately stores its operand at the current memory address contained in the stack pointer. The stack pointer is then incremented by the size of the pushed operand. Thus, the stack "grows" into increasing memory address space. A POP instruction first decrements the stack pointer by the size of the popped operand (to point to the last pushed operand) and then fetches the data from the top of the stack.

Program Counter

The program counter (PC), register r15, contains the 32-bit memory address of the currently executing instruction. The PC is referenced by all program control instructions, including all function calls and returns.

FIGURE 5-4   WE 32100 Microprocessor Stack

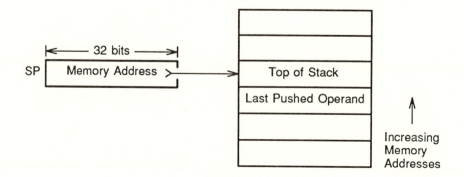

Flag Register

Bits 18 through 21 of register r11, the processor status word (PSW) register (see Figure 5-5), contain the standard negative (N), zero (Z), overflow (V), and carry (C) condition flags (as described in Section 2.2). Generally these flags reflect the result of the most recently executed instruction. All conditional program-control instructions check one or more of these flags before executing a jump, branch, or return instruction.

Program Register Model - Special Purpose Registers

The *WE* 32100 Microprocessor special-purpose register group is called the high-level language register group (see Figure 5-6). This group consists of the frame pointer (register r9) and argument pointer (register r10). Although both registers may be used as general-purpose data and address registers, they are typically reserved for pointing to high-level language variable and argument stacks, respectively.

Frame Pointer

The frame pointer (FP), register r9, points to a beginning stack location in which the local variables of the currently running program, procedure, or function are stored. The FP is automatically changed by SAVE and RESTORE instructions used in calling and returning from program subroutines, functions, and procedures.

FIGURE 5-5   Condition Flags

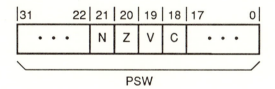

FIGURE 5-6   High-Level Language Register Group

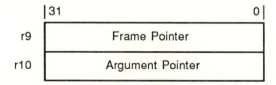

Argument Pointer

The argument pointer (AP), register r10, points to a beginning stack location in which arguments passed into the currently running program, procedure, or function have been pushed. The AP is automatically altered by calling and returning from program subroutines, functions, and procedures in which arguments have been passed.

System Model Register Set

The system model register set for the *WE* 32100 Microprocessor is comprised of three registers: register r11, the processor status word; register r13, the process control block pointer; and register r14, the interrupt stack pointer (see Figure 5-7). These three registers contain addresses that may be read at any time, but that may be written only when the operating system is in control.

Processor Status Word

The processor status word (PSW), register r11, contains status information about the microprocessor and the current task. The PSW also contains four condition code flags discussed under Program Register Model. In general, the PSW changes as a whole only when a task switch occurs, and can be written only by operating system level instructions.

Process Control Block Pointer

The process control block pointer (PCBP), register r13, points to the starting address of the process control block for the current process. The process control block is a data structure in external memory that contains the hardware context of a process when the process is not running (a process is synonymous with a task). This context consists of the initial and current contents of the PSW, PC, and SP; the last contents of r0 through r10; boundaries for an execution stack; and block move specifications (and possible memory specifications) for the process. The PCBP may be written only by operating system level instructions.

Interrupt Stack Pointer

The interrupt stack pointer (ISP), register r14, contains the 32-bit memory

FIGURE 5-7   System Model Register Set

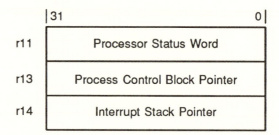

address of the top of the interrupt stack. This stack is used when an interrupt request is received and by the call process (CALLPS) and return to process (RETPS) instructions. The ISP may be written only by operating system level instructions.

5.2 Data Types

The data types supported by the WE 32100 Microprocessor are byte, halfword, word, floating point (word, double word, and double-extended word) and bit field data. Floating-point data is provided only when the WE 32106 Math Acceleration Unit (MAU) coprocessor is used with the WE 32100 Microprocessor. The instruction set provides that bytes, halfwords, and words can be interpreted as either signed or unsigned quantities.

A byte is an 8-bit quantity that may appear at any address. Bits are numbered from right to left within a byte; starting with zero, the least significant bit (LSB); and ending with 7, the most significant bit (MSB). See Figure 5-8.

A halfword is a 16-bit quantity that may appear at any address divisible by two. Bits are numbered from right to left starting with zero, the LSB, and ending with 15, the MSB. See Figure 5-9.

A word is a 32-bit quantity. Data words may appear at any address divisible by four. Bits are numbered from right to left starting with zero, the LSB, and ending with 31, the MSB. See Figure 5-10.

FIGURE 5-8   Byte Data

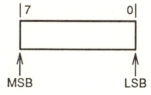

FIGURE 5-9   Halfword Data

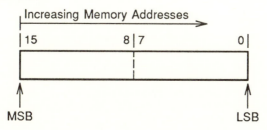

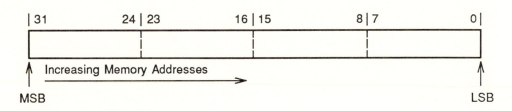

```
| 31          24 | 23          16 | 15          8 | 7          0 |
|                |                |               |              |
```

↑ Increasing Memory Addresses ⟶   ↑

MSB   LSB

FIGURE 5-10   Word Data

Floating-point data types may appear at any address in memory divisible by four. Figures 5-11a through 5-11c show the floating-point data types supported by the *WE* 32106 MAU.

Each of these four numeric data types may be interpreted as either a signed or unsigned quantity, with signed data represented in two's complement form.

A bit field is a sequence of 1 to 32 bits extracted from a byte, halfword, or word data. The bit field is specified by the address of the data containing the field, an offset and a width. The offset, from 0 to 31, identifies the starting bit in the word containing the bit field. This bit becomes the LSB of the selected field. The width, also a number from 0 to 31, specifies the size of the field. The number of bits in the extracted field is one more than the width value. Figure 5-12 illustrates a bit field extracted from a word using an offset of 6 and a width of 9. Notice that the extracted field contains ten bits, one more than the width.

FIGURE 5-11a   Single-Precision Floating-Point Data Type

Bit Field

31	30 23	22 0
Sign	Exponent	Fraction

FIGURE 5-11b   Double-Precision Floating-Point Data Type

Bit Field

63	62 52	51 0
Sign	Exponent	Fraction

FIGURE 5-11c   Double-Extended Floating-Point Data Type

Bit Field

95 80	79	78 64	63	62 0
Unused	Sign	Exponent	J	Fraction

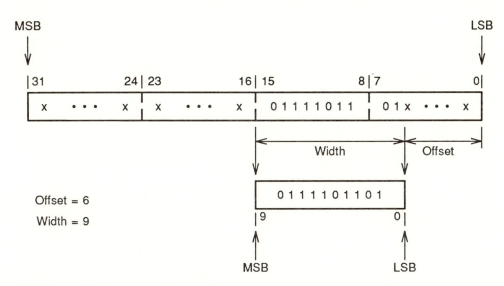

FIGURE 5-12   Extraction of a Bit Field

Bit fields do not extend across word boundaries. If the selected width requires bits beyond the MSB of the word being used, the extraction of bits continues by wrapping around to the LSB.

Sign and Zero Extension

All CPU operations are performed on 32-bit quantities even though an instruction may specify a byte or halfword operand. The *WE* 32100 Microprocessor reads in the correct number of bits for the operand and extends the data automatically to 32 bits. It uses *sign extension* when reading signed data or halfwords, and *zero extension* when reading unsigned data or bytes (or bit fields that contain less than 32 bits). The data type of the source operand determines how many bits are fetched and what type of extension is applied. This default extension can be changed using the expanded-operand type mode described in Section 5.4. For sign extension, the value of the MSB is replicated to fill the high-order bits to form a 32-bit value. In zero extension, zeros fill the high-order bits. Figure 5-13 illustrates sign and zero extension.

Data Storage in Memory

Memory locations consist of a series of 8-bit (byte) locations for storing data. Halfwords occupy two consecutive memory locations and words occupy four consecutive memory locations. Boundary restrictions apply to the starting location

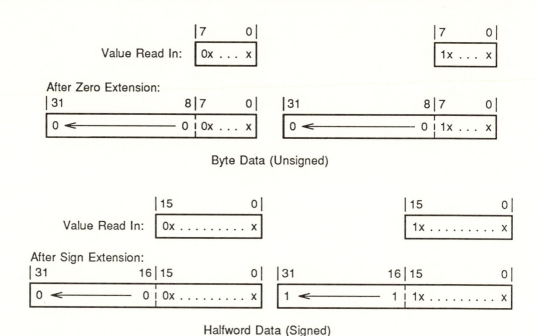

FIGURE 5-13   Extending Data to 32 Bits

of halfwords and words. Halfwords may be stored only at addresses divisible by 2, and words only at addresses divisible by 4. The microprocessor generates a fault if these boundaries are violated.

Figure 5-14 illustrates the storage of word data in memory. As illustrated, the hexadecimal word, 0x12345678, is stored with the lower-order bytes at higher-order addresses. (Notice Intel assembler notation uses a trailing H to designate a hexadecimal number, whereas AT&T assembler notation designates a hexadecimal number by a leading 0x.) All data stored in memory follow this format. For example, the hexadecimal halfword data, 0xEEFF, would be stored in memory with the lower-order byte, 0xFF, at the next higher-byte address than the location containing the byte, 0xEE.

All arithmetic, logical, data transfer, and bit field operations yield results that are 32 bits in length. For byte and halfword operations stored in memory, only the lower 8-bits or 16-bits, respectively, of the result are retained.

Register Data Storage

All data stored in a register is a full 32 bits, regardless of the instruction or data type. For all CPU operations, including register storage, the *WE* 32100 Microprocessor reads in the correct number of bits for the operand and extends the data automatically to 32 bits. Halfword operands, assumed to be signed data,

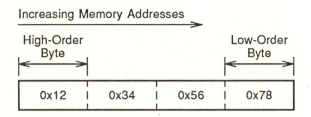

FIGURE 5-14   Word Storage in Memory

are sign-extended to 32 bits. When storing byte operands into a register, unsigned data is assumed and zero extension is used. Intermediate results of all operations in the CPU are always 32 bits. If the results of an operation are stored in a register, the processor writes all 32 bits to the register.

When a register is specified as the source of a byte operand, the low-order 8 bits (bits 0-7) of the register are fetched and zero-extended to 32 bits. The zero extension may be changed to a sign extension using the expanded operand type addressing mode described in Section 5.4. When a register is used as the source of a halfword operand, the low-order 16 bits (bits 0-15) of the register are fetched and sign-extended to 32 bits. Again, the extension may be changed to zero using an expanded operand type addressing mode.

5.3 Instruction Set

A *WE* 32100 Microprocessor instruction consists of a one-byte or two-byte opcode followed by at most four operands. In assembly language, a mnemonic (such as ADDW) replaces the opcode and is followed by its operands. This is represented as

mnemonic operand_1, operand_2, operand_3, operand_4

The assembler requires at least one space after the mnemonic and commas must be used to separate the operands.

The complete *WE* 32100 CPU instruction set consists of six functional groups: data transfer, arithmetic, logical, program control, coprocessor, and stack and miscellaneous instructions. This section contains a description of each group and a listing of the mnemonics within each group. The next section presents the addressing modes available to describe instruction operands.

Data Transfer Instructions

The data transfer instructions permit the transfer of data to and from registers and memory. Most of these instructions have three types indicated by the last character in the mnemonic: a B refers to a byte operand, an H to a halfword operand, and a W to a word operand. For example, the mnemonic MOVB is an

TABLE 5-1 Data Transfer Instruction Group

Instruction	Mnemonic	Operands	Description
Move:			
Move byte	MOVB	src,dst	src → dst
Move halfword	MOVH	src,dst	src → dst
Move word	MOVW	src,dst	src → dst
Move address (word)	MOVAW	src,dst	&src → dst
Move complemented byte	MCOMB	src,dst	NOT src → dst
Move complemented halfword	MCOMH	src,dst	NOT src → dst
Move complemented word	MCOMW	src,dst	NOT src → dst
Move negated byte	MNEGB	src,dst	–src → dst
Move negated halfword	MNEGH	src,dst	–src → dst
Move negated word	MNEGW	src,dst	–src → dst
Move version number	MVERNO		PVN → r0
Swap (Interlocked):			
Swap byte interlocked	SWAPBI	dst	dst ⟷ r0
Swap halfword interlocked	SWAPHI	dst	dst ⟷ r0
Swap word interlocked	SWAPWI	dst	dst ⟷ r0
Block Operations:			
Move block of words	MOVBLW		(See Note 1)
Field Operations:			
Extract field byte	EXTFB	w,off,src,dst	FD(off,w,src) → dst
Extract field halfword	EXTFH	w,off,src,dst	FD(off,w,src) → dst
Extract field word	EXTFW	w,off,src,dst	FD(off,w,src) → dst
Insert field byte	INSFB	w,off,src,dst	src → FD(off,w,dst)
Insert field halfword	INSFH	w,off,src,dst	src → FD(off,w,dst)
Insert field word	INSFW	w,off,src,dst	src → FD(off,w,dst)
String Operations:			
String copy	STRCPY		(See Note 2)
String end	STREND		(See Note 3)
Notations:			

&src – address of source operand

PVN – processor version number (–128 to +127)

w – field width (number of bits minus 1)

TABLE 5-1 Data Transfer Instruction Group (Continued)

Notations: Continued

off – number of bits offset from bit 0

FD(off,w,src or dst) – bit field of src or dst comprised of w+1 bits, starting from the offset-numbered bit.

Notes

1. The operation of the block move instruction is:

   MOVBLW   (%r0)→(%r1)   (memory-to-memory word move)

   r0+4→r0, r1+4→r1, r2-1→r2

   Repeat above while r2 > 0.

2. The operation of the string copy instruction is:

   STRCPY   (%r0)→(%r1)   (memory-to-memory byte move)

   r0+1→r0, r1+1→r1

   Repeat above until (%r0)=0 (zero byte is moved also, but addresses are not incremented).

3. The operation of the string end instruction is:

   STREND   r0+1→r0

   Repeat until (%r0)=0.

Notice (%rn) denotes the memory operand whose address is contained in register n.

---

instruction to move a byte of data, while the mnemonic MOVW is an instruction to move a word of data. Table 5-1 lists all the instructions within the data transfer group. Notice for two-operand instructions the source operand is listed before the destination operand. This is the opposite of the notation used by Intel for the 80386 CPU.

Arithmetic Instructions

The *WE* 32100 Microprocessor arithmetic instructions are listed in Table 5-2. These instructions perform arithmetic operations on data in registers and memory. The type of the operand is specified by the last alphabetic character of the mnemonic (B for byte, H for halfword, and W for word) and, unless overridden by an expanded-operand type, applies to each operand in the instruction. Two-address arithmetic instructions have both a source operand (src) and a destination operand. Three-address instructions have two source operands (src1, src2) and a destination operand. Some arithmetic instructions also contain a count operand (count).

If the result of an arithmetic operation is too large to be represented in 32 bits, the high-order bits are truncated and the processor issues an integer-overflow exception.

TABLE 5-2 Arithmetic Instruction Group

Instruction	Mnemonic	Operands	Description
Add:			
Add byte	ADDB2	src,dst	dst+src→dst
Add halfword	ADDH2	src,dst	dst+src→dst
Add word	ADDW2	src,dst	dst+src→dst
Add byte, 3-address	ADDB3	src1,src2,dst	src1+src2→dst
Add halfword, 3-address	ADDH3	src1,src2,dst	src1+src2→dst
Add word, 3-address	ADDW3	src1,src2,dst	src1+src2→dst
Subtract:			
Subtract byte	SUBB2	src,dst	dst − src→dst
Subtract halfword	SUBH2	src,dst	dst − src→dst
Subtract word	SUBW2	src,dst	dst − src→dst
Subtract byte, 3-address	SUBB3	src1,src2,dst	src2 − src1→dst
Subtract halfword, 3-address	SUBH3	src1,src2,dst	src2 − src1→dst
Subtract word, 3-address	SUBW3	src1,src2,dst	src2 − src1→dst
Increment:			
Increment byte	INCB	dst	dst+1→dst
Increment halfword	INCH	dst	dst+1→dst
Increment word	INCW	dst	dst+1→dst
Decrement:			
Decrement byte	DECB	dst	dst − 1→dst
Decrement halfword	DECH	dst	dst − 1→dst
Decrement word	DECW	dst	dst − 1→dst
Multiply:			
Multiply byte	MULB2	src,dst	dst*src→dst
Multiply halfword	MULH2	src,dst	dst*src→dst
Multiply word	MULW2	src,dst	dst*src→dst
Multiply byte, 3-address	MULB3	src1,src2,dst	src1*src2→dst
Multiply halfword, 3-address	MULH3	src1,src2,dst	src1*src2→dst
Multiply word, 3-address	MULW3	src1,src2,dst	src1*src2→dst
Divide:			
Divide byte	DIVB2	src,dst	dst/src→dst
Divide halfword	DIVH2	src,dst	dst/src→dst
Divide word	DIVW2	src,dst	dst/src→dst

TABLE 5-2 Arithmetic Instruction Group (Continued)

Instruction	Mnemonic	Operands	Description
Divide: (Continued)			
Divide byte, 3-address	DIVB3	src1,src2,dst	src2/src1→dst
Divide halfword, 3-address	DIVH3	src1,src2,dst	src2/src1→dst
Divide word, 3-address	DIVW3	src1,src2,dst	src2/src1→dst
Modulo:			
Modulo byte	MODB2	src,dst	rem(dst/src)→dst
Modulo halfword	MODH2	src,dst	rem(dst/src)→dst
Modulo word	MODW2	src,dst	rem(dst/src)→dst
Modulo byte, 3-address	MODB3	src1,src2,dst	rem(src2/src1)→dst
Modulo halfword, 3-address	MODH3	src1,src2,dst	rem(src2/src1)→dst
Modulo word, 3-address	MODW3	src1,src2,dst	rem(src2/src1)→dst
Arithmetic Shift:			
Arith left shift word	ALSW3	count,src,dst	src*(2*(count AND 0x1F))→dst
Arith right shift byte	ARSB3	count,src,dst	src/(2*(count AND 0x1F))→dst
Arith right shift halfword	ARSH3	count,src,dst	src/(2*(count AND 0x1F))→dst
Arith right shift word	ARSW3	count,src,dst	src/(2*(count AND 0x1F))→dst

Note rem(x/y) denotes the remainder of x divided by y.

Logical Instructions

Logical instructions perform logical operations on data in registers and memory. Most logical instructions have one of three types as specified by the last character of the mnemonic: B for byte, H for halfword, and W for word. A mnemonic's type determines the type of each operand in the instruction, unless the expanded-operand type mode changes an operand's type.

Table 5-3 lists all the *WE* 32100 Microprocessor logical instructions. Two-address logical instructions have both a source and a destination operand. Three-address instructions have two source operands and a destination operand. Some logical instructions also contain a count operand.

TABLE 5-3 Logical Instruction Group

Instruction	Mnemonic	Operands	Description
AND:			
AND byte	ANDB2	src,dst	dst AND src→dst
AND halfword	ANDH2	src,dst	dst AND src→dst
AND word	ANDW2	src,dst	dst AND src→dst
AND byte, 3-address	ANDB3	src1,src2,dst	src1 AND src2→dst
AND halfword, 3-address	ANDH3	src1,src2,dst	src1 AND src2→dst
AND word, 3-address	ANDW3	src1,src2,dst	src1 AND src2→dst
Exclusive OR (XOR):			
Exclusive OR byte	XORB2	src,dst	dst XOR src→dst
Exclusive OR halfword	XORH2	src,dst	dst XOR src→dst
Exclusive OR word	XORW2	src,dst	dst XOR src→dst
Exclusive OR byte, 3-address	XORB3	src1,src2,dst	src1 XOR src2→dst
Exclusive OR halfword, 3-address	XORH3	src1,src2,dst	src1 XOR src2→dst
Exclusive OR word, 3-address	XORW3	src1,src2,dst	src1 XOR src2→dst
OR:			
OR byte	ORB2	src,dst	dst OR src→dst
OR halfword	ORH2	src,dst	dst OR src→dst
OR word	ORW2	src,dst	dst OR src→dst
OR byte, 3-address	ORB3	src1,src2,dst	src1 OR src2→dst
OR halfword, 3-address	ORH3	src1,src2,dst	src1 OR src2→dst
OR word, 3-address	ORW3	src1,src2,dst	src1 OR src2→dst
Compare or Test:			
Compare byte	CMPB	src1,src2	src2–src1
Compare halfword	CMPH	src1,src2	src2–src1
Compare word	CMPW	src1,src2	src2–src1
Test byte	TSTB	src	src–0
Test halfword	TSTH	src	src–0
Test word	TSTW	src	src–0
Bit test byte	BITB	src1,src2	src1 AND src2
Bit test halfword	BITH	src1,src2	src1 AND src2
Bit test word	BITW	src1,src2	src1 AND src2
Clear:			
Clear byte	CLRB	dst	0→dst
Clear halfword	CLRH	dst	0→dst
Clear word	CLRW	dst	0→dst

TABLE 5-3 Logical Instruction Group (Continued)

Instruction	Mnemonic	Operands	Description
Rotate or Logical			
Rotate word	ROTW	count,src,dst	↻ src→dst
Logical left shift byte	LLSB3	count,src,dst	src*2*(count AND 0x1F)→dst
Logical left shift halfword	LLSH3	count,src,dst	src*2*(count AND 0x1F)→dst
Logical left shift word	LLSW3	count,src,dst	src*2*(count AND 0x1F)→dst
Logical right shift word	LRSW3	count,src,dst	src/(2*(count AND 0x1F))→dst

Notation:

↻ denotes rotate right by the number of bit positions specified by count
ANDed with 0x1F.

Program Control Instructions

The jump, branch, and subroutine transfer instructions constitute the WE 32100 CPU program control group. These instructions change the program sequence, but generally do not alter the flags.

Jump instructions are always unconditional, but both conditional and unconditional branch and return instructions are provided. Unconditional transfers change the contents of the PC to the value specified. Conditional transfers first examine the status of the processor's flags to determine if the transfer should be executed.

Branch instructions can be one of two types as specified by the last character of the mnemonic: byte displacement (B) and halfword displacement (H). A mnemonic's type determines if an 8-bit or a 16-bit displacement is embedded in the instruction. This displacement is read, sign-extended to 32 bits, and the result is added to the program counter (PC) to compute the target address. The symbol y is used to denote this displacement address in the descriptions of the program control instruction group (Table 5-4). Unlike branch instructions which add an offset to the contents of the PC, a jump instruction includes a 32-bit address that replaces the PC's entire value.

In addition to altering the contents of the PC, as done by the branch and jump instructions, a subroutine call instruction also saves the PC's value for reinstatement later by a return instruction. A jump to subroutine (JSB) instruction saves the address of the next instruction on the stack at the location identified by the SP, increments the SP by 4, and then alters the PC. A return from subroutine (RSB) instruction decrements the SP by 4, retrieves the saved address from the stack, and writes it to the PC.

Procedure call (CALL) and return (RET) instructions are special transfer instructions that facilitate high-level language function (C language) or procedure (PASCAL) calls. Each function is provided with a register-save area. This register-save area is used for storing the calling function's frame pointer (FP), argument pointer (AP), return PC value, and the contents of registers r3 through r8, when requested. The SAVE and RESTORE instructions control the number of the user registers that will be saved and restored. These instructions explicitly manipulate four registers:

1. PC - The CALL instruction saves the old PC as the return address and sets the PC to the first executable instruction of the function being called. The return (RET) instruction restores the PC to the return address (the address of the next executable instruction of the calling function).

2. SP - These instructions adjust the SP automatically to point to the top of the stack whenever they store or retrieve items.

3. FP - The SAVE instruction sets the FP to the address just above the saved registers. The FP accesses a region on the stack that stores temporary (or automatic) variables for the function.

4. AP - The call instruction adjusts the AP to the starting address of a list of arguments for the function.

The calling function contains a CALL instruction. The SAVE instruction should be the first statement of the called function. For a return, a RESTORE and a RET appear in the function being exited. For example, a typical procedure call and save sequence is:

```
        PUSHW arg1              /* push three arguments */
        PUSHW arg2
        PUSHW arg3
        CALL offset,func1       /* call function */
          .
          .                     /* other instructions */
          .
func1: SAVE %r3                  /* save r3 through r8 */
```

This sequence of instructions starts with the pushing of three arguments onto the stack. Each push increments the SP by 4. The CALL instruction automatically saves the old pointers. The SAVE statement is then executed, automatically saving registers r3 through r8 by pushing them onto the stack. The SP and FP are adjusted for each push. Figure 5-15 shows the stack after this call and save sequence.

To return to the calling program, the function func1 must contain the following instructions:

```
func1: SAVE %r3          /* save r3 through r8 */
       .
       .                 /* other instructions */
       .
       RESTORE %r3       /* restore r3 through r8 */
       RET               /* return to main function */
```

The restore instruction retrieves registers r3 through r8 from the stack. It must have the same operand as the original SAVE; otherwise, the return (RET) cannot restore the correct AP and PC. Both instructions decrement the SP by 4 as they pop the register contents from the stack.

FIGURE 5-15   Stack After a CALL and SAVE Sequence

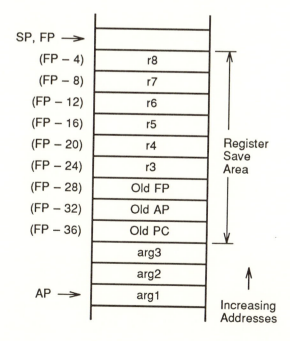

TABLE 5-4 Program Control Instruction Group

Instruction	Mnemonic	Operands	Description
Unconditional Transfer:			
Branch with byte displacement	BRB	disp8	$PC+y \rightarrow PC$
Branch with halfword displacement	BRH	disp16	$PC+y \rightarrow PC$
Jump	JMP	dst	$\&dst \rightarrow PC$
Conditional Transfers:			
Branch on carry clear byte	BCCB	disp8	if(C=0) $PC+y \rightarrow PC$
Branch on carry clear halfword	BCCH	disp16	if(C=0) $PC+y \rightarrow PC$
Branch on carry set byte	BCSB	disp8	if(C=1) $PC+y \rightarrow PC$
Branch on carry set halfword	BCSH	disp16	if(C=1) $PC+y \rightarrow PC$
Branch on overflow clear, byte displacement	BVCB	disp8	if(V=0) $PC+y \rightarrow PC$
Branch on overflow clear, halfword displacement	BVCH	disp16	if(V=0) $PC+y \rightarrow PC$
Branch on overflow set, byte displacement	BVSB	disp8	if(V=1) $PC+y \rightarrow PC$
Branch on overflow set, halfword displacement	BVSH	disp16	if(V=1) $PC+y \rightarrow PC$
Branch on equal byte	BEB	disp8	if(Z=1) $PC+y \rightarrow PC$
Branch on equal halfword	BEH	disp16	if(Z=1) $PC+y \rightarrow PC$
Branch on not equal byte	BNEB	disp8	if(Z=0) $PC+y \rightarrow PC$
Branch on not equal halfword	BNEH	disp16	if(Z=0) $PC+y \rightarrow PC$
Branch on less than byte (signed)	BLB	disp8	if(N=1 AND Z=0) $PC+y \rightarrow PC$
Branch on less than halfword (signed)	BLH	disp16	if(N=1 AND Z=0) $PC+y \rightarrow PC$
Branch on less than byte (unsigned)	BLUB	disp8	if(C=1) $PC+y \rightarrow PC$
Branch on less than halfword (unsigned)	BLUH	disp16	if(C=1) $PC+y \rightarrow PC$
Branch on less than or equal byte (signed)	BLEB	disp8	if(N=1 OR Z=1) $PC+y \rightarrow PC$
Branch on less than or equal halfword (signed)	BLEH	disp16	if(N=1 OR Z=1) $PC+y \rightarrow PC$
Branch on less than or equal equal byte (unsigned)	BLEUB	disp8	if(C=1 OR Z=1) $PC+y \rightarrow PC$

TABLE 5-4 Program Control Instruction Group (Continued)

Instruction	Mnemonic	Operands	Description
Branch on less than or equal halfword (unsigned)	BLEUH	disp16	if(C=1 OR Z=1) PC+y→PC
Branch on greater than byte (signed)	BGB	disp8	if(N=0 AND Z=0) PC+y→PC
Branch on greater than halfword (signed)	BGH	disp16	if(N=0 AND Z=0) PC+y→PC
Branch on greater than byte (unsigned)	BGUB	disp8	if(C=0 AND Z=0) PC+y→PC
Branch on greater than halfword (unsigned)	BGUH	disp16	if(C=0 AND Z=0) PC+y→PC
Branch on greater than or equal byte (signed)	BGEB	disp8	if(N=0 OR Z=1) PC+y→PC
Branch on greater than or equal halfword (signed)	BGEH	disp16	if(N=0 OR Z=1) PC+y→PC
Branch on greater than or equal byte (unsigned)	BGEUB	disp8	if(C=0) PC+y→PC
Branch on greater than or equal halfword (unsigned)	BGEUH	disp16	if(C=0) PC+y→PC
Return on carry clear	RCC	–	if(C=0) stack→PC
Return on carry set (signed)	RCS	–	if(C=1) stack→PC
Return on overflow clear	RVC	–	if(V=0) stack→PC
Return on overflow set (signed)	RVS	–	if(V=1) stack→PC
Return on equal (unsigned)	REQLU	–	if(Z=1) stack→PC
Return on equal (signed)	REQL	–	if(Z=1) stack→PC
Return on not equal (unsigned)	RNEQU	–	if(Z=0) stack→PC
Return on not equal (signed)	RNEQ	–	if(Z=0) stack→PC
Return on less than (signed)	RLSS	–	if(N=1 AND Z=0) stack→PC
Return on less than (unsigned)	RLSSU	–	if(C=1) stack→PC
Return on less than or equal (signed)	RLEQ	–	if(N=1 OR Z=1) stack→PC
Return on less than or equal (unsigned)	RLEQU	–	if(C=1 OR Z=1) stack→PC
Return on greater than (signed)	RGTR	–	if(N=0 AND Z=0) stack→PC

TABLE 5-4 Program Control Instruction Group (Continued)

Instruction	Mnemonic	Operands	Description
Return on greater than (unsigned)	RGTRU	–	if(C=0 AND Z=0) stack→PC
Return on greater than or equal (signed)	RGEQ	–	if(N=0 OR Z=1) stack→PC
Return on greater than or equal (unsigned)	RGEQU	–	if(C=0) stack→PC
Subroutine Transfer:			
Branch to subroutine, byte displacement	BSBB	disp8	PC→stack,PC+y→PC
Branch to subroutine, halfword displacement	BSBH	disp16	PC→stack, PC+y→PC
Jump to subroutine	JSB	dst	PC→stack, &dst→PC
Return from subroutine	RSB	–	stack→PC
Procedure Transfer:			
Save registers	SAVE	%rn	FP,rn–r8→stack new SP→FP
Restore registers	RESTORE	%rn	stack→FP,rn-r8
Call procedure	CALL	src,dst	AP,PC→stack &src→AP,&dst→PC
Return from procedure	RET		stack→AP,PC

Coprocessor Instructions

Coprocessor instructions implement the software interface between the CPU and any attached coprocessors. All *WE* 32100 CPU coprocessor instructions have an 8-bit opcode followed by one word, which is transmitted on the data bus and interpreted by the coprocessor. This word is not used by the CPU. If no coprocessor responds to the transmitted word, an external memory fault occurs.

After the word following the opcode is transmitted, the source operands, if any, are fetched from memory. The CPU then waits until the "coprocessor done" signal is asserted, after which the CPU attempts to read a word. For invalid accesses, an external memory fault occurs; otherwise bits 18 through 21 of the word are copied into bits 18 through 21 (flag register) of the PSW. The resulting operand, if any, is then written to memory. (This process is illustrated by an example in Section 9.1).

Coprocessor instructions can have from zero to two operands. The operands may be of three data types as specified by the last character of the mnemonic: single-word (S), double-word (D), and triple-word (T). All operands must start on an address evenly divisible by four (a word boundary). Table 5-5 lists the coprocessor instructions for the *WE* 32100 Microprocessor.

TABLE 5-5 Coprocessor Instruction Group

Instruction	Mnemonic	Operand(s)	Description*
Coprocessor operation	SPOP	word	word,PSW
Coprocessor operation read single	SPOPRS	word,src	word,read,PSW
Coprocessor operation read double	SPOPRD	word,src	word,read,PSW
Coprocessor operation read triple	SPOPRT	word,src	word,read,PSW
Coprocessor operation single 2-address	SPOPS2	word,src,dst	word,read,PSW, write
Coprocessor operation double 2-address	SPOPD2	word,src,dst	word,read,PSW, write
Coprocessor operation triple 2-address	SPOPT2	word,src,dst	word,read,PSW, write
Coprocessor operation write single	SPOPWS	word,dst	word,PSW,write
Coprocessor operation write double	SPOPWD	word,dst	word,PSW,write
Coprocessor operation write triple	SPOPWT	word,dst	word,PSW,write

* Operations described are word, read, PSW, and write.

word – word written to coprocessor (to command register if MAU is used).

read – source operand (src) is read from *WE* 32100 Microprocessor and used by coprocessor.

PSW – result of coprocessor operation reflected in the flag bits (auxiliary status register of MAU transferred to PSW, if MAU used).

write – result of coprocessor operation written to destination operand (dst).

Stack and Miscellaneous Instructions

The stack instructions given in Table 5-6 are used to manipulate the stack. The push and pop instructions always process a word and alter the SP. The push instructions always have a source operand; the pop instructions have a destination operand.

Miscellaneous instructions include those that alter the machine state or have some effect on the cache memory. The breakpoint instruction results in a breakpoint-trap exception and transfers control to the operating system for the appropriate exception handler. The NOP instructions come in 1-, 2-, or 3-byte lengths. Cache flushes invalidate any instructions within the instruction cache.

Table 5-6 Stack and Miscellaneous Instruction Groups

Instruction	Mnemonic	Operands	Description
Stack Operations:			
Push address word	PUSHAW	src	&src→stack
Push word	PUSHW	src	src→stack
Pop word	POPW	dst	stack→dst
Miscellaneous:			
No operation, 1 byte	NOP		No operation
No operation, 2 byte	NOP2		No operation
No operation, 3 byte	NOP3		No operation
Breakpoint trap	BPT		Breakpoint trap exception generated
Cache flush	CFLUSH		All instruction cache entries marked invalid
Extended opcode	EXTOP	byte	Reserved opcode exception generated

5.4 Addressing Modes

An assembly language instruction for the *WE* 32100 Microprocessor consists of a mnemonic (such as, ADDW, MOVH, or INCB) followed by up to four operands. Each operand is physically located in either a microprocessor register, a memory location, an input/output port, or directly within the instruction. Machine-coded instructions may appear at any byte address in memory and are stored as a one-byte or two-byte opcode followed by up to four operands. Figure 5-16 illustrates the general format of an assembly instruction as it is stored in memory.

Each individual operand shown in Figure 5-16 consists of a descriptor byte, followed by up to four bytes of data (see Figure 5-17). The descriptor byte defines an operand's addressing mode and register field. Bytes that follow the descriptor byte contain any data required by the address mode. This data is stored with lower-order bytes located at lower-order addresses. For example, the hexadecimal value 0x12345678 would be stored as illustrated in Figure 5-18.

Notice that operand data stored within an instruction, as shown in Figure 5-18, is the reverse of the data storage within a memory location shown in Figure 5-14.

FIGURE 5-16 Instruction Storage in Memory

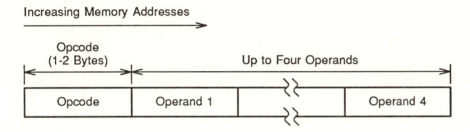

FIGURE 5-17 Operand Format

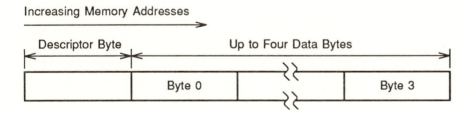

FIGURE 5-18 Storing Immediate Operand Data

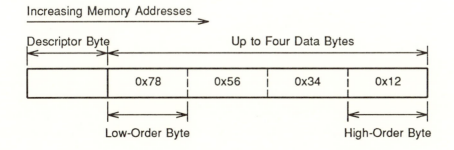

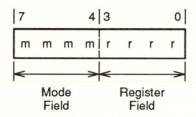

FIGURE 5-19   Descriptor Byte Format

Figure 5-19 illustrates the format of the descriptor byte, which consists of two 4-bit fields. The mode field, mmmm, contains a number between 0 and 15 that determines the operand's addressing mode. The register field, rrrr, contains a number from 0 through 15, representing register r0 through r15.

Table 5-7 lists all mode field values (0-15) and a brief description of the corresponding addressing mode. These modes are listed by type (immediate, absolute, register, etc.) in Table 5-8, along with the valid combinations of mode and register field values for each type.

TABLE 5-7 Addressing Modes

Mode Field Value	Addressing Mode	Description
0-3	Immediate (Positive Literal)	The register field bits are concatenated with the two low-order mode field bits to form an unsigned 6-bit immediate data.
4	Register or Word Immediate	The operand is contained in one of the 16 registers. If 15 is specified in the register field, this becomes the word immediate mode.
5	Register Deferred or Halfword Immediate	The register specified in the register field contains the operand's address. If 15 is specified in the register field, this becomes the halfword immediate mode.
6	Displacement (FP Short Offset) or Byte Immediate	The FP (register r9) is implicitly referred to by this mode. Register field bits are used as an offset and are added to the FP to form the operand's address. This addressing mode is an optimized case of the register deferred mode, produced by the assembler. If 15 is specified in the register field, this becomes the byte immediate mode.

TABLE 5-7 Addressing Modes (Continued)

Mode Field Value	Addressing Mode	Description
7	Displacement (AP Short Offset) or Absolute	The AP (register r10) is implicitly referred to by this mode. Register field bits are used as an offset and are added to the AP to form the operand's address. This addressing mode is an optimized case of the register deferred mode, produced by the assembler. If 15 is specified in the register field, this mode becomes the absolute mode, and the four bytes following the descriptor's byte contain the operand's address.
8	Displacement (Word)	The four bytes following the descriptor byte are added to the contents of the register specified in the register field. The sum forms the address of the operand.
9	Displacement (Word Deferred)	The four bytes following the descriptor byte are added to the contents of the register specified in the register field. The sum forms the address of a pointer, which contains the operand's address.
A	Displacement (Halfword)	The two bytes following the descriptor byte are added to the contents of the register specified in the register field to form the operand's address.
B	Displacement (Halfword Deferred)	The two bytes following the descriptor byte are added to the contents of the register specified in the register field. The sum forms the address of a pointer, which contains the operand's address.
C	Displacement (Byte)	The byte following the descriptor byte is added to the contents of the register specified in the register field to form the operand's address.
D	Displacement (Byte Deferred)	The byte following the descriptor byte is added to the contents of the register specified in the register field. The sum forms the address of a pointer, which contains the operand's address.
E	Expanded Operand or Absolute Deferred	This mode is used to modify the data type of an operand. If 15 is specified in the register field, this becomes the absolute deferred mode.
F	Immediate (Negative Literal)	The register field bits are concatenated with the mode field bits to form a negative literal in the range −1 to −16.

TABLE 5-8 Addressing Modes by Type

Mode	Mode Field	Register Field	Bytes *
Immediate:			
Positive literal	0-3	15	1
Word immediate	4	15	5
Halfword immediate	5	15	3
Byte immediate	6	15	2
Negative literal	15	0-15	1
Absolute:			
Absolute	7	15	5
Absolute deferred	14	15	5
Register:			
Register	4	0-14	1
Register deferred	5	0-10, 12-14	1
Displacement From a Register:			
FP short offset	6	0-14	1
AP short offset	7	0-14	1
Word displacement	8	0-10, 12-15	5
Word displacement deferred	9	0-10, 12-15	5
Halfword displacement	10	0-10, 12-15	3
Halfword displacement deferred	11	0-10, 12-15	3
Byte displacement	12	0-10, 12-15	2
Byte displacement deferred	13	0-10, 12-15	2
Special Mode:			
Expanded operand type	14	0-14	2-6

* Maximum bytes per operand excluding opcode.

Register Mode

Any operand located directly in one of the microprocessor's registers is accessed using the register address mode. This mode is indicated in assembly language with the percent symbol (%). For example, the instruction INCW %r2 causes the 32-bit contents of register r2 to be incremented by one.

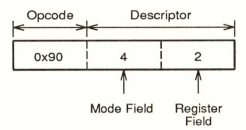

FIGURE 5-20   Register Mode Example

The general syntax, mode, and register fields used to signify the register addressing mode are:

syntax: %rn   where n is a register number
mmmm: 4
rrrr: 0 to 14

Using this information, the instruction INCW %r2 is stored in memory as shown in Figure 5-20.

Register Deferred Mode

Deferred addressing mode involves indirect addressing using pointers. A pointer is either a register or a memory location containing an address. Figure 5-21 illustrates the relationship between the address contained in a pointer and the operand ultimately obtained. The term deferred is used to describe this procedure because the operand obtained is deferred, or delayed, by going to the pointer first for an address. The address contained in the pointer is then used to access the desired operand.

When deferred addressing is used and the pointer is one of the microprocessor's registers, the addressing mode is referred to as register deferred mode. This addressing mode is designated in assembly language by the use of parentheses around the pointer register.

For example, the instruction MOVW (%r2),%r3 causes the CPU to regard the data in register r2 as an address. The contents of the memory location having this address will be copied into register r3. Notice that this instruction uses two operands, each with its own addressing mode. Although register deferred mode

FIGURE 5-21   Deferred Addressing Using a Pointer

225

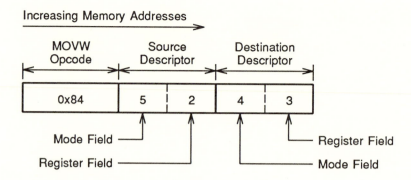

FIGURE 5-22   Register Deferred Mode Example

was used for the source operand and register mode was used for the destination operand, any other valid addressing modes could have been used.

The general syntax, mode, and register fields for a register deferred mode operand are:

syntax: (%rn)   where n is a register number
mmmm: 5
rrrr: 0 to 10, 12 to 14

Using this information, the instruction MOVW (%r2),%r3 is stored in memory as shown in Figure 5-22.

Displacement Mode

The displacement mode forms an operand's address by adding an offset to the contents of a register. For example, the instruction MOVB 0x30(%r2),%r3 copies the contents of a memory location into register r3. The source operand's memory address is calculated as the contents of register r2 plus an offset of 0x30 (see Figure 5-23).

FIGURE 5-23   Example of MOVB 0x30 (%r2),%r3

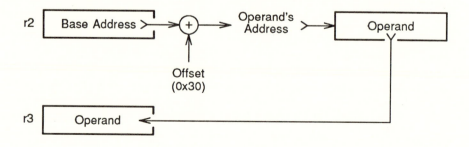

The general syntax, and valid register fields for a displacement mode operand are:

> syntax: offset(%rn)   where n is a register number
> mmmm: 8, 10, or 12   (word, halfword, or byte offset)
> rrrr: 0 to 10, 12 to 15

Using the appropriate mode and register fields, the instruction MOVB 0x30 (%r2),%r3 is stored in memory as shown in Figure 5-24.

The offset used in the displacement mode may be either a byte (8 bits), halfword (16 bits), or word (32 bits), or an expression yielding such a value. Two's complement, negative offsets are also valid. Negative byte and halfword offsets are first sign-extended to 32 bits before being used to obtain the operand's final address. This sign extension converts a negative byte or halfword into its equivalent 32-bit counterpart.

When the displacement mode is used with registers FP and AP, only a short offset between 0 and 14 may be used. This facilitates storage of a shortened instruction format in memory. The mode fields, when the frame and argument registers are used in the displacement mode, are 6 and 7, respectively. The short offset (0-14) is stored in the register field and extra bytes for an offset are not included in the stored instruction.

Deferred Displacement Mode

The deferred displacement mode uses the contents of the address calculated in the displacement mode as a pointer which contains the address of the desired operand. Consider the example shown in Figure 5-25. For a typical displacement

FIGURE 5-24   A Displacement Mode Source Operand

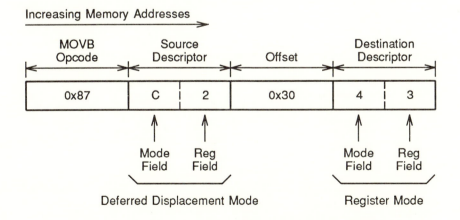

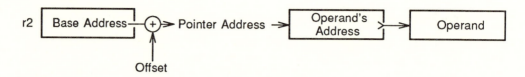

FIGURE 5-25 Deferred Displacement Addressing

mode, the operand would be located in the first memory address calculated. In deferred displacement mode, the content of this location is the address of the desired operand.

The deferred displacement mode is indicated to the assembler by the use of an asterisk before the offset. For example, the instruction INCW *0x30 (%r2) adds one to the contents of a memory location whose address is contained within a pointer. The address of the pointer is the contents of register r2 plus 0x30.

The general syntax, mode field, and register field for a deferred displacement mode operand is:

syntax: *expr (%rn)
mmmm: 9, 11, or 13   (word, halfword, or byte offset)
rrrr: 0-10, 12-15

Using this information, the instruction MOVB *0x30 (%r2),%r3 is stored in memory as shown in Figure 5-26.

FIGURE 5-26 A Deferred Displacement Mode Source Operand

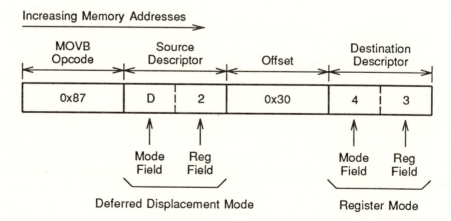

Immediate Mode

In the immediate addressing mode, the operand is contained within the instruction. The ampersand symbol is used to indicate this addressing mode to the assembler. For example, the instruction MOVB &0x50,%r6 copies the immediate data, 0x50, into register r6. The & symbol signifies that the data immediately following is to be treated as immediate data. The % symbol indicates that the register mode is being used for the destination operand.

The general syntax, valid mode, and register fields for the immediate addressing mode are:

syntax: &data (word, halfword, or byte data)

mmmm: 4, 5, or 6

rrrr: 15

A mode field of 4 indicates that the immediate data is 32 bits long, while mode fields of 5 and 6 are used for 16-bit and 8-bit immediate data, respectively. Figure 5-27 illustrates the storage of the instruction MOVW &0x12345678,%r2 in memory. This instruction causes the immediate data, 0x12345678, to be placed into register r2.

Notice in Figure 5-27 that the immediate data is stored in memory with lower order bytes stored at lower order addresses. This is true for all immediate data. For example, the 16-bit immediate data 0xABCD would be stored as 0xCDAB, with the byte containing 0xCD stored at the immediately lower address than the byte containing 0xAB.

The immediate mode also has a short storage form for positive immediate data between 0 and 63, and negative data between –1 and –16. In these two cases, the immediate data is stored directly within the descriptor byte.

FIGURE 5-27 A 32-Bit Immediate Source Operand

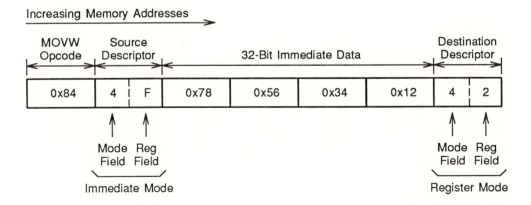

Absolute Mode

In absolute mode, the address of the desired operand is contained directly within the instruction. The dollar symbol is used to indicate this addressing mode to the assembler. For example, the instruction MOVB $0x2E04,%r0 moves the byte starting at location 0x2E04 into register r0. The general syntax, mode, and register fields for the absolute address mode are:

> syntax: $expr (expr must evaluate to a byte, halfword, or word)
> mmmm: 7
> rrrr: 15

The instruction MOVB $0x2E04,%r0 is stored in memory as shown in Figure 5-28.

The memory address in Figure 5-28 is stored as a 32-bit address with lower order bytes stored in lower order memory addresses.

Absolute Deferred Mode

In the absolute deferred mode, the address contained within the instruction is used as a pointer to a word containing the address of the operand. As in all deferred modes, an asterisk is used to indicate deferred addressing to the assembler.

For example, the instruction MOVB *$0x2E04,%r0 uses the data starting at memory location 0x2E04 as the address of the source operand. The general syntax, mode, and register fields for this deferred mode are:

> syntax: *$expr (expr must evaluate to a byte, halfword, or word)
> mmmm: 14
> rrrr: 15

FIGURE 5-28   An Absolute Mode Source Operand

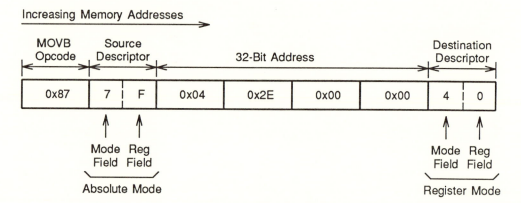

The instruction MOVB *$0x2E04,%r0 is stored in memory as illustrated in Figure 5-29.

Expanded Operand Mode

The expanded operand mode changes the type of an operand. For example, using this mode, a signed byte located in a register could be converted to an unsigned halfword stored in memory.

The expanded operand mode does not affect the length of immediate operands, but does affect whether they are treated as signed or unsigned. The expanded operand mode does not affect the treatment of literals. In assembly language, the syntax of this mode is

{type}operand

where operand is an operand having any address mode except an expanded operand mode. When the expanded operand mode is used, type overrides the operand's normal data type, except as noted above. The new type remains in effect for the operands that follow in the instruction unless another expanded operand mode overrides it. Table 5-9 lists the syntax for type.

The expanded operand mode requires two descriptor bytes as shown in Figure 5-30. The first byte identifies the expanded operand mode and the new type, while the second is the descriptor byte for the address mode. The type field contains the value of the new type (see Table 5-9). The second byte contains the mode field (mmmm) and the register field (rrrr) for the address mode. This byte is the descriptor byte for the new address mode.

FIGURE 5-29   An Absolute Deferred Mode Source Operand

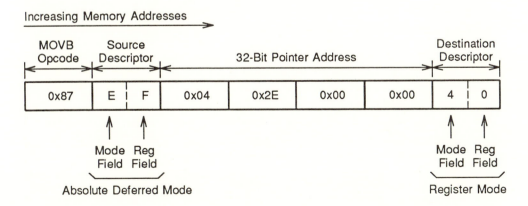

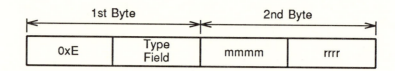

FIGURE 5-30   Expanded Operand Mode Descriptor Bytes

TABLE 5-9 Options for Type in Expanded Operand Mode

Type	Syntax	Type Field*
Signed byte	byte or sbyte	E7
Signed halfword	half or shalf	E6
Signed word	word or sword	E4
Unsigned byte	ubyte	E3
Unsigned halfword	uhalf	E2
Unsigned word	uword	E0

* Type fields E1, E5, E8-EE are reserved data types. Type field EF is an absolute deferred data type.

For example, the following instruction converts a signed byte into an unsigned halfword:

MOVB {sbyte}%r0,{uhalf}4(%r1)

The first operand has a register addressing mode; the second operand a byte displacement addressing mode. The instruction reads bits 0 through 7 from register 0, extends the sign bit (7) through 16 bits, and writes an unsigned halfword. The instruction is stored in memory as illustrated in Figure 5-31.

FIGURE 5-31   Expanded Operand Mode Example

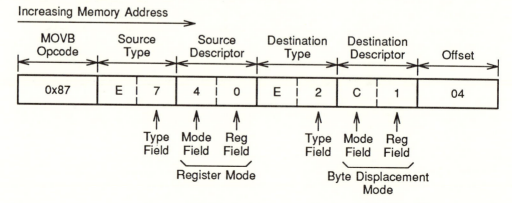

5.5 AT&T *WE* 32200 Microprocessor Enhancements

The *WE* 32200 Microprocessor, or CPU, offers system improvements over the *WE* 32100 Microprocessor while maintaining upward code compatibility. These new features are:

• An additional sixteen 32-bit registers to increase data storage in the CPU.

• Seven new addressing modes, including auto-incrementing and decrementing, and indexed addressing with displacement or scaling.

• Twenty new instructions which are primarily loop control operations for more efficient string manipulation, and support for processing of binary coded decimal (BCD) data.

• A faster and more secure quick interrupt.

• Improved normal-exception handling.

• 16-Bit dynamic bus sizing and arbitrary byte alignment.

Our discussion in this section is limited to the additional registers, the new addressing modes, and a summary of the new instructions. For further information consult the *AT&T WE 32200 Microprocessor Information Manual* (see Appendix D).

As previously discussed, the AT&T *WE* 32100 Microprocessor has both general-purpose registers (r0 through r8) and special-purpose registers (r9 through r15).The *WE* 32200 Microprocessor adds sixteen more general-purpose registers (r16 through r31) to this basic set. These new registers may be used for accumulating, addressing, or temporary data storage. However, the upper eight registers (r24 through r31) are privileged registers and can be written to only in kernel mode. The sixteen new registers can be used in all addressing modes other than the expanded operand, literal, or short offset modes; for these cases, either no register or a special-purpose register is implied by the mode.

The *WE* 32100 CPU addressing modes are summarized in Table 5-7, and the mode and register field codes comprising the descriptor byte are presented in Table 5-8. The seven new addressing modes for the *WE* 32200 CPU are:

• auto predecrement
• auto postdecrement
• auto preincrement
• auto postincrement

• indexed with byte displacement
• indexed with halfword displacement
• indexed with scaling

Notice from Table 5-8 that not all mode and register field combinations have been used for the *WE* 32100 Microprocessor coding. For example, register r11, the processor status word (PSW), is not used with the register deferred mode (mode field 5) or with any of the displacement modes (mode fields 8 through 13). To maintain compatibility with the *WE* 32100 CPU, the designers of the *WE* 32200 CPU assigned the unused combinations of register field 11 and mode fields 5, 10, 11, 12, and 13 to handle the additional registers as well as the new addressing modes. A second descriptor byte either identifies a mode and register, or a pair of registers used for the particular mode. Table 5-10 shows the two-byte descriptor format for the various cases.

TABLE 5-10 Descriptors for New *WE* 32200 CPU Registers and Modes

| | Two-Byte Descriptor Formats | | | |
| | Byte 1 | | Byte 2 | |
Mode	Mode Field	Register Field	Mode/Register Field	Register Field
	(4-bits)	(4-bits)	(4-bits)	(4-bits)
Register	12	11	4	0-15 *
Register deferred	12	11	5	0-15 *
Word displacement	12	11	8	0-15 *
Word displacement deferred	12	11	9	0-15 *
Halfword displacement	12	11	10	0-15 *
Halfword displacement deferred	12	11	11	0-15 *
Byte displacement	12	11	12	0-15 *
Byte displacement deferred	12	11	13	0-15 *
			(3-bits)	(5-bits)
Auto predecrement	5	11	0	0-31 **
Auto postdecrement	5	11	2	0-31 **
Auto preincrement	5	11	4	0-31 **
Auto postincrement	5	11	6	0-31 **
			(4-bits)	(4-bits)
Indexed with byte displacement	10	11	0-15 **	0-15 *
Indexed with halfword displacement	11	11	0-15 **	0-15 *
Indexed with scaling	13	11	0-15 **	0-15 *

* Add 16 to register code (specifies r16-r31).
** The new addressing modes cannot be used with r11 (PSW) or r15 (PC).

Observe that when the first descriptor byte is 0xCB (mode = 12, register = 11) one of eight original *WE* 32100 CPU modes is selected by the first 4 bits of byte 2. The lower 4 bits define one of the 16 upper registers (r16 through r31) which contain the operand or operand address. A code of 0x5B for the first descriptor byte, along with the first 3 bits of the second byte (actually only the first two bits are used), defines one of the four autoincrementing or autodecrementing modes; the lower 5 bits of the second byte then identify any one of the 32 registers used in this mode. For the indexed modes, the first byte alone (0xAB, 0xBB, or 0xDB) defines the mode. Both a register from the set r0 to r15 and one from the set r16 to r31 are used with these modes. The entire second descriptor byte is therefore required to define the two registers.

Each of the new *WE* 32200 CPU addressing modes, with examples of their use, is described below.

Auto Pre/Post Increment/Decrement

For the four auto modes, any register from r0 to r31, except r11 (PSW) and r15 (PC) is used as a pointer. The operand size may be byte, halfword, or word. The register is either incremented or decremented by 1 for a byte operand, 2 for a halfword operand, and 4 for a word operand. If preincrement/predecrement is used, the register is first incremented or decremented by the appropriate number, after which the register contains the starting address of the operand. For the postincrement/postdecrement case, the specified register is used as a pointer to the operand; after the operation is performed, the register is then incremented or decremented by 1, 2, or 4.

Figure 5-32 shows an example of the coding of an operation involving auto-postdecrementing. The instruction

    MOVB (%r19)-,%r7

causes a byte at memory address contained in register r19 to be moved to register r7; the byte is zero extended to 32-bits (bits 31 to 8 of r7 are replaced by zeroes). After the move, register r19 is decremented by 1, so that it then points to the address one below that of the operand used with the move instruction.

The general syntax for the autoaddressing modes is:

    syntax: -(%rx)   auto-predecrement
            (%rx)-   auto-postdecrement
            +(%rx)   auto-preincrement
            (%rx)+   auto-postincrement

where x is a register number in the range 0 to 31.

The instruction code contains the MOVB opcode (0x87), followed by the first byte of the source descriptor, 0x5B, which corresponds to any of the four

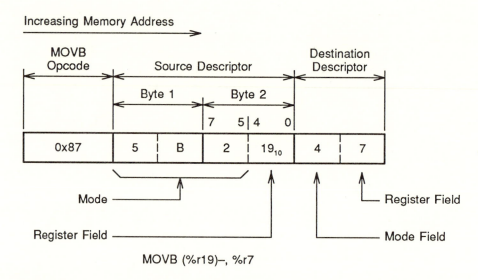

FIGURE 5-32   Auto-Postdecrement Mode Example

autoaddressing modes. The second source descriptor byte contains 2 (010) which defines the postdecrement mode followed by the 5-bit register identifier, 19_{10} (10011). The fourth byte is the destination descriptor, which identifies the register mode (mode 4) used with register 7.

Indexed Register Modes

The indexed register modes with byte or halfword displacement add the sum of two specified registers (i.e., a base and an index register) to the byte or halfword offset. The sum is then used as the operand address. The base register is one of the upper sixteen registers, r16 to r31, and the index register is one of the lower sixteen registers, r0 to r15 (except for PSW and PC). These modes are analogous to the base index relative mode of the INTEL 80386 CPU. The index register mode with scaling multiplies the content of the index register by 1, 2, or 4 depending on the operand size (byte, halfword, or word respectively). It then adds the scaled result to the base register content, and the resulting address points to the operand. Thus it is comparable to the INTEL 80386 CPU base index mode with automatic scaling.

The general syntax for the index modes is:

syntax: expr(%rn,%rm)   Indexed with byte displacement
       expr(%rn,%rm)   Indexed with halfword displacement
       %rm[%rn]   Indexed with scaling

where:
1. expr must evaluate to a byte, halfword, or word
2. m is a register number in the range 0 to 15 (except for PSW and PC), and
3. n is a register number in the range 16 to 31.

Figures 5-33, 5-34, and 5-35 show examples of the three indexed modes used with an add operation. The instruction

ADDW2 %r0,0x17(%r6,%r18)

illustrated in Figure 5-33 adds the content of register r0 to the word in memory addressed by

r18	+	r6	+	0x17
(base)		(index)		(byte displacement)

The sum replaces the memory word. Notice the byte displacement is sign-extended to 32-bits, and in accordance with data storage format for the *WE* 32100/32200 CPU, the operand address formed points to the highest order byte.

The code consists of five bytes, which include the opcode for ADDW2 (0x9C) and the source descriptor for register mode (4) and register (0). The third byte, 0xAB, defines the *indexed with byte displacement* mode, and the fourth byte specifies the index and base registers (0x62). Notice the base register code of 2 is added to 16 to identify r18. A fifth byte is required for the byte displacement, 0x17.

FIGURE 5-33   Indexed Register (Byte Displacement) Mode Example

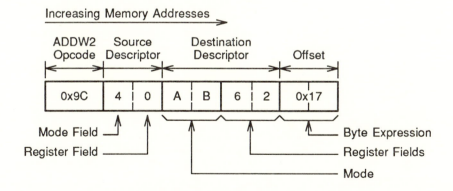

ADDW2 %r0, 0x17(%r6, %r18)

The instruction

ADDW2 %r0,0x1723(%r6,%r18)

shown in Figure 5-34 performs the same addition operation as for the previous example, except that the displacement from the base plus index address is of word length (0x1723). The code is identical except that the third byte is changed to 0xBB to identify indexed with halfword displacement mode, and an extra byte is required to accommodate the larger displacement size.

The final example, shown in Figure 5-35, uses the indexed mode with scaling. The instruction

ADDH2 %r18[%r9],%r1

adds a memory-based halfword to the lower 16-bits of register r1, and stores the result in r1 (sign extended to 32-bits). The memory operand address in this case is

$$\underset{\text{(base)}}{\text{r18}} \quad + \quad \underset{\text{(scale)}}{2} \quad * \quad \underset{\text{(index)}}{\text{r9}}$$

The scale factor of 2 corresponds to the halfword operand size. The instruction code requires four bytes — one for the instruction opcode (0x9E for ADDH2), two for the source descriptor, and one for the destination descriptor (register mode 4, with register r1). The source descriptor bytes are 0xDB, identifying the index register mode with scaling, followed by 0x92, which specifies the index register (r9) and the base register (r18, again formed by the code number 2 added to 16).

The new *WE 32200* CPU nonsystem instructions are listed in Table 5-11.

FIGURE 5-34   Indexed Register (Halfword Displacement) Mode Example

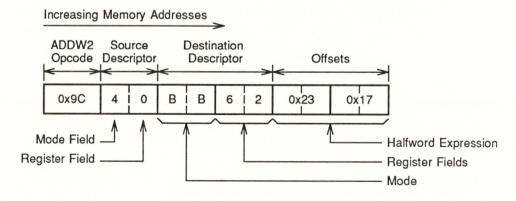

ADDW2 %r0, 0x1723 (%r6, %r18)

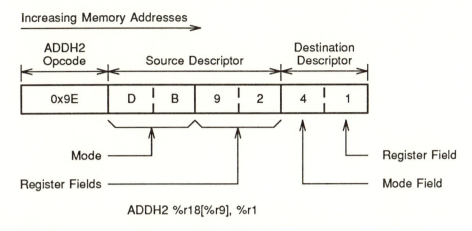

FIGURE 5-35   Example of Indexed Register Mode with Scaling

These include packed decimal (BCD) operations, decrement and test instructions, and a compare and swap operation. Relevant to BCD operations is the fact that the *WE* 32200 CPU has an additional flag bit. In addition to the negative (N), zero (Z), overflow (V), and carry/borrow (C) flag bits, which were part of the *WE* 32100 CPU PSW, the *WE* 32200 CPU has an extended carry/borrow (X) flag. This flag is bit 26 of the PSW, a previously unused bit position. This bit is set if there is a carry or borrow from a BCD arithmetic operation on two BCD digits.

TABLE 5-11 Additional *WE* 32200 Microprocessor Instructions

Instruction	Mnemonic	Operands	Description
Packed Decimal:			
Add packed byte 2-address	ADDPB2	src,dst	dst+src+X→dst
Add packed byte 3-address	ADDPB3	src1,src2,dst	src1+src2+X→dst
Clear X bit of PSW	CLRX		0→X
Pack BCD halfword	PACKB	src,dst	u(src)→p(dst)
Set X bit of PSW	SETX		1→X
Subtract packed byte 2-address	SUBPB2	src,dst	dst−src−X→dst
Subtract packed byte 3-address	SUBPB3	src1,src2,dst	src2−src1−X→dst
Unpack BCD byte	UNPACKB	src1,src2,dst	u(src1,src2)→p(dst)
Decrement and Test:			
Decrement, test, and branch byte	DTB	dst,disp8	dst−1→dst if (dst>0)
Decrement, test, and branch halfword	DTH	dst,disp16	PC+y→PC

239

TABLE 5-11 Additional WE 32200 Microprocessor Instructions (Continued)

Instruction	Mnemonic	Operands	Description
Test equal, decrement, and test byte	TEDTB	dst,disp8	if not equal
Test equal, decrement, and test halfword	TEDTH	dst,disp16	if(dst > 0) dst—1→dst PC+y→PC else dst–1→dst
Test greater, decrement, and test byte	TGDTB	dst,disp8	if less than or equal
Test greater, decrement, and test halfword	TGDTH	dst,disp16	if(dst > 0) dst—1→dst PC+y→PC else dst–1→dst
Test greater or equal, decrement, test byte	TGEDTB	dst,disp8	if less than
Test greater or equal, decrement, test halfword	TGEDTH	dst,disp16	if(dst > 0) dst—1→dst PC+y→PC else dst–1→dst
Test not equal, decrement, test byte	TNEDTB	dst,disp8	if equal
Test not equal decrement, test halfword	TNEDTH	dst,disp16	if (dst > 0) dst—1→dst PC+y→PC else dst–1→dst

| **Compare and Swap:** | | | |
| Compare and swap word | CASWI | src1,src2,dst | if (dst=src2) src1→dst else dst→src2 |

Notes:
1. **Pack and Unpack Operations:**
       p(dst) - packed destination data
    u(src) or u(src1,src2) - unpacked source data

PACKB: Before   After
           src = n d1 n d2   dst = d1 d2
              (halfword)   (byte)

UNPACKB: Before   After
           src1 = d1 d0   src2 = d3 d2   dst = d3 d1 d2 d0
              (byte)   (byte)   (halfword)

where d0 to d3 represent 4-bit decimal digits (BCD) and n is any arbitrary 4-bit number.

2. **Test Operations:**
   y - operand sign-extended to 32-bits, used as displacement address.

5.6 Chapter Highlights

1. The program model register set of the AT&T *WE* 32100 Microprocessor consists of nine general-purpose registers, a stack pointer, a program counter, a flags register, an argument pointer, and a frame pointer. Except for the flags register, which consists of four bits of the 32-bit processor status register, all registers in the program model set are 32-bits wide.

2. Although both the argument pointer and frame pointer registers may be used as general-purpose registers, they are usually reserved for pointing to high-level language argument and variable stack areas. Arguments passed to a subprogram are pushed on a stack, with the address of the top-of-stack placed into the argument pointer. Similarly, the frame pointer is used to point to the stack area used for storing local variables of the currently running program.

3. The *WE* 32100 Microprocessor system model register set consists of a processor status register, a process control block pointer, and an interrupt stack pointer. All three of these 32-bit registers are used to contain addresses that may be read at any time, but may be written only when the operating system is in control.

4. The *WE* 32100 Microprocessor supports byte (8-bit), halfword (16-bit), word (32-bit), and bit field data. Floating-point data is supported by the *WE* 32106 Math Acceleration Unit (MAU). The CPU instruction set provides that all data can be interpreted as either signed or unsigned quantities.

5. Data stored within memory is assumed by the CPU to be stored with its lower-order bytes at higher-order addresses. All data stored in a register is 32-bits wide, regardless of the instruction or data type. If less than 32 bits is accessed from memory, signed data is sign-extended to 32 bits and unsigned data is zero-extended to 32 bits.

6. The instruction set of the *WE* 32100 Microprocessor consists of data transfer, arithmetic, logical, program control, coprocessor, and stack manipulation instruction groups.

7. An individual *WE* 32100 Microprocessor assembly language instruction consists of an optional label field, a mnemonic, and up to four operands. Multioperand instructions require that the destination operand be the last operand listed.

8. Machine language instructions are encoded using either a one-byte or two-byte opcode followed by addressing mode information for up to four operands. Each operand is encoded using a single descriptor byte and up to four additional data

bytes. The descriptor byte defines the operand's addressing mode and register field. The additional bytes contain any required immediate data. Immediate data within an instruction is stored with lower-order bytes located at lower-order addresses.

9. The AT&T *WE* 32200 Microprocessor offers system improvements over the *WE* 32100 Microprocessor while maintaining upward code compatibility. Enhancements include sixteen additional general-purpose CPU registers, additional addressing modes and instructions, improved interrupt and exception handling, 16-bit dynamic bus sizing, and arbitrary byte alignment.

10. The seven additional addressing modes offered by the *WE* 32200 Microprocessor include automatic preincrement and predecrement, automatic postincrement and postdecrement, indexed with byte and halfword displacement, and indexed with scaling. Twenty additional instructions are primarily for loop control operations, and provide more efficient string manipulation and support for processing of BCD data.

Exercises

1a. List the registers that comprise the *WE* 32100 Microprocessor program register set and the functions that can be performed by these registers.
1b. List the registers that comprise the *WE* 32100 Microprocessor system register set and the functions that these registers perform.

2. List the data types supported by the *WE* 32100 Microprocessor.

3a. What is a descriptor byte? What information does this byte provide?
3b. How many descriptor bytes are required in a two-operand instruction?

4a. Describe how the 32-bit data 0xABEF19CC would be stored in memory starting at address 0x1620.
4b. Describe how the 32-bit immediate operand 0xABEF19CC would be stored within an instruction assuming that the operand's descriptor byte is located at memory address 0x187F.

5a. How many addressing modes are provided by the *WE* 32100 CPU?
5b. List the mode field values corresponding to absolute, immediate, register, and register-deferred addressing modes.

6. The opcodes for the *WE* 32100 Microprocessor MOVB, MOVH, and MOVW instructions are 0x87, 0x86, and 0x84, respectively. Using these opcodes determine the bit encoding for the following instructions:
6a. MOVW %r2,%r3
6b. MOVB %r6,%r7
6c. MOVH (%r5),%r3
6d. MOVH (%r3),%r5
6e. MOVW &0x738291AB,%r5
6f. MOVW &0x738291AB,(%r5)

7. Using the opcodes given in Exercise 6, determine the bit encodings for the following instructions.
7a. MOVW $0xAC1900DD,%r3
7b. MOVW $0xAC1900DD,(%r3)
7c. MOVH *$0xAC1900DD,%r2
7d. MOVH *$0xAC1900DD,(%r2)
7e. MOVB 0x20(%r3),(%r4)
7f. MOVB *0x20(%r3),(%r4)
7g. MOVW *0xAB(%r2),$0x1960AAEE
7h. MOVW &0xAC186500,$0x19890000
7i. MOVH &0x12345678,*$0x12345678

8. Identify the operand-addressing modes used for the source and destination operands used in each instruction encoded in Exercise 7.

9. The opcodes for the *WE* 32100 CPU two-operand ADD instructions, ADDB2, ADDH2, and ADDW2, are 0x9F, 0x9E, and 0x9C, respectively. Using this information, determine the bit encoding for the following instructions:
9a. ADDB2 %r0,%r3
9b. ADDH2 (%r0),%r3
9c. ADDH2 %r0,(%r3)
9d. ADDW2 &0x19AB,%r2
9e. ADDW2 &0x19AB,(%r2)
9f. ADDB2 %r2,0xA(%r5)
9g. ADDB2 %r4,*0xA(%r5)
9h. ADDH2 $0xFFEE,(%r6)
9i. ADDW2 *$1950ABDF,%r1
9j. ADDW2 49(%r3),*$0x110

10. Write assembly language instructions to perform the following operations:
10a. Move the number 0xFFEE into r2.
10b. Move the number 0xAAEF into the memory location whose address is in register r5.
10c. Add the word located at memory address 0x1960 to register r6.
10d. Shift the contents of register r1 one bit to the left.
10e. Multiply the lower 16-bits of register r3 by the lower 16-bits of register r4.

11. Assuming that 8-bit codes for the characters Hello World! are stored in memory starting at location 0x1690, write one or more instructions to individually perform the following operations:

11a. Move a copy of the characters into memory starting at location 0xAACD.

11b. Move a reverse copy of the characters into memory starting at location 0xAACD.

11c. Load the last four characters (rld!) into register r6.

12a. An array of ten signed 16-bit integers is stored in memory starting at address 0xAB190000. Write a sequence of *WE* 32100 CPU assembly language instructions to sum the ten elements, allowing sufficient room for a sum greater than 16-bits.

12b. Modify the instructions written in Exercise 12a so that the sums of the positive and negative elements are produced individually.

13. An array of nonzero, 16-bit unsigned integers is stored in memory starting at address 0x1620. A trailing value of zero is used to indicate the end of the list. Write a sequence of *WE* 32100 CPU assembly language instructions to sum the numbers in the list. Terminate when the zero value is accessed. Assume that the sum does not exceed 32-bits.

14. The unsigned 16-bit operands, 0xAB60 and 0x1162, are to be multiplied. Write a series of *WE* 32100 CPU assembly language instructions to load these operands into the lower 16 bits of registers r2 and r3, respectively, and generate their product in register r3.

15a. Write a series of *WE* 32100 CPU assembly language instructions to locate the maximum value in a set of twenty-five 32-bit signed integers. The first integer is stored in memory at address 0x6000.

15b. Modify the instructions written for Exercise 15a to locate the minimum value.

16. Write a series of *WE* 32100 CPU assembly language instructions to produce the cube of a signed 8-bit integer number located in the lower 8-bits of register r2. The result should be placed in register r3.

17. The binary and ASCII codes for the digits 0 through 9 are listed in Table 5-12. To convert the binary code for these digits to the corresponding ASCII code requires adding a constant value to the digit's binary value. Using this information, write a series of *WE* 32100 CPU assembly language instructions to convert a binary number (representing 0-9) stored in the lower 8 bits of register r1 into its equivalent ASCII representation.

18. The binary and ASCII codes for the hexadecimal digits A through F are listed in Table 5-13. To convert the binary code for these digits to the corresponding ASCII code requires adding a constant value to each digit's binary value. Using this information, write a series of *WE* 32100 CPU assembly language instructions to convert a binary number, represented by the hexadecimal digits A to F, into its equivalent ASCII representation. Assume that the binary number is initially stored in the lower 8 bits of register r2.

19. Using the results of Exercises 17 and 18, write a series of *WE* 32100 CPU assembly language instructions to convert the binary representation of the hexadecimal digits 0

through F into their equivalent ASCII codes. (Hint: Recall that the decimal digit and letter codes require different values to be added for proper conversion to ASCII).

TABLE 5-12 Binary and ASCII Digit Codes (0 - 9)

Digit	Binary	ASCII Binary	ASCII Hex
0	00000000	011 0000	0x30
1	00000001	011 0001	0x31
2	00000010	011 0010	0x32
3	00000011	011 0011	0x33
4	00000100	011 0100	0x34
5	00000101	011 0101	0x35
6	00000110	011 0110	0x36
7	00000111	011 0111	0x37
8	00001000	011 1000	0x38
9	00001001	011 1001	0x39

TABLE 5-13 Binary and ASCII Digit Codes (A - F)

Digit	Binary	ASCII Binary	ASCII Hex
A	00001010	100 0001	0x41
B	00001011	100 0010	0x42
C	00001100	100 0011	0x43
D	00001101	100 0100	0x44
E	00001110	100 0101	0x45
F	00001111	100 0110	0x46

MOTOROLA MC68020 Microprocessor

Chapter Six

6.1   Register Sets
6.2   Data Types
6.3   Addressing Modes
6.4   Instruction Set
6.5   Instruction Encoding
6.6   Chapter Highlights

This chapter presents the register sets, data types, addressing modes, instruction set, and the instruction formats supported by the MOTOROLA MC68020 Microprocessor (CPU).

6.1 Register Sets

Figure 6-1 illustrates the complete set of MOTOROLA MC68020 CPU user-accessible registers. Due to the inherently different functions performed by the program and system model register sets, each of these sets is described separately.

Program Model Registers

The program model register set consists of eight general-purpose data registers, seven address registers, a user stack pointer, a program counter, and a condition code register. Each of these registers performs a function almost identical to the registers in the generic program model register set described in Chapter 2.

General-Purpose Data Registers

The MOTOROLA MC68020 CPU has eight general-purpose data registers, named D0 through D7. Each of these 32-bit registers may be used interchangeably as data registers for bit field (1 to 32 bits), byte (8-bit), word (16-bit), long-word (32-bit), and quadword (64-bit) operations.

When used for byte or word data, only the low-order 8 bits or 16 bits, respectively, of a data register are used (see Figure 6-2). Unlike the INTEL 80386 CPU, which identifies the low-order 8 and 16 bits of its 32-bit general-purpose registers with individual register names to identify register operand sizes, Motorola uses the same register name regardless of the operand size. For the MOTOROLA MC68020 CPU, the register operand size is either explicitly designated as part of the instruction or implicitly defined by the operation performed. This is the same approach taken by the AT&T 32-bit CPU. As with the INTEL 80386 CPU, only the designated bits of the general-purpose registers are affected and any remaining higher-order bits remain unchanged.

General-Purpose Address Registers

The seven 32-bit general-purpose address registers, named A0 through A6, are used to store operand addresses. Both 16-bit and 32-bit addresses can be loaded and manipulated in these address registers. When 16-bit addresses are used, the 16-bits are sign extended to 32 bits before any operation is performed.

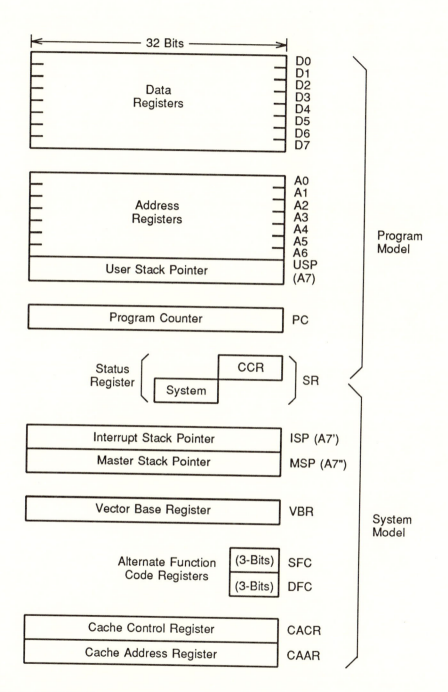

FIGURE 6-1   MOTOROLA MC68020 Microprocessor Register Set

Bit:	31		16	15		8	7		0
D0									
D1									
D2									
D3									
D4									
D5									
D6									
D7									

FIGURE 6-2   MC68020 Microprocessor General-Purpose Data Registers

User Stack Pointer

The user stack pointer, named A7, is a 32-bit address register used for holding the address of the current user stack. As shown in Figure 6-3, the stack pointer points to the current "top of stack" location by containing the address of the last operand pushed on the stack. As with the Intel stack, the Motorola stack "grows downward", expanding into decreasing memory address areas.

Program Counter

The 32-bit program counter (PC) contains the memory address of the currently executing instruction or, on instruction completion, the starting address of the next instruction.

Condition Code Register

The condition code register (CCR) consists of the low-order byte of the the 16-bit system status register (SR). Of this byte, only the low-order five bits are

FIGURE 6-3 MC68020 Stack "Grows Downward" into Memory

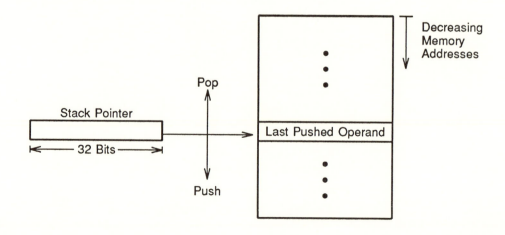

used as flag bits and the remaining three high-order bits are always cleared (0). Figure 6-4 illustrates the condition code register and Table 6-1 lists the function of each flag.

TABLE 6-1 Condition Flag Description

Symbol	Name	Bit	Description
C	Carry Flag	0	Set (1) on a high-order carry or borrow; otherwise cleared (0).
V	Overflow Flag	1	Set (1) if the result of a monitored operation is either too large a positive number or too small a negative number to fit in the destination; otherwise cleared (0).
Z	Zero Flag	2	Set (1) if the result of a monitored operation is zero; otherwise cleared (0).
N	Negative Flag	3	Made equal to the MSB of the result of a monitored operation (0 if positive, 1 if negative).
X	Extend Flag	4	Set by arithmetic operations to the same state as the carry flag.

System Model Registers

The system model register set consists of a status register, an interrupt stack pointer, a master stack pointer, a vector base register, two alternate code function registers, a cache control register, and a cache address register (see Figure 6-1). Except for the status and alternate code function register, all the system registers are 32-bits long.

FIGURE 6-4 Condition Code Register

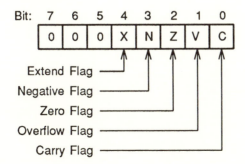

Status Register

The 16-bit status register is shown in Figure 6-5. Bits 0 through 7 of this register constitute the condition code register (CCR) of the program model register set. The remaining bits (8 through 15) are used for system status purposes and consist of three interrupt priority mask bits (I0, I1, and I2), two trace mode bits (T0 and T1), a supervisor/user state bit (S), and a master/interrupt state bit (M).

The two trace bits permit instruction traces according to the assignments listed in Table 6-2.

TABLE 6-2 Tracing Permissions

Bit Settings		
T1	T0	Description
0	0	Tracing disabled
0	1	Trace on change of execution flow
1	0	Trace on each instruction execution
1	1	Reserved for future use

The S bit determines whether the CPU is in supervisor (S = 1) or user (S = 0) mode. In user mode, the user stack pointer (USP) is active and any references to register A7 by the programmer refer to the USP. When the S bit is set, indicating supervisor mode, the M bit is also active and determines the stack pointer register used by the system. For S = 1 and M = 0, a reference to register A7 refers to the interrupt stack pointer (ISP). For S = 1 and M = 1, references to

FIGURE 6-5   The Status Register

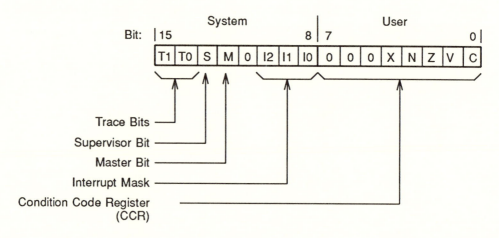

A7 refer to the master stack pointer (MSP).

Master and Interrupt Stack Pointers

Both the master stack pointer (MSP) and the interrupt stack pointer (ISP) registers are 32-bits wide. The MSP points to the top of the current supervisor stack area; the ISP points to the top of the current interrupt stack area. Both registers are active only when the CPU is in supervisor mode (S bit of the status register is 1) and both are referenced as register A7. The selection between the registers is determined by the setting of the status register's M bit as previously described.

Vector Base Register

The vector base register is a 32-bit address register containing the address of the memory exception vector table. Entries in the memory exception table point to individual vector tables.

Alternate Code Function Register

The two 3-bit alternate code function registers permit the supervisor to access multiple address spaces for both source and destination operands. The contents of the source function code (SFC) determine the address space accessed by an instruction for memory source operands. The contents of the destination function code (DFC) determine the address space accessed by the current instruction for memory destinations. Table 6-3 lists the bit encodings used by both of these registers.

TABLE 6-3 Alternate Function Code Assignments

Bit Settings	Selected Address Space
0 0 0	Reserved for future use
0 0 1	User data space
0 1 0	User program space
0 1 1	Reserved for future use
1 0 0	Reserved for future use
1 0 1	Supervisor data space
1 1 0	Supervisor program space
1 1 1	Reserved for future use

Cache Control and Address Registers

The MOTOROLA MC68020 CPU uses an on-chip memory cache for improving processor performance. The cache consists of 64 locations, each of which is 64 bits long. Within each cache location two items — a partial address, and a valid (V) bit flag — are stored. When the cache is enabled and an instruction fetch request is made, the CPU first checks the cache for the instruction before accessing external memory. If there is a match and the cache valid (V) bit is set for the referenced cache entry, this entry is used and no external memory fetch is employed.

The cache is controlled by the CPU's internal control unit and a user has no direct method of either reading or writing individual cache entries. The cache control register (CACR) does provide the user with the means of determining how the cache entries will be used. As illustrated in Figure 6-6, the 32-bit CACR contains four flag bits that can be set or cleared under user control. They are defined as:

Enable (E) Bit: When set (1), the cache is enabled for all instructions. When cleared (0), the cache is disabled and external memory accesses are used for all instruction fetches.

Freeze (F) Bit: When set (1) and the cache is enabled, cache misses are not permitted to replace cache entries whose valid (V) bit is set (1).

Clear Entry (CE) Bit: When set (1), the valid (V) bit for the selected cache entry is cleared (0). The index value for the selected entry (a number from 0 to 63) is contained within the cache address register (CAAR).

Clear (C) Bit: When set (1), the valid (V) bit for all cache entries is cleared (0), which invalidates all entries in the cache. This operation is used by software to clear the cache whenever a task switch occurs.

The cache address register (CAAR) is used only in conjunction with the clear entry (CE) bit of the cache control register. As shown in Figure 6-7, bits 2 through

FIGURE 6-6   Cache Control Register (CACR)

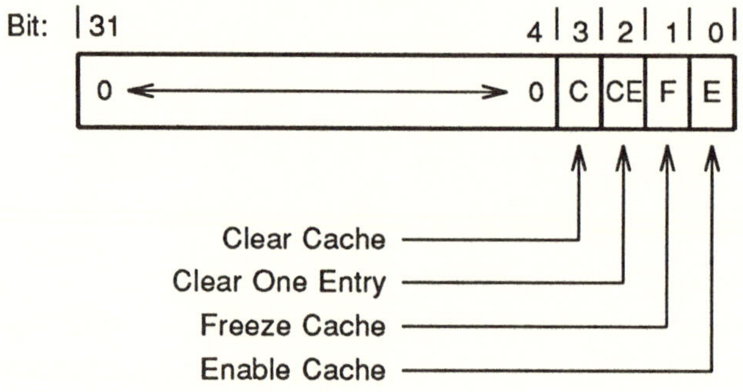

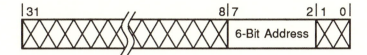

FIGURE 6-7 Cache Address Register (CAAR)

7 of the CAAR contain the address (from 0 to 63) of the cache entry whose V bit is to be cleared. Addresses are loaded into the CAAR using the MOVEC (move control register) instruction described in Section 6.4.

6.2 Data Types

The data types supported by the MOTOROLA MC68020 CPU are byte, word, long word, packed and unpacked binary coded decimal (BCD), individual bits, and bit fields. Floating-point data is provided only when a numeric coprocessor, such as the MOTOROLA MC68881 Floating-Point Coprocessor, is used with the CPU. When addressing data located in memory, the MC68020 CPU associates lower memory addresses with higher-order data bytes.

A byte is an 8-bit quantity that may be stored at any memory address or as the lower 8-bits of any data register. Bits within a byte are numbered from right to left starting with zero, the least significant bit (LSB), and ending with 7, the most significant bit (MSB). This is illustrated in Figure 6-8.

A word is a 16-bit quantity that may be stored at any memory address or as the lower 16-bits of any data register. Figure 6-9 shows the storage of a word in memory as accessed by the MOTOROLA MC68020 CPU. As illustrated, the high-order byte is located at the low-order address, and bits within each byte are numbered from right to left. Although the MC68020 CPU can access words at any byte address, the most efficient data transfers occur for words stored starting at even byte addresses.

A long word is a 32-bit quantity that may be stored at any memory address or in any 32-bit register. Figure 6-10 shows the storage of a long word in memory as accessed by the CPU. As illustrated, higher-order bytes are located at lower-order addresses, and bits within each byte are numbered from right to left. Although the MC68020 CPU can access long words located at any byte starting address, the most efficient data transfers occur for long words stored at addresses that are divisible by four.

Decimal arithmetic is supported by the MOTOROLA MC68020 CPU using binary coded decimal (BCD) data formats and instructions for processing data in these formats. BCD data can be manipulated by the MC68020 CPU in both packed and unpacked formats. In unpacked format each decimal digit is encoded using the   lower   four

FIGURE 6-8   Byte Data Stored in Memory

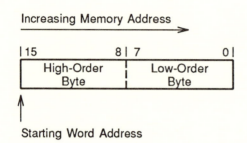

FIGURE 6-9   Word Data Stored in Memory

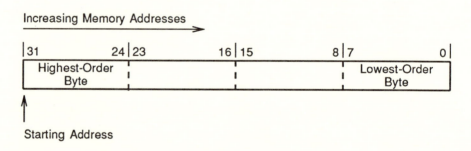

FIGURE 6-10   Long Word Data Stored in Memory

the lower 4 bits of a byte, as illustrated in Figure 6-11. Using this format, for example, the decimal number 682247 would require six bytes of storage. In packed decimal format, shown in Figure 6-12, each byte is used to store two decimal digits. For example, the decimal number 682247 stored in packed BCD format requires three bytes of storage. In both formats the most significant digit (MSD) is associated with the lowest memory address and the least significant digit (LSD) with the highest memory address.

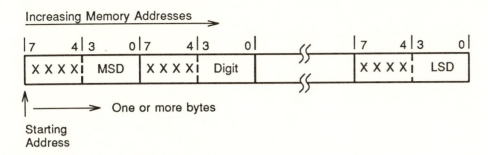

FIGURE 6-11 Unpacked BCD Data Stored in Memory

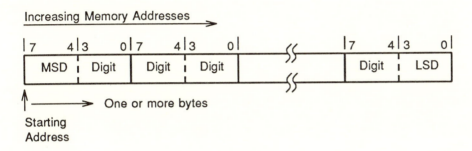

FIGURE 6-12 Packed BCD Data Stored in Memory

The last two data types supported by the MOTOROLA MC68020 CPU are bit fields and individual bits. As illustrated in Figure 6-13, individual bits in memory are located by specifying a byte address and a bit number within the addressed byte. The bit number corresponds to the conventional bit numbering system employed by Motorola: the LSB of the byte is bit 0 and the MSB is bit 7.

A bit field is a sequence of 1 to 32 bits that is specified by a byte starting address, an offset, and a width. The offset can be any value between -2^{31} and 2^{31}

FIGURE 6-13 Bit Datum in Memory

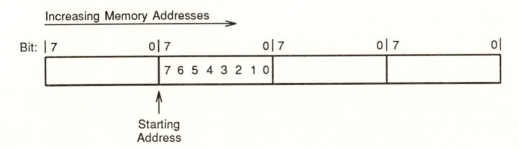

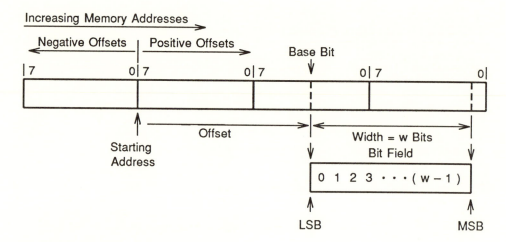

FIGURE 6-14 Specification of a Bit Field

and identifies the leftmost (base) bit of the bit field. This bit becomes the LSB of the selected field. The width, a number between 1 and 32, specifies the size of the field (see Figure 6-14). As shown in Figure 6-14, a field specified with a width of w has bits numbered within the field from 0 to w–1.

6.3 Addressing Modes

The MOTOROLA MC68020 CPU uses straightforward addressing modes in which an operand or its address is contained within either an instruction or a general-purpose register. Specifically, seven basic addressing mode types are defined for the MC68020 CPU. These are:
- Absolute Addressing
- Immediate Addressing
- Register Direct Addressing
- Register Indirect Addressing
- Indexed Register Indirect Addressing
- Memory Indirect Addressing
- Program Counter Relative Addressing

Within each of these seven major address mode categories, the individual variations listed in Table 6-4 can be constructed. The operand address determined using one of the valid addressing modes is referred to as an *effective address*.

TABLE 6-4 Addressing Mode Variations

Addressing Mode	Variation
Absolute	Short address (16 bits) Long address (32 bits)
Immediate	None
Register direct	Data register direct Address register direct
Register indirect	Address register indirect Address register indirect with postincrement Address register indirect with predecrement Address register indirect with displacement
Indexed register indirect	Address register indirect with index and an optional 8-bit, 16-bit, or 32-bit immediate displacement
Memory indirect	Memory indirect postindexed Memory indirect preindexed
Program counter relative	Program counter indirect with displacement Program counter indirect with index and an optional 8-bit, 16-bit, or 32-bit immediate displacement Program counter memory indirect postindexed Program counter memory indirect preindexed

Absolute Addressing Mode

In absolute addressing mode, an operand's address is included directly within the instruction. This mode is indicated in assembly language by listing the address within parentheses. Any address or value prefixed by a dollar sign ($) designates a hexadecimal number. For example, the instruction

NEG ($AB271562)

uses absolute addressing to identify the data starting at hexadecimal address AB271562 as the desired operand for the negate instruction (the negate instruction causes its operand to be subtracted from zero).

The size of an operand, regardless of the addressing mode, is assumed to be 32 bits unless an optional size modifier is specified. Size modifiers are designated by appending a period, followed by either a B for byte, W for word, or L for long word (32 bits) to the mnemonic contained within the instruction. For example, the instruction

NEG.B ($AB27FE42)

negates the byte located at hexadecimal address AB27FE42 and the instruction

NEG.W ($AB27FE42)

negates the word starting at the same address. The size modifier L is the default value assumed by the MC68020 CPU and may be omitted for 32-bit data.

Immediate Addressing Mode

In immediate addressing mode, the operand, as opposed to the operand's address, is contained within the instruction. This mode is indicated by including a pound sign (#) in front of the immediate data. For example, the instruction

MOV.W #$FEAB,($CD16E423)

uses both the absolute and immediate addressing modes. The mnemonic MOV denotes the move instruction, which causes the contents of a source operand to be copied into a destination operand. In Motorola assembly language, the source operand is always the first operand and the destination is the second operand listed. Thus, the above move instruction causes the immediate hexadecimal data FEAB, the source operand, to be moved into the 16 bits of memory starting at hexadecimal address CD16E423. As before, the size modifier W designates that the operands are considered as word data.

Register Direct Addressing Mode

In register direct addressing, the operand is the contents of either a data or address register (see Figure 6-15).

This mode is indicated in assembly language by listing the register name containing the operand directly in the instruction. For example, the instruction

NEG.L D0   or   NEG D0

uses the register direct addressing mode to identify the 32-bit (long word) contents of register D0 as the operand for the negate instruction. In the absence of a size modifier, the default value L is assumed by the processor. Similarly, the instruction

NEG.B D0

FIGURE 6-15   A Register Direct Operand

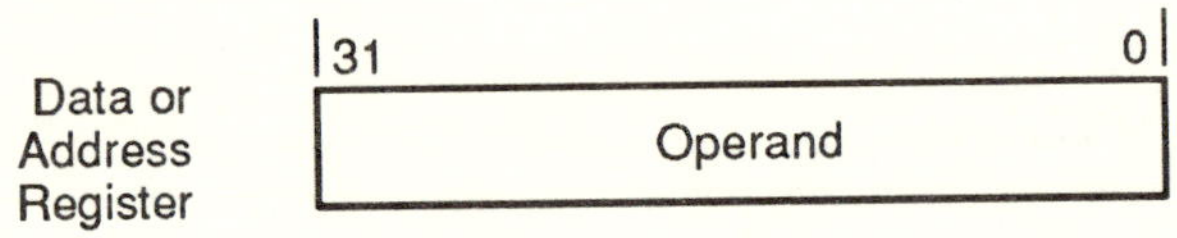

uses the lowest byte of register D0 as its operand, and the instruction

NEG.W D0

uses the low-order word of register D0 as its operand.

Register Indirect Addressing Mode

In register indirect addressing mode, the address of the operand is contained within an address register (A0 through A7). The desired operand is located by first going to the address register for the address, and then using this address to locate the operand (see Figure 6-16). As illustrated, the address register used in this mode is also referred to as a *pointer* register, because its contents, an address, are used to "point to" the desired operand.

The register indirect addressing mode is indicated by enclosing the register name containing the operand within parentheses. For example, the instruction

NEG.L (A5)

uses indirect register addressing to locate the operand for the negate instruction. In this single operand instruction, register A5 is identified as a pointer register, the contents of which is the address of the final operand. Upon completion of this instruction, the contents of the long word (32 bits) whose address is contained in register A5 is changed to its negated value. Similarly, the instruction

NEG.B (A5)

negates the byte pointed to by the 32-bit address in register A5, and the instruction

NEG.W (A5)

negates the word pointed to by the 32-bit address in register A5.

Register Indirect Variations

Motorola provides the capability within register indirect mode to postincrement, predecrement, and add a displacement value to the address contained within the address register. Descriptions of these variations to the basic register indirect mode follow.

FIGURE 6-16   Register Indirect Addressing

A Pointer Register (A0–A7) | Operand's Address > → Operand (in Memory)

Register Indirect Mode with Postincrement

In register indirect mode the address in the pointer register is automatically incremented by the byte size of the operand after the operand is accessed. This mode is indicated by including the *postfix operator* (+) after the designation of the pointer register. For example, the assembly language instruction

NEG.W (A5)+

causes both the word operand, whose address is located in address register A5, to be negated and then the address in A5 to be incremented by two (the byte size of a word). Similarly, the instruction

NEG.L (A5)+

causes the address in register A5 to be incremented by four, which is the byte size of a long word, and the instruction

NEG.B (A5)+

causes the address in register A5 to be incremented by 1. In each case, the address has been incremented correctly for the data type referenced.

This automatic incrementing of addresses is extremely useful when cycling through an array of elements, starting from the first element, because it permits the current element to be accessed using a pointer register while correctly adjusting the address in the register to point to the next element in the array.

Register Indirect Mode with Predecrement

In register indirect mode with predecrement, the address in the pointer register is automatically decremented by the byte size of the operand before its address is used to locate the desired operand. This mode is indicated by including the prefix operator (–) before the designation of the pointer register. For example, the assembly language instruction

NEG.L –(A5)

causes the address in register A5 to be decremented by the byte size of a long word (four) before the address is used to locate the 32-bit operand to be negated. The automatic decrementing of addresses is extremely useful when cycling through an array of elements in reverse order.

Register Indirect Mode with Displacement

In register indirect mode with displacement, the address of the operand is the sum of the address in the address register and a 16-bit integer displacement value (see Figure 6-17). This mode is indicated in assembly language by including

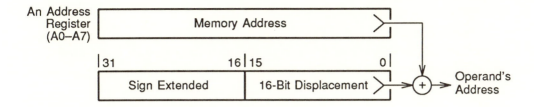

FIGURE 6-17   Register Indirect With Displacement

the displacement value within the parentheses enclosing the address register name, separating the two items with a comma. For example, the instruction

NEG.W ($1625,A5)

adds the 16-bit hexadecimal number 1625 to the address in register A5, and uses this address to locate a word operand. As shown in Figure 6-17, the 16-bit displacement value is automatically sign-extended to 32 bits before it is added to the address in the designated address register.

Indexed Register Indirect Addressing Mode

In indexed register indirect addressing mode, the address of the operand is determined as the sum of an address in an address register and a value in an index register. Any data or address register can be used as an index register. Additionally, an optional displacement value can be added to the sum of the addresses in the address and index registers. This displacement value can be either an 8-bit, 16-bit, or 32-bit immediate value. Figure 6-18 illustrates the components used to obtain the final operand address.

As shown in Figure 6-18, the value in the index register can be multiplied by 1, 2, 4, or 8 before it is added into the address calculation. This permits the index value to represent an offset in either bytes, words, long words, or quad words.

Register indirect addressing mode is indicated in assembly language by enclosing the displacement, address register, and scaled index register, in that order, within parentheses. For example, the instruction

NEG ($AFCE1950, A0, A3)

designates the immediate hexadecimal value AFCE1950 as a displacement, the A0 register as the primary address register, and the A3 register as the index register. To scale the value in the index register, the register name is followed by an asterisk (*) and the scale factor. For example, the instruction

NEG ($AFCE1950, A3, A6*2)

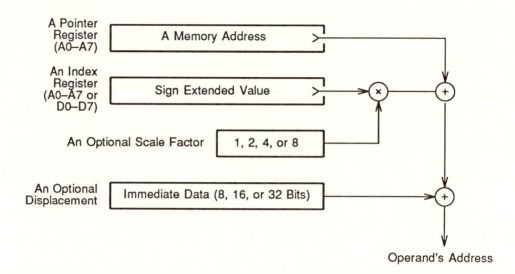

FIGURE 6-18   Indexed Register Indirect Addressing with Optional Offset

uses the A6 register as an index register and multiplies the value in the register by two before using it with the contents of the primary address register, A3, and the immediate displacement to compute the operand's address. All 8-bit and 16-bit displacement values are automatically sign-extended to 32 bits prior to their use in the final address determination.

The size of the index register value is assumed to be 32 bits unless an optional word size (W or L only) is appended to the index register name (index register values may only be 16 bits or 32 bits; 8-bit index registers are not allowed). For example, the instruction

NEG ($AFCE, A5, A2.W*2)

specifies register A5 as the primary address register and A2 as the index register. The W appended to the index register name further specifies that its low-order 16 bits are to be used. These bits are automatically sign extended to 32 bits prior to being multiplied by the indicated scale factor of 2.

Memory Indirect Addressing Mode

In postindexed memory indirect addressing, the contents of an address register and an optional sign-extended 16-bit or 32-bit displacement value are added to form an initial address. The contents of this initial address are themselves an address to which an additional sign extended 16-bit or 32-bit displacement and scaled index value may be added to yield the address of the desired operand (see Figure 6-19).

Notice the addressing used in this mode is essentially a double indirect address mode. In assembly language notation, the initial displacement and primary address register must be separated by a comma and enclosed within brackets. The bracketed displacement/address pair is then included within parentheses with an index register and a further immediate 16-bit or 32-bit displacement value. For example, the instruction

MOV.B ([$AE16,A5],A2.W*2,$19AC),D0

uses the memory indirect mode to locate the source operand for the move instruction. In this case an initial pointer address is obtained as the sum of the contents of registers A5 and the sign-extended displacement AE16. The contents of this address are then added to the sign-extended value of the low order word in register A2 (scaled by 2) plus the sign-extended value of the immediate hexadecimal value 19AC. Due to the byte modifier (B) appended to the MOV mnemonic, only a single byte is accessed from the calculated address. This byte is then copied into the lowest byte of the destination, register D0.

Another memory indirect mode called preindexed allows the scaled index value to be used in the first address calculation illustrated in Figure 6-19 rather than in the second address calculation. This variation is obtained by including the index register within the brackets used to define the "inner" displacement

FIGURE 6-19 Memory Indirect Addressing (Postindexed)

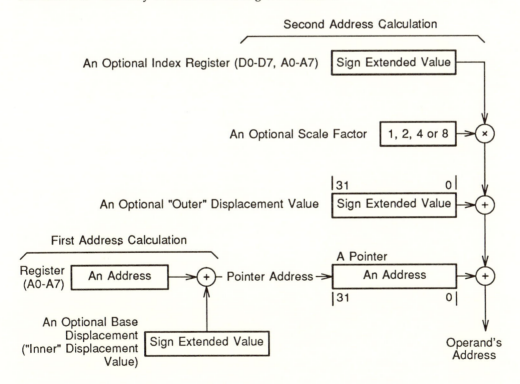

and primary address registers. For example, the source operand in the instruction

MOV.B ([$AE16,A5,A2.W*2],$19AC),D0

is located by first adding the contents of register A5 and the sign-extended immediate displacement value AE16 with the scaled and sign-extended value in the index register A2. The result of this calculation is the address of a pointer. The address in this pointer is then added to the optional sign extended "outer" displacement to yield the address of the desired operand. This address, as before, is used to access a byte of data, which is then moved into the lowest order byte of register D0.

Program Counter Relative Addressing Modes

The program counter relative addressing modes are one-to-one counterparts to other register and memory indirect modes with the program counter register replacing the address registers normally associated with these modes. For example, the instruction

NEG.W ($AE25,PC)

can be used to negate the word located AE25 bytes beyond the address contained within the program counter. Table 6-5 lists the available program counter relative modes and their counterparts within the addressing modes previously presented.

TABLE 6-5 Correspondence Between PC-Relative Addressing Modes and Addressing Modes Using General-Purpose Address Registers

Program Counter Relative Mode	Counterpart
PC Indirect with optional 16-bit displacement	Address Register Indirect with optional 16-bit displacement
Index PC Indirect with optional 8-bit, 16-bit, or 32-bit displacement	Index Register Indirect with optional 8-bit, 16-bit, or 32-bit displacement
Postindexed PC Memory Indirect	Postindexed Memory Indirect
Preindexed PC Memory Indirect	Preindexed Memory Indirect

The advantage of using the program counter within the addressing modes listed in Table 6-5 is that it allows operands to be addressed directly within the code space of a program, relative to the PC, rather than addressed within a separate data space typically associated with the general-purpose address registers. This is especially useful for encoding smaller programs where all data and code can be contained within a single memory segment because it eliminates the requirement for an additional address register to point to the data area.

6.4 Instruction Set

This section presents the complete set of MOTOROLA MC68020 CPU instructions. The MC68020 instruction set consists of six basic functional groups: data transfer, arithmetic, logical, bit management, program and system control, and multiprocessor instructions. A description of each instruction and a list of mnemonics are presented.

In their most general form, MC68020 instructions can manipulate, at most, two operands. Such instructions consist of a mnemonic followed by two operands, where the first operand is the source operand and the second operand is the destination operand. Unlike the INTEL 80386 CPU, both operands may be memory resident. The MC68020 instruction set is also highly orthogonal, which means that the majority of instructions can use any addressing mode to designate an operand.

Notation

Describing the MC68020 instruction set requires a consistent set of notations to indicate the addressing modes and registers that can be used by each instruction. Table 6-6 lists the notation used by Motorola for defining general

TABLE 6-6 MC68020 CPU General Operand Notation

Symbol	Meaning
An	An address register (A0-A7)
d	A displacement value
Dn	A data register (D0-D7)
dst	Destination operand
d8	An 8-bit displacement value
d16	A 16-bit displacement value
d32	A 32-bit displacement value
<ea>	An effective operand address determined using a valid addressing mode
imm	Immediate integer data
list	A list of registers, e.g., A1-A4
Rn	A data or address register
src	Source operand
#<data>	Immediate integer data

operands that can be used by an instruction. Table 6-7 lists the symbols used to designate specific registers. The notations contained in Tables 6-6 and 6-7 are sufficient for describing the majority of instructions. However, additional notation will be introduced as required for specialized instructions.

TABLE 6-7 Specific MC68020 CPU Register Notation

Symbol	Meaning
CCR	Condition code register
DFC	The destination function code register
Rc	Any control register (CAAR, CACR DFC, ISP, MSP, USP, SFC, VBR)
SFC	The source function code register
SP	The active stack pointer
SSP	The supervisor stack pointer
USP	The user stack pointer

Data Transfer Instructions

The data transfer instructions permit transferring data between the CPU registers internal to the MC68020 chip, between registers and memory, and directly between memory locations. Most of these instructions have three types indicated by appending a period and either the letters B, W, or L to the mnemonic: a B refers to a byte (8-bit) operand, a W to a word (16-bit) operand, and an L to a long-word (32-bit) operand. For example, the mnemonic

MOVE.B

is an instruction to move a byte of data while the mnemonic

MOVE.W

is an instruction to move a word of data. A default data size of 32 bits is assumed by the processor in the absence of a size modifier.

Table 6-8 lists all the instructions within the data transfer group. Included are the operand syntax, operand size, and a brief description of the operation performed.

Arithmetic Instructions

The MC68020 arithmetic instructions consist of both integer arithmetic operations and binary-coded decimal operations. Table 6-9 lists the integer arithmetic instructions, which consist essentially of addition, subtraction, multiplication, division, comparison, and negation instructions. These

TABLE 6-8 Data Transfer Instruction Group

Instruction	Mnemonic	Operand Syntax	Operand Size	Description
Exchange registers	EXG	Rn,Rn	32	Rn ⟷ Rn
Load effective address	LEA	<ea>,An	32	<ea> → An
Link and allocate	LINK	An,#<d>	16,32	SP – 4 → SP; An → (SP); SP → An; SP + d → SP
Move data	MOVE	<ea>,<ea>	16,32	<ea> → <ea>
Move address	MOVEA	<ea>,An	16,32 →32	<ea>→ An
Move multiple registers	MOVEM	list,<ea> <ea>,list	16,32 16,32 →32	list of registers → dst src→ list of registers
Move peripheral data	MOVEP	Dn,(d16,An) (d16,An),Dn	16,32 16,32	src → dst src → dst
Move quick	MOVEQ	#<data>,Dn	8 → 32	imm → Dn
Push effective address	PEA	<ea>	32	SP-4 → SP; <ea> → (SP)
Unlink	UNLK	An	32	An → SP; (SP) → An; SP+4 → SP

instructions perform arithmetic operations on data in both registers and memory locations and may be used with byte, word, and long word data by appending a B, W, or L size modifier, respectively, to the operation's mnemonic. A data size of 32 bits is assumed in the absence of a size modifier.

Additional notation is required for division operations to specify the dividend, quotient, and remainder registers. For multiplication operations, additional notation is needed to specify the high and low order 32 bits of the product. The notation used is:

• Dq - designates a data register used as the destination for the quotient of a division and is the source for the lower order 32 bits of the dividend.

• Dr - designates a data register used as the destination for the remainder of a division and is the source of the high-order 32 bits of the dividend. If Dr is the same as Dq, no remainder is returned and the register contains the quotient only.

• Dh - designates a data register used as the destination for the high order 32 bits of a multiplication result.

• Dl - designates a data register used as the destination for the low order 32 bits of a multiplication result.

TABLE 6-9 Integer Arithmetic Operations

Instruction	Mnemonic	Operand Syntax	Operand Size	Description
Add	ADD	Dn,<ea> <ea>,Dn	8,16,32 8,16,32	src + dst → dst
Add address	ADDA	<ea>,An	16,32	src + dst → dst
Add immediate	ADDI	#<data>,<ea>	8,16,32	imm + dst → dst
Add quick	ADDQ	#<data>,<ea>	8,16,32	imm + dst → dst
Add extended	ADDX	Dn,Dn –(An),–(An)	8,16,32 8,16,32	src + dst + X flag → dst
Clear an operand	CLR	<ea>	8,16,32	0 → dst
Compare	CMP	<ea>,Dn	8,16,32	dst – src
Compare address	CMPA	<ea>,An	16,32	dst – src
Compare immediate	CMPI	#<data>,<ea>	8,16,32	dst – imm
Compare memory	CMPM	(An)+,(An)+	8,16,32	dst – src
Compare registers	CMP2	<ea>,Rn	8,16,32	Compare Rn to an upper and lower bound
Signed divide	DIVS.W	<ea>,Dr:Dq	32/16 → 16:16	dst/src→ dst (unsigned)
	DIVS.L	<ea>,Dr:Dq	64/32 → 32:32	
	DIVSL.L	<ea>,Dr:Dq	32/32 → 32:32	
	DIVS.L	<ea>,Dq	32/32 → 32	
Unsigned divide	DIVU	Same as DIVS	Same as DIVS	dst/src → dst (signed)
	DIVUL.L	Same as DIVSL.L	Same as DIVSL.L	
Sign extend	EXT.W EXT.L EXTB.L	Dn Dn Dn	8 → 16 16 → 32 8 → 32	extend sign

TABLE 6-9 Integer Arithmetic Operations (Continued)

Instruction	Mnemonic	Operand Syntax	Operand Size	Description
Signed multiply	MULS.W	<ea>, Dn	16*16 → 32	src*dst→ dst (signed)
	MULS.L	<ea>,Dl	32*32 → 32	
	MULS.L	<ea>,Dh:Dl	32*32 → 64	
Unsigned multiply	MULU	Same as MULS	Same as MULS	src*dst→ dst (unsigned)
Negate	NEG	<ea>	8,16,32	0 – dst → dst
Negate with carry	NEGX	<ea>	8,16,32	0 – dst – X flag → dst
Subtract binary	SUB	<ea>,Dn Dn,<ea>	8,16,32 8,16,32	dst – src → dst
Subtract address	SUBA	<ea>,An	16,32	dst – src → dst
Subtract immediate	SUBI	#<data>,<ea>	8,16,32	dst – imm → dst
Subtract quick	SUBQ	#<data>,<ea>	8,16,32	dst – imm → dst (3-bit)
Subtract with extend	SUBX	Dn,Dn	8,16,32	dst – src – X flag → dst

Binary Coded Decimal Instructions

In addition to the integer arithmetic instructions listed in Table 6-9, binary coded decimal (BCD) addition, subtraction, and negation operations are available with the MC68020 CPU. Also provided are a PACK instruction, which converts ASCII and EBCDIC numeric data into BCD, and an UNPACK instruction for performing the opposite conversion. Table 6-10 lists the available BCD operations.

Logical, Shift, and Rotate Instructions

The logical AND, OR, EOR, and NOT instructions permit bit-by-bit logical operations on 8-bit, 16-bit, and 32-bit operands. The AND, OR, and EOR instructions also have immediate forms for use with immediate data. Right and left shift instructions are also provided, in both signed (arithmetic) and unsigned (logical) forms. Rotate instructions, with and without carry, are also included in the instruction set. The shift and rotate instructions can be applied to 8-bit, 16-bit, and 32-bit register operands and include a shift count from 1 to 8. When applied to memory operands, these instructions operate on word data and only permit single-bit shifts and rotates. See Table 6-11 for a summary of the logical, shift, and rotate instructions.

TABLE 6-10 Binary Coded Decimal Arithmetic Operations

Instruction	Mnemonic	Operand Syntax	Operand Size	Desciption
Add BCD	ABCD	Dn,Dn –(An),–(An)	8 8	Add as BCD numbers using the extend bit
Negate BCD	NBCD	<ea>	8	Negate with extend
Pack	PACK	Dn,Dn,#<data> –(An), –(An),#<data>	16→8	Unpacked BCD +imm → packed BCD
Subtract BCD	SBCD	Dn,Dn –(An),–(An)	8 8	Subtract as BCD numbers using the extend bit
Unpack	UNPK	Dn,Dn,#<data> –(An), –(An),#<data>	8→16	Packed BCD + imm→ unpacked BCD

TABLE 6-11 Logical, Shift, and Rotate Operations

Instruction	Mnemonic	Operand Syntax	Operand Size	Description
AND logical	AND	<ea>,Dn Dn,<ea>	8,16,32 8,16,32	dst AND src → dst
AND immediate	ANDI	#<data>,<ea>	8,16,32	dst AND imm→ dst
Exclusive OR	EOR	Dn,<ea>	8,16,32	dst EOR src → dst
Exclusive OR immediate	EORI	#<data>,<ea>	8,16,32	dst EOR imm→ dst
Complement	NOT	<ea>	8,16,32	NOT dst → dst
Inclusive OR	OR	<ea>,Dn Dn,<ea>	8,16,32 8,16,32	dst OR src → dst
Inclusive OR immediate	ORI	#<data>,<ea>	8,16,32	dst OR imm→ dst
Test Operand	TST	<ea>	8,16,32	dst – 0
Arithmetic shift left	ASL	Dn,Dn #<data>,Dn <ea>	8,16,32 8,16,32 16	– – –
Arithmetic shift right	ASR	Dn,Dn #<data>,Dn <ea>	8,16,32 8,16,32 16	– – –

TABLE 6-11 Logical, Shift, and Rotate Operations (Continued)

Instruction	Mnemonic	Operand Syntax	Operand Size	Decription
Logical shift left	LSL	Dn,Dn	8,16,32	–
		#<data>,Dn	8,16,32	–
		<ea>	16	–
Logical shift right	LSR	Dn,Dn	8,16,32	–
		#<data>,Dn	8,16,32	–
		<ea>	16	–
Rotate left	ROL	Dn,Dn	8,16,32	–
		#<data>,Dn	8,16,32	–
		<ea>	16	–
Rotate left with carry	ROXL	Dn,Dn	8,16,32	–
		#<data>,Dn	8,16,32	–
		<ea>	16	–
Rotate right	ROR	Dn,Dn	8,16,32	–
		#<data>,Dn	8,16,32	–
		<ea>	16	–
Rotate right with carry	ROXR	Dn,Dn	8,16,32	–
		#<data>,Dn	8,16,32	–
		<ea>	16	–
Swap register words	SWAP	Dn	32	$Dn(31{:}16) \longleftrightarrow Dn(15{:}0)$

Bit Management Instructions

The bit management instructions consist of two individual groups: bit manipulation and bit field operations. The bit manipulation operations allow the programmer to test, set, clear, and change individual bits in either register or memory locations. Register and memory operands can only be 32 and 8 bits, respectively. The operand's bit number can be specified as either immediate data or as the contents of a data register. Table 6-12 lists the four bit manipulation instructions.

The bit field instructions allow the insertion, extraction, and testing of variable length bit fields of up to 32 bits. The starting bit position and field width are specified by including these items, within braces, after the effective address of the operand containing the desired field. Table 6-13 lists the bit field operations supported. Before performing the indicated operations, all of these instructions copy the bit field's MSB to the condition code register's N flag and set the CCR's Z flag to the complement of the bit-by-bit inclusive OR of the field's bits.

Program and System Control Instructions

The MC68020 control instructions consist of individual program and system control groups. The program control group consists of conditional,

TABLE 6-12 Bit Manipulation Operations

Instruction	Mnemonic	Operand Syntax	Description
Bit test and change	BCHG	Dn,<ea> #<data>,<ea>	$\bar{b} \rightarrow b, Z$
Bit test and clear	BCLR	Dn,<ea> #<data>,<ea>	$\bar{b} \rightarrow Z,$ $0 \rightarrow b$
Bit test and set	BSET	Dn,<ea> #<data>,<ea>	$\bar{b} \rightarrow Z,$ $1 \rightarrow b$
Bit test	BTST	Dn,<ea> #<data>,<ea>	$\bar{b} \rightarrow Z$

TABLE 6-13 Bit Field Operation

Instruction	Mnemonic	Operand Syntax	Description
Bit field change	BFCHG	<ea>{offset;width}	Complement all bits in the field
Bit field clear	BFCLR	<ea>{offset;width}	Clear all bits in the field
Bit field extract signed	BFEXTS	<ea>{offset;width},Dn	Bit field $\rightarrow$ Dn sign extended
Bit field extract unsigned	BFEXTU	<ea>{offset;width},Dn	Bit field $\rightarrow$ Dn zero extended
Bit field find first one	BFFFO	<ea>{offset;width},Dn	Position of first 1 in field $\rightarrow$ Dn
Bit field insert	BFINS	Dn,<ea>{offset;width}	Dn $\rightarrow$ bit field
Bit field set	BFSET	<ea>{offset;width}	Set all bits in the field
Bit field test	BFTST	<ea>{offset;width}	MSB $\rightarrow$ N flag if (all field bits =0) 1$\rightarrow$Z flag else 0$\rightarrow$Z flag

unconditional, and return instructions as listed in Tables 6-15a, 6-15b, and 6-15c, respectively. These instructions alter the normal sequence of instruction execution, but generally do not alter the flag bits in the condition register. The "cc" notation used in Table 6-15a refers to the valid conditions given in Table 6-14 and must be replaced by one of the conditional mnemonics listed.

TABLE 6-14 Valid Conditional Tests

Conditional Mnemonic (cc)	Meaning
CC	Carry flag is clear
CS	Carry flag is set
EQ	Equal to
F	Always false
GE	Greater than or equal to (as signed operands)
GT	Greater than (as signed operands)
LE	Less than or equal to (as signed operands)
LS	Lower or the same as (unsigned operands)
LT	Less than (as signed operands)
MI	Minus (operand is negative)
NE	Not equal to
OC	Overflow flag is clear
OS	Overflow flag is set
PL	Plus (operand is positive or zero)
T	Always true

TABLE 6-15a Conditional Program Control Operations

Instruction	Mnemonic	Operand Syntax	Operand Size	Description
Branch on condition	Bcc	<label>	8,16,32	If (cc) then PC + d → PC
Decrement and branch	DBcc	Dn,<label>	16	If (NOT(cc)) then Dn − 1 → Dn; If Dn <> −1 PC + d → PC
Set on condition	Scc	<ea>	8	If (cc) then 1s → dst, else 0s → dst

TABLE 6-15b Unconditional Program Control Operations

Instruction	Mnemonic	Operand Syntax	Operand Size	Description
Branch always	BRA	\<label\>	8,16,32	PC + d → PC
Branch to subroutine	BSR	\<label\>	8,16,32	SP − 4 → SP PC → (SP) PC + d → PC
Call module	CALLM	#\<data\>,\<ea\>	None	Save module state on stack; load new state from dst
Jump	JMP	\<ea\>	None	dst → PC
Jump to subroutine	JSR	\<ea\>	None	SP − 4 → SP PC → (SP) dst → PC
No operation	NOP	None	None	–

TABLE 6-15c Return Program Control Operations

Instruction	Mnemonic	Operand Syntax	Operand Size	Description
Return & de-allocate parameters	RTD	#\<d\>	16	(SP) → PC SP + 4 + d → PC
Return from module	RTM	Rn	None	Reload module state from stack; load Rn with data area pointer
Return and restore condition code	RTR	None	None	(SP) → CCR SP + 2 → SP (SP) → PC SP + 4 → SP
Return from subroutine	RTS	None	None	(SP) → PC SP + 4 → SP

The system control instructions are presented in Tables 6-16a, 6-16b, and 6-16c. These instructions consist of privileged, trap generating, and condition code register operations, respectively.

TABLE 6-16a Privileged System Control Operations

Instruction	Mnemonic	Operand Syntax	Operand Size	Description
AND immediate with status register	ANDI	#<data>,SR	16	imm AND SR → SR
Exclusive OR immediate with status register	EORI	#<data>,SR	16	imm EOR SR → SR
Move status register	MOVE	<ea>,SR SR,<ea>	16 16	src → SR SR → dst
Move user stack pointer	MOVE	USP,An An,USP	32 32	USP → An An → USP
Move control register	MOVEC	Rc,Rn Rn,Rc	32 32	Rc → Rn Rn → Rc
Move address space	MOVES	Rn,<ea> <ea>,Rn	8,16,32 8,16,32	Rn → dst src → dst
OR immediate with status register	ORI	#<data>,SR	16	imm OR SR → SR
Reset external devices	RESET	None	None	assert $\overline{\text{RESET}}$ line
Return from exception	RTE	None	None	(SP) → SR SP + 2 → SP (SP) → PC SP + 4 → SP
Load status register and stop	STOP	#<data>	16	imm → SR and then stop

TABLE 6-16b Trap Generating System Control Operations

Instruction	Mnemonic	Operand Syntax	Operand Size	Description
Breakpoint	BKPT	#vector	None	If $\overline{\text{DSACK}}$ is asserted, execute returned instruction, else trap is an illegal instruction
Check data register	CHK	<ea>,Dn	16,32	If Dn < 0 or Dn > (ea) Trap to vector 6
Check register	CHK2	<ea>,Rn	8,16,32	Compare Rn to upper and lower bound located at <ea>

TABLE 6-16b Trap Generating System Control Operations (Continued)

Instruction	Mnemonic	Operand Syntax	Operand Size	Description
Take illegal instr. trap	ILLEGAL	None	None	Trap to vector 4
Trap	TRAP	#vector	None	Trap to vector
Trap on condition	TRAPcc	None	None	If (cc) then trap to vector 7
		#vector	16,32	If (cc) then trap to vector
Trap on overflow	TRAPV	None	None	If (V=1) trap to overflow exception

TABLE 6-16c Condition Code Register Control Operations

Instruction	Mnemonic	Operand Syntax	Operand Size	Description
AND immediate with CCR	ANDI	#<data>,CCR	8	imm AND CCR → CCR
Exclusive OR immediate with CCR	EORI	#<data>,CCR	8	imm EOR CCR → CCR
Move CCR	MOVE	<ea>,CCR	16	src → CCR
		CCR,<ea>	16	CCR → dst
OR immediate with CCR	ORI	#<data>,CCR	8	imm OR CCR → CCR

Coprocessor Instructions

The MC68020 coprocessor instructions consist of four types: a general instruction (cpGEN), conditional instructions (cpBcc, cpDBcc, cpScc, cpTRAPcc), a coprocessor context save instruction (cpSAVE), and a coprocessor context restore instruction (cpRESTORE). The general instruction is used to implement any general-purpose instruction defined for a coprocessor and always consists of at least two words. The first word is used to identify the coprocessor; the second word is the coprocessor's command word.

The conditional coprocessor instructions permit program control based on conditions evaluated by the coprocessor. Coprocessor context save and restore instructions are privileged instructions that may only be operated in privileged mode. In multitasking environments, these instructions permit the saving and restoring of the coprocessor's context while it is executing either a general or conditional instruction. Table 6-17a lists the specific coprocessor operations supported by the MC68020 CPU.

TABLE 6-17a Coprocessor Control Operations

Instruction	Mnemonic	Operand Syntax	Operand Size	Description
Branch on coprocessor condition	cpBcc	<label>	16,32	If (cpcc) then PC + d → PC
Decrement & branch on coprocessor condition	cpDBcc	<label>	16	if (NOTcpcc) then Dn – 1 → Dn, then if Dn <> –1 PC + d → PC
Coprocessor general function	cpGEN	User Defined	User Defined	operand → coprocessor
Coprocessor restore	cpRESTORE	<ea>	None	restore coprocessor state from <ea>
Coprocessor save	cpSAVE	<ea>	None	save coprocessor state to <ea>
Set on coprocessor condition	cpScc	<ea>	8	if (cpcc) then 1s → dst; else 0s→ dst
Trap on coprocessor	cpTRAPcc	None #<data>	None 16,32	if (cpcc) then trap to vector 6

In addition to coprocessor instructions, three MC68020 instructions provide read-modify-write of bus cycles with any general-purpose processor. These are in Table 6-17b.

TABLE 6-17b Read-Modify-Write Multiprocessor Operations

Instruction	Mnemonic	Operand Syntax	Operand Size	Description
Compare and swap operand	CAS	Dn1,Dn2,<ea>	8,16,32	dst – Dn1 if Z flag =1 Dn2 → dst; else dst→ Dn1
	CAS2	Dn1:Dn2, Dn3:Dn4, (Rn1):(Rn2)	16,32	dual operand CAS
Test and Set Operand	TAS	<ea>	8	dst – 0 1 → dst bit 7

6.5 Instruction Encoding

Each MOTOROLA MC68020 Microprocessor instruction contains sufficient information to identify both the operation to be performed and the location of any required operands. Instructions may be stored in memory at any byte address and consist of at least one 16-bit word and at most eleven words (see Figure 6-20).

The first word of the instruction is called the operation word and designates the length of the instruction, the operation code (opcode), and addressing information needed to locate required operands. The remaining words are used, when needed, to specify additional source and destination operand information. Within the general instruction format illustrated in Figure 6-20, Motorola identifies three individual instruction encoding formats:

Single Effective Address Format: This format encodes an instruction within a single operation word. All single operand instructions and the majority of double operand instructions in which both operands or their addresses reside in registers, can be encoded using a single word format. Exact bit assignments within the operation word are instruction dependent.

Brief Extension Word: This format is used to encode an operand's addressing information using a single extension word. This extension word is in addition to the operation word required for all instructions. In single and double operand instructions either none, one, or both operands may be encoded individually in a brief extension word format.

Full Extension Words(s): This format uses up to five extension words to encode an operand's addressing information. These extension words are in addition to the operation word required for all instructions. In single and double operand instructions either none, one, or both operands may individually be encoded using a full extension word format.

Single Effective Address Instruction Format

Figure 6-21 illustrates the encoding format of a single effective address instruction format. This format is used for the majority of all single and

FIGURE 6-20   Instruction Format

Primary Operation Word	Brief Extension Word*	Full Source Extension	Full Destination Extension
Opcode and Address Mode	Index and 8-Bit Displacement	0 to 5 words	0 to 5 words

* Not present if both full source and full destination extensions are used.

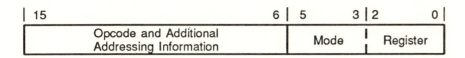

FIGURE 6-21   Single Effective Address Instruction Format

double operand instructions that use either address or data registers for each operand.

As illustrated in Figure 6-21, the low-order six bits of the operation word in the single effective address format are collectively referred to as the effective address field. This field is composed of a 3-bit register field, used to specify a register, and a 3-bit mode field, used to specify an addressing mode. Table 6-18 lists the bit encodings for the mode and register fields.

The register numbers indicated in Table 6-18 use a straight 3-bit encoding for both data and address registers, as listed in Table 6-19. The distinction between

TABLE 6-18 Effective Address Encoding Summary

Addressing Mode	Mode Field	Register Field
Data register direct	000	Register number
Address register direct	001	Register number
Address register indirect	010	Register number
Address register indirect with postincrement	011	Register number
Address register indirect with predecrement	100	Register number
Address register indirect with displacement	101	Register number
Address register and memory Indirect with index	110	Register number
Absolute address (16-bits)	111	000
Absolute address (32-bits)	111	001
PC indirect with displacement	111	010
PC and PC memory indirect with index	111	011
Immediate data	111	100
Reserved for future use	111	101
Reserved for future use	111	110
Reserved for future use	111	111

the address and data registers referred to by the register number listed in Table 6-19 is determined by the addressing mode.

TABLE 6-19 Register Numbers

Register Name	Register Number
A0 and D0	000
A1 and D1	001
A2 and D2	010
A3 and D3	011
A4 and D4	100
A5 and D5	101
A6 and D6	110
A7 and D7	111

Using Tables 6-18 and 6-19, instructions having the single effective address instruction format can be illustrated. For example, the assembly instruction

NEG.W D5

is encoded as shown in Figure 6-22. This instruction uses the direct register addressing mode using register D5. As illustrated in Figure 6-22, the direct register addressing mode is indicated by a 000 mode field, and a register field encoding of 101 specifies register D5. Also shown is the operand size field for the NEG instruction. For instructions that can operate on either byte, word, or long word data, a size field is always present. The size field uses the encoding listed in Table 6-20.

TABLE 6-20 Size Field Encodings

Size Field Encoding	Meaning
00	Designates a byte operand
01	Designates a word operand
10	Designates a long word operand

The single effective address format is also used to encode double operand instruction. For example, the instruction

ADD.B (A5),D2

adds the byte pointed to by register A5 to the lowest byte of register D2. The encoding of this instruction, as specified by Motorola, is illustrated in Figure 6-23.

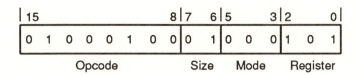

FIGURE 6-22 Machine Encoding of NEG.W D5

The S/D field in the ADD instruction determines whether the mode and register fields specify the source or destination operand. A zero (0) in this field, as shown in Figure 6-23, specifies that the mode and register (Reg) fields contain source operand information; a one (1) specifies that these fields contain destination information. For the encoding shown in Figure 6-23, the source operand is specified by the mode and register fields of the encoded instruction. A mode field of 010, as listed in Table 6-18, designates address register indirect mode, and a register field of 101 specifies register A5 as the address register.

The ADD instruction requires that at least one of the operands, source or destination, must be a data register (see Table 6-9). The encoding for this data register is assigned to the operation word bits 9, 10, and 11. An encoding of 010 in these bits specifies register D2 (see Table 6-19) as the data register for this instruction. Finally, the size bits for the ADD instruction, using the codes listed in Table 6-20, specify the operand's data size. In this case, since a byte operand is specified by the size modifier (B) in the assembly instruction, the correct encoding for the size field is 00.

As an additional example of the ADD instruction encoding consider the assembly instruction

ADD.B D2,(A5)

This instruction uses direct register addressing for the source operand and indirect address register addressing for the destination operand. The encoding of this instruction is identical to that shown in Figure 6-23 except that the S/D bit would be 1.

FIGURE 6-23 Machine Encoding of ADD.B (A5), D2

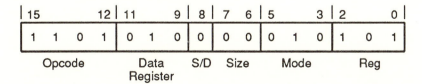

Brief Extension Word

Figure 6-24 illustrates the encoding format of the brief extension word used when either a single index register or an immediate 8-bit displacement value is present in the instruction. The fields shown in Figure 6-24 are defined in Table 6-21.

TABLE 6-21 Brief Extension Word Field Definitions

Field	Description	Encoding
D/A	Index register type	0 designates a data register 1 designates an address register
Register	Index register number	Encoded as per Table 6-19
W/L	Word/long word size	0 designates a sign extended word index register value 1 designates a long word index register value
Scale	Scale factor size	00 designates a factor of 1 01 designates a factor of 2 10 designates a factor of 4 11 designates a factor of 8
Displacement	Immediate value	Any 8-bit signed value

A brief extension word, when it is present, is always in addition to the operation word represented by the single effective address instruction format. The brief extension word simply contains additional information that cannot be encoded within the 16 bits of the primary operation word format. For example, the instruction

NEG.B ($AF,A5,A2.W*2)

uses indirect memory addressing with A5 as the primary address register. In addition to the primary address register, the instruction specifies an immediate hexadecimal displacement value of AF, and designates A2 as a 16-bit index register (due to the W size specifier) whose value is to be scaled by 2. The machine

FIGURE 6-24 Brief Extension Word Format

15	14 12	11	10 9	8	7 0
D/A	Register	W/L	Scale	0	Displacement

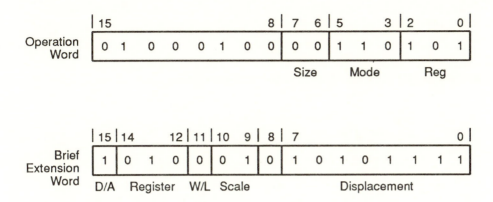

FIGURE 6-25   Machine Encoding of NEG.B ($AF, A5, A2.W*2)

encoding of this instruction is illustrated in Figure 6-25.

Due to the index and displacement included in this instruction, a brief extension word is required in addition to the operation word. The encoding of the operation word is straightforward and uses the same format as designated for single effective address instructions. For the particular addressing mode used by this instruction, a mode field of 110 is required (see Table 6-18) and the register field value of 101 designates register A5 (see Table 6-19). The opcode and size fields illustrated are encoded as previously described for the negate instruction.

The second word of the encoded instruction specifies the additional index and displacement data designated by the assembly language instruction. As given in Table 6-21, a D/A encoding of 1 specifies an address register is used as an index register, and the 010 in the register field designates A2 as this register. The W/L encoding of 0 specifies that the lower 16 bits of the index register are to be used (automatically sign-extended to 32 bits) and the scale field indicates a scale factor of 2. Finally, the displacement field of 10101111 corresponds to the immediate displacement value of AF designated in the assembly instruction.

Full Extension Word Format

A full extension word format is required to encode instructions using the memory or register indirect addressing modes when either 16-bit or 32-bit displacement values are included. As with the brief instruction word format, the extension words are required in addition to the operation word that is present in all MC68020 machine instructions. In the case of full extension words, the additional information contains the longer displacements that cannot be accommodated within the shorter brief word format. Figure 6-26 illustrates the full extension word format. The fields shown are described in Table 6-22. Notice the first four fields listed are the same as those used in the brief extension word format.

TABLE 6-22 Full Extension Word Field Definitions

Field	Description	Encoding
D/A	Index register type	0 designates a data register 1 designates an address register
Register	Index register number	Encoded as per Table 6-19

W/L	Word/long word size	0 designates a sign-extended word
		    index register value
		1 designates a long word
		    index register value

Scale	Scale factor size	00 designates a factor of 1 01 designates a factor of 2 10 designates a factor of 4 11 designates a factor of 8
BS	Base suppress	0 designates a base displacement 1 designates no base displacement

BD Size	Base displacement
	    size
		00 is a reserved code
		01 designates no displacement
		10 designates a word displacement
		11 designates a long word
		    displacement

I/IS	Index/indirection	Used in conjunction with the IS
		    field to designate indirection
		    options (see Table 6-23)

FIGURE 6-26   Full Extension Word Format

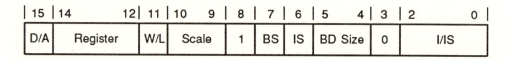

15	14 12	11	10 9	8	7	6	5 4	3	2 0
D/A	Register	W/L	Scale	1	BS	IS	BD Size	0	I/IS

Base (Inner) Displacement (0, 1, or 2 words)

Outer Displacement (0, 1, or 2 words)

TABLE 6-23 Index/Indirection Selection Summary

IS	I/IS	Encoded Options
1	000	No memory indirection
(No	001	Memory indirect mode with no outer displacement
Index		
Register	010	Memory indirect mode with outer word displacement
Present)		
	011	Memory indirect mode with outer long word displacement
	100-111	Reserved for future use
0	000	No memory indirection
(Index	001	Preindexed memory indirect mode with no outer displacement
Register		
is	010	Preindexed memory indirect mode with outer word displacement
Present)		
	011	Preindexed memory indirect mode with outer long word displacement
	100	Reserved for future use
	101	Postindexed memory indirect mode with no outer word displacement
	110	Postindexed memory indirect mode with outer word displacement
	111	Postindexed memory indirect mode with outer long word displacement

6.6 Chapter Highlights

1. The program model register set of the MOTOROLA MC68020 Microprocessor (CPU) consists of eight general-purpose data registers, seven address registers, a user stack pointer, a program counter, and a condition code register. Except for the 8-bit condition code register, each of these registers is 32-bits wide.

2. The MC68020 system model register set consists of a status register, an interrupt stack pointer, a master stack pointer, a vector base register, two alternate code function registers, a cache control register, and a cache address register.

3. The MC68020 CPU supports byte (8-bit), word (16-bit), long word (32-bit), packed and unpacked BCD, individual bit, and bit field data. Floating-point data is supported by a separate MOTOROLA MC68881 Floating-Point Coprocessor. The CPU instruction set provides that all data can be interpreted as either signed or unsigned quantities.

4. The MC68020 CPU assumes data stored within memory is stored with its lower-order bytes at higher-order addresses. Although byte, word, and long word data can be stored starting at any byte address, more efficient data transfers occur when words are stored at even byte addresses and long words at addresses evenly divisible by four.

5. The addressing modes supported by the MC68020 CPU include absolute, immediate, register direct, register indirect, indexed register indirect, memory indirect, and program counter relative addressing.

6. The instruction set of the MC68020 CPU consists of data transfer, arithmetic, logical, bit management, program and system control, coprocessor, and multiprocessor instructions.

7. An individual MC68020 assembly language instruction consists of a label field, a mnemonic, and up to two operands. In two operand instructions the source operand is always listed before the destination operand.

8. Machine language instructions are encoded using at least one 16-bit word and at most 11 words. The majority of instructions in which operands or their addresses are stored in registers are encoded using a 16-bit single effective address format. Up to five additional extension words may be required for each operand requiring immediate data.

Exercises

1a. List the registers that comprise the MOTOROLA MC68020 Microprocessor program model register set and the functions that can be performed by these registers.
1b. List the registers that comprise the MC68020 system model register set and the functions that these registers perform.

2. List the data types supported by the MOTOROLA MC68020 Microprocessor.

3. Describe how the 32-bit hexadecimal data $ABEF19CC would be stored in memory starting at address $1880.

4a. What is meant by the term effective address?
4b. List the complete set of components that can be included in an effective address.
4c. Determine the individual components required to form an effective address for a memory operand specified using indexed register indirect addressing.
4d. List the seven basic addressing modes supported by the Motorola MC68020 Microprocessor.

4e. Are memory-to-memory addressing modes supported by the MC68020 instruction set?

5a. Define what is meant by an orthogonal instruction set.
5b. What are the requirements for an instruction set to be defined as completely orthogonal?

6. The format, opcode, and field definitions for the MC68020 MOVE instruction are illustrated on Figure 6-27. Using the information provided in this figure, determine the bit encoding for the following instructions:
6a. MOV.B D2,D3
6b. MOV.W D6,D7
6c. MOV.L D1,D4
6d. MOV ($CF,A3,A5.W*2),D6
6e. MOV.W #$AE,D5
6f. MOV.L #$738291AB,(A6)

7. Using Figure 6-27, determine the bit encoding for the following instructions:
7a. MOV.L D4,($AF62,A5)
7b. MOV.W (A6),($FE,A3,A5.W)
7c. MOV.W ($FE,A2,A5),($C1,A1,A4)
7d. MOV.W ($FE,A2,A5.W),($C1,A1,A4.W*8)
7e. MOV.B #$AB,($FB,A6,A3)
7f. MOV.B #$AB,($FB,A6,A3.W*4)
7g. MOV ($FDAE,A5,A2),($19A4,A6,A3)
7h. MOV ([$19CE,A2,A3],$ACEE),([$18FA,A4],A5,$17AB)

8. Identify the operand addressing modes used for the source and destination operands in each instruction encoded in Exercise 7.

9. The format for various MC68020 ADD instructions are illustrated in Figure 6-28. Using this information, determine the bit encoding for the following instructions:
9a. ADD.B D2,D2
9b. ADD.L D5,(A6)
9c. ADD.L #1953FFEE,D5
9d. ADD.L #738291AB,(A6)
9e. ADD.L D4,($AF62,A5)
9f. ADD.W (A6),($FE,A3)
9g. ADD.W (A6),($FE,A2,A5)
9h. ADD.W (A6),($FE,A2,A5.W)
9i. ADD #$16AB,($FB,A6)
9j. ADD #$16AB,($FB,A6,A2.W)
9k. ADD ($FDAE,A5,A2),($19A4,A6,A3)
9l. ADD ([$19CE,A2,A3],$ACEE),([$18FA,A4],A5,$17AB)

10. Write MC68020 assembly language instructions to perform the following operations:
10a. Move $FFEE into A6.
10b. Move the number $AAEF into D4.
10c. Move the number $19 into A1.

a. Instruction Format

15	14	13 12	11		6	5		0
0	0	Size	Destination			Source		
			Register	Mode		Mode	Register	

b. Instruction Fields

Size Field - Specifies the size of the operand to be moved.

       01   –   Byte operation.

       11   –   Word operation.

       10   –   Long operation.

Destination Effective Address field - Specifies the destination location. Only data alterable addressing modes are allowed. These are:

Address Mode	Mode	Register	Address Mode	Mode	Register
Dn	000	reg. number:An	(xxx).W	111	000
An	–	–	(xxx).L	111	001
(An)	010	reg. number:An	#<data>	–	–
(An)+	011	reg. number:An			
–(An)	100	reg. number:An			
(d16,An)	101	reg. number:An	(d16 ,PC)	–	–
(d8,An,Xn)	110	reg. number:An	(d8 ,PC,Xn)	–	–
(bd,An,Xn)	110	reg. number:An	(bd,PC,Xn)	–	–
([bd,An,Xn],od)	110	reg. number:An	([bd,PC,Xn],od)	–	–
([bd,An],Xn,od)	110	reg. number:An	([bd,PC],Xn,od)	–	–

Source Effective Address Field - Specifies the source operand. All addressing modes are allowed. These are:

Address Mode	Mode	Register	Address Mode	Mode	Register
Dn	000	reg. number:Dn	(xxx).W	111	000
An *	001	reg. number:An	(xxx).L	111	001
(An)	010	reg. number:An	#<data>	111	100
(An)+	011	reg. number:An			
-(An)	100	reg. number:An			
(d16 ,An)	101	reg. number:An	(d16,PC)	111	010
(d8,An,Xn)	110	reg. number:An	(d8 ,PC,Xn)	111	011
(bd,An,Xn)	110	reg. number:An	(bd,PC,Xn)	111	011
([bd,An,Xn],od)	110	reg. number:An	([bd,PC,Xn],od)	111	011
([bd,An],Xn,od)	110	reg. number:An	([bd,PC],Xn,od)	111	011

* For byte size operation, address register direct is not allowed.

FIGURE 6-27 MOVE Instruction Formats

A. Instruction Format

15	14	13	12	11 9	8 6	5 0
1	1	0	1	Register Dn	Opmode	Effective Address
						Mode | Register

B. Instruction Fields

Register Field - Specifies any of the eight data registers.
Opmode field - Given by:

Byte	Word	Long	Operation
000	001	010	<ea> + <Dn> → <Dn>
100	101	110	<Dn> + <ea> → <ea>

Effective Address Field - Determines addressing mode.

a. If the location specified is a source operand, then all addressing modes are allowed. These are:

Address Mode	Mode	Register
Dn	000	reg. number:Dn
An *	001	reg. number:An
(An)	010	reg. number:An
(An)+	011	reg. number:An
−(An)	100	reg. number:An
(d16,An)	101	reg. number:An
(d8,An,Xn)	110	reg. number:An
(bd,An,Xn)	110	reg. number:An
([bd,An,Xn],od)	110	reg. number:An
([bd,An],Xn,od)	110	reg. number:An

Address Mode	Mode	Register
(xxx).W	111	000
(xxx).L	111	001
#<data>	111	100
(d16,PC)	111	010
(d8,PC,Xn)	111	011
(bd,PC,Xn)	111	011
([bd,PC,Xn],od)	111	011
([bd,PC],Xn,od)	111	011

* Word and Long only.

b. If the location specified is a destination operand, then only alterable memory addressing modes are allowed These are:

Address Mode	Mode	Register
Dn	−	−
An	−	−
(An)	010	reg. number:An
(An)+	011	reg. number:An
-(An)	100	reg. number:An
(d16,An)	101	reg. number:An
(d8,An,Xn)	110	reg. number:An
(bd,An,Xn)	110	reg. number:An
([bd,An,Xn],od)	110	reg. number:An
([bd,An],Xn,od)	110	reg. number:An

Address Mode	Mode	Register
(xxx).W	111	000
(xxx).L	111	001
#<data>	−	−
(d16,PC)	−	−
(d8,PC,Xn)	−	−
(bd,PC,Xn)	−	−
([bd,PC,Xn],od)	−	−
([bd,PC],Xn,od)	−	−

FIGURE 6-28   ADD Instruction Formats

10d. Add the byte contents of memory location $ACE4 to register D5.

10e. Multiply the lower 16 bits of D2 by the lower 16 bits of D3.

11. Assuming that 8-bit codes for the characters Hello World! are stored in memory starting at location $1690, write a series of instructions to perform the following operations individually :

11a. Move a copy of the characters into memory starting at location $AACD.

11b. Move a reverse copy of the characters into memory starting at location $AACD.

12a. An array of ten signed 16-bit integers is stored in memory starting at address $AB190000. Write a sequence of MC68020 assembly language instructions to sum the ten elements. Provide sufficient room for a sum greater than 16 bits.

12b. Modify the instructions written in Exercise 12a so that the sums of the positive and negative elements are produced individually.

13. An array of nonzero, 16-bit unsigned integers is stored in memory starting at address $1620. A trailing value of zero is used to indicate the end of the list. Write a sequence of MC68020 assembly language instructions to sum the numbers in the list and terminate when the zero value is accessed. Assume that the sum does not exceed 32 bits.

14. The unsigned 32-bit operands, $AB601988 and $11623587, are to be multiplied. Write a series of MC68020 assembly language instructions to load these operands into registers D2 and D3, respectively, and generate a 64-bit product in D4 and D3.

15a. Write a series of MC68020 assembly language instructions to locate the maximum value in a set of twenty-five 32-bit signed integers. The first integer is stored in memory at address $6000.

15b. Modify the instructions written for Exercise 15a to locate the minimum value.

16. Write a series of MC68020 assembly language instructions to produce the cube of a signed 8-bit integer number located at memory location $1623ABCC. The instructions should use indirect memory addressing with A6 as an address register. The result should be placed in register D3.

17. The binary and ASCII codes for the digits 0 through 9 are listed in Table 6-24. To convert the binary code for these digits to the corresponding ASCII code requires adding a constant value to the digit's binary value. Using this information, write a series of MC68020 assembly language instructions to convert a binary number, representing 0 through 9, stored in the lower 8 bits of register D0 to its equivalent ASCII representation.

18. The binary and ASCII codes for the hexadecimal digits A through F are listed in Table 6-25. To convert the binary code for these digits to the corresponding ASCII code requires adding a constant value to the digit's binary value. Using this information, write a series of MC68020 assembly language instructions to convert a binary number, represented by the hexadecimal digits A to F, to its equivalent ASCII representation. Assume that the binary number is initially stored in the lower 8 bits of register D0.

TABLE 6-24 Binary and ASCII Digit Codes (0 - 9)

Digit	Binary	ASCII (Binary)	ASCII (Hex)
0	00000000	011 0000	$30
1	00000001	011 0001	$31
2	00000010	011 0010	$32
3	00000011	011 0011	$33
4	00000100	011 0100	$34
5	00000101	011 0101	$35
6	00000110	011 0110	$36
7	00000111	011 0111	$37
8	00001000	011 1000	$38
9	00001001	011 1001	$39

TABLE 6-25 Binary and ASCII Digit Codes (A - F)

Digit	Binary	ASCII (Binary)	ASCII (Hex)
A	00001010	100 0001	$41
B	00001011	100 0010	$42
C	00001100	100 0011	$43
D	00001101	100 0100	$44
E	00001110	100 0101	$45
F	00001111	100 0110	$46

19. Using the results of Exercises 17 and 18, write a series of MC68020 assembly language instructions for converting the binary representation of the hexadecimal digits 0 - F to their equivalent ASCII codes. (Hint: Recall that the binary number and letter codes required different values to be added for proper conversion to ASCII.)

Interfacing

Part Three

Memory Interfacing

Chapter Seven

7.1   Memory Devices
7.2   Address Decoding and Buffering
7.3   Timing
7.4   DRAM Interfacing
7.5   Memory Management Revisited
7.6   Chapter Highlights

Previous chapters concentrated on 32-bit microprocessor features. The objective of this and subsequent chapters is to present techniques for interfacing the CPU to memory, input/output devices, and coprocessors. This chapter deals with memory interfacing and begins with a survey of memory devices. Address decoding, buffering, and timing are discussed and examples illustrating these important interfacing topics are presented. Special considerations required for dynamic random access memory (DRAM) interfacing are also presented, as are the use of high-speed cache memory and memory management units.

7.1 Memory Devices

As introduced in Chapter One, the 1970s saw the development of MOS LSI memory devices that started with modest 1000-bit size devices. Today, development is proceeding on single chips able to store as many as one million bits. These memory devices are categorized as either read/write memory, more commonly called random access memory (RAM), or read-only memory (ROM). Since ROMs are also randomly accessed devices, implying equal access time to data at any location, the term RAM is actually a misnomer. Nevertheless, it is used to refer to devices for which the data can be conveniently written as well as read.

RAM is also distinguished from ROM by the fact that it is a volatile memory. The data is preserved only so long as power is applied. In contrast, ROMs retain their content even when power is removed. Before microcomputers, RAMs were used as general-purpose storage devices in larger computers as well as in other digital systems. ROMs were used mostly as logic function generators, replacing logic gate structures. As microcomputers evolved, ROMs became the vehicle for storing the application programs of dedicated controllers and, more recently, the operating systems and language translators of more powerful machines.

Read Only Memories

The nonvolatility of ROM makes it useful in applications that require information to be stored for long periods of time. The first ROMs contained cell arrays in which the data (zeros and ones) were entered by the manufacturer during the fabrication process. The process of writing the contents to ROM has become known as programming the ROM. As the creation of the metallization interconnect mask needed for this process was costly, a user would only contract with a ROM manufacturer for large volume applications.

As an alternative, manufacturers developed a user-programmable ROM, called a PROM. Early PROMs used fusible links which could be melted with special PROM programming, or PROM burning, hardware. This proved more cost effective for the user with low volume applications, even though an error in the programming often rendered the chip useless.

As microcomputers began to use ROM for program storage, the need arose for a more flexible device which would allow for changes during the program development and debugging phase of the system design.

Pioneered by Intel, the mid-1970s saw the advent of the ultraviolet erasable PROM (or EPROM). The EPROM came in a standard package, but had a quartz covered window to allow chip exposure to ultraviolet light. Erasure time was about 15 minutes, and required removal of the device from its circuit board.

The electrically erasable PROM (EEPROM) evolved in the 1980s. Since it can be programmed and erased electrically in several milliseconds without removal from its circuit board, it is in a sense a nonvolatile RAM. However, like other ROMs, it is generally used to store information for extended time. The disadvantages of an EEPROM are that it is more expensive than the EPROM, and is limited to about ten thousand erasure and reprogramming operations. In contrast, EPROMs can be reprogrammed virtually indefinitely.

Read/Write Memories

Read/write memories (RAMs) allow a location to be written as well as read in a fraction of a microsecond, much faster than even the electrically erasable ROM (EEPROM). Thus, RAMs are used when data has to be changed often and rapidly. Two major categories of RAMs are static RAM (SRAM) and dynamic RAM (DRAM). SRAMs store their information using the traditional bistable flip-flop cell. The flip-flop retains its content (zero or one) so long as power is applied to it; reading or transferring its output elsewhere does not change its content. Its input(s) must be activated in the appropriate way to change it, that is, write new data to it.

The DRAM is based on a transistor-capacitor cell that takes up much less chip space than an SRAM flip-flop. This allows fabrication of larger memories on the same size chip. Also, since the bit value is stored as capacitor charge rather than the state of a flip-flop, much less power is needed to store and hold the charge than to maintain the flip-flop's state. However, the DRAM's capacitive charge dissipates itself in time and refresh circuitry is required to restore the charge. This circuitry adversely affects the cost per cell, or per bit, of a low capacity DRAM but is less significant for larger memory capacities. This cost is a result of the refresh process that involves reading and rewriting groups of memory locations at a time. The refreshing typically must be done every few milliseconds. Another disadvantage of DRAM is the lower switching speed of its capacitive cell, as compared to the SRAM's flip-flop cell.

During the 1970s, most microprocessor applications required only modest sized memories, and SRAM was the favored choice. Now that 16-bit and 32-bit CPUs are in the marketplace, their larger memory addressing capability has resulted in a shift that makes using DRAM more economical. As will be discussed later, the use of caches with 32-bit CPUs is an attempt to give the designer the best of both worlds. The cache is typically a small-sized, fast SRAM designed to store routines and data blocks that are accessed repeatedly. The remaining routines and data are stored in the slower, large sized DRAM, which reduces overall memory cost.

Memory Structure

Memory devices have provisions for address, data, and control lines. The size of a memory chip is specified as the number of storage addresses and the number of bits stored at each location. If N is the number of address lines, and M is the number of bits stored at each address, the memory size is $2^N \times M$ total bits. For example, a device with 10 address lines and 4 data bits per address is 1024 x 4 bits. For convenience, the term 1K is used to denote 1024 (2^{10}). Thus, 2048 (2^{11}) is 2K, 4096 (2^{12}) is 4K, and so on. The number of bits at each location (M) determines the number of data lines that must be provided by the memory device.

To save on pins, many memory chips combine data in and data out on the same pins (bidirectional data I/O). The exception is generally RAM devices with a 1-bit data size. Here, providing separate data in and data out pins only adds one pin, and saves the chip designer the need to provide internal chip circuitry to prevent data read out of a location from conflicting with data to be written to the same address. Conversely, DRAMs typically save pins by sharing their address inputs between the high-order and low-order bits (for an N bit address, N/2 pins are provided).

The disadvantage of shared address pins is that the time to access an address is increased and more interfacing hardware is required to multiplex the high and low sets of address lines. The data pins on ROMs are for data out, since it is a read only device. But PROMs typically employ those same pins for writing in data when the device is programmed.

A block diagram of a typical read/write memory device is shown in Figure 7-1. The memory address register (MAR) and memory data register (MDR) are typically part of the bus interface unit of the CPU, and provide temporary storage of the address and data respectively. The N-bit address provided by the MAR is decoded inside the memory chip to provide access to 2^N locations in the array. The MDR lines are physically connected to the corresponding bit positions of all 2^N locations.

Data to be written to a location must be first placed into the MDR before being transferred to memory, whereas data read out from the addressed location is transferred to the MDR from memory. Structurally, a ROM may be viewed in the same way except that only the read operation is permitted. Since address and data lines are shared by many devices, including I/O as well as memory, control lines are required to ensure that only the proper device or devices are accessed each time. Also, control must be provided to enable the desired operation - either read or write. Otherwise, the data bus can experience a conflict between data being read out of a location at the same time an attempt is made to write new data from the same lines into the addressed location.

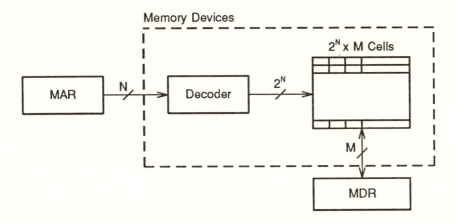

FIGURE 7-1 General Memory Structure

The control lines generally include one or more chip select (CS) pins (sometimes called chip enable - CE), and a read/write (R/$\overline{\text{W}}$) or write enable ($\overline{\text{WE}}$) pin for RAMs. A separate output enable (OE) or output disable (OD) pin may exist, providing an additional degree of control. The chip select must be asserted to allow access to the addressed location, but data is not actually read out until OE is active. Additionally, PROMs often include either a separate or a shared program (PGM) pin to which high voltage pulses are applied as required by the programming process. Figure 7-2 illustrates a typical SRAM structure.

The speed of a memory device is characterized by its access time. For a read operation, the read access time is the delay between the presentation of an address to the memory chip and valid content read out to the data lines. Write access time is the delay from presentation of an address to the memory chip to valid

FIGURE 7-2 Typical 1K x 4 SRAM

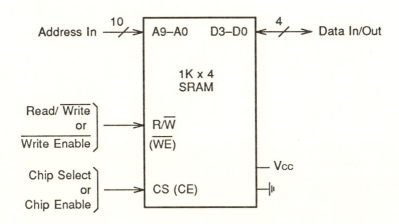

data written to that location. The memory interface designer must be concerned with additional timing specifications involving the memory device's control signals, as well as delay times of decoding and other logic placed between the CPU and memory. These considerations are dealt with in Section 7.3. Nevertheless, access time alone is useful in a relative speed comparison between memory devices.

Device Examples

EPROMs

The Intel EPROM family provides a good illustration of the orderly evolution of EPROM devices. Table 7-1 summarizes the size and access time characteristics of EPROMs ranging from 16K to 1M bit capacity (1M = 1K x 1K = 2^{20} = 1048576).

TABLE 7-1 EPROM Characteristics

Device	Pins	Address Lines	Bit Capacity	Organization	Maximum Access Time (ns)
2716	24	11	16K	2K x 8	450 (350 for 2716-1)
2732A	24	12	32K	4K x 8	250 (200 for 2732A-2)
2764A	28	13	64K	8K x 8	250 (180 for 2764A-1)
27128A	28	14	128K	16K x 8	250 (200 for 27128A-2)
27256	28	15	256K	32K x 8	250 (170 for 27256-1)
27512	28	16	512K	64K x 8	250 (170 for 27512-170V05)
27010	32	17	1M	128K x 8	200

Notice all the EPROMs are byte wide (data size of M = 8) and the number of address lines, N, ranges from 11 for the 2716 (2^{11} = 2048 = 2K) to 17 for the 27010 (2^{17} = 128K). The 8-bit data width has made interfacing of these devices to 8-bit CPUs very straightforward. Since most 16-bit and 32-bit CPUs also address bytes rather than larger size words, these EPROMs are suited to the newer CPUs as well.

Figure 7-3 illustrates the pinouts for the 24-pin, 28-pin, and 32-pin EPROM packages. Notice pin compatibility has been maintained between larger capacity and smaller capacity devices having the same package configuration and dimensions. In addition to the address and data lines discussed previously, chip enable and output enable control pins are provided. The output enable ($\overline{OE}$) pin, not present on Intel's earliest EPROMs, provides a separate degree of control from chip enable. As access times have decreased, the possibility that two data accesses may interfere with each other has increased. This occurs when the currently accessed device places data on the bus before the data from the previously accessed device has been transferred to the CPU. Proper use of the output enable pin prevents this.

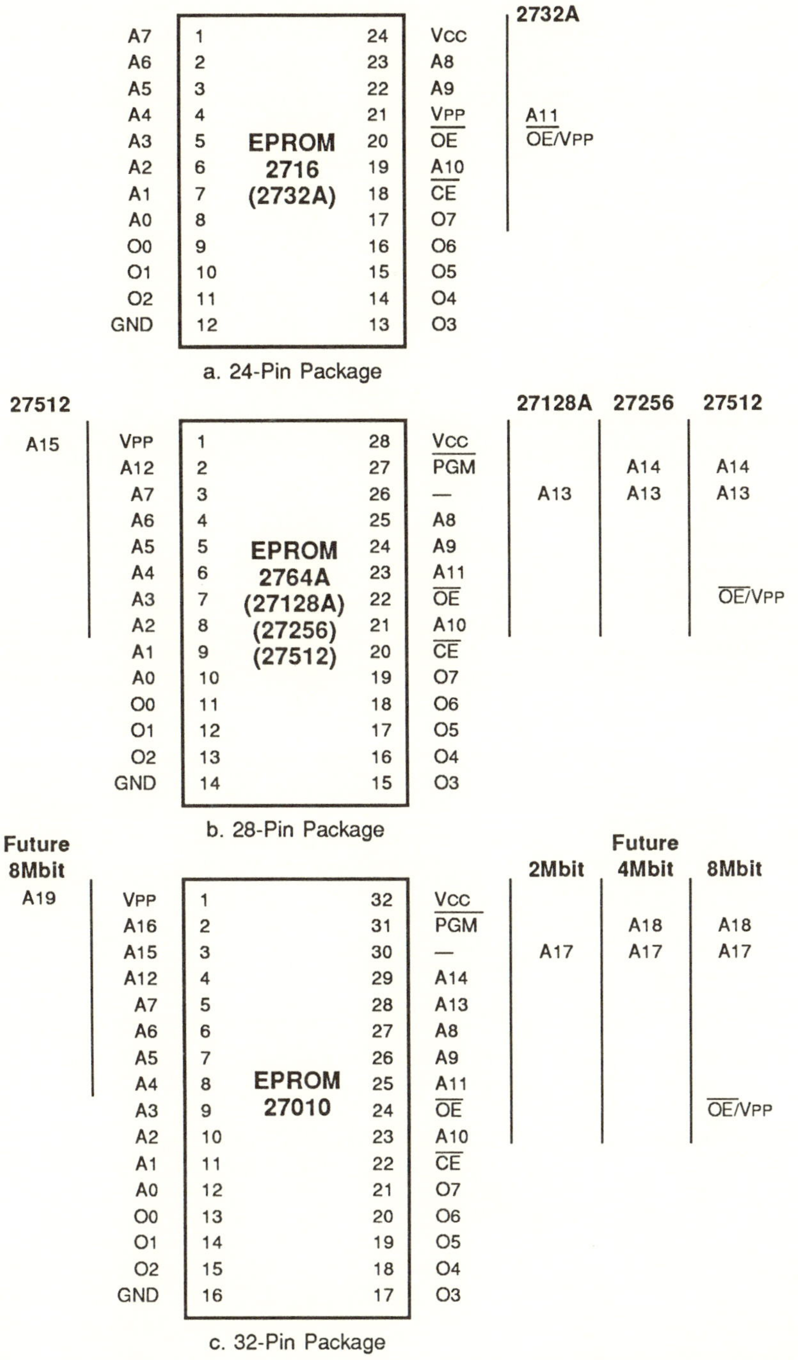

2732A

A7	1	24	Vcc
A6	2	23	A8
A5	3	22	A9
A4	4	21	VPP
A3	5	20	OE̅
A2	6	19	A10
A1	7	18	CE̅
A0	8	17	O7
O0	9	16	O6
O1	10	15	O5
O2	11	14	O4
GND	12	13	O3

EPROM 2716 (2732A)

2732A: A11, OE̅/VPP

a. 24-Pin Package

27512 — A15

27128A, 27256, 27512

VPP	1	28	Vcc
A12	2	27	PGM
A7	3	26	—
A6	4	25	A8
A5	5	24	A9
A4	6	23	A11
A3	7	22	OE̅
A2	8	21	A10
A1	9	20	CE̅
A0	10	19	O7
O0	11	18	O6
O1	12	17	O5
O2	13	16	O4
GND	14	15	O3

EPROM 2764A (27128A) (27256) (27512)

27128A: A13
27256: A14, A13
27512: A14, A13, OE̅/VPP

b. 28-Pin Package

Future 8Mbit — A19

2Mbit, 4Mbit, Future 8Mbit

VPP	1	32	Vcc
A16	2	31	PGM
A15	3	30	—
A12	4	29	A14
A7	5	28	A13
A6	6	27	A8
A5	7	26	A9
A4	8	25	A11
A3	9	24	OE̅
A2	10	23	A10
A1	11	22	CE̅
A0	12	21	O7
O0	13	20	O6
O1	14	19	O5
O2	15	18	O4
GND	16	17	O3

EPROM 27010

2Mbit: A17
4Mbit: A18, A17
8Mbit: A18, A17, OE̅/VPP

c. 32-Pin Package

Key:

A0–A_{N–1}	Address Inputs (A0 is LSB)		PGM	Program (input)
O0–O7	Data Outputs (inputs for programming)		VPP	Programming Voltage
CE̅	Chip Enable (input)		Vcc	Supply Voltage
OE̅	Output Enable (input)		GND	Ground

FIGURE 7-3 EPROM Pinouts

A separate voltage input (VPP) is provided for programming, and a programming pin ($\overline{PGM}$) may also exist. To maintain pin compatibility, it was necessary for some devices to place $\overline{OE}$ and VPP on a shared pin, and/or to eliminate $\overline{PGM}$. Figure 7-3c also illustrates how Intel plans to continue upward mobility by maintaining pin compatibility from their largest EPROM device to date, the 27010, to even larger EPROMs (2M, 4M, and 8M bit sizes).

To illustrate control signal and power requirements, the specifications for the 1M-bit 27010 EPROM are given in Table 7-2.

TABLE 7-2 Intel 27010 EPROM Control and Power Requirements

Mode of Operation	$\overline{CE}$	$\overline{OE}$	$\overline{PGM}$	VPP (in V)	Vcc (in V)
Read	L	L	x	x	5
Output Disable	L	H	x	x	5
Standby	H	x	x	x	5
Programming	L	H	L	12.5 to 13	6 to 6.5
Program Verify	L	L	H	12.5 to 13	6 to 6.5
Program Inhibit	H	x	x	12.5 to 13	6 to 6.5

Where: L - Low, H - High, x - Don't care (could be H or L)

The programming voltage values (VPP) listed are nominal specifications and also apply to the 2764A, 27128A, 27256, and 27512 EPROMs. The earlier 2716 and 2732A EPROMs required a higher VPP (20 to 25 V) and a VCC of 5 V. The time required to program the newer devices has significantly decreased compared to earlier ones, despite their larger sizes. From the table it can be observed that one method of programming an EPROM is to set $\overline{OE}$ high, $\overline{PGM}$ low, and repeatedly present the chip enable ($\overline{CE}$) pin with a low-going pulse for all addresses and corresponding data values to be written (an exception is that an active high pulse is required for the 2716). As an alternative, low-going pulses can be presented to $\overline{PGM}$ with $\overline{CE}$ held low and $\overline{OE}$ high. Since the $\overline{PGM}$ pin doesn't exist on all devices, using $\overline{CE}$ has the advantage of allowing creation of a "universal" EPROM programmer to handle various size devices.

A standard programming algorithm recommended for the smaller devices involves applying a 50 ms nominal width pulse for each address to be written. After writing to all locations, a verification routine is performed (reading each location and comparing it to the original data). Since verification time is negligible, the total programming time is

50 ms/byte x 2K bytes = 102.4 s

for writing the entire 2716 EPROM, and twice as long (more than three minutes) for all the locations in a 2732A EPROM. As a result, the development of larger capacity EPROMs has necessitated the development and use of algorithms with significantly reduced programming time. Intel developed a technique for production environments that involves applying an initial pulse of only 100 us for each address, followed by an immediate verification of the data written. The pulse is re-applied a maximum of 25 times before the device is assumed to have failed (is nonprogrammable). This "quick-pulse programming algorithm" has decreased programming time by a factor of nearly 100 for the larger capacity devices. For example, the entire 128K bytes of a 27010 EPROM can be programmed in under 15 seconds using this approach. By slightly increasing VPP and VCC over their values used with other algorithms, greater programming energy is provided. As a result, a study has shown that the majority of EPROM bytes are actually verified after only one 100 us pulse, and more than 90% after three pulses.

A variation on this method, called the "intelligent programming algorithm," keeps track of how many pulses were required to write a byte that could be verified, and then applies a single pulse of three times the total duration of the previously applied pulses to the same location. For example, if a byte is verified after five 100 μs pulses, an additional

$$3 \times 5 \times 100 = 1500 \ \mu s$$

pulse is applied. This "overprogramming" provides a safety margin, and has been a standard industry method for several years. Interestingly, overprogramming by too great a factor can actually decrease retention, due to "electrical stressing" of other cells in the same row or column of the programmed bit in physical memory. The tradeoff between providing a safety margin to improve long term data retention and the overstressing of other bits is of more concern in a production environment where a number of EPROMs may be programmed in parallel. Normal variation among devices will require different numbers of pulses to verify corresponding bits. Trying to program for the worst-case device results in increasing overall programming time and risks stressing the other devices. Intel claims that their algorithm allows the programming of as many as 20 devices in parallel without any overstressing.

RAMs

To illustrate both static and dynamic RAM structures, a representative sample of current devices is presented. Table 7-3 summarizes the size and access time characteristics of selected SRAM and DRAM devices.

In contrast to 8-bit wide EPROM devices, RAMs come in various data sizes - typically 1, 4, or 8 bits per word. Using 1-bit-wide or 4-bit-wide RAMs presents no problem when interfacing to a CPU; the appropriate number of devices can be paralleled to achieve an 8-bit (or larger) word size. Table 7-3 illustrates the points made earlier that higher-bit capacity is achievable with DRAMs, but that SRAM speeds are higher (at least when comparing the 1-bit and 4-bit wide

TABLE 7-3 SRAM and DRAM Characteristics

Device	Technology	Pins	Bit Capacity	Organization	Maximum Access Time (ns)*
SRAM:					
2149	NMOS	18	4K	1K x 4	35 - 55
2147A	NMOS	18	4K	4K x 1	25 - 45
446	CMOS	24	16K	2K x 8	150 - 450
4016	NMOS	24	16K	2K x 8	120 - 250
4314	MIX-MOS	20	16K	4K x 4	35 - 55
4311	MIX-MOS	20	16K	16K x 1	35 - 55
4364	MIX-MOS	28	64K	8K x 8	120 - 200
4464	CMOS	28	64K	8K x 8	150 - 200
4362	MIX-MOS	22	64K	16K x 4	45 - 70
4361	MIX-MOS	22	64K	64K x 1	40 - 70
43256	MIX-MOS	28	256K	32K x 8	100 - 150
DRAM:					
41416	NMOS	18	64K	16K x 4	120 - 200
4164	NMOS	16	64K	64K x 1	100 - 120
41464	NMOS	18	256K	64K x 4	100 - 150
41256	NMOS	16	256K	256K x 1	120 - 200
44256	NMOS	20	1M	256K x 4	100 - 150
411000	NMOS	18	1M	1M x 1	100 - 150

* The access time range specifies maximum values for the different versions of each device.

devices). The pin diagrams in Figure 7-4 show that, in addition to data and address lines, all SRAMs have at least one chip select and a write enable. The 8-bit wide devices also have a separate output enable pin. The 8K x 8 4364 SRAM also has both a low-active and a high-active chip enable that must be activated to select the device. It is interesting to note that the 2K x 8 446 SRAM is pin compatible with the 2716 EPROM, and that the 8K x 8 SRAM (4364) can be replaced by the same capacity 2764A EPROM. This allows the designer the convenience of using RAM for initial program development, and to replace it easily with nonvolatile EPROM later. Also, common data input/output lines are used for all devices except those of 1-bit width, where separate data in and data out costs only one pin (as pointed out previously).

The pin diagrams in Figure 7-5 show that the DRAMs all feature the shared high and low address pins as discussed earlier. The chip select is replaced by separate row-address-strobe ($\overline{RAS}$) and column-address-strobe ($\overline{CAS}$) pins, which route each half of the full address to the appropriate place internally.

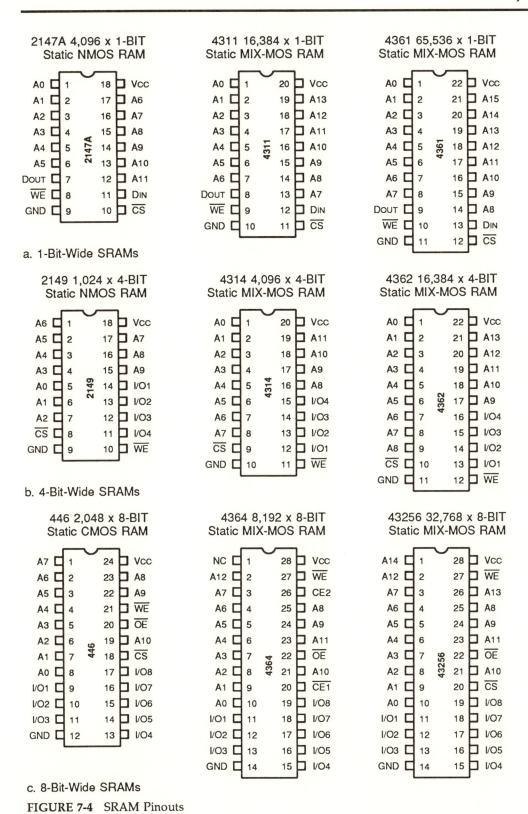

a. 1-Bit-Wide SRAMs

b. 4-Bit-Wide SRAMs

c. 8-Bit-Wide SRAMs

FIGURE 7-4   SRAM Pinouts

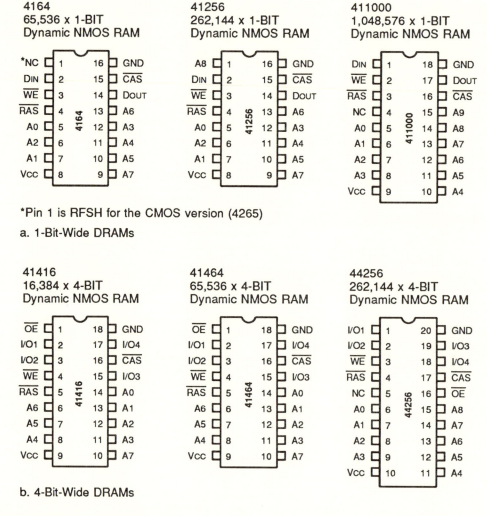

4164
65,536 x 1-BIT
Dynamic NMOS RAM

*NC	1	16	GND
DIN	2	15	$\overline{CAS}$
$\overline{WE}$	3	14	DOUT
$\overline{RAS}$	4	13	A6
A0	5	12	A3
A2	6	11	A4
A1	7	10	A5
VCC	8	9	A7

41256
262,144 x 1-BIT
Dynamic NMOS RAM

A8	1	16	GND
DIN	2	15	$\overline{CAS}$
$\overline{WE}$	3	14	DOUT
$\overline{RAS}$	4	13	A6
A0	5	12	A3
A2	6	11	A4
A1	7	10	A5
VCC	8	9	A7

411000
1,048,576 x 1-BIT
Dynamic NMOS RAM

DIN	1	18	GND
$\overline{WE}$	2	17	DOUT
$\overline{RAS}$	3	16	$\overline{CAS}$
NC	4	15	A9
A0	5	14	A8
A1	6	13	A7
A2	7	12	A6
A3	8	11	A5
VCC	9	10	A4

*Pin 1 is RFSH for the CMOS version (4265)

a. 1-Bit-Wide DRAMs

41416
16,384 x 4-BIT
Dynamic NMOS RAM

$\overline{OE}$	1	18	GND
I/O1	2	17	I/O4
I/O2	3	16	$\overline{CAS}$
$\overline{WE}$	4	15	I/O3
$\overline{RAS}$	5	14	A0
A6	6	13	A1
A5	7	12	A2
A4	8	11	A3
VCC	9	10	A7

41464
65,536 x 4-BIT
Dynamic NMOS RAM

$\overline{OE}$	1	18	GND
I/O1	2	17	I/O4
I/O2	3	16	$\overline{CAS}$
$\overline{WE}$	4	15	I/O3
$\overline{RAS}$	5	14	A0
A6	6	13	A1
A5	7	12	A2
A4	8	11	A3
VCC	9	10	A7

44256
262,144 x 4-BIT
Dynamic NMOS RAM

I/O1	1	20	GND
I/O2	2	19	I/O3
$\overline{WE}$	3	18	I/O4
$\overline{RAS}$	4	17	$\overline{CAS}$
NC	5	16	$\overline{OE}$
A0	6	15	A8
A1	7	14	A7
A2	8	13	A6
A3	9	12	A5
VCC	10	11	A4

b. 4-Bit-Wide DRAMs

FIGURE 7-5 DRAM Pinouts

7.2 Address Decoding and Buffering

Three main factors must be considered when interfacing a CPU to memory:

1. Address decoding and CPU control signals
2. Buffering needs
3. Timing.

The first two factors are discussed in this section, with main emphasis on address decoding and CPU control signals in the interface. Timing considerations are the subject of Section 7.3.

Recall that memory devices have address and data lines, as well as chip select or chip enable inputs. In general, memory device data lines are connected directly to the data bus (with buffering possibly provided between the CPU and the bus); and the memory device address lines are connected directly to the lowest order bits supplied by the CPU to the address bus. The higher order CPU address bits are decoded to provide the chip enables when more than one memory device or bank of devices is used. This prevents accessing locations in more than one device (or bank) at the same time. The examples presented assume ROM or SRAM devices which provide separate pins for all N memory address lines, or DRAM devices with N/2 multiplexed address lines. DRAM interfacing is discussed more fully in Section 7.4. The proper control of other memory device functions, such as read/write for RAM and output enable are discussed later in this section.

Let us first illustrate the concepts of address decoding using a CPU with a 16-bit address bus. This was characteristic of the earlier 8-bit microprocessors (INTEL 8080 CPU, MOTOROLA MC6800 CPU, ZILOG Z-80 CPU), which were limited to addressing 64K (2^{16}) bytes of memory. The same concepts apply to 32-bit CPUs having a 32-bit address bus. If you were to choose either a single 64K x 8 memory device (27512 EPROM), a 64K x 4 device (41464 DRAM), or a 64K x 1 device (4361 SRAM), no address decoding would be required. Since all 64K CPU addresses issued would select a byte, a nibble (4 bits), or a single bit from one device, the chip select or enable could be made permanently active (grounded).

Where the memory device word size is smaller than the CPU word size, a bank of memory devices can be paralleled. Figure 7-6 illustrates this using 64K x 8, 64K x 4, and 64K x 1 devices. Note that for the 4-bit and 1-bit word sizes, the address inputs and chip selects of all devices are tied together, but the data pins are connected to separate data bus lines. In the case of a 1-bit-wide device, it was noted earlier that, typically, separate data in and data out pins are provided. This necessitates some external control logic, such as a tristate gate, to properly interface the two pins to a single bidirectional data bus line. This is illustrated later as part of the discussion of read/write control.

Address Decoders

Decoders are devices which take N inputs and provide all switching combinations among the inputs. This results in 2^N outputs, only one of which is active at a time. The logic function is basically an ANDing one, with certain inputs being inverted first. Since most decoders provide a low-active rather than high-active output, the function is logically equivalent to a NAND. Figure 7-7 illustrates the gating required to implement 1-of-2 (1/2), 2-of-4 (2/4), and 3-of-8 (3/8) line decoders. A high-active enable is provided, which requires an additional input (EN) to each gate. If EN is inactive (low), then all 2^N decoder outputs are inactive (high); but if EN is active (high), one of the outputs is activated (low).

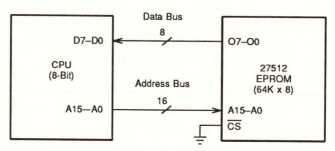

a. One 64K x 8 Memory Device

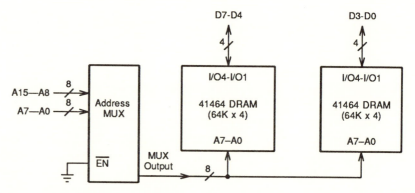

b. Two 64K x 4 Memory Devices (41464)

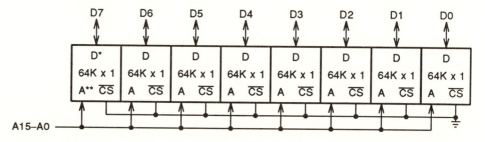

* Separate DIN and DOUT pins need to be gated on to a single bidirectional data line.
** A is A15–A0.

c. Eight 64K x 1 Memory Devices (4361)

FIGURE 7-6   Direct Interface of CPU to Memory

Decoder devices are readily available in these sizes, as well as 4-of-16 (4/16) lines. Enables may be low rather than high active, and multiple enables may be provided allowing for separate degrees of control.

Figure 7-8 illustrates the use of decoders to divide the address space into smaller blocks. When the highest order bits are inputs to the decoder, each output

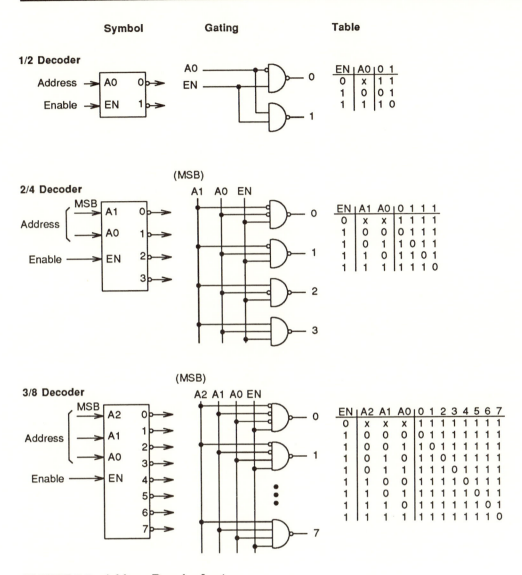

Symbol	Gating	Table

1/2 Decoder

EN	A0	0	1
0	x	1	1
1	0	0	1
1	1	1	0

2/4 Decoder

EN	A1	A0	0	1	1	1
0	x	x	1	1	1	1
1	0	0	0	1	1	1
1	0	1	1	0	1	1
1	1	0	1	1	0	1
1	1	1	1	1	1	0

3/8 Decoder

EN	A2	A1	A0	0	1	2	3	4	5	6	7
0	x	x	x	1	1	1	1	1	1	1	1
1	0	0	0	0	1	1	1	1	1	1	1
1	0	0	1	1	0	1	1	1	1	1	1
1	0	1	0	1	1	0	1	1	1	1	1
1	0	1	1	1	1	1	0	1	1	1	1
1	1	0	0	1	1	1	1	0	1	1	1
1	1	0	1	1	1	1	1	1	0	1	1
1	1	1	0	1	1	1	1	1	1	0	1
1	1	1	1	1	1	1	1	1	1	1	0

FIGURE 7-7   Address Decoder Logic

is active for a range of consecutive addresses for which the high-order bits have a specific value. For example, if A15 and A14 enter a 2/4 decoder, the output lines are activated for the addresses:

A15	A14	A13	Active A12	A11 ... A0	Decoded Output	Address Range (Hex)
0	0	x	x	x ... x	0	0000 - 3FFF
0	1	x	x	x ... x	1	4000 - 7FFF
1	0	x	x	x ... x	2	8000 - BFFF
1	1	x	x	x ... x	3	C000 - FFFF

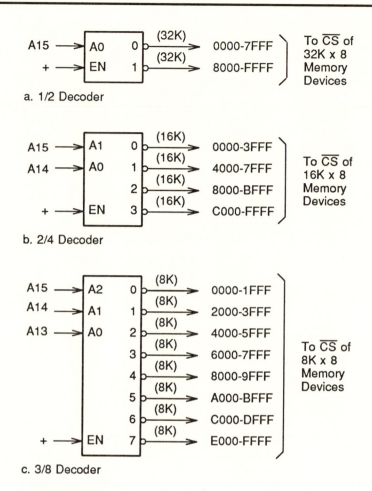

a. 1/2 Decoder

b. 2/4 Decoder

c. 3/8 Decoder

FIGURE 7-8 Decoded Addresses

The decoder has divided the total 64K address space into four sequential blocks, each having 16K addresses.

Figure 7-9 shows how the decoded addresses can be used to chip select various size devices that might be used in an application. Although the use of larger sized devices reduces the decoding hardware interconnections, the larger devices are more costly and not always readily available. In addition, decoding is needed to distinguish ROM addresses from RAM addresses.

In cases where small size memory devices would require a decoder with a large number of outputs, smaller decoders can be cascaded. Cascading creates an additional time delay that is generally not a problem with slower 8-bit and 16-bit system designs, but that can be significant at the higher clock rates of 32-bit CPUs. To understand this concept, consider Figure 7-10. Notice how the decoder enable (EN) input is used with gating to effectively decode the highest order address bits before the decoder itself handles the next lower bits. In Figure 7-10a,

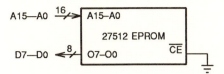

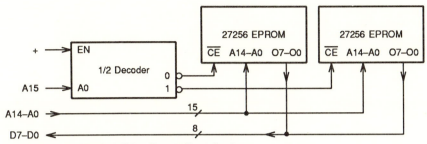

a. 64K Bytes of EPROM Using One 64K x 8 Device

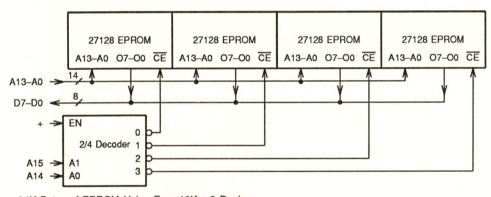

b. 64K Bytes of EPROM Using Two 32K x 8 Devices

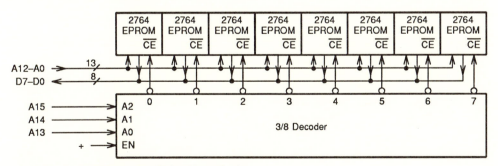

c. 64K Bytes of EPROM Using Four 16K x 8 Devices

d. 64K Bytes of EPROM Using Eight 8K x 8 Devices

FIGURE 7-9   Chip Selects from Decoded Addresses

313

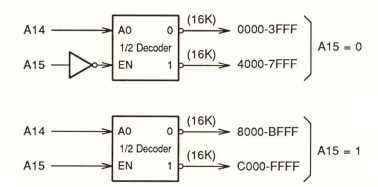

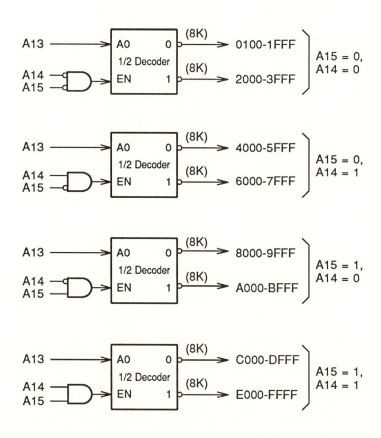

a. Decoding Highest Order Address with an Enable Input

b. Decoding The Two Highest Order Addresses Using an Enable Input

FIGURE 7-10   Activating Decoder Enable Inputs

the highest address is "decoded" first by either applying A15 or its complement directly to EN. If $\overline{A15}$ is used, the highest address bit must be 0 to enable the 1/2 decoder and the valid addresses are 0000 to 7FFF (a total of 32K addresses). The decoding of the next highest address bit, A14, by the 1/2 decoders serves to further divide the addresses into 16K blocks. The net result is that a single 2/4 decoder can be replaced by two 1/2 decoders and an inverter gate.

In Figure 7-10b, the two highest address bits, A15 and A14, are gated to the enables and A13 is the input to each 1/2 decoder. The AND gates (with either noninverted or inverted inputs) are equivalent to a 2/4 decoder in that they first subdivide the 64K address space by 4, resulting in four groups of 16K addresses. The 1/2 decoders then use A13 to further divide each 16K range into two 8K groups. The advantage of this approach is that a system might not utilize all the existing memory but may wish to reserve the remaining memory in case of future expansion. For example, if a system only uses two 8K devices for a total of 16K addresses, only the first decoder of Figure 7-10b need be used along with its gate to EN. Only addresses 0000 to 3FFF are decoded, since the gate to EN prevents any higher address from activating a decoder output. As memory is added to the system, the additional decoders with their own enabling gate can be inserted, without the need to modify the first decoder circuit. The use of gates to generate the enable rather than a separate decoder chip is advantageous when the overall design has resulted in some spare gates being available. Less board space is used, compared to the alternative of adding another decoder chip.

This approach also illustrates another important point, incomplete decoding. If you wanted to design only a 16K system comprised of 8K devices without concern for expansion, the first decoder of Figure 7-10b could be used with the gate removed and EN tied high. The addresses 0000 to 3FFF would still be decoded properly, but higher addresses would also be decoded onto the same lines. This is because A15 and A14 no longer affect the decoder; only A13 is actually decoded. Thus, addresses in the ranges 0000-1FFF, 4000-5FFF, 8000-9FFF, and C000-DFFF are all decoded onto output line 0; the remaining four address ranges are decoded onto line 1. This address overlap is of no consequence if the system only uses the lowest 16K addresses (or another 16K range starting at 4000, 8000, or C000 for that matter). Future expansion will require controlling the EN input of the first decoder to "free up" the other addresses needed. The concept of incomplete decoding, which clearly saves hardware cost, is particularly important in designing interfaces for 32-bit CPUs. With a 32-bit address bus available, it is unlikely that any system in the foreseeable future is going to require the full 4G (2^{32}) byte addresses. Thus, the highest order address bits need not be used in the decoding. Examples of 32-bit CPU address decoding are presented later.

Cascaded decoders are particularly useful when memory devices of varying sizes are to be used in the same system. This is illustrated in Design Example 7-1.

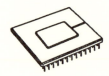

Design Example 7-1

Decoder System For Mixed Capacity Memory Devices

Problem: A 64K memory system consists of four EPROM devices. The sizes of the individual chips (or banks) are 32K x 8 (27256), 16K x 8 (27128A), 8K x 8 (2764A), and 8K x 8 (2764A). Design a decoding system to provide the required chip selects.

Solution: The decoding system consists of three 1/2 decoders arranged as shown in Figure 7-11. Notice the first decoder divides the 64K space into two 32K ranges; one output provides the chip select for the 32K device, and the other output enables a second decoder which divides the upper 32K address range into two 16K spaces. A third level decoder then creates two 8K ranges from the upper 16K space, in the same manner.

An alternative approach to the solution for Design Example 7-1 is to use a larger decoder to divide to the smallest size range, 8K in this case. Then appropriate outputs can be "encoded" using ORing to recreate a larger range of addresses. Figure 7-12 illustrates this for Design Example 7-1. The 3/8 decoder creates eight 8K nonoverlapping address ranges. If either outputs 0, 1, 2, or 3 are activated, the 4-input gate provides a low-active chip select. Any address in the lower 32K space will therefore select the 32K device. Likewise, the 2-input gate activates the 16K device if either line 4 or 5 is selected; lines 6 and 7 need no further decoding since they represent 8K addresses each. The alternative solution

FIGURE 7-11   Address Decoding for Design Example 7-1

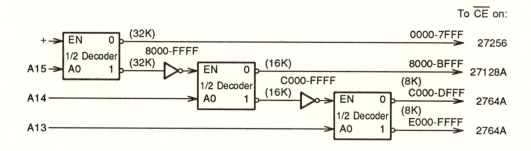

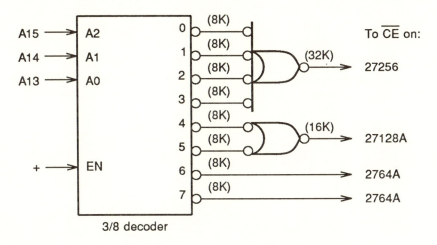

FIGURE 7-12 Alternative Address Decoding for Design Example 7-1

uses a larger size decoder and requires external gates, but has somewhat less delay time.

Address Decoding for 32-bit CPUs

As indicated previously, the techniques presented for address decoding apply to larger CPUs as well. The difference is that a larger address bus exists and decoding starts with an address bit of higher order than A15 (assuming of course a memory system exceeding 64K addresses). Each 32-bit CPU discussed in this textbook has a 32-bit address bus and a 32-bit data bus. In theory, the decoding can begin with address line A31. However, a real system consists of far less than 4G (2^{32}) byte addresses; thus, the highest address bits can be ignored (incomplete decoding).

An important point to understand about most 16-bit and 32-bit CPUs is that they still address memory bytes rather than 16-bit or 32-bit quantities. That is, each byte is assigned a separate address, as was the case for 8-bit CPUs. However, to take advantage of the larger data bus, the interface must provide for access to one or more addresses at a time. Four individual bytes, each having its own address, must be accessed and have their individual 8-bits of data placed on different sections of the 32-bit data bus simultaneously. This is done by paralleling 8-bit wide memory devices (or banks of devices) onto the wider data bus. However, rather than simply tying all the chip selects to a common decoded address line, as shown earlier, proper control must be provided to accommodate CPU operations for various data sizes. The CPUs are generally provided with special "data size" control pins to assist in this task. Some operations will only require 8 bits of data, some will require 16 bits, and some the entire 32 bits permissible by the CPU.

317

To illustrate this concept, consider the 16-bit INTEL 8086 CPU, the earliest member of Intel's 16-bit and 32-bit families. The 8086 CPU has a 20-bit address, with the low 16 bits being shared with the 16 data lines. Figure 7-13a illustrates how the address lines are latched and the data lines buffered to provide separate buses in a typical system. The 8086 CPU issues an address latch enable (ALE) signal which is asserted when the shared lines are outputting an address rather than data; ALE is used to enable the address latches.

In contrast, the low active data enable ($\overline{DEN}$) pin provides an enable of the data buffers, and a data transmit/receive (DT/ $\overline{R}$) pin provides direction control. A low active bus high enable ($\overline{BHE}$) signal is also supplied by the 8086 CPU to provide control of the high byte of the data bus. When $\overline{BHE}$ is not asserted, the high eight data lines are effectively isolated from the 8086 CPU's internal data bus. The lowest order address bit, A0, serves the same purpose for the lower data byte.

Figure 7-13b illustrates how $\overline{BHE}$, in conjunction with A0, can be used to control a 16-bit wide memory array. The lower memory bank contains the odd addressed bytes; the upper memory bank the even addressed bytes. As shown in Table 7-4, the 8086 CPU permits both byte and 16-bit word operations to be performed independent of whether the data starts on an even or odd address. Notice the lowest address line directly entering the memory devices is A1, since A0 is used to control the chip selects of the even addressed bank.

TABLE 7-4 Summary of INTEL 8086 CPU Data Operations

Transfer	$\overline{BHE}$	A0	Active Data
Even addressed byte	1	0	D7-D0
Odd addressed byte	0	1	D15-D8
Even addressed 16-bit word	0	0	D15-D0
Odd addressed 16-bit word	0	1	D15-D8 (Bus Cycle 1)
	1	0	D7-D0 (Bus Cycle 2)

Observe that data bytes and 16-bit words starting on an even address can be transferred in a single bus cycle, but that 16-bit words starting at an odd address ("misaligned" data) must be transferred one byte at a time. Notice the 8086 CPU, like the 80386 CPU, stores its data with the least significant byte at the lowest address. Thus, in the case of an odd addressed 16-bit word, the least significant byte is transferred first over the upper data bus, and then the most significant byte over the low data bus. The CPU ensures that the bytes are directed to or from the appropriate half of the internal 16-bit registers involved in the transfer, in a manner transparent to the programmer.

The INTEL 80386 CPU design built upon the 8086 concept of a bus enabling control signal by eliminating the lowest two address lines and replacing them

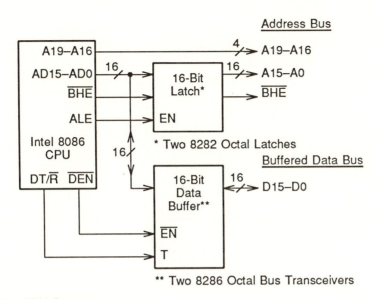

a. Intel 8086 CPU System

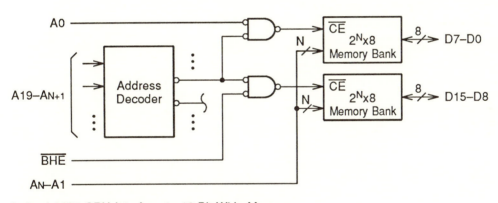

b. Intel 8086 CPU Interface to 16-Bit Wide Memory

FIGURE 7-13   INTEL 8086 CPU Byte and 16-bit Word Data Transfer

with four byte enables ($\overline{BE3}$-$\overline{BE0}$). This allows ease of hardware control for 8-bit, 16-bit, and 32-bit operations. Figure 7-14 shows how each byte enable is gated to a decoded address to control access to each byte of the 32-bit data bus. In this case, a full 32-bit double word corresponds to four successive addresses, so that the lowest address bit entering the memory devices directly is now A2. The address space is appropriately viewed as 2^{30} double words of 32-bits each, which is equivalent, in total size, to 2^{32} bytes.

319

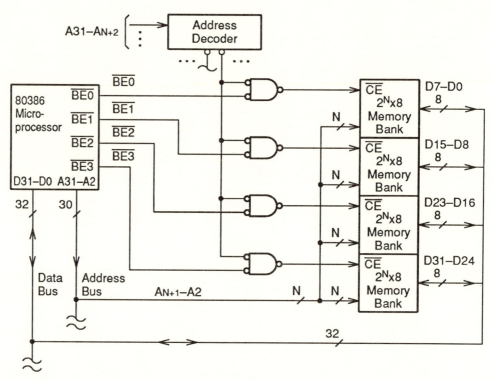

FIGURE 7-14   80386 CPU Byte, 16-Bit Word, and 32-Bit Double-Word Transfer

As with the 8086 CPU, data transfer for the 80386 CPU permits the data to be stored at any address in the total address space. It also performs the transfer in one bus cycle if the data is properly "aligned"; otherwise a second cycle is required. For the 80386 CPU, an aligned address is divisible by 4 (address = 4N, where N is any integer); therefore, data is aligned if it is contained between the addresses 4N and 4N + 3. As a result, a 32-bit word must start at address 4N to be properly aligned, a 16-bit data word may start at 4N, 4N + 1, or 4N + 2 (but not 4N + 3), and a byte may start at any address. Table 7-5 summarizes all the cases. Notice a bus cycle may result in a 24-bit transfer as well, but only as part of the transfer of a misaligned 32-bit double word.

Notice the byte enables ($\overline{BE3}$-$\overline{BE0}$) provided by the 80386 CPU simplify the interfacing considerably, in the same way as did $\overline{BHE}$ of the 8086. For the 80386 CPU, there are cases where the lowest address bits A1 and A0 may be required. An interface to a "standard" bus, such as MULTIBUS I or MULTIBUS II, which are discussed in Chapter Nine, would require both addresses; another use of byte enables involves a feature called dynamic bus sizing.

Dynamic Bus Sizing

Dynamic bus sizing allows the 80386 CPU to be connected to either a 32-bit or a 16-bit data bus for memory or I/O data transfer. This is accomplished by having an address decoding circuit or a device itself activate the 80386

TABLE 7-5 Summary of INTEL 80386 Data Operations

Transfer	Starting Address	First Bus Cycle BE3	BE2	BE1	BE0	Active Data	Second Bus Cycle BE3	BE2	BE1	BE0	Active Data
32 Bit	4N	0	0	0	0	D31-D0					
16 Bit	4N+2	0	0	1	1	D31-D16					
	4N+1	1	0	0	1	D23-D8					
	4N	1	1	0	0	D15-D0					
Byte	4N+3	0	1	1	1	D31-D24					
	4N+2	1	0	1	1	D23-D16					
	4N+1	1	1	0	1	D15-D8					
	4N	1	1	1	0	D7-D0					
32 Bit	4N+1	1	1	1	0	D7-D0	0	0	0	1	D31-D8
	4N+2	1	1	0	0	D15-D0	0	0	1	1	D31-D16
	4N+3	1	0	0	0	D23-D0	0	1	1	1	D31-D24
16 Bit	4N+3	1	1	1	0	D7-D0	0	1	1	1	D31-D24

control input ($\overline{BS16}$) on any bus cycle involving a 16-bit data operation. All transfers then physically occur on the lower half of the 32-bit bus over lines D15-D0. Dynamic bus sizing is advantageous in situations where certain sections of memory need not be accessed at very high speed, and the use of 16-bit wide rather than 32-bit wide devices may reduce chip count. Another advantage is that I/O software compatibility with earlier 16-bit CPUs can be maintained.

When a 16-bit bus is used instead of the full 32-bits, all odd addressed 16-bit data require two bus cycles. Also, 32-bit data may still be transferred, but, depending on alignment, will take either two or three bus cycles. For a 32-bit operation involving only the upper half of the bus (D31-D16), the same transfer via the 16-bit bus uses the lower half instead (D15-D0). For transfers requiring both upper and lower halves of the data bus, an extra cycle is required because the lower half is used for both transfers. For the 16-bit bus interface, the 80386 CPU needs to generate the signals equivalent to the 8086 bus high enable ($\overline{BHE}$) and bus low enable (A0). Additionally, A1 is needed to provide the lowest order address bit directly to the device.

Table 7-6 shows the result of the relationships of data size and starting address to generating byte enables for both the 32-bit and 16-bit bus cases.

Figure 7-15 shows the design of simplified gate logic to generate the two low address bits and $\overline{BHE}$ for the 16-bit bus used with the 80386. Figure 7-16 shows how the 80386 CPU can be interfaced to 16-bit wide devices (rather than 32-bit wide devices) and to a standard bus.

TABLE 7-6 80386 Byte Enables and Equivalent
8086 Signals

80386 Byte Enables				Equivalent 8086 Signals		
$\overline{BE3}$	$\overline{BE2}$	$\overline{BE1}$	$\overline{BE0}$	$\overline{BHE}$	A1	A0
0	0	0	0	0	0	0
0	0	0	1	0	0	1
0	0	1	0	x	x	x*
0	0	1	1	0	1	0
0	1	0	0	x	x	x*
0	1	0	1	x	x	x*
0	1	1	0	x	x	x*
0	1	1	1	0	1	1
1	0	0	0	0	0	0
1	0	0	1	0	0	1
1	0	1	0	x	x	x*
1	0	1	1	1	1	0
1	1	0	0	0	0	0
1	1	0	1	0	0	1
1	1	1	0	1	0	0
1	1	1	1	x	x	x**

* Transfer of noncontiguous bytes does not occur.
** No data transfer.

Notes:
1. $\overline{BHE}$ is low when D15–D8 is active.
2. A1 is low for even addressed 16-bit words.
3. A0 is low when D7–D0 is active.

The MOTOROLA MC68020 CPU and AT&T *WE* 32100 CPU also feature data transfer of various widths. Unlike the INTEL 80386 CPU, which presents decoded byte enable bits to external hardware, these two CPUs issue a 2-bit data size indicator (SIZ1-SIZ0 for the MOTOROLA MC68020 CPU and DSIZE1-DSIZE0 for the AT&T *WE* 32100 CPU). The details are given in Table 7-7.

TABLE 7-7 MOTOROLA MC68020 CPU and AT&T *WE* 32100
CPU Data Sizing Bits

MOTOROLA MC68020 CPU Data Sizing			AT&T *WE* 32100 CPU Data Sizing		
SIZ1	SIZ0	Width	DSIZE1	DSIZE0	Width
0	1	8 bit	1	1	8 bit
1	0	16 bit	1	0	16 bit
1	1	24 bit	0	0	32 bit
0	0	32 bit	0	1	64 bit

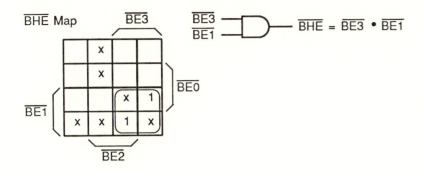

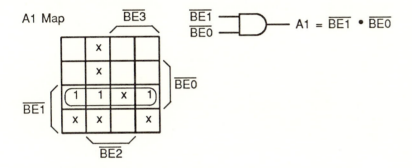

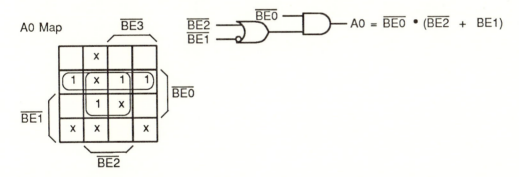

FIGURE 7-15   Generating 80386 Low Address Bits and Byte High Enable for a 16-Bit Bus

Logic can be designed which takes the lowest two address bits and the data size indicator bits and generates the equivalent INTEL 80386 CPU byte enable signals ($\overline{BE3}$-$\overline{BE0}$). The details of the design using the MOTOROLA MC68020 CPU are left as an exercise (see Exercise 11).

323

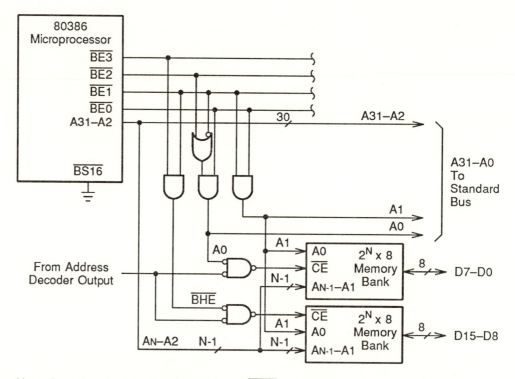

Note: Asserting the bus size control input ($\overline{BS16}$) assures data transfer over the lower half of the data bus (D15–D0)

FIGURE 7-16   INTEL 80386 CPU Interface to 16-Bit Device and Standard Bus

Read/Write Control

As we have seen, address decoding schemes have the objective of providing chip selects (or chip enables) for one device or bank of devices at a time. In addition, proper control must be provided to distinguish between read and write operations. This prevents data read out of an addressed location conflicting with new data to be written to that location. Also, additional control must be provided for those CPUs which separate memory and I/O address spaces. The 80386 CPU is an example of such a CPU (recall the discussion of IN and OUT instructions in Section 4.5). Otherwise, a memory access could also result in reading or writing an I/O device since a common address bus is used.

As shown in Figure 7-17, the CPU typically provides this control on anywhere from 1 to 4 lines. Intel CPUs, as well as the ZILOG Z-80 CPU, are examples of microprocessors that feature separate I/O instructions. The Motorola and AT&T CPUs use memory-mapped I/O, where the I/O device appears to the CPU as addressable memory along with ROM and RAM. Thus, CPUs with memory mapped I/O only have to provide read/write control; those with separate I/O

324

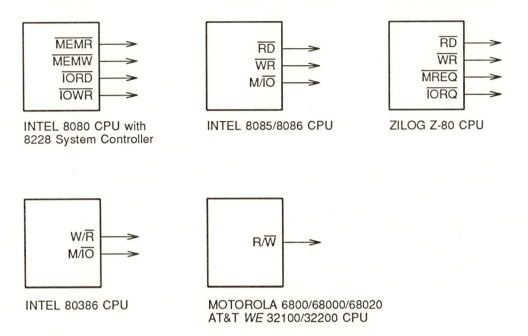

FIGURE 7-17 CPU Read/Write Control of Memory and I/O

must provide at least one additional pin to distinguish between a memory and an I/O operation.

The 8-bit INTEL 8080 Microprocessor did not provide the required interface control signals directly from the CPU. When used with an INTEL 8228 System Controller, it supplies separate memory read, memory write, I/O read, and I/O write lines. The other CPUs shown either provide separate low active read and write control pins or a shared pin (usually R/$\overline{\text{W}}$, or W/$\overline{\text{R}}$ for the 80386 CPU). Those that permit use of separate I/O addressing also have an M/$\overline{\text{IO}}$ pin or, in the case of the Z-80 CPU, separate memory request ($\overline{\text{MREQ}}$) and I/O request ($\overline{\text{IORQ}}$) lines. Simple gating can convert the outputs provided by one CPU to those supplied by another, which might be required to interface the CPU to a standard bus.

When interfacing to memory or I/O, the control signals are generally tied to device control pins such as write enable ($\overline{\text{WE}}$) or output enable ($\overline{\text{OE}}$). Additionally, the same lines may be used to enable the address decoder. This is particularly true of the memory request or shared M/$\overline{\text{IO}}$ line. Figure 7-18 shows the use of the control lines in interfacing to a typical memory device. The only logic required is inverters for those CPUs where either the read/write control or the memory or I/O selection is on a shared pin.

Additional control must be provided when the memory devices have separate data in and data out pins. Recall this is typically the case for 1-bit wide RAMs. Figure 7-19 shows how a read/write line from the CPU can be used to control direction flow and avoid bus contention. If the memory chip tristates its data out

a. INTEL 8080 CPU Based System ($\overline{\text{IORD}}$ and $\overline{\text{IOWR}}$ used for I/O control)

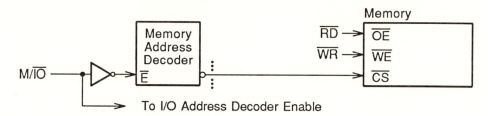

b. INTEL 8085/8086 CPU Based System

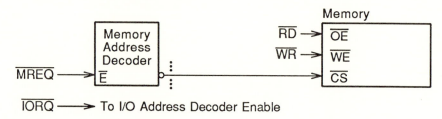

c. ZILOG Z-80 CPU Based System

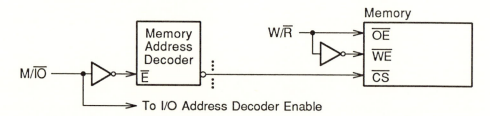

d. INTEL 80386 CPU Based System

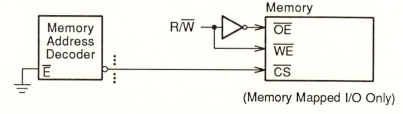

e. MOTOROLA 6800/68000/68020 CPU and AT&T *WE* 32100/32200 CPU Based System

FIGURE 7-18   Use of Control Lines in Memory Interfacing

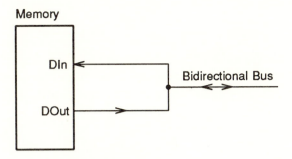

a. Internal Control Provided

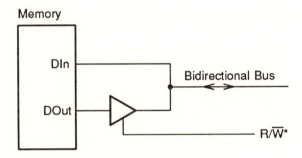

b. External Control with a Single Gate

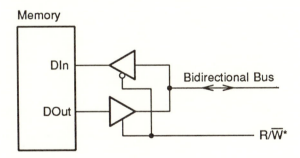

c. External Control with Two Gates

*If using INTEL 80386 CPU, invert W/$\overline{R}$ line.

FIGURE 7-19   Interface of Separate Data In/Out Pins to Bidirectional Bus

line when data is not being output, the data out and data in pins can simply be tied. A safer way is to provide one or two external tristates to control the data flow as shown. Separate write control also ensures correct operation for CPUs that may not provide the proper internal tristating.

Buffering

Binary digital logic offers the advantage that a device need only distinguish between one of two voltage levels. Using the positive logic convention, the lower voltage corresponds to logic 0 and the higher voltage to logic 1. The actual voltage may vary somewhat and still remain within an acceptable range for that logic level.

A potential problem exists when a logic device has its output or outputs connected to several other devices. In this configuration the outputting logic device is referred to as the driver and the other devices are called loads. The number of loads connected determines the amount of current which a driver must either supply or absorb, depending on the logic level at the driver's output. When too many loads are connected to a given driver, the current required may exceed the driver's rated value. For this case, the resulting voltage is no longer guaranteed by the device manufacturer to be within the proper range for the required logic level. The insertion of special devices, called buffers, between the driver and the loads often solves the problem. Buffers basically enhance the current capability of the driver. The loads now see the buffers as the drivers, and the buffers are chosen with a higher output current rating than the original drivers.

The maximum number of loads that a driver can accommodate without buffering is called the fanout. A given logic device generally has four voltage and four current value specifications. The four cases result from the fact that the device may be used as either a driver or as a load, and that the logic level may be either low (logic 0) or high (logic 1). Using standard notation, the eight values are:

Parameter	Description
V_{OL}	Maximum output voltage, low case (driver)
I_{OL}	Maximum output current, low case (driver)
V_{OH}	Minimum output voltage, high case (driver)
I_{OH}	Maximum output current, high case (driver)
V_{IL}	Maximum input voltage, low case (load)
I_{IL}	Maximum input current, low case (load)
V_{IH}	Minimum input voltage, high case (load)
I_{IH}	Maximum input current, high case (load)

The voltage levels must be below a specified maximum value to be considered a low, and above a specified minimum level for a high. Current specifications are all given as maximum values. A driver supplies (sources) current to the load in the high case, and absorbs (sinks) current from the load in the low case. The current values specified for load devices are a guarantee that they will not require more than that value, although a given load could require less. The maximum driver current is also a guarantee that the device can source or sink up to the specified value of current. These values all represent worst case assumptions in terms of voltage and current levels. Thus, a given design is guaranteed to provide acceptable voltages provided the fanout is not exceeded. If the fanout is exceeded, the design may or may not work.

Table 7-8 presents voltage and current specifications for typical gate devices in the standard TTL, low-power Schottky TTL (LSTTL), and CMOS families of logic. Currents entering a device are listed as positive, and currents leaving a device are negative.

TABLE 7-8 Voltage and Current Specifications

Voltage or Current	Logic Family			Unit
	TTL	LSTTL	CMOS	
VOL	0.4	0.5	0.4	V
IOL	16	8	0.36	mA
VOH	2.4	2.7	4.6	V
IOH	− 0.4	− 0.4	− 0.36	mA
VIL	0.8	0.8	1.5	V
IIL	− 1.6	− 0.4	− 0.001	mA
VIH	2.0	2.0	3.5	V
IIH	0.04	0.02	0.001	mA

Figure 7-20 shows a driver connected to several loads, and identifies the voltages and currents for both the low and high cases. The output voltage from the driver and the input voltages to the loads would be the same except that noise may enter the system at the interconnection point.

From Table 7-8, notice the load input voltage VIL for the low case is higher than the guaranteed driver output VOL. This means that some noise can enter the system which would add to the driver output voltage, and still be at an acceptable level for the load to recognize it as a low. The difference in these voltage levels that maintain the low state without triggering the logic circuit to the high state is called the noise immunity. Likewise, VOH for a given logic family is in all cases higher than VIH; thus in the high case a certain noise immunity is provided as well. Noise in the high case can decrease VOH by a certain amount before the load fails to recognize it as a high.

Voltage-level related problems may arise when a driver from one family is connected to loads from a different family. For example, the minimum VIH required by a CMOS load exceeds the guaranteed minimum VOH provided by a TTL or LSTTL driver (see Example 2).

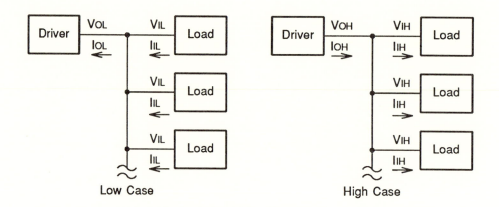

Note: All voltages are measured with respect to ground.

FIGURE 7-20   Device Voltages and Currents for Low and High Cases

Recall that voltage values are guaranteed only so long as fanout is not exceeded. Since it is apparent that for N loads the driver current required is N times the load current, the allowable fanout is the ratio of driver current to load current. Since the low and high case are considered independently, the fanout is then the smaller of the ratios I_{OL}/I_{IL} and I_{OH}/I_{IH} (ignoring signs).

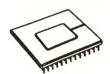

Sample Calculations

Device Fanouts and Noise Immunity Calculations for Combinations of Driver and Load Families

Example 1. TTL Driver, TTL Loads

Low Case:

$$\text{Fanout} = I_{OL}(TTL) / I_{IL}(TTL) = 16 \text{ mA} / 1.6 \text{ mA} = 10$$
$$\text{Noise Immunity} = V_{IL}(TTL) - V_{OL}(TTL) = 0.8 \text{ V} - 0.4 \text{ V} = 0.4 \text{ V}$$

High Case:

$$\text{Fanout} = I_{OH}(TTL) / I_{IH}(TTL) = 0.4 \text{ mA} / 0.04 \text{ mA} = 10$$
$$\text{Noise Immunity} = V_{OH}(TTL) - V_{IH}(TTL) = 2.4 \text{ V} - 2.0 \text{ V} = 0.4 \text{ V}$$

For both cases, notice that a maximum of 10 TTL loads can be connected to a TTL driver and noise immunity is 0.4 V.

Example 2. LSTTL Driver, CMOS Loads

Low Case:

Fanout = IOL(LSTTL) / IIL(CMOS) = 8 mA / 0.001 mA = 8000

Noise Immunity = VIL(CMOS) − VOL(LSTTL) = 1.5 V − 0.5 V = 1.0 V

High Case:

Fanout = IOH(LSTTL) / IIH(CMOS) = 0.4 mA / 0.001 mA = 400

Noise Immunity = VOH(LSTTL) − VIH(CMOS) = 2.7 V − 3.5 V = −0.8 V

Notice up to 400 loads can be accommodated due to the limited current requirements of CMOS loads. The low case yields a noise immunity of 1.0 V; however, a CMOS load may require at least 3.5 V in the high case and an LSTTL driver output may be as low as 2.7 V. The negative noise immunity indicates that buffering is required, independent of the number of loads connected.

Example 3. CMOS driver, TTL loads

Low Case:

Fanout = IOL(CMOS) / IIL(TTL) = 0.36 mA / 1.6 mA = 0.225

Noise Immunity = VIL(TTL) − VOL(CMOS) = 0.8 V − 0.4 V = 0.4 V

High Case:

Fanout = IOH(CMOS) / IIH(TTL) = 0.36 mA / 0.04 mA = 9

Noise Immunity = VOH(CMOS) − VIH(TTL) = 4.6 V − 2.0 V = 2.6 V

In this example, a noise immunity of 0.4 V for the low case and 2.6 V for the high case is quite acceptable. While a CMOS driver can handle up to 9 loads for the high case, clearly it is unable to drive a single TTL load in the low case. Buffering is needed.

The examples highlight that bipolar logic families, such as TTL, have greater drive capability than do MOS logic families. CMOS is often chosen because of its very low power dissipation; however, its particularly low current drive capability often necessitates buffering. Buffering is generally required when a microprocessor, usually an MOS device, drives loads which are either bipolar logic or have current requirements comparable to one or more bipolar devices. The buffering needs of microprocessor systems must be analyzed carefully since data, address, and control lines may all have different current and voltage specifications.

Voltage and Current Specifications for 32-Bit Microprocessors

Table 7-9 shows the specifications for the INTEL 80386 CPU, MOTOROLA MC68020 CPU, and AT&T *WE* 32100 CPU used as drivers. Values are shown for the data and address lines only. Differences exist for certain control signals.

TABLE 7-9 Microprocessor Voltage and Current Specifications

Voltage or Current	INTEL 80386 CPU*	MOTOROLA MC68020 CPU	AT&T WE 32100 and 32200 CPU	Unit
VOL	0.45	0.5	0.4	V
IOL	4	3.2	3.5	mA
VOH	2.4	2.4	2.4	V
IOH	−1	−0.4	−3.5	mA

* Based on preliminary data.

Since the voltage levels are nearly identical with those of typical bipolar devices, there is several tenths of a volt noise immunity when one of these CPUs is interfaced to a TTL or LSTTL type device. Buffering is therefore not required from a voltage standpoint. Current drive for the address and data lines of these CPUs is somewhat better than that of the typical CMOS device shown earlier. However, only a limited number of TTL load equivalents can be driven from these buses in the low case. For example, the INTEL 80386 CPU can sink 4 mA in the low case while a TTL load may source as much as 1.6 mA. Therefore, only two TTL loads can be driven by the 80386 CPU even though the high case supports 25 loads (1 mA/0.04 mA). To drive more than two TTL loads requires buffering.

7.3 Timing

A complete timing analysis requires that timing waveforms and specifications be studied carefully. In its most basic form, timing analysis reduces to answering the question of whether a memory device is fast enough to read or write data within the time frame allowed by the CPU. If the memory is too slow, the system will not work reliably and either must operate at a lower clock rate or the CPU's time frame must be lengthened by inserting wait states. CPUs are constantly achieving higher clock rates and memory devices have tried to keep pace with the subsequent reductions in access times. To take advantage of the high clock rates achievable with 32-bit CPUs while keeping memory costs reasonable, techniques such as address pipelining or the use of high-speed temporary storage (called cache memory) are used.

Read and Write Cycles

Figure 7-21 illustrates a typical CPU timing diagram for both a memory read and memory write operation. The intent here is to define critical timing parameters; the actual waveforms for a particular CPU are referenced to the system's clock signal(s). As is done on most manufacturer's data sheets, the address and data buses are represented by two parallel lines. The actual address or data bit values are not relevant, the concern being whether address or data appearing on the lines at any time is valid. Recall from Chapter One, crosshatched lines indicate unknown or invalid address or data. The assumption is that the CPU has a single read/write pin with a high signifying a read operation. For the INTEL 80386 CPU, a high logic level denotes a write operation and the waveform for R/$\overline{W}$ in Figure 7-21 has to be inverted. For earlier CPUs with separate low active read ($\overline{RD}$) and write ($\overline{WR}$) lines, only the R/$\overline{W}$ waveform shown for the memory read cycle has to be inverted. For CPUs with separate I/O addressing available, the M/$\overline{IO}$ pin is held high to access memory as opposed to I/O.

Both a read cycle and a write cycle begin with the CPU issuing a memory address. Shortly after, the read/write line goes high to identify a read cycle, or low to signify a write cycle. The CPU's data bus is then configured to bring data into the CPU for a read operation, or to send data out when writing to memory.

For a read, the CPU expects valid data from the addressed memory location to be present on the data bus. This data is required within a time tACC after the

FIGURE 7-21 Typical CPU Timing for Read and Write Operations (Using Intel Notation)

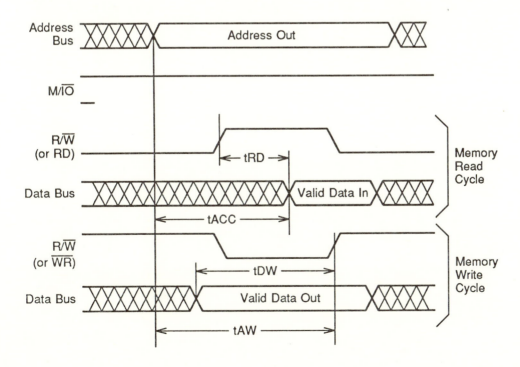

address has been sent out. The CPU also must receive the data no later than tRD after the read/write line has been activated; otherwise it may not be able to latch the data before the read/write line is deactivated again. The access time (tACC) is the maximum amount of time the memory device has to respond to the address, decode it internally, and read the data out onto the data bus. A problem exists if the memory's access time exceeds tACC; even if the memory access time is below tACC, other factors must be checked. For example, several of the address lines are generally decoded externally. Depending on decoder delays and the memory timing specifications involving maximum delay from chip select to valid data read out on the data bus, the actual memory access time may exceed the tACC specification. Also, if tRD is too small, the delay in activating the memory device's output enable could increase effective access time, although this is not too likely.

For a write operation the address out is generally followed by valid data being presented to the data bus by the CPU. The read/write line is then brought low to activate a write. The memory must latch the data before read/write goes high again. This corresponds to the data write time (tDW) starting from the time data is valid. Alternatively, the address write time (tAW) is measured from address out to read/write being deactivated.

Timing Examples

As an example of an initial timing analysis, consider the problem of reading data from a ROM or RAM device into the 80386 CPU. Ignoring the address decoding, this first example calculates the worst case time from when the CPU's address is sent out to when data is required by the CPU on the bus. Figure 7-22

FIGURE 7-22   80386 Timing for Basic Read Cycle

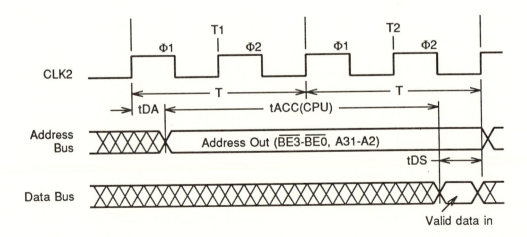

shows the timing relationships of the address and data buses referenced to the system clock. The timing parameters are:

tDA = Delayed Address Time
tDS = Data-in Setup Time
T = System Clock Period

Both minimum and maximum values of tDA are usually specified in the manufacturer's data sheets. The maximum value must be used for worst case analysis, since it represents the latest time we can expect a valid address to be sent out (although the CPU may send it sooner). Data setup time is given as a minimum value, indicating that it must be present on the bus no later than that time prior to the end of the cycle to guarantee a valid read. The *INTEL 80386 Advance Information Data Sheet* (current at the time of this publication) gives the following specifications for the two CPU clock rates available:

Parameter	Value for 16 MHz Clock	Value for 20 MHz Clock
tDA	38 ns (max)	32 ns (max)
tDS	10 ns (min)	10 ns (min)
T	62.5 ns [1/(16 MHz)]	50 ns [1/(20 MHz)]

The CPU access time for the worst case is the time from address out to data in. The memory access time cannot exceed this. For the 80386 CPU, this access time is

$$tACC(CPU) = 2T - tDA - tDS$$

For the values specified, the maximum access time is

$$tACCmax(16 \text{ MHz}) = 2(62.5) \text{ ns} - 38 \text{ ns} - 10 \text{ ns} = 77 \text{ ns at 16 MHz},$$

and

$$tACCmax(20 \text{ MHz}) = 2(50) \text{ ns} - 32 \text{ ns} - 10 \text{ ns} = 58 \text{ ns at 20 MHz}.$$

Typical access times for Intel EPROM and RAM devices were given in Section 7.1. Access times are on the order of 200 ns to 250 ns for EPROMs, and about 100 ns for DRAM. Only 1-bit and 4-bit SRAMs have access times below 50 ns. Thus, for most memory devices, the use of wait states or some other technique is required to avoid read or write errors when running at the CPU clock rate.

For write operations with the 80386 (not shown in the diagrams), valid data out is available about midway through state T1 and remains on the bus until the end of T2. Since W/$\overline{R}$ is also active until the end of T2, the parameters tAW and tDW (shown in Figure 7-21) are sufficiently large, so that in most cases the read access time will be the more critical one.

When address decoding is used with the appropriate CPU control signals, the additional delays may significantly increase the memory's effective access time. Design Example 7-2 illustrates this point as well as the address decoding techniques discussed previously in Section 7.2.

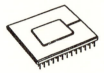

Design Example 7-2

Interfacing EPROM to the INTEL 80386 Microprocessor

a. Interface the INTEL 80386 CPU to 1M byte of EPROM, using 27256-1 EPROMs. This memory is to occupy the lowest 1M addresses (00000000 to 000FFFFF).

b. Assuming a 16 MHz clock rate, calculate the worst case access time. Is this acceptable?

Solution: The 27256-1 EPROM is a 32K x 8 EPROM with 15 address inputs, a chip enable ($\overline{CE}$), and an output enable ($\overline{OE}$) pin. Figure 7-23 shows the waveforms for the 27256-1 and the worst case time delay specifications. Only the access time tACC was used in previous calculations for worst case access time. Notice from the specifications in the figure that the delay from chip enable to valid data out (tCE) may be as large as tACC. This can create a problem. Some of the address lines from the CPU are to be decoded causing a decoding delay that will result in the EPROM's chip enable being activated after the address out time. This corresponds to the time when the EPROM's address pins are presented with a valid address. Thus, the time to valid data out may be longer than tACC. Also, some time is required after the output enable is activated before valid data appears, so that its effect on the access time must also be determined.

The memory interface is shown in Figure 7-24. Individual delay times are shown in parentheses. The delay times for 80386 CPU outputs represent the latest times those signals are activated with respect to the beginning of the first bus cycle T1 as shown in Figure 7-22. The delay times shown at the input lines of the 27256-1 EPROM are the maximum delays before valid data out can be guaranteed. Typical TTL devices are assumed, resulting in 10 ns gate delays and

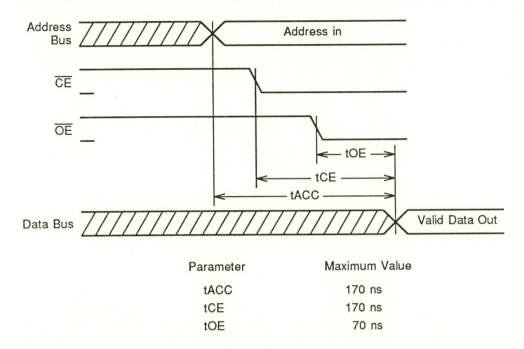

Parameter	Maximum Value
tACC	170 ns
tCE	170 ns
tOE	70 ns

FIGURE 7-23 Timing Waveform for Reading a 27256-1 EPROM

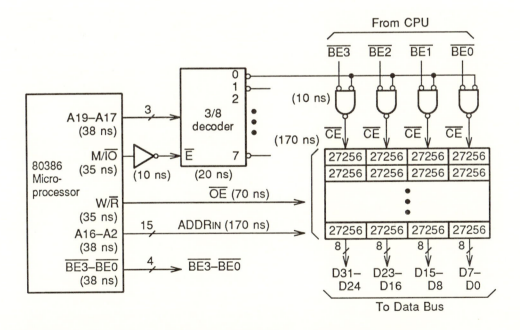

FIGURE 7-24 Interfacing the INTEL 80386 CPU to 1M byte of EPROM

337

a 20 ns decoder delay (recall that a decoder is basically a two-level gate circuit). The various paths produce these worst case results:

Address in (A16-A2) to data out:	$38 + 170 = 208$ ns
M/$\overline{\text{IO}}$ to chip enable in to data out:	$35 + 10 + 20 + 10 + 170 = 245$ ns
W/$\overline{\text{R}}$ to output enable to data out:	$35 + 70 = 105$ ns

The chip enable path is obviously the most critical. The net effect is that the EPROM's access time has been increased to

$$170 \text{ ns} + (245 - 208) \text{ ns} = 207 \text{ ns}$$

Compared to the previously calculated 80386 CPU access time of 77 ns at 16 MHz, we see that the difference of 130 ns corresponds to slightly more than two clock cycles, where

$$\text{One clock cycle at 16 MHz} = 1/(16 \text{ MHz}) = 62.5 \text{ ns}$$

Since the EPROM access time greatly exceeds the CPU's access requirements, read or write errors are likely to occur. Address pipelining and wait state insertion are techniques commonly used to solve this timing problem.

80386 CPU Address Pipelining

Address pipelining is an option provided by the 80386 CPU that enables it to operate at a clock rate that would otherwise be too high for the memory being used. This is accomplished by outputting the address and control signals for a given bus cycle during the previous cycle. The CPU access time is thereby lengthened, and the memory device's own access time can be correspondingly longer. Pipelined or nonpipelined address timing is selected on a cycle by cycle basis by the 80386's next address ($\overline{\text{NA}}$) input. Since current address and control signals are replaced before the end of the given bus cycle, address latches should be used in systems with pipelined addressing.

Figure 7-25 illustrates waveforms from the *Intel 80386 Advance Information Data Sheet* for both nonpipelined and pipelined operations. In the nonpipelined case in Figure 7-25a, the time from address out to data read in is nominally four CLK2 cycles, or two system clock cycles (T1 and T2). As discussed earlier, the actual CPU access time is reduced by the worst case address delay and data setup times. For the pipelined address case, shown in Figure 7-25b, the access time is increased by one system clock cycle. This is observed as the difference between address valid for CYCLE 2 (the start of VALID 2 address and control signals) and data in for CYCLE 2 (called IN2 on the data bus). The memory and interface circuitry receive the address and control signals near the start of T2P of CYCLE 1, and have T1P and most of T2P of CYCLE 2 to read the data. Note that after a bus state where no bus request has been made (a bus idle state), the first

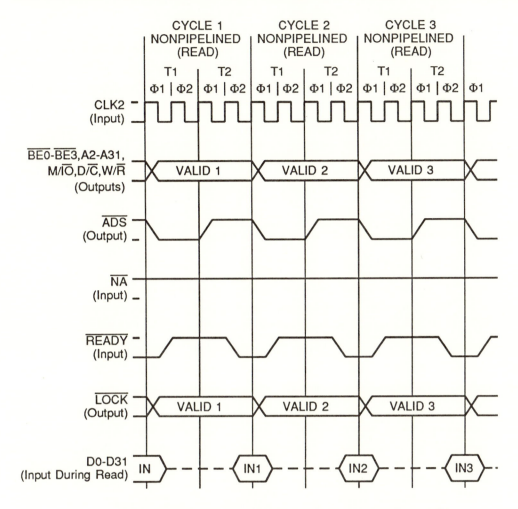

Note: Fastest nonpipelined bus cycles consist of T1 and T2

FIGURE 7-25a Fastest Read Cycles with Nonpipelined Address Timing

read or write cycle must be a nonpipelined cycle; a pipelined address cannot be sent out during a bus idle cycle. In a system containing both "fast" memory which does not require pipelined address timing and "slow" memory which does, it is advantageous to use pipelining for all devices. In this case, if a fast memory access is followed by a pipelined cycle to the slower memory, the slower memory has the extra cycle to respond. This would not be the case if the faster memory access was done with a nonpipelined cycle, since the CPU does not know which device the next bus cycle accesses. If two successive fast memory accesses are performed with pipelined cycles, the extra time is provided even though not needed; however, no processor time is lost.

The first timing example in this section calculated the CPU access times for a read operation and considered only address delay and data setup requirements.

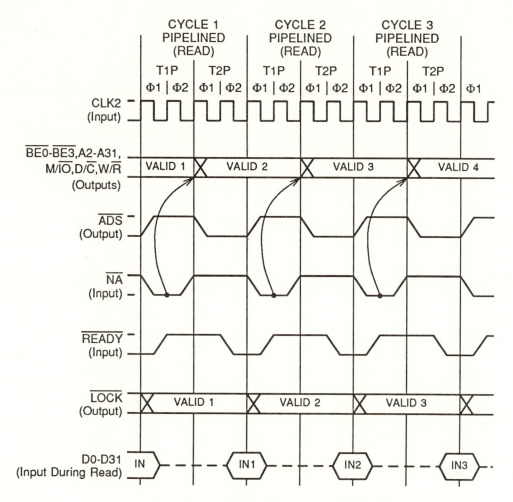

CYCLE 1
PIPELINED
(READ)

CYCLE 2
PIPELINED
(READ)

CYCLE 3
PIPELINED
(READ)

Fastest pipelined bus cycles consist of T1P and T2P

FIGURE 7-25 (b) Fastest Read Cycles with Pipelined Address Timing

The results were 77 ns at a 16 MHz clock rate and 58 ns at a 20 MHz clock rate. If these cycles were pipelined instead, the increase in access time would be one system clock period (62.5 ns at 16 MHz or 50 ns at 20 MHz). The CPU read access times for pipelined address cycles are therefore 139.5 ns at 16 MHz, and 108 ns at 20 MHz. Typical EPROMs are still too slow, but SRAM would be suitable.

Wait States

Most microprocessors offer the use of wait states as another alternative to using a slower clock. Wait states require extra hardware for a memory or I/O device to "inform" the CPU when it has completed the read or write operation, which is offset by the advantage that only certain bus cycles are slowed down.

In contrast, a slower clock increases all bus cycles thereby lowering the overall system throughput in proportion to the clock rate reduction.

Wait states are basically additional clock cycles added to the bus cycle. The CPU generally has one or more input pins which must be activated by external logic to generate a wait state. Multiple wait states are generated by keeping the input(s) active as long as required by the device's timing needs. Wait states are generally more crucial for I/O device accesses as opposed to memory operations, since I/O devices often require more response time than the slowest of memory devices. However, the impact of I/O wait states on overall system performance is relatively small since most programs require more memory accesses than I/O accesses. For this reason the designers of the ZILOG Z-80 Microprocessor chose to insert automatically one wait state into every I/O read and write cycle; extra hardware is needed only if additional wait states are to be provided for I/O accesses.

As pointed out for the INTEL 80386 CPU, pipelined address timing has the effect of adding one clock cycle to the CPU access time. It is equivalent to inserting one wait state but without the same degree of reduction in system throughput. There is some reduction with pipelining when nonpipelined cycles are required (after bus idle cycles). The results of a sample simulation performed by Intel are given in Table 7-10. The impact of pipelining, use of wait states, and reduced clock frequency on system performance are given in the table. All factors are relative to a 16 MHz clock, with no address pipelining, and zero wait states (corresponding to a performance of 1.00).

TABLE 7-10 INTEL 80386 CPU - Effects of Pipelining, Wait States, and Clock Frequency on System Performance

Wait States	16 MHz		12.5 MHz	
	No Pipelining	Pipelining	No Pipelining	Pipelining
0	1.00	0.91	0.78	0.71
1	0.81	0.76	0.64	0.59
2	0.66	0.63	0.52	0.49
3	0.57	-	0.45	-

Notice from the simulation results that one wait state reduces performance by 19%, whereas pipelining only incurs a 9% reduction. The penalty for using pipelining decreases to 5% or 6% when one or two wait states have also been provided. The reduction in performance due to reduced frequency is exactly proportional to the frequency reduction itself, namely

$$(16 - 12.5) / 16 = 22\%$$

Reducing clock speed is an acceptable alternative in certain applications. Observe from Table 7-10 that a 12.5 MHz system without any wait states yields higher performance than a 16 MHz system with two wait states (independent of pipelining). Since the hardware cost of providing wait states would also be saved, it might appear that the reduced clock rate is a better approach. However, a critical issue is whether the memory devices have enough time to respond, a point that the performance table does not address. To determine the effect of wait states, pipelining, and clock frequency on access time, let us again consider the critical CPU access time for reading operations. This was

$$tACC(CPU) = 2T - tDA - tDS$$

where:

    T = clock period
    tDA = maximum address delay
    tDS = minimum data setup

With N wait states inserted, the access time becomes

$$tACC(CPU) = (2 + N)T - tDA - tDS$$

for the nonpipelined case. Since pipelining adds one more clock cycle, the access time for the pipelined case is then

$$tACC(CPU) = (3 + N)T - tDA - tDS.$$

From the INTEL 80386 CPU specifications,

    at 16 MHz: T = 62.5 ns, tDA = 38 ns, tDS = 10 ns
    at 12.5 MHz: T = 80 ns,   tDA = 45 ns, tDS = 12 ns

The values for 16 MHz were used previously to calculate access time; the address delay and data setup values for 12.5 MHz were taken from the specifications from a 12 MHz version of the 80386 CPU (since the two frequencies are very close). Using these values and the access time formulas, Table 7-11 summarizes the CPU access times for the various conditions.

Now we can see clearly that reducing the clock rate without wait states or pipelining increases the access time window from 77 ns to 103 ns. Alternatively, adding two wait states at 16 MHz allows us to accommodate memory devices on the order of 200 ns access time (ignoring the effect of decoding delays). Another important factor supporting the use of wait states is that the cost of wait state circuitry is negligible when compared with the potential memory cost savings resulting from using slower devices. For example, Table 7-11 suggests that at a higher clock rate, such as 20 MHz, the CPU can run with a 60 ns memory without wait states, or with a 100 ns memory with one wait state inserted (subject to a more careful analysis, of course). For systems with large memory requirements, cost dictates the use of DRAM as opposed to more costly SRAM. DRAMs are available with 60 ns access time, but they are three to four times more costly than 100 ns DRAMs. While inserting a wait state decreases system performance by under 20%, the reduction in memory cost is on the order of 75%.

TABLE 7-11 INTEL 80386 CPU Read Access Time - Effects of Pipelining, Wait States, and Clock Frequency

Wait States	16 MHz		12.5 MHz	
	No Pipelining	Pipelining	No Pipelining	Pipelining
0	77 ns	139 ns	103 ns	183 ns
1	139 ns	202 ns	183 ns	263 ns
2	202 ns	264 ns	263 ns	343 ns
3	264 ns	326 ns	343 ns	423 ns

Wait State Circuit

A simple shift register circuit can be used to generate the required input to place a typical CPU into a wait state. A longer register can be used to generate multiple wait states. For example, the 80386 CPU requires its $\overline{\text{READY}}$ input to be activated every time a new bus cycle is to commence (at the end of T2 of the current cycle). If $\overline{\text{READY}}$ is held high at the end of T2, a wait state will follow (a repeated "T2"). $\overline{\text{READY}}$ is sampled at the end of each wait state and when it is found low, the CPU enters T1 of the next bus cycle.

Figure 7-26 shows the waveforms required for repeated access to a device requiring a single wait state; Figure 7-27 shows the circuit used to implement the wait state generator. Note that the 82384 clock generator's CLK output provides a convenient clock for the positive edge-triggered flip-flops. During accesses which do not require wait states, the address decoder output is high and the shift register state (reading from left to right) is 11; the NAND gate keeps the $\overline{\text{READY}}$ line activated for the 11 state. Since the address status ($\overline{\text{ADS}}$) output from the 80386 CPU is always activated by a new bus cycle, it is convenient to use it along with the address decoder output to strobe a 0 into the shift register at the start of a cycle requiring the wait state. The register state is then 01 at the start of T2 and $\overline{\text{READY}}$ is pulled high; since $\overline{\text{ADS}}$ is deactivated after T1, a 1 enters the register and the 0 shifts right midway through T2. Since the state is now 10 through the end of T2, $\overline{\text{READY}}$ remains high and a WAIT state is entered. However, on the next clock the register returns to the 11 state and $\overline{\text{READY}}$ is low again; a new bus cycle thus commences after a single wait state.

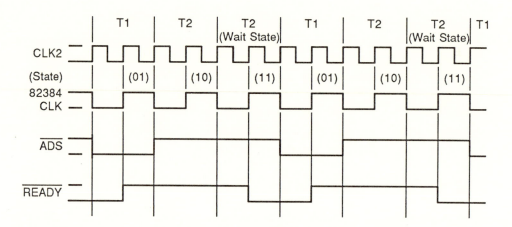

FIGURE 7-26 80386 Waveforms for a Single Wait State Insertion

Figure 7-28 shows the relevant signals required for wait state generation with the MOTOROLA MC68020 CPU and AT&T *WE* 32100 CPU. Designing wait state generators for these CPUs is left as an exercise (see Exercise 22).

Cache Systems

The analysis of timing considerations in this section has emphasized the problem faced using 32-bit microprocessors at high clock rates - namely to provide a large amount of memory at reasonable cost to achieve high system performance. We have seen that the use of wait states or address pipelining for the 80386 CPU can help reduce memory cost but with a reduction in system performance. Another cost effective solution is to provide a cache memory system. As discussed in Section 7.1, a cache is a relatively small-sized but high-speed memory (typically SRAM), placed between the CPU and a larger-sized but slower memory (typically DRAM). The concept is similar to the use of semiconductor memory (ROM and RAM) as the main memory in a computer and disk for auxiliary storage. Programs execute from the faster main memory, while the lower-cost auxiliary memory provides the bulk of the storage for the system. As programs and data are needed,

FIGURE 7-27 Single Wait-State Generator for INTEL 80386 Microprocessor

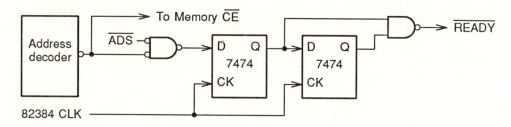

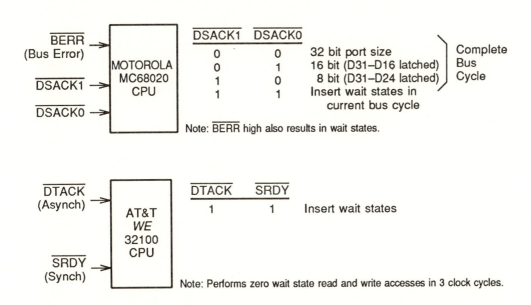

FIGURE 7-28 MOTOROLA MC68020 CPU and AT&T WE 32100 CPU Wait State Control Inputs

they are transferred to main memory and then run (often as part of memory management). This results in high system performance at reasonable cost. Similarly, a semiconductor memory system itself can provide high performance, with a small-capacity cache using fast but expensive SRAM. At the same time the system can achieve economy if the bulk of the storage is in less expensive, though slower, DRAM.

In the case of cache memory, its size must be reasonably small compared to the total amount of main memory; otherwise, the economy of its use is lost. On the other hand, the cache system design must provide a high degree of likelihood that the opcodes and data to be accessed at a given time reside in the cache; otherwise system performance is compromised. As is usually the case, cost and performance are factors that are traded off; a larger size cache will provide increased performance, but at higher cost.

Fortunately, the nature of computer programs helps the cache designer in trying to achieve both goals. Most programs spend a high percentage of time reaccessing the same code (such as when in a loop), and the same data locations as well. Thus, the first time a program or data location is addressed, it must be accessed from the lower-speed memory and brought to the cache, incurring an initial time penalty. Subsequent accesses to the same code or data are then done via the faster cache memory, hopefully resulting in saving time overall. Since the cache is of limited capacity, it often fills and some of its contents have to be changed as new memory locations are accessed from the slower memory. The objective is to have the code and data most likely to be needed at a given time

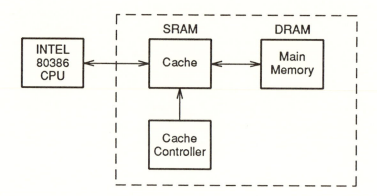

FIGURE 7-29   Cache Memory System

available in the cache; most accesses can then use the fast cache rather than the slower DRAM.

When code or data is accessed from the cache, a cache "hit" has occurred; if it is accessed from the lower-speed main memory, a cache "miss" has occurred. Cache effectiveness is measured by a factor called the hit rate, which is simply the percentage of accesses that find the code or data in the cache. The hit rate is a function of several factors - the cache size (a major factor), the algorithm used for determining which location(s) to replace when the cache is full, and the nature of the program being run at the time. Performance is also affected to some degree by the method used for organizing the cache, as this relates to the speed with which the CPU can determine whether a code or data value does, in fact, reside in the cache. A reasonably high hit rate is crucial to justify the use of a cache.

As stated previously, there is a penalty to be paid each time an item is not found in the cache. The time needed to check the cache and then access the information from the slower memory adds one or two clock cycles to the total access time as compared to a system without cache. Therefore, too low a hit rate can actually degrade rather than improve overall system performance. Hit rates of less than 50% to 60% generally do not enhance system performance. As a practical matter, the cache must be at least 4K bytes in size to be useful for 32-bit CPUs with several Mbytes of main memory.

As shown in Figure 7-29, a cache memory system consists of a fast SRAM cache, the slower DRAM main memory, and cache controller logic. It is not within the scope of this text to detail the design of a cache controller; instead we outline the common schemes used in implementing cache systems, and survey developments such as caches built into the CPU or into a memory management unit (on-chip cache).

Since programs reference code, data, and stack contents in different parts of the address space of main memory, a cache is generally filled with noncontiguous blocks of information. To improve the hit rate, a cache controller partitions main memory into blocks; a 4 byte or 8 byte block size is typical for a 32-bit CPU.

When the controller moves one item to the cache, it moves the entire block containing that item using a blockfetch (or equivalent) instruction. Of course, much of a program's time is spent accessing code from sequential locations, so that the entire block's contents is very likely to be used anyway. A larger size block reduces overhead time for cases where program loops are not encountered often. However, larger block sizes reduce the overall number of blocks that can fit into a cache, and also increase the likelihood that code or data words may not be used (since they were located further from the item associated with the transfer).

A fully associative cache can hold as many blocks as will fit into the cache, independent of where the blocks were located in the main memory. Since none of the original block addresses need be related to one another, the cache must store the entire address of each block as well as the block itself. A code or data request from memory would require the cache controller to compare the requested address with all block addresses in the cache. Once a match is found, the data from the cache is sent to the CPU. While this scheme is flexible in that any block can be stored in the cache, the address compare operation is slow for the typical number of blocks used and may be expensive to implement as well.

In contrast to the fully associative cache, where each main memory block can occupy any cache location, a direct-mapped cache represents the opposite extreme; each block can only occupy one cache location. This results in only one address comparison being needed to determine if the requested data is in the cache. A direct-mapped cache address has two fields - a cache index field to specify a block location within the cache, and a tag field to distinguish that block from any others that are assigned to the same cache location.

For example, consider a 64K byte cache with a 4 byte block size that is to be used in an 80386 CPU-based system with 16M bytes of main memory. Since cache blocks are generally stored at aligned addresses (divisible by 4 in this case), there are 16K (64K/4) cache block locations. The cache index field is therefore 14 bits with 2 additional bits needed to select a byte from the 4-byte block. Since the ratio of main memory to cache size is 256 (16M/64K), any of 256 main memory blocks can occupy a single cache block location. This requires an 8-bit tag field to identify the appropriate block. Since the cache address requires a total of 24 bits (the same as if a single byte were to be selected directly from the 16M byte main memory), the remaining 8 bits of the 80386 32-bit address can be used to decode the cache subsystem from the remaining system memory. Note, if a fully associative cache were used in this example, a total of 16K address comparisons would be needed.

Since the direct-mapped cache does not have the flexibility of the fully associative cache in placing blocks anywhere in the cache, the performance is somewhat lower; however, the direct-mapped cache controller logic is much simpler, thus reducing cost.

The set associative cache represents a compromise between the extremes of the fully associative and direct-mapped caches. This type of cache has several sets or groups (typically two or four) of direct mapped caches that operate in parallel. There are two or four locations in the cache where each block will be stored, requiring the controller to make two or four comparisons to determine in which block, if any, the requested data is located. Adding to the complexity is the fact that whenever information is to be placed in the cache, which block is to receive the information must be decided. However, the hit rate for the set associative cache is higher than for the direct-mapped cache. A 2-way set associative cache contains half as many block locations but allows two blocks for each location. The index field is thus reduced from 16 bits to 15 bits, and the extra bit is added to the tag field.

Cache controller logic must address the issue of cache updating as well. Since cache information represents a copy of what is in main memory, provisions must be made to ensure that if one copy is changed, the old data is not used. For example, if a CPU operation writes data to the cache, the same data must be written to main memory. Copying cache data immediately to memory is simple, but requires time and causes increased bus traffic. This can be significant in multiprocessing systems. Performance can be improved by buffering write accesses to main memory; the CPU can then begin a new cycle before the write cycle to main memory is completed.

Another problem arises when caches are used in a system where more than one device has access to main memory, as in multiprocessing or direct memory access (DMA) systems. When new data is written to main memory by one device, such as a second CPU or DMA controller, the cache maintained by its CPU will contain "old" data. This can be overcome by techniques involving routing all memory access through the cache, designating shared memory as noncacheable (since shared memory is never copied into cache, all accesses to shared memory are cache misses), or by purging cache data periodically (cache flushing) to reduce the possibility of using old data. When shared memory is used, software can offset the reduction in hit rate by using a string move instruction to copy data between noncacheable and cacheable memory. Also, an altered bit (sometimes called a valid bit) is often appended to the tag field; this bit flags the case where cache and corresponding main memory data do not agree.

Table 7-12 shows the results of an Intel study on cache system performance. As noted before, the results verify the fact that a 1K size cache actually degrades system performance as a result of a hit rate well below 50%. Improvement is apparent as cache size increases, although it is rather marginal beyond a 32K size. The performance increase is also marginal for the 2-way associative cache as compared to a direct mapped cache of the same size.

The INTEL 82385 Cache Controller provides a cache directory and cache management logic to support an external 32K byte cache for an 80386 CPU running at either 16 or 20 MHz. Although the directory structure maps the entire 80386 physical address space (4 Gbytes) into the cache, areas of memory can be set aside as noncacheable. You have the option of organizing the memory as a

TABLE 7-12 Cache System Performance

Size (Bytes)	Cache Configuration		Cache Performance	
	Type	Block Bytes	Hit Rate (%) (Note 1)	Performance Ratio (Note 2)
1K	Direct	4	41	0.91
8K	Direct	4	73	1.25
16K	Direct	4	81	1.35
32K	Direct	4	86	1.38
32K	2-way associative	4	87	1.39
32K	Direct	8	91	1.41
64K	Direct	4	88	1.39
64K	2-way associative	4	89	1.40
64K	4-way associative	4	89	1.40
64K	Direct	8	92	1.42
64K	2-way associative	8	93	1.42
128K	Direct	4	89	1.39
128K	2-way associative	4	89	1.40
128K	Direct	8	93	1.42

Notes:

1. Hit rate compared to 100% for two clock cycle SRAM access.

2. Performance ratio compared to 1.00 for four clock cycle pipelined DRAM access.

direct-mapped or a 2-way set associative cache, with hit rates obtainable up to 99%.

Other Examples of Cache Implementation

Another approach to the concept of a cache is to build one directly into the CPU. This has the advantage of allowing the CPU to search for the information in the cache without need for external access, thus freeing the bus for other system bus masters. The MOTOROLA MC68020 CPU provides an on-chip direct mapped 256 byte cache for instruction words only. The newer MC68030 CPU also provides a second independently-operating 256 byte data cache that allows both instructions and data to be accessed at the same time. While the MC68020 CPU organizes its instruction cache into 64 blocks of 4 bytes each, both MC68030 caches are set up as 16 blocks of 16 bytes each; Motorola claims a significant improvement in hit rate as a result of the larger block size.

When the MC68020 CPU fetches an instruction, it simultaneously accesses the cache (if enabled) and external memory. It then checks the cache index and tag bit fields of the address, as well as a valid bit and the FC2 function code output of the MC68020 CPU (which identifies whether the instruction is a supervisor or user). If a hit occurs, the process takes 2 clock cycles as opposed to the normal

3 cycles required for an external access. A miss results in the external cycle being completed, and the new instruction is transferred to the cache (provided the freeze bit in the CPU's cache control register is inactive). An external cache for both instructions and data can be provided to further improve system performance.

A small external cache (less than 4K size) is not worthwhile since the hit rate is generally too low to achieve improved performance. Of course, for an internal cache, any nonzero hit rate represents an improvement if access to cache and main memory is simultaneous. The wider block size of the MC68030 CPU and its ability to have its bus controller selectively "burst fill" the cache (using a look-ahead or block fetch approach) have produced the following simulated results:

	Hit Rate		
	Instruction Cache	Data Cache	Overall
Burst filling not used	45%	36%	41%
Burst filling used	80%	48%	70%

Since 32-bit microprocessor systems perform virtual to physical address translation via a memory management unit, maintaining high performance at ever increasing clock frequencies is even more difficult. If a physical cache is used, time is lost even for hits, since each address must first be translated before determining whether the accessed code or data is in the cache. Some high-end system designers are settling for a virtual rather than physical cache to improve performance; however, data integrity in multiprocessor systems becomes an issue in this case (memory management issues such as these are discussed in Section 7.5). The AT&T WE 32200 CPU, the successor to the WE 32100 CPU, is supported with a separate MMU chip (the AT&T WE 32201 MMU) which includes a physical 4K byte 2-way associative data cache. Early studies indicate that this cache can support zero wait state accesses up to clock rates of 30 MHz. Its hit rate of at least 85% is equivalent to that of an 8K byte direct-mapped cache. Multiple MMUs can be employed with a minimum of interfacing logic being required, if increased system performance is desired. It is estimated that the use of four MMUs to quadruple the cache size to 16K can produce a hit rate as high as 95% for an AT&T WE 32200 Microprocessor system.

7.4 DRAM Interfacing

Dynamic RAM (DRAM) has greater density, consumes less power, and is less costly per bit than static RAM (SRAM). However, DRAM requires more complex support circuitry than does SRAM. Generally, this support must include address multiplexing, refreshing to preserve memory contents, and arbitration between refresh cycles and read/write cycles. This section discusses implementation of these additional requirements with standard logic components and with DRAM controller chips.

Address Multiplexing, Reading and Writing DRAMs

DRAM manufacturers have kept device package size down by providing shared address pins requiring that an address be entered in two steps. It is convenient to envision a 1-bit-wide DRAM as a two-dimensional square array of single storage cells, each cell being defined by a row and a column. The lower half of the address is called the row address, and the upper half the column address. A 4-bit-wide DRAM can be viewed in the same way, except that a full address defines a group of four cells (a 4-bit memory "word").

Consider the 64K x 1 INTEL 2164A DRAM. This device is pin compatible with the 4164, and comes packaged in a 16-pin DIP with one pin unused. The pins include eight address inputs, separate data in and data out pins, a write enable ($\overline{WE}$) input, row and column strobe ($\overline{RAS}$ and $\overline{CAS}$) inputs, and +5 V and ground. Figure 7-30 shows the read and write cycle relationship of the row and address strobes to the contents of the address bus. The row address is latched by the DRAM on the falling edge of $\overline{RAS}$; the column address is latched on the falling edge of $\overline{CAS}$. Thus, valid row and column addresses are present before the respective strobes are activated. Refreshing may also use $\overline{RAS}$.

Since the CPU's 32 address lines are available simultaneously, multiplexing must be provided to select either the low or high address at the appropriate time. $\overline{CAS}$ (Figure 7-30) can be used to perform the multiplexer select functions since it is inactive when the row address is present, and active for the column address. Notice the total read or write cycle time (tRC) is the time between successive falling edges of $\overline{RAS}$. The minimum tRC specification for the INTEL 2164A-15 DRAM is 260 ns; for the 2164A-20 DRAM it is 330 ns.

Figure 7-31 shows a multiplexer arrangement using two 74157 quad 2-to-1 line multiplexers. The sixteen address lines A0-A15 are multiplexed onto the eight address lines A0-A7 which go directly to the DRAM. The $\overline{CAS}$ strobe must be

FIGURE 7-30 2164 DRAM Timing for Read and Write Cycles

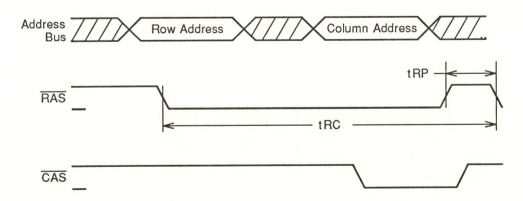

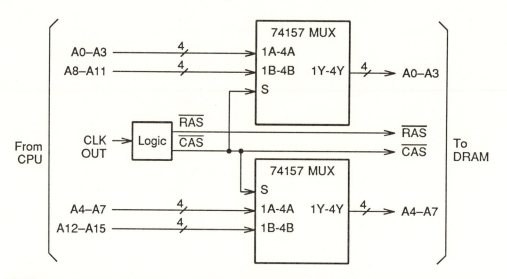

FIGURE 7-31 Using Multiplexers to Provide DRAM Address Inputs

generated from logic tied to the CPU clock. Initially, when $\overline{CAS}$ is inactive, multiplexer section A is selected and the low address (A0-A7) is latched into the DRAM as the row address. When $\overline{CAS}$ is brought low, multiplexer section B is selected and the high address (A8-A15) is latched into the DRAM as the column address.

The row and column address strobes ($\overline{RAS}$ and $\overline{CAS}$) control read and write operations in addition to latching in the row and column addresses. During read cycles, the DRAM data output(s) are enabled only when both $\overline{RAS}$ and $\overline{CAS}$ are active. For write cycles, both $\overline{CAS}$ and $\overline{WE}$ must be active for write data to be latched by the DRAM. DRAMs such as the 2164A have a separate read-modify-write cycle. During this cycle, data is first read, presumably modified by the CPU, and written back to DRAM in only slightly more time than required for an individual read or write cycle.

DRAM Refreshing

A DRAM transistor-capacitor cell is refreshed by periodically reading the bit value, amplifying the capacitor charge with sense amplifier circuitry, and recharging the capacitor to its initial state. Typically, the DRAM must be refreshed every few milliseconds to prevent data loss. Since each column of a DRAM has its own sense amplifier, refresh can be performed on an entire row at a time. Since DRAMs usually have an equal number of rows and columns, a DRAM with twice as many rows and columns as another DRAM has four times the bit capacity, but only takes twice as long to refresh. Typically, a 16K device configured as 128 rows by 128 columns has its 128 rows refreshed every 2 ms; a 64K device configured as 256 rows and 256 columns will then have its 256 rows refreshed every 4 ms.

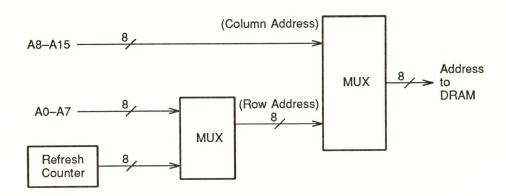

FIGURE 7-32 Additional Multiplexing Required for DRAM Refreshing

Refresh can be performed with a $\overline{RAS}$ only refresh cycle, where only the row addresses are sent. Since $\overline{CAS}$ is never activated, no data is read or written. Additionally, any memory operation will refresh the row accessed. No refresh cycles are required in applications where it is certain that the entire memory is accessed every 2 ms.

Refresh may be done on either a distributed, burst, or "hidden" basis. Assume that we have a device with 128 rows. On a distributed basis, a single row is refreshed every 15 microseconds; on a burst basis, all of the rows are refreshed simultaneously every 2 ms. A "hidden" refresh performs the refresh at the same time the first opcode of an instruction is being decoded. However, if there are long time periods when code is not fetched, such as during DMA transfers, data can be lost.

Figure 7-32 illustrates the additional multiplexing logic required for refresh. A refresh counter provides the addresses of the rows to be refreshed. The actual refresh counter and multiplexer select control logic depend on the refresh method being implemented.

Interleaved DRAM Banks

DRAMs require an idle time between successive accesses to precharge. If the idle time is too short, data can be lost. Referring to Figure 7-30, the $\overline{RAS}$ precharge time (tRP) is the time the row address strobe is inactive before the next access begins. The specifications call for a tRPmin of 100 ns for the 2164A-15 DRAM and 120 ns for the 2164A-20 DRAM. These times take up 30% and 40% of the minimum cycle times (tRC). This is a significant factor, particularly in view of the previous discussion of timing at high CPU clock rates (Section 7.3).

A solution to this problem is to interleave memory so that successive memory accesses are likely to be directed to different banks of DRAMs. This allows one bank of DRAMs to perform the current access while the other bank precharges. The second access does not have to be delayed, unless the same bank happens to be accessed twice in succession.

353

Since program code, stack, and data array locations tend to be accessed sequentially, the DRAM can be arranged so that adjacent addresses are in different banks. Two banks of DRAM can be provided for a 32-bit CPU - one for even-addressed 32-bit double words, and one for odd-addressed 32-bit double words. Then, all sequential 32-bit accesses can be performed without waiting for the DRAMs to precharge. Even in the worst case, where successive accesses are random, 50% of the accesses will not need to wait for DRAMs to precharge.

Precharge time is also avoided when idle bus cycles occur between accesses, since the most recently accessed DRAM bank can precharge during the idle time. The next access to either bank can then begin immediately.

To understand how interleaved memory can be implemented for the 80386, refer to Figure 7-14. The memory bank shown is selected for any of the externally decoded 2^N addresses. For interleaved memory, A_{N+2} (the least significant bit input to the address decoder) can be replaced by A_2. The ($A_{N+1} - A_2$) direct inputs to the memory bank become ($A_{N+2} - A_3$). This bank is then selected by alternate 32-bit addresses, and a second bank tied to an adjacent address decoder output is selected for the remaining addresses.

INTEL 80386 CPU performance studies verify the advantage of interleaving. For example, use of 200 ns DRAM at 12 MHz or 150 ns DRAM at 16 MHz requires three wait states for successive read or write accesses from the same bank. Use of pipelined address timing would not speed up the cycle, because the DRAM controller must allow the DRAMs to precharge before starting the new access. If the memory were interleaved, two wait states are required for the nonpipelined case and only one if pipelining were used. These results ignore the effects of DRAM refresh cycles and data bus buffering.

Depending on system size and the memory devices available, an interleaved system may require more chips. For example, a 1M byte DRAM requirement for a 32-bit CPU could be implemented as a single bank of eight 256K x 4 44256 DRAMs. Interleaving the banks requires going to a smaller capacity device. The number of address inputs is an even number due to address pin multiplexing. Therefore, the next size down is the 64K x 4 41464 DRAM. This now requires four times as many devices. On the other hand, a 2M byte system could use two banks of eight 256K x 4 DRAMs, and the banks could be interleaved without increasing the device count. Larger systems with multiple memory banks are more flexible when it comes to configuring the system without adding memory devices.

DRAM Controller Devices

The need for complex DRAM control logic has resulted in the development of special purpose DRAM controller devices. Generally, these devices provide address multiplexing, refresh timing and counter circuitry, generation of row and column address strobes, some degree of address decoding, and other control functions.

Intel has a series of controllers that meet the needs of DRAMs used at a variety of CPU clock rates. The INTEL 8203 64K DRAM Controller handles 16K and 64K DRAMs, and is compatible with the 8085, 8086, and 8088 CPUs. The 40-pin 8203 device multiplexes 14 address inputs to 7 outputs. When used with 16K DRAM, two bank select inputs are decoded to four row address strobe outputs ($\overline{\text{RAS0}}$–$\overline{\text{RAS3}}$), which latch the row address into the selected bank. One of two banks can be selected if the 8203 DRAM controller is operating in 64K mode. In this case, the second bank select input and two $\overline{\text{RAS}}$ outputs become address pins, providing the required 16 address inputs and 8 multiplexed outputs. Column address strobe ($\overline{\text{CAS}}$) and write enable ($\overline{\text{WE}}$) outputs drive the corresponding DRAM array inputs. DRAM distributed refresh can be generated internally by the on-chip refresh timer; a refresh cycle is requested every 10 to 16 us, insuring refresh of all DRAM rows every 2 ms (128 cycles) or every 4 ms (256 cycles). Alternatively, externally generated "hidden" refresh can be requested via a REFRQ input to the 8203 DRAM controller.

The 68-pin INTEL 8207 Dual-Port DRAM Controller provides DRAM control of 16K, 64K, and 256K devices, and supports 8086, 80186, and 80286 CPUs running as high as 10 MHz. A dual-port interface allows independent memory access from two separate buses. The 18 address inputs and 9 multiplexed outputs accommodate 256K DRAM; pins are left unused for smaller sized DRAMs. DRAM can be divided into as many as four banks, each having its own $\overline{\text{RAS}}$ and $\overline{\text{CAS}}$ pair of strobes. This permits interleaved memory organization, with the advantage of overlapped access and precharge. Each port of the 8207 device is programmable under control of the port control (PCTL) and program data input (PDI) pins. Each port can be programmed to run synchronous or asynchronous to the CPU clock, to adjust to different speeds and bus structures, to use any of four different refresh options, and to provide error checking and correction (ECC) capability.

The 82C08 CHMOS DRAM controller provides control for 64K and 256K DRAMs in high-performance microcomputer systems and is available in a 48-pin DIP or a 68-pin PLCC. The 82C08 device is the CHMOS version of the 8208 device and is pin compatible with it. The 82C08 device is available for use at 8, 10, 16, or 20 MHz clock rates. Up to 1 Mbyte of memory can be directly addressed without external drivers. Two memory banks can be supported by separate $\overline{\text{RAS}}$ and $\overline{\text{CAS}}$ signals. The 18 address in and 9 multiplexed address output lines accommodate 256K DRAMs. The 82C08 device has a power down mode, with programmable memory refresh that uses battery backup, resulting in reduced power supply demand. Another improvement over the 8208 device is the shortening of the timing requirements for $\overline{\text{WE}}$ and $\overline{\text{CAS}}$, which eliminates the need for external bus latches. An internal refresh interval counter and address counter support all DRAM refresh options. The 9-bit address counter can refresh 128 rows every 2 ms, 256 rows every 4 ms, or 512 rows every 8 ms. A refresh period programming option allows faster refresh (256 rows every 2 ms).

Figure 7-33 contains the signal names for the pins on the 82C08 device. Notice pins PDI and WE/PCLK. These two pins control the setting of the nine

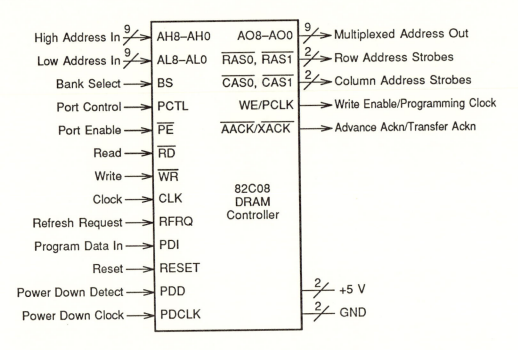

FIGURE 7-33 INTEL 82C08 DRAM Controller Signal Diagram

user-selectable options that program the controller. The shared WE/PCLK pin functions as PCLK immediately after a RESET, and is used to clock serial programming data into the PDI pin. After programming is completed, the pin provides the write enable ($\overline{WE}$) to the DRAMs. Also, the state of the port enable ($\overline{PE}$) input pin, determined by a decoded address, initiates a memory cycle request. The operating parameters for the 82C08 device, given in Table 7-13, are established using programming data bits PD0-PD8.

TABLE 7-13 INTEL 82C08 DRAM Controller Programming Bit Definitions

Bit	Name	Function (Low/High Case)
PD0	CFS	Slow/fast processor cycle
PD1	S	Asynchronous/synchronous operation
PD2	RFS	Slow (150 ns)/fast (100 ns) RAM
PD3	RB	One/two memory banks
PD4,PD5	CI1,CI0	Two-bit refresh count interval*
PD6	PLS	Short/long refresh period
PD7	FFS	Slow/fast CPU frequency
PD8	X	Advance/transfer acknowledge

*The higher the number, the more frequent is the refreshing.

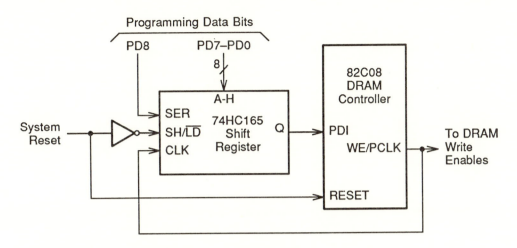

FIGURE 7-34 Using a Shift Register to Enter Programming Data
into the INTEL 82C08 DRAM Controller

Figure 7-34 illustrates the entry of programming data into the controller. The 74HC165 shift register has asynchronous loading capability. The PD0-PD8 programmed data bits are tied either to ground (low) or to +5 V (high), depending on the user-selected function in each case. The shift register is parallel loaded with bits PD0 to PD7 on reset; the controller supplies the PCLK clocking signal to shift data into the PDI pin (starting with PD0). On the first clock pulse, PD8 is shifted in as PD0 is shifted out to the controller; the remaining bits are shifted on subsequent clock pulses. For certain applications it may be necessary to reset all the bits to zero (a low frequency case using slower RAMs), or set the bits to all ones (for a high frequency case with fast RAMs). For either of these cases, the shift register output is not used and the DRAM controller PDI pin is permanently grounded or tied to +5 V. When using a clock frequency of 16 MHz or higher, the shifting of all ones to PDI (rather than permanently tying it to +5 V) may apply.

Figure 7-35 shows the configuration needed for noninterleaved and interleaved memory control. The RB programming bit, in conjunction with the bank select (BS) controller input, configures the system for one or two banks. The default programming case (PDI is tied high) defines two banks; this allows memory to be interleaved saving DRAM precharge time. For RB = 0, BS must also be 0, and both sets of $\overline{RAS}$ and $\overline{CAS}$ are activated at the appropriate times. As shown in Figure 7-35a, the single bank, called bank 0, can be divided into two 16-bit arrays to equalize loading. The entire 32-bit bank is activated in one memory cycle. To interleave memory as shown in Figure 7-35b, RB must be programmed to 1. Then BS = 0 activates $\overline{RAS0}$ and $\overline{CAS0}$, selecting bank 0. When BS = 1, bank 1 is selected by activation of $\overline{RAS1}$ and $\overline{CAS1}$ instead. The lowest order address bit, A2 in the case of the 80386, provides the bank select input to the controller. This results in the desired alternate bank selection for sequential 32-bit double word accesses.

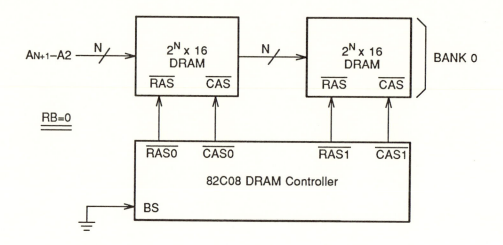

a. Noninterleaved Memory

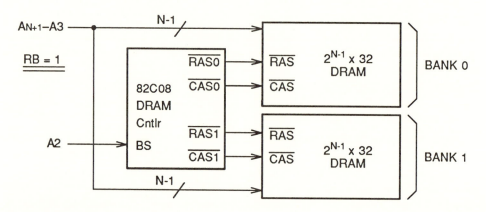

b. Interleaved Memory

FIGURE 7-35 INTEL 82C08 DRAM Controller Configured for Noninterleaved and Interleaved 32-Bit Memory Banks

The AT&T *WE* 32103 DRAM Controller (DRAMC) provides DRAM with address multiplexing, access and cycle time, management, and refresh control. It is available in 10 MHz, 14 Mhz, and 18 MHz versions supplied in a 125 pin, ceramic pin-grid-array package. Figure 7-36 shows a functional block diagram of the controller. The twenty address inputs and ten multiplexed outputs permit interfacing to DRAMs up to 1M in size. A bidirectional 8-bit data bus allows peripheral mode data transfer to and from a set of registers; the registers are programmed to specify memory and other system parameters. The two bank address inputs (BANKAD0 and BANKAD1) select one of four banks, and select

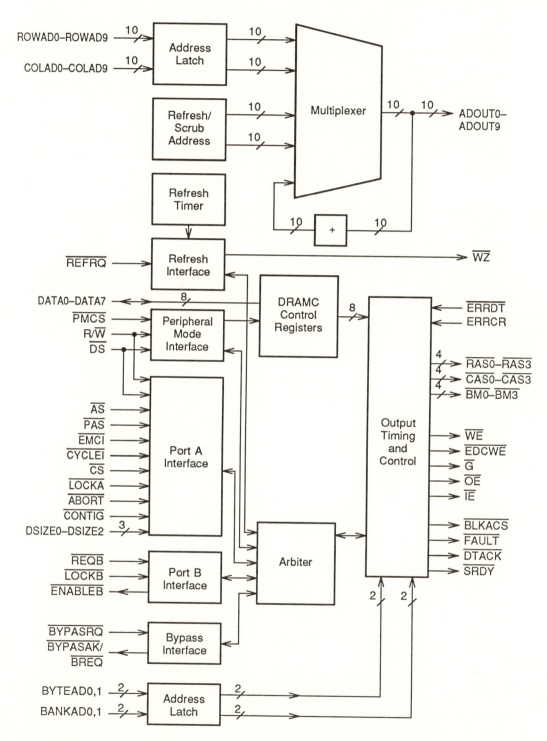

FIGURE 7-36 *WE 32103 DRAM Controller Functional Block Diagram*

359

which column address strobes ($\overline{CAS0}$-$\overline{CAS3}$) are to be asserted. Four row address strobes ($\overline{RAS0}$-$\overline{RAS3}$) are also provided. Two byte address inputs (BYTEAD0-BYTEAD1) generate four byte mark outputs ($\overline{BM0}$-$\overline{BM3}$), which select the bytes to be written to memory during partial and full word writes. All bytes are asserted for read operations, independent of data size. The three data size inputs (DSIZE0-DSIZE2) specify transactions of 0 to 3 bytes, as well as half, full, double, triple, and quad 32-bit words.

The DRAMC provides more efficient operation at high speed by allowing the controller to be configured for early access initiation. This permits a memory access to begin before chip select ($\overline{CS}$) is asserted; however, data strobe ($\overline{DS}$) must be asserted before column addresses are strobed via $\overline{CAS0}$-$\overline{CAS3}$. Additionally, data output drivers are not enabled and an acknowledge is not sent to the CPU until $\overline{CS}$ is received by the controller. Early access initiation results in some "false starts," but access is terminated quickly if $\overline{CS}$ does not arrive when expected. As a result, DRAM timing specifications are not violated. Overall, this is a benefit since most bus operations are, in fact, memory accesses.

The DRAMC can also start a memory access before a virtual address is translated to a physical address, if an MMU is in the system (MMUs are discussed in the next section). The DRAMC provides full support for error detection and correction (EDC) devices, supports dual-port memory configuration (using two controllers, however), and can drive up to 88 DRAM devices without external buffering.

The DRAMC has eleven 8-bit memory-mapped registers that can be accessed in peripheral mode. The registers, selected by four of the column address inputs, establish the system and refresh configurations, $\overline{RAS}$ and $\overline{CAS}$ timing, acknowledge and data timing, and provide fault and startup indicators, and fault addresses.

Figure 7-37 shows the interconnections between the AT&T WE 32103 DRAM Controller and DRAM, for both 1-bit-wide and 4-bit-wide devices. Four memory banks (without EDC) are assumed. Sixteen low active AND gates (equivalent to NOR) provide column address strobes to each bank, and byte markers to each 8-bit width of DRAM in the 32-bit wide bank. The controller provides input enable ($\overline{IE}$) and output enable ($\overline{OE}$) signals to drive tristate buffers; also, an output $\overline{G}$ is available for those DRAMs with bidirectional I/O. As shown, the manufacturer recommends single gate control of data out for the 1-bit-wide case. For 4-bit-wide DRAMs, bidirectional data I/O buffering is also shown; it is convenient to use both $\overline{IE}$ and $\overline{OE}$ to provide separate control for both directions and thereby ensure an absence of bus contention. Additional control is provided by connecting $\overline{G}$ to the $\overline{OE}$ inputs on the 4-bit wide DRAMs.

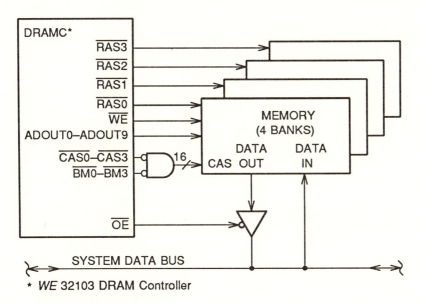

a. 1-bit-wide DRAM

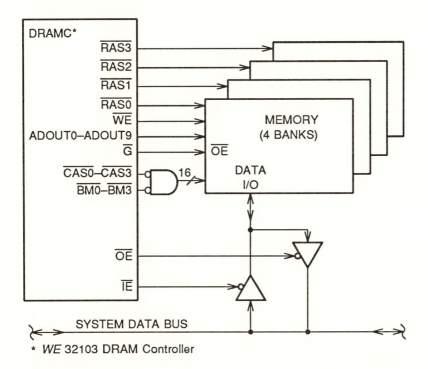

b. 4-bit-wide DRAM

FIGURE 7-37   AT&T *WE* 32103 DRAM Controller - Memory Interconnection for
1-Bit-Wide and 4-Bit-Wide Devices

7.5 Memory Management Revisited

As described in Chapter Two, memory management of computer systems has two important purposes:

1. Increased flexibility resulting from virtual to physical address mapping, and

2. System protection provided by access restrictions in a multiuser environment.

Recall that early microcomputer applications featured limited memory size in a single-user environment. Memory management became a necessity when memory-addressing capability went beyond the 64K byte limitation imposed by a 16-bit address bus. It is indispensable with 32-bit CPUs that can address gigabytes of memory and operate in a multiuser environment. The address translation feature of memory management gives the appearance that there is virtually unlimited memory at a user's disposal. The amount of physical memory may be much smaller, consisting of RAM and ROM main memory and auxiliary disk memory. Memory management is then responsible for swapping code and data between main memory and disk in a transparent manner without seriously reducing system performance. This permits the programmer to reference large amounts of code and data regardless of which resides in main memory at a given time.

System protection, as opposed to address translation, is often the primary reason for providing memory management because access to code and data in a multiuser environment can be controlled. This protects both operating system and user software from unauthorized access. Generally, several levels of access to areas of code and data are provided. For example, a system may allow execution of code only, or read privilege as well as code execution, or both read and write privileges as well as code execution. It may be advantageous in an application to prevent writing to certain areas of user memory to protect a user program from itself. Protection facilitates the partitioning of virtual memory into local (user private) space, and global or shared space for interrupt routines, library functions, and other system software.

Segmented and Paged Addressing

Computer systems have long found it convenient to subdivide memory into smaller, more manageable blocks. For example, the DEC PDP-8 Minicomputer addressed 4K memory locations. To specify operand addresses conveniently with a limited size code word, the PDP-8 Minicomputer divided memory into blocks, called pages, of 128 locations each. Using 7 bits, an instruction which referenced memory specified an offset address relative to the start of the page. An 8th bit denoted whether page 0 was being referenced (the lowest addressed page in memory), or the current page on which the instruction resided. The 8-bits could be viewed as a virtual address, which the CPU then translated to a physical address (the actual location on the referenced page). The 8-bit MOTOROLA MC6800 Microprocessor featured a mode called page 0 addressing. Data on the lowest address page could be referenced with an 8-bit address instead of a full 16-bit address. For the MC6800 CPU, a page comprised 256 rather than 128 locations. For current 32-bit CPUs, a page typically denotes several K locations; the actual size is dependent on the microprocessor and may be of fixed or variable size.

As memory addressing capability grew, it became convenient to first subdivide the large memory size into variable-sized blocks called segments, and then further partition the segments into pages. The INTEL 8086 CPU, from which the 80386 CPU evolved, has an external 20-bit address bus permitting addressing of up to 1M byte of physical memory. The four internal segment registers of the 8086 CPU include a code register, a stack register, a data segment register, and an extra data segment register. A segment starts at an address divisible by 16 and may be as large as 64K locations. The content of the appropriate 16-bit segment register, with four zeros appended to it, is the first or lowest address of the segment. An instruction provides an offset (relative) address within the segment.

How the INTEL 8086 CPU translates its offset address to the physical address sent to the bus is best reviewed with an example. Assume the appropriate segment register contains hex address 1234, and the offset address provided by the instruction is hex 2143. The physical address is determined by adding the offset address to the starting segment address. This is done as follows:

$$
\begin{array}{ll}
1\,2\,3\,4\,0 & \text{Segment register with four zeros appended} \\
+\,0\,2\,1\,4\,3 & \text{Offset address} \\
\hline
1\,4\,4\,8\,3 & \text{Physical 20-bit address.}
\end{array}
$$

The 8086 architecture limits access to one of only four segments, or 256K (4 x 64K) locations assuming nonoverlapping maximum-size segments. Since the bus permits access to 1M locations, only one-fourth of the space is accessible at a given time. To access the remaining space, the physical segments need to be relocated by reinitializing the appropriate segment register. Of course, a time penalty is incurred whenever this becomes necessary.

It is evident that simple paging or segmenting of addresses, as done by earlier microprocessors, is inadequate for the needs of 32-bit CPUs. These 32-bit systems have larger memory requirements, higher clock rates, and the need for system protection in a multiuser environment. The 32-bit CPUs presented in this text all use a common approach to memory management, although the details differ. The address translation is somewhat indirect in that the virtual address provided by an instruction results in accessing the appropriate information in a segment

363

descriptor table in memory. The descriptor table contains the protection attributes of the code or data accessed; it may also contain the physical address, or a pointer to a page descriptor table if memory segments are further subdivided into pages.

Using both segmentation and paging, an operating system can organize and manage code and data in an efficient manner. For example, different-sized segments can be allocated first to various user programs and data structures. However, the operating system may have difficulty finding room in physical RAM for a very large segment at a given time. Even if room existed, the time to transfer the entire segment might seriously affect system performance. Providing paging beneath segmentation permits the system to split a large segment into smaller fixed-size pages. Portions of a segment can then be swapped into RAM as needed. Individual pages need not even occupy contiguous memory locations since the system keeps track of their whereabouts via the page descriptor table (although system performance improves if pages can be moved sequentially, without interruption for reinitializing addresses).

Memory Management Implementations

Memory management hardware can be included on the CPU chip, as done with the INTEL 80386 CPU and MOTOROLA MC68030 CPU. Separate memory management units (MMUs) may be used in conjunction with the CPU; examples include the MOTOROLA MC68851 MMU designed for the MOTOROLA MC68020 CPU, the AT&T *WE* 32101 MMU for the AT&T *WE* 32100 CPU, and the AT&T *WE* 32201 MMU for the AT&T *WE* 32200 CPU. Since the process of accessing descriptor tables can be time consuming, the need to maintain performance at high clock rates has resulted in descriptor caches being included with memory management hardware. The argument made previously about program and data locality when discussing cache memory, applies here as well. If a large number of sequential accesses are limited to the same segment or page, having the descriptor information in the CPU, or MMU where used, saves valuable access time to external memory.

The remainder of this section surveys the memory management hardware used with the 32-bit CPUs. Where an external MMU is available, the interface to the CPU is shown. Details of the address translation and protection mechanisms have already been presented in Chapters Two and Three.

INTEL 80386 CPU Memory Management

The INTEL 80386 CPU performs memory management internally with the aid of segmentation and paging units that operate in parallel with other CPU hardware. A 48-bit virtual or logical address is comprised of a 16-bit segment register address concatenated to a 32-bit offset provided by the instruction. The code, data, and stack segment registers are supplemented by three extra data segment registers (as opposed to a single extra one for the 8086 CPU). The segment register acts as a segment selector by pointing to an entry in a segment descriptor table. A descriptor consists of two 32-bit double words, and a task may have as many as 16K segments defined at a time. Since the offset address is 32-bits wide, a segment size may be anywhere from 1 to 4G bytes. In contrast, a page is always 4K bytes in size.

Figure 7-38a shows how the virtual address (called a logical address by Intel) is converted to a linear address. If paging is not used, the linear address becomes the physical address; otherwise it is used by the paging unit as illustrated in Figure 7-38b. Two levels of memory-based page descriptors are used. A 1K entry page directory maps into a 1K entry page table, which in turn maps into the physical pages in memory. Since each page is 4K bytes in size, a single page directory maps 4G bytes (1K x 1K x 4K bytes), the entire linear address space.

Referencing memory-based page information for each physical address translation seriously degrades performance. To avoid this, the 80386 CPU includes on-chip a four-way set-associative page descriptor cache, called a translation look-aside buffer (TLB). The TLB contains the most recently used linear addresses along with their translated physical addresses. The cache is 4K bits, allowing room for 32 descriptor entries. The internal cache can therefore hold the mapping information for 128K bytes (32 x 24K bytes) of memory. Simulations show that this size cache produces a hit rate exceeding 98%, meaning that fewer than 2% of the address translations need to access the memory-based descriptor tables. Paging does not add any processing time for the hit case, since TLB look-up and translation are performed during the second phase of the same clock as the linear address calculation. Figure 7-38c illustrates the functioning of the on-chip TLB.

MOTOROLA MC68020 and MC68030 CPU Memory Management

Unlike the INTEL 80386 CPU, the MOTOROLA MC68020 CPU was not designed with on-chip memory management hardware. The MOTOROLA MC68851 Paged Memory Management Unit (PMMU) is a separate memory manager used with the MC68020 CPU or with other 32-bit CPUs. The MC68851 PMMU acts as a coprocessor when used with the MC68020 CPU, allowing the execution of special-purpose instructions that supplement the CPU's instruction set. (Chapter Nine presents coprocessing in more detail). The extra instructions basically facilitate the movement of data to and from PMMU registers, allow access to address translation tables, and enable manipulation of an on-board cache. Segmentation is not employed, but flexibility is maintained by allowing page sizes to vary from 256 bytes to 32K bytes. The PMMU contains a fully associative 64-entry cache to ensure efficient address translation.

The MC68851 PMMU is available in a 132-lead PGA package; a signal diagram is shown in Figure 7-39. The logical and physical addresses use separate groups of 24 lines each for the upper 3 bytes, and 8 common lines for the lowest order byte; full 32-bit logical and 32-bit physical addresses are thereby supported. The data bus, in conjunction with the SIZ0 and SIZ1 transfer size signals, provide dynamic bus sizing, enabling transfer of 8-bit, 16-bit, 24-bit, or 32-bit PMMU data during a bus cycle. A function code provided by the CPU identifies the processor state (e.g., code or data, user or system) for the current cycle. Most of the

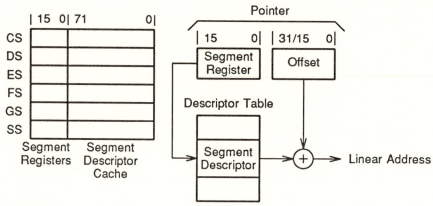

a. Segmentation

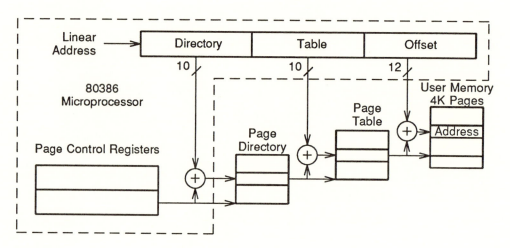

b. Paging

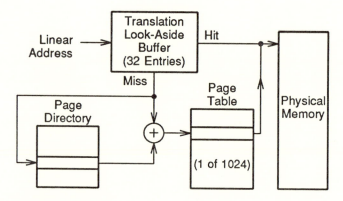

c. Page Descriptor Cache

FIGURE 7-38   Intel 80386 Segmentation and Paging

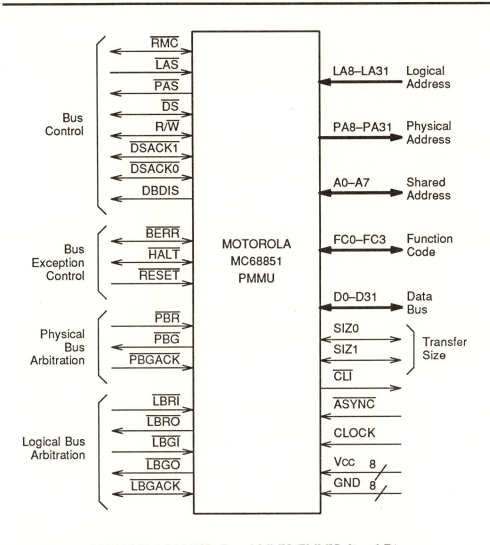

FIGURE 7-39   MOTOROLA MC68851 Paged MMU (PMMU) Signal Diagram

remaining PMMU pins perform bus control or arbitration functions. The PMMU clock rate need not match that of the CPU; however, a version of the MC68851 PMMU exists that runs at 16.67 MHz, corresponding to the maximum clock speed for the MC68020 CPU.

Figure 7-40 shows a basic interface between the MC68020 CPU and MC68851 PMMU. The logical address (notice Motorola also refers to the virtual address as a logical address) to the PMMU is supplied by the CPU, and the physical address is decoded and supplied to the memory devices. The CPU and PMMU data lines are tied, as are the transfer size signals. Three of the four bits of the function code (FC0-FC2) are supplied by the CPU; the fourth bit (FC3) is an indicator of DMA access in progress. The MC68020 CPU supplies the bus control signals read-modify-write cycle ($\overline{\text{RMC}}$), logical address strobe ($\overline{\text{LAS}}$), data strobe ($\overline{\text{DS}}$),

367

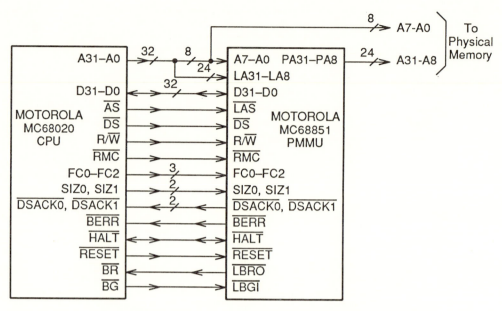

FIGURE 7-40   MOTOROLA MC68020 CPU and MC68851 PMMU Interface

read/write (R/$\overline{\text{W}}$), and accepts data transfer size and acknowledge ($\overline{\text{DSACK0}}$, $\overline{\text{DSACK1}}$) directly. The three bus exception control lines, reset, halt, and bus error ($\overline{\text{BERR}}$) also interface directly. Finally, logical bus arbitration can be provided to establish which system device is the bus master at a given time. The PMMU's logical bus request out ($\overline{\text{LBRO}}$) is connected to the bus request ($\overline{\text{BR}}$) input of the MC68020 CPU, to allow the PMMU to request ownership of the bus. The logical bus grant in ($\overline{\text{LBGI}}$) can be provided directly from the MC68020 CPU bus request ($\overline{\text{BR}}$), to inform the PMMU that the CPU will release bus ownership at completion of the current bus cycle.

The MC68851 PMMU requires about 45 ns for virtual-to-physical address translation. As noted earlier in Section 7.3 on timing, this amount of delay becomes significant for systems operating at clock rates exceeding 20 MHz. Motorola therefore decided to incorporate the PMMU on-chip when designing the more advanced MC68030 CPU; the translation time is effectively reduced to zero by translating the next address during the current bus cycle. The PMMU used on-chip is a subset of the MC68851, but retains all its functionality. It also supports multiple page sizes from 256 bytes to 32K bytes. Its address translation cache can handle only 22 descriptor entries as opposed to the 64 allowed by the MC68851 PMMU; nevertheless, hit rates are claimed to exceed 98% for 1K byte pages, and 99% for 4K byte pages (at least for small numbers of users and small programs). Note that MMU descriptor caches, in contrast to data/instruction caches, need not be very large to achieve high hit rates. This is the result of a single descriptor being able to reference a relatively large block of memory (a segment or page). Thus, program and data locality results in misses only when going off the segment (or page).

Memory Management for the AT&T *WE* 32100/32200 CPU

The AT&T *WE* 32101 MMU and *WE* 32201 MMU were designed to interface to the *WE* 32100 CPU and *WE* 32200 CPU, respectively. The *WE* 32101 MMU is available in 10 MHz, 14 MHz, and 18 MHz versions, and is packaged in either a 132-pin rectangular or 125-pin square, ceramic PGA package. The *WE* 32201 MMU operates at 24 MHz and is packaged in a 133-pin square, ceramic PGA package. These MMUs support both segmented and paged memory. Both MMUs organize the total address space into four 1G byte sections, and then into segments which may be as large as 128K bytes. Further subdivision into pages is optional. The *WE* 32101 MMU uses fixed 2K byte-sized pages so that segments may contain as many as 64 pages. In contrast, a *WE* 32201 MMU segment can accommodate either sixty-four 2K byte pages, thirty-two 4K byte pages, or sixteen 8K byte pages.

The internal register architecture of both MMUs is similar. They consist of two section RAM areas, each of which contains four 32-bit words. These describe the base address and length (number of entries) of the segment descriptor table for each section of external memory. Four other internal registers keep track of the current MMU state; they are the configuration register, virtual address register, fault code register, and fault address register. The *WE* 32201 MMU also contains several registers used with its more extensive onboard caching.

The *WE* 32101 MMU has two caches - a direct-mapped 32-entry segment descriptor cache (SDC), and a two-way set associative 64-entry page descriptor cache (PDC). Each descriptor is 64-bits in length and is divided into four parts, one corresponding to each section of virtual memory. The *WE* 32201 MMU PDC is the same size as that for the *WE* 32101 MMU, although it is a fully associative configuration. The SDC is an 8-entry direct-mapped configuration, but is augmented by a 16-entry fully-associative ID number cache. The main improvement provided by the the *WE* 32201 MMU is the addition of a 4K byte, two-way set associative cache for both data and instructions. As stated previously, AT&T claims that this size physical cache is accessible, with no wait states, for clock rates up to 30 MHz. A hit rate of 85% is claimed, which is equivalent to that for an 8K byte direct-mapped cache. The hit rate for the descriptor caches is estimated to be 99.8% .

The signal diagram for the AT&T *WE* 32101/32201 MMU is shown in Figure 7-41. They have the same pin assignments except for the comments given below the diagram. Note that the 32-bit virtual and physical addresses are on a completely shared address bus (in contrast to the MOTOROLA MC68851 MMU, where separate logical and physical address lines are used for 24 of the 32 bits). When $\overline{VAD}$ is asserted, a virtual address is received from the CPU. Alternatively, when $\overline{PAS}$ is asserted, a physical address is sent to the bus. When the MMU chip select ($\overline{MCS}$) is asserted, the MMU is treated as a memory-mapped peripheral, allowing descriptors and other data to be transferred to/from the MMU via the bidirectional data bus.

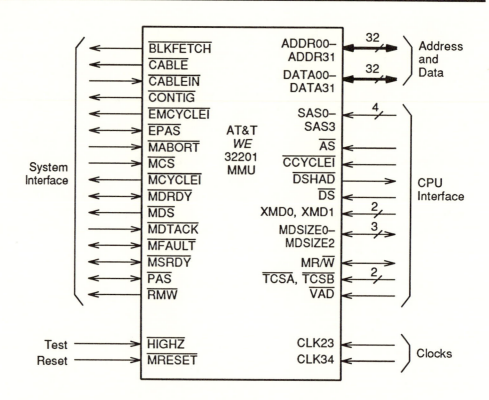

Note: $\overline{\text{BLKFETCH}}$, $\overline{\text{CABLEIN}}$, and MDSIZE2 not available on *WE* 32101 MMU.

FIGURE 7-41 AT&T *WE* 32101/32201 MMU Signal Diagram

There are other pins and signals that you should notice. The execution level signals (XMD0, XMD1) signify one of the four levels of privilege (kernel, executive, supervisor, and user). The MMU data size pins (MDSIZE0-MDSIZE2) allow operations on various data sizes ranging from 1 to 16 bytes. For the *WE* 32101 MMU, only two data-size pins are provided, limiting data options to 1, 2, 4, or 8 bytes. Four access status bits (SAS0-SAS3) indicate the type of transaction to be performed. Examples include address fetch, instruction fetch, instruction prefetch, support processor operation, and interrupt acknowledge.

Figure 7-42 illustrates the basic interface between the AT&T *WE* 32201 MMU and the *WE* 32200 CPU. The interface between the *WE* 32101 MMU and the *WE* 32100 CPU is identical, except for the absence of one data size pin (the *WE* 32100 CPU to *WE* 32101 MMU interface shows DSIZE0-DSIZE1 connected to MDSIZE0-MDSIZE1; the connection of DSIZE2 to MDSIZE2 only applies to the *WE* 32200 CPU/*WE* 32201 MMU interface). Also, the connection from the CPU output CYCLEI (asserted when a bus transaction is initiated) is not used by the *WE* 32101 MMU.

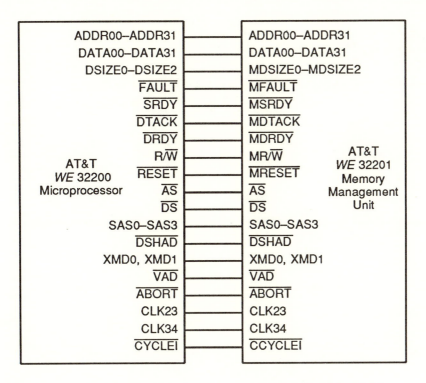

FIGURE 7-42 AT&T *WE* 32200 CPU Interface to a Single *WE* 32201 MMU

Multiple MMUs can be interfaced to a single CPU with little extra logic. This results in increasing the overall cache size and performance. The MMU translation chip select inputs ($\overline{TCSA}$, $\overline{TCSB}$) permit as many as four MMUs to be configured. Figure 7-43 illustrates the connections required for configurations containing two and four MMUs. Address bits ADDR29 and ADDR28 are used in the decoding.

7.6 Chapter Highlights

1. Microcomputer memory systems use read/write memory (RAM) and read-only memory (ROM) devices. RAM is volatile and its contents are lost when power is removed. RAM is used for nonpermanent storage of programs and data. RAMs are either the static (SRAM) or dynamic (DRAM) type. SRAMs storage is based on flip-flops; DRAMs work on a charge storage principle. DRAMs are less costly than SRAMs but are slower and require refreshing to prevent loss of contents. ROM is nonvolatile and does not lose its contents when power is removed. ROMs are either permanent or erasable. The permanent type are programmed during manufacture and their contents cannot be changed. Erasable ROM devices

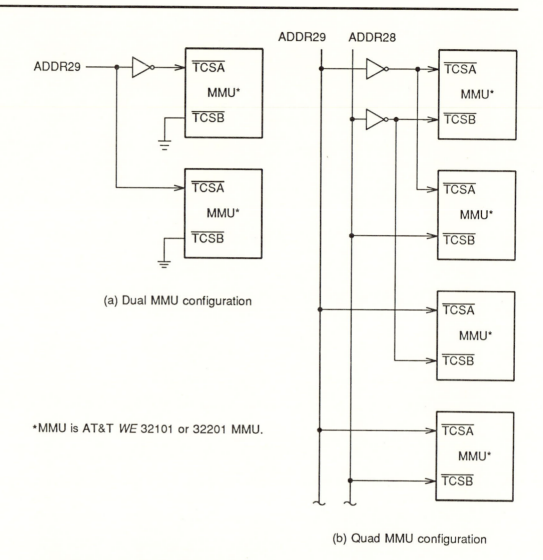

(a) Dual MMU configuration

*MMU is AT&T *WE* 32101 or 32201 MMU.

(b) Quad MMU configuration

FIGURE 7-43   Multiple MMU Configurations

(EPROMs and EEPROMs) can be reprogrammed and are useful during microcomputer system development.

2. SRAM bit capacities range from 4K to 256K bits; DRAM sizes range from 64K to 1M bits. Most RAM devices are 1-bit or 4-bits wide, with a few 8-bit SRAMs available. Typical DRAM access times are between 100 and 200 ns, while the fastest SRAMs can be accessed in 25 ns to 35 ns. Current EPROMs can address from 2K to 128K 8-bit locations, for a total capacity of 16K to 1M bits, with typical read access times of several hundred ns.

3. The hardware designer interfacing a CPU to memory needs to provide address decoding, determine the need for buffering, and ensure that timing specifications are met.

4. External address decoding logic provides the chip select (or chip enable) inputs to the physical memory devices. Incomplete decoding reduces hardware requirements when the CPU addressing capability exceeds the physical memory size, but often at the expense of ease of system expansion.

5. The INTEL 80386 CPU simplifies the interface to a 32-bit data bus by providing four individual byte enable ($\overline{BE3}$-$\overline{BE0}$) control outputs. The 80386 CPU performs operations on 8-bit, 16-bit, or 32-bit sized data regardless of address alignment; however, extra bus cycles are required for misaligned data. The MOTOROLA MC68020 CPU and the AT&T *WE* 32100 CPU issue data size indicator bits, rather than byte enables, for use by interfacing logic.

6. The CPU provides read and write control outputs that are generally connected to the corresponding output enable and write enable pins of the memory devices.

7. Buffering is required when a driver device is unable to meet the voltage level required for a load device to distinguish between a logic 0 or 1. The driver's voltage level specifications are not guaranteed if its current drive capability is exceeded by excessive loading. Buffering devices that provide sufficient current drive are needed in cases where fanout is exceeded. MOS devices, such as CPUs, have lower drive capability than bipolar devices (TTL). Therefore, buffering is generally required on the CPU's data bus when interfacing to devices which are equivalent to several bipolar loads.

8. Timing analysis must ensure that data read from memory is available within the CPU's data read time in order to be latched by the processor. Likewise, the memory must be able to latch the data within the CPU's data write time. Analysis should include the effect of external decoder delays.

9. The INTEL 80386 CPU provides address pipelining to allow memory additional time to read and write data. This is accomplished by overlapping the address and control signals for the next bus cycle with those of the current cycle.

10. Wait state insertion permits selected read and write cycles to be lengthened without reducing the clock rate. This is done to accommodate slow memory or I/O devices. Although adding wait states slightly reduces performance, it can significantly reduce system costs by enabling substitution of less costly slower DRAM for more expensive faster SRAM.

11. Cache is a small high-speed memory, usually SRAM, between the CPU and larger DRAM main memory. Overall system performance is enhanced when frequently accessed code and data is placed in a cache of sufficient size (typically at least 4K bytes for a 32-bit CPU with several Mbytes of main memory). In this case, the likelihood of the accessed information residing in the cache (called the hit rate) should exceed 50% to 60%; a lower hit rate generally results in a degradation of performance. Studies show that 32K or 64K bytes of cache result in an 85% to 90% hit rate. Cache controller devices, as well as on-CPU or on-MMU caches, are also used to maintain performance at very high clock rates.

12. DRAM controller logic provides row and column address strobing, and satisfies timing requirements for DRAM refreshing. Single-chip DRAM controllers provide required address multiplexing and strobing, refresh timing, as well as counter circuitry and address decoding.

13. DRAMs require an idle time to precharge between accesses. Interleaved DRAM banks therefore improve performance by allowing one bank to perform the current access while the other bank precharges. Since code and data tend to be accessed sequentially, decoding logic can be configured so that adjacent addresses are in different banks.

14. Memory management hardware provides virtual to physical address translation and system protection in a multiuser environment. The memory management unit (MMU) may be incorporated on the CPU (such as the INTEL 80386 CPU and MOTOROLA MC68030 CPU), or is provided as a separate device interfaced to the CPU (such as the MOTOROLA MC68851 PMMU, AT&T *WE* 32101 MMU, and AT&T *WE* 32201 MMU).

Exercises

Advanced problems are indicated with an asterisk (*).

1. How many address lines (N) and how many data lines (M) are connected to the following devices?
1a. 2764A EPROM
1b. 4362 SRAM
1c. 41256 DRAM

2. What is the memory device bit size and organization for the following numbers of address and data lines?

2a. N = 12 , M = 4
2b. N = 16, M = 8
2c. N = 22, M = 1

3a. Show how the gating and truth table for the 2/4 decoder (see Figure 7-7) is modified if the enable line is low active, rather than high active.
3b. Show the symbol, gating, and truth table for a 4/16 size decoder.

4. Assume the availability of 22 address lines, ranging from A21 to A0.
4a. What is the total range of addresses in hex?
4b. Using the highest order address lines, show how the addresses are decoded by 1/2, 2/4, and 3/8 size devices (as in Figure 7-8).
4c. Show the decoding provided by a 4/16 size device.

5. Assuming 22 address lines available (A21-A0), show decoding and the connections to memory devices (as in Figure 7-9) for the following requirements. The decoding need not be complete.
5a. 256K bytes EPROM using 27512 devices.
5b. 2M bytes EPROM using 27010 devices.

6. Repeat Exercise 5 assuming complete decoding is required. Use the highest-order address lines to enable the decoders, as illustrated in Figure 7-10.

7. Cascade the proper size decoders (see Figure 7-11) to implement an EPROM system using the device sizes shown below. The addressing is sequential, starting with all zeros. The decoding should be complete to allow for expansion. Address lines A21 to A0 are available.

    1M byte EPROM
    512K byte EPROM
    256K byte EPROM
    256K byte EPROM
    2M byte expansion space

8. Repeat Exercise 7 for the following EPROM configuration:

    1M byte EPROM
    1M byte EPROM
    512K byte EPROM
    512K byte EPROM
    256K byte EPROM
    256K byte EPROM
    256K byte EPROM
    256K byte EPROM

9. Implement the EPROM configuration of Exercise 7 using a single decoder with ORing as illustrated in Figure 7-12.

10. Repeat Exercise 9 implementing the EPROM configuration of Exercise 8.

11.* Design gating logic that takes the MOTOROLA MC68020 CPU's two-bit size indicator (SIZ1, SIZ0) and two lowest address bits (A1, A0), and generates the INTEL 80386 CPU's equivalent byte high enable signals ($\overline{BE3}$-$\overline{BE0}$). The table below defines the relationship between an internal multiplexer in the MC68020 CPU, and its external data bus.

Operand format:

	Long Word				Word		Byte
Byte	op0	op1	op2	op3	op2	op3	op3
Data Bus	D31–D0				D31–D16		D31–D24

Transfer	Size		Address		External Data Bus			
Size	SIZ1	SIZ0	A1	A0	D31–D24	D23–D16	D15–D8	D7–D0
Byte	0	1	x	x	op3	op3	op3	op3
Word	1	0	x	0	op2	op3	op2	op3
	1	0	x	1	op2	op2	op3	op2
3 byte	1	1	0	0	op1	op2	op3	op0
	1	1	0	1	op1	op1	op2	op3
	1	1	1	0	op1	op2	op1	op2
	1	1	1	1	op1	op1	op2	op1
Long word	0	0	0	0	op0	op1	op2	op3
	0	0	0	1	op0	op0	op1	op2
	0	0	1	0	op0	op1	op0	op1
	0	0	1	1	op0	op0	op1	op0

12. Using the voltage and current loading data from Tables 7-8 and 7-9, determine the high and low fanouts and maximum number of loads that can be connected to the CPU for each case. Is voltage buffering needed for any of the cases?

12a. LSTTL loads driven by the INTEL 80386 CPU

12b. LSTTL loads driven by the AT&T WE 32100 CPU

12c. CMOS loads driven by the MOTOROLA MC68020 CPU

13. Design an INTEL 80386 CPU interface (see Figure 7-24) to the following memory configuration:

    1M double words of EPROM starting at hex address 00000000
        using 27010 EPROMs,
    64K double words of SRAM starting at hex address F0000000
        using 43256 SRAMs.

The decoding need not be complete.

14. Repeat Exercise 13 assuming complete decoding is required. This means that all 32 address lines must be used.

15. Add appropriate read/write control to the design of Exercise 14.

16. Repeat the design of Exercise 14 using the
16a. MOTOROLA MC68020 CPU
16b. AT&T WE 32100 CPU.

17. Analyze the path timing delays for your design in Exercise 14a. Utilizing the access time for the EPROM used, determine the highest clock rate at which the INTEL 80386 CPU can be run without the need for wait states. Ignore any pipelining effects.

18.* If you have access to the appropriate timing specification information, analyze your timings for the MOTOROLA MC68020 CPU and AT&T WE 32100 CPU designs in Exercise 16. Determine the highest clock rate at which these CPUs can be run with zero wait states.

19. An INTEL 80386 CPU based system uses 27256-1 EPROMs (the faster version of the 27256). If no pipelining is used, determine from the information in Table 7-11 how many wait states must be inserted if the CPU's clock rate is
19a. 12.5 MHz
19b. 16 MHz
19c. 20 MHz.

20. Repeat Exercise 19 assuming that pipelining is used.

21. An INTEL 80386 CPU is to be run at 16 MHz with zero wait states. If RAM devices of at least 64K bit size are to be used in the system, which devices from Table 7-3 appear to be acceptable
21a. without pipelining?
21b. with pipelining?

22.* Referring to Figures 7-26 to 7-28, design a single wait state generator for the
22a. MOTOROLA MC68020 CPU
22b. AT&T WE 32100 CPU.

23.* Design an interface between the INTEL 80386 CPU and 256K bytes of DRAM (64K double words). Use address multiplexers, the 82C08 DRAM controller, and 41464 DRAM devices. Analyze timing and wait state requirements for both 16 MHz and 20 MHz clock rates. Assume no interleaving.

24.* Repeat Exercise 23 for an INTEL 80386 CPU based system that requires 2M bytes of DRAM. Use 41256 DRAM devices, and provide address interleaving. Since these DRAM devices are 1-byte wide it will be necessary to use tristate gates on the data lines.

25. Referring to Figures 7-36 and 7-37, show the interfacing of the AT&T WE 32103 DRAM Controller to four banks of 411000 DRAM devices.

I/O Interfacing

Chapter Eight

8.1   Overview of Data Transfer Techniques
8.2   Programmed I/O
8.3   Interrupts
8.4   Direct Memory Access (DMA)
8.5   Interfacing to Parallel I/O
8.6   Serial I/O Interfacing
8.7   Chapter Highlights

This chapter discusses data transfer techniques and hardware interfacing between the CPU and I/O devices. Programmed I/O, interrupt controlled I/O, and direct memory access (DMA) are presented with sample programs, timing analysis, and descriptions of single-chip controller devices that implement these data transfer techniques. Parallel transmission using a programmable peripheral interface (PPI) device is presented followed by signal formats for serial transmission. The use of a universal synchronous/asynchronous receiver transmitter (USART) for serial transmission is also examined.

8.1 Overview of Data Transfer Techniques

Many of the memory interfacing concepts discussed in Chapter Seven apply to I/O devices as well because address decoding logic must also be provided for I/O device selection. Due to the wide variety of I/O device specifications, timing and loading considerations are even more diverse than for memory system design. Also, I/O devices can differ significantly in signal format requirements. Some devices communicate directly with the CPU in parallel, some devices may require a serial data format, and others may provide or accept only analog rather than digital data.

The transmission needs of I/O devices and peripherals cover a wide range. A low speed ASCII terminal operating at 300 bits/s transfers (300/8) bytes/s, or approximately 40 bytes/s. In contrast, consider an 80 column by 24 row video terminal with 10 lines of character dots and spaces per row. A typical display refreshed at a 60 Hz rate requires approximately 20000 character codes [(80 x 24 x 10) bytes] to be fetched every 1/60 of a second. This results in a data rate of 1.2 Mbytes/s (20K x 60 bytes/s). Current memory device access times range from about 25 ns to 450 ns; therefore the difference between the slowest and fastest memory devices exceeds a factor of 20. This is nowhere near the difference between a 40 bytes/s and a 1.2 Mbytes/s I/O device.

Several different I/O data transfer techniques are used to handle the wide range of I/O device speeds. These techniques can be broadly categorized into programmed I/O, interrupt, controlled I/O, and direct memory access (DMA). The remainder of this section gives an overview of these techniques. A detailed description of each is presented in subsequent sections.

An additional consideration for hardware and software designers is whether the system uses memory-mapped I/O as opposed to "I/O mapped I/O" (sometimes called accumulator-based I/O). Any system can be configured so that I/O devices appear to the CPU as an extension of memory. The advantage is that any memory instruction automatically becomes an I/O instruction if the I/O device's address is properly referenced. This gives the software designer a much larger repertoire of instructions to use than would be available otherwise.

Accumulator-based I/O can be used with machines that feature separate input (such as IN) and output (such as OUT) instructions; generally, the data transfer occurs between the CPU's accumulator and the I/O device. Usually, the advantage of simpler address decoding results from using a separate I/O address space, as opposed to memory mapped I/O. For the 32-bit CPUs featured in this textbook, the INTEL 80386 CPU is the only one which offers the choice of memory-mapped or accumulator based I/O. Since the MOTOROLA MC68020/MC68030 CPU and AT&T WE 32100/32200 CPU do not include separate I/O instructions, only memory-mapped I/O can be used with these CPUs.

Programmed I/O

Often during the course of program execution it is desired to transfer data between an I/O device and the CPU's memory. The data will either be read from memory and written to an output device, or read from an input device and written to memory.

The transfer of data under program control is an example of what is called programmed I/O. The time required for this transfer obviously is influenced by the size of the data block, the CPU's clock rate, and the efficiency of the program segment that accomplishes the transfer. If this time is acceptable to the device and to the overall system performance, programmed I/O is a logical choice.

Although the data transfer may be under program control, the system designer can implement the request for transfer via either hardware or software. Under software control, the device may be continually or periodically "polled" by the CPU to determine its readiness for data transfer. Figure 8-1 illustrates this concept. If the hardware approach is used, the device indicates its readiness by activating an interrupt control input on the CPU. In either case, data transfer is accomplished by a program. We will use the term programmed I/O only for the case where the transfer request, as well as the data transfer itself, is under software control. Where the request is initiated by hardware, the technique will be called interrupt-controlled I/O.

Interrupt Controlled I/O

Interrupt mechanism details differ for the various CPUs, but there are certain fundamental concepts common to all cases. Section 8.3 details the interrupt mechanisms for the Intel, AT&T and Motorola 32-bit CPUs featured in this textbook. Figure 8-2 illustrates how the interrupt process typically works. The CPU continually senses its interrupt request line(s). When a request is made, the current instruction is completed before the CPU responds. Many CPUs can handle two types of interrupts, maskable and nonmaskable. As discussed in Section 3.4, the nonmaskable interrupt request must always be accepted, whereas maskable interrupt requests can be ignored depending on the processor's state. An interrupt

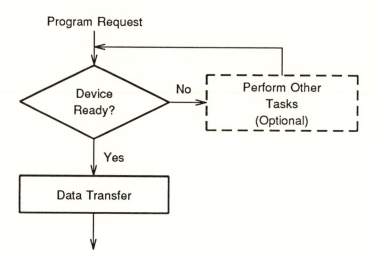

Program Request

Device Ready?

No

Perform Other Tasks (Optional)

Yes

Data Transfer

FIGURE 8-1 Programmed I/O Mechanism

enable flag bit, usually controllable by the programmer, determines whether a maskable interrupt request is accepted or ignored. Thus, maskable interrupts are either enabled or disabled; in contrast, a nonmaskable interrupt is always enabled.

A nonmaskable interrupt or a maskable interrupt with interrupt enabled results in the data transfer being done as part of a special subprogram called an interrupt service routine (see Figure 8-2). Since an interrupt request is generated by external hardware, it can occur at any time. The main program is often in the middle of a task when an interrupt occurs. This necessitates a mechanism for saving important CPU register data before proceeding with the interrupt service routine. This is required since some or all of the same registers are likely to be used in the data transfer.

The various CPUs differ in the way they handle the saving and later restoring of register data and other processor status information during interrupts. The details of how the system finds its way to the appropriate memory location to start executing the service routine is also dependent on the CPU being used.

Early 8-bit CPUs, with limited register and status information, typically responded to interrupts in a simple manner. Users of the INTEL 8080/8085 CPU and the ZILOG Z-80 CPU usually used special restart (RST) instructions that directed the program to the appropriate memory location containing the service routine. The instruction code is generated either by external logic or, in some cases, with the INTEL 8085 CPU or ZILOG Z-80 CPU, automatically via internal CPU hardware. This technique, called vectoring, is characterized by each interrupting device having its own restart instruction that identifies it as the interrupt requester. The ZILOG Z-80 CPU features an interrupt mode which allows access to a vector table of addresses, a more convenient way to handle multiple device situations. This approach is similar to that used by 32-bit CPUs.

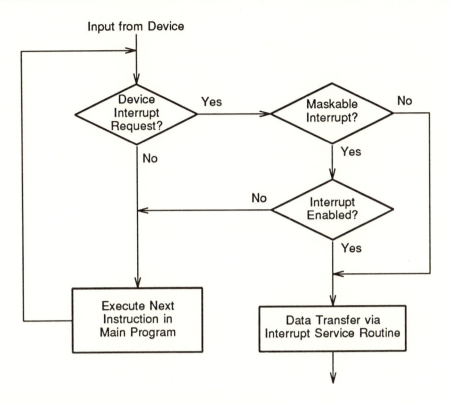

FIGURE 8-2 Interrupt-Controlled I/O Mechanism

The 8-bit CPUs also require the user to save and restore registers with the individual instructions, PUSH and POP. Current CPUs approach this in a more sophisticated manner with automatic register set saves and restores to reduce the task switching time, often a critical factor in high performance applications.

Direct Memory Access

In contrast to programmed I/O and interrupt-controlled I/O, direct memory access (DMA) is a method of hardware-controlled data transfer between a device and memory. Similar to the manner in which an interrupt is initiated, the device requests attention by activating a DMA request input to the CPU. A DMA acknowledge output issued by the CPU activates external logic, often a single-chip DMA controller. The CPU then tristates its buses, allowing direct communication between memory and the device. During this time the CPU is in a "hold" state. It resumes execution of code when the controller logic deactivates the DMA request after a single data item or a block of data has been transferred. Alternatively, DMA transfer may occur during idle clock cycles when only internal CPU operations take place. This method is referred to as cycle stealing or hidden DMA.

The main advantage of DMA over software-controlled data transfer is speed. For example, the video terminal discussed earlier in this section requires a transfer rate of 1.2M bytes/s to satisfy its refresh requirement. Let us assume that data is being transferred under software control without the benefit of a block move instruction. A typical program segment would include at least four operations inside a loop: load the accumulator from memory, output it to the device, decrement a block size count, and jump back and repeat as long as the count exceeds zero. Assume that for a typical CPU such a segment requires 20 clock cycles to accomplish this single-byte transfer. An 8-bit CPU operating at a clock rate from 2 MHz to 4 MHz requires from 5 to 10 microseconds to accomplish this transfer. Therefore, the effective maximum data transfer rate (assuming 4 MHz) is only 1/(5 microseconds), or 0.2 Mbytes/s.

The video terminal requirements can be handled with 80386 software running at a 20 MHz clock rate. An I/O operation preceded by a repeat prefix (such as REP OUTS) can transfer data between memory and a device in 6 clock cycles per item moved. This ignores overhead cycles involved in initializing address and block size. Assuming byte-wide data, a rate of

$$20 \text{ MHz}/6 = 3.33 \text{ Mbytes/s}$$

is possible. If you can take advantage of the larger data widths, the rate is doubled for a 16-bit width, and quadrupled if the entire 32-bit bus is used. On the other hand, the overhead time can become significant for smaller block size transfers, particularly if task switching time is also a factor.

The alternative of using DMA with relatively fast static RAM allows each byte to be transferred in a time approximately equal to the memory access time (ignoring DMA controller delay). Thus, for 50 ns SRAM, a data rate of

$$1/(50 \text{ ns}) \text{ or } 20 \text{ Mbytes/s}$$

is possible. Although the video terminal requirements might be satisfied with a software approach, the higher rates achievable with DMA are advantageous in virtual memory systems. In these systems there is a need for very rapid data transfer between memory and disk as part of the CPU's memory management.

8.2 Programmed I/O

It is the responsibility of the program to initiate the data transfer between the CPU and an external device when using programmed I/O. In certain cases, the external device may be assumed to be ready at all times for a data exchange. If intervening tasks do not provide sufficient delay to allow the CPU to slow down to the device's transfer rate, it may be necessary to insert a programmed delay between successive transfers. For most I/O situations, the device indicates its readiness for transfer via a status flag bit. The CPU inputs and tests this flag bit, and performs the transfer only when the bit has been asserted. Multiple devices can be handled and the software can easily implement a desired device priority.

Data Transfer Without Status Checking

When using programmed I/O, certain devices may always be ready for data exchange when requested by the program. For example, a 7-segment display can always receive information without waiting. The 80386 instruction sequence

```
MOV AL,SEGON
OUT SEVSEG,AL
```

loads the lower eight bits of the accumulator (AL) with the pattern that lights the appropriate segments of the display. The byte corresponding to the pattern is symbolically referred to as SEGON. The byte is then sent to the decoded output port with the symbolic address SEVSEG (representing an 8-bit port address). The program can update the display as often as desired, since the display is always ready to receive new information. Some minimum data hold time is needed since the display is being viewed by the human eye.

The need for program delay is more evident when the output device is a printer. Assume that a printer can accept up to 100 characters per second. An 80386 program segment that loads AL and outputs the character code (ASCII) to be printed must be followed by a 1/100 second delay routine, to ensure that characters sent to the printer are not lost. Consider Program 8-1.

 *Program 8-1*

Delay Subroutine for a 100 Character/Second Printer

```
              MOV       AL,ASCII
              OUT       PRTR,AL
              CALL      DELAY
              :
              :                    ;   Clock Cycles
DELAY:        MOV       CX,NUM
LOOP:         DEC       CX         ;   2
              JNZ       LOOP       ;   8
              RET
```

The delay subroutine, or procedure, uses the 16-bit CX register as a counter. After its value is initialized, the counter is decremented repeatedly and tested until it reaches zero. Control then returns to the main program. The initial counter

385

value, symbolically called NUM, must be chosen to achieve the desired delay. Most of the time is spent in LOOP where the decrement and conditional jump are repeatedly executed. The DEC operation takes 2 clock cycles, and the jump takes (7 + m) cycles when the condition is met; that is, when the program branches back to LOOP. The variable m is the number of components of the instruction to which the program branches, a consequence of the CPU having to empty and reload its prefetch queue. The entire displacement, if any, and the entire immediate data, if any, count as one component, as does each of the other instruction bytes and prefix(es). For this case, it is assumed that the DEC instruction is assembled into its shortest form, a 1-byte instruction. Since there is no displacement nor immediate data, m is 1, and the conditional jump requires 8 cycles.

A total of 10 clock cycles are required for each decrement and test of the counter (as long as it is not zero). The approximate duration of the subroutine is 10n clock cycles, and the value of n corresponds to NUM, the initial counter value. If the 80386 is operating at 20 MHz, its

$$\text{Clock Period} = 1/(20 \text{ MHz}) = 50 \text{ ns}$$

and n must be chosen to satisfy

$$(10)(n) \times (50 \text{ ns}) = 0.01 \text{ s}$$

Thus,

$$n = 0.01 \, / \, [(10) \times (50 \times 10^{-9})] = 20000$$

Since a 16-bit number can be as large as decimal 65535, the choice of the 16-bit CX counter was appropriate. The programmer can also choose an 8-bit register for shorter delays, or a 32-bit register if longer delays are required for an application.

In general, the time taken for assembly language code to execute can be determined by adding the clock cycle counts for each instruction. (These counts are found in the manufacturer's literature.)

Status Checking

To avoid the possibility of the CPU attempting to perform an I/O data transfer before the device is ready for it, a device status flag bit is often built into the device. The hardware interface and accompanying software can then treat this status bit as data from an input device; the bit can be continually or periodically checked, and the data transfer (in or out) performed only when the status bit has been asserted.

Figure 8-3 illustrates a hardware interface between the 80386 CPU and a single-output device. The status flag bit can be read in via input port "STAT"; if asserted (high), the data can be sent out via output port "DEV". Since M/$\overline{\text{IO}}$ must

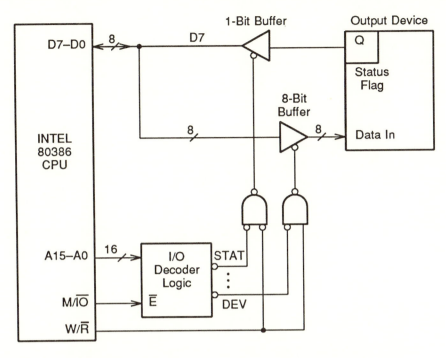

FIGURE 8-3 INTEL 80386 CPU Interface to Output Device With Status Flag

be low, the address decoder outputs are asserted only for I/O operations, as opposed to memory operations. The 80386 output, W/$\overline{R}$, ensures the correct operation (read or write); the same address "STAT" can then be used for an output device as well, and "DEV" may also address a separate input peripheral. The status bit can be connected to any data line; D7 was chosen arbitrarily for this example.

Program 8-2 again illustrates the transfer of a single byte of data, but only after the device has indicated its readiness by asserting the status flag.

 *Program 8-2*

Transfer of a Single Byte of Data

```
CHECK:    IN       AL,STAT      ; Read in status flag
          TEST     AL,80H       ; Compare to 1
          JNZ      TRNSFR       ; Transfer data if ready (1)
          :
          :                     ; Perform other tasks
          :                     ; (optional)
          :
          JMP      CHECK        ; Repeat status check
TRNSFR:   MOV      AL,DATA      ; Load and output data byte
          OUT      DEV,AL
```

387

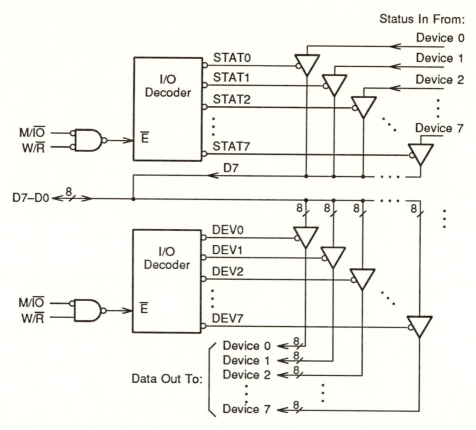

FIGURE 8-4   80386 CPU Interface to Multiple Output Devices - Status Bits Read Individually

The IN instruction reads the status flag to bit 7 of AL, and the TEST operation performs a logical AND between AL and binary 10000000. This operation masks the remaining bits read in, since their values are unknown. If the status bit read in has value 0, the result is all zeros, and the CPU's zero flag bit is set. When the device is ready, the status bit has value 1, and a nonzero condition results. In that case, the program branches to TRNSFR and the byte at symbolic location DATA is written to the output device.

When more than one device is capable of handling data transfer, the individual status bits must be read in. A device priority can be established easily by having the software check the status of the highest priority device first, and transfer data if the status bit is asserted. The remaining devices can then be checked in their order of priority. Figure 8-4 shows a configuration of up to eight output devices for which one status bit is read in at a time to line D7. For convenience, separate decoder devices are shown for the input and output operations.

Program 8-3 assumes the device priority is Device 0 to Device 7, with 0 having the highest priority. Each device's status is checked, and a byte of data is transferred if that device is ready. The next higher priority device is then checked, independent of whether any previous device has been served. Thus, if multiple devices indicate readiness at the same time, they will be recognized in the order of priority. After all devices are checked, other tasks may be performed and then the device status testing repeated.

Program 8-3

Transfer of Data with Prioritized Devices

```
CHECK0:   IN     AL,STAT0      ; Read device 0 status
          TEST   AL,80H        ; Test it
          JZ     CHECK1        ; Test next device if not
          CALL   TRSFR0        ;   ready
CHECK1:   IN     AL,STAT1      ; Repeat for device 1
          TEST   AL,80H
          JZ     CHECK2
          CALL   TRSFR1
CHECK2:   IN     AL,STAT2      ; Repeat for device 2
          :
          :
          :
CHECK7:   IN     AL,STAT7      ; Repeat for device 7
          TEST   AL,80H
          JZ     OTHER
          CALL   TRSFR7
OTHER:    :
          :                    ; Perform other tasks
          :
          JMP    CHECK0        ; Start over
TRSFR0:   MOV    AL,DATA0      ; Transfer data to
          OUT    DEV0,AL       ;   device 0
          RET
TRSFR1:   MOV    AL,DATA1      ; Transfer data to
          OUT    DEV1,AL       ;   device 1
          RET
TRSFR2:   :
    :     :
    :     :
TRSFR7:   MOV    AL,DATA7      ; Transfer data to
          OUT    DEV7,AL       ;   device 7
          RET
```

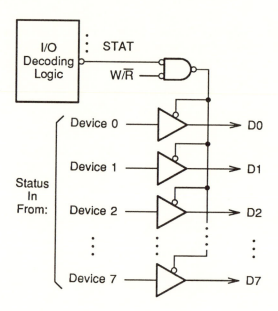

FIGURE 8-5 80386 CPU Interface to Multiple Output Devices - All Status Bits Read in at Once

An alternative approach exists which results in software reduction and faster operation. If the status flag input buffering is modified as shown in Figure 8-5, a single input operation from address STAT will read in all the status bits at once onto data lines 0 to 7.

Program 8-4 takes advantage of the paralleling of the status flag bits; it also employs indexed addressing of sequentially stored data bytes, and indirect addressing of the output ports. This permits the use of a more efficient looping procedure for both the status checking and data byte transfer operations.

Program 8-4

Alternative Data Transfer With Prioritized Devices

```
START:    MOV    CX,8            ; Set device number count
          MOV    DX,DEV0-1       ; Set device port address
          MOV    ESI,TABLE- 1    ; Set data table address
CHECK:    INC    DX              ; Update addresses for
          INC    ESI             ;    next device
          IN     AL,STAT         ; Read in all status flags
          ROR    AL,1            ; Current status flag
          JNC    NEXT            ;    replaces carry bit
          CALL   TRNSFR          ; Transfer byte if ready
```

(Continued)

```
NEXT:     DEC      CX                  ; Update device counter
          JNZ      CHECK               ; Check next device
            :
            :                          ; Perform other tasks
            :
          JMP      START               ; Start over
TRNSFR:   MOV      AL,(SI)             ; Transfer data byte to
          OUT      (DX),AL             ;    corresponding device
          RET
```

Register CX is used as a counter, keeping track of the number of devices remaining to be checked. DX contains the device address, which now may be 8 or 16 bits. Using all the outputs of a standard decoder allows the device addresses to be sequential, and the next device is pointed to by simply incrementing DX. Note that the indirect form of the output instruction is used in the single data transfer subroutine here. The operation

OUT (DX),AL

outputs the byte in AL to the device corresponding to the 16-bit port address in DX. Source index register, SI, points to an 8-byte data table containing the individual bytes to be transferred to the devices. By organizing the data as well as the device addresses sequentially, the data corresponding to each device can be conveniently fetched as each status flag is asserted. The data table is organized as:

Memory Address	Data Byte Stored
TABLE	Device 0 data
TABLE+1	Device 1 data
:	
:	
:	
TABLE+7	Device 7 data

8.3 Interrupts

The examples in the previous sections illustrate that programmed I/O using status bits incurs some degree of software overhead to check device status before performing data transfer. In many situations the extra time does not degrade system performance, particularly if other tasks can be performed between device status checks. A good example of this is a system whose main responsibility is the monitoring of a keyboard and display. The system can alternately scan the keyboard and refresh the display. A "key down" signifies a keyboard ready condition; the response is usually to update the display by writing output data corresponding to the code of the key. Since the time between successive inputs to a keyboard is relatively long, most of the time is spent in display refresh. The minimum time a key is held down is also relatively long so that it is unlikely that the routine will miss the request for data transfer.

There are situations where the overhead of monitoring device status significantly degrades system performance. A related problem is the case where the device's status flag is asserted for a very short interval, which may not allow the system sufficient time to perform other necessary tasks without the risk of missing the device's status flag assertion. In such situations, interrupt-controlled I/O is generally preferred over programmed I/O.

One penalty that interrupt-controlled I/O incurs is that additional hardware may be required to identify a device and point the main program to the appropriate interrupt service routine. Another is the increased difficulty in the debugging of software that is subject to being interrupted at random times. The programmer must ensure that the proper tasks are carried out regardless of when the interrupt service routine is handled.

Interrupt Control Signals

Recall that interrupt requests are either the maskable or nonmaskable variety. CPUs differ in their mechanisms for accepting requests and in issuing acknowledgments to external logic. Often, the external logic must supply an identifier to the data bus to direct the program to the appropriate interrupt service routine. An interrupt acknowledge signal acts as an enable, placing this identifier on the data bus only after an interrupt request has been accepted by the CPU.

It is useful at this point to profile the interrupt mechanism of some early CPUs, particularly in how it influenced the design of the INTEL 80386 CPU. Figure 8-6 shows the relevant signals that provide request and acknowledge capability for several CPUs.

The earliest CPU shown, the INTEL 8080 CPU, has the most primitive interrupt capability. A single maskable interrupt request (INT) is provided. Its companion support controller chip, the 8228 System Controller, issues an interrupt acknowledge ($\overline{\text{INTA}}$).

The ZILOG Z-80 CPU also provides a nonmaskable interrupt request ($\overline{\text{NMI}}$) in addition to the maskable request, but does not supply the interrupt acknowledge ($\overline{\text{INTA}}$) directly. The control output $\overline{\text{M1}}$ is only asserted at the start of a new instruction (opcode fetch operation). In contrast, $\overline{\text{IORQ}}$ is only asserted by an input or output instruction, well after the opcode fetch operation. An interrupt acknowledge is provided indirectly by asserting both $\overline{\text{M1}}$ and $\overline{\text{IORQ}}$ in

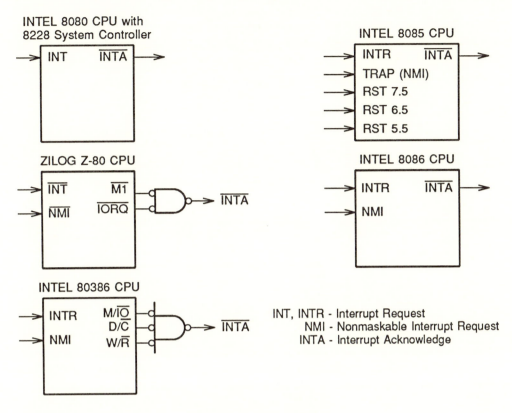

FIGURE 8-6   Interrupt Control Signals for Various CPUs

response to an interrupt request that has been accepted. By ANDing these signals, a single $\overline{\text{INTA}}$ is generated since there is no other condition that asserts both $\overline{\text{M1}}$ and $\overline{\text{IORQ}}$. The 32-bit CPUs use a similar technique by outputting status bits, with one of the codes corresponding to interrupt acknowledge.

Since the INTEL 8085 CPU was intended to replace the 8080 CPU and eliminate the need for the 8228 support device, $\overline{\text{INTA}}$ is provided directly by the CPU. The 8085 CPU also provides a nonmaskable interrupt (NMI) called TRAP, and three other maskable requests (RST 7.5, RST 6.5, RST 5.5). The RST inputs are called *direct vectored interrupts*, since internal CPU logic, rather than external hardware, assists in the transferring of the program to the service routine. Although the INTEL 8085 CPU has more interrupt inputs than the ZILOG Z-80 CPU, the Z-80 CPU has the flexibility of being placed in one of three modes (called Modes 0, 1, and 2) by software. This allows the single maskable interrupt ($\overline{\text{INT}}$) to be handled in different ways, the details of which will be discussed shortly.

The INTEL 8086 and 80386 CPUs are similar to the ZILOG Z-80 CPU in that they have one maskable interrupt request (INTR) and an NMI. The 8086 CPU, like the 8085 CPU, provides $\overline{\text{INTA}}$ directly from the chip. However, the 80386 CPU does not have an output $\overline{\text{INTA}}$ pin. Rather, its acknowledge is provided in a similar way to the ZILOG Z-80 CPU, in that outputs that provide bus cycle definition are all low only when an interrupt has been accepted. Normally when both M/$\overline{\text{IO}}$ and W/$\overline{\text{R}}$ are low, data/control (D/$\overline{\text{C}}$) is high, indicating an I/O data read operation. Since all three outputs are not normally low, this condition is used to define the interrupt acknowledge bus cycle type.

Transferring Control to Interrupt Service Routines

As part of the interrupt acknowledge bus cycle, information must be provided to the CPU as to the location of the routine to service the interrupt request. This is necessary since the normal opcode fetch of the next instruction will not occur. The reason for this can be seen easily for the 80386 CPU by noting the states of the bus cycle definition signals (see Figure 8-18 for complete bus cycle status definitions):

M/$\overline{\text{IO}}$	D/$\overline{\text{C}}$	W/$\overline{\text{R}}$	Bus Cycle Type
0	0	0	Interrupt acknowledge
1	0	0	Memory code read

Recalling that memory interfacing is designed so that memory devices will be enabled only when M/$\overline{\text{IO}}$ is high (logic 1), code will not be read during an interrupt acknowledge cycle. Thus, either CPU logic or external logic must take over and provide the data bus with the needed information.

When an INTEL 8080/8085 CPU or ZILOG Z-80 CPU (for Mode 0 operation) accept a maskable request, it expects external hardware to provide the next opcode. In the absence of an interrupt controller device (such as the INTEL 8259A Programmable Interrupt Controller), a special restart (RST) instruction is the most convenient substitute.

The RST instruction's binary opcode (11xxx111) allows as many as eight I/O devices to be uniquely identified (since each "x" may be 0 or 1). When executed, RST calls a subroutine at binary address xxx000 (corresponding to hex addresses 00, 08, 10, 18, 20, 28, 30, and 38). By providing a separation of 8 bytes, jump instruction codes can be inserted at these locations to transfer the program to the start of the appropriate routine to service the requesting device.

Since the RST instructions act as subroutine calls, the program counter is saved on the stack, and is later restored by terminating the service routine with a return instruction. However, the programmer is responsible for saving and later restoring other register contents as part of the interrupt routine. In addition, acceptance of an interrupt automatically disables further maskable requests, so that an enable interrupt instruction is generally inserted just prior to the return to the main routine.

The INTEL 8085 CPU and ZILOG Z-80 CPU also are capable of what previously was called direct vectored interrupt, where internal CPU hardware automatically transfers control to a specific address. For example, the 8085 CPU's nonmaskable interrupt (TRAP) vectors the program to address 24H, and the other maskable request inputs (RST 5.5, RST 6.5, RST 7.5) direct it to 2CH, 34H, and 3CH, respectively. These addresses interleave with those provided by the RST instructions, still allowing enough space (4 bytes) to insert a jump instruction. The ZILOG Z-80 CPU's nonmaskable interrupt ($\overline{\text{NMI}}$) branches to 66H, and the maskable interrupt ($\overline{\text{INT}}$) for Mode 1 operation to 38H.

Mode 2 operation of the ZILOG Z-80 CPU avoids the need to reserve low end memory addresses by accessing the service routine indirectly via a look-up table. The combination of a byte from an internal interrupt register, accessible to the programmer, and a byte supplied by external hardware, forms a 16-bit memory address that points to the start of a table of service routine starting addresses. The table, as well as the routines, can be placed anywhere in the addressable 64K byte memory space.

The look-up table concept was used by the 8086 CPU designers, and is central to the interrupt handling mechanisms of the Intel 32-bit CPU. The 8086 also features software interrupt capability. An INT instruction includes a code byte which specifies one of 256 vector locations. A separate interrupt-on-overflow (INTO) instruction causes interrupt only if the overflow flag bit is asserted. In addition, if a trap (T) flag bit is asserted, the 8086 CPU operates in single-step mode. In this mode, the 8086 executes a software interrupt after each instruction.

Software interrupts have higher priority than both the nonmaskable and maskable external interrupts. An 8086 software interrupt can occur in another way - by an attempt to divide by zero (executing the divide instruction with a zero divisor).

The 32-bit CPUs "interrupt" for a variety of abnormal conditions; recall that these conditions are referred to as exceptions. Differences in how interrupts and exceptions are handled will be discussed later.

The 8086 CPU's vector table is shown in Figure 8-7. Recall from the discussion of memory management in Section 2.3 that the 8086 CPU's physical instruction address is computed from the code segment (CS) base value and the offset address placed in the instruction pointer (IP). Since both are 16-bit values, four bytes are assigned to each vector. Of course, the current CS and IP values are saved on the stack before being replaced by the values from the table. This enables the service routine to return to the point of interrupt in the main program.

The nonmaskable and special software interrupts are identified by vectors 0 to 4, which must be stored at the low end of physical memory. Vectors 32 through 255 are available for external maskable interrupts; software interrupts can also access the same vectors. For external interrupts, interrupt logic must provide the vector number. This number is then multiplied by 4 to obtain the vector's starting address. For software interrupts, the vector number is generally part of the instruction; otherwise default vector 3 is used.

Like its 8086 CPU predecessor, the 80386 CPU handles maskable interrupts via the INTR pin, and nonmaskable interrupts on the NMI pin. As with the 8086 CPU, its interrupt enable and trap flag bits allow for the masking of interrupts and single-step operation, respectively. Whereas the 8086 CPU only handled a

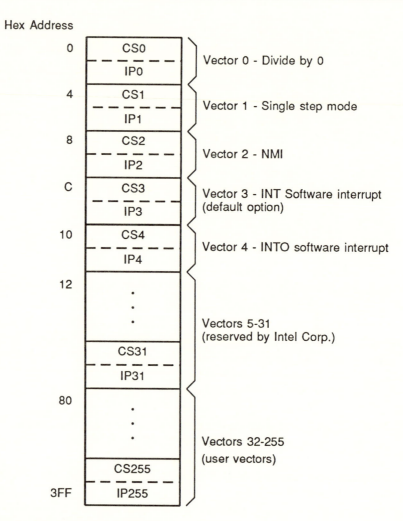

FIGURE 8-7   8086 CPU Vector Table

divide-by-zero exception, the 80386 CPU can handle a variety of exceptions classified as faults, traps, and aborts (described in Section 3.5). Faults are either detected before or during execution of an instruction, with the instruction restarted if detected during execution. In contrast, traps are reported after the instruction is completed, and aborts indicate severe errors for which the instruction causing the exception can't be located.

The 80386 vector identifiers, which are 8-bit numbers from 0 to 255 summarized in Table 3.2, are repeated in Table 8-1.

As for the 8086 CPU, vectors numbered above 31 can identify maskable interrupts via INTR if external hardware supplies the identifier byte, or software interrupts of the form

INT n

TABLE 8-1 80386 Interrupt and Exception Vector Identifiers

Identifier	Type of Interrupt or Exception
0	Divide error (fault)
1	Debug traps or faults
2	NMI
3	Software interrupt - default case
4	Software interrupt on overflow (INTO)
5	Bounds check (fault) - BOUND instruction
6	Invalid opcode (fault)
7	Coprocessor not available (fault)
8	Double fault (abort)
9	Coprocessor segment overrun (abort)
10	Invalid TSS (fault)
11	Segment not present (fault)
12	Stack exception (fault)
13	General protection (fault or abort)
14	Page fault
15	(Reserved)
16	Coprocessor error (fault)
17–31	(Reserved)
32–255	Available for external or software interrupts

where n is an 8-bit number. However, unlike the 8086 CPU which requires that the vector table be stored at the low end of memory, the 80386 CPU in protected mode permits the table to be placed anywhere in the physical space. As discussed in Chapter 3, this table is referred to as an interrupt descriptor table (IDT), and each descriptor is an 8-byte quantity. The IDT register (IDTR), which locates the descriptor in the physical address space, is accessible via the instructions which load and store the IDT (LIDT, SIDT).

Recall there are three types of interrupt service descriptors: task gates, trap gates, and interrupt gates. Task gates save all registers and load in a new set, whereas trap and interrupt gates save only the flag register, code segment, and instruction pointer. The task gate is therefore more convenient for the programmer if other register contents must be saved. However, it wastes time in those cases where register data need not be preserved. Trap and interrupt gates differ only in that further interrupts are disabled by an interrupt gate, but not by a trap gate.

The format of a single descriptor is:

Relative Address	16 Bits
0	Offset (LO)
+2	Selector
+4	Attributes
+6	Offset (HI)

The 16-bit selector defines the segment. The 32-bit offset allows transfer to an interrupt routine at any point in the segment. The attributes include bits identifying privilege level and number of parameters transferred to the new procedure.

Multiple Device Interrupt Handling

When more than one device is capable of interrupting a program in progress, a mechanism must be provided to identify the requesting device and to establish priority in the event more than one device at a time is vying for attention. One approach, called software polling, provides a single vector which branches the software to the same place regardless of which device caused the interrupt. The software then checks the individual device status bits (the interrupt request lines) starting with the highest priority peripheral. Upon finding an asserted status bit, control is transferred to the appropriate service routine.

Figure 8-8 shows the hardware interface between a maximum of eight devices and an 80386 CPU. Notice only the low byte of the data bus is used, with each device assigned its own bit on the data bus. As many as 32 devices can be accommodated with this approach if the entire data bus is used. Even more can be handled if additional decoding logic is provided, although, in this case, single-chip interrupt controllers (to be discussed later) would be preferred.

For both the single and multiple device case, the maskable interrupt request enters via INTR and the interrupt vector is gated to the data bus only on acknowledgment ($\overline{\text{INTA}}$). The flexibility of this approach is increased by providing external interrupt masking capability for as many devices as desired. Data can be written to the latch that masks interrupt requests from those devices corresponding to the zeros in the byte. For those devices which external logic allows an interrupt, a request from any one (or more) enters INTR. Assuming the CPU's internal interrupt flag is asserted, $\overline{\text{INTA}}$ permits the entry of the 8-bit vector. Recall only numbers from 32 to 255 are permitted because vectors 0 to 31 are reserved for the CPU.

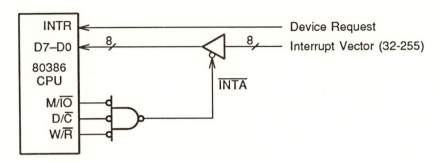

a. Single Device

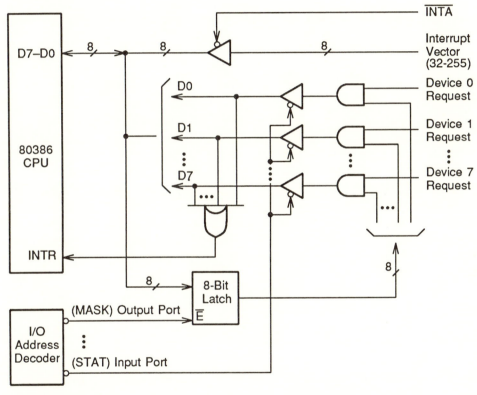

b. Multiple Devices

FIGURE 8-8   Interrupt Logic for INTEL 80386 CPU Software Polling Technique

Program 8-5 illustrates how the interrupting device can be identified. The location called INTERR is assumed to be the location to which the appropriate descriptor transfers control. It is assumed arbitrarily that device 0 has highest priority, device 1 next highest, etc.; also, interrupts from devices 3 through 7 will not be recognized.

Program 8-5

Identifying the Interrupting Device

```
          :              :
          :              :
     (main routine)
          :              :
          :              :
          MOV       AL,07H    ; Mask devices 3-7
          OUT       MASK,AL
          STI                 ; Enable interrupts
                        :
                        :
INTERR:   IN        AL,STAT   ; Read device status bits
          MOV       ECX,0     ; Setup counter
INTSHF:   ROR       AL,1      ; Test current status bit
          JC        INTJMP
          INC       ECX       ; Update counter
          JMP       INTSHF    ; Repeat until asserted
                              ;    status bit found
INTJMP    ROL       ECX,2     ; Multiply count by 4
          MOV       ESI,TABLE ; Access look-up table
          ADD       ESI,ECX   ;    and branch to service
          JMP       ESI       ;    routine
                        :
                        :
```

The table of interrupt service routine (ISR) addresses and the routines themselves are set up as:

Memory Address	Memory Contents (ISR Addresses)
TABLE	INT0
TABLE+4	INT1
TABLE+8	INT2
:	:
:	:
TABLE+28	INT7

400

<u>Structure of Interrupt Service Routines</u>

INT0:   :
                                         :
                                        IRET

INT1:   :
                                         :
                                        IRET

      :
      :
      :

INT7:   :
                                         :
                                        IRET

The above example illustrates the use of interrupt logic at the gate and latch level, and a software approach to identifying the requesting device. Although the example has tutorial value, the approach is costly in terms of the circuit board space required. Also, the time required for the software to identify the device and then branch to the appropriate ISR is relatively long. A preferred approach is to provide each device with the means of supplying its own vector when its interrupt is acknowledged. A priority arrangement can be configured by "daisy chaining" the devices, which in essence passes the acknowledge through to a device only after higher priority devices have received but not responded to it. A single-chip interrupt controller is designed to provide the needed capabilities.

Programmable Interrupt Controller

The INTEL 8259A Programmable Interrupt Controller (PIC), available in a 28-pin package, is designed to support the Intel families of 8-bit, 16-bit, and 32-bit CPUs. The 8259A PIC can handle the needs of up to eight I/O devices. By cascading a master controller PIC with up to eight slave PICs, as many as 64 I/O devices can be accommodated. If necessary, a three-level controller scheme can be configured for systems with more than 64 devices. The PIC's main functions are to provide an interrupt request to the CPU if any device needs service, accept the acknowledgment from the CPU, assign priorities, arbitrate cases where simultaneous requests occur, and provide the required vectoring information to the data bus.

The 8259A PIC can be programmed to specify a variety of parameters, one of which is whether the CPU is an 8080/8085 CPU or an 8086 CPU family member (8086/80286/80386 CPU) is being used. When used with an 8080 or 8085 CPU, the PIC issues a CALL instruction in response to an interrupt acknowledge. This is a 3-byte instruction which includes a 16-bit address (a full address for these 8-bit machines), allowing the service routine to start anywhere in memory. Recall that without a PIC, interrupt hardware generally supplies a 1-byte RST code. This involves the use of locations at the low end of memory in the vectoring process which is often inconvenient since system initialization routines are generally placed there as well. For the case of a CPU in the 8086 family, the PIC supplies the 1-byte vector needed to access the descriptor table. Recall that values of 32 to 255 can be used to avoid conflict with descriptors for special interrupts and exceptions. The PIC requires that vectors for multiple devices be numbered sequentially, but this is not a serious limitation.

Figure 8-9 shows an 8259A PIC interfaced to the 80386 CPU; in this case, only a single PIC is required. The data bus lines (D7-D0) permit control words to be written to the PIC and vector information to be read by the CPU. Individual lines are provided to as many as 8 devices to accept their interrupt request status (IR7-IR0). The cascade (CAS2-CAS0) and slave program/enable buffer ($\overline{SP}/\overline{EN}$) lines are generally used for multiple PIC configurations only. Interrupt request (INT), interrupt acknowledge ($\overline{INTA}$), chip select ($\overline{CS}$), and read and write control ($\overline{RD},\overline{WR}$) are provided as well.

Finally, address input A0 to the PIC is generally provided by the lowest order CPU address bit, excluding those used to distinguish data word size. That is, address line A0 is used for the 8-bit 8080/8085 CPU. In contrast, A1 is used for the 16-bit 8086 CPU, and A2 for the 32-bit 80386 CPU. This ensures that a byte written to the PIC uses the low eight data bus lines (D7-D0), provided the PIC addresses are aligned. Recalling the discussion of byte alignment in Section 7.2, addresses are restricted to 2N and 2N + 2 for the 8086 CPU; only addresses 4N and 4N + 4 are valid for the 80386 CPU. In this case, N must be an even integer to ensure that the lower address corresponds to the PIC's A0 input being 0. To further clarify this, consider the 80386 CPU; its A2 input provides the PIC's A0. Since the lower address (4N) must result when A2 = 0, the address must be divisible by 8.

Two to four initialization command words (ICWs) must be written to the 8259A PIC to program it. The ICWs are usually set by an initialization routine and are not changed. Additional operation command words (OCWs) can also be written to set various modes and invoke other features. In contrast to the ICWs, the OCWs are often changed during the course of interrupt processing.

The PIC is assigned two I/O addresses differing by 4 as a result of the decoded address input to $\overline{CS}$ and the address input from A2. When a command is sent to the lower address (A2 = 0), and bit 4 = 1, it is interpreted as initialization command word 1 (ICW1). Subsequent ICWs are written to the higher address, for which A2 = 1. For a single PIC in an 8080/8085 system, only two ICWs are written (ICW1, ICW2). A multiple PIC configuration requires a third command (ICW3), and use with an 8086 CPU necessitates a separate command (ICW4). As many as three OCWs may follow the ICWs (OCW1 to OCW3). OCW1 is written

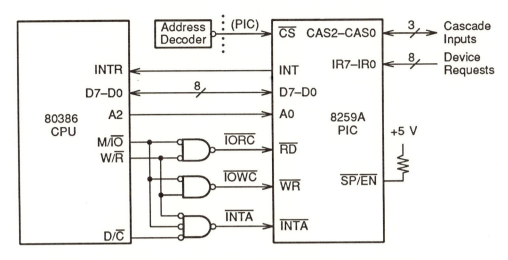

FIGURE 8-9   Intel 8259A PIC Signal Diagram and Interface to 80386 CPU

to the higher address following the last ICW. Commands written to the lower address, for which bit 4 = 0, are interpreted as OCW2 if bit 3 = 0 as well, or OCW3 if bit 3 = 1.

A partial description of the command word formats is given in Table 8-2. Only those bits relevant to the use of a single PIC with an 8086 family CPU are presented. For a full presentation of the formats, consult the *INTEL 8259A Programmable Interrupt Controller Data Sheet*.

TABLE 8-2 INTEL 8259A PIC Command Word Formats

Command Word	A0	D7	D6	D5	D4	D3	D2	D1	D0
ICW1	0	x	x	x	1	LTIM	x	1	1
ICW2	1	T7	T6	T5	T4	T3	x	x	x
ICW3	1	x	x	x	x	x	x	x	x
ICW4	1	0	0	0	0	0	x	AEOI	1
OCW1	1	M7	M6	M5	M4	M3	M2	M1	M0
OCW2	0	x	x	x	0	0	x	x	x
OCW3	0	0	x	x	0	1	x	x	x

Bit Descriptions:

LTIM	1 - Level triggered; 0 - edge triggered.
T7—T3	Interrupt vector address bits.
AEOI	1 - Auto end of interrupt; 0 - normal EOI.
M7—M0	Device interrupt masks.
x	Bits relevant to 8080/8085 systems, cascade mode operation, or other special features.

Program 8-6 initializes the 8259A PIC to handle interrupts up to eight devices, with the same assumptions as for the example illustrating the software polling technique (see Figure 8-8 and Program 8-5).

Program 8-6

Initializing the 8259A PIC to Handle Interrupts For Up to Eight Devices

```
MOV   AL,1BH        ; ICW1: Single PIC, level triggering
OUT   P8259,AL
MOV   AL,80H        ; ICW2: Vectors starting at 128 used
OUT   P8259+4,AL
MOV   AL,03H        ; ICW4: Auto end-of-interrupt mode
OUT   P8259+4,AL
MOV   AL,0F8H       ; OCW1: Set masks for devices 3 to 7
OUT   P8259+4,AL
```

Bit 4 of the first word sent to symbolic address P8259 is 1, and is interpreted as ICW1. This byte informs the PIC that it is in single rather than multiple mode, implying that ICW3 does not exist. It also signifies an 8086 family CPU, and the PIC therefore expects ICW4. The remaining command words are written to the higher address, and are interpreted as ICW2, ICW4, and OCW1 respectively. ICW2 assigns the eight devices successive vector addresses starting arbitrarily at 128. ICW4 places the PIC in an automatic end-of-interrupt mode, which is appropriate as long as a nested multilevel interrupt structure is not required within a single 8259A PIC.

The operation command word allows the PIC to perform the same function as the 8-bit latch and the AND gates shown in Figure 8-8; that is, individual device requests can be masked. Again, the byte written in this example masks devices 3 to 7, leaving only requests for 0, 1, or 2 to be recognized. Notice the PIC automatically prioritizes the devices from 0 to 7, with 0 having the highest priority. During the processing of an interrupt the PIC allows only higher priority devices to break in, provided that the CPU's internal interrupt flag has been enabled by software. The acknowledgment of an interrupt typically disables further interrupts. The other operation command words, OCW2 and OCW3, permit rotation of priorities and special masking modes.

MOTOROLA MC68020 CPU Interrupt Handling

Interrupt handling by the MOTOROLA MC68020 CPU is part of the more general category of exception processing. Like the INTEL 80386 CPU, a vector table of 256 32-bit addresses is set up in memory with a starting address provided

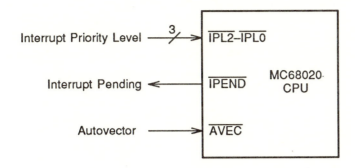

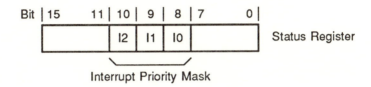

FIGURE 8-10   MOTOROLA MC68020 CPU Interrupt Signals and Status Register
Priority Bits

by the vector base register (VBR). Figure 8-10 shows the relevant interrupt signals
and status register bits of the MC68020 CPU. Unlike the 80386, this CPU has
built-in logic to handle multiple devices. The interrupt priority pins ($\overline{\text{IPL2-IPL0}}$)
indicate the complement of the encoded priority level of the device requesting
interrupt. Level 0 (all pins are high) corresponds to no interrupts requested, and
level 7 (all pins low) is a nonmaskable input with the highest priority. Levels 1
to 6 represent maskable requests responded to only if the level exceeds the current
priority in the status register (as identified by status bits I2, I1, and I0). If that
condition is met, or if a nonmaskable interrupt has been recognized, an
acknowledgment is sent out in the form of an interrupt pending ($\overline{\text{IPEND}}$) signal.
The level number is also sent out on address lines A3-A1.

Figure 8-11 illustrates how up to seven device requests can be encoded directly
to provide the inputs to the MC68020 CPU's interrupt priority pins. The 74148
device is an 8-to-3 priority encoder; its truth table shows that not only is the
device request properly encoded, but the outputs are the same even when a lower
priority device issues a request simultaneously. The encoder, along with program
control of the status register's priority bits, enables device prioritizing as well as
dynamic control of the masking of interrupt requests of devices below a certain
priority level.

74148 Function Table

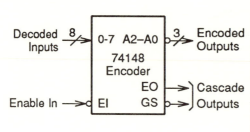

Inputs									Outputs				
EI	0	1	2	3	4	5	6	7	A2	A1	A0	GS	EO
H	x	x	x	x	x	x	x	x	H	H	H	H	H
L	H	H	H	H	H	H	H	H	H	H	H	H	L
L	x	x	x	x	x	x	x	L	L	L	L	L	H
L	x	x	x	x	x	x	L	H	L	L	H	L	H
L	x	x	x	x	x	L	H	H	L	H	L	L	H
L	x	x	x	x	L	H	H	H	L	H	H	L	H
L	x	x	x	L	H	H	H	H	H	L	L	L	H
L	x	x	L	H	H	H	H	H	H	L	H	L	H
L	x	L	H	H	H	H	H	H	H	H	L	L	H
L	L	H	H	H	H	H	H	H	H	H	H	L	H

H = High; L = Low; x = Don't Care

a. 8-to-3 Priority Encoder

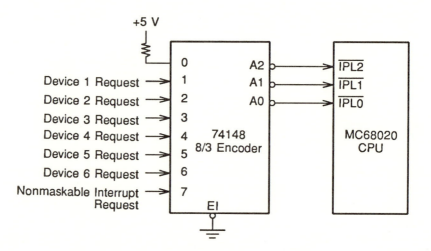

b. Encoder Interface to MOTOROLA MC68020 CPU

FIGURE 8-11 Encoding of Device Interrupt Requests to MOTOROLA MC68020 CPU

Of the 256 vectors provided, the first 64 are reserved for a variety of exceptions and for future use. Included are vector numbers 25-31, which are used as Level 1-7 interrupt autovectors, respectively. This allows a device the option of requesting internal generation of the vector number during the acknowledge cycle. The device does this by asserting the MC68020 CPU's autovector ($\overline{\text{AVEC}}$) input shown in Figure 8-10. The alternative is to have the device supply its own vector; the remaining 192 vector numbers (64-255) are available to the user for this purpose. Autovectoring has the advantage of reducing hardware costs, since device logic to generate the vector externally is not needed.

Finally, several steps occur during the processing of interrupts and other exceptions. In addition to determining the vector number and using it to locate the vector's memory address, the status register is saved and then changed to place the CPU in its supervisory mode. For interrupts, the priority mask is updated as well. The program counter, status register, and vector offset are saved on the supervisory stack. For certain types of exceptions, additional processor state information is also placed on what is defined as the exception stack frame.

AT&T *WE* 32100 CPU Interrupt Handling

The AT&T *WE* 32100 CPU has an interrupt mechanism similar to that of the MOTOROLA MC68020 CPU, but provides a larger number of priority levels. As a result, a larger vector table is employed as well. Another difference is that the AT&T CPU offers the option of a "quick" interrupt as opposed to a full interrupt. For the case of a quick interrupt, only the program counter (PC) and processor status word (PSW) are saved. The full interrupt is treated as a task switch, whereby the entire program control block (PCB) is replaced and later restored. Recall that the PCB consists of both initial and current values of the PC, PSW, and SP. Additionally, it includes most of the remaining *WE* 32100 CPU registers, as well as stack bound and block move information. Thus, a full interrupt is more flexible, but slower than a quick interrupt. This is a result of the extra time required for a complete task switch to save and later restore the additional information.

Figure 8-12 shows the *WE* 32100 CPU interrupt input lines and the PSW bits related to interrupt and other exception conditions. A separate nonmaskable input ($\overline{\text{NMINT}}$) is provided with four encoded priority inputs ($\overline{\text{IPL3}}$-$\overline{\text{IPL0}}$). As with the MOTOROLA MC68020 CPU, if all $\overline{\text{IPL}}$ inputs are high, no interrupt request is pending. For the remaining 15 levels, the inverted $\overline{\text{IPL}}$ inputs are compared to the PSW's IPL field and an interrupt is acknowledged only if the requested device's level is higher than the PSW's field value. An interrupt option input ($\overline{\text{INTOPT}}$) provides a fifth bit, which increases the number of devices that can be handled with direct encoding logic.

Although no single interrupt acknowledge output pin is provided, a unique status access code (SAS3-SAS0) of 1011 denotes an interrupt acknowledge state. In addition, the combination of the inverted $\overline{\text{INTOPT}}$ bit and 4-bit priority level is sent out on address lines A6-A2. The *WE* 32100 CPU distinguishes the nonmaskable interrupt from all others by outputting zeros on all 32 address lines. External decoding hardware can be provided for any interrupting device that requires an acknowledgment. The WE 32100 CPU also provides the same autovectoring option as the MOTOROLA MC68020 CPU via its $\overline{\text{AVEC}}$ input.

The *WE* 32100 CPU, unlike the INTEL 80386 CPU and MOTOROLA MC68020 CPU, must use the low end of memory for exception and interrupt vector tables. However, pointers are used for part of the table, thereby increasing flexibility. The exception conditions are subdivided into normal, reset, process, and stack types. The normal exceptions are the largest class, including such conditions as integer zero-divide, illegal or privileged opcode, integer overflow, and external

407

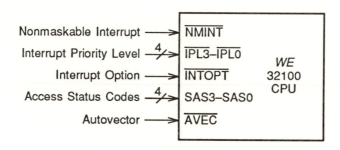

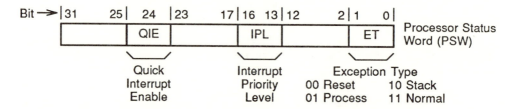

$\overline{IPL3}-\overline{IPL0}$: 1111 - no interrupts requested
$\overline{NMINT}$: Nonmaskable interrupt (autovector 0)
SAS3-SAS0: 1011 - interrupt acknowledge

FIGURE 8-12 AT&T *WE* 32100 CPU Interrupt Signals and Related Status Register Bits

memory fault. A 32-bit normal exception pointer must be placed at address 0; it addresses the base of a table which contains the PSW and PC values corresponding to each particular normal exception handler. For the other types of exceptions, process control block pointers (PCBPs) at hex addresses 80, 84, and 88 define the reset, process, and stack exception PCBs, respectively.

Above these pointers reside the full interrupt and quick interrupt vector tables. The 1K byte full interrupt table consists of 256 32-bit PCBPs. Vector 0 is reserved for the nonmaskable interrupt handler, and 1-31 are pointers to the other autovector handlers. Vectors 32-255 are available for the device-supplied vectors. The quick interrupt table is structured in the same way, except that each table entry is a PC/PSW pair rather than a PCBP. This gives an additional speed advantage to quick interrupt processing, since a level of indirection is removed. However, the quick interrupt vector table requires two 32-bit words for each handler for a total of 2K bytes.

In summation, the 32-bit CPUs have provided more sophisticated interrupt and exception processing, as compared to earlier machines. The INTEL 80386 CPU, MOTOROLA MC68020 CPU, and AT&T *WE* 32100 CPU all utilize vector tables to achieve this flexibility. Whereas the MOTOROLA MC68020 CPU and AT&T *WE* 32100 CPU provide a multilevel interrupt structure internally, an INTEL 80386 system generally requires an INTEL 8259A programmable interrupt controller or equivalent hardware.

8.4 Direct Memory Access (DMA)

The various data transfer techniques described earlier in this chapter differ in the way the request for service and the actual transfer are handled. Programmed I/O can be considered a technique in which the device request and the transfer are software controlled; the device is polled by the software to determine its readiness. In interrupt-controlled I/O, the device requests attention through hardware; some time is saved since the software need not poll the device periodically. However, the data transfer itself is still under software control and is thereby limited by the CPU's clock rate and instruction repertoire.

Another factor is the increased difficulty encountered in software debugging created by the presence of an interrupt mechanism. This is because an interrupt can occur at any point in the main program. The interrupt service routine must be verified at all entry points in the main program, hardly an insignificant task.

In contrast to the other techniques, during DMA the device request and the data transfer are handled by hardware. DMA potentially offers the highest data transfer rate as a result of the nonintervention of software. However, DMA control requires more external hardware than either programmed or interrupt-controlled I/O. Fortunately, this resulted in the development of sophisticated DMA controller devices. This section discusses the ways in which DMA is implemented, and the characteristics of typical DMA controllers.

CPU Bus Request and Acknowledge Signals

DMA capability is provided with 8-bit, 16-bit, and 32-bit CPUs. A typical CPU has an input called bus request or bus hold request, and a corresponding output that acknowledges the request to relinquish the bus. When an asserted bus request has been acknowledged, the address lines, data lines, and many of the control lines are "floated" (tristated). This allows the DMA controller to control the buses and facilitates the actual transfer. When the transfer is completed, the CPU's bus request is deactivated and control of the buses returns to the CPU.

Figure 8-13 shows the request and acknowledge signals for the three 32-bit CPUs. For the INTEL 80386 CPU, the device issues a bus request through the DMA controller to HOLD (asserted for a high). HOLD is a level-sensitive synchronous input. The subsequent assertion (high) of the 80386 CPU's HLDA output indicates that the CPU has relinquished control of its local buses, and has been placed in a bus hold acknowledge state. When the device has completed its operation, it relinquishes the bus to the CPU by negating the HOLD signal.

The AT&T *WE* 32100 CPU has the same two functional lines, but also provides for the case where the CPU is not the bus arbiter, such as when used as a slave processor in a multiprocessing application. As bus arbiter, it accepts the bus request input (low) to $\overline{BUSRQ}$, and acknowledges it with a low output to $\overline{BRACK}$. When the *WE* 32100 CPU is not the arbiter, the directions of the two lines are

409

reversed. The CPU can then request bus control by outputting a low to $\overline{\text{BUSRQ}}$. The current arbiter then acknowledges transfer of control to the CPU via $\overline{\text{BRACK}}$, which is now an input. A separate bus arbiter ($\overline{\text{BARB}}$) input pin (not shown) is held low if the WE 32100 CPU is to be the bus arbiter. If $\overline{\text{BARB}}$ is held high, the CPU is not the arbiter and must therefore request access to use the bus.

In contrast to the Intel and AT&T CPUs, the MOTOROLA MC68020 CPU features 3-line rather than 2-line bus control. For typical operation, a bus request ($\overline{\text{BR}}$) from the device through the DMA controller is granted by the CPU ($\overline{\text{BG}}$), indicating the bus will be available at the end of the current bus cycle. The device then negates $\overline{\text{BR}}$ and acknowledges that it has become the bus master by asserting the $\overline{\text{BGACK}}$ input. $\overline{\text{BG}}$ is then negated by the CPU, and the device maintains bus control until it negates $\overline{\text{BGACK}}$.

The extra level of acknowledgment allows for some additional flexibility in bus arbitration. For example, if several devices are capable of becoming bus masters, their requests would be logically ORed by the controller to $\overline{\text{BR}}$. If one device has had its request granted, it negates its bus request. However, if another device issues a request within a few clock cycles after the negation of $\overline{\text{BG}}$, another bus grant will be asserted. This allows external arbitration circuitry to select another bus master before the current device has completed using the bus. This is analogous to allowing a higher priority device's interrupt routine to be called before another service routine has been completed.

DMA Transfer Modes

DMA controller hardware is often flexible enough to be able to handle transfers between two blocks of memory or between two peripherals, as well as between memory and a device. Thus, the following four types of transfers are actually possible:

1. Input device to memory
2. Memory to output device
3. Memory to memory
4. Input device to output device

If the system hardware is configured so that the I/O devices are memory mapped, all data transfers are treated as memory to memory.

One way to classify a DMA transfer is in terms of simultaneous or one cycle operation versus sequential or two cycle operation. One cycle operation allows faster transfer by performing reading and writing simultaneously. Data is essentially transferred directly from source to destination without being held in a DMA controller register. For the more conventional sequential operation, the data is read into the DMA controller during the first cycle and written to the destination during a second cycle. Note that each cycle corresponds to a bus cycle, but under certain circumstances could be longer.

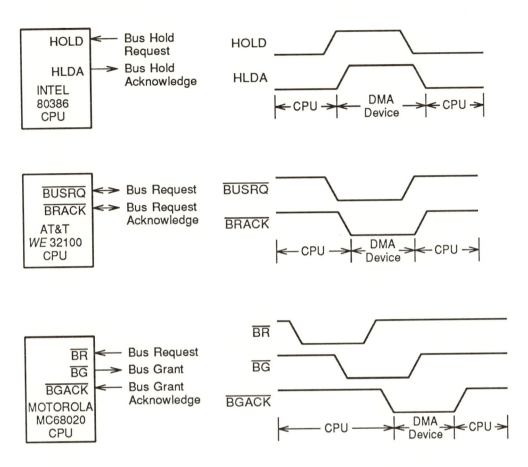

FIGURE 8-13   DMA Request and Acknowledge Lines for 32-bit CPUs

DMA transfers are also classified by their mode of operation. In single mode, the DMA controller transfers a single byte (or longer word) after gaining control. Control is then relinquished until the device is "ready" again.

In contrast, either a burst or block mode is more efficient for devices with high-speed data buffers. In the case of burst mode (also called demand mode), data continues to be transferred by the controlling DMA controller until the device's "ready" is no longer asserted. Control is then returned to the CPU. For the case of an output device, burst mode allows the buffer to be filled very rapidly by the controller and the device can then read it from the buffer at its own rate.

Block mode is very similar, except that the DMA controller retains control until an entire block of data is transferred. If the device's buffer fills during the transfer, the controller simply waits for "ready" to be reasserted before relinquishing the bus. Block transfer is efficient for high-speed devices that can generally keep pace with the DMA controller.

Another mode of DMA transfer used is referred to as cycle stealing or hidden DMA. This mode takes advantage of the clock cycles during the normal fetching and execution of instructions where the system buses are idle. Only internal operations take place during this time. The controller can "steal" one or more clock cycles and allow DMA operations during this time, without the formality of requesting the bus from the CPU. This is an efficient means of transferring small amounts of data over time, as opposed to a burst approach.

Introduction to Single-Chip DMA Controllers

As indicated previously, the DMA approach to data transfer requires more hardware than either the programmed or interrupt-controlled I/O methods. This is because DMA is hardware controlled; programmed and interrupt-controlled I/O are software controlled. Consider a block transfer involving memory. At least two CPU registers are required to keep track of the current address and block size. The program is responsible for incrementing (or decrementing) the values after each transfer. In the absence of software control, clearly the DMA hardware must include these registers with incrementing capability (counters). It must also provide the logic to sense the end of the block operation and issue the appropriate signal to enable the CPU to regain bus control. Coupling this to the need for logic to handle other DMA operation modes and multidevice requests (separate channels), it is apparent that DMA control hardware can be extremely complex.

The INTEL 8237A High-Performance Programmable DMA Controller, the INTEL 82258 Advanced DMA Coprocessor, and the AT&T WE 32104 DMA Controller (DMAC) share some common characteristics. (Figure 8-14 shows a typical single channel DMA controller.) All three are programmable and can handle up to four devices on independent channels. A request input from, and an acknowledgment output to, the device is provided for each channel. A single DMA request is sent to, and an acknowledgment received from, the CPU. The address and data bus lines, connected to the system bus, facilitate data transfer and enable data to be read from and written to the DMA registers. The chip select input allows the controller to be assigned device or memory addresses. All three DMA controllers have read and write control lines used with decoded addresses to access the DMA registers. Each controller has its own clock input (CLK) that is generally tied to the system clock.

INTEL 8237A High-Performance Programmable DMA Controller

The 40-pin INTEL 8237A DMA Controller (DMAC) is a 4-channel DMA controller designed for INTEL 8080/8085 CPU-based systems. Interfacing to an 8-bit data bus, it can be cascaded easily to handle more channels. The 8237A DMAC contains two 16-bit registers enabling each channel to have 64K address and word count capability. It is capable of transfers between memory and between a device and memory. Versions are available that operate at 3, 4, and 5 MHz. The 5 MHz version is able to perform transfers at a rate of up to 1.6M bytes/sec.

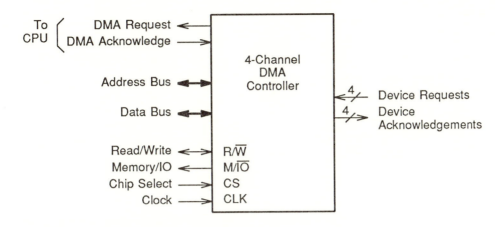

FIGURE 8-14   Typical Single-Chip DMA Controller

The 8237A DMAC goes from the idle state to the active state when it receives a DMA request. Depending on the type of transfer, it may take as long as seven active states to complete the transfer (each state corresponds to one clock period). In contrast, a compressed timing option permits transfer time to be as short as two clock cycles. Transfers involving I/O were previously called the one-cycle type, with data bypassing the DMA controller. Memory-to-memory transfers require separate rather than simultaneous read and write operations (2-cycle type).

The 8237A DMAC is programmable for either single, block, or demand mode transfer. In addition to read and write, each of the three modes can perform a verify operation. Another software selectable option is fixed versus rotating priority. Under fixed priority, the priority is always channel 0 (highest) to channel 3 (lowest). If any channel is recognized, interference from other channels is prevented until service is completed. Under the rotating priority scheme, the last channel serviced becomes the lowest priority channel, with the others rotating accordingly.

The 8237A registers include 16-bit base registers which store the original values of the address and word count. As indicated previously, the current values are stored as well. The selected channel and other options are programmed by writing to 8-bit command, mode, and request registers. Any channel's DMA request can be disabled by setting an appropriate bit in a separate mask register. Finally, an 8-bit status register can be read from the 8237A DMAC.

The 8237A DMA controller, along with its interface to a CPU and the system buses, is shown in Figure 8-15. The DMA request and acknowledge lines and the read/write control functions are similar to those of the typical DMA controller (see Figure 8-14). The 8-bit data and high byte of the 16-bit address share the DMA controller's data bus lines (DB7-DB0); this necessitates latching of the high address as shown. Notice the four lowest address lines (A3-A0) are also inputs to the controller, allowing selection of any of the internal registers.

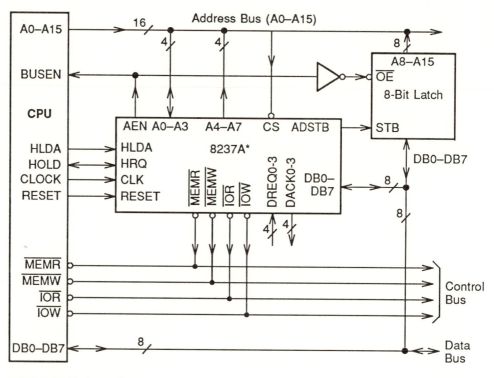

*8237A DMA Controller

FIGURE 8-15   INTEL 8237A DMA Controller System Interface

INTEL 82258 Advanced DMA Coprocessor

The INTEL 82258 Advanced DMA (ADMA) Coprocessor is a 16-bit DMA processor designed to support the 8086, 80186, and 80286 CPUs; it is also compatible with the 80386 CPU. Like the 8237A DMAC, it supports four independently programmable channels. Channel 3 can be used as a multiplexer channel, supporting up to 32 subchannels. This flexibility allows one channel to handle a large number of low-speed and medium-speed devices. Maximum transfer rates of 8M bytes/s for an 8 MHz 80286 system and 4M bytes/s for an 8 MHz 8086 system are achievable. An automatic data assembly/disassembly feature enables interfacing of 16-bit CPUs with 8-bit peripherals, or 8-bit CPUs with 16-bit peripherals. The presence of 24-bit address and byte count registers results in a 16M byte addressing range and a 16M byte block transfer capability.

The 82258 ADMA Coprocessor supports both 1-cycle and 2-cycle transfers, as well as fixed or rotating channel priority. In addition to being able to be set to a mode corresponding to the particular CPU used, the DMA processor can be programmed to be either in a local or a remote mode. In local mode it shares the local bus and all support devices with the CPU. In remote mode it is the sole local bus master and interfaces to the CPU via the system bus (using a bus arbiter,

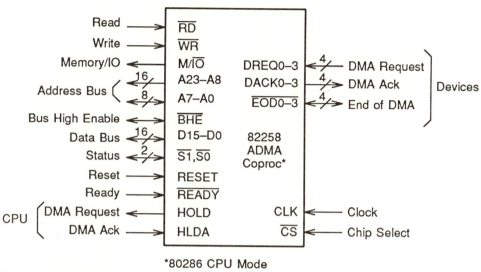

*80286 CPU Mode

Ack – Acknowledge

FIGURE 8-16   INTEL 82258 Advanced DMA Coprocessor Signal Diagram

such as an 82289 Bus Arbiter); this enables the 82258 ADMA Coprocessor to operate in parallel with the CPU. This concept is discussed further with coprocessors and multiprocessing in Chapter Nine.

Data transfers are controlled through channel command blocks in external memory with a 24-bit command pointer residing in the 82258 ADMA Coprocessor. These blocks are loaded into internal channel registers on receiving a channel start command from the CPU. A command chaining feature allows sequential execution of the command blocks. Such commands as conditional and unconditional STOP and JUMP enable the performing of complex DMA sequences. Command chaining gives the 82258 device the characteristics of a coprocessor, allowing it to do independent I/O processing and thus save CPU time. Likewise, data chaining enables data to be scattered to or gathered from separate memory locations, a useful feature for demand paging.

The signal diagram for the 82258 ADMA Coprocessor operating in 80286 CPU mode is shown in Figure 8-16. The low eight address lines (A7-A0) are inputs when registers are being addressed. The upper data bus (D15-D8) is used only if $\overline{BHE}$ is asserted; otherwise, for an 8-bit bus, only the lower data lines (D7-D0) are used. Each channel has the usual request and acknowledge line, as well as an end of DMA ($\overline{EOD}$) pin for added flexibility. As inputs, they can be asserted asynchronously from an external source to cause termination of a running DMA. As outputs, they can be used to interrupt the CPU or provide status information to the peripheral.

Figures 8-17 and 8-18 illustrate a portion of the logic required to interface the 32-bit 80386 CPU to the 82258 16-bit advanced DMA coprocessor. Figure 8-17 shows how the device's DMA request, issued by the 82258 device's HOLD output,

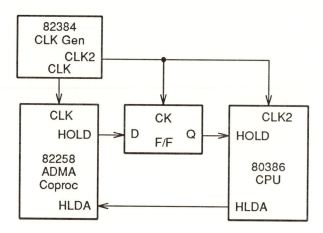

FIGURE 8-17   Synchronization of DMA Request to 80386 CPU Clock

is synchronized to CLK2. This is necessary to meet the synchronous setup and hold times of the 80386 CPU. The design of gating logic to convert the CPU's bus cycle status to that required by the 82258 ADMA Coprocessor is shown in Figure 8-18. The outputs $\overline{S1}$ and $\overline{S0}$ are then equivalent to those produced by an 80286 CPU. Additional logic is required to produce a completely 80286-compatible interface to the 82258 ADMA Coprocessor. For example, the logic in Figure 7-15, shows the conversion of the 80386 CPU's byte enable outputs ($\overline{BE3}$-$\overline{BE0}$) to address bits A1 and A0 and bus high enable ($\overline{BHE}$). Use of these signals with an 80286-compatible bus controller and bus arbiter, and the design of wait-state generator logic to satisfy 80386 CPU requirements are discussed in the *INTEL 80386 Hardware Reference Manual*.

Intel's announced 32-bit 82380 DMA controller is designed to interface directly to the 80386 CPU without any external logic (as required with the 82258). The 82380 DMAC also provides other system functions, including DRAM refresh, interrupt, and hardware timers. Featuring eight independently programmable channels, it can transfer data at a rate equal to the full bus bandwidth of the 80386 CPU - 40 Mbytes/s at 20 MHz.

AT&T *WE* 32104 DMA Controller

The AT&T *WE* 32104 DMA Controller (DMAC) is a 32-bit memory mapped device, packaged in a 133-pin PGA package. In addition to providing access to the full width of a 32-bit data bus, it provides a separate peripheral bus to decouple 8-bit I/O devices from the system bus. The DMAC is available in 10 MHz, 14 MHz, and 18 MHz versions. At the 18 MHz frequency it can perform memory/peripheral transfers at rates of up to 7.8 Mbytes/s (with burst mode), and memory-to-memory transfers at a rate up to 14.4 Mbytes/s.

Bus Cycle Status Definitions

80386 CPU				82258 ADMA Coproc			
M/$\overline{\text{IO}}$	D/$\overline{\text{C}}$	W/$\overline{\text{R}}$	Bus Cycle Type	M/$\overline{\text{IO}}$	$\overline{\text{S1}}$	$\overline{\text{S0}}$	Bus Cycle Initiated
0	0	0	Interrupt acknowledge	0	0	0	Read I/O vector
0	0	1	(Does not occur)	0	1	1	(None)
0	1	0	I/O data read	0	0	1	Read from I/O
0	1	1	I/O data write	0	1	0	Write to I/O
1	0	0	Memory code read	1	0	1	Read from memory
1	0	1	Halt/shutdown	1	0	0	(None)
1	1	0	Memory data read	1	0	1	Read from memory
1	1	1	Memory data write	1	1	0	Write to memory

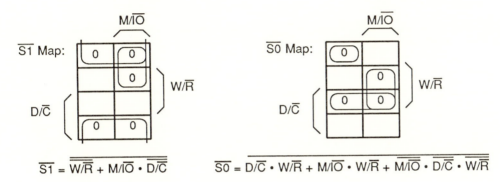

$$\overline{\text{S1}} = \overline{\text{W/}\overline{\text{R}}} + \text{M/}\overline{\text{IO}} \cdot \overline{\text{D/}\overline{\text{C}}}$$

$$\overline{\text{S0}} = \text{D/}\overline{\text{C}} \cdot \text{W/}\overline{\text{R}} + \text{M/}\overline{\text{IO}} \cdot \text{W/}\overline{\text{R}} + \overline{\text{M/}\overline{\text{IO}}} \cdot \overline{\text{D/}\overline{\text{C}}} \cdot \overline{\text{W/}\overline{\text{R}}}$$

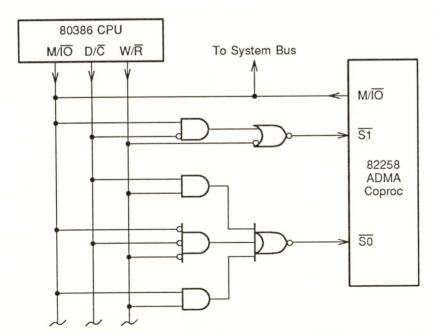

FIGURE 8-18   80386 CPU Status Definition Interface Logic to 82258 Advanced ADMA Coprocessor

417

As with the Intel devices just discussed, this DMAC also handles four independent channels (fixed priority, with Channel 0 assigned the highest). The internal register set consists of 32-bit source and destination address registers, and a 16-bit transfer count register (block size count). Thus, a single DMA operation can transfer up to 64K bytes of data. The location of the block in memory can be anywhere in the 4G address space, which typifies the addressing capability of the 32-bit CPUs. System bus operand sizes of 8, 16, 32, 64, or 128 bits may be handled.

The DMAC can be programmed for either burst or cycle steal mode operation. A burst length bit in a device control register allows setting the burst length to one, which in effect places it in the single mode. Both the peripheral and system buses can be serviced at the same time, and different channels can be on each bus. Other features include request chaining, interrupt, and bus exceptions. The DMAC can be configured to interrupt the CPU upon completion of a channel's operation by setting a bit in a mode register for that channel. The controller supplies an interrupt vector and expects an interrupt acknowledge cycle when interrupts are enabled. Any one of four types of bus exceptions can force the DMAC to terminate the current bus cycle when the associated signal is asserted. These exceptions include fault, retry, relinquish and retry, and reset.

The AT&T *WE* 32104 DMA Controller was designed to interface to the *WE* 32100 CPU with a minimum of external logic. Figure 8-19 illustrates this configuration; only chip select decoding and interrupt controller logic is required. The separate peripheral bus connected to the I/O devices includes a bus request and chip select for each channel (equivalent to DMA request and acknowledge), eight peripheral data lines, a 5-bit address, and a single peripheral bus read/write pin. Among the matching CPU/DMAC signals are the DMA request ($\overline{\text{BUSRQ}}$) and acknowledge ($\overline{\text{BRACK}}$), the 3-bit data size indicator (DSIZE0-DSIZE2), and the exception signals ($\overline{\text{FAULT}}$, $\overline{\text{RETRY}}$, $\overline{\text{RRREQ}}$, $\overline{\text{RRRACK}}$, and $\overline{\text{RESET}}$).

The interrupt controller logic is straightforward, although some details are omitted from the diagram. If the interrupt feature is set when programming the DMAC, an interrupt request ($\overline{\text{INTRQ}}$) is encoded into a relatively high priority interrupt (IPL2-IPL0, with IPL3=0) upon completion of the DMA operation. If acknowledged, the *WE* 32100 CPU outputs an access status code (SAS3-SAS0) of 1011 which is gated to enable the 3-to-8 line decoder. Recall that all zeros are output on the address bus as well. The $\overline{\text{INTACK}}$ line, from output line 0 of the decoder, enables the interrupt controller and provides the acknowledge to the DMAC. Now that DMA has been completed, the devices can issue their own direct interrupt requests (via DIRQ4 to DIRQ1). The controller output, $\overline{\text{IRQ}}$, is now encoded and again presented to the CPU on its priority pins IPL2-IPL0.

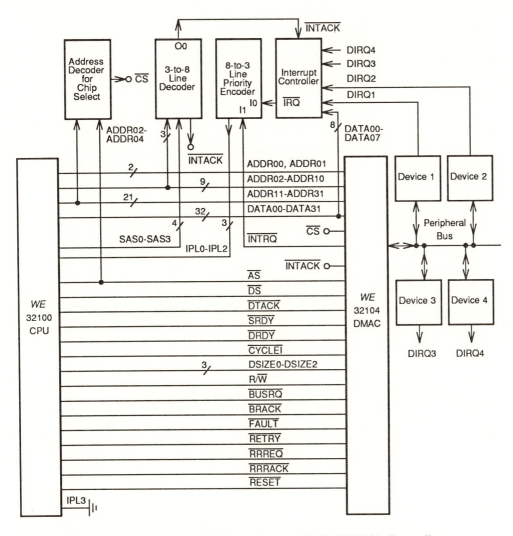

FIGURE 8-19 AT&T *WE* 32100 CPU Interface to *WE* 32104 DMA Controller

8.5 Interfacing to Parallel I/O

Data transfer is usually performed in parallel to take advantage of the CPU's inherent parallel data format. Alternatively, serial data transmission may be more efficient for longer distance transfer or for I/O devices requiring a serial format such as modems or serial printers.

This section focuses on the use of a versatile programmable peripheral interface (PPI) device, the INTEL 8255A PPI. Originally developed for use with the 8-bit 8080 CPU, the PPI has been widely used with other 8-bit and 16-bit CPUs as well. We show how one or more 8255A PPIs can be interfaced to the 80386 to provide a parallel interface to either an 8-bit, 16-bit, or 32-bit I/O bus.

The simplicity of the PPI results in ease of programming. We demonstrate how to set it up to operate in a basic I/O mode, as well as in an interrupt support mode. Finally, a brief overview of the IEEE-488 bus parallel interface standard is presented.

8255A PPI Basic Operation

The 8255A PPI, and the faster 8255A-5, are available in either a 40-pin DIP or 44-pin plastic leaded chip carrier (PLCC) package. The signal diagram and basic operation table are shown in Figure 8-20. Each PPI provides an interface to eight data lines from the CPU (D7-D0), and to three independent 8-bit I/O ports (called Ports A, B, and C). The typical control lines for read ($\overline{RD}$), write ($\overline{WR}$), chip select ($\overline{CS}$), and reset functions are provided. Two address inputs (A1,A0) enable selection of one of the three ports, as well as an internal control register for programming purposes.

Note that the 8255A PPI is a MOS rather than a TTL device. Its current drive capability is limited and additional buffering may be required. Specifically, all three I/O port specifications have limiting values of

$$I_{OL} = 1.7 \text{ mA}$$
$$I_{OH} = 200 \text{ }\mu\text{A}.$$

Therefore, the 8255A PPI can drive only one standard TTL load or four standard LSTTL loads. In contrast, recall that a standard TTL driver can handle up to 10 TTL loads.

As indicated by the basic operation table, the data bus is enabled when $\overline{CS}$ and either $\overline{RD}$ or $\overline{WR}$ is asserted (low). A read operation from an input device transfers the selected port data to the data bus. Conversely, the CPU's data is transferred to the selected port when writing to an output device. The control word register (write only) corresponds to the highest of the four addresses.

Interfacing the Intel 8255A PPI to the 80386 CPU

The Intel, AT&T, and Motorola 32-bit CPUs are capable of transferring either 8-bit, 16-bit, or 32-bit data. The INTEL 8255A PPI, on the other hand, was designed as an 8-bit I/O interface device. Therefore, to take advantage of the wider data bus requires paralleling 8255A PPIs. To accomplish this, we use the approach shown in Section 7-2 for interfacing to memory banks of 16-bit and 32-bit widths. The 32-bit interface of Figure 8-21 can be used to handle transfers for all three bit widths. Notice the 80386 bus enable lines, gated to the decoded address, generate the PPI chip selects in a manner similar to the memory interface in Figure 7-14. Also, the standard I/O read and write control signals ($\overline{IORC}$, $\overline{IOWC}$) are derived as shown for the interrupt controller interface in Figure 8-9.

The full 32-bit CPU data bus is interfaced to three 32-bit I/O ports by paralleling four PPI chips. The two lowest address bits from the 80386 CPU, A3

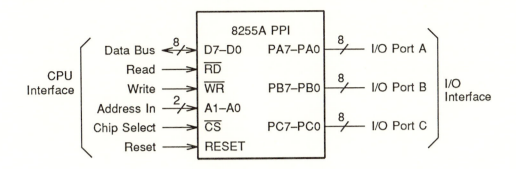

8255A PPI Basic Operation

A1	A0	$\overline{RD}$	$\overline{WR}$	$\overline{CS}$	Operation	
0	0	0	1	0	Port A → Data Bus	Input
0	1	0	1	0	Port B → Data Bus	(Read)
1	0	0	1	0	Port C → Data Bus	
1	1	0	1	0	Illegal Condition	
0	0	1	0	0	Data Bus → Port A	Output
0	1	1	0	0	Data Bus → Port B	(Write)
1	0	1	0	0	Data Bus → Port C	
1	1	1	0	0	Data Bus → Control Register	
x	x	x	x	1	Data Bus Disabled	
x	x	1	1	0	(Tristated)	

Note: If RESET is high, the control register is cleared and all ports are set to input mode

FIGURE 8-20   INTEL 8255A PPI Signal Diagram and Basic Operation

and A2, provide the PPI's address inputs (A1, A0). As a result, the addresses of the 32-bit ports and the 32-bit control register are separated by four. Assume that the symbolic address AD8255 represents xxxx0000, where xxxx is the actual values of address bits A7-A4, which have been decoded. The port and control addresses then become

Port A	AD8255
Port B	AD8255 + 4
Port C	AD8255 + 8
Control Register	AD8255 + 12

Notice the two low order bits of AD8255 are not used. Recall the 80386 CPU can handle any size data transfer starting at any address; however, alignment of 16-bit and 32-bit data results in fewer bus cycles being required for the transfer.

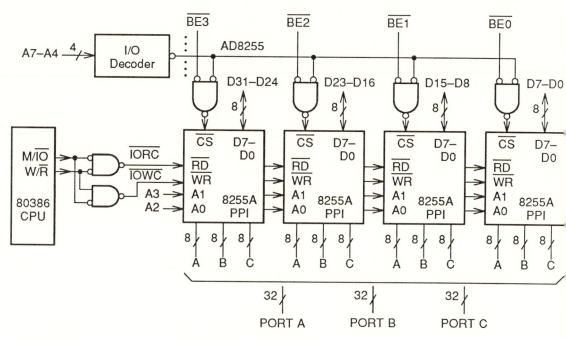

FIGURE 8-21   Interface of Intel 80386 to 32-bit I/O Ports

If dealing with I/O devices that handle either 8-bit or 16-bit data widths, the hardware cost is reduced by using the configuration of Figure 8-21 with either three or two of the PPIs removed. For the 8-bit case only, the rightmost 8255A PPI (connected to D7-D0) remains. Adding the PPI to its left results in three 16-bit ports tied to data lines D15-D0. If this is done, alignment is more critical to insure that 8-bit or 16-bit data is transferred on the low order data lines. Specifically for the 8-bit case, data bytes must be read from or written to memory locations divisible by 4. If two 8255A PPIs are retained, 16-bit data must be aligned with even addresses (divisible by 2).

An alternative approach to interfacing to 8-bit and 16-bit ports is illustrated in Figure 8-22. This scheme takes advantage of the 80386 CPU's dynamic bus sizing feature. Recall that asserting $\overline{BS16}$ causes all transfers to be automatically routed to the lower half of the data bus (D15-D0). Also, the 80386 CPU outputs the four byte enables ($\overline{BE3}$-$\overline{BE0}$) in lieu of the two low address bits (A1,A0). The logic derived using Figure 7-15, and shown in Figure 8-22a, generates those address bits and the "8086-like" bus high enable ($\overline{BHE}$) required for the 16-bit bus interface.

Figure 8-22b shows the interface to 16 bit I/O buses. This interface is similar to that shown in Figure 7-16 and requires an asserted 80386 16-bit bus size control input ($\overline{BS16}$). The derived $\overline{BHE}$ and A0 (byte high and byte low enables, respectively) control the PPI chip selects, and A1 becomes the low order direct

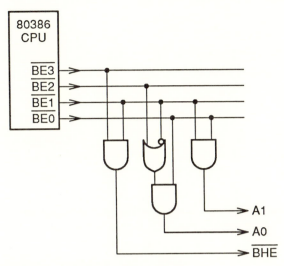

a. Generation of Standard Bus Signals

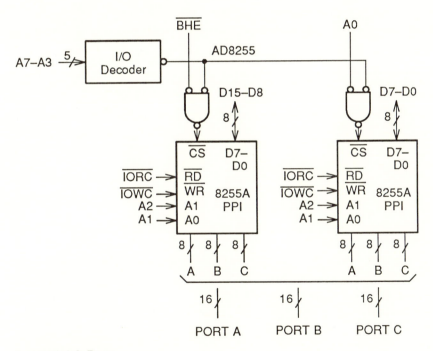

b. 16-Bit I/O Ports

Note: 80386 CPU $\overline{BS16}$ must be asserted.

FIGURE 8-22   Interface of INTEL 80386 CPU to 16-bit I/O Ports

423

addressing bit. The port and control addresses are now

Port A	AD8255
Port B	AD8255 + 2
Port C	AD8255 + 4
Control Register	AD8255 + 6

It is again desirable that addresses be aligned, meaning that AD8255 be even for this case. If the PPI connected to D15-D8 is removed, the remaining configuration can handle byte transfers, as long as they are aligned with even addresses. The advantage of using the 16-bit rather than the 32-bit bus configuration is that fewer I/O addresses are required for each device. This is because addresses are separated by two rather than by four. On the other hand, a system with 32-bit wide memory or I/O that also uses the 32-bit bus interface requires additional logic to assert the $\overline{BS16}$ line only at the appropriate times.

Programming the 8255A PPI for Basic I/O Mode

Prior to transferring data via one of the ports, the 8255A PPI must be programmed to set the mode of operation and the port directions. This is done by writing one byte to the control register. Note that if the 8255A PPI's RESET is asserted (high), the control register is cleared and all ports are set to the input mode. Figure 8-23a shows the mode definition format for the control byte; when the leading bit is 1, the remaining 7 bits define the mode and port directions. The three modes of operation and their main characteristics are:

Mode 0: Basic I/O
- Two 8-bit and two 4-bit data ports
- Any port can be used as input or output
- Outputs are latched; inputs are not latched.

Mode 1: Strobed I/O
- Two groups each containing one 8-bit data port and one 4-bit port for data port control/status
- Data ports can be used as input or output
- Both inputs and outputs are latched.

Mode 2: Strobed Bidirectional Bus I/O (One Group Only)
- One 8-bit bidirectional bus port and 5-bit port for data port control/status
- Both inputs and outputs are latched.

For convenience, the high 4 bits of Port C (PC7-PC4) with 8-bit Port A are referred to as Group A. The low 4 bits of Port C (PC3-PC0) with 8-bit Port B constitute Group B. Notice, from the mode definition format, that one group can

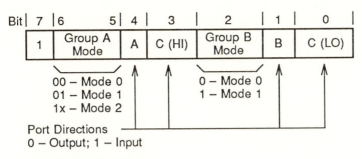

a. Mode Definition Format

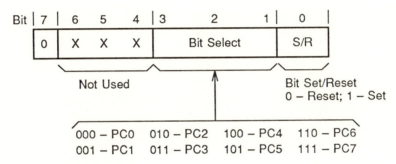

b Bit Set/Reset Format

FIGURE 8-23   INTEL 8255A PPI Control Byte Formats

operate in one mode and the other group in a different mode. However, only Group A can operate in Mode 2. For Modes 0 and 1, each data port can be programmed as an input or output port; to reverse the direction a new byte must be written to the control register. In contrast, Mode 2 operation permits Port A to transfer data in either direction, without further modification to the control register.

When the leading bit of the control byte is a 0, a bit set/reset operation is performed rather than a mode and port direction set. As shown in Figure 8-23b, the low 4 bits permit setting or resetting one of the eight Port C lines; separate control writes must be performed if more than one bit is to be initialized. This feature is most useful in setting certain control/status functions for Mode 1 or Mode 2 operation. In these modes, Port C bits are used for controlling and providing status for data ports A and B. One of the control/status functions to be discussed is the use of an 8255A output as an interrupt request to the CPU. The request from a particular device can be inhibited or enabled by using the Port C bit set/reset feature on an associated interrupt enable flag bit (INTE) in the PPI.

For the first example, it is assumed that data transfer can be accomplished by programmed I/O without the need for status checking; that is, the device is always ready to read or write data. To illustrate 8255A PPI operation in basic I/O mode 0, assume the 32-bit configuration of Figure 8-21 (or a reduced subset of it for interfacing to 16-bit or 8-bit ports). The segments of Program 8-7 first set the control word and read data from an input device into memory. The same size data, perhaps processed by the CPU, is then transferred to an output device. Port A is used for the input device and Port B for the output device. Although Port C is not used, it will be programmed as an output port.

Recall the four addresses corresponding to this configuration are:

Port A	AD8255
Port B	AD8255 + 4
Port C	AD8255 + 8
Control Register	AD8255 + 12

To avoid data alignment problems assume that the decoded address, corresponding to AD8255, is divisible by 4. Corresponding to the mode definition format of Figure 8-23a, the control byte must be configured as:

Bit →	7	6	5	4	3	2	1	0
Value →	1	0	0	1	0	0	0	0

where the control byte bit assignments (for bit 7 = 1) are:

Bit 0 - C(LO) Out	Bit 3 - C(HI) Out
Bit 1 - B Out	Bit 4 - A In
Bit 2 - Group B, Mode 0	Bits 5 and 6 - Group A, Mode 0

The first two instructions initialize the control byte. Notice only one output operation is required to enter the control byte, independent of the port size. The wider data bus for the 16-bit and 32-bit cases, as compared to the 8-bit port size, results in the simultaneous loading of all 8255A control registers with the required number, 90H. The third and fourth instructions read the data into the CPU via Port A, and store it in memory. DATA8 refers to a single location, whereas DATA16 and DATA32 symbolically represent 2 and 4 sequential addresses, respectively. After processing, the last two instructions result in the writing of the data to the output device connected to Port B.

Section 8.2 showed how programmed I/O can also handle a device with a status flag that indicates its readiness for data transfer. Figure 8-24 illustrates how such a device can be interfaced to the 80386 CPU through an 8255A PPI. Since the status bit is supplied by the device and must be tested by the CPU, it must be connected to an input port. An 8-bit output device is assumed. In Figure 8-24a, the status bit is read via input port A, and data is transferred via output port B.

The routine in Program 8-8 is analogous to Program 8-2 in Section 8.2. The status is inputted and tested periodically until it is asserted (device ready); then a data byte is written out.

Program 8-7

Program Segment to Initialize the Control Byte and Transfer Data

8-Bit Port Size	16-Bit Port Size	32-Bit Port Size
MOV AL,90H	MOV AX,9090H	MOV EAX,90909090H
OUT AD8255+12,AL	OUT AD8255+12,AX	OUT AD8255+12,EAX
IN AL,AD8255	IN AX,AD8255	IN EAX,AD8255
MOV DATA8,AL	MOV DATA16,AX	MOV DATA32,EAX
:	:	:
:	:	:
	(process data)	
:	:	:
:	:	:
MOV AL,DATA8	MOV AX,DATA16	MOV EAX,DATA32
OUT AD8255+4,AL	OUT AD8255+4,AX	OUT AD8255+4,EAX

Program 8-8

PPI Data Byte Transfer to a Peripheral Device with a Status Flag

```
          MOV    AL,90H          ; Set control word
          OUT    AD8255+12,AL    ; Mode 0, A-in, B-out
CHECK:    IN     AL,AD8255       ; Read status on Port A
          TEST   AL,80H
          JNZ    TRNSFR          ; Transfer when ready
          :
          :                      ; Perform other tasks
          :
          JMP    CHECK           ; Repeat status check
TRNSFR:   MOV    AL,DATA8        ; Transfer data byte
          OUT    AD8255+4,AL     ;    via port B
```

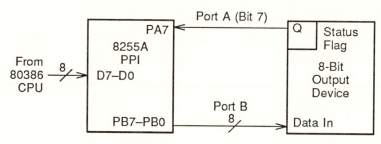

a. Separate Status and Data Port

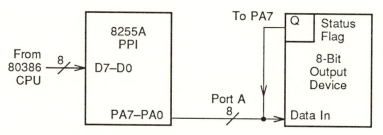

b. Combined Status and Data Port

FIGURE 8-24   Interfacing the INTEL 8255A PPI to Output Device with Status Flag

As an alternative, the status bit can be tied to a line on the same port used to transfer the data. This frees the second port for use by another 8-bit device. The versatility of the 8255A PPI permits the port direction to be changed at any time, at the expense of some additional software, of course. Figure 8-24b shows this modification. Program 8-8 still performs the status check for this new configuration; however, Port A has been programmed as an input port. It is therefore necessary to write a new control byte to change it to an output port before actually transferring the data. The only modification is:

```
TRNSFR:    MOV      AL,80H          ; Reset control bit 5
           OUT      AD8255+12,AL    ; Now port A is output
           MOV      AL,DATA8        ; Transfer data byte
           OUT      AD8255,AL       ;   via port A
```

AD8255 is again the decoded base address of the 8255A PPI, aligned as necessary; DATA8 contains the byte to be sent out. A note of caution: programming the control word generally resets all bits of those ports used as outputs. Therefore, depending on the application, it may be necessary to rewrite 1s to certain output lines before proceeding.

8255A PPI Strobed I/O Mode used with Interrupt

We conclude our discussion of the 8255A PPI by illustrating how strobed I/O mode (Mode 1) can be used to provide interrupt capabilities. The strobed bidirectional bus mode (Mode 2) is not covered; if you are interested, consult the *INTEL 8255A PPI Data Sheet*. As noted earlier, the basic I/O mode (Mode 0) treats Ports A, B, and C as independent ports; in fact, Port C can be split into two independent 4-bit ports. When Mode 1 is invoked, however, Ports A and B are independent data ports; most of the Port C lines are then reserved for providing status and control functions to support the data ports. These lines can be used to provide "handshaking" between the device and the CPU, including the generating of an interrupt request.

From the mode definition format of Figure 8-23a, we see that either Group A or Group B can be placed into Mode 1, with the other in Mode 0. Alternatively, both groups can be in Mode 1 if two devices require handshaking. Also, each data port can be directed as an input or an output port. Figure 8-25 shows the handshaking control provided for both the input and output cases. Notice the low 3-bits of Port C (PC0-PC2) are always used to control data Port B, whether Port B is used for input or output. In contrast, PC3-PC5 provides control when Port A is configured as an input port and a different set of Port C bits (PC3, PC6, PC7) controls output Port A. This also results in PC6 and PC7 being free for I/O when Port A is an input, with PC4 and PC5 available to the user when Port A is an output. This minor confusion is compounded by the fact that PC3, which controls Port A is actually part of Group B. However, the other control bits are in the "right" group.

The three control functions for each data port include an 8255A output which can be used to provide an interrupt request (INTR) to the CPU. A second function is also an 8255A output, which either acknowledges to an input device the loading of data into the PPI's input latch (IBF), or informs an output device that the CPU has written data to the specified port ($\overline{OBF}$). The third signal is an input to the PPI which strobes data from an input device to the input latch ($\overline{STB}$), or enables the PPI's tristate output buffer to send data to an output device ($\overline{ACK}$).

Figure 8-26 shows the status byte format for Port C. In comparing this to the control functions just discussed, we see that the lines used to strobe data in or out ($\overline{STB}$ or $\overline{ACK}$) also serve as interrupt enables (INTE) for the appropriate port. Two 8255A interrupt enable flag bits, one associated with each port, can be easily programmed by the user. The bit set/reset format is a convenient way to do this without affecting other Port C bit values. When INTE is reset (0), the interrupt request output (INTR) corresponding to that port is inhibited. Therefore, the PPI has the necessary hardware to enable or disable each device's interrupt request. In Section 8.3, external hardware was shown (see Figure 8-8) to provide this capability in conjunction with device polling software.

The following example illustrates the application of the 8255A strobed I/O mode, and of the bit set/reset control word format. Consider the interface of the 80386 CPU via a PPI to an output device, as illustrated in Figure 8-27. The device

429

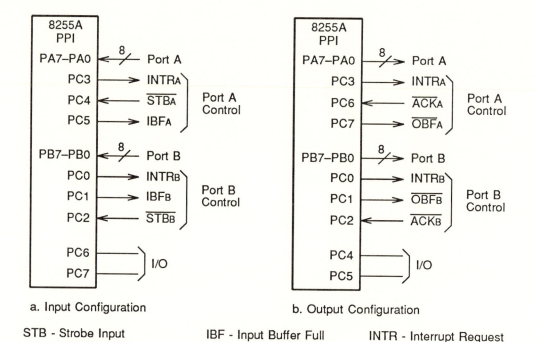

FIGURE 8-25   INTEL 8255A PPI Mode 1 Control Functions

is assumed to have handshaking ability in the form of a strobe input and an acknowledge output ($\overline{\text{READY}}$). Our previous examples have not considered the strobe input control. A parallel printer is an actual example of a device with this handshaking control. In fact, the typical printer has two separate outputs, one indicating the status of its buffer (BUSY/$\overline{\text{READY}}$), and the other acknowledging the receipt of data, ($\overline{\text{ACK}}$). Notice from Figure 8-27 that Port B

FIGURE 8-26   INTEL 8255A PPI Mode 1 Status Byte Format

Bit	7	6	5	4	3	2	1	0
	I/O	I/O	IBF$_A$	INTE$_A$	INTR$_A$	INTE$_B$	IBF$_B$	INTR$_B$

a. Input Configuration

Bit	7	6	5	4	3	2	1	0
	$\overline{\text{OBF}_A}$	INTE$_A$	I/O	I/O	INTR$_A$	INTE$_B$	$\overline{\text{OBF}_B}$	INTR$_B$

b. Output Configuration

430

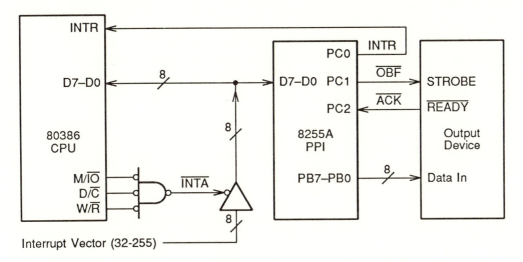

FIGURE 8-27   Use of INTEL 8255A PPI Interrupt Mode to Output Data

has been chosen arbitrarily as the output data port; therefore, the low 3 bits of Port C (PC0-PC2) provide the necessary control. After an interrupt is recognized by the CPU, the 80386 CPU generates the interrupt acknowledge ($\overline{\text{INTA}}$) and the interrupt vector is placed on the data bus.

Program 8-9 shows how to set the device's interrupt mask (INTE), and provide an interrupt service routine to transfer a byte to the device.

Program 8-9

Setting the Interrupt Mask and Providing Interrupt Service Routine for Peripheral Device Interfaced to an 8255A PPI

```
MOV     AL,84H          ; Set control word
                        ;   (1xxxx10x)
OUT     AD8255+12,AL    ; Group B in Mode 1, Port B - out
MOV     AL,05H          ; Bit set/reset format
                        ;   (0 xxx 010 1)
OUT     AD8255+12,AL    ; Set Port B INTE (PC2)
                        ;   enable device request
STI                     ; Enable 80386 CPU interrupt
:                       ; Continue main routine
:                       ; Interrupt occurs when
:                       ;   device is ready for
:                       ;   new data
```

(Continued)

431

```
                    :
          MOV       AL,04H              ; (0 xxx 010 0)
          OUT       AD8255+12,AL        ; Disable device request
                    :                   ; Main routine continues,
                    :                   ;    ignoring device ready
                    :
INTERR:             :                   ; Interrupt routine
                    :
                    :
          MOV       AL,DATA8            ; Output data byte
          OUT       AD8255+4,AL         ;    to Port B
                    :
                    :
                    :
          IRET                          ; Return to main routine
                                        ;    (re-enables 80386 CPU
                                        ;    interrupt)
```

To understand how the hardware and software function, refer to Figure 8-27 and to the timing diagram in Figure 8-28. The 8255A PPI is first set to Mode 1 operation for Group B, with B defined as an output port. The interrupt flag for Port B is then enabled by explicitly setting PC2. When STI is executed, the interrupt mechanisms of both the PPI and CPU permit an interrupt request. Since the 8255A PPI's INTR output is initially high, an interrupt immediately occurs and results in the transfer of one byte from memory location DATA8 to the output device. The device's STROBE input is deactivated (low) during the transfer, and the device now controls the occurrence of the next transfer by pulsing its $\overline{READY}$ output. When $\overline{READY}$ is asserted (low), STROBE is again asserted; when $\overline{READY}$ returns to a high and STROBE is still asserted, a new interrupt is generated.

The program segment also illustrates how the device can be ignored in favor of a higher priority activity. This is done simply by resetting PC2, the INTE flag for Port B. Recall that this does not affect the 80386 interrupt enable. If other device requests were logically ORed to the CPU's INTR, they would still be recognized as a result of the STI instruction. Other requests are masked while an interrupt is being serviced. Also notice the interrupt return instruction (IRET), among other things, has the effect of reasserting the 80386 CPU's interrupt enable flag. This makes it unnecessary to re-execute the STI instruction before returning from interrupt, an operation necessary with earlier CPU's (INTEL 8080 CPU, ZILOG Z-80 CPU).

IEEE-488 Parallel Data Transfer Standard Bus - A Brief Overview

The IEEE-488 bus was developed by the Hewlett-Packard Corporation in the early 1970s for use in interfacing their instruments. The IEEE adopted it in 1975

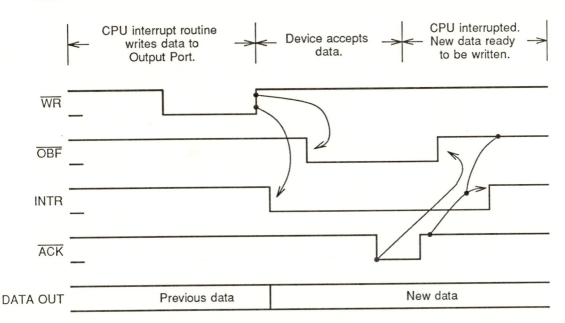

FIGURE 8-28   Timing for INTEL 8255A PPI Mode 1 Strobed Output

as a general-purpose instrumentation bus (GPIB). A revised standard, released in 1978, allows as many as 15 devices in close proximity to engage in 8-bit parallel, bidirectional communications. A total cable length of 20 meters is permitted, with no more than 2 meters per device. The maximum data transfer rate is 1M bytes/s, although total cable length at that rate should not exceed 15 meters.

The GPIB consists of the 16 signal lines:

Data Group:
   8 I/O lines (DIO1-DIO8)

Data Transfer Control Group:
   Data valid (DAV)
   Not ready for data (NRFD)
   Not data accept (NDAC)

Interface Management Group:
   Interface clear (IFC)
   Attention (ATN)
   Service request (SRQ)
   Remote enable (REN)
   End or identify (EOI)

Each device on the GPIB must be in at least one of the following three classes (some devices may perform two or three of the functions):

Talker – Transmits data onto the bus
Listener – Receives data from the bus
Controller – Manages operation of the bus.

A simple system could consist of a single talker and a single listener, without the need for a controller. When more devices are present, a controller is programmed to schedule and monitor tasks, set up the devices to perform these tasks, and interpret the results. For a single listener system, the handshaking scheme uses the three lines of the data transfer control group. The DAV line is controlled by the talker, while NRFD and NDAC are provided from the listener.

The following sequence illustrates initiation of the data transfer process. DAV is asserted when NDAC is asserted, NRFD is not, and the talker sends valid data to the bus. In response, the listener asserts NRFD to signify data acceptance and no further data should be transmitted.

As for the interface management signal group, ATN is used to distinguish between command and data mode. In command mode, the controller drives the data lines. In data mode, a talker transmits information to any number of listeners. IFC is generally used at startup to place all devices into an idle state, preparing for controller initialization. The SRQ line allows devices to request service via the controller (interrupt). The controller can remotely enable or disable devices via the REN line. Finally, EOI either can be used by a talker to indicate transfer of a data block, or to identify an interrupting device to the controller when in interrupt mode. Thus, the kinds of handshaking and interrupt features discussed in this chapter are provided by this interface standard.

As one would expect with a widely accepted standard, several LSI devices have been developed to handle the GPIB's functional protocol. For example, talker/listener functions can be handled by the INTEL 8291A GPIB Talker/Listener or the MOTOROLA 68488 GPIB Talker/Listener. The INTEL 8292 GPIB Controller was developed for those systems requiring controller functions.

Although the IEEE-488 bus standard was not intended for the high speed data disk/memory data transfers required in 32-bit CPU systems, it provides a useful parallel 8-bit I/O standard for instrumentation applications that can be employed with either 8-bit, 16-bit, or 32-bit CPUs.

8.6 Serial I/O Interfacing

Serial transmission has always offered an economical approach when digital data must be transferred over a distance. It has become even more important in recent years due to the popularity of remote access to computers via telephone lines. An important application for powerful 32-bit microprocessors is serving as the central facility in a multiuser environment. Individual terminals, perhaps having their own CPU as well, will be able to communicate with the host computer.

In this section we discuss the signal formats typically used for serial asynchronous and synchronous modes of communication, as well as the conversion of digital data to a form suitable for transmission over telephone lines. The problem of interfacing a serial I/O device to the CPU's parallel data bus is examined, and a software approach to serial/parallel conversion is illustrated. Finally, the use of standard universal (synchronous)/asynchronous receiver transmitter (UART or USART) devices in the interface is examined.

Serial Signal Formats

As was emphasized previously, the 32-bit CPUs discussed in this text are capable of processing data of various sizes (8-bit, 16-bit, 32-bit and larger bit widths). Serial transmission generally involves character information which is byte oriented. For example, most terminals used today feature the full set of alphabetic, numeric, and control characters encoded in the American Standard Code for Information Interchange (ASCII). The so-called "full ASCII" set comprises a total of 128 characters, requiring therefore a 7-bit code (since $2^7 = 128$). Older terminals with fewer characters used a subset of ASCII, and were generally coded with 6 bits. On the other hand, a full 8-bit code may be used to represent up to 256 data items.

An additional bit, called a parity bit, is often generated and appended to the data code. The purpose of a parity bit is to provide limited error detection capability. The subject of error detection and correction is an extensive one; generally, the more bits used for this purpose the greater the protection against errors. The single parity bit is chosen either to result in an even number of 1s (even parity) or an odd number of 1s (odd parity) in the extended code word. The extended word includes the parity bit as well.

For example, if even parity is used on 7-bit ASCII characters, each byte transmitted contains an even number of 1s (none, 2, 4, 6, or 8). If a single bit is corrupted by the transmission and is thereby misinterpreted at the receiver (a 0 is received as a 1, or a 1 as a 0), the result is a byte with an odd number of 1s. This allows the receiver to detect any single-bit error, although it cannot correct it since the bit causing the error cannot be identified. In this case, provided the proper handshaking exists, the receiver simply requests retransmission of the character. Multiple bit errors are less likely, but any odd number of bit errors can be detected. However, an even number of errors results in the number of 1s remaining even and the receiver thinks a valid character has been sent. In the case of odd parity selection, a single-bit or any odd number of bit errors result in an even number of 1s and a request for retransmission.

Data may be transmitted in blocks of characters rather than as individual characters. For this case, hardware is usually provided that calculates a checksum, or provides a cyclic redundancy check (CRC) for the entire block. Basically, these techniques perform arithmetic and a check on an entire data block that results in detecting most single-bit and multiple-bit errors. If an error is detected, then the entire block is retransmitted. The advantage to these techniques is that the desired protection is provided without the considerable overhead associated with appending a parity bit to every data byte. This concept is discussed in more detail later.

The data and parity bits comprising each character, or block of characters, must be supplemented with additional information to ensure synchronization between transmitter and receiver. This information, plus the bit ordering and transmission duration, defines the serial communications protocol. Serial data is transmitted in either asynchronous or synchronous form, and the protocol is very dependent on which mode is used. In synchronous transmission a clock waveform is transmitted with the data on a separate line. This allows large blocks of characters to be transferred sequentially, with only synchronizing information before and after the entire block. In contrast, asynchronous transmission, characterized by the absence of the clock, necessitates including start and stop bit information with each character to keep the transmitter and receiver in sync. This adds 20% to 30% of overhead per character (even when excluding the parity bit), resulting in asynchronous being slower than synchronous transmission. However, synchronous protocols, which include the separate clock line, generally require more hardware as compared to asynchronous operation.

Figure 8-29 shows three popular serial protocols. The format shown in Figure 8-29a is typical for asynchronous transmission. The line is held at the logic 1 level (called a "mark") in between data transmissions. A logic 0 bit (called a "space") is sent prior to each character; this start bit synchronizes the receiver to the transmitter. All the data bits are then sent starting with the least significant bit, followed by the parity bit (if used). The receiver keeps track of how many data and parity bits have been transmitted, so that it will not mistake a data transition from a logic 1 to a logic 0 as a new start bit. After all data and parity bits have been transmitted, a mark serving as a stop bit is transmitted. Some older electromechanical teletypes use 1 1/2 or 2 stop bits to allow these slower devices more time for synchronization.

There may be a long time before the next character is sent, in which case the line simply remains in the mark state until the next start bit appears. On the other hand, the next character could follow immediately. By providing at least one stop bit, the receiver can then synchronize to the transition from a mark to a space, to identify the start of the next character.

IBM developed two popular synchronous protocols called binary synchronous communication (BISYNC) and serial data link control (SDLC). These signal formats are illustrated in Figures 8-29b and 8-29c, respectively. BISYNC, referred to as a byte or character oriented protocol, uses several special ASCII codes to

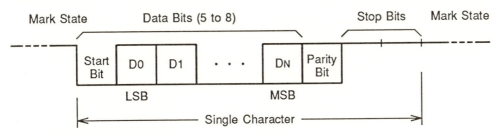

a. Asynchronous Serial Data

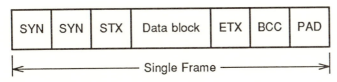

b. Synchronous Serial Data – BISYNC Protocol

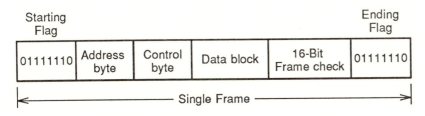

c. Synchronous Serial Data – SDLC Protocol

FIGURE 8-29   Serial Data Formats

control the data transfer. The data block is placed between control characters, analogous to asynchronous data being surrounded by start and stop bits. Preceding the block are two sync characters (SYN) followed by a start-of-text (STX) character. The data characters may be 7-bit ASCII with the eighth bit used for parity, or 8-bit data representation without parity. Following the data block is an end-of-text (ETX) character. Error detection and possibly correction is provided by one or more block check characters (BCC) that perform additional parity, checksum, or CRC. One or more end of frame (PAD) characters of all 1s are supplied prior to the next data frame. These are analogous to the mark state between asynchronous characters on a serial line.

BISYNC was developed in 1968 as a protocol for point-to-point communication, which assumes that a physical transmission link has been previously established between transmitter and receiver. Its use has been extended to systems with multiple terminals or computers having access to the same physical link. In contrast, SDLC (initially released in 1974) was designed to handle systems with one or more host computers networked to many terminals. The protocol, among other things, contains an address field (one byte) which enables selection of a particular transmitter and receiver within the network. The physical link is thus established by the transmission operation.

SDLC is a bit-oriented protocol, meaning that its data block can have any format, not necessarily consisting of an integral number of bytes. Each frame is enclosed within synchronization flag bytes (binary 01111110). The unique flag byte permits the receiver to detect the end of the frame, regardless of how many bits are in the data block. The flag value is unique in that it has six successive 1s. To avoid confusing a data byte with a flag byte, the transmitter always inserts a binary 0 after five consecutive 1s appearing anywhere in the data block, and the receiver strips the 0 away. Also included in the frame is a control byte and two bytes used for error detection purposes. SDLC is a subset of high-level data link control (HDLC), an international synchronous protocol.

Data Transmission Standards and Modems

The obvious advantage of serial communications is that the data path requires a cable with only two or three conductors, one of which is the common ground. Communication is classified as either simplex, half duplex, or full duplex. Simplex operation assumes one device is a transmitter only and the other a receiver only; thus, communication occurs in one direction only over a single line. For duplex operation, either device can send or receive. Communication can take place in both directions, but not at the same time on a single line (half duplex), or simultaneously if a second data line is available (full duplex). Clearly, full duplex is the fastest and most versatile operation, but at the expense of an extra conductor.

In addition to the minimum requirements for data and ground lines, some applications require separate lines providing handshaking functions (analogous to device ready and acknowledge signals). It became evident years ago that standards would be needed to insure compatibility among data communication equipment. The standards that evolved not only define which data and handshaking signals are required, but also specify such things as their logic voltage levels, maximum data rates, and cable requirements (maximum lengths and connector types). Data rates are generally specified in terms of baud, which is usually, but not always, equivalent to bits per second. Generally, terminals and modems handle baud rates ranging from 300 to 20000 baud. Data rates are discussed later in conjunction with modems.

The RS-232C Interface Standard developed by the Electronics Industry Association in the 1960s has been the most widely used standard for asynchronous serial communications. RS-232C was developed to standardize the interface required when a remote terminal communicated with a computer (generally a mainframe) via telephone lines. A device known as a modem (short for modulator/demodulator) is required to translate between the binary digital format used by the computer and the analog voice lines required for telephone line transmission. The standard, therefore, actually governs the terminal/modem

438

interface. According to this standard, devices are classified as either data terminal equipment (DTE) or data communication equipment (DCE). Terminals obviously are in the DTE category, as are printers; modems are classified as DCEs. On the other hand, a microcomputer can be a DTE if it is interfaced to a modem, or a DCE if it controls a printer.

RS-232C voltage levels use negative logic, meaning that the higher of the two voltages is associated with logic 0 rather than with logic 1. The logic 0 level must be a positive voltage, typically between 10 and 12 volts. In contrast, logic 1 is a negative voltage, generally from –10 V to –12 V. Guaranteed levels are:

	RS-232C Receiver	RS-232C Transmitter
logic 1	–3 V (maximum)	–5 V (maximum)
logic 0	+3 V (minimum)	+5 V (minimum)

A transmitter is guaranteed to output a voltage more negative than –5 volts for a logic 1, while a receiver will interpret its input as a logic 1 provided the voltage is more negative than –3 volts. Hence, 2 volts of noise immunity is provided; the same amount is provided for the logic 0 case.

Recall from the discussion of loading in Chapter Seven that TTL has a noise immunity of only 0.4 volts. The higher immunity specified by RS-232C allows communication over longer distance than if TTL levels were used. The noise resulting from capacitive effects is a function of data rate. TTL can be used if cable lengths do not exceed 5 to 10 feet for moderate data rates (1200 to 4800 baud). In contrast, RS-232C interfaces using 1000 to 2000 foot cables are common at moderate data rates, although the maximum specified line length is only 50 feet at the highest data rate (20000 baud). If TTL devices are to be made RS-232C-compatible, readily available level translating devices such as a MOTOROLA MC1488 Line Driver and MC1489 Line Receiver can be used.

The standard RS-232C connector contains 25 pins, although not all of them are typically used in a given application. Separate data transmit and receive pins are provided, so that an application not requiring handshaking would use only those two pins as well as a common signal ground. The additional pins have handshaking and other modem control functions. The most commonly used pins in RS-232C interfaces are:

Pin Number	Function
2	Transmit data
3	Receive data
4	Request to send ($\overline{\text{RTS}}$)
5	Clear to send ($\overline{\text{CTS}}$)
6	Data set ready ($\overline{\text{DSR}}$)
7	Signal ground
20	Data terminal ready ($\overline{\text{DTR}}$)

The handshaking signals consist of two pairs. Refer to Figure 8-30. When a modem is used as the DCE, the respective modem pins are tied to comparable ones from the computer or terminal (the DTE). A UART or USART device, discussed later, provides these connections on the DTE side. $\overline{DTR}$ is output by the DTE when it is ready to communicate and prepares the modem to be connected and begin transmitting, and $\overline{DSR}$ acknowledges that the modem is on and not in test mode. Similarly $\overline{RTS}$ is output by the DTE when it is ready and turns the modem's transmitter on and off for half duplex operation. In response, $\overline{CTS}$ indicates that the modem is ready to transmit. If a computer were used as a DCE with a printer or terminal (handshaking is not required and the modem is not used), the pairs of lines can be shorted on both sides as shown in Figure 8-30. This permanently enables the DTE and DCE.

Figure 8-30 also shows that the transmit and receive data lines from the DTE must be reversed before being connected to a DCE. A modem's internal wiring provides this reversal and permits a standard straight-through cable to be used. In the absence of a modem, a *null modem* cable that simply reverses pins 2 and 3 at the opposite ends must be used.

The RS-422A, RS-423A, and RS-449 standards have been added since the introduction of the RS-232C standard. The RS-449 standard specifies the functional and mechanical characteristics for an interface used with either the RS-422A or RS-423A electrical standard. RS-449 offers an advantage over RS-232C in that higher data rates over longer cables can be handled. For example, RS-422A can operate as high as 10M baud with a 40 foot cable; a 4000 foot line can be used at a lower data rate of 100K baud. The disadvantage of RS-449 is that a larger and more expensive 37-pin connector is required, with a separate 9-pin secondary channel connector being required for some applications. RS-232C is the most prevalent serial data transmission standard today, but RS-449 may replace it in the future.

Modems are needed to convert serial data from the form required by the DTE to that which can be communicated over telephone lines. DTE digital signals require much higher bandwidths than are available on a telephone line designed to carry voice transmissions at audio frequencies. Voice telephone lines are designed to handle frequencies in the range of 300 to 3300 Hz. Modems are classified as either originate modems, used to originate the call at the DTE end, or as answer modems, used to answer the call at the remote computer. Depending on the direction of transmission, one modem converts the digital signals to audio tones (modulation) before transmitting them over the telephone line. The other modem performs the demodulation required to change the audio tones on the telephone line back to digital form. These restored digital signals are now ready for processing by the DTE or the host computer.

For relatively low data rates, the modem converts the 0s and 1s to two different sine-wave frequencies in the audio range. This technique, called frequency shift keying (FSK), requires two sets of frequencies if full duplex operation is used.

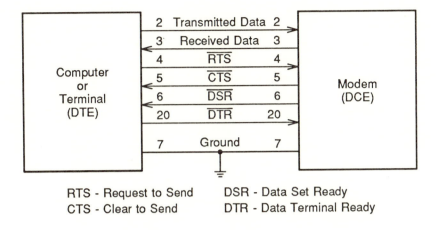

RTS - Request to Send   DSR - Data Set Ready
CTS - Clear to Send   DTR - Data Terminal Ready

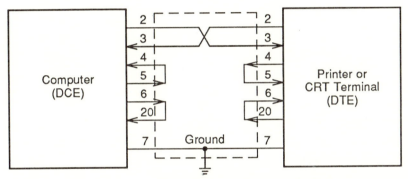

"Null modem" cable – No handshaking provided

FIGURE 8-30   Typical RS-232C Interfaces Between Data Communication and Data Terminal Devices

For example, the Bell 103 300-baud modem assigns the following frequencies:

| | Transmit | | Receive | |
	Space	Mark	Space	Mark
Originate Modem	1070 Hz	1270 Hz	2025 Hz	2225 Hz
Answer Modem	2025 Hz	2225 Hz	1070 Hz	1270 Hz

The frequencies distinguishing the two logic levels are separated by 200 Hz. Devices such as tone detectors or phase locked loops are able to easily distinguish between the two frequencies and output the appropriate voltage level corresponding to logic 0 (space) or logic 1 (mark). The originate modem transmits at the lower frequencies and receives at the higher frequencies; the reverse is true for the answer modem.

For FSK, each bit corresponds to a frequency and the baud rate and bit/s rate are the same. A problem with this technique is that the highest data rate is constrained by the lowest frequency used. For example, the popular 1200 bit/s rate could not be used with FSK and Bell 103 frequency assignments since the time duration of a single bit is less than a full period of the 1070 Hz tone.

Techniques involving modulation of the phase or amplitude of the tones rather than the frequency are used to overcome this limitation. Phase shift keying (PSK) varies the phase of a single frequency sine-wave. If 90 degrees of phase shift can be detected by the demodulator, two bits at a time can be represented by one of four phase shifts:

Phase Shift (Degrees)	Bit Pattern Represented
0	01
90	00
180	10
270	11

The pattern is arbitrary; the particular one shown is defined for the 1200-baud Bell 212A modem. The advantage of this technique over FSK is that the bit/s rate is actually double that of the fundamental or carrier frequency of the transmission (since two bits are represented by each tone). If the transmitter and receiver are more sophisticated, eight different phase shifts could be used to represent three bits at a time. This would yield a data rate that is triple the baud rate.

It is also possible to combine amplitude and phase modulation to further increase the data rate. Quadrature amplitude modulation (QAM) uses four amplitude levels with four different phases; the resulting 16 combinations enable representing 4 bits of data at a time. For example, a 1200 Hz baud rate becomes a 4800-bit/s data rate. The price paid for the higher data rate of PSK or QAM over FSK is increased control circuitry complexity.

Serial Interfacing - A Software Approach

Before discussing the serial interface hardware device, the UART/USART, it is instructive to show how software is used to provide the required format for asynchronous serial data. Consider the simple interface shown in Figure 8-31. This figure could easily represent the transmission of ASCII character codes from memory to a serial printer. The code bytes are to be converted to a serial stream of bits and sent out over a single data line. Data line D0 is chosen arbitrarily as the serial line. The output port can be provided by an 8255A PPI or a comparable device (only one I/O line is required). The device corresponds to the symbolic port address SERDEV.

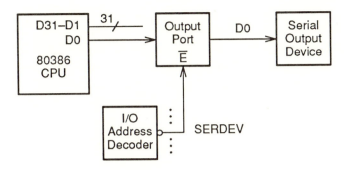

FIGURE 8-31 Serial Interface Without UART

Program 8-10 loads a character code from symbolic memory address ASCII, converts it to asynchronous serial format, and transmits it to SERDEV at a 2400 baud rate. The character code contains 8-bits, including a parity bit if any. A single stop bit will be provided. The program is written for the 80386 CPU.

Program 8-10

Asynchronous Serial Transmission via Software

```
            MOV      DL,10            ; Set counter to number of bits
            MOV      AL,ASCII         ; Load character code
            SAL      AL,1             ; Prepare to send start bit (0)
MORE:       OUT      SERDEV,AL        ; Transmit to device
            CALL     DELAY            ; Adjust to baud rate
            RCR                       ; Position next bit
            STC                       ; Set carry flag (stop bit)
            DEC      DL
            JNZ      MORE             ; Done after stop bit(s)
            :
            :
            :
            :                         ; Clock Cycles
DELAY:      MOV      CX,833
LOOP:       DEC      CX               ; 2
            JNZ      LOOP             ; 8
            RET
```

The bit counter is set to 10, which includes the start and stop bit and the data/parity bits. After loading the character into AL, it is shifted left by one position. The low order bit (D0) is cleared (0) by this operation, and corresponds to the start bit. The least significant data bit is then in bit position 1, and is rotated into position D0 during the first loop (via RCR). On subsequent passes, data bits corresponding to D1, D2, ..., D7 are output to the device in that order. Note the highest order bit (D7) was initially shifted by SAL into the carry flag. The rotate right instruction (RCR) includes the carry in the rotate, so that D7 will follow D6 out as required. By setting the carry flag (STC) after each rotate, any bits following D7 will be 1s. Thus, one or more stop bits follow D7. Only one stop bit is provided in this example since the bit counter reaches zero at that point. If the serial device requires two stop bits, the bit counter is initialized to 11 (decimal) instead; no other changes are required.

The delay routine was described in Section 8.2. Assuming a 20 MHz clock, the initial value n must satisfy

$$(10)(n) \times 50 \text{ ns} = 1 \ / \ 2400 \text{ s}$$

Thus

$$n = 1 \ / \ [(10)(50 \times 10^{-9})(2400)] = 10^4 \ / \ 12$$
$$n = 833$$

A similar routine can be written to input a character (from the keyboard of a serial printer for example), convert it to parallel, and store it in memory. Additional routines can be provided to do such things as check parity and other types of errors relating to loss of character synchronization. The UART or USART devices (described next) provide the hardware capability for serial/parallel conversion and detection of various types of errors.

Serial Interfacing - the INTEL 8251A USART

The INTEL 8251A USART is a programmable communication device capable of either asynchronous or synchronous full-duplex operation. Transmission rates up to 19.2K baud for asynchronous, or 64K baud for synchronous operation, can be accommodated. It is packaged in a 28-pin DIP, has an 8-bit data bus, and was designed for use with the INTEL 8080, 8085, and 8086 CPUs. The following overviews the features of this device, and illustrates programming it for transmission of data from the 80386 to a serial device.

Figure 8-32 shows a block diagram and the external signals of the 8251A USART. The device includes a parallel data bus buffer, a serial transmit buffer and control, a serial receive buffer and control, and other logic to handle read/write and modem control. A master clock input (CLK), generally supplied by the system clock generator, provides internal device timing. The maximum clock rate is about 3.1 MHz. Separate transmit and receive clock inputs ($\overline{TxC}$, $\overline{RxC}$) control the transmission and reception rates, and are set to a multiple of the desired baud rate. Data is transferred via the parallel data bus (D7-D0) interfaced to the CPU bus and the serial I/O lines (TxD, RxD) connected to the device(s).

Other control lines signal the CPU that the transmitter is ready to accept data (TxRDY), or that the USART contains a character ready to be input to the CPU (RxRDY). A transmitter empty line (TxE) indicates if the USART has any characters to send. These lines need not be used unless the appropriate control is desired. Similarly, the modem control lines provide the kind of handshaking discussed earlier when the serial device is communicating with a remote CPU. Finally, SYNDET/BRKDET enables the checking for sync characters when in synchronous mode and indicates a break condition in asynchronous mode (when the receiver remains low through two consecutive stop bit sequences, which include start, data, and parity bits).

The read/write lines control the transfer of data, as well as control and status information. The type of information and direction of transfer are:

$C/\overline{D}$	$\overline{RD}$	$\overline{WR}$	$\overline{CS}$	Operation
0	0	1	0	Receive buffer data $\rightarrow$ data bus
0	1	0	0	Data bus $\rightarrow$ transmit buffer data
1	0	1	0	Status $\rightarrow$ data bus
1	1	0	0	Data bus $\rightarrow$ control
x	1	1	0	Data bus disabled (tristated)
x	x	x	1	Data bus disabled (tristated)

Notice the data bus is enabled only when chip select and either read or write is asserted. The control/data input ($C/\overline{D}$) determines whether the information transferred is data or a control/status byte.

Programming the 8251A USART is similar conceptually to that for the 8255A PPI discussed in Section 8.5. Control information is first written to the USART to set the parameters of operation, after which data can be transmitted or received. By tying one of the low order system address lines to $C/\overline{D}$, two separate addresses define either control and data transfer. Unlike the 8255A PPI, this USART permits the reading in of a status byte at the same address as the control information (since $C/D = 1$ for both cases). Another difference is that the control information is programmed by executing two successive writes, the first being treated as a mode instruction and the second as a command instruction.

Figure 8-33 shows the formats for the mode and command instruction, as well as that of the status byte. For asynchronous operation, the mode instruction sets the number of stop bits appropriate for the I/O device being used; the number of data bits and type of parity are also defined. The low 2-bits set a baud rate factor. This factor may be 1, 16, or 64 in asynchronous mode. The factor defaults to 1 when synchronous mode is chosen (bit values = 00), and the other bits have a different meaning as well.

The frequency of the transmit and receive clock inputs ($\overline{TxC}$, $\overline{RxC}$) must be set to the desired baud rate multiplied by the selected factor. For example, the

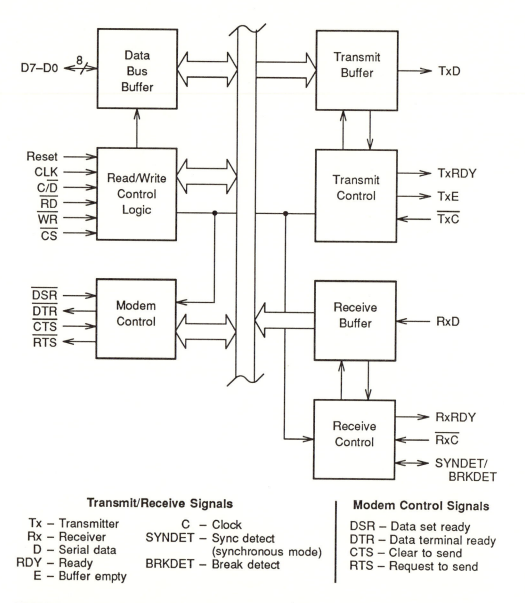

FIGURE 8-32 Block Diagram of INTEL 8251A USART

frequency of $\overline{TxC}$ and $\overline{RxC}$ for 2400 baud and a baud rate factor of 64 is

$$2400 \times 64 = 153.6 \text{ kHz}$$

The significance of the baud rate factor is that the transmit and receive clocks are generally provided by the system clock output which has gone through a divider chain of counters. If the system clock frequency is much higher than the baud rate, a higher baud rate factor is usually advantageous in that it reduces the hardware counter circuitry.

Individual bits of the command instruction byte, the format of which is shown in Figure 8-33b, may or may not be significant depending on the application. Two important bits are TxEN and RxEN. These enable the transmitter and receiver, respectively. Since the mode and command instructions are written to the same address, there must be a means of distinguishing them. Upon reset, the first write to that address is treated as a mode byte. Subsequent writes are command bytes unless the internal reset bit (IR) of the command instruction is

FIGURE 8-33 8251A USART Control and Status Format

a. Mode Instruction Format (First Control Byte)

Bit	7 6	5 4	3 2	1 0
Bit Values:	Stop Bit(s)	Parity	Data Bits	Baud Rate Factor
00	Invalid	None	5 bits	Synchronous Mode
01	1 bit	Odd	6 bits	CLOCK/1
10	1-1/2 bits	None	7 bits	CLOCK/16
11	2 bits	Even	8 bits	CLOCK/64

b. Command Instruction Format (Second Control Byte)

Bit	7	6	5	4	3	2	1	0
	EH	IR	RTS	ER	SBRK	RxEN	DTR	TxEN
	Enter Hunt Mode *	Internal Reset	Request to Send	Error Reset	Send Break Character	Receiver Enable	Data Terminal Ready	Transmitter Enable

* Not used with async.

c. Status Byte Format

Bit	7	6	5	4	3	2	1	0
	DSR	SYNDET/ BRKDET*	FE	OE	PE	TxE*	RxRDY*	TxRDY

Framing Overrun Parity

Error Flags

* Same as 8251A USART pins

Exceptions: 1. DSR is complement of pin value $\overline{DSR}$

2. TxRDY is same only for $\overline{CTS}$ low and TxEN high: otherwise TxRDY = 0.

asserted (1). This returns the USART to the mode format for the next control write. If the mode parameters are to be initialized once and never changed, then the IR command bit can be permanently cleared (0). The other bits are not used in the following example. Consult the *Intel 8251A USART Data Sheet* for details on the remaining bit functions.

The status byte includes five bits that are virtually identical to USART signals and three error flag indicators. In addition to parity errors, framing and overrun errors can be detected. A framing error occurs when a stop bit is not in the proper position. An overrun occurs when a new character has been received before the previous one was removed from the internal shift register (hardware which performs the serial/parallel conversion). In this case, the previous character is unavoidably lost. Software, particularly for the data receive operation, can include the testing of these bits and the subsequent transfer to error handling routines, if necessary.

We now illustrate how the 8251A USART control information can be programmed and a block of data transmitted to a serial output device. Figure 8-34 shows a possible interface between the 80386 CPU and the 8251A USART. Once again, the device is I/O mapped and the read and write control signals ($\overline{\text{IORC}}$, $\overline{\text{IOWC}}$) are generated as in previous examples in this chapter. The lowest address bit from the CPU, A2 in this case, provides the control/data select (C/$\overline{\text{D}}$).

FIGURE 8-34   Interfacing the 80386 CPU to Serial Device(s) via an 8251A USART

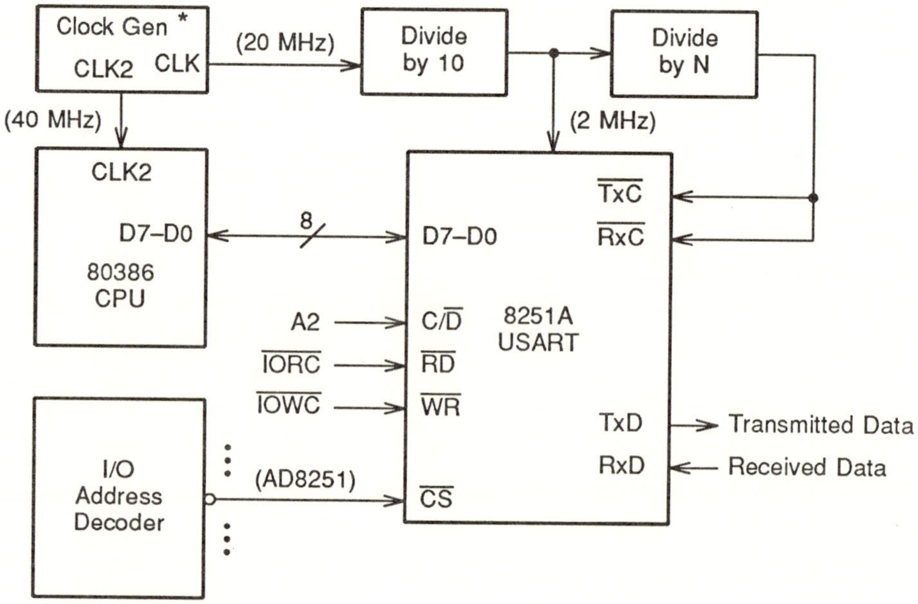

* 82384-20 Clock Generator.

The decoded address, symbolized by AD8251, is again assumed to be aligned (a multiple of 4). The 82384 clock generator, used with the 80386, provides the required CLK2 to the CPU (at twice the clock frequency). A separate CLK output provides the actual clock frequency used with peripherals such as the 8251A. Since the USART's maximum clock rate is limited to about 3 MHz, a divide by 10 counter is inserted to reduce the 20 MHz frequency to 2 MHz. (A standard TTL 7490 counter does the job.) The factor N required for the counter chain will be calculated shortly.

Program 8-11 sets the USART for asynchronous operation with a terminal requiring only one stop bit operating at 2400 baud. Even parity and a baud rate factor of 64 are assumed. A data block, stored starting at TABLE, and of SIZE not to exceed 64K bytes, is to be transmitted serially.

Program 8-11

Setting the 8251A USART for Asynchronous Operation

```
          MOV     AL,7BH          ; Program mode instruction
          OUT     AD8251+4,AL     ; (01 11 10 11)
          MOV     AL,05H          ; Program command instruction
          OUT     AD8251+4,AL     ; (x0 x0 x1 x1)
          MOV     EBX,TABLE       ; Initialize block address
          MOV     CX,SIZE         ;    and size
WAIT:     IN      AL,AD8251+4     ; Input status byte
          TEST    AL,04H          ; Wait for transmitter empty
          JNZ     WAIT
          MOV     AL,[EBX]        ; Transmit current byte
          OUT     AD8251,AL
          INC     EBX
          DEC     CX
          JNZ     WAIT            ; Repeat for entire data block
          MOV     AL,04H          ; Send end of text control
          OUT     AD8251,AL       ;    character
           :
           :
           :
```

The factor N, by which the USART's CLK input must be divided to generate $\overline{TxC}$ and $\overline{RxC}$, must satisfy the following relationship:

$$2 \text{ MHz} / N = 2400 \text{ baud} \times 64$$

Thus

$$N = (2 \times 10^6) / (2400 \times 64) = 13.002$$

A divide-by-13 circuit can be implemented with a 7493 TTL divide-by-16 counter wired to reset after 13 clocks.

When operating in synchronous mode, the 8251A can supply and detect one or two SYN characters, which provide support (at least) for a BISYNC-like protocol. Intel introduced three devices having advantages over the 8251A USART in that they support higher speeds and/or handle the standard synchronous protocols. The three 40-pin devices are:

- INTEL 8273 Programmable HDLC/SDLC Protocol Controller
- INTEL 8274 Multi-Protocol Serial Controller (MPSC)
- INTEL 82530 Serial Communications Controller (SCC)

Unlike the 8251A PPI, the 8273 protocol controller supports the bit-oriented HDLC and SDLC protocols; however, it is limited to 64K baud synchronous transfers. The 8274 MPSC supports BISYNC as well as the bit-oriented protocols; moreover, it features two independent full duplex transmitters and receivers which can operate at up to 880K baud. It also has provision for four independent DMA channels, and can be interfaced with the 8237 DMA controller. Both the 8273 DMAC and 8274 MPSC can operate at a maximum clock rate of 4 MHz.

The 82530 SCC, like the 8274 MPSC, provides two independent channels, supports both the byte-oriented and bit-oriented synchronous protocols, and has DMA capability. A 6 MHz version is available.

Additional details on the operation and use of the devices presented in this chapter are available in their individual Intel data sheets.

8.7 Chapter Highlights

1. In contrast to memory devices which have access times comparable to one another, I/O data transfer rates may differ greatly among devices. As a result, one of several data transfer schemes are used, depending largely on the required data transfer rate. These techniques include programmed I/O, interrupt, and direct memory access (DMA).

2. Programmed I/O is a technique whereby the software may test the status of a device, or of multiple devices, to determine whether the device is ready for a data transfer. The transfer is also done under software control. Hardware interrupt

permits a CPU to engage in other tasks until a device signals the CPU of its readiness by activating an interrupt request pin on the CPU. System performance may be enhanced since the CPU need not spend time repeatedly sensing the device's ready status. Although the request is now hardware initiated, the transfer is software controlled via an interrupt service routine.

3. In contrast to programmed I/O and interrupt, DMA offers the most potential for handling data transfers at high rates. In this case, a hardware-initiated DMA request from the device results in direct data transfer between device and memory under the control of special DMA hardware. Since hardware controls both the request and the actual DMA transfer, throughput is constrained only by hardware delays rather than by the CPU clock rate and instruction execution times.

4. When using programmed I/O, one can assure data transfer after the device is ready by testing a device's status bit. Alternatively, sufficient delay can be inserted into the program to assure that the CPU is not too fast for the device (such as when interfaced to a terminal with a known baud rate). Multiple device status bits can be tested in the order of device priority to handle simultaneous requests.

5. Interrupts are either of the maskable or nonmaskable type. CPU software can be set up to ignore maskable requests, while nonmaskable interrupts are always accepted. Depending on the mechanism or interrupt mode set for a particular CPU, transfer of program control to an interrupt service routine may be done directly by internal CPU hardware. Alternatively, the transfer is handled indirectly via a memory table of service routine addresses that correspond to multiple interrupting devices.

Device priority can be established either by software or by hardware (daisy chaining). For 32-bit CPUs, interrupts are a special case of the more general exception processing, where exceptions may also include various faults (divide by zero error or invalid opcode) as well as those induced by software interrupt instructions.

6. A programmable interrupt controller device, such as the INTEL 8259A PIC, conveniently handles multiple interrupting devices. It provides the interrupt request to the CPU when any device requests service, accepts an acknowledgment from the CPU for the maskable case, assigns priorities, handles simultaneous requests, and provides the required vectoring information to the data bus to enable transfer to the appropriate service routine. The controller can also be programmed to mask certain device requests selectively while allowing other devices to interrupt at a particular time.

7. The need for relatively complex hardware to control DMA has resulted in the development of DMA controller devices. Since the CPU architecture is not available during DMA, the hardware includes address registers and a block size counter. Current DMA controllers are capable of handling multiple devices and

transferring data using various modes of operation. For slower devices, a single byte (or larger size data) may be transferred whereupon the DMA controller relinquishes control until a device "ready" is received. For devices with high speed data buffers, a large data block is transferred at once. Higher data rates can be achieved by programming a one-cycle transfer between memory and I/O (reading and writing during the same cycle). A 32-bit DMA controller designed for the INTEL 80386 CPU can transfer data at a rate of 40 Mbytes/s for a 20 MHz clock.

8. The INTEL 8255A PPI is a general-purpose, 8-bit, programmable peripheral interface (PPI) device. Multiple PPIs can be used to handle the requirements of 16-bit or 32-bit parallel data transfer operations. A basic I/O mode is sufficient for many applications, and a strobed I/O mode is available for use with interrupt. In the basic I/O mode, two 8-bit and two 4-bit ports can be independently directed as input or output ports. An IEEE-488 parallel data transfer bus standard permits 8-bit bidirectional communication among several devices in close proximity to each other at a rate as high as 1M bytes/s.

9. Serial, rather than parallel, communication is more economical over long distances. Transmission of data may be done asynchronously or in synchronism with a separately transmitted clock signal. Asynchronous characters must be appended with start and stop bits which reduce the effective data bit transfer rate. A synchronous protocol such as binary synchronous communication (BISYNC) transfers entire character blocks with only a small number of control and addressing information appended. Bit-oriented synchronous protocols, such as serial data link control (SDLC), are similar except that the data field formats are not necessarily byte oriented.

10. The RS-232C format was developed to standardize the interface required when a computer communicates asynchronously with a remote terminal via telephone lines. Modems provide the translation between the computer's digital signal format and that used by analog voice lines for telephone line transmission. Using the RS-232C standard, communication is limited to a distance of 50 feet when operating at a data rate of 20000 baud; however, distances of 1000 to 2000 feet can be accommodated at lower data rates (1200 to 4800 baud). For relatively low data rates, modems use frequency shift keying (FSK), which involves converting digital 0 and 1 levels into two distinct audio frequencies. Phase shift keying (PSK) and quadrature amplitude modulation (QAM) are more suitable for higher data rates, but require more complex equipment.

11. The INTEL 8251A Universal Synchronous/Asynchronous Receiver-Transmitter (USART) is a programmable device capable of full-duplex operation at up to 19200 baud (64000 baud in synchronous mode). The USART provides the parallel-to-serial conversion required when interfacing a CPU to a serial terminal. It can be programmed to set the number of data bits and stop bits for asynchronous operation, as well as the type of parity used. Other communication

controller devices introduced more recently support higher speeds and a wider variety of synchronous protocols.

Exercises

Advanced Exercises are indicated by an asterisk (*).

1. Modify the time delay routine in Program 8-1 (Section 8.2), assuming a lower clock rate of 16 MHz and a slower output rate of 10 characters per second. This requires the use of a 32-bit register as a counter. Note the 32-bit decrement requires the same number of clock cycles as does the 16-bit decrement.

2. Repeat Exercise 1 using the MOTOROLA MC68020 CPU instruction set. Consult the *MC68020 32-Bit Microprocessor User's Manual* for instruction timing information.

3. Repeat Exercise 1 using the AT&T *WE* 32100 Microprocessor instruction set. Consult the *AT&T WE 32100 Microprocessor Information Manual* for instruction timing information.

4. Modify the interface hardware in Figure 8-3 and the device status testing routine in Program 8-2 (Section 8.2) for a device that is an input device rather than an output device. Assume the status bit is placed on line D0 instead of D7, and the data transfer is 16-bits rather than 8-bits wide.

5. Repeat Exercise 4 using a MOTOROLA MC68020 CPU in place of the INTEL 80386 CPU.

6. Repeat Exercise 4 using an AT&T *WE* 32100 CPU in place of the INTEL 80386 CPU.

7. Compare the relative speed of the two routines of Programs 8-3 and 8-4 (Section 8.2) for checking the status of multiple devices, assuming the status of the lowest-priority device (Device 7) is the only one asserted. Consult the *INTEL 80386 Programmer's Reference Manual* for instruction timing information.

8. Without changing the interrupt logic for software polling shown in Figure 8-8, modify the routine for identifying the interrupting device in Program 8-5 (Section 8.3) to meet the requirements:

    Devices 1, 2, 4, and 6 are to be masked.
    Priority is reversed (Device 7 has highest priority).

9. Repeat Exercise 8 using an INTEL 8259A Programmable Interrupt Controller to interface the CPU to the devices. Show how the device requests are connected to the 8259A in order to establish the desired priority. Additionally, modify the 8259A initialization routine in

Program 8-6 (Section 8.3) to meet the new device masking requirements.

10. Assume that devices 1 to 6 have their interrupt requests encoded and connected to the MOTOROLA MC68020 CPU as shown in Figure 8-11. Specify the MC68020 instruction required to set its status register if the two lowest-priority device requests are to be masked.

11.* Design an AT&T *WE* 32100 CPU interrupt controller circuit to handle up to 16 I/O devices.

12. Design gate logic to interface the MOTOROLA MC68020 CPU to the INTEL 82258 DMA Controller. Figure 8-18 shows the logic required for the INTEL 80386 CPU.

13. Repeat Exercise 12 using the AT&T *WE* 32100 CPU.

14. Figure 8-21 shows the interface between the INTEL 80386 CPU and a 32-bit port using the 8255A programmable peripheral interface device.
14a. Design the I/O address decoder if AD8255 = 40H (the address of Port A).
14b. Repeat 14a for the 16-bit port interface in Figure 8-22.

15. Modify the appropriate routine from Program 8-7 (Section 8.5) to meet the following requirements:

> 8255A Basic I/O Mode 0.
> Port A input, Port B input, Port C output.
> Input 32-bit data via Port B.
> After processing, output 32-bit data via Port C.

16. A matrix keyboard permits a large number of keys to be interfaced to a processor using relatively few data lines. Figure 8-35 shows how a maximum of 64 keys (sufficient for a full ASCII keyboard) can be configured as an 8x8 matrix and interfaced to the INTEL 80386 CPU via two of the three ports available with an 8255A PPI.

As illustrated by the smaller 3 x 3 matrix keyboard on the left of Figure 8-35, the rows and columns are normally not connected together. The pressing of a key connects the appropriate row and column together. Since the columns are tied to +5 V through pull-up resistors, each column line is normally high (logic 1). A column line is brought low (logic 0) only when a key is pressed, provided its row line is low.

Write a routine to properly initialize the 8255A PPI, and then wait in a loop until any key is pressed. This simply requires outputting a low to all row lines simultaneously, followed by reading and testing the column lines to determine if any are low. Assume that keyboard rows 1-8 (from the top) are connected to lines PA0-PA7, respectively, and that columns 1-8 (from the left) input to lines PB0-PB7, respectively.

17a.* Modify the routine of Exercise 16 to also enable identification of the row and column corresponding to the key pressed (assuming only one key is down). This can be accomplished by a keyboard "scan" procedure, where one row at a time is brought low and the columns sensed. A register can be used to save the row identifier, and a second register the column identifier.
17b.* To the routine in 17a, add a subroutine that actually calculates a number from 0 to

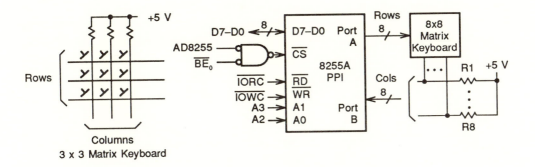

FIGURE 8-35   Matrix Keyboard Interface to an Intel 80386 CPU

63 to uniquely identify the position of the key pressed. Such a calculation is useful when this number is used as an offset to an address table. Each table entry points to a routine corresponding to the function identified by the key.

18.* Figure 8-36 shows an interface to a display consisting of eight 7-segment arrays. This display can be used to show a 32-bit address or data value in hexadecimal. Displays of this type are typically multiplexed to reduce the number of data lines required. As a result, only one array is selected at a time (only one array select line is asserted).

To maintain visibility of the display, the software asserts each select line in sequence, outputs the appropriate segment select bits to display the desired character, and then repeats the process often enough to avoid visible flickering. This requires a refresh rate of at least 30 Hz, which is generally not a problem for such a small sized display. The current requirements of the display's LEDs require buffering, which has been omitted from the diagram for convenience.

Write a routine to properly initialize the 8255A PPI and continually display the hex number 13579BDF. Assume that the segment select lines are high active (i.e., a logic 1 lights the appropriate bar); that a high is also required to enable the appropriate array select line; that the segment select lines a-g are connected to lines PA0-PA6, respectively (PA7 is not used); and that arrays 1-8 (starting from the left) are tied to lines PB0-PB7, respectively. Note that to avoid a "spillover" effect, routines of this type should blank each display before selecting the next array. Otherwise, lit segments of the previous character may be visible on the next array as well.

19.* Figure 8-37 illustrates a possible interface to a single line display of 24 alphanumeric characters. A 14-segment array is used permitting display of all numeric and uppercase alphabetic characters with reasonable clarity.

19a. Complete the details of the interface, using the entire 32-bit data bus with four 8255A PPI devices (as was shown in Figure 8-21). Arbitrarily assign the 8255A port outputs to the array and segment select lines.

19b. Write a routine to initialize the 8255A PPI and display a one line message of your choice. Start with the assumption that the message is stored sequentially in memory in the form of ASCII codes. Provide a look-up table to convert ASCII to the 14-segment array outputs required for each character.

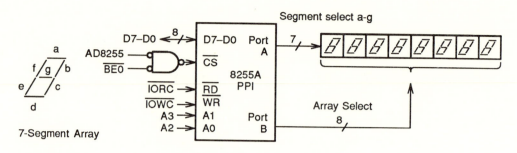

FIGURE 8-36   Interface to an Array of 7-Segment Displays

20. Modify the hardware of Figure 8-27 and the software in Program 8-9 (Section 8.5) to use Port B of the INTEL 8255A to transfer data from an input device to the 80386 CPU via interrupt mode 1.

21. Modify Program 8-10 (Section 8.6) to input a serial character from a keyboard, convert it to a parallel code, and store it in memory.

22. Redesign the INTEL 80386 CPU interface to the 8251A USART shown in Figure 8-34 and modify Program 8-11 (Section 8.6) to meet the following requirements for the terminal:

    19200 baud
    2 stop bits
    No parity.

FIGURE 8-37   Interface to an Array of 14-Segment Displays

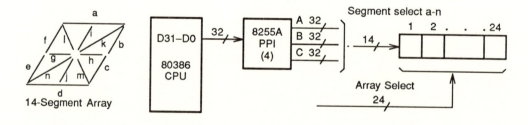

Coprocessors
and
Multiprocessing

Chapter Nine

9.1   Coprocessors
9.2   Multiprocessing
9.3   Chapter Highlights

This chapter presents coprocessors and multiprocessing. Numeric processors and their interface to the CPU are featured. Programming examples illustrate the transfer of control between coprocessor and CPU and the problems associated with multiple CPUs sharing the same resources. The use of standard multiprocessing system buses is discussed.

9.1 Coprocessors

The peripheral support devices discussed in Chapter Eight were designed to support data transfer to or from an I/O device. Most of these interface devices are generally programmed for operation by the CPU's software, and cannot execute any instructions of their own. In contrast, some support devices are classified as either independent processors or coprocessors. One example, briefly described in Section 8.4, is the INTEL 82258 Advanced DMA Coprocessor. Another example is the INTEL 8089 I/O Processor, designed to provide high speed DMA capability for two independent I/O channels when used with an 8086 or 8088 CPU. These devices differ from other DMA controllers in that they can fetch and execute a routine stored as a channel command or control block in external memory. Thus, the independent processor or coprocessor device supplements the CPU's instructions with a set of its own. The distinction between coprocessor and independent processor relates to resource sharing. A coprocessor generally shares memory and other system resources with the CPU. On the other hand, an independent processor executes its instructions from private memory not accessible to the CPU; it may also have other resources such as its own I/O bus that are physically separate from the CPU system bus.

An Overview of Coprocessor Operation

A device like the 8089 I/O processor was designed to increase the efficiency of an 8086/8088 system by removing the burden of I/O processing from the CPU. The I/O processor does this by assuming all the responsibilities of data transfer including device setup and programmed I/O, as well as DMA operation. Its instruction set is oriented to I/O operations, but it features arithmetic and logic, branching, and searching, as well as data transfer operations. After the CPU has prepared the control blocks for the task to be performed, it relinquishes control via an interrupt-like signal, allowing the 8089 I/O processor to fetch and execute instructions from the channel program. The 8089 I/O processor issues an interrupt request or updates a status location in memory to notify the CPU that it has completed its task.

The 8089 I/O processor, coupled to the CPU, provides distributed processing. In this case the 8089 I/O processor is dedicated to I/O processing while the 8086 or 8088 CPU can concentrate on higher level tasks. When the 8089 I/O processor shares the bus interface with the host CPU, the configuration is said to be a local one and the 8089 I/O processor operates as a coprocessor. Use of the bus is arbitrated by connecting a request grant pin of the 8086/8088 CPU with that of the 8089 I/O processor. Although only one processor has use of the bus at a time, both can still perform their tasks in parallel and thereby improve system performance.

A further increase in performance, at the expense of additional hardware, can be attained by using a remote rather than a local configuration with one or more CPUs. Each CPU may have its own independent processor as well as a coprocessor. Additionally, each I/O processor, acting as an independent processor, may have access to its own I/O devices via a local I/O bus, and can communicate with a CPU on a shared system bus as well. However, access to the system bus requires bus arbiter and controller hardware, as well as address latches and data transceivers. Issues involving the use of more than one CPU are discussed in the next section.

A coprocessor, like an independent processor, has its own set of instructions to supplement that of the CPU. However, it provides instructions that are not part of the CPU's instruction set, which would otherwise require the writing of separate routines to perform the equivalent operation. Arithmetic coprocessors are the most widely used coprocessors and are the focus of our attention. The coprocessors typically supplement the CPU's repertoire of arithmetic instructions by handling floating-point operations, as well as providing trigonometric and logarithmic functions. Unlike the independent processor, an arithmetic coprocessor does not execute a stream of instructions. Rather, the instructions are included in the CPU's program and are therefore fetched and decoded by the CPU in the normal manner. If the opcode indicates that it is a coprocessor rather than a CPU operation, the instruction is transferred to the coprocessor. After execution of the one instruction by the coprocessor, control is returned to the CPU. However, while the coprocessor is executing its instructions, the CPU can also execute code in parallel.

Numeric Coprocessors for the INTEL 80386 CPU

Three numeric coprocessors have been developed to support members of the Intel 8086 CPU family. The 8087 Numeric Data Coprocessor was designed to support 8086 systems, whereas the 80287 Numeric Processor Extension is the numeric coprocessor for the 80286 CPU. Both coprocessors have versions that can run at a clock rate as high as 10 MHz. The 80287 device, although designed for a 16-bit CPU, can also operate with the 80386 CPU. However, to ease the interfacing problem and provide higher performance for the 32-bit CPU, Intel has developed the 80387 Numeric Coprocessor Extension. The 80387 coprocessor, which can perform at 25 MHz, is about 5 to 6 times faster than the 8087 or 80287 coprocessors. As one might expect, the numeric coprocessors have a similar degree of upward compatibility as do the respective CPUs which they support.

Both the 8087 and 80287 coprocessors include a 16-bit data bus as part of their 40-pin package. In contrast, the 80387 coprocessor, with its 32-bit data bus, is available in a 68-pin ceramic PGA package. Each coprocessor supports seven data types:

- 16-bit, 32-bit, and 64-bit integers
- 32-bit, 64 bit, and 80-bit floating point
- 18-digit binary coded decimal (BCD)

The internal register architectures include an 8-register stack, with each register having 80 bits. Each register is supplemented by a 2-bit tag register that indicates whether the data in the register is valid, zero, a special value, or empty. In addition, there are 16-bit control, status, and tag word registers, and 32-bit instruction and data pointers (48-bit pointers for the 80387).

The numeric coprocessors add about 70 instructions to the CPU's repertoire. The 80387 coprocessor has a few additional instructions not available with the 8087/80287 coprocessors. The arithmetic operations include add, subtract, multiply, and divide on the various data types. Additional features include square root, scale adjust (using powers of 2), modulo division, round off (real to integer), exponent and fractional extract, absolute value, and sign change. Transcendental functions include tangent and arc tangent (for angles in the range of 0 to 45 degrees), and limited exponentiation and logarithm capability. Data transfer and data comparison operations exist, as do generations of special numerical constants (e.g., 0.0, 1.0, and log 2 using natural or decimal base). Finally, a group of processor control instructions enable manipulation of the control and status registers, and the saving and restoring of the numeric coprocessor's state (in conjunction with subroutines or interrupt service routines using the coprocessor).

Figure 9-1 shows an interface between the 80386 CPU and the 80287 coprocessor. An 80387 coprocessor interface is illustrated by Figure 9-2. The most obvious differences in the interfaces are that the 80287 coprocessor uses only the lower 16-bits of the data bus and requires data buffering, as well as latching of certain address and control lines. The 80387 coprocessor can be connected directly to the CPU; an optional wait state generator (not shown) and separate 80387 clock generator are the only external hardware that would be used in a specific case. The additional hardware is needed when the 80287 coprocessor is used because it cannot reside directly on the 80386 CPU's very high speed local bus. Controller logic for the local bus is required to generate the necessary read and write cycle timings, as well as the 80287 coprocessor's chip select timings.

After a reset, the 80386 CPU samples its $\overline{\text{ERROR}}$ input pin during initialization. The 80387 $\overline{\text{ERROR}}$ output pin is asserted by a reset, whereas that pin of the 80287 coprocessor remains deactivated. As a result, the 80386 CPU can determine which coprocessor is being used, whereupon it sets the ET bit of its control register zero (CR0). Certain 80387 instructions deactivate its $\overline{\text{ERROR}}$ pin so that it can be used for its main function, that of denoting an error status. When the 80287 coprocessor has been identified as the coprocessor present, the 80386 CPU automatically converts 32-bit memory transfers to 16-bit 80287 transfers (and vice versa). The

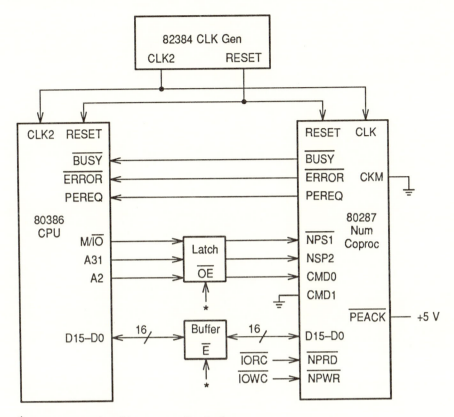

* Provided by local bus controller logic.

FIGURE 9-1   INTEL 80386 CPU with 80287 Numeric Processor Extension

transfers are routed to the lower half of the data bus, and do not require the $\overline{BS16}$ control input of the 80386 CPU to be asserted. (Recall the discussion of dynamic bus sizing in Section 7.2.)

When the 80386 CPU fetches an opcode for which the first five bits are 11011, it interprets it as a special escape (ESC) instruction. The remaining bit fields of the instruction define the particular coprocessor instruction, operands, etc. Notice ESC is only a convenient reference for the entire class of coprocessor instructions.

The mnemonics of all the coprocessor instructions start with "F" (for floating point). Since no other 80386 instruction mnemonics start with F, the assembler automatically provides the ESC code. After testing emulation mode and context change flag bits and the $\overline{ERROR}$ pin (to determine whether the coprocessor detected an error in the previous ESC instruction), the instruction is sent to the coprocessor.

The 80386 CPU also automatically generates one or more I/O cycles using I/O command address 800000F8H (when reading a control or status register, or writing an opcode) and data address 800000FCH (when reading or writing data). Since an I/O address is ordinarily 8 or 16 bits, resulting in the high-order bits

(A31-A16) always being low, these coprocessor addresses lie outside the range of the programmed I/O address space. This removes the need for address decoding. It should be noted that if the 80386 is in emulation mode (resulting from the system asserting the EM bit of control register CR0), the ESC opcode will generate a coprocessor not available fault. This can be used to execute software which emulates the numeric coprocessor operations, where no coprocessor is actually present.

As seen from the interface diagrams, the coincidence of A31 high and M/$\overline{\text{IO}}$ low activates both numeric processor select lines ($\overline{\text{NPS1}}$, NPS2). No programmed I/O address or memory address will therefore select the coprocessor. By connecting the lowest available address line (A2) to the coprocessor's command line (CMD0 for the 80287, $\overline{\text{CMD0}}$ for the 80387), the command and data addresses are only four locations apart. Read and write control is provided directly to the 80387 by the write/read bus cycle (W/$\overline{\text{R}}$) and address strobe ($\overline{\text{ADS}}$) lines from the 80386. In contrast, the 80287's numeric processor read and write inputs ($\overline{\text{NPRD}}$, $\overline{\text{NPWR}}$) are supplied by $\overline{\text{IORC}}$ and $\overline{\text{IOWC}}$, which are derived from the CPU's W/$\overline{\text{R}}$ and M/$\overline{\text{IO}}$ outputs (see Figure 8-9).

The processor extension request (PEREQ) and busy status ($\overline{\text{BUSY}}$) connections between CPU and coprocessor provide a degree of handshaking. PEREQ signals the 80386 that the 80287/80387 coprocessor is ready to transfer data. $\overline{\text{BUSY}}$ is asserted so long as the coprocessor is executing an instruction. PEREQ is always deactivated before $\overline{\text{BUSY}}$. Since data transfer occurs asynchronous to the 80386 CPU's instruction execution, both processors can be executing instructions in parallel. This is advantageous since many 80386 instructions can be performed in the time required for certain individual coprocessor instructions. On the other hand, in particular situations the CPU may need to wait for a result from the coprocessor. The 80386 WAIT instruction serves this purpose. When executed, it simply waits until the $\overline{\text{BUSY}}$ line is no longer active before proceeding. Thus, it prevents the CPU from executing code until the coprocessor has finished its work.

As shown, both coprocessors can operate from the CLK2 output of the 82384 clock generator designed for the 80386 CPU. The 80287 coprocessor can alternatively be clocked by the 82384 CLK output or by a dedicated oscillator. When operating from the 82384 clock generator, the 80287 clock mode pin (CKM) must be grounded; the coprocessor's internal circuitry then divides the system clock frequency by three. The 80387 coprocessor is designed to run either synchronously or pseudo-synchronously with the 80386 CPU. With the synchronous interface, shown in Figure 9-2, the 80387 coprocessor can achieve its maximum speed (25 MHz). In both modes, the CLK2 signal is connected to the 80387 coprocessor's 386CLK2 pin. CKM is high for the synchronous mode. In pseudo-synchronous mode, CKM is low and a second frequency source provides an input to a separate 387CLK2 pin (not shown) on the 80387 coprocessor.

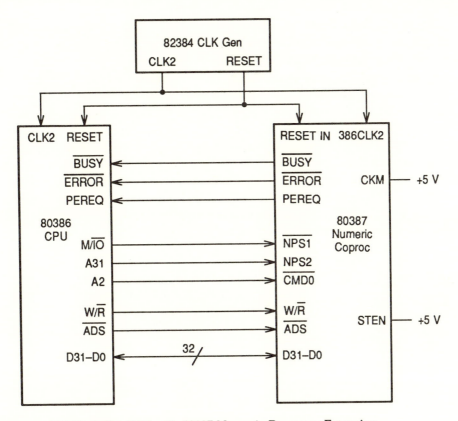

FIGURE 9-2 INTEL 80386 CPU with 80387 Numeric Processor Extension

Numeric Coprocessor for the MOTOROLA MC68020 CPU

The MOTOROLA MC68881 Floating-Point Coprocessor is designed to be used with the MOTOROLA M68000 Microprocessor family. Although primarily intended as a coprocessor to the MC68020 CPU, it can be used as a peripheral processor with earlier members of the MC68000 family or with non MC68000 CPUs. The MC68020 CPU, like the INTEL 80386 CPU, has a coprocessor interface that can recognize special instruction codes as coprocessor operations and initiate the proper actions. In fact, the MOTOROLA MC68020 CPU is similar to the INTEL 80386 CPU on the assembler level in that it recognizes mnemonics starting with an F as coprocessor instructions. If the MC68881 coprocessor is used as a peripheral with CPUs that cannot recognize this coprocessor interface protocol, special instruction sequences must be provided. This is done by providing a trap handling routine (recall that a trap is a type of exception). The instructions starting with F then invoke the trap handler which emulates the required protocol.

The MC68881 coprocessor is available in a 68-pin PGA package, and in either a 12.5 MHz or 16.67 MHz version. Like Intel's numeric devices, it supports integer, floating-point (up to 80 bits), and BCD data formats. It also features eight 80-bit floating-point data registers, along with 32-bit control, status, and instruction

463

address registers. The latter register holds the main processor memory address of the last floating-point instruction executed and is used in exception handling. In addition, several 16-bit and 32-bit coprocessor interface registers handle communication between the CPU and the MC68881 coprocessor. The additional 46 instructions feature 35 arithmetic operations, including a full complement of trigonometric and transcendental functions. The 22 numerical constants available include pi, e, and powers of 10.

The MC68881 coprocessor can be used with any CPU on an 8-bit, 16-bit, or 32-bit data bus. Figure 9-3 illustrates its interface to the MC68020 CPU for the three bus sizes. The common connections shown in Figure 9-3a include the address and data strobe lines ($\overline{AS}$, $\overline{DS}$), read/write (R/$\overline{W}$), and addresses A4-A1 for coprocessor register selection. Table 9-1 determines the connections shown in Figures 9-3b, 9-3c, and 9-3d for the various size buses.

TABLE 9-1 MC68881 Coprocessor Data Alignment for Various Port Sizes

Port Size	$\overline{SIZE}$	A4	A1	A0	$\overline{DSACK1}$	$\overline{DSACK0}$	Active Data
32 Bits	1	0	x	1	0	1	D31–D16
	1	1	x	1	0	0	D31–D0
16 Bits	1	0	x	0	0	1	D31–D16
	1	1	0	0	0	1	D31–D16
	1	1	1	0	0	1	D15–D0
8 Bits	0	0	x	0	1	0	D31–D24
	0	0	x	1	1	0	D23–D16
	0	1	0	0	1	0	D31–D24
	0	1	0	1	1	0	D23–D16
	0	1	1	0	1	0	D15–D8
	0	1	1	1	1	0	D7–D0

where: 1 - High; 0 - Low

The port size is determined by the coprocessor's $\overline{SIZE}$ and A0 inputs. The port size is 32 bits when both are high (1). However, A4 must also be high to address the coprocessor's 32-bit data registers. For A4 low, only 16-bit registers are addressed and only the upper half of the 32-bit bus is actually used.

For the 16-bit port size ($\overline{SIZE}$ high and A0 low), the data can be transferred via the MC68881 coprocessor's upper 16 data lines (D31-D16), or lower 16 lines (D15-D0), depending on A1. The connections shown ensure that the data always resides on the MC68020 CPU's upper 16 data lines. Actually, the lower 16 lines can be used as an alternative since both halves of the MC68020 CPU's data bus transfer the operand if it is aligned at an even address (when A0 from the CPU is also low).

When $\overline{\text{SIZE}}$ is low, the port size is 8 bits, independent of the coprocessor's A0 input. As Table 9-1 shows, the byte may be transferred over any of the four groups of eight data lines, depending on the coprocessor's address inputs. Thus, all four groups must be tied together to form an 8-bit port bus. The connection is shown to the MC68020 CPU's upper eight data lines, although any of the groups could be used (since an 8-bit operand is replicated on all four sets of MC68020 data lines). Notice the data size acknowledge lines ($\overline{\text{DSACK1}}$,$\overline{\text{DSACK0}}$) are connected for all three configurations. However, the table shows that $\overline{\text{DSACK0}}$ is never asserted for the 16-bit case, so that its connection is optional. Likewise, when an 8-bit bus is used, the $\overline{\text{DSACK1}}$ connection need not be made since it also remains inactive (high).

It is also useful to observe that some degree of dynamic bus sizing is provided by the coprocessor (recall the discussion in Section 7.2). This results from A4 distinguishing between 16-bit and 32-bit registers. Additional dynamic sizing can be implemented by designing logic to provide the coprocessor's $\overline{\text{SIZE}}$ and A0 inputs, as opposed to keeping them at a fixed logic level (see Exercise 1 at the end of this Chapter).

Math Accelerator Units for the AT&T *WE* 32100 and 32200 CPUs

AT&T has a numerical coprocessor for its 32-bit CPU designated the *WE* 32106 Math Acceleration Unit (MAU). The *WE* 32106 MAU was designed to interface directly to the 32-bit data bus of the WE 32100 CPU. It is available in either a 100 or 125 pin ceramic PGA package, in 10 MHz, 14 MHz, and 18 MHz versions. Like the Intel and Motorola coprocessors discussed, it provides up to 80-bit precision capability for floating-point operations. As with the MOTOROLA MC68881 Numeric Coprocessor, it can be operated in either peripheral or coprocessor mode. The MAU's 23 instructions provide add, subtract, multiply, divide, remainder, negate, absolute value, square root, compare, move, and rounding-to-integral value functions.

The *WE* 32206 MAU, designed for the *WE* 32200 CPU, is upwardly compatible with the *WE* 32106 MAU. It is available in a 125 pin PGA package. The *WE* 32206 MAU adds the trigonometric sine, cosine, and arctangent functions, and the stored constant pi to the *WE* 32106 MAU instruction set. The internal architecture of both MAUs consists of 32-bit auxiliary status, command, and data registers (ASR, CR, DR). In addition, the *WE* 32106 MAU has four operand registers (F0-F3) and the *WE* 32206 MAU has eight (F0-F7); the operand registers are 96-bits wide, although only 80-bits are used.

Figure 9-4 emphasizes the ease of interfacing either MAU to its companion processor. The corresponding data, control, and status signals are provided on both devices. Of particular note is that a $\overline{\text{DONE}}$ signal sent by the MAU signals the completion of the coprocessor operation. This is analogous to the $\overline{\text{BUSY}}$ issued by the INTEL 80287/80387 Numeric Processor Extension to the INTEL 80386 CPU.

465

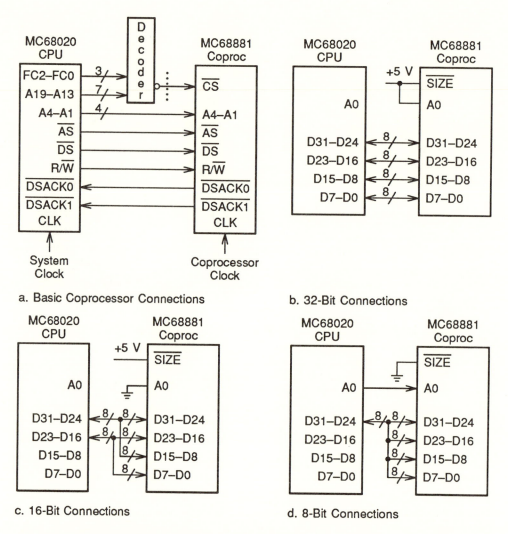

a. Basic Coprocessor Connections

b. 32-Bit Connections

c. 16-Bit Connections

d. 8-Bit Connections

FIGURE 9-3   MOTOROLA MC68020 CPU/68881 Coprocessor Interface Via 32-Bit, 16-Bit, and 8-Bit Data Buses

Programming Example Using the AT&T *WE* 32106 Math Accelerator Unit

The *WE* 32106 MAU will now be used to illustrate a numeric coprocessor carrying out a floating-point operation. The *WE* 32100 CPU contains the ten coprocessor instructions given in Table 9-2.

If the CPU issues any one of these SPOP instructions, a coprocessor broadcast access status code is issued (0101 on lines SAS3-SAS0). Note the SPOP prefix is analogous to the escape (ESC) issued by the INTEL 80386 CPU to the INTEL 80287/80387 Numeric Processor Extension, although the opcodes in this case do not all start with the same bit sequence. During this coprocessor broadcast the address strobe ($\overline{AS}$) output of the *WE* 32100 CPU (normally asserted at the start of an instruction fetch) is not issued during this transaction. As

466

TABLE 9-2 AT&T *WE* 32100 CPU Coprocessor Instructions

Mnemonic	Opcode (Hex)	Instruction
SPOP	32	Coprocessor operation
SPOPRS	22	Coprocessor operation read single
SPOPRD	02	Coprocessor operation read double
SPOPRT	06	Coprocessor operation read triple
SPOPWS	33	Coprocessor operation write single
SPOPWD	13	Coprocessor operation write double
SPOPWT	17	Coprocessor operation write triple
SPOPS2	23	Coprocessor operation single 2-address
SPOPD2	03	Coprocessor operation double 2-address
SPOPT2	07	Coprocessor operation triple 2-address

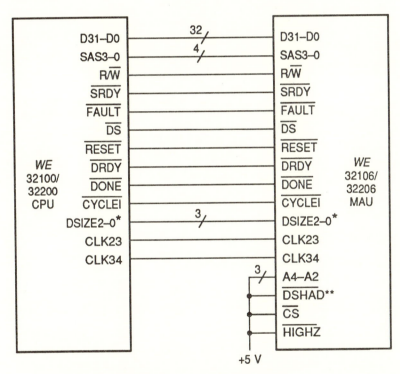

* For *WE* 32200 CPU and *WE* 32206 MAU only.

** To MMU's $\overline{\text{DSHAD}}$ output for systems with *WE* 32101/32201 MMU.

FIGURE 9-4   *WE* 32100/32200 CPU Interface to 32106/32206 MAU

a result, memory is not accessed. All coprocessor instructions follow the opcode with a 32-bit word sent to the MAU's command register (CR). The CR fields, shown in Table 9-3, include an ID number and opcode for the MAU, and identifiers for as many as three operands.

Command Register

8 Bits	9 Bits	5 Bits	3 Bits	3 Bits	4 Bits
ID	Unused	Opcode	op1	op2	0p3

Field

TABLE 9-3 AT&T *WE* 32106 MAU Command Register Format

Field	Description
ID	All zeros for MAU
Opcode	Selects one of 23 MAU instructions
op1, op2	Source operand locations 0-3 F0–F3 4-6 Memory (coprocessor mode) or DR (peripheral mode) single, double, or triple word 7 No operand
op3	Destination operand location and precision 0-3 F0–F3, single precision (32-bits) 4-7 F0–F3, double precision (64 bits) 8-B F0–F3, double extended precision (80 bits) C-E Memory (coprocessor mode) or DR (peripheral mode) single, double, or triple word F No operand

The CPU's coprocessor instructions include zero, one, or two operands following the broadcasted command word. The assembler syntax is of the form

SPOPxx *word*,<src>,<dst>

where *word* refers to the 32-bit command word, src to the source operand, and dst to the destination operand. The arrow symbols, <>, indicate that src and dst are optional fields. The operands and associated operations for all of the coprocessor instructions are in Table 9-4.

From Tables 9-3 and 9-4, we see that the particular SPOP mnemonic defines the number of operands (0, 1, or 2), the operand size (32, 64, or 80 bits), and whether the operation is a read, a write, or both. Notice the coprocessor operations are limited to one source and one destination operand, although several of the MAU's floating-point instructions deal with three operands. For a three operand

TABLE 9-4 AT&T *WE* **32100 CPU Coprocessor Operations**

Mnemonic	Operand(s)	Operation
SPOP	None	No operands
SPOPRS,SPOPRD,SPOPRT	src *	Read **
SPOPWS,SPOPWD,SPOPWT	dst *	Write **
SPOPS2,SPOPD2,SPOPT2	src,dst *	Read and write (2 address) **

  * All addressing modes except register, literal, or immediate.
** Operation(s) performed on single (S), double (D), or triple (T) words, where a word is 32-bits.

instruction, an operation is performed on source operands op1 and op2, and the result is placed into destination op3. Table 9-5 shows the operations corresponding to specific MAU instructions.

The CR *word* following the SPOP mnemonic defines the MAU instruction to be performed and the location of the operand(s). The location is either one of the four MAU operand registers or external memory. In the case of memory, most of the *WE* 32100 CPU addressing modes can be used. However, due to the two operand limitation imposed by the SPOP instruction format, only two operands at most can reference memory for the three operand MAU instructions. The extra source operand requires use of an MAU operand register. (This restriction would not apply if the MAU were used with a processor supporting three memory-based operands for its coprocessor protocol instructions).

The complete process involved in performing an MAU operation is:

Step 1 - *word* written to CR of MAU (coprocessor broadcast access status)

Step 2 - (optional) *src* read (coprocessor data fetch access status)

Step 3 - coprocessor executes instruction and asserts CPU's $\overline{\text{DONE}}$ input upon completion

Step 4 - Condition code bits from MAU's ASR copied to CPU's PSW register (coprocessor status fetch access status)

Step 5 - (optional) *dst* written (coprocessor data write access status)

Note that four of the bits in the MAU's status register are flag conditions that match the positions of the negative, zero, overflow, and carry flag bits in the CPU's status register. Thus, Step 4 of the process outlined updates the CPU status to reflect the result of the MAU operation.

The instruction sets for the *WE* 32106 and 32206 MAUs are summarized in Table 9-5.

Floating-point numbers consist of a sign bit, exponent bits, and fraction bits (see Appendix A for details). Table 9-6 gives the number of exponent and fraction bits used by the *WE* 32106/32206 MAU, and the range of floating-point numbers for the different precisions.

TABLE 9-5 AT&T *WE* 32106/32206 MAU Instruction Set

Instruction	Mnemonic	Opcode (Hex)	Operation
Data Transfer Group			
Move	MOVE	07	op3 ← op1
Move from ASR	RDASR	08	op3 ← ASR
Move to ASR	WRASR	09	ASR ← op1
Load DR	LDR	18	DR ← op1
Arithmetic Group			
Absolute value	ABS	0C	op3 ← |op1|
Add	ADD	02	op3 ← op1+op2
Subtract	SUB	03	op3 ← op2-op1
Multiply	MUL	06	op3 ← op1*op2
Divide	DIV	04	op3 ← op2/op1
Remainder	REM	05	op3 ← rem(op2/op1)
Square root	SQRT	0D	op3 ← sqrt(op1)
Negate	NEG	17	op3 ← −(op1)
Round to integral value	RTOI	0E	op3 ← integer(op1)
Logical Group			
Compare	CMP	0A	*
Compare with exceptions	CMPE	0B	*
Compare with flags swapped	CMPS	1A	*
Compare with exceptions and flags swapped	CMPES	1B	*
Conversion Group			
Convert decimal to floating point	DTOF	11	op3 ← float(decimal op1)
Convert floating point to decimal	FTOD	12	op3 ← decimal(float op1)
Convert floating point to integer	FTOI	0F	op3 ← integer(float op1)
Convert integer to floating point	ITOF	10	op3 ← float(integer op1)
Transcendental Group *(WE 32206 MAU only)*			
Sine	SIN	1C	op3 ← sin(op1)
Cosine	COS	1D	op3 ← cos(op1)
Arc tangent	ATAN	1E	op3 ← atan(op1)
Pi	PI	1F	op3 ← Pi
Miscellaneous Group			
Extract result on fault	EROF	14	op3 ← DR
No operation	NOP	13	none

* Set flags according to comparison of op1 with op2 (op1 and op2 are unchanged)

TABLE 9-6 Range of Floating Point Number Representation for the AT&T *WE* 32106/32206 MAU

Precision	Number of Bits		Approximate Range (Normalized Numbers)
	Exponent	Fraction	
Single	8	23	2^{-126} to 2^{128}
Double	11	52	2^{-1022} to 2^{1024}
Double extended	15	63	2^{-16382} to 2^{16384}

Note that for double-extended precision, an explicit bit (i.e., integer bit) is used. The fraction and explicit bits together can represent numbers in the range:

$$0 \text{ to } [2 - (2^{-63})]$$

In addition to floating-point numbers, the MAUs can represent integers in the range

$$-2^{31} \text{ to } 2^{31}$$

and binary coded decimal (BCD) numbers in the range

$$-10^{18} \text{ to } 10^{18}$$

The following example illustrates the addition of two floating-point double-precision numbers (64 bits each). Assume the two numbers are initially in memory and the result is also to be written to memory. Although the floating-point ADD instruction handles three operands, only two operands at most can be memory based (as discussed earlier). Therefore, two MAU instructions are required. First, an operand must be read from memory into an MAU operand register. Then the second instruction can fetch the second operand from memory, add it to the first (already in the MAU), and write the floating-point sum back into memory. The two SPOP instructions embedded in the *WE* 32100/32200 CPU's program accomplish the task.

Assembly Language Instructions	Hex Code
SPOPRD CRWORD1,FPNUM1	02 CRWORD1 src
SPOPD2 CRWORD2,FPNUM2,FPSUM	03 CRWORD2 src dst

Notes on symbolic names:

1. CRWORD1 and CRWORD2 are command register values adhering to the format of Table 9-3.
2. FPNUM1 and FPNUM2 are the two floating-point values to be added, and FPSUM is the result.

The first instruction is a read double SPOP (SPOPRD), since only a source double word memory operand is to be read. The second instruction must read the second operand, and write the result of the MAU operation back into memory. Since both source and destination operands are double precision, a double 2-address SPOP is used (SPOPD2). In the assembled hex code, the opcode (see Table 9-2) and command register word is followed by source and destination operand codes which depend on the addressing mode.

The 64-bit operands FPNUM1, FPNUM2, and FPSUM correspond to the source operands (op1 and op2) and destination operand (op3), respectively. They represent the two floating-point numbers and the resulting sum. For this exercise, we are only concerned with the command register words CRWORD1 and CRWORD2. The 32-bit codes for these two words are:

CRWORD1

	8 Bits	9 Bits	5 Bits	3 Bits	3 Bits	4 Bits
Field	00000000	000000000	00111	101	111	0100
	MAU ID	Unused	Opcode MAU MOVE	op1 Memory (Double Word)	op2 No Operand	op3 F0 Register (Double Precision)

CRWORD2

	8 Bits	9 Bits	5 Bits	3 Bits	3 Bits	4 Bits
Field	00000000	000000000	00010	000	101	1101
	MAU ID	Unused	Opcode MAU ADD	op1 F0 Register	op2 Memory (Double Word)	op3 Memory (Double Word)

The control words are therefore set to hexadecimal

CRWORD1 = 00001EF4
CRWORD2 = 0000085D

To understand the bit values assigned to the various fields, refer to the CR format in Table 9-3. The ID must be all zeros to select the MAU, as opposed to any other coprocessor that may be in the system. Unused bits are arbitrarily set to zero also. The 5-bit MAU opcode is obtained from Table 9-5. MOVE is coded as 07 (00111 in binary), and ADD is 02 (00010 in binary).

The operand fields are coded in accordance with whether an MAU register or memory is the source (or destination). Note that the destination (op3) field of Table 9-3 has an extra bit, as compared to the fields for the source operands. This enables specification of the precision when writing the result to an MAU register (F0-F3). For this example, which uses all double-precision operands, the MOV operation fetches op1 from memory (code = 5 = 101) to replace op3 in MAU register F0 (code = 4 = 0100). Since no other source operand exists, the op2 field is coded as 7, or binary 111. This data then becomes op1 for the ADD instruction. The ADD fetches op1 from F0 (code = 0 = 000) and op2 from memory (code = 5 = 101), adds them, and writes op3 to memory (code = D = 1101).

9.2 Multiprocessing

The Intel, AT&T and Motorola 32-bit CPUs discussed in this text have extensive provisions for multitasking that enable rapid switching (often via interrupt) between tasks or processes. The tasks take turns using the CPU in a time-shared fashion. This improves overall performance by allowing, for example, one task to perform computations while the other is handling I/O (such as waiting for a device ready indicator). Performance is not the only issue, however. If the execution of tasks were not interleaved in time, a lengthy computation in one task could result in input data used by a second task not being sensed in time and thereby lost. In a multiuser environment with a high CPU clock rate and multitasking, the system appears to each user to be a dedicated CPU. Too many users can result in noticeable time delays, a reminder of the interleaved operation of the system.

Even in a single CPU multitasking environment only one task can be handled at a time since only one instruction can execute at a time. As indicated in Section 9.1, an independent processor or coprocessor can carry out its own instructions at the same time the CPU is executing code. A system with two or more processors executing instructions simultaneously is called a multiprocessing system. Using a coprocessor with a CPU is only one example of a multiprocessing system. Such a system may include more than one CPU and possibly coprocessors as well. There are a variety of possible configurations, depending on the degree to which memory and I/O resources are shared and whether the processors work independent of one another.

The ever declining cost of single-chip CPUs makes it economical to use multiple processors in a system as compared to the use of a more complex CPU in a centralized approach. The use of multiprocessors also allows efficient system configuration and ease of expansion. In contrast, the centralized approach may result in costly and unneeded capability. Tracing a hardware failure in a centralized system is usually more difficult. In a multiprocessing system, replacing the failed processor is less expensive. On the other hand, the multiprocessing system designer must contend with the problems of bus contention and interprocessor communications.

Resource Sharing in Multitasking and Multiprocessing

In a multitasking environment, different tasks share the same CPU as well as other hardware resources. Consider the situation where two tasks are manipulating the same block of memory or I/O data, and either task may interrupt the other before completion. Generally it is necessary to provide control of this shared resource. Errors can result if the interrupting task is allowed to access the shared data block while the interrupted task is in the midst of processing that block. This can be accomplished in software with the aid of special flag bits called semaphores, which are defined by the programmer and used to reserve a shared resource. Control of the shared resource is more complex in a multiprocessor situation. With only one CPU, switching between tasks cannot occur in the middle of an instruction. However, with independently running processors it is possible for tasks controlled by different CPUs to test a semaphore simultaneously and together gain access to the shared resource. It is then necessary, with the aid of hardware, to lock out all but one CPU from the resource.

To illustrate the software approach when only a single CPU is used, consider using a single semaphore referenced by the symbolic address FLAG. Assume that the resource is free for FLAG=1, and is in use when FLAG=0. Two tasks, where either task can be interrupted by the other, could be set up as:.

	Task 1			**Task 2**	
TASK1:	:		TASK2:	:	
CHECK1:	TEST	FLAG,1	CHECK2:	TEST	FLAG,1
	JZ	CHECK1		JZ	CHECK2
	MOV	FLAG,0		MOV	FLAG,0
	:			:	
(Task 1 accesses shared data block)			(Task 2 accesses shared data block)		
	:			:	
	MOV	FLAG,1		MOV	FLAG,1
	:			:	

Notice the TEST instruction performs a bit-by-bit logical ANDing of the source and destination operands without altering either one. Thus if FLAG=1, the result of

TEST FLAG,1

produces 1, a nonzero condition. When the resource is in use, FLAG = 0 and the test operation produces a zero result. The jump-on-zero instruction, therefore, keeps the task in the loop until the resource is free.

Assuming FLAG has been initialized to 1 and Task 1 is executed first, it gains access to the shared data. Before doing so it clears FLAG (to 0) to prevent Task 2 from accessing the block until Task 1 has completed its manipulation of the data. If Task 2 interrupts during this time, it keeps looping back to CHECK2 until another interrupt occurs and Task 1 completes its processing. FLAG is then set (1) again to allow Task 2 access to the data.

A problem occurs with this scheme if Task 1 is executed with FLAG=1 and Task 2 interrupts during the JZ instruction. In this case, the instruction will be completed, giving Task 1 access to the data when its routine later resumes at that point. However, the switch is made before FLAG has been cleared, and therefore Task 2 also gains access to the data. Now, an interrupt occurring before Task 2 has completed its access can cause problems, since Task 1 will proceed to manipulate the data.

One way to overcome this problem is to provide separate semaphores for each task. Before a task accesses the data, it can clear its own flag and test the other processor's flag to determine if the shared resource is available. The tasks would be modified as:

	Task 1			**Task 2**	
TASK1:	:		TASK2:	:	
	:			:	
CHECK1:	MOV	FLAG1,0	CHECK2:	MOV	FLAG2,0
	TEST	FLAG2,1		TEST	FLAG1,1
	JZ	CHECK1		JZ	CHECK2
	:			:	
(Task 1 accesses shared data block)			(Task 2 accesses shared data block)		
	:			:	
	MOV	FLAG1,1		MOV	FLAG2,1
	:			:	

By clearing its own flag before testing the other's flag, an interrupting task cannot access the shared data until the current task has completed its processing of the data. Setting its own flag after completing data manipulation then allows the next task access to that data. Unfortunately, this approach can trigger the opposite problem created by the single flag method, namely that of simultaneously locking out both tasks from the data. For example, assume Task 1 commences with FLAG2 set (giving Task 1 access) and an interrupt occurs during the first MOV instruction. Thus, Task 1 has cleared its own flag (preventing access by Task 2) but it has been interrupted before testing FLAG2. Task 2 then begins by clearing its own flag (FLAG2). Since both flags are now cleared, neither task can exit from its loop and access the data.

The following routine prevents both tasks from accessing the data block simultaneously, and also prevents both from being denied entry. A single flag is used, with the key being the use of the data exchange instruction (XCHG).

	Task 1			**Task 2**	
TASK1:	:		TASK2:	:	
	MOV	AL,0		MOV	AH,0
CHECK1:	XCHG	AL,FLAG	CHECK2:	XCHG	AH,FLAG
	TEST	AL,AL		TEST	AH,AH
	JZ	CHECK1		JZ	CHECK2
	:			:	
(Task 1 accesses shared data block)			(Task 2 accesses shared data block)		
	:			:	
	MOV	FLAG,1		MOV	FLAG,1
	:			:	

In this case, each task saves FLAG in a separate 8-bit register (using AL and AH) and clears its value via the single XCHG instruction. The saved value is then tested. If one task interrupts the other during or after the exchange, and before the end of its data block access, the interrupting task is blocked (since FLAG=0 is passed to it). Using separate registers prevents both tasks from being blocked. If only AL or AH were used, a task switch during XCHG or TEST would result in the interrupting task clearing that register. Thus, FLAG and its saved value would both be 0 and neither task could exit from its testing loop.

As pointed out, if the tasks are running on separate processors, a task switch can occur in the middle of an instruction. For the routine shown, the exchange instruction requires two bus cycles - one for reading FLAG from memory and the second for writing AL to it. Suppose both CPUs happen to be testing the semaphore and have fetched the exchange instructions at the same time. It is possible for Task 1 to then use the first available bus cycle to read FLAG=1, and then Task 2 (running on the other CPU) to read the same value of FLAG on the next bus cycle. Succeeding cycles then result in writing 0 from AL to FLAG for Task 1 and from AH to FLAG for Task 2. However, it is now too late since AL of the first CPU and AH of the second CPU are both replaced by 1 (the original value of FLAG). The TEST instruction then results in both tasks exiting the loop and concurrently accessing the shared data.

The solution to this problem lies in the use of the 80386 $\overline{\text{LOCK}}$ output signal. In a multiprocessing environment, this signal can be used to ensure that the 80386 CPU has exclusive use of any shared memory (to be illustrated). This signal is asserted by the LOCK instruction (opcode 11110000). It is also asserted automatically when the processor is engaged in special activities, such as acknowledging interrupts or loading descriptors. The LOCK instruction may precede various bit testing and arithmetic/logic operations as well as the exchange instruction (XCHG), for which one of the operands is in memory. An undefined opcode trap occurs if LOCK precedes an instruction other than an allowable one. Ordinarily the assembler requires a LOCK prefix preceding the instruction. However, the use of the XCHG instruction for testing semaphores is extremely important in a multiprocessing situation, as illustrated by the previous example. As a result, the 80386 also asserts the $\overline{\text{LOCK}}$ signal automatically when XCHG is executed, regardless of whether the LOCK prefix is used.

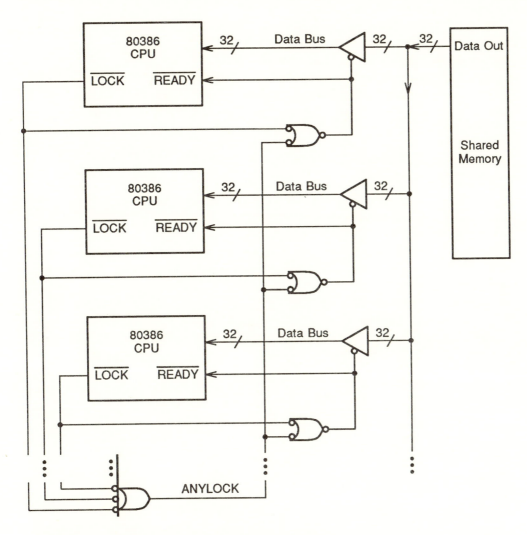

FIGURE 9-5   Multiprocessing Control Logic Example

Figure 9-5 illustrates conceptually the use of the $\overline{\text{LOCK}}$ signal in controlling access to shared memory. When the processor controlling the bus at a given time asserts its $\overline{\text{LOCK}}$ signal, ANYLOCK is high and the $\overline{\text{LOCK}}$ outputs from the other CPUs are negated. The outputs from the 2-input low active OR gates (logically equivalent to a high active AND) inhibit all tristate gates, except the one tied to the data bus of the processor in control. Therefore, no other processor can read data until the controlling one has finished executing its instruction. Although data is locked out of the other processors, it is necessary to place them in wait states; otherwise they will complete their instruction cycles and proceed to access the next one (recall the discussion of wait states in Section 7.3).

By tying the tristate gate control input to the $\overline{\text{READY}}$ input of each CPU, all but the controlling processor remains in a wait state. When the controlling

477

processor's instruction has completed, its $\overline{LOCK}$ output is negated. ANYLOCK then goes low enabling all the tristate gates giving all CPUs access to memory. Similar tristate gate logic can be provided to control memory writing as well.

Applying this hardware to the previous software example, recall that FLAG is read by the current task as part of the XCHG instruction. The automatic assertion of its $\overline{LOCK}$ signal prevents tasks of other CPUs from reading the same location until the FLAG value is cleared by completion of the exchange operation.

Multiprocessing with Local and System Buses

A powerful multiprocessing system results when several processors, each with its own local bus and private resources, are interconnected to a system bus supporting shared resources. The system bus provides a standard interface through which components from different manufacturers can be integrated, permitting modular expansion. The concept of a standard bus has been widely used in single processor systems, permitting the rapid integration of CPU, memory, and I/O boards which are predesigned to match the standard interface. Design time is considerably reduced. A disadvantage is in the cost of special features that may be provided on the available boards but are not used in the designer's application. The INTEL MULTIBUS Bus and MOTOROLA VMEbus bus are popular industry standards that support 16-bit and 32-bit CPUs.

INTEL MULTIBUS I

The INTEL MULTIBUS Bus is a 16-bit multiprocessing system bus originally developed to support the 8086. The MULTIBUS I is a revised 16-bit standard designed to handle the additional addressing capability of the 80286 CPU. Interrupt and DMA handling are also supported. Details of the protocols for this system bus are not provided here, but are available in Intel's *MULTIBUS I Architecture Reference Book*. One method of providing an interface between the 80386 CPU and the MULTIBUS I is to use an 80286 CPU-compatible interface as shown in Figure 9-6. Figure 9-6 does not show the local bus interface and local resources. The blocks shown perform the following functions:

• **A0/A1 Logic:** Converts the 80386 CPU byte high enables ($\overline{BE3}$-$\overline{BE0}$) to the low two addresses (A1,A0). The logic to provide this was shown in Figure 7-16.

• **Address Decoder:** Determines whether the bus cycle requires a MULTIBUS I access.

• **Address Latch:** Connects directly to 80386 address pins A23-A2 and to the low-two addresses, A1 and A0. The MULTIBUS I bus allows up to 24 address lines.

• **Data Transceivers:** Connect directly to 80386 data pins D15-D0. The MULTIBUS I bus allows up to 16 data lines.

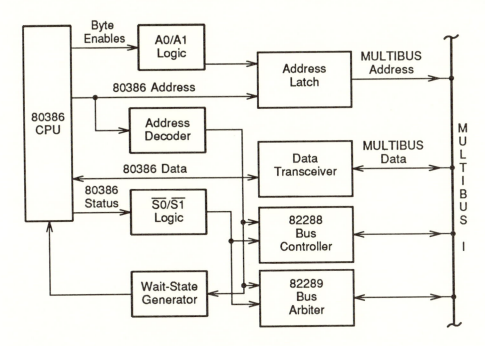

FIGURE 9-6   Intel 80386 CPU/MULTIBUS I Interface

• $\overline{\text{S0}/\text{S1}}$ **Logic:** Converts 80386 status outputs to 80286 CPU-compatible status signals. The logic to provide this was shown in Figure 8-18.

• **Wait State Generator:** Controls the length of the 80386 bus cycle via the $\overline{\text{READY}}$ signal (see Section 7.3 for a discussion of wait states).

• **82288 Bus Controller:** This 20-pin device generates command signals for the MULTIBUS I. (See the *INTEL 82288 Bus Controller Data Sheet* for its operational details.)

• **82289 Bus Arbiter:** This 20-pin device resolves bus control contention between the 80386 and other processors (i.e., MULTIBUS masters). (See the *INTEL 82289 Bus Arbiter Data Sheet* for its operational details.)

The 82289 bus arbiter, included with each subsystem, prevents the bus controller from accessing the system bus when its subsystem does not control the bus. Upon receiving control, the arbiter enables the bus controller and address latches to drive the MULTIBUS I. When a read or write operation is completed, MULTIBUS I issues the acknowledgment signal used to activate the $\overline{\text{READY}}$ inputs of all the processors allowing them to complete their current bus cycles.

One interesting aspect of MULTIBUS I is that to maintain compatibility between 8-bit, 16-bit, and 32-bit systems, all single-byte data transfers must be performed on the lower eight data lines. Recall from Section 7.2 that 80386 byte transfers can take place over data lines D31-D24, D23-D16, D15-D8, or D7-D0 depending on the starting address (see Table 7-5). However, MULTIBUS I supports only 16-bit data size at most. Therefore, the interface logic should provide $\overline{BS16}$ to the 80386 CPU, which is asserted for all MULTIBUS I cycles. Also recall, all data transfers are automatically routed to the lower half of the data bus (D15-D0) when the 80386 CPU is placed in the 16-bit mode. The only additional logic that must be supplied is the logic required to swap bytes between D15-D8 and D7-D0, so as to meet MULTIBUS I requirements.

The hardware of Figure 9-7 provides the required byte swapping logic. The bus high enable ($\overline{BHE}$) and low address bit (A0) are generated by the logic derived in Figure 7-15 and implemented in Figure 7-16. When the address is stable, the 82288 bus controller asserts an address latch enable (ALE) output. As a result, the latched $\overline{BHE}$ and A0 enable the appropriate transceiver(s) (back-to-back tristate gates) when data to be transferred is made available.

The transceiver enable logic implements the requirements shown in Table 7-4. For byte transfers, either $\overline{BHE}$ = 1 and A0 = 0 (for an even-addressed byte) or $\overline{BHE}$ = 0 and A0 = 1 (for an odd-addressed byte). For either case, in Figure 9-7, transceiver 1 connecting lines D15-D8 is disabled. This ensures that those MULTIBUS I lines are not used in the transfer. For the even-addressed byte, A0 = 0 activates transceiver 3 and transfer takes place via the 80386 CPU's D7-D0 lines. In contrast, for an odd-addressed byte (where A0=1) the 80386 CPU has active data on D15-D8. Thus, transceiver 2 is activated and data is routed between the upper eight data lines of the 80386 CPU and the lower 8 lines of MULTIBUS I.

For 16-bit odd-addressed data, an odd-addressed byte is transferred first followed by an even-addressed byte during a second bus cycle. Thus, both transfers again only use the D7-D0 lines of MULTIBUS I. Finally, transfer of 16-bit even addressed data is not affected by this circuit. For this case $\overline{BHE}$ = 0 and A0 = 0, resulting in transceivers 1 and 3 both being active, and both upper and lower bytes transferred at once.

INTEL MULTIBUS II

MULTIBUS II was designed to support 8-bit, 16-bit, and 32-bit processors. Designed for higher speed performance than MULTIBUS I, it can handle data transfer rates as high as 40 Mbytes/s. This bus standard has added multiprocessing support over that provided by MULTIBUS I, improved reliability, and features better cost versus performance. MULTIBUS II includes the following specialized Intel buses: parallel system bus, local bus extension, serial system bus, multichannel DMA I/O bus, and system expansion I/O bus. The DMA and system expansion I/O buses are brought forth directly from MULTIBUS I architecture. The parallel system bus permits interprocessor data transfer and communication up to the highest rate. The local bus extension is designed for quick access to off-board memory. A bus extension can support either two

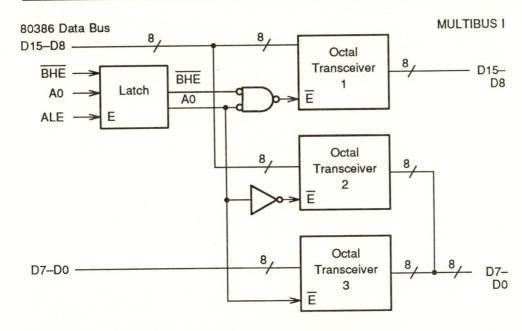

FIGURE 9-7 Byte-Swapping Logic for INTEL MULTIBUS I Interface

processing subsystems plus four memory subsystems, or one processing subsystem with five memory subsystems. For larger memory requirements, more than one bus extension can be used with a MULTIBUS II system. The serial system bus provides a lower cost alternative to the parallel system bus, where the high performance of the parallel bus is not required. The serial bus can support up to 32 bus agents distributed over a distance as large as 10 meters. The intelligence of the interface, combined with the error detection capability provided, enables the serial bus to match the parallel bus's reliability.

VMEbus

The VMEbus was an outgrowth of the MOTOROLA VERSAbus Bus, the backplane of an early MC68000 development system. Motorola, as well as many other vendors, provides a variety of board products that interface to this bus. In addition, AT&T has developed a 32-bit VMEbus single-board computer, which includes the WE 32100 CPU, WE 32101 MMU, WE 32106 MAU, up to 256K bytes of EPROM/ROM, 1M byte DRAM, two serial ports, three timer/counters and interrupt hardware. The functional structure of the VMEbus can be divided into four categories, each consisting of a bus along with associated functional modules. The categories are summarized as:

Data Transfer: Transfers take place over the data transfer bus (DTB), which consists of 32 data lines, address lines, and associated control signals. Functional modules called masters, slaves, interrupters, and interrupt handlers use the DTB to transfer data between each other. Bus timer and interrupt-acknowledge daisy chain driver modules also assist the transfers.

481

DTB Arbitration: For a system configured with more than one master or interrupt handler, orderly transfer of DTB control is provided. The control transfer is coordinated by arbitration bus modules called requesters and arbiter.

Priority Interrupt: The lines of this bus are used by interrupter modules to request service from interrupt handlers. The interrupt requests can be prioritized into a maximum of seven levels.

Utilities: The utility bus provides clocking, initialization, and failure detection. Included are two clock lines, single lines providing system reset, system fail and power fail indicators, and serial data transfer.

On the data transfer bus, masters use address lines A31-A2 to select a four-byte data group starting at an address divisible by 4 (address 4N, where N is an integer). Four additional lines ($\overline{DS1}$, $\overline{DS0}$, A1, and $\overline{LWORD}$) select those byte locations of the group which are accessed. This permits transfers of 1, 2, 3, or 4 bytes at a time. Table 9-7, patterned after Table 7-5 showing 80386 data operations, summarizes the requirements for the four additional signals.

Notice the VMEbus data transfer protocol is consistent with that used by both the MOTOROLA MC68020 CPU and AT&T WE 32100 CPU. When more than one byte is transferred, the byte at the lowest address is transferred over the highest eight data lines, and likewise for the other bytes. This is opposite to the protocol of the INTEL 80386 CPU, where the lower-order data lines are associated with the lower addresses. Table 9-8 specifies the relationship of the individual bytes of the group to the data lines used for the transfer.

TABLE 9-7 VMEbus Signal Requirements for Data Operations

Transfer	Starting Address	$\overline{DS1}$	$\overline{DS0}$	A1	$\overline{LWORD}$	Active Data
32-Bit Word	4N	0	0	0	0	D31–D0
24-Bit Word	4N	0	1	0	0	D31–D8
	4N+1	1	0	0	0	D23–D0
16-Bit Word	4N	0	0	0	1	D15–D0
	4N+1	0	0	1	0	D23–D8
	4N+2	0	0	1	1	D15–D0
Byte	4N	0	1	0	1	D15–D8
	4N+1	1	0	0	1	D7–D0
	4N+2	0	1	1	1	D15–D8
	4N+3	1	0	1	1	D7–D0

Figure 9-8 illustrates an approach to designing an INTEL 80386 CPU module which interfaces to the protocol of the VMEbus. The control logic to generate the four VMEbus control signals ($\overline{DS1}$, $\overline{DS0}$, A1, and $\overline{LWORD}$) can be implemented

TABLE 9-8 VMEbus Data Transfer Protocol Summary

Transfer	Starting Address	Data Lines Used in Transfer*			
		D31–D24	D23–D16	D15–D8	D7–D0
32-Bit Word	4N	0	1	2	3
24-Bit Word	4N	0	1	2	
	4N+1		1	2	3
16-Bit Word	4N			0	1
	4N+1		1	2	
	4N+2			2	3
Byte	4N			0	
	4N+1				1
	4N+2			2	
	4N+3				3

* The numbers 0, 1, 2, and 3 represent:

0 - Byte at address 4N   2 - Byte at address 4N+2

1 - Byte at address 4N+1   3 - Byte at address 4N+3

by matching the requirements of Table 7-5 to those of Table 9-7 for the various data sizes and alignments. As discussed, the INTEL 80386 CPU and VMEbus reverse the order of the data bytes. By connecting the D31-D24 lines to D7-D0, and D23-D16 to D15-D8, the number of octal transceivers and enabling logic is reduced. Note that two additional transceivers are required to provide byte swapping between D15-D8 and D7-D0 (analogous to the MULTIBUS I interface shown in Figure 9-7). An examination of the requirements shows the necessity of these transceivers. Transfers of 8-bit or 16-bit data, confined to addresses 4N and 4N+1, only utilize the lower 16 data lines (D15-D0) of both the INTEL 80386 CPU and VMEbus. This maintains the upward compatibility with 16-bit systems. The details of designing the control logic are left as an exercise (see Exercise 7).

9.3 Chapter Highlights

1. A coprocessor is a device which generally shares memory and I/O system resources with the CPU and supplements the CPU's instructions with a set of its own. Arithmetic or numeric coprocessors typically supplement the CPU's arithmetic instructions with floating-point operations, as well as trigonometric and logarithmic functions. The coprocessor instructions are part of the program written for the CPU. When the program is run, control is passed by the CPU to

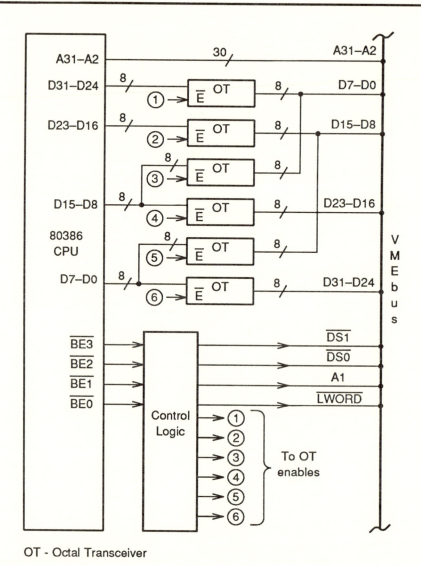

OT - Octal Transceiver

FIGURE 9-8 Interfacing the INTEL 80386 CPU to the VMEbus

and from the coprocessor as each coprocessor instruction is encountered.

2. Numeric coprocessors have been designed for the INTEL 80386 CPU and the MOTOROLA MC68020 CPU. The INTEL 80387 Numeric Processor Extension, derived from the earlier 8087 and 80287 numeric coprocessors, interfaces directly with the 80386 CPU and can run at 20 MHz. Up to 64-bit integer, 80-bit floating point, and 18-digit binary coded decimal (BCD) data is supported. An escape (ESC) prefix on an instruction's opcode identifies to the 80386 CPU one of about 70 coprocessor instructions. The MOTOROLA MC68881 Floating-Point Coprocessor interfaces to the MC68020 CPU, or can be used with any other CPU

on an 8-bit, 16-bit, or 32-bit data bus. Its data support and protocol are similar to that of the INTEL 80387 Numeric Processor Extension; it features 46 instructions, and is available in 12.5 MHz and 16.67 MHz versions.

3. The AT&T *WE* 32106 and 32206 Math Accelerator Units (MAUs) were developed for the *WE* 32100 and 32200 CPUs, respectively. The *WE* 32106 MAU is available in 10 MHz, 14 MHz, and 18 MHz versions. Like the Intel 80387, it can handle up to 80-bit size data (called double-extended precision).

An MAU instruction is invoked when the CPU issues one of ten coprocessor operation instructions. These instructions distinguish the number of operands (0 to 2), whether the operation performs a read or write (or both), and the operand size. A total of 23 MAU instructions are available.

4. In a multitasking environment, different tasks or processes share the same CPU, as well as other hardware resources. Multiprocessing systems, on the other hand, take advantage of the declining cost of microprocessors by providing several CPUs, and possibly coprocessors as well. This decentralized approach can result in more efficient use of the system's shared resources and easier tracing of hardware failure, but introduces problems of bus contention and interprocessor communications. The system designer must configure the hardware and software to ensure that a task carried out by one CPU does not attempt to access a shared resource such as a memory data block when another CPU's task, running concurrently, is processing that data block.

5. The power of multiprocessing systems is achieved when several CPUs, with their own local bus and private resources, are interconnected to a "standard" system bus supporting shared resources. A standard bus interface permits the designer to easily integrate matching CPU, memory, and I/O boards. The INTEL MULTIBUS I and II and the MOTOROLA VMEbus bus are industry standards that support 16-bit and 32-bit CPUs.

Exercises

Advanced problems are indicated by an asterisk (*).

1.* Using the MOTOROLA MC68020 CPU data size outputs (SIZ1, SIZ0) and the information in Table 9-1, design gating logic to provide dynamic bus sizing for the interface to the MC68881 numeric coprocessor. This means providing a single interface, controlled by SIZ1 and SIZ0, to replace the 32-bit, 16-bit, and 8-bit connections shown in Figures

9-3b, 9-3c, and 9-3d. Use octal transceivers (eight back-to-back tristate gates) to control the data line flow.

2. Using the information on the AT&T WE 32106/32206 MAU instructions presented in Tables 9-2 to 9-5, specify the assembly language instruction(s) and hex code(s) required to take the square root of a double-precision floating-point number. Determine the numerical value of the command register (CR) word(s) required. The source operand resides in memory and the destination operand is to be placed in memory as well.

3. Repeat Exercise 2 for the AT&T WE 32206 MAU sine trigonometric operation for a single-precision floating-point operand.

4. Repeat Exercise 2 for a divide operation involving three memory based triple-precision operands.

5.* An INTEL 80387 Numeric Processor Extension (coprocessor) is interfaced to an 80386 CPU. Obtain and study the 80387 instructions and duplicate the floating-point addition example, presented for the AT&T WE 32106/32206 MAU, in Section 9.1.

6.* Repeat Exercise 5 for the Motorola MC68881 Floating-Point Coprocessor interfaced to a MC68020 CPU.

7.* Design the control gating logic required to complete the INTEL 80386 CPU/VMEbus interface shown in Figure 9-8.

Appendices

A. Numeric Data Formats
B. Digital Logic
C. Microprocessor Signal Description
D. Manufacturers' Addresses
E. Acronyms and Abbreviations
F. Answers to Selected Exercises

Appendix A   Numeric Data Formats

All the 32-bit microprocessors and associated math coprocessors considered in this textbook are capable of manipulating numbers encoded in unsigned integer, signed integer, floating-point, and binary coded decimal (BCD) binary formats. The representation of numbers in each of these formats is presented in this appendix.

Unsigned Integers

An unsigned decimal integer is encoded using any multiple of 8 bits, where each bit position represents an increasing power of two. In this format, the least significant bit position represents the value 2^0, the next higher bit represents the value 2^1, and so on. Figure A-1 shows both the powers of two and the values represented by each bit position. The individual powers of 2 are called weights. Determining the decimal value of any unsigned binary number simply requires summing the weights corresponding to the 1s in the binary number. For example, the decimal number represented by the binary sequence

   11001010

is found by adding the weights

   $128 + 64 + 8 + 2$

which equal

   202_{10}

Notice the largest decimal number that can be represented using 8 bits is 255_{10}. This is the sum of all the weights shown in Figure A-1 and represents the number $(2^8 - 1)$. For larger unsigned binary words, such as 16-bit and 32-bit unsigned numbers, the format used for an 8-bit binary number is simply extended. Figure A-2 shows the individual bit weights for an unsigned 16-bit binary word. Here

FIGURE A-1   8-Bit Unsigned Binary Integer Format

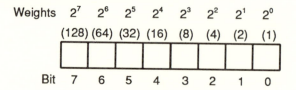

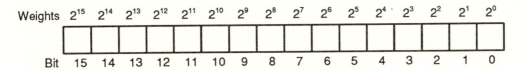

Weights 2^{15} 2^{14} 2^{13} 2^{12} 2^{11} 2^{10} 2^{9} 2^{8} 2^{7} 2^{6} 2^{5} 2^{4} 2^{3} 2^{2} 2^{1} 2^{0}

Bit   15   14   13   12   11   10   9   8   7   6   5   4   3   2   1   0

FIGURE A-2   16-Bit Unsigned Binary Integer Format

the highest weight, again corresponding to the most significant bit (MSB), is 32768 (2^{15}). The largest unsigned decimal number that can be represented using 16 binary bits is 65535 ($2^{16} - 1$). For a 32-bit word, the highest bit weight is 2,147,483,648 (2^{31}), and the largest unsigned decimal number that can be represented is 4,294,967,295 ($2^{32} - 1$).

Signed Integers

The most prevalent encoding of signed integers uses a weighted sign format, also referred to as a two's complement representation. In this format, the weights assigned to all bits are identical to the weights used for unsigned integers with one exception: the weight assigned to the MSB is the negative of the weight associated with the MSB of an equivalent length unsigned integer. Figure A-3 illustrates the weighted sign format for an 8-bit signed number.

As with unsigned binary numbers, determining the decimal value of a weighted sign binary number requires summing the weights corresponding to the 1s in the binary number. For example, the decimal number represented by the 8-bit weighted sign number

11001010

is found by adding the weights

$-128 + 64 + 8 + 2$

which equal

-54_{10}

For larger signed binary words, such as 16-bit and 32-bit signed numbers, the format used for an 8-bit binary number is simply extended. Figure A-4 shows

FIGURE A-3   8-Bit Signed Binary Integer Format

Weights -2^7 2^6 2^5 2^4 2^3 2^2 2^1 2^0

(−128) (64) (32) (16) (8) (4) (2) (1)

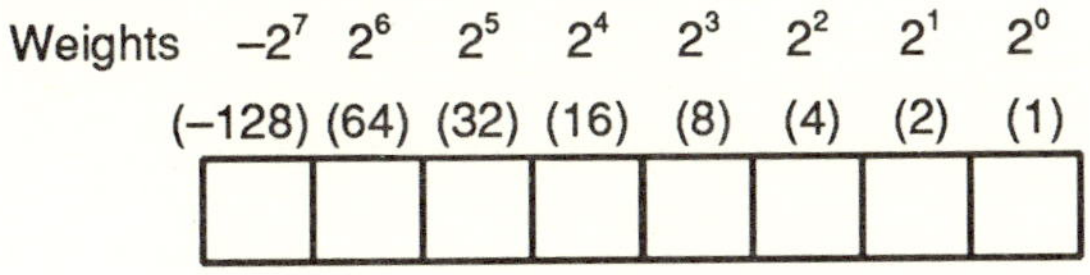

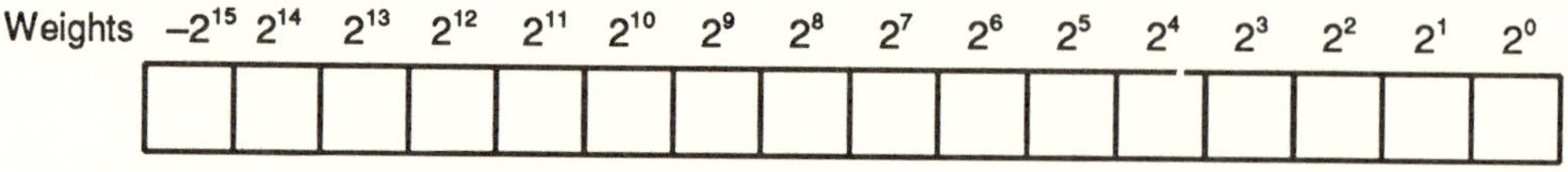

Weights	-2^{15}	2^{14}	2^{13}	2^{12}	2^{11}	2^{10}	2^{9}	2^{8}	2^{7}	2^{6}	2^{5}	2^{4}	2^{3}	2^{2}	2^{1}	2^{0}

FIGURE A-4 16-Bit Signed Binary Integer Format

the individual bit weights for an signed 16-bit binary word. Here the MSB weight is –32768. For a 32-bit word, the signed MSB weight is –2,147,483,648 (-2^{31}).

Notice the weighted sign format allows both positive and negative numbers to be represented. Any weighted sign number whose MSB is 0 always represents a positive (or zero) number because all of the remaining bits have positive weights. Similarly, since the magnitude of the negative weight assigned to the MSB is always one larger than the sum of all the remaining positive weights, any weighted sign binary number whose MSB is a 1 must represent a negative number.

The largest positive value that can be represented by an N bit two's complement number is ($2^{N-1} - 1$); the most negative number is -2^{N-1}. For example the most positive number that can be represented using an 8-bit two's complement format is +127 ($2^{7} - 1$); the most negative number is –128 (-2^{7}).

An interesting and useful feature of weighted sign numbers is that higher bit length representations of a number can be determined easily once a smaller bit length representation has been found. This is accomplished by extending the value of the MSB to the desired number of bits. For example, the 8-bit representation of the number –125 is 10000011 (–128 + 2 + 1). The 16-bit representation of –125 is determined easily by extending the MSB value eight places to the left, yielding 1111111110000011. Similarly, the 32-bit weighted sign representation of this number is also determined easily by further extending the MSB 16 more places to the left. Since the MSB determines the sign of the binary number, positive or negative, this operation is also referred to as sign extension. For positive numbers, sign extension is the same as adding leading zeros to the number.

It should be noted that although the term *two's complement representation* is widely used in microprocessor literature, this term is a misnomer. Two's complement is not a binary representation, but is a method for determining the weighted sign binary representation of negative numbers. The method involves determining the unsigned binary representation of the number's magnitude. This positive representation is then complemented, bit-by-bit, to yield its one's complement representation. Adding one to the one's complement number results in the final weighted signed representation.

Floating-Point Numbers

Noninteger numbers are referred to as floating-point numbers. Like their decimal counterparts that use a decimal point to separate the integer and fractional parts of a number, floating-point binary numbers use a binary point for the same purpose. Consider the binary number 1011.11. The digits to the left of the binary point (1011) represent the integer part of the number and the digits to the right of the binary point (11) represent the fractional part.

A code similar to decimal scientific notation is used when storing floating-point binary numbers. The number is separated into a mantissa and exponent. The following examples illustrate floating-point binary numbers expressed using this notation.

Binary Notation	Binary Scientific Notation
1010.	1.01 exp 11
−10001.	−1.0001 exp 100
.001101	1.101 exp −11
−.000101	−1.01 exp −100

In binary scientific notation, the term exp stands for exponent. The binary number preceding the exp term is the mantissa and the binary number following the exp term is the actual exponent value. Except for the number zero, the mantissa always has a single leading 1 followed immediately by its binary point. The exponent represents a power of 2 and indicates the number of places the binary point should be moved in the mantissa to obtain the conventional binary notation. If the exponent is positive, the binary point is moved to the right. If the exponent is negative, the binary point is moved to the left. For example, the exponent 11 in the number

1.01 exp 11

means move the binary point three places to the right, so that the number becomes 1010. The −11 exponent in the number

1.101 exp −11

means move the binary point three places to the left, so that the number becomes

.001101

In storing floating-point numbers, the sign, mantissa, and exponent are stored individually within separate fields.

Single-precision (32 bit), double-precision (64 bit), and extended-precision (80 bit) floating-point data formats are defined by IEEE Standard 754-1985 to have

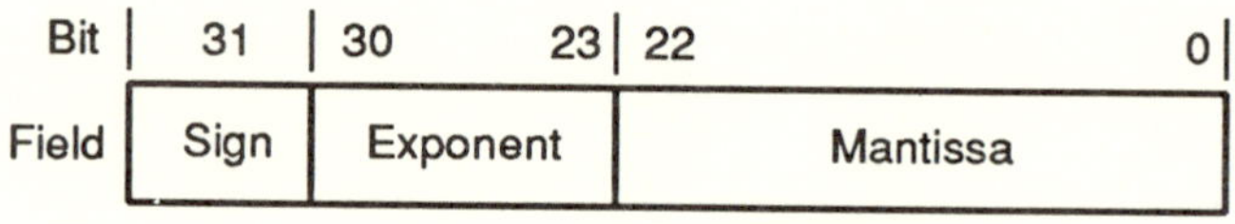

Bit	31	30	23	22	0
Field	Sign	Exponent		Mantissa	

FIGURE A-5 Single-Precision Floating-Point Data Format

the characteristics given in Table A-1. The format for a single-precision floating-point number is illustrated in Figure A-5.

TABLE A-1 IEEE Standard 754-1985 Floating-Point Specifications

Data Format	Sign Bits	Mantissa Bits	Exponent Bits
Single-Precision	1	23	8
Double-Precision	1	52	11
Extended-Precision	1	64	15

The sign bit shown in Figure A-5 refers to the sign of the mantissa. Unlike the signed integer format, the floating-point sign bit is not weighted. A sign bit of 1 represents a negative number; a zero represents a positive value. Since all mantissas, except for the number zero, have a leading 1 followed by their binary points, these two items are never stored explicitly. The binary point implicitly resides immediately to the left of mantissa bit 22, and a leading 1 is always assumed. The binary number zero is specified by setting all mantissa and exponent bits to 0. For this case, the implied leading mantissa bit is also zero.

The exponent field contains an exponent that is biased by 127. For example, an exponent of 5 would be stored using the binary equivalent of the number 132 (127 + 5). Using eight exponent bits, this is coded as 10000100. The addition of 127 to each exponent allows negative exponents to be coded within the exponent field without the need for an explicit exponent sign bit. For example, the exponent −11, which corresponds to −3, would be stored using the binary equivalent of +124 (127 − 3).

Figure A-6 illustrates the encoding of the decimal number −59.75 as a single-precision floating point number. The sign, exponent, and mantissa bits are determined as follows:

The binary equivalent of

$$-59.75_{10}$$

is

$$-111011.11$$

Sign	Exponent	Mantissa
1	10000100	11011110000000000000000

FIGURE A-6 Single-Precision Floating-Point Representation of -59.75_{10}

Expressed in binary scientific notation this becomes

   -1.1101111 exp 101

The minus sign is signified by setting the sign bit to 1. The mantissa's leading 1 and binary point are omitted and the mantissa field is encoded as

   11011110000000000000000

The exponent field encoding is obtained by adding the exponent value of 101 to 1111111, which is the binary equivalent of the 127_{10} bias value.

$$
\begin{array}{rcl}
1\,1\,1\,1\,1\,1\,1 & = & 127_{10} \\
+\,1\,0\,1 & = & +\,5_{10} \\
\hline
1\,0\,0\,0\,0\,1\,0\,0 & = & 132_{10}
\end{array}
$$

Binary Coded Decimal (BCD) Numbers

In binary coded decimal representation, each decimal digit is stored using the four-bit binary code given in Table A-2. Unpacked BCD numbers store one encoded BCD digit in the lower four bits of each byte, with the upper four bits generally zero-filled. For example, the decimal number 85 requires two bytes of storage and is coded as illustrated in Figure A-7.

TABLE A-2 BCD Number Equivalents

Decimal Digit	BCD Code
0	0000
1	0001
2	0010
3	0011
4	0100
5	0101
6	0110
7	0111
8	1000
9	1001

Zero Fill	8	Zero Fill	5
0000	1000	0000	0101

FIGURE A-7 The Storage of 85_{10} in Unpacked BCD Format

In packed BCD format each byte is used to store two BCD digits. In packed BCD representation, the number 85_{10} is encoded in a single byte as

10000101

The upper four bits contain the BCD code for the decimal digit 8 and the lower four bits contain the BCD code for the decimal digit 5. Larger decimal numbers would, of course, require more bytes of storage, with each two consecutive decimal digits packed into a single byte. Decimal numbers having an odd number of digits are encoded with the most significant digit unpacked.

Appendix B   Digital Logic

This appendix provides background information on the operation of the logic devices used in the interfacing examples in Part Three of this textbook. The fundamentals of switching algebra operation, truth table representation for logic functions, and the implementing of logic functions using AND, OR, and NOT logic gates are presented. Additionally, NAND and NOR functions are presented, along with equivalence-of-logic symbols resulting from the properties of complementation. Examples of two-level switching function implementation with one gate type, such as (NAND/NAND) are presented, along with logic function simplification with the aid of Karnaugh maps. The presentation of an exhaustive treatment of the underlying theory of switching algebra and minimization techniques is not intended; these subjects are treated comprehensively in many textbooks on logic design or digital circuits.

Two-level gate logic is used to illustrate the implementation of encoding and multiplexing functions. The use of single-level gating to provide decoding is detailed in Section 7.2 and, therefore, is not repeated.

The basic set-reset flip-flop, constructed with NAND or NOR gates, is used to provide the basis for understanding the concept of information storage in static type memory. Synchronization of flip-flops to an external clock is also discussed. Implementation of the latch and edge-triggered D-type flip-flop devices, used in several examples in Chapters 7 and 8, is illustrated. The flip-flop building block is then used to introduce shift register and counter structures.

Switching Algebra and Fundamental Gate Circuits

Switching algebra is an outgrowth of Boolean algebra, a body of mathematical theory developed long before the advent of switching circuits. In switching algebra, variables and functions are two-valued (logic 0 or logic 1) to conform to the binary number representation of digital signals. The framework of the algebra is embodied in the definitions of fundamental operations and rules of combination. For convenience, switching variables are denoted by a single letter such as X or Y. The text, of course, is replete with switching variables with all kinds of designations for address, data, and control lines such as A31, D3, $\overline{CE}$, $\overline{BHE}$. Thus, X and Y can represent an input or output signal from any physical device. The operations and rules of combination are presented in Table B-1.

Notice " = " means equality, so that either side can replace the other. For convenience

$$X \bullet Y$$

TABLE B-1 Switching Algebra Operations and Rules of Combination

Operation	Symbol	Example	Rules of Combination
AND	$\bullet$	$X \bullet Y$	$0 \bullet 0 = 0$ $0 \bullet 1 = 0$ $1 \bullet 0 = 0$ $1 \bullet 1 = 1$
OR	$+$	$X + Y$	$0 + 0 = 0$ $0 + 1 = 1$ $1 + 0 = 1$ $1 + 1 = 1$
NOT	$-$	$\overline{X}$	$\overline{0} = 1$ $\overline{1} = 0$

is written as

$$XY$$

without ambiguity. In the absence of parentheses, AND has precedence over OR for multiple operations. Therefore, an operation such as

$$X + (Y \bullet Z)$$

can be written as

$$X + YZ$$

This is analogous to the implied precedence of multiplication over addition in ordinary algebra. Also, NOT has the highest precedence. Therefore, an expression such as

$$\overline{X}Y + Z$$

performs the NOT operation first, AND second, and finally OR.

We see that the names of the operation derive from the condition for which the operation results in a value of 1. Thus,

- $X \bullet Y$ is 1 only if both X AND Y are 1s
- $X + Y$ is 1 if either X OR Y (or both) has value 1
- NOT X is 1 only if X is 0.

If these conditions are not met, the result of the operation is 0. Notice OR implies "inclusive" OR, as opposed to the "exclusive" OR operation which results in a 1 only if X or Y is 1, but not if both are 1s. The NOT operation is also referred to as "invert" or "complement," since the operation always produces the opposite value.

As in ordinary algebra, we can refer to a single or multiple operation as a function of the variables involved. Examples of functions are:

$$f1\ (X,Y) = X + \overline{Y}$$
$$f2\ (X,Y,Z) = (\overline{X} + Y)\ Z$$
$$f3\ (W,X,Y,Z) = W\ X + W\ \overline{Y}\ Z + \overline{W}\ \overline{X}\ Y\ \overline{Z}$$

Since each variable has a value of 0 or 1, and every operation results in one of those two values, it is clear that no matter how complex the function, its value is either 0 or 1 as well. Since individual variables with different names are assumed independent, there are 2^N different combinations of values for N variables. These combinations, along with the resulting value of the function for each combination, can be presented in a tabular form called a truth table. Examples of truth tables for the functions given above are shown in Table B-2. It is customary, though not necessary, to tabulate the variable values in ascending numerical order. The binary values range from all zeros to all ones. The equivalent decimal numbers, ranging from 0 to $(2^N - 1)$, are shown to the left of each table. You can verify the value of the function for each combination.

TABLE B-2 Truth Tables for Two, Three, and Four Variable Switching Functions

No.*	X	Y	f1	No.*	X	Y	Z	f2	No.*	W	X	Y	Z	f3
0	0	0	1	0	0	0	0	0	0	0	0	0	0	0
1	0	1	0	1	0	0	1	1	1	0	0	0	1	0
2	1	0	1	2	0	1	0	0	2	0	0	1	0	1
3	1	1	1	3	0	1	1	1	3	0	0	1	1	0
				4	1	0	0	0	4	0	1	0	0	0
				5	1	0	1	0	5	0	1	0	1	0
				6	1	1	0	0	6	0	1	1	0	0
				7	1	1	1	1	7	0	1	1	1	0
									8	1	0	0	0	0
									9	1	0	0	1	1
									10	1	0	1	0	0
									11	1	0	1	1	0
									12	1	1	0	0	1
									13	1	1	0	1	1
									14	1	1	1	0	1
									15	1	1	1	1	1

* Decimal number.

Notice the function

$$f1\ (X,Y)$$

can be read as

X OR (NOT Y)

which means f1 has a value of 1 if X is 1 or if NOT Y is 1, (X is 1 or Y is 0, or both). Likewise,

f2 (X,Y,Z) = [(NOT X) OR Y] AND Z

means f2 is 1 only if Z is 1 and either X is 0 or Y is 1. The function

f3 (W,X,Y,Z)

evaluates to 1 under any of the following conditions:

W = 1 AND X = 1
W = 1 AND Y = 0 AND Z = 1
W = 0 AND X = 0 AND Y = 1 AND Z = 0

From the truth table for f3, observe its value is 1 for 6 of the 16 combinations of binary values for the four variables. Since these logic functions have values that depend only on the particular combination of variables, and not upon time, they are called combinational functions (or combinatorial functions). In contrast, logic functions dependent on both current and previous values of logic variables (functions with the property of "memory") are called sequential functions. The difference will become clear when we introduce basic flip-flop circuits later.

The definitions and rules of combination for switching algebra can lead to a large number of algebraic rules or theorems. We will limit our discussion to a small number of rules that permit us to understand the techniques used to reduce or manipulate the form of switching functions. These techniques provide economy and flexibility in switching circuit design. The following rules can be shown to be valid for all cases:

1. $XY + XZ = X(Y + Z)$
2. $XY + X\overline{Y} = X$
3. $\overline{X + Y} = \overline{X}\,\overline{Y}$
4. $\overline{XY} = \overline{X} + \overline{Y}$

Rule 1 is the familiar associative law from ordinary algebra, which permits "factoring out" a common term. It can be reasoned that the condition

(X AND Y) OR (X AND Z)

produces the same results as

X AND (Y OR Z)

In either case, the result is 1 only if both X and Y are 1, both X and Z are 1, or if all three variables are 1.

Rule 2 forms the basis of logic simplification using a map technique, to be discussed shortly. Clearly,

(X AND Y) OR (X AND NOT Y)

is equivalent to " X regardless of Y" or just plain X. The result is the replacement of the switching function on the left side by a simpler one. Another way to view this rule is to notice that factoring permits writing it as

$$XY + X\overline{Y} = X(Y + \overline{Y})$$

The expression

X AND (Y OR NOT Y)

has the value 1 if X = 1 and either Y or $\overline{Y}$ has value 1. Since either Y or $\overline{Y}$ always has value 1 (they are complements), the expression can depend only on X.

Rules 3 and 4 are called complementation theorems, and serve to alter, rather that simplify, the form of a switching function. These are proven easily with the aid of Table B-3 which contains the truth tables for each operation. The corresponding expressions for rules 3 and 4 are identical for all possible values of X and Y.

TABLE B-3 Verification of Complementation Theorems

X	Y	X+Y	$\overline{X+Y}$	XY	$\overline{XY}$	$\overline{X}$	$\overline{Y}$	$\overline{X}\,\overline{Y}$	$\overline{X}+\overline{Y}$
0	0	0	1	0	1	1	1	1	1
0	1	1	0	0	1	1	0	0	1
1	0	1	0	0	1	0	1	0	1
1	1	1	0	1	0	0	0	0	0
Rule	→		↑ 3		↑ 4			↑ 3	↑ 4

Gates are digital circuits that perform a logic function according to the rules of switching algebra. Physically, the circuit distinguishes between two voltage levels. Using a convention known as positive logic, a relatively low voltage corresponds to a logic 0, and a higher voltage to a logic 1. Figure B-1 shows the standard logic gate symbols for AND, OR, and NOT circuits. The small circle at the output side of the inverter (NOT gate) denotes complementation. It is also common practice to place the circle at the input side; since the gate has a single input, there is no logical difference.

The NAND and NOR logic functions are contractions of NOT(AND) and NOT(OR). Therefore, the NAND is shown with the AND gate symbol with an inverted output; this of course is equivalent to the AND gate followed by a NOT gate (inverter). Likewise, NOR is OR followed by invert. The designer can get the equivalent of two logical operations with these gates, and their versatility makes them very popular.

Although the gates are shown with two inputs, all except the NOT gate can have more than two inputs. In general, the AND output is high (logic 1) and the NAND is low (logic 0) only when all inputs are high. On the other hand, the OR output is high if at least one input is high, while the NOR output is low for the same condition.

The complementation theorems, rules 3 and 4, lead to the logic gate equivalences shown in Figure B-2. The NAND and NOR equivalences implement the theorem directly. The AND and OR equivalences produce an inverted output from NAND and NOR, respectively. Notice the conversion of AND and OR also use the fact that NOT (NOT X) is the same as X, and likewise for Y.

The use of alternative symbols often conveys the intent of a gate more clearly. For example, if all the inputs and the output of an AND gate represent high-active enabling signals, the output can be viewed as being enabled only if all inputs are enabled. On the other hand, the examples presented in the interfacing chapters make it clear that far more device functions are enabled by a low-active signal than by a high-active one.

When dealing with the AND gate, the statement that the output is high only if all inputs are high is equivalent to saying that the output is low if at least one input is low. Thus, if the inputs and output represent low-active enables, the function is really an "ORing" of inputs. The equivalent symbol is therefore that of an OR, with both inputs and output inverted. The use of this symbol then reminds the designer that it is really an OR condition - active output if one or more inputs are active. Likewise the OR gate implements an AND condition when dealing with low-active signals. The same discussion applies to NAND and NOR gates as well, except that the outputs are inverted. Thus, a NAND gate "ANDs" high-active signals to produce a low-active output. Alternatively, it "ORs" low-active signals and yields a high-active output. NOR can be described in a similar way.

Combinational logic functions can be implemented directly from the algebraic form of the functions by cascading AND, OR, and NOT gates. Figure B-3 illustrates this for the three functions used in an earlier example. For convenience, the circuits were redrawn with the NOT gate symbol replaced by a small circle

Gate Symbols

Truth Tables

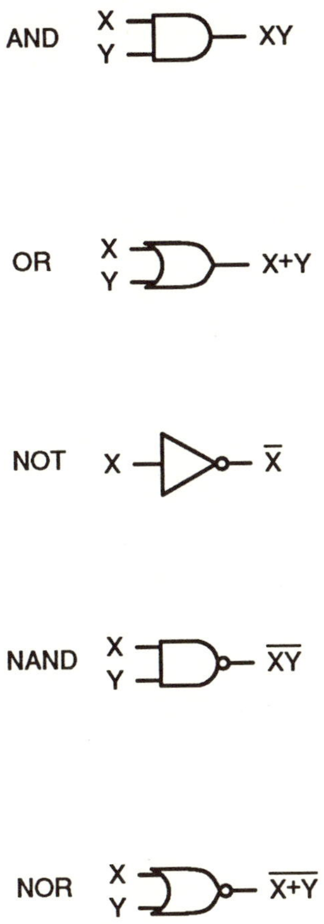

X	Y	XY
0	0	0
0	1	0
1	0	0
1	1	1

X	Y	X+Y
0	0	0
0	1	1
1	0	1
1	1	1

X	$\overline{X}$
0	1
1	0

X	Y	$\overline{XY}$
0	0	1
0	1	1
1	0	1
1	1	0

X	Y	$\overline{X+Y}$
0	0	1
0	1	0
1	0	0
1	1	0

FIGURE B-1   Basic Logic Gates

at the appropriate input to the AND or OR gate. This is common practice and has been used with logic diagrams shown in the interfacing chapters. The inverter may not actually be needed, since often both the true and complemented forms of a signal are available on separate lines.

The function f3 is an example of a form of a function called a sum of products (SOP). This name is derived from the ordinary algebraic interpretation of such a function. In terms of logic operations, the function is actually an ORing of AND terms. Ignoring the initial inversion of the input variables (W, X, Y, and Z), the function has been implemented with one level of AND gates whose outputs are tied to a second-level OR gate. The significance of such a two-level circuit is that no signal represented by a true or an inverted variable name passes through more than two gates before it reaches the output. Thus, the effect of any change in the

501

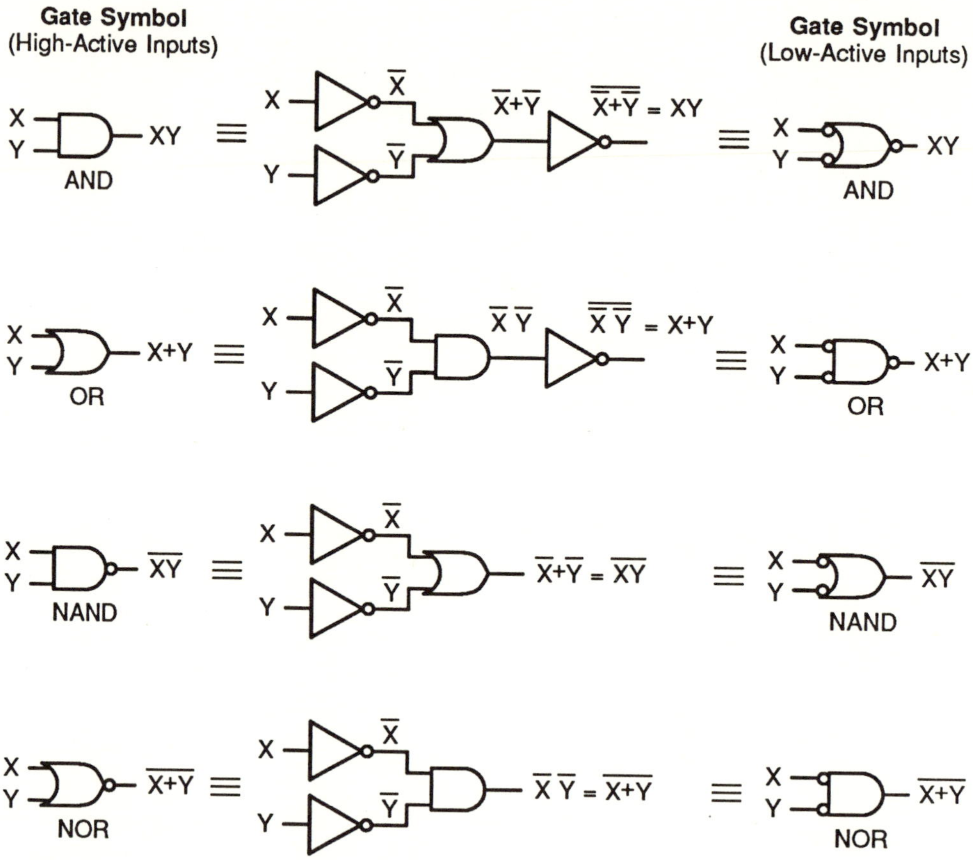

Gate Symbol
(High-Active Inputs)

Gate Symbol
(Low-Active Inputs)

FIGURE B-2 Logic Equivalence

value of a variable reaches the output in no more than the time equivalent to two gate delays.

To contrast this form of a function with a non-SOP form, note that the factoring rule of algebra permits us to rewrite f3 as:

$$f3 = WX + W\overline{Y}Z + \overline{W}\,\overline{X}YZ$$
$$f3 = W(X + \overline{Y}Z) + \overline{W}\,\overline{X}Y\overline{Z}$$

This form of f3 is implemented in Figure B-4. Although the algebraic description of the function may look more compact, the gate implementation is not necessarily "simpler." The net effect is that two 3-input gates have been replaced by three 2-input gates. More importantly, certain signals ($\overline{Y}$ and Z) must pass through four gates to reach the output. The maximum delay in the output's response to an input change is now double that for the two-level circuit implementation.

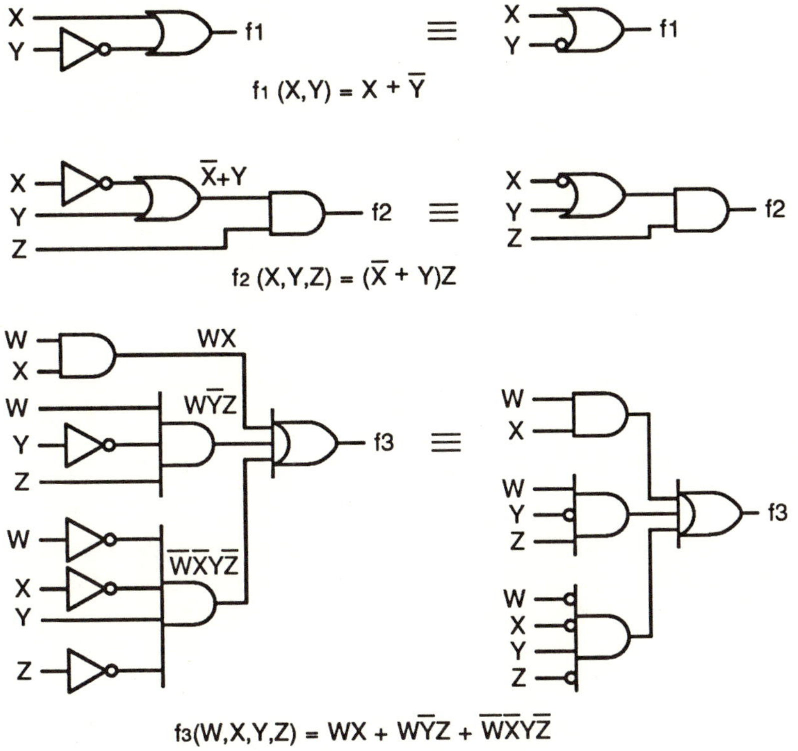

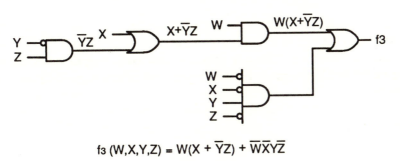

$$f_1 (X,Y) = X + \overline{Y}$$

$$f_2 (X,Y,Z) = (\overline{X} + Y)Z$$

$$f_3(W,X,Y,Z) = WX + W\overline{Y}Z + \overline{W}\overline{X}\overline{Y}\overline{Z}$$

FIGURE B-3 Gate Implementation Using AND/OR Logic

Figure B-5 illustrates the conversion of 2-level AND/OR logic to a single gate type (NAND in this case). The inverting of the outputs of the first level AND gates results in NAND gates (see Figure B-2), as does the inversion of the inputs to the second level OR gate. From a logical standpoint, double inversions on a single line cancel out (since the complement of $\overline{X}$ is X), and the function therefore has not been changed. The advantage of the conversion is that only one type of gate need be used. Since integrated circuit gate packages generally feature several gates of one type on a chip, overall package count is usually reduced in this way.

FIGURE B-4 Alternative Implementation Using a NonSOP Form of Function f3

$$f_3 (W,X,Y,Z) = W(X + \overline{Y}Z) + \overline{W}\overline{X}Y\overline{Z}$$

503

$$f_3 (W,X,Y,Z) = WX + W\overline{Y}Z + \overline{W}\overline{X}Y\overline{Z}$$

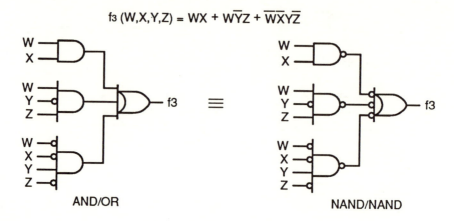

FIGURE B-5   Conversion of Two-Level AND/OR to NAND/NAND Logic

A NAND gate can even function as a NOT gate by using only one input and tying the other input(s) to +5 V (logic 1). If the inverted form of the variables are not available, they can be generated by NAND gates.

Use of Karnaugh Maps in Gate Logic Reduction

The truth table description of a switching function provides a starting point for reducing that function to a minimum two-level form. The function can be expressed in a standard SOP form from direct examination of the truth table. For example, referring to the function f1 shown in Table B-2, we can state:

f1 = 1	only if	X = 0	AND	Y = 0	
	OR	X = 1	AND	Y = 0	
	OR	X = 1	AND	Y = 1	

Written algebraically

$$f1 (X,Y) = \overline{X}\,\overline{Y} + X\overline{Y} + XY$$

Another notation for this expression is

$$f1 (X,Y) = \Sigma (0, 2, 3)$$

which expresses the fact that f1 has a value of 1 for any of the variable combinations corresponding to numbers 0, 2, and 3 in Table B-2. Since each truth table entry represents a condition on all the variables, each product term of the standard SOP form includes each variable in either true or complemented form.

In a similar fashion, the standard forms of the other two functions shown in

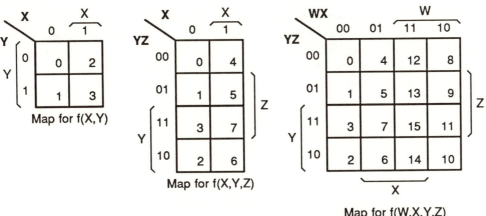

FIGURE B-6   Two, Three, and Four Variable Karnaugh Map Formats

Table B-2 can be expressed as:

$$f2\ (X,Y,Z) = \overline{X}\,\overline{Y}Z + \overline{X}YZ + XYZ$$
$$f2\ (X,Y,Z) = \Sigma\ (\ 1,\ 3,\ 7\ )$$

and

$$f3\ (W,X,Y,Z) = \overline{W}\,\overline{X}Y\overline{Z} + W\overline{X}\,\overline{Y}Z + WX\overline{Y}\,\overline{Z} + WX\overline{Y}Z + WXY\overline{Z} + WXYZ$$

$$f3\ (W,X,Y,Z) = \Sigma\ (\ 2,\ 9,\ 12,\ 13,\ 14,\ 15\ )$$

A Karnaugh map is actually a graphical version of a truth table. Figure B-6 shows the Karnaugh map formats for functions of 2, 3, and 4 variables. Like a truth table, the layout is somewhat arbitrary, but the nonascending numerical ordering used on the 3 and 4 variable maps (00, 01, 11, 10) has a purpose that will be discussed shortly. Each smaller square on the map identifies a combination of variables, as does a row of the truth table. The entry in a square is a 0 or a 1, depending on the value of the function for that combination. A third entry is possible, a "don't care" condition generally denoted by an "x" entry. Don't care means that the particular combination of variables is not important because it either does not occur or the function can take on either value if it does occur. Thus, the "x" entry denotes either 0 or 1.

As previously illustrated, each entry of 1 for the value of the function identifies a standard product term included in the standard SOP form. Likewise, a map square with an entry of 1 is associated with a standard product term. The objective of map simplification is to visually group standard terms together in an optimum manner so as to obtain a minimum set of reduced product terms.

We now illustrate the various ways that standard product terms may be combined to form reduced product terms. The groups are referred to as subcubes.

Note that the regions identified as W, X, Y, or Z around the edges of the maps of Figure B-6 denote those rows or columns corresponding to a value of 1 for that variable. Those rows and columns outside that region then correspond to the complemented variable. For example, on a 4-variable map, the second and third columns represent X and the first and fourth columns $\overline{X}$.

The nonascending ordering 00, 01, 11, 10 used on the maps results in the numbers identifying two adjacent squares (either horizontally or vertically) differing in only one bit position. Since this pattern is circular (10 and 00 also differ by one bit), squares at corresponding edges also must be considered adjacent. Thus, a map with four squares in a row or column must be visualized as wrapping around itself. As an example, for the 4- variable map format, square 0 is obviously adjacent to square 1 and to square 4. However, wrapping the map around both horizontally and vertically means that square 0 is also adjacent to squares 2 and 8. In binary, this means that 0000 is adjacent to 0001, 0010, 0100, and 1000. In each case the adjacent square's number differs in only one bit position from 0000.

Adjacent squares with entries of 1 can be grouped together as shown in Figure B-7. The two adjacent squares on the 2-variable map form a subcube of size 2, which lies entirely in the region $\overline{X}$ (outside of region X). The grouping of these two squares, individually representing $\overline{X}\,\overline{Y}$ and $\overline{X}Y$, is equivalent to the valid algebraic identity

$$\overline{X}\,\overline{Y} + \overline{X}Y = \overline{X}(\overline{Y} + Y) = \overline{X}$$

This is the simplification theorem 2 presented earlier with $\overline{X}$ used in place of X. The forming of the various sized subcubes shown in the figure is based on this same rule. For example, squares 2 and 10 of the 4-variable map combine to form

$$\overline{W}\,\overline{X}Y\overline{Z} + W\overline{X}Y\overline{Z} = \overline{X}Y\overline{Z}\,(\overline{W} + W) = \overline{X}Y\overline{Z}$$

For this example, we are reminded that the two squares are adjacent as a result of the wrap-around property of the map. You should be able to visualize the resulting subcube entirely inside $\overline{X}$ and Y and $\overline{Z}$, thus representing the term

$$\overline{X}Y\overline{Z}$$

Notice the subcube is neither inside W nor $\overline{W}$ (it crosses the boundary). This signifies that W is, in fact, the variable eliminated by grouping the two standard product terms. Regardless of the size of the map, the forming of a size 2 subcube results in the elimination of one variable from the standard product term.

The remaining examples in Figure B-7 illustrate larger-sized subcubes that can be formed. Size 4 subcubes are either shaped as a 2-by-2 square or as a 4-by-1 or 1-by-4 rectangle. As noted from the map examples, two variables are removed in each case. For example, consider that the subcube representing

$$\overline{W}X$$

on one of the 4-variable maps is a result of grouping squares 4, 5, 6, and 7 together. Since the vertical grouping crosses the boundaries of both the Y and Z regions, those two variables have been removed. Algebraically, we have

$$\overline{W}X\overline{Y}\,\overline{Z} + \overline{W}X\overline{Y}Z + \overline{W}XY\overline{Z} + \overline{W}XYZ$$
$$\quad\;\;(4) \qquad\quad (5) \qquad\quad (6) \qquad\quad (7)$$
$$= \overline{W}X(\overline{Y}\,\overline{Z} + \overline{Y}Z + Y\overline{Z} + YZ)$$
$$= \overline{W}X[\overline{Y}(\overline{Z} + Z) + Y(\overline{Z} + Z)]$$
$$= \overline{W}X(\overline{Y} + Y)(\overline{Z} + Z)$$

Again, since ORing a variable with its complement always results in a value of 1, both

$$\overline{Y} + Y \text{ and } \overline{Z} + Z$$

can be eliminated. The result is

$$\overline{W}X$$

as expected. Proper grouping of squares on the map, and identification of the region of the resulting subcubes, removes the need for this algebraic manipulation.

A size 8 subcube may appear on a 4-variable map as a 4-by-2 or 2-by-4 rectangle. This results in eliminating three of the four variables, leaving only one. You can verify the results of the two examples shown in Figure B-7.

To find a minimum SOP form for a combination function, subcubes must be formed in an optimum way. All the squares with 1s inserted must all be grouped in at least one subcube, and the resulting function is a logical ORing of all the product terms represented by the subcubes. We have seen that the larger the size of a subcube, the more variables are eliminated. The objective is to use as large subcubes as possible, but as few as possible, to cover all the squares with 1s.

Sometimes these objectives appear to conflict, as illustrated by the example in Figure B-8. The subcube composed of squares 1, 3, 5, and 7 is the largest on the map and so it is tempting to use it. However, notice each of those squares is also needed to form a maximum size group with another square (1 with 0, 3 with 11, 5 with 13, and 7 with 6). Since these four size 2 subcubes are sufficient to cover all the squares with 1s, the size 4 subcube would add an unnecessary term to the minimum SOP form.

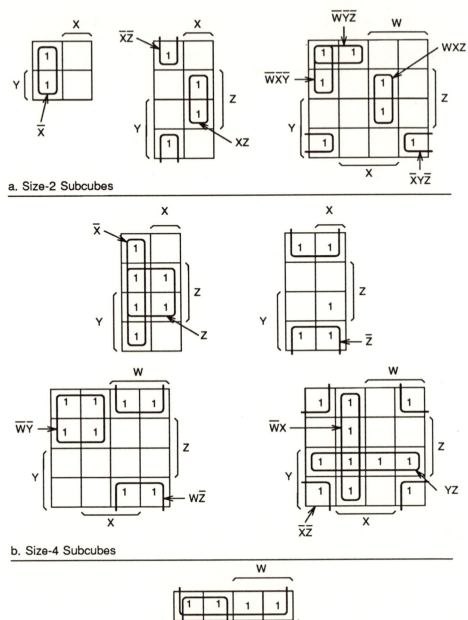

a. Size-2 Subcubes

b. Size-4 Subcubes

c. Size-8 Subcubes

FIGURE B-7 Examples of Map Subcubes

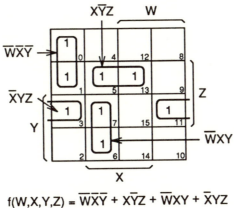

$$f(W,X,Y,Z) = \overline{W}\overline{X}\overline{Y} + X\overline{Y}Z + \overline{W}XY + \overline{X}YZ$$

Note: Subcube formed by squares 1,3,5,7 and representing $\overline{W}Z$ is not essential.

FIGURE B-8   Map Example with Nonessential Subcube

The minimum SOP form is desirable. It leads to implementing the function with a minimum 2-level gating circuit using only NAND type gates. Figure B-9 illustrates the implementation of the function

$$f (X, Y, Z) = \Sigma (0, 3, 4, 6)$$

with 2-level NAND/NAND logic. Notice the standard product term corresponding to 3 ($\overline{X}YZ$) is not adjacent to any other square on the map containing a 1; thus the standard term appears in the solution.

Figure B-10 shows an alternative approach to the design by working with the complement of the function instead of the function itself. That is, the conditions which result in $f = 0$ are the same as those for which $\overline{f} = 1$. By forming subcubes for the squares with 0s (in this case, squares 1, 2, 5, and 7), we form the minimum SOP of $\overline{f}$. An inverter is required to recomplement $\overline{f}$ to obtain f. This inverter of course adds delay, but in certain examples it may still reduce the overall circuit. However, for this example the minimum SOP form for $\overline{f}$ is no "simpler" than that for f. Actually the use of the complementary map can also lead to a 2-level implementation with NOR/NOR; the details of this are left for you to pursue.

In Figure B-11, a four-variable function has been minimized by forming subcubes of sizes 2, 4, and 8. The subcube of size 8 results in a product term with only one variable. Although a first level gate is not actually needed (since W enters the second level NAND), a double inversion is shown just to maintain the 2-level structure. Actually, in this situation, a buffer (a gate with no logic function) is often provided to keep the delays and current drive capability consistent with the rest of the circuit.

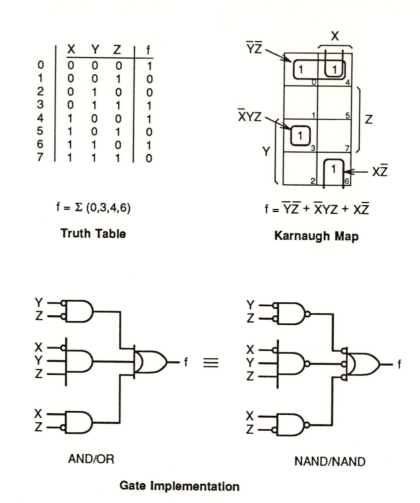

	X	Y	Z	f
0	0	0	0	1
1	0	0	1	0
2	0	1	0	0
3	0	1	1	1
4	1	0	0	1
5	1	0	1	0
6	1	1	0	1
7	1	1	1	0

$f = \Sigma\,(0,3,4,6)$

Truth Table

$f = \overline{Y}\overline{Z} + \overline{X}YZ + X\overline{Z}$

Karnaugh Map

AND/OR   NAND/NAND

Gate Implementation

FIGURE B-9 Two-Level Gate Design - Example 1

Simplification with maps which have don't care entries is illustrated by an example in Section 7.2. Figures 7-15 and 7-16 show the maps and the logic required to convert the INTEL 80386 CPU byte-enable inputs ($\overline{BE3}$-$\overline{BE0}$) to those signals required by a 16-bit data bus, such as MULTIBUS I bus (signals A1, A0, $\overline{BHE}$). The maps have several don't care entries which reflect the fact that certain combinations of byte enable are irrelevant (where no bytes or noncontiguous bytes would be transferred). Notice on the maps in Figure 7-15, that only the "x" squares which can be grouped with the 1s to form larger subcubes are covered. The remaining "x" squares are ignored (treated as squares with 0s and therefore not covered). Thus the proper use of don't care conditions can only help to further minimize a function, or at worst not add any terms or variables.

Although Karnaugh maps have been used for functions of five or six variables by placing four variable maps side by side (representing a third dimension), it

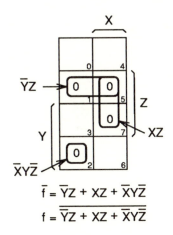

$$\bar{f} = \bar{Y}Z + XZ + \bar{X}Y\bar{Z}$$

$$f = \overline{\bar{Y}Z + XZ + \bar{X}Y\bar{Z}}$$

Karnaugh Map (Zero Squares Grouped)

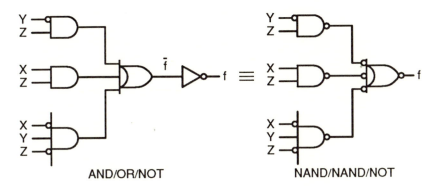

AND/OR/NOT   NAND/NAND/NOT

Gate Implementation

FIGURE B-10   Two-Level Gate Design - Example 2

becomes more difficult to visualize subcube patterns. Mapping is therefore a quick technique for simplifying functions of a very small number of variables. For larger numbers of variables, computer-aided minimization and other techniques involving use of special logic functions (adders, multiplexers, etc.) are used.

Examples of Logic Gate Implementation

A number of examples presented in the chapters on memory and I/O interfacing utilized standard decoding, encoding, or multiplexing devices. Although these logic functions have long been available on devices, it is instructive to show their implementation with fundamental logic gates. Examples such as these serve to enhance the understanding of the process of logic design with gates, and of the coding and multiplexing operations themselves.

The logic to implement decoding was discussed in Section 7.2, and is not repeated here. Figure 7-7 illustrates the gate implementation of 1-to-2, 2-to-4, and

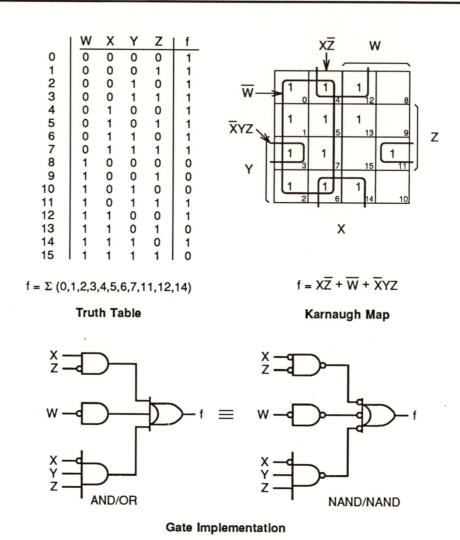

	W	X	Y	Z	f
0	0	0	0	0	1
1	0	0	0	1	1
2	0	0	1	0	1
3	0	0	1	1	1
4	0	1	0	0	1
5	0	1	0	1	1
6	0	1	1	0	1
7	0	1	1	1	1
8	1	0	0	0	0
9	1	0	0	1	0
10	1	0	1	0	0
11	1	0	1	1	1
12	1	1	0	0	1
13	1	1	0	1	0
14	1	1	1	0	1
15	1	1	1	1	0

$f = \Sigma\,(0,1,2,3,4,5,6,7,11,12,14)$

Truth Table

$f = X\overline{Z} + \overline{W} + \overline{X}YZ$

Karnaugh Map

Gate Implementation

FIGURE B-11   Two-Level Gate Design - Example 3

3-to-8 size decoders with an enable input. A single-level NAND circuit provides low-active outputs for all combinations of input variable values. The function would, of course, be AND if the outputs were to be high active (the selected line is high, and all other lines remain low).

Figure B-12 shows the implementation of a multiplexer (MUX) which selects one of several data lines and outputs its value (a parallel to serial converter). In general, there are N select bits for 2^N data lines. The derivation of gate logic is shown for N = 1 and N = 2. For each case, a modified truth table, referred to as a logic table, describes which data input appears at the output for each select combination. The logic equation and gate circuit follow from the table. Clearly, any size multiplexer can be implemented with two level AND/OR (or equivalent

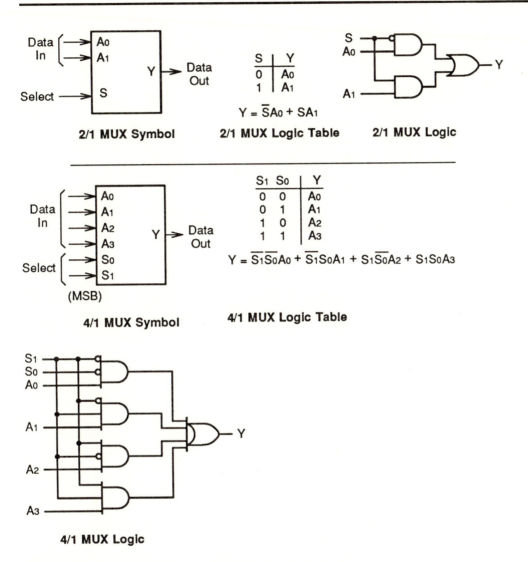

FIGURE B-12   Multiplexer Logic Design Example With Gates

NAND/NAND) logic. The 74157 multiplexer, used in examples in the text, consists of four 2-to-1 multiplexer circuits with a common enable input. Sizes of 4-to-1, 8-to-1, and 16-to-1 are also available in the TTL logic family.

Figure B-13 illustrates the gate design of a priority encoder circuit where 2^N inputs, one of which is active (high) at a time, are encoded into an N-bit number. As for the multiplexer examples, gate logic is shown for N = 1 and N = 2 (2-to-1 and 4- to-2 encoder sizes). The outputs are all low for the case where the encoder is enabled and only input Y0 is active, since Y0 encodes into all 0s. Notice the outputs also are all low for the cases where the enable is inactive (low) and no decoded input line is active. An actual encoder chip, such as the 74148 8-to-3 line priority encoder, has additional cascade outputs that allow it to distinguish between the disabled, no active decoded input, and lowest priority line active cases. A block diagram and logic table for the 74148 are shown in Figure 8-11, which includes the cascade signals E0 and GS.

If more than one decoded input is active at a time, the encoder selects the higher numbered one; thus it is called a priority encoder. For example, the output of the 4-to-2 encoder is binary 10 (decimal 2) if Y2 is active, as long as Y3 is inactive. It does not matter whether Y1 or Y0 is active, since Y2 has a higher priority than either. The logic equations and resulting gate implementation for the examples shown are derived from the table, making optimum use of don't care entries. Notice the logic for the encoded outputs appears to be independent of the lowest priority input, Y0. However, if the cascade output signals were provided (as for the 74148), Y0 would be used. This is left for you to pursue.

Basic Flip-Flop Circuits

A flip-flop, the fundamental building block of static memory, is able to store a bit value indefinitely. Figure B-14 shows how two gates can be configured to provide this capability. The bit value is read out at the Q output, with a complementary output $\overline{Q}$ also being available. The bit value is controlled by writing to the R and S input lines. R corresponds to writing a zero (reset state) and S to writing a one (set state).

When NOR gates are cross-coupled as shown, a logic 1 (high) written to the appropriate line places the device in the desired state. This is evident from the fact that the NOR gate outputs a 0 if either input is 1. Thus, R = 1 results in Q = 0 (the reset state). If S = 0, then both inputs to the lower NOR gate are 0 and the output $\overline{Q} = 1$, as expected. Since the circuit is clearly symmetrical, the condition S = 1 and R = 0 produces the opposite result. In this case Q = 1, $\overline{Q}$ = 0, and the device is set.

The key to recognizing the memory property of the circuit is that the NOR gate with the active (high) input has two 1s entering it, and the other NOR inputs two 0s. Removing the active high input (changing it from 1 to 0) does not affect either output since the second input to that gate remains high. The output of that NOR gate then remains low, and the flip-flop state has not changed. Thus, the case R = 0 and S = 0 can result in either the reset or set state, depending on its previous state (when either R or S was 1). This ability of the circuit to "remember" and hold its previous state gives it the property of memory. In contrast, the class of combinational circuits discussed previously always produce the same output(s) for a given input condition, independent of the previous history of input changes.

It should be evident that activating both R and S at the same time (R = 1 and S = 1) leads to an undesired result. A 1 to an input of both NOR gates results in both outputs being 0. Since Q and $\overline{Q}$ are no longer complementary, the state of the flip-flop is indeterminate. Due to this limitation, the RS flip-flop is not widely used; rather, a more versatile JK device is preferred. The JK circuit, not discussed here because of its relative complexity, permits the flip-flop to be set or reset by

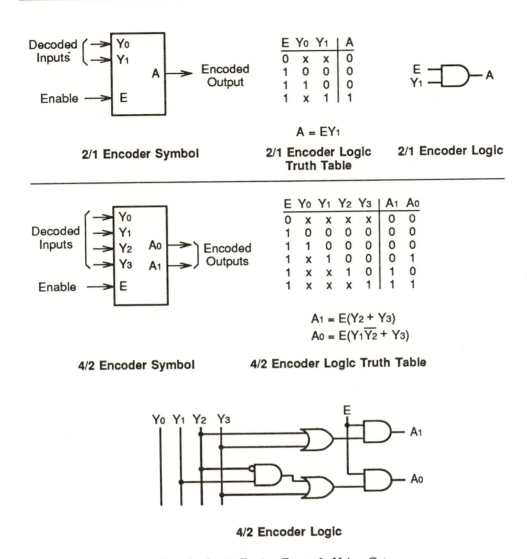

Decoded Inputs
Enable → E

A → Encoded Output

E	Yo	Y1	A
0	x	x	0
1	0	0	0
1	1	0	0
1	x	1	1

$$A = EY_1$$

E
Y1 —— A

2/1 Encoder Symbol

2/1 Encoder Logic Truth Table

2/1 Encoder Logic

Decoded Inputs
Enable → E

Ao → Encoded Outputs
A1 →

E	Yo	Y1	Y2	Y3	A1	Ao
0	x	x	x	x	0	0
1	0	0	0	0	0	0
1	1	0	0	0	0	0
1	x	1	0	0	0	1
1	x	x	1	0	1	0
1	x	x	x	1	1	1

$$A_1 = E(Y_2 + Y_3)$$
$$A_0 = E(Y_1\overline{Y_2} + Y_3)$$

4/2 Encoder Symbol

4/2 Encoder Logic Truth Table

Yo Y1 Y2 Y3   E

A1

Ao

4/2 Encoder Logic

FIGURE B-13   Priority Encoder Logic Design Example Using Gates

the individual inputs (as for the RS type). However, activating both inputs simultaneously causes the flip-flop to be complemented. This property of inverting or "toggling" the state is a very useful one in designing counters, and will be discussed further.

Figure B-14 also illustrates the use of an alternative RS flip-flop implementation using cross-coupled NAND gates. Using the alternative NAND symbol (invert, then OR) and double complementing the outputs as shown, it is noted that the circuit is nearly identical to the NOR gate type. The only difference is that the R and S inputs are inverted first. This device will either set or reset on a logic 0 (low) rather than on a logic 1 (high). This flip-flop is therefore referred to as a low-active RS type. Like the first device, it holds its previous state when both

515

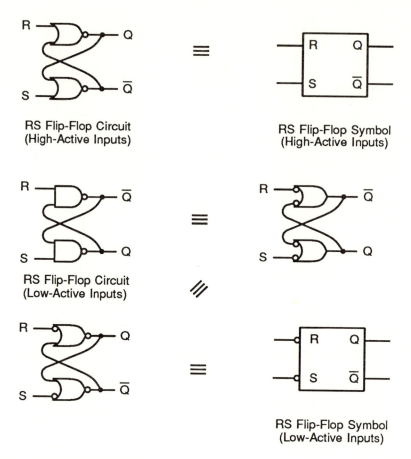

RS Flip-Flop Circuit
(High-Active Inputs)

RS Flip-Flop Symbol
(High-Active Inputs)

RS Flip-Flop Circuit
(Low-Active Inputs)

RS Flip-Flop Symbol
(Low-Active Inputs)

FIGURE B-14 RS Flip-Flop Circuits

inputs are inactive (high), and does not permit both inputs to be asserted (low) at the same time.

Figure B-15 shows the difference in the response of the high-active and low-active devices. In both cases the flip-flop is first placed into the set state (Q = 1) from an unknown initial state by asserting S, and then the reset state (Q = 0) by asserting R. For the high-active device, the activating signal is brought from low to high, and then low again. For the low-active device, the transition is high to low to high. The current state is held when both inputs are deactive. In addition, R is not asserted until after S is deactivated, thus avoiding the forbidden condition where both inputs are active at the same time.

In any digital system it is advantageous to have all flip-flops respond to input changes at the same time (synchronously). This is particularly true for devices such as shift registers, where flip-flop inputs are tied to the outputs of other flip-flops. The use of a separate synchronizing clock signal is therefore prevalent. The clock signal is generally a symmetrical sequence of high and low voltages

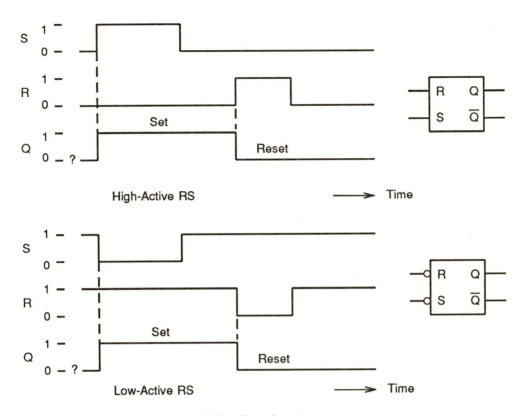

FIGURE B-15 Waveforms for RS Flip-Flop Circuits

(alternating 1s and 0s) at a particular repetition rate, or frequency. The first circuit of Figure B-16 shows conceptually how a clock input (CK) can be added to a high-active RS flip-flop. By logically ANDing both the external R and S inputs to CK, the clock input must be active (high) for any state transition to occur. For CK low, the flip-flop's R and S inputs are both low, and the current state is held. When CK is high, the external R and S inputs enter the flip-flop's respective inputs, and normal set-reset operation occurs.

The first waveform of Figure B-17 shows how the clock signal controls the state change. The sequence is S active followed by R active, as was used previously. The difference here is that the output Q does not change until the clock input is high. Thus, the state change is synchronized to the clock rather than to the R and S inputs. Some flip-flops invert the clock signal, in which case a low rather than high clock input is required for the device to perform its function. For these devices, the symbol includes a small circle at the clock input (analogous to the inversion symbols for the low-active RS flip-flop using NAND gates).

The remaining diagrams in Figure B-16 introduce two important concepts - the implementation of a D-type storage flip-flop, and the difference between a level-sensitive and an edge-triggered flip-flop. As shown, one type of D flip-flop can be implemented with a clocked RS and an inverter. The single input called D is applied to the set input and its complement to the reset input. As a result, one of the inputs is always asserted while the other is negated (deactive). Upon an active (high) clock, D = 1 results in Q = 1 (set) and D = 0 causes Q = 0 (reset). The device therefore stores the D input that is present when CK goes high and holds (latches) its value when CK is brought low.

A latch is suitable for many applications, but in some situations, such as shift registers, it is necessary to hold the D input value that is present when the clock is asserted, even if the input changes while the clock remains active. The simple latch circuit shown is not capable of this because basically it is a level-sensitive device. That is, the flip-flop responds to its D input and outputs its value on Q as long as CK is high. The last circuit in Figure B-16 implements a D flip-flop which transfers the D input to the Q output only at the time CK goes from low to high. That value is then held until the next low-to-high transition of CK, whereupon Q takes on the value of D at that time. Since the transition is "triggered" only by the positive going direction of the clock (low to high), the device is called a positive edge-triggered flip-flop.

The second set of waveforms in Figure B-17 illustrate the difference between the latch and edge-triggered type of D flip-flop. The response differs during those clock phases where D changes while CK is high (time periods 1, 4, and 5). The latch output follows the changes in D and holds the last value of D prior to CK going low. In contrast, the edge-triggered device ignores changes that occur while CK is high; changes in Q take place only at the positive edge of each clock, the value being held until the next positive edge. It is left for you to verify this waveform for the edge-triggered circuit implementation shown in Figure B- 16.

Flip-flops often have other features such as direct clear (reset) or direct preset (set). These inputs override all other inputs, including CK, and permit the device to be asynchronously reset or set. These features are useful for placing the flip-flop in an initial state such as to reset it before the sequence of input changes commences. The circuit implementation of direct clear and preset is a subject for you to pursue.

Examples of Flip-Flop Implementation

Since a flip-flop stores a single bit value, an M-bit register consists of M flip-flops. If clocked flip-flops are used, the clock inputs are generally tied together to the external clock source. For D-type flip-flops, the data can be synchronously read on the Q outputs or written to via the D inputs. If direct clear (or preset) is provided, these lines are generally tied together to an external signal permitting the value in the register to be initialized (for example, to all 0s).

Special functions can be implemented if the inputs to certain flip-flops are provided by the outputs of others, rather than by external inputs. Shift registers and counters are examples of such functions, the concepts of which can be easily demonstrated. Figure B-18 shows the cascading of D flip-flops to implement a

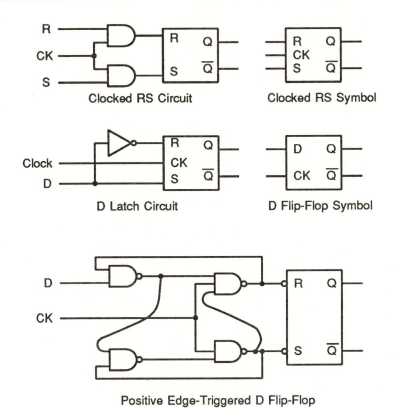

Positive Edge-Triggered D Flip-Flop

FIGURE B-16 Clocking and D Flip-Flop Circuits

simple serial-in, parallel-out shift register. Although only a 3-bit register is shown, the structure can be extended to any length; the only practical problem is delay in storage of a long sequence. The sequence of inputs for this example (110) is stored as Q1 each time the clock is active, with the previous Q1 shifting right to Q2, and the previous Q2 to Q3. After three clock pulses, the serial data has entered and the 3-bits (110) are available as parallel outputs Q3, Q2, and Q1, respectively. It is assumed that the shift register initially contains 000, as a result of initialization via direct clear (or by other means).

As stated earlier, an edge-triggered rather than a latching type flip-flop must be used to implement a shift register. It should now be evident why. If latches were used, each bit shifted into a flip-flop would be immediately shifted to the one on its right. This occurs because the latch's output responds to changes at its input as long as its clock input is active. As a result of unequal circuit delays, it is inevitable that bits would be lost in this case (bit shifted in before previous value has been shifted out). The edge-triggered device ensures that there is only one transition per clock cycle. Since there is gate delay before each flip-flop's Q output responds to its D-input, the new value of Q is not available until after the

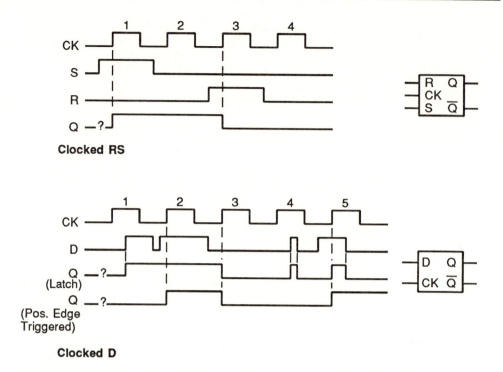

Clocked RS

Clocked D

FIGURE B-17 Waveforms for Clocked Flip-Flop Circuits

positive clock edge has occurred. This bit value is therefore ignored by the next flip-flop until the positive edge of the next clock pulse.

In contrast to registers that store data values provided to their inputs, counters keep track of the number of pulses presented on a single input line ("count" them). Most counters are either up-counters or down-counters, in that each succeeding input results in incrementing or decrementing the count by 1. For an up-counter, whenever 1 is added to a number stored, the least significant bit is always complemented. Subsequent bits are then complemented if a carry bit is generated in the previous position. This type of algorithm lends itself to a storage device which complements or "toggles" its value for each new input.

Figure B-19 shows how an edge-triggered D flip-flop can be used as a toggling device, or T flip-flop. By connecting the complementary output $\overline{Q}$ back to D and applying the input to CK, the D input and flip-flop state Q are complementary. Each positive edge of the input pulse then clocks the device, and the next state is the complement of the current state. In comparing the output waveform Q to the input waveform D, we see that Q toggles on every positive edge of the input but remains constant at the negative edge. Thus, Q is a signal at half the repetition rate, or frequency, of the input. Each value of Q also can be viewed as being equal to the previous value incremented by 1 (or decremented by 1 for that matter), no carry being generated. The toggle flip-flop is therefore referred to as a divide-by-2 circuit, or alternatively as a modulo-2 counter. Notice again,

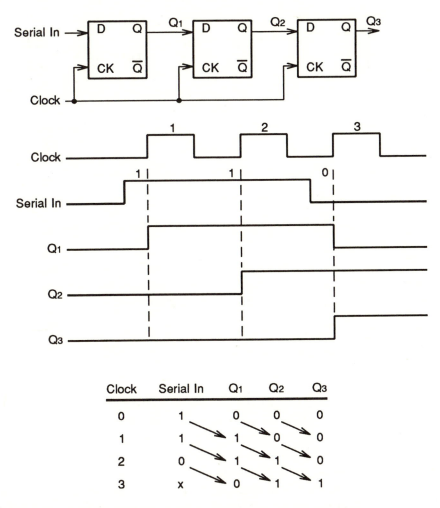

Clock	Serial In	Q1	Q2	Q3
0	1	0	0	0
1	1	1	0	0
2	0	1	1	0
3	x	0	1	1

FIGURE B-18 3-Bit Shift Register Using Edge-Triggered D Flip-Flops

edge-triggered rather than latching devices must be used to avoid toggling more than once per clock phase.

When M toggle flip-flops are cascaded, the result is a divide by 2^M circuit, or a modulo 2^M counter. Figure B-20 illustrates this circuit for $M = 3$. To achieve an upward count, each bit must be incremented by 1 when a carry is generated by the previous addition. This means complementing the lowest order bit on every input, and complementing the remaining bits on a 1 to 0 transition of the corresponding next lower order bit. Since each flip-flop toggles on a 0 to 1 transition of its T input, the inverted value of the lower order bit must be used. Therefore, in each case the $\overline{Q}$ output provides the T input of the next higher order bit. Q1 toggles each time the input goes from 0 to 1, Q2 toggles for Q1 going from 1 to 0, and Q3 toggles on the 1 to 0 transition for Q2. The number stored as Q3,Q2,Q1 reflects the number of inputs from the last time the count was reset

521

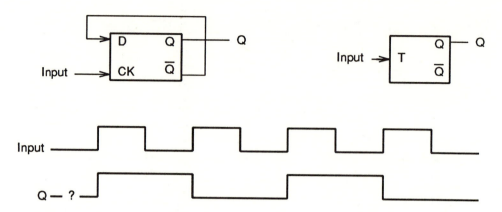

FIGURE B-19   Toggle Flip-Flop Using Positive Edge-Triggered D-Type

to 000; after eight successive input pulses (2^M in general), the count repeats itself. Also note that each succeeding flip-flop divides the previous output frequency by 2. Thus, if the input frequency is given by f

Q1 frequency = f / 2
Q2 frequency = f / 4
Q3 frequency = f / 8

One disadvantage of the cascade approach shown is that the clocking is basically asynchronous rather than synchronous, since each flip-flop is clocked after the previous one has changed state. This can lead to significant delay times for large counts. These counters are often referred to as ripple counters, as the count, in effect, "ripples" through one stage at a time.

Divide by N counters, where N is not necessarily a power of 2, are used in many applications. For example, the interface between the INTEL 80386 CPU and INTEL 8251 USART (see Figure 8-34) features divide-by-10 and divide-by-13 counters. The factor of 10 was arbitrarily chosen to reduce the CPU clock frequency to a value within the range of allowable USART rates; the factor of 13 provides additional reduction to match the transmit and receive baud rate requirements. The TTL-series of devices features relatively simple up-counters which divide by factors of 10, 12, and 16. These devices (the 7490, 7492, and 7493, respectively) can be wired easily to divide by half of their maximum value since they cascade a single toggle flip-flop (divide by 2) to the remaining counter stages.

One approach to implementing divide-by-N counters is to use the divide-by-2^M ripple structure shown with flip-flops having a direct clear provision, and provide a gate to logically AND the appropriate Q and $\overline{Q}$ outputs. The output of this gate can be used to directly clear all flip-flops, thus resetting the counter prematurely to all 0s. The 7490 and its companion counters can be used in this fashion. Thus, the divide-by-13 required by the USART interface example can be implemented with a 7493, which is capable of dividing by up to 16. Alternatively,

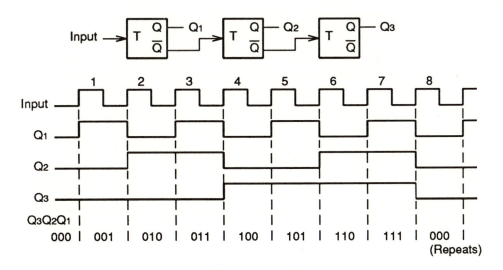

FIGURE B-20   3-Bit Up Counter Using Toggle Flip-Flops

there is a structured approach to designing synchronous counters which are inherently faster and can implement any arbitrary sequence of states. The disadvantage is that more external gating is required than for the ripple counters, and the simplification of gating requires use of Karnaugh maps or an equivalent technique. The subject of divide-by-N counter design is an extensive one. If you are interested in the details, consult a textbook on logic design.

Appendix C Microprocessor Signal Descriptions

This appendix contains functional signal diagrams and signal descriptions for the INTEL 80386 CPU, the AT&T *WE* 32100/32200 CPU, and the MOTOROLA MC68020 CPU. The signals are grouped functionally.

INTEL 80386 Microprocessor Signal Descriptions

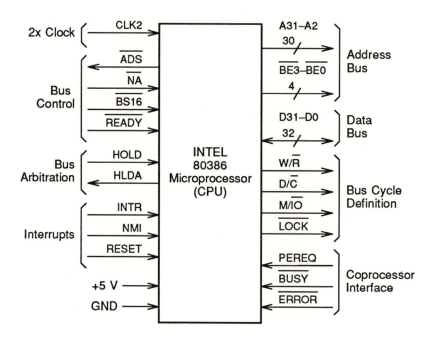

INTEL 80386 Microprocessor Functional Signal Groups

TABLE C-1 INTEL 80386 Microprocessor Signal Descriptions

Designation (Name)	Direction	Description
Data Bus		
D31–D0 (Data)	Input/ Output	Bidirectional data lines.

TABLE C-1 INTEL 80386 Microprocessor Signal Descriptions (Continued)

Designation (Name)	Direction	Description
Address Bus		
A31–A2 (Address)	Output	Provide memory or I/O port addresses.
$\overline{BE3}$–$\overline{BE0}$ (Byte Enables)	Output	Indicates transferred bytes of 32-bit data bus.

Enable	Byte Transferred
$\overline{BE3}$	D31–D24
$\overline{BE2}$	D23–D16
$\overline{BE1}$	D15–D8
$\overline{BE0}$	D7–D0

Designation (Name)	Direction	Description
Bus Cycle Definition		
W/$\overline{R}$ (Write/Read)	Output	Distinguishes between read and write cycles.
D/$\overline{C}$ (Data/Control)	Output	Distinguishes between data and control cycles.
M/$\overline{IO}$ (Memory/IO)	Output	Distinguishes between memory and input/output cycles.
$\overline{LOCK}$ (Lock)	Output	Distinguishes between locked and unlocked bus cycles.
Bus Control		
$\overline{ADS}$ (Address Status)	Output	Indicates valid address and bus cycle definition signals. Asserted during T1 and T2P bus states.
$\overline{NA}$ (Next Address Request)	Input	Requests address pipelining when system can accept new address and bus cycle definition signals, before end of current cycle.
$\overline{BS16}$ (Bus Size 16)	Input	Allows connection to both 32-bit and 16-bit data buses. When asserted, only lower half of data bus (D15–D0) is used.
$\overline{READY}$ (Transfer Acknowledge)	Input	Indicates completion of current bus cycle and acceptance (for read) or provision of data (for write).
Bus Arbitration		
HOLD (Bus Hold Request)	Input	Indicates device other than 80386 CPU requires bus mastership. Remains asserted while another device is a local bus master.
HLDA (Bus Hold Acknowledge)	Output	Indicates 80386 CPU has relinquished control of local bus in response to assertion of HOLD.

TABLE C-1 INTEL 80386 Microprocessor Signal Descriptions

Designation (Name)	Direction	Description
Interrupts		
INTR (Maskable Interrupt Request)	Input	Interrupt request that can be masked by interrupt flag (IF) bit. If accepted, two interrupt acknowledge bus cycles occur, after which the 8-bit interrupt vector on D7–D0 is latched to identify the interrupt source.
NMI (Nonmaskable Interrupt Request)	Input	Interrupt request that cannot be masked by software. Pointer to interrupt routine is Vector 2 of 80386 interrupt vector table. No acknowledge cycles occur.
RESET (Reset)	Input	Places processor in known state with instruction execution starting at hex physical address FFFFFFF0. Reset has priority over all other inputs.
Coprocessor Interface		
PEREQ (Coprocessor Request)	Input	Indicates coprocessor request to 80386 CPU for data operand transfer between memory and coprocessor.
$\overline{BUSY}$ (Coprocessor Busy)	Input	Indicates coprocessor is still executing an instruction and cannot accept another.
$\overline{ERROR}$ (Coprocessor Error)	Input	Indicates type of error caused by coprocessor instruction that is not masked by coprocessor's control register. If asserted, the 80386 CPU generates exception 16 to access an error handler.

AT&T *WE* 32100/32200 Microprocessor Signal Descriptions

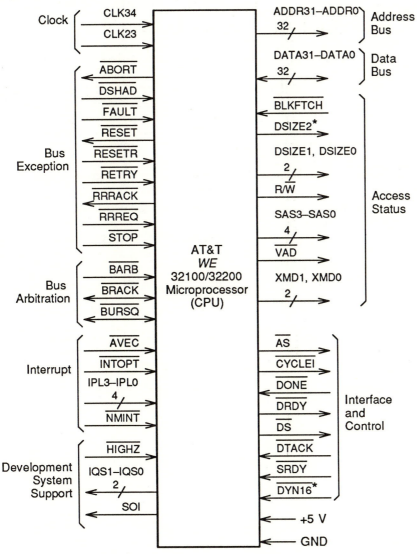

WE 32200 Microprocessor Signal Only.

AT&T *WE* 32100/32200 Microprocessor Functional Signal Groups

TABLE C-2 AT&T *WE* 32100/32200 Microprocessor Signal Descriptions

Designation (Name)	Direction	Description
Data Bus		
DATA31–DATA0 (Data)	Input/ Output	Bidirectional data lines.
Address Bus		
ADDR31–ADDR0 (Address)	Output	Provides memory addresses or addresses of memory-mapped I/O ports. ADDR6–ADDR2 indicates interrupt acknowledge level during an interrupt acknowledge operation.
Access Status		
$\overline{\text{BLKFTCH}}$ (Block Fetch)	Input	Indicates memory is designed to handle a double-word (64 bit) block fetch.
DSIZE2–DSIZE0 (Data Size) (*WE* 32200 CPU Only)	Output	Indicates data size for current bus transaction.

DSIZE2	DSIZE1	DSIZE0	Transaction Size
0	0	0	Three-byte (24 bits)
0	0	1	Zero-byte (probe)
0	1	0	Reserved
0	1	1	Reserved
1	0	0	Word (32 bits)
1	0	1	Double-word (64 bits)
1	1	0	Halfword (16 bits)
1	1	1	Byte (8 bits)

Designation (Name)	Direction	Description
R/$\overline{\text{W}}$ (Read/Write)	Output	Distinguishes between read and write cycles.
SAS3–SAS0 (Access Status Code)	Output	Identifies type of bus cycle.

SAS3	SAS2	SAS1	SAS0	Bus Cycle Type
0	0	0	0	Move translated word
0	0	0	1	Coprocessor data write
0	0	1	0	Autovector interrupt acknowledge
0	0	1	1	Coprocessor data fetch
0	1	0	0	Stop acknowledge
0	1	0	1	Coprocessor broadcast
0	1	1	0	Coprocessor status fetch
0	1	1	1	Read interlocked
1	0	0	0	Address fetch
1	0	0	1	Operand fetch
1	0	1	0	Write
1	0	1	1	Interrupt acknowledge
1	1	0	0	Instruction fetch after PC discontinuity
1	1	0	1	Instruction prefetch
1	1	1	0	Instruction fetch
1	1	1	1	No operation

TABLE C-2 AT&T *WE* 32100/32200 Microprocessor Signal Descriptions (Continued)

Designation (Name)	Direction	Description
Access Status		

DSIZE1–DSIZE0 (Data Size) (*WE* 32100 CPU Only)	Output	Indicates data size for current bus transaction.
		
		DSIZE1 DSIZE0 Transaction Size
		  0 0 Word (32 bits)
		  0 1 Double-word (64 bits)
		  1 0 Halfword (16 bits)
		  1 1 Byte (8 bits)

$\overline{\text{VAD}}$ (Virtual Address)	Output	Indicates whether address bus contains virtual or physical address.

XMD1–XMD0 (Execution Mode)	Output	Indicates current processor execution mode.
		
		XMD1 XMD0 Mode
		  0 0 Kernel
		  0 1 Execution
		  1 0 Supervisor
		  1 1 User

Interface and Control		
$\overline{\text{AS}}$ (Address Strobe)	Output	Indicates valid physical address on address bus.
$\overline{\text{CYCLEI}}$ (Cycle Initiate)	Output	Indicates start of bus transaction to external devices.
$\overline{\text{DONE}}$ (Coprocessor Done)	Input	Indicates completion of coprocessor operation.
$\overline{\text{DRDY}}$ (Data Ready)	Output	Indicates processor acting as a bus master has not detected any bus exceptions ($\overline{\text{FAULT}}$, $\overline{\text{RETRY}}$, and $\overline{\text{RRREQ}}$ signals) during current bus transaction.
$\overline{\text{DS}}$ (Data Strobe)	Output	Indicates coprocessor or slave device can drive the data bus (for read operation) or that CPU has placed data on the bus (for write operation).
$\overline{\text{DTACK}}$ (Data Transfer Acknowledge)	Input	Asserted by coprocessor or slave to acknowledge data transfer.
$\overline{\text{SRDY}}$ (Synchronous Ready)	Input	Terminates read or write operation. If not asserted by fifth clock state of read or write cycle, and $\overline{\text{DTACK}}$ was not asserted during previous clock state, wait state cycles are inserted until either signal is asserted.
$\overline{\text{DYN16}}$ (Dynamic 16-Bit Port Acknowledge) (*WE* 32200 CPU Only)	Input	Informs *WE* 32200 CPU it is reading or writing 16-bit port, using the upper 16 data lines (D31–D16). Ignored if $\overline{\text{DSHAD}}$ asserted.

TABLE C-2 AT&T *WE* 32100/32200 Microprocessor Signal Descriptions (Continued)

Designation (Name)	Direction	Description
Bus Exception		
$\overline{\text{ABORT}}$ (Access Abort)	Output	Indicates access ignored by memory. Occurs as a result of program counter discontinuity with an instruction cache hit or alignment fault.
$\overline{\text{DSHAD}}$ (Data Bus Shadow)	Input	Used by MMU to remove the processor from data bus.
$\overline{\text{FAULT}}$ (Fault)	Input	Indicates occurrence of a fault condition. Signal ignored if $\overline{\text{DSHAD}}$ is asserted.
$\overline{\text{RESET}}$ (Reset Acknowledge)	Output	Indicates processor recognition of external reset request or internal reset exception.
$\overline{\text{RESETR}}$ (Reset Request)	Input	Used to reset system.
$\overline{\text{RETRY}}$ (Retry)	Input	Causes processor to terminate current bus transaction and retry it when signal is negated.
$\overline{\text{RRRACK}}$ (Relinquish and Retry Request Acknowledge)	Output	Asserted in response to a relinquish and retry bus exception when the processor has released bus.
$\overline{\text{RRREQ}}$ (Relinquish and Retry Request)	Input	Causes termination of bus transaction, and processor's release of the bus.
$\overline{\text{STOP}}$ (Stop)	Input	Halts execution of further instructions. One or two more instructions may be executed after assertion as a result of pipelining.
Bus Arbitration		
$\overline{\text{BARB}}$ (Bus Arbiter)	Input	Must be asserted if processor is arbiter or master of the bus.
$\overline{\text{BRACK}}$ (Bus Request Acknowledge)	Input/ Output	As an input, indicates that processor's bus request has been recognized and processor may take possession of the bus. As output, indicates that another device has requested the bus and the processor has released the bus.
$\overline{\text{BUSRQ}}$ (Bus Request)	Input/ Output	As input, indicates that another device is requesting the bus. As an output, indicates that processor is requesting the bus.
Interrupt		
$\overline{\text{AVEC}}$ (Autovector)	Input	If asserted during interrupt request, interrupt vector number is generated from interrupt option ($\overline{\text{INTOPT}}$) and priority level inputs (IPL3–IPL0). If not asserted, vector number must be supplied by the interrupting device.
$\overline{\text{INTOPT}}$ (Interrupt Option)	Input	Latched along with interrupt priority level inputs (IPL3–IPL0) during an interrupt acknowledge transaction. Inverted signal is sent out on ADDR6 of address bus.

TABLE C-2 AT&T *WE* 32100/32200 Microprocessor Signal Descriptions (Continued)

Designation (Name)	Direction	Description
Interrupt		
IPL3–IPL0 (Interrupt Priority Level)	Input	Indicates encoded priority level of device requesting interrupt. Level 0 has highest priority and level 14 lowest. Level 15 indicates no interrupts are pending. These interrupts are masked unless requested level with 4 bits inverted is higher than interrupt priority level (IPL) field of the processor status word (PSW).
$\overline{\text{NMINT}}$ (Nonmaskable Interrupt)	Input	Interrupts processor regardless of priority level in IPL field. This interrupt is treated as an autovector interrupt with vector number 0.
Development System Support		
$\overline{\text{HIGHZ}}$ (High Impedance)	Input	When asserted, all processor output pins are placed in high impedance state. This signal is intended for testing purposes.
IQS1–IQS0 (Instruction Queue Status)	Output	Identifies processor instruction queue activity. **IQS1 IQS0 Activity** 0 0 Discard four bytes 0 1 Discard one byte 1 0 Discard two bytes 1 1 No discard during cycle
$\overline{\text{SOI}}$ (Start of Instruction)	Output	Indicates processor's internal control has fetched next instruction's opcode. Due to pipelining, it is not an indication that current instruction execution has completed.
Clock		
CLK34 (Clock)	Input	Provides internal clock signal (along with CLK23) for instruction execution. Falling edge of this signal indicates beginning of a machine cycle.
CLK23 (Clock)	Input	Clock input at same frequency as CLK34 and leading it by 90 degree phase angle.

Motorola MC68020 Microprocessor Signal Descriptions

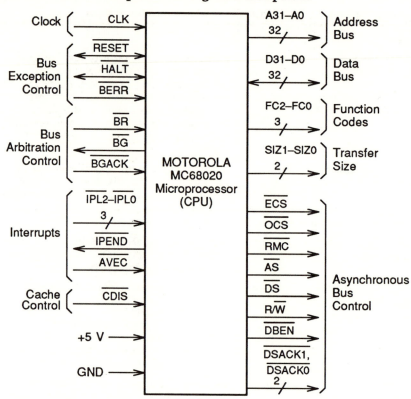

MOTOROLA MC68020 Microprocessor Functional Signal Groups

TABLE C-3 MOTOROLA MC68020 Microprocessor Signal Descriptions

Designation (Name)	Direction	Description
Data Bus		
D31–D0 (Data)	Input/ Output	Bidirectional data lines.
Address Bus		
A31–A0 (Address)	Output	Provide memory addresses or addresses of memory-mapped I/O ports.
Clock		
CLK (Clock)	Input	Provides internal clock signal used for instruction execution.

TABLE C-3 MOTOROLA MC68020 Microprocessor Signal Descriptions (Continued)

Designation (Name)	Direction	Description
Function Codes		
FC2–FC0 (Function Codes)	Output	Identify processor state and address space of current bus cycle.

FC2	FC1	FC0	Cycle Type
0	0	0	Reserved for future use
0	0	1	User data space
0	1	0	User program space
0	1	1	User defined
1	0	0	Reserved for future use
1	0	1	Supervisor data space
1	1	0	Supervisor program space
1	1	1	CPU space

Designation (Name)	Direction	Description
Transfer Size		
SIZ1–SIZ0 (Size)	Output	Indicates number of operand's bytes transferred during a bus cycle.

SIZ1	SIZ0	Size
0	0	Long word (32 bits)
0	1	Byte (8 bits)
1	0	Word (16 bits)
1	1	3 Bytes (24 bits)

Asynchronous Bus Control

Designation (Name)	Direction	Description
$\overline{ECS}$ (External Cycle Start)	Output	Indicates start of a new bus cycle.
$\overline{OCS}$ (Operand Start Cycle)	Output	Indicates start of an operand transfer or instruction prefetch bus cycle.
$\overline{RMC}$ (Read-Modify-Write Cycle)	Output	Indicates read-modify-write cycle. Can be used as a bus lock signal.
$R/\overline{W}$ (Read/Write)	Output	Distinguishes between read and write cycles.
$\overline{DBEN}$ (Data Buffer Enable)	Output	Provides enable to external data buffers, permitting $R/\overline{W}$ to change without causing external buffer contention.
$\overline{DSACK1}$, $\overline{DSACK0}$ (Data Transfer and Size Acknowledge)	Output	Indicates data transfer is complete and I/O port size (8, 16, or 32 bits).

$\overline{DSACK1}$	$\overline{DSACK0}$	Result
1	1	Insert wait states in current bus cycle
1	0	Complete cycle: 8-bit port
0	1	Complete cycle: 16-bit port
0	0	Complete cycle: 32-bit port

TABLE C-3 MOTOROLA MC68020 Microprocessor Signal Descriptions (Continued)

Designation (Name)	Direction	Description
$\overline{\text{AS}}$ (Address Strobe)	Output	Indicates valid function code, address, size, and R/$\overline{\text{W}}$ state is on bus.
$\overline{\text{DS}}$ (Data Strobe)	Output	Indicates a coprocessor or slave device can drive the data bus (for read cycle) or that MC68020 CPU has placed valid data on the data bus (for write cycle).
Bus Exception Control		
$\overline{\text{RESET}}$ (Reset)	Input/ Output	As input, used as system reset and initiates reset exception processing. As output, asserts reset to external devices but is not affected internally.
$\overline{\text{HALT}}$ (Halt)	Input/ Output	As input, stops all processor bus activity at end of current bus cycle. As output, indicates to external devices that processor has stopped due to a double bus fault condition.
$\overline{\text{BERR}}$ (Bus Error)	Input	Indicates bus cycle problem resulting from nonresponding devices, interrupt vector number acquisition failure, illegal accesses determined by MMU, or other application dependent errors. $\overline{\text{BERR}}$, along with $\overline{\text{HALT}}$ determines if current bus cycle should be rerun or aborted with a bus error.
Bus Arbitration Control		
$\overline{\text{BR}}$ (Bus Request)	Input	Indicates a device other than the MC68020 CPU requires bus mastership.
$\overline{\text{BG}}$ (Bus Grant)	Output	Indicates MC68020 CPU will release bus at end of current bus cycle.
$\overline{\text{BGACK}}$ (Bus Grant Acknowledge)	Input	Acknowledges another device has become bus master.
Interrupt Control		
$\overline{\text{IPL2}}$–$\overline{\text{IPL0}}$ (Interrupt Priority Level)	Input	Indicates encoded priority level of device requesting interrupt. Level 7 is highest priority and cannot be masked. Level 0 indicates that interrupts have been requested. Indicates encoded priority level ($\overline{\text{IPL2}}$–$\overline{\text{IPL0}}$) is higher than current level of status register's interrupt mask, or that a nonmaskable interrupt has been recognized.
$\overline{\text{AVEC}}$ (Autovector)	Input	Requests internal generation of the vector number during interrupt acknowledge cycle.
Cache Control		
$\overline{\text{CDIS}}$ (Cache Disable)	Input	Dynamically disables on-chip cache.

Appendix D Manufacturers' Addresses

Manufacturer's provide specifications and technical information in the form of data sheets, application notes, manuals, and product catalogs. These can be obtained by contacting the manufacturers directly at:

Intel Literature Sales
P.O. Box 58130
Santa Clara, CA 95052-8130
(800) 548-4725

AT&T Technologies
555 Union Blvd.
Allentown, Pa. 18103
(800) 372-2447

Motorola, Inc.
3501 Ed Bluestein Blvd.
Austin, Texas 78762
(512) 928-6000

Appendix E Acronyms and Abbreviations

AF	auxilary carry flag
AH	accumulator (high)
AL	accumulator (low)
ALE	address latch enable
ALU	arithmetic and logic unit
AP	argument pointer
ARPL	adjust requested privilege level
AS	address strobe
ASCII	American Standard Code for Information Interchange
ATN	attention
AVEC	autovector
BARB	bus arbiter
BCC	block check characters
BCD	binary coded decimal
BE	byte enable
BERR	bus error
BHE	bus high enable
BISYNC	binary synchronous communication
BR	bus request
BS	bank select
BUSY	busy status
CAAR	cache address register
CACR	cache control register
CAS	column-address-strobe
CCR	condition code register
CE	chip enable
CF	carry flag
CHMOS	complementary HMOS
CK	clock input
CKM	clock mode pin
CMOS	complementary metal-oxide semiconductor
CPL	calling privilege level

CPU	central processing unit
CR	command register
CRC	cyclic redundancy check
CS	code segment, chip select
CTS	clear to send
DAV	data valid
D/C	data/control
DCE	data communication equipment
DEN	data enable
DF	direction flag
DFC	destination function code
DIP	dual in-line package
DIRQ	direct interrupt request
DMA	direct memory access
DMAC	direct memory access controller
DPL	descriptor privilege level
DRAM	dynamic RAM
DS	data segment
DSR	data set ready
DST	destination operand
DTE	data terminal equipment
DTR	data terminal ready
DT/R	data transmit/receive
EEPROM	electrically erasable PROM
EFLAGS	extended flags register
EIP	extended instruction pointer
EM	emulation
EOD	end of direct memory access
EOI	end or identify
EPROM	erasable PROM
ES	extra segment
ESP	extended stack pointer
ET	extension type
ETX	end-of-text
FP	frame pointer

FSK	frequency shift keying		LAS	logical address strobe
			LBGI	logical bus grant in
GDT	global descriptor table		LCCC	leadless ceramic chip carrier
GDTR	global descriptor table register		LDT	local descriptor table
GE	global enable		LDTR	local descriptor table register
GPIB	general purpose instrumentation bus		LE	local enable
			LEA	load effective address
			LED	light emitter diode
HDLC	high-level data link control		LIDT	load interrupt descriptor table
HMOS	high-performance MOS		LIFO	last-in-first-out
			LSB	least significant bit
IC	integrated circuit		LSI	large scale integrated
ICE	in-circuit emulator			
ICW	initialization command word		MAR	memory address register
IDT	interrupt descriptor table		MAU	math acceleration unit
IDTR	interrupt descriptor table register		MCS	MMU chip select
IE	input enable		MDR	memory data register
IEEE	Institute of Electrical and Electronic Engineers		MIPs	millions of instructions per second
			MMU	memory management unit
IF	interrupt enable flag		MOS	metal-oxide semiconductor
IFC	interface clear		MP	math present
INT	interrupt request (also INTR)		MPSC	multi-protocol serial controller
INTA	interrupt acknowledge		MREQ	memory request
INTE	interrupt enable		MSB	most significant bit
INTO	interrupt-on-overflow		MSI	medium scale integrated
INTOPT	interrupt option input		MSP	master stack pointer
I/O	input/output			
IOPL	input/output privilege level		NA	next address
IORC	input/output read control		NDAC	not data accept
IORQ	input/output request		NMI	nonmaskable interrupt request
IOWC	input/output write control		NMINT	nonmaskable input
IP	instruction pointer		NMOS	n-type MOS
IPEND	interrupt pending		NRFD	not ready for data
IPL	interrupt priority level		NT	nested task
IR	internal reset			
IRET	interrupt return instruction		OCW	operation command word
ISP	interrupt stack pointer		OD	output disable
ISR	interrupt service routine		OE	output enable
			OF	overflow flag
JEDEC	Joint Electronic Device Engineering Council		PC	program counter

PCB	process control block	SDC	segment descriptor cache
PCBP	process control block pointer	SDLC	serial data link control
PDBR	page descriptor base register	SF	sign flag
PDC	page descriptor cache	SFC	source function code
PDE	page directory entry	SI	strobe input
PE	protection enable	SIB	scale, index, and base
PEREQ	processor extension request	SIDT	store interrupt descriptor table
PF	parity flag	SOP	sum of products
PG	paging flag	SP	stack pointer
PGA	pin grid array	SP/EN	slave program/enable buffer
PGM	program pin	SR	status register
PIC	programmable interrupt controller	SRAM	static RAM
		SRC	source operand
PLCC	plastic leaded chip carrier	SRQ	service request
PMMU	paged MMU	SS	stack segment
PMOS	p-type MOS	SSI	small-scale integrated
PPI	programmable peripheral interface	SSP	supervisor stack pointer
		SSR	system status register
PROM	programmable ROM	STX	start-of-text
PSK	phase shift keying		
PSW	program status word	TCS	translation chip select
		TF	trap enable flag
QAM	quadrature amplitude modulation	TLB	translation look-aside buffer
		TR	task register
Qword	quadword	TS	task switch
		TSS	task state segment
RA	return address	TxC	transmit clock input
RAM	random access memory		
RAS	row-address-strobe	UART	universal asynchronous receiver transmitter
REN	remote enable		
RF	resume flag	USART	universal synchronous/asynchronous receiver transmitter
R/M	register/memory		
RMC	read-modify-write cycle	USP	user stack pointer
ROM	read-only memory		
RTS	request to send	VBR	vector base register
R/W	read/write	VLSI	very large scale integrated
RxC	receive clock input	VM	virtual 8086 mode
SCC	serial communications controller	ZF	zero flag

Appendix F Answers To Selected Exercises

Chapter One

1a. Accept input, provide output, store information (programs and data), perform arithmetic and logic operations, and control the overall operation and sequencing of operations

2b. Asynchronous

2c. Synchronous

4. 2^{16} = 65,536 addressable bytes

5. 2^{20} = 1,048,576 addressable bytes = 524,288 words (16 bits)

6. 2^{24} = 16,777,216 addressable bytes = 8,388,608 words (16 bits)

7. 2^{32} = 4,294,967,296 addressable bytes = 2,147,483,648 words (16 bits)

      = 1,073,741,814 double words (32 bits)

9. tDATVC34H   16

   tDSHDATX   18

   tC34HDRYH   20

   tC34HASL   9

   tADDVASL   4

   tASLADDV   5

10. 1 = tC34HDSL   2 = tDSLDSH   3 = tDATVDSL

Chapter Two

1a. A computer's architecture refers to the structure, arrangement, and interaction of its hardware components.

3a. Addressing mode refers to the manner in which an instruction specifies an operand's address.

5. Exceptions are internal CPU detected errors. Interrupts are externally generated requests for CPU attention.

7a. The CPU registers that are accessible to assembly language applications programmers compare the program model register set.

7b. General-purpose data and address registers, instruction pointer (program counter), stack pointer, and flag register.

9. Negative, zero, overflow, and carry flags.

13a. AB9C7

13b. 3EAB4

13c. 14A20

13d. F3AB0

15. The D bit sets the default operand and offset address bit width, which allows the 32-bit 80386 CPU to emulate the 16-bit 80286 CPU.

17c. All three addresses (logical, linear, and physical) are the same.

Chapter Three

1a. The TSCB is a data structure used to store the hardware context of a task.

3. At the start of the task, the task must disable all interrupts by setting appropriate flag bits. Any maskable interrupt requests will then be ignored by the CPU.

5. The second task can alter its own in-use flag; since both in-use flags are set neither task can access the common data area - it is permanently locked from both tasks

7. Returns from call gates are typically not protected by privilege level checking. Thus, the return to the higher privilege level provides an unprotected entry into it from the lower privilege level.

9a. Stack

9b. A stack is not provided for task calls.

9c. No.

Chapter Four

3. Memory content → AB   EF   19   CC
   Byte Address   → 1623 1622 1621 1620

5a. An operand's offset address.

5b. A base address, scaled index, and displacement.

7. Long form: 11000111 00 000 011 0001 1001 0111 1010 0000 0000 0000 0000
Short form: 10111 011 0001 1001 0111 1010 0000 0000 0000 0000

9a. 10001011 00 000 100 00 001 011

9b. 10001011 00 000 100 01 001 011

9c. 10001011 10 000 011 1110 1110 1111 1111 0000 0000 0000 0000

Note: a mod value of 10 specifies four displacement bytes

11a. MOV AX,0FFEEH

11b. MOV BX,0AAEFH

11c. MOV AL,19

13a.
```
          MOV EBX,0AB190000H    ; Load starting address
          MOV ECX,0AH           ; Load table size
          MOV EAX,0             ; Start with zero sum
   AGAIN: ADD EAX,[EBX]
          INC EBX
          INC EBX
          LOOP AGAIN            ; Sum in EAX
```

15a. MOV AX,0AB60H
    MOV BX,3587H
    MUL AX,BX

15b. Upper 16-bits of the 32-bit product are in DX. Lower 16-bits of the 32-bit product are in AX.

Chapter Five

3b. Two.

6a. 1000 0100 0100 0010 0100 0011

6b. 1000 0111 0100 0110 0100 0111

6c. 1000 0110 0101 0101 0100 0011

6d. 1000 0110 0101 0011 0100 0101

6e. 1000 0100 0100 1111 1010 1011 1001 0001 1000 0010 0111 0011 0100 0101

6f. 1000 0100 0100 1111 1010 1011 1001 0001 1000 0010 0111 0011 0101 0101

9a. 1001 1111 0100 0000 0100 0011

9b. 1001 1110 0101 0000 0100 0011

9c. 1001 1110 0100 0000 0101 0011

9d. 1001 1100 0101 1111 1010 1011 0001 1001 0100 0010

9e. 1001 1100 0101 1111 1010 1011 0001 1001 0101 0010

9f. 1001 1111 0100 0010 1100 0101 1010 0000

9g. 1001 1111 0100 0010 1101 0101 1010 0000

9h. 1001 1110 0111 1111 1110 1110 1111 1111 0000 0000 0000 0000 0101 0110

9i. 1001 1100 1110 1111 1101 1111 1010 1011 0101 0000 0001 1001 0100 0001

9j. 1001 1100 1100 0011 0011 0001 1110 1111 0001 0000 0000 0001 0000 0000 0000 0000

10a. MOVH &0xFFEE,%r2

10b. MOVH &0xAAEF,(%r5)

10c. ADDW2 $0x1960,%r6

10d. LLSW3 1,%r1,%r1

10e. MULH2 %r3,%r4 or MULH2 %r4,%r3

12.   MOVW &0xAB190000,%r0
            MOVB &0xA,%r1
            MOVW &0,%r3
     AGAIN: ADDW2 (%r0),%r3
            ADDW2, &2,%r0
            DECB %r2
            BNEB AGAIN

Chapter Six

2. Byte (8 bits), word (16 bits), long word (32 bits), packed and unpacked BCD, individual bits, and bit fields. Quad words (64 bits) are only used in multiply and divide operations.

5a. A highly orthogonal instruction set is one in which the majority of instructions can use all of the addressing modes supported by the CPU.

5b. A completely orthogonal instruction set is one in which all instructions can use all addressing modes supported by the CPU.

7a. 0010 101 101 000 100 ← instruction word
    10101111 01100010 ← displacement

7b. 0011 011 110 010 110 ← instruction word
    11010000 11111110 ← brief destination extension word

7c. 0011 001 110 110 010 ← instruction word
    11011000 11111110 ← brief source extension word
    11001000 11000001 ← brief destination extension word

7g. 0010 110 110 110 101 ← instruction word
    10101001 00100000 ← full source extension word
    11111101 10101110 ← base displacement
    10111001 00100000 ← full destination extension word
    00011001 10100100 ← base displacement

10a. MOV.W #$FFFE,A6

10b. MOV.W #$AAEF,D0

10c. MOV.B #$19,A1

10d. ADD.B ($ACE4),D5

10e. MULS.W D2,D3

```
12a.          MOV.W #$AB190000,A0
              MOV.B #$A,D0
              MOV.W #0,D2
   AGAIN:     ADD.W (A0)+,D2
              DBNE D0,AGAIN
```

Chapter Seven

1a. N = 13, M = 8
1b. N = 14, M = 4
2a. 16K bits organized as 4K x 4
3a. EN inputs to all four gates must be inverted. Table values for EN are also inverted (1,0,0,0,0)
4a. 4M addresses from 000000 to 3FFFFF.
4b. 2/4 decoder: A21 to A1 input, A20 to A0 input

Decoder Output	Address Range
0	000000-0FFFFF
1	100000-1FFFFF
2	200000-2FFFFF
3	300000-3FFFFF

12a.	Low Case	High Case
Fanout	10	50
Noise Margin	0.35	0.4

Maximum number of loads without buffering = 10
19a. One wait state.
20a. No wait states.

Chapter Eight

1. Use ECX in place of CX, with NUM = 160000.
4. Replace TEST AL, 80H with TEST AL, 01H
   Replace TRNSFR: MOV AL, DATA with TRNSFR: IN AL, DEV
                         OUT DEV, AL   MOV DATA; AL
8. Replace MOV AL, 07H with MOV AL, 0A9H
Replace ROR AL, 1 with ROL AL, 1
15. In program for 32-Bit Port Size:
Replace MOV EAX, 90909090H with MOV EAX, 92929292H
Replace IN EAX, AD8255 with IN EAX, AD8255+4
Replace OUT AD8255+4, EAX with OUT AD8255+8, EAX
22. N = $2 \times 10^6/(19200 \times 64) = 104 = 13 \times 8$
Add divide-by-8 counter after divide-by-13 in Figure 8-34.
In Program 8-11, replace MOV AL,7BH with MOV AL, 0CFH

Chapter Nine

2. Single instruction required.
Assembly language instruction: SPOPD2 CRWORD FPNUM, FPSQRT
Hex Codes: SPOPD2 = 03
           CRWORD = 000036FD

Index

Aborts, 103
Access time, 23, 30, 301, 334
Address bus, 9, 309
Address decoding, 308
Address hold time, 30
Address pipelining, 43, 338
Address registers, 52
Address set-up time, 29
Address-size prefix byte, 153
Addressing modes, 45
Addressing modes (AT&T CPU)
  absolute, 230
  absolute deferred, 230
  auto increment/decrement, 235
  deferred displacement, 227
  displacement, 226
  expanded operand, 231
  immediate, 229
  indexed, 236

  register, 224
  register deferred, 225
Addressing modes (Intel CPU)
  based index, 136
  based index relative, 137
  immediate, 129
  memory, 130
  register, 128
  register indirect, 132
  register relative, 133
    base relative, 136
    direct indexing, 135
    stack frame relative, 136
Addressing modes (Motorola CPU)
  absolute, 259
  immediate, 260
  indexed register indirect, 263
  memory indirect, 264
  program counter relative, 266

register direct, 260
register indirect, 261
 with displacement, 262
 with postincrement, 262
 with predecrement, 262
Aligned data, 320
Alternate code function register
 (Motorola), 253
ALU, 6
Applications privilege level, 86
Architecture, 4
Argument pointer, 202, 214
Asynchronous transmission, 436

Base register, 131
Binary coded decimal, (BCD)
 packed, 127, 239, 256, 494
 unpacked, 127, 255, 493
BISYNC, 436
Bit field, 127
Bit string, 127
Breakpoint, 120
Buffering, 328
Bus arbiter (82289), 479
Bus cycles, 27
 read cycle, 27, 333, 351
 write cycle, 31, 333, 351
Bus high enable signal, 318
Bus interface control (AT&T CPU), 198
Bus interface unit, 43
Buses, 8
 address bus, 9, 309
 control bus, 10
 data bus, 8, 317
 IEEE-488 bus, 432
 local bus, 478
 MULTIBUS I, 478
 MULTIBUS II, 480
 PDP-11 UNIBUS Bus, 11
 system bus, 478
 VMEbus, 481

Byte enable signals, 319

Cache, 344
 address register (Motorola), 254
 control register (Motorola), 254
 controller, 348
 direct mapped, 347
 fully associative, 347
 hit rate, 346
 index field, 347
 set associative, 347
 tag field, 347
Call gate, 95
Call instruction, 96, 213, 276
Cascaded decoders, 312
Chip enable signal, 301
Chip select signal, 301
Clock generator (82384), 27
Clock signals, 24
CMOS, 32, 329
Code segment register, 58, 115
Column address strobe, 306, 351
Computer architecture, 4
Condition code register (Motorola), 250
Control bus, 10
Control registers (Intel), 119
Control unit, 6
Coprocessors, 458
 I/O processor (8089), 458
 MAU (AT&T), 47, 465
 numeric, 47, 459
Counters, 520
CPU, 7
Cycle time, 24

Data access time, 30, 301, 334
Data bus, 8, 317
Data hold time, 30
Data registers, 52
Data segment registers, 58, 115
Data set-up time, 30, 335

Data transfer, 380

Data types, 123, 203, 255

Debug registers (Intel), 120

Decode unit, 43

Decoders, 309

Delay routine, 385

Delay time, 22

Demand paging, 77

Device density, 34

Device status, 386

Digital logic,
  counters, 520
  decoders, 309
  encoders, 405, 513
  flip-flop circuits, 514
  gate circuits, 499
  Karnaugh maps, 504
  multiplexers, 309, 351, 512
  shift registers, 343, 518
  switching algebra, 495

DIP, 15

Direct mapped cache, 347

DMA, 383, 409

DMA controller, 412, 416

DMA coprocessor (82258), 414

DMA transfer techniques,
  block mode, 411
  burst mode, 411
  cycle stealing, 412
  one cycle, 410
  two cycle, 410

DRAM, 299
  controller, 354
  interfacing, 350
  precharge time, 353
  refresh, 352

Drive capability, 34, 328

Dynamic bus sizing, 320

Dynamic relocation, 60

EEPROM, 299

Effective address, 130, 258

Encoders, 405, 513

EPROM, 299

Escape instruction, 461

Exceptions, 102
  aborts, 103
  faults, 103
  programmed, 104
  traps, 103

Execution unit, 43, 198

Executive privilege level, 86

Extended flags register (Intel), 116

Extended instruction pointer (Intel), 115

Fabrication, 32

Fanout, 34, 328

Far pointer (Intel), 125

Faults, 103

Fetch unit, 42, 198

Flag bits
  carry, 57
  negative, 56
  overflow, 57
  zero, 57

Flag register, 55, 201

Flip-flop circuits, 514

Floating point numbers, 125, 204, 469, 490

Fragmentation, 75

Frame pointer, 201, 214

Framing error, 448

Frequency shift keying (FSK), 440

Fully associative cache, 347

Gate descriptors
  call gate, 95
  interrupt gate, 95, 100, 397
  task gate, 95, 397
  trap gate, 95, 397

Gate circuits, 499

Gate instruction, 87

General-purpose registers,

AT&T CPU, 199
Intel CPU, 113
Motorola CPU, 248
Global descriptor table register
(Intel), 73, 116

Hit rate, 346
Hold time, 23

I/O interfacing techniques,
direct memory access (DMA), 383, 409
interrupt controlled I/O, 381, 391
programmed I/O, 381, 384
serial I/O, 434
I/O processor (8089), 458
I/O unit, 6
IEEE-488 bus, 432
Index register, 131
Input instructions, 158, 388
Instruction encoding,
Intel CPU, 139
Motorola CPU, 280
Instruction pointer, 53
Instruction prefix byte, 153
Instruction set (AT&T), 207
additional 32200 instructions, 239
arithmetic, 209
coprocessor, 218
data transfer, 208
logical, 211
program control, 213
stack and miscellaneous, 220
Instruction set, (Intel), 156
arithmetic, 164
data transfer, 156
high-level language support and
systems, 178
logical, shift, and rotate, 170
program control, 173
string/character translation, 175
Instruction set (Motorola)

arithmetic, 268
binary coded decimal (BCD), 271
bit management, 273
coprocessor, 278
data transfer, 268
logical, shift, and rotate, 271
program and system control, 273
Integers,
signed, 123, 489
unsigned, 123, 488
Integrated circuit, 15
Intelligent programming algorithm, 305
Interleaving
DRAM, 353
tasks, 46
Interlevel system calls, 98
Interrupt
acknowledge, 392
gates, 100
maskable, 100, 392
nonmaskable, 100, 392
software, 104, 396
Interrupt controlled I/O, 381, 391
Interrupt descriptor table register (Intel), 116
Interrupt gate, 95, 100, 397
Interrupt register, 61
Interrupt stack pointer, 202, 253
Intralevel system calls, 97

Karnaugh maps, 504
Kernel privilege level, 86

LCCC package, 16
Linear address, 75, 79, 365
Local bus, 478
Local descriptor table register (Intel), 72, 116
Lock instruction, 476
Logical address, 71, 365

Main controller (AT&T), 198
Maskable interrupt, 100, 392

Master stack pointer (Motorola), 253
MAU (AT&T), 47, 465
Memory
    cache, 344
    RAM, 299
    ROM, 298
Memory address lines, 300, 351
Memory address register (MAR), 300
Memory data register (MDR), 300
Memory interfacing, 298
Memory management, 61, 362
Memory unit, 6
Microcomputer, 12
Microprocessor, 12
    AT&T CPU, 16, 50, 198, 233, 350, 370
    Intel CPU, 17, 49, 111
    Motorola CPU, 17, 51, 248, 349, 368
MMU, 63, 364
Modem, 440
ModR/M byte, 143
MOS, 32
MULTIBUS I, 478
MULTIBUS II, 480
Multitasking, 45
Multiplexers, 309, 351, 512
Multiprocessing, 473

Near pointer (Intel), 125
Noise immunity, 34, 329, 439
Nonmaskable interrupt, 100, 392
Null modem cable, 440
Numeric coprocessor, 47, 459

Opcode, 45, 139
Operand-size prefix byte, 152
Output enable/disable signals, 301
Output instructions, 158, 385
Override prefix bytes, 150
    address-size, 153
    instruction, 153
    operand-size, 152

    segment override, 151
Overrun error, 448

Packaging, 15
    DIP, 15
    LCCC package, 16
    PGA package, 18
Packed BCD, 127, 239, 256, 494
Page directory base register (Intel), 80, 93
Paged MMU (Motorola), 365
Paging, 77, 364
Parallel I/O, 419
Parity bit, 435
PGA package, 18
Physical address, 9, 63, 365
Pipelining, 43, 45, 338
Pop operation, 54
Power dissipation, 33
Precharge time, 353
Prefetched instructions, 45
Privilege levels, 86
    applications, 86
    executive, 86
    kernel, 86
    supervisor, 86
Procedure call instruction, 214
Process control block pointer (AT&T), 202
Processor exceptions, 103
Processor status word (AT&T), 202
Program address space, 62
Program counter, 53, 200, 250
Program delay, 385
Program model registers, 50, 112
    AT&T CPU, 199
    Intel CPU, 112
    Motorola CPU, 248
Programmable DMA controller (8237A), 412
Programmable interrupt controller (8259A), 401
Programmable peripheral interface (8255A), 419
    basic I/O mode, 424
    basic operation, 420

interfacing to 80386 CPU, 420

strobed I/O mode, 429

Programmed exceptions, 104

Programmed I/O, 381, 384

Programming signal, 304

PROM, 298

Protected mode 58, 71

Pulse width, 24

Push operation, 54

Queue, 45

Quick interrupt, 407

Quick pulse programming algorithm, 305

RAM, 299

Read cycle, 27, 333, 351

Read/write signal, 301

Real address space, 62

Real mode, 58, 62, 66

Refresh (DRAM), 352

Register sets, 48, 112, 199, 248

program model, 50, 112, 199, 248

system model, 60, 116, 202, 251

Repeat prefix, 177

Return from procedure, 99, 214

Return instruction, 99,213,276

ROM, 298

Row address strobe, 306, 351

RS-232C interface standard, 438

RS-449 interface standard, 440

SDLC, 436

Segment descriptor table, 71

Segment override prefix byte, 151

Segment registers, 58, 115

code, 58,115

data, 58,115

stack, 58,115

Segmentation, 63, 69, 363

Semaphores, 474

Serial I/O interfacing, 434

Set associative cache, 347

Set-up time, 22

Shift registers, 343, 518

SIB byte, 149

Sign extension, 205

Signal descriptions,

AT&T CPU, 527

Intel CPU, 524

Motorola CPU, 532

Signal groups, 15

Signed integers, 123, 489

Software interrupt, 104, 396

Software polling, 398

Speed-power product, 34

SPOP prefix, 466

SRAM, 299

Stack, 54, 214

Stack operations,

pop, 54

push, 54

Stack pointer, 54, 200

Stack segment register, 58, 115

Status register, 61, 252

Supervisor privilege level, 86

Switching algebra, 495

Switching speed, 33

Synchronous transmission, 436

BISYNC, 436

SDLC, 436

System bus, 478

System calls,

interlevel, 98

intralevel, 97

System model registers, 60

AT&T CPU, 202

Intel CPU, 116

Motorola CPU, 251

Task, 45, 87

Task gate, 95, 397

Task register, 61, 90, 116

Task state,
control block, 87
control block pointer, 88
segment, 88
segment descriptor, 88
Task switches, 92
Test registers, 123
Timing
conventions, 18
definitions, 20
memory cycle
address hold, 30
address set-up, 29
data access, 30, 301, 334
data hold, 30
data set-up, 30, 335
reference points, 24
standard intervals, 22
access time, 23
cycle time, 24
delay time, 22
hold time, 23
pulse width, 24
set-up time, 22

Trap gate, 95, 397
Traps, 103
Tristate gate, 11, 327
TTL, 329

UNIBUS Bus, 11
Unpacked BCD, 127, 255, 493
Unsigned integers, 123, 488
USART (8251A), 444
User stack pointer, 250

Vector base register (Motorola), 253
Virtual address, 63, 365
Virtual mode, 117
VMEbus, 481

Wait states, 340
Write cycle, 31, 333, 351
Write enable signal, 301

XCHG instruction, 476

Zero extension, 205